WEBSTER'S NEW ENGLISH LANGUAGE THESAURUS

Thesaurus text based on *Roget's New Millennium*™
Concise Thesaurus from Thesaurus.com

Published by
The Popular Group, LLC
1700 Broadway
New York, NY 10019

Publishing Consultant: Charles M. Levine
Design and Composition: Charlotte Staub

FOR LEXICO
Edited by Barbara Ann Kipfer, Ph.D.
Executive Editor: Brian Kariger

ISBN: 1-59027-078-9

Printed in the United States of America

9 8 7 6 5 4 3 2 1

A

abandon *verb.* desert, discontinue, disown, ditch, drop, duck, dump, dust, leave, quit, relinquish, slide, strand, surrender, vacate, walk, withdraw, yield

abandoned *adjective.* **1** alone, deserted, discarded, dissipated, dropped, eliminated, empty, forsaken, jilted, left, outcast, rejected, relinquished, shunned, stranded, unoccupied, vacant, vacated **2** amoral, corrupt, depraved, dissolute, evil, immoral, incorrigible, lewd, licentious, loose, shameless, sinful, uncontrolled, uninhibited, unprincipled, wanton, wicked, wild

ability *noun.* **1** aptitude, bent, capability, command, competence, comprehension, expertise, facility, intelligence, knack, might, potentiality, power, proficiency, skill, strength, talent, understanding **2** adroitness, bent, capability, cleverness, competence, craft, deftness, flair, gift, ingenuity, intelligence, knack, proficiency, savvy, skill, skillfulness, strength, talent

able *adjective.* **1** able, adept, adequate, adroit, alert, bright, cleft, cunning, effortless, fitted, good, intelligent, powerful, qualified, ready, smart, strong, worthy **2** accomplished, agile, artful, deft, efficient, expert, gifted, intelligent, keen, learned, practiced, prepared, qualified, savvy, sharp, skilled, skillful, talented

abolish *verb.* cancel, dissolve, end, eradicate, erase, expunge, extinguish, invalidate, kill, negate, obliterate, overthrow, prohibit, repeal, repudiate, scrub, undo, vacate

abolition *noun.* annihilation, cancellation, destruction, dissolution, elimination, end, ending, eradication, negation, obliteration, overthrow, overturning, repeal, repudiation, subversion, suppression, termination, withdrawal

absolute *adjective.* **1** consummate, downright, entire, free, full, infinite, outright, plenary, pure, sheer, simple, thorough, total, unabridged, unadulterated, unlimited, unqualified, unrestricted **2** actual, categorical, conclusive, consummate, decide, decisive, definite, exact, factual, fixed, genuine, infallible, positive, precise, sure, unambiguous, undeniable, unquestionable

absolutely *adverb.* actually, categorically, conclusively, decidedly, decisively, def, definitely, doubtless, easily, exactly, positively, precisely, really, surely, truly, unambiguously, unconditionally, unquestionably

absorption *noun.* assimilation, consumption, digestion, exhaustion, fusion, imbibing, impregnation, incorporation, ingestion, inhalation, intake, osmosis, penetration, reception, retention, saturation, suction, taking in

abstraction *noun.* absorption, aloofness, brooding, consideration, contemplation, daydreaming, detachment, entranced, musing, pensiveness, pondering, preoccupation, reflecting, reflection, remoteness, reverie, thinking, trance

absurd *adjective.* cool, crazy, dizzy, flaky, fool, foolish, idiotic, illogical, inane, ludicrous, monkey, preposterous, sappy, senseless, silly, stupid, unreasonable, wacky

absurdity *noun.* applesauce, bull, crap, farce, flapdoodle, folly, foolishness, illogicality, illogicalness, incongruity, insanity, irrationality, jazz, jive, ludicrousness, ridiculousness, silliness, stupidity

abundant *adjective.* abounding, ample, copious, exuberant, filled, full, generous, heavy, lavish, liberal, mucho, overflowing, plenty, profuse, rich, rolling in, sufficient, teeming

abuse *noun.* **1** corruption, crime, debasement, delinquency, desecration, exploitation, fault, injustice, misconduct, misdeed, mishandling, misuse, offense, perversion, prostitution, sin, wrong, wrongdoing **2** blame, castigation, censure, curse, curses, derision, insults, libel, opprobrium, quinine, reproach, scolding, screwing, signifying, slander, swearing, upbraiding, vilification

abuse *verb.* **1** corrupt, damage, harm, hose, hump, impair, maltreat, mar, misuse, molest, pollute, ruin, spoil, taint, total, victimize, violate, wax **2** cap, chop, derogate, dig, discount, knock, minimize, offend, rag, ride, run down, signify, slam, slap, smear, sound, swipe, trash

accent *noun.* accentuation, articulation, beat, cadence, emphasis, enunciation, force, inflection, intonation, meter, modulation, pitch, pronunciation, rhythm, stroke, timbre, tonality, tone

accept *verb.* **1** acknowledge, acquiesce, agree, assent, bear, bear with, bow, endure, live with, recognize, respect, stand, stomach, suffer, swallow, take, tolerate, yield to **2** accede, acknowledge, acquiesce, admit, adopt, affirm, approve, assent, assume, bear, buy, comply, go for, okay, recognize, sign, stroke, undertake

acceptable *adjective.* adequate, close, cool, delightful, fair, hip, ice, kosher, okay, passable, pleasing, respectable, sharp, standard, sufficient, swell, tolerable, welcome

acceptance *noun.* accepting, acknowledgement, acquiring, admission, compliance, cooperation, having, nod, obtaining, okay, permission, receipt, reception, recognition, securing, taking, undertaking, yes

accepted *adjective.* accustomed, acknowledged, authorized, chosen, confirmed, conventional, in, kosher, normal, orthodox, popular, recognized, sanctioned, standard, straight, universal, usual, welcomed

access *noun.* admission, admittance, approach, avenue, connection, contact, course, door, entrance, entry, in, introduction, key, passage, path, road, route, way

accident *noun.* blow, calamity, casualty, collision, crack-up, disaster, event, fender-bender, fluke, hazard, misadventure, misfortune, mishap, setback, shunt, smash, total, wrack-up

accommodate *verb.* **1** accord, adapt, adjust, agree, comply, conform, coordinate, correspond, fit, harmonize, integrate, make consistent, modify, proportion, reconcile, settle, tailor, tune **2** aid, assist, avail, benefit, bow, favor, furnish, gratify, humor, oblige, pamper, serve, submit, suit, supply, support, sustain, yield

accompany *verb.* attend, chaperon, conduct, consort, convoy, date, draft, drag, escort, follow, guard, guide, lead, shadow, show about, squire, tailgate, usher

accomplish *verb.* achieve, arrive, attain, conclude, consummate, do, effect, finish, fulfill, gain, hit, manage, perform, produce, reach, realize, score, win

accomplished *adjective.* able, adept, brainy, consummate, cool, cultivated, expert, gifted, hip, masterly, polished, practiced, proficient, savvy, sharp, skillful, talented, with it

accord *noun.* accordance, concert, concord, concurrence, conformity, congruence, correspondence, deal, good vibrations, harmony, okay, pact, rapport, reconciliation, sympathy, treaty, unanimity, understanding

accordingly *adverb.* appropriately, consequently, correspondingly, duly, equally, ergo, fitly, hence, in consequence, properly, proportionately, respectively, so, subsequently, suitably, then, therefore, thus

account *noun.* **1** annual, bulletin, chronicle, detail, explanation, history, lowdown, make, narration, narrative, picture, recital, report, score, story, tab, take, version **2** balance, bill, book, books, charge, check, computation, cuff, inventory, ledger, reckoning, record, register, report, score, statement, tab, tally

accumulation *noun.* accretion, addition, agglomeration, aggrandizement, aggregation, buildup, chunk, collecting, collection, growth, heap, hunk, intensification, mass, multiplication, pile, stack, stock

accuracy *noun.* carefulness, certainty, closeness, correctness, definiteness, efficiency, exactness, faultlessness, incisiveness, mastery, meticulousness, preciseness, precision, sharpness, skill, skillfulness, veracity, verity

accurate *adjective.* **1** authentic, careful,

concrete, correct, defined, deft, discriminating, distinct, explicit, judicious, literal, meticulous, rigid, scrupulous, sharp, skillful, solid, strict **2** absolute, authentic, certain, conclusive, correct, definite, faultless, final, infallible, official, straight, strict, true, truthful, undeniable, undisputed, unimpeachable, valid

accuse *verb.* allege, apprehend, attack, attribute, betray, blame, brand, censure, cite, complain, denounce, finger, frame, impute, name, sue, summon, tax

achieve *verb.* accomplish, acquire, conclude, deliver, discharge, dispatch, effectuate, end, gain, obtain, perform, procure, produce, resolve, sign, win, wind up, work out

achievement *noun.* acquisition, act, completion, consummation, deed, effort, enactment, execution, exploit, feat, fulfillment, hit, masterpiece, production, realization, success, triumph, victory

acknowledge *verb.* **1** accede, accept, acquiesce, agree, allow, approve, attest to, certify, defend, endorse, grant, own, ratify, recognize, subscribe to, support, uphold, yield *verb.* **2** accede, accept, acquiesce, allow, avow, come clean, concede, confess, crack, declare, fess up, grant, open up, own, own up, profess, recognize, yield

acquire *verb.* achieve, amass, annex, buy, collect, cop, earn, gain, hustle, lock up, obtain, pick up, procure, promote, secure, snag, take, win

acquisition *noun.* **1** accretion, achievement, acquiring, addition, attainment, buy, gaining, learning, prize, procurement, property, purchase, pursuit, recovery, redemption, retrieval, salvage, winning **2** achievement, allowance, benefit, bonus, dividend, donation, fortune, gain, gift, grant, income, inheritance, net, premium, prize, riches, security, wealth

act *noun.* **1** amendment, clause, code, commitment, decree, enactment, judgment, law, measure, order, ordinance, resolution, statute, subpoena, summons, verdict, warrant, writ **2** affectation, attitude, bit, fake, feigning, front, performance, phony, pose, posture, pretense, put-on, sham, show, stall, stance, stunt, sweet talk

act *verb.* **1** accomplish, achieve, begin, consummate, cook, develop, do, function, intrude, move, perk, persist, practice, preside, serve, tick, transport, undertake **2** appear, behave, carry, carry out, comport, conduct, do, enact, execute, exert, function, operate, perform, react, represent oneself, seem, serve, strike **3** burlesque, characterize, dramatize, enact, ham, mug, parody, perform, personate, play, play role, portray, pretend, rehearse, represent, simulate, star, strut

acting *noun.* depiction, dramatizing, enacting, enactment, feigning, hamming, imitating, imitation, pantomime, performing, playing, portrayal, posing, pretending, pretense, seeming, theatre, theatricals

action *noun.* **1** activity, alacrity, bit, business, flurry, happening, life, liveliness, occupation, pipeline, plan, power, process, proposition, reaction, spirit, vigor, vivacity **2** achievement, blow, commission, dealings, doing, effort, execution, exertion, exploit, feat, handiwork, move, operation, procedure, step, thrust, transaction, undertaking

active *adjective.* **1** alive, bustling, efficacious, flowing, hasty, impelling, mobile, movable, moving, operating, pushing, rapid, restless, rushing, speeding, streaming, turning, walking **2** aggressive, agile, animated, daring, dashing, determined, dynamic, forceful, industrious, intense, inventive, jumping, keen, lively, perky, pushing, resolute, sharp

activity *noun.* act, avocation, bit, deed, enterprise, entertainment, hobby, interest, labor, occupation, pastime, project, scene, scheme, stunt, trip, undertaking, works

actor *noun.* amateur, artist, barnstormer, character, clown, comedian, entertainer, extra, foil, ham, idol, lead, performer, player, stand-in, star, thespian, villain

actual *adjective.* absolute, authentic, categorical, certain, concrete, confirmed, hard, kosher, physical, positive, realistic, substantial, substantive, tangible, true, truthful, undeniable, verified

acute *adjective.* **1** astute, canny, clever, discerning, discriminating, incisive, ingenious, intense, intuitive, judicious, keen, observant, penetrating, piercing, sensitive, sharp, smart, subtle **2** cutting, distressing, excruciating, exquisite, fierce, keen, overpowering, overwhelming, piercing, poignant, powerful, racking, severe, sharp, shooting, stabbing, sudden, violent

add *verb.* affix, annex, ante, augment, boost, build up, continue, hike, hook on, include, pad, pyramid, reply, snowball, speed up, spike, supplement, tag

addition *noun.* accretion, additive, adjunct, aggrandizement, annex, appendix, bells, bonus, boost, dividend, extra, gain, hike, raise, reinforcement, rise, supplement, wing

address *verb.* **1** approach, bespeak, call, deliver, discourse, discuss, give speech, greet, hail, lecture, memorialize, orate, pitch, pontificate, sermonize, spout, stump, talk **2** apply, concentrate, devote, dig, direct, give, go at, go for, hammer away, peg away, pitch into, plug, throw, to, try, turn, turn to, undertake

adequate *adjective.* able, acceptable, all right, capable, comfortable, commensurate, competent, decent, equal, fait, passable, requisite, satisfactory, sufficient, sufficing, suitable, tolerable, unexceptional

adequately *adverb.* abundantly, acceptably, appropriately, capably, competently, copiously, decently, enough, fairly well, fittingly, modestly, pleasantly enough, presentably, satisfactorily, sufficiently, suitably, tolerably, well enough

adjust *verb.* **1** accommodate, adapt, alter, arrange, compose, conform, dispose, fit, fix, modify, order, reconcile, redress, regulate, settle, suit, tailor, tune **2** accommodate, align, balance, connect, correct, fit, fix, focus, grind, improve, overhaul, polish, regulate, repair, service, set, sharpen, square **3** accord, allocate, arrange, clarify, conclude, conform, coordinate, doctor, fiddle with, fine tune, grade, modify, organize, reconcile, regulate, settle, sort, straighten

adjustment *noun.* alteration, arrangement, balancing, conformance, fitting, fixing, mending, ordering, organization, organizing, orientation, readjustment, redress, regulating, regulation, repairing, setting, turning

administration *noun.* **1** authority, directing, direction, dispensation, distribution, enforcement, execution, governing, government, guidance, jurisdiction, legislation, order, oversight, policy, power, regulation, rule **2** advisers, chairman, commander, consulate, department, embassy, executives, feds, general, headquarters, legislature, management, officers, president, stewards, superintendents, supervisors, upstairs

administrative *adjective.* central, controlling, deciding, decisive, directing, governing, governmental, jurisdictional, legislative, management, managerial, managing, official, presiding, regulatory, ruling, supervising, supervisory

administrator *noun.* authority, captain, chairman, commander, consul, dean, exec, governor, head, inspector, leader, minister, official, overseer, premier, president, producer, supervisor

admirable *adjective.* attractive, cool, crack, dream, exquisite, fine, good, great, greatest, heavy, keen, meritorious, rare, smashing, solid, valuable, wonderful, worthy

admiration *noun.* affection, approval, deference, delight, esteem, estimation, favor, fondness, glorification, idolatry, liking, love, pleasure, praise, recognition, regard, wonder, worship

admire *verb.* adore, applaud, appreciate, approve, cherish, commend, credit, esteem, glorify, hail, honor, idolize, praise, prize, revere, treasure, value, worship

admissible *adjective.* acceptable, applicable, appropriate, fair, fitting, justifiable, legal, logical, okay, permissible, pertinent, possible, rational, reasonable, relevant, suitable, tolerable, worthy

admission *noun.* accession, acknowledgment, admittance, affirmation, allowance, assent, assertion, averment, concession, confirmation, declaration, deposition, disclosure, profession, revelation, statement, testimonial, testimony

admit *verb.* **1** accept, bless, buy, concede, enter, entertain, grant, harbor, house, initiate, introduce, let, lodge, permit, receive, sign, suffer, take **2** accord, agree, bare, concede, confide, declare, disclose, expose, let, own, permit, proclaim, recite, recognize, relate, spill, tell, yield

adopt *verb.* accept, affirm, appropriate, approve, assent, assume, embrace, endorse, follow, imitate, maintain, ratify, seize, select, support, tap, use, utilize

adoption *noun.* acceptance, approbation, appropriation, approval, assumption, choice, confirmation, embracement, embracing, enactment, endorsement, espousal, following, maintenance, ratification, selection, support, taking on

advance *noun.* **1** advancement, betterment, boost, break, breakthrough, buildup, development, enrichment, gain, growth, increase, progress, promotion, rise, step, up, upgrade, upping **2** accommodation, allowance, credit, deposit, down payment, floater, grubstake, hike, increase, jawbone, loan, prepayment, rise, score, scratch, stake, take, touch

advance *verb.* **1** accelerate, achieve, conquer, cream, dispatch, drive, gain ground, go ahead, hasten, launch, march, proceed, progress, promote, propel, quicken, speed, storm **2** allege, ballyhoo, benefit, boost, cite, encourage, foster, further, introduce, offer, propose, puff, push, serve, spot, submit, suggest, thump **3** boost, develop, elevate, enlarge, get fat, grade, grow, improve, multiply, pan out, prefer, prosper, raise, strike gold, thrive, up, upgrade, uplift

advanced *adjective.* avant-garde, break, breakthrough, excellent, exceptional, extreme, first, foremost, forward, higher, late, leading, liberal, old, precocious, progressive, radical, unconventional

advantage *noun.* aid, asset, break, eminence, favor, gain, gratification, interest, lead, leeway, leverage, power, prestige, prevalence, resources, superiority, supremacy, wealth

adventure *noun.* chance, contingency, emprise, enterprise, experience, exploit, feat, happening, hazard, incident, jeopardy, occurrence, peril, scene, speculation, trip, undertaking, venture

adverse *adjective.* conflicting, contrary, detrimental, inimical, injurious, inopportune, negative, opposed, opposing, opposite, ornery, reluctant, repugnant, stuffy, unfortunate, unfriendly, unlucky, unwilling

advertising *noun.* announcing, ballyhoo, blasting, broadcasting, buildup, displaying, exhibiting, exhibition, exposition, hoopla, pitch, plug, proclamation, promoting, promotion, publicity, puff, spread

advice *noun.* admonition, advisement, aid, caution, consultation, input, judgment, lesson, opinion, persuasion, proposal, proposition, steer, suggestion, teaching, tip, view, word

advise *verb.* **1** advocate, caution, commend, counsel, direct, encourage, enjoin, guide, instruct, move, prepare, prescribe, prompt, recommend, steer, suggest, tout, warn **2** acquaint, apprise, break in, clue, clue in, fill in, inform, make known, notify, post, report, show, tell, tip, tip off, update, warn

advocate *noun.* apostle, attorney, backer, campaigner, champion, counsel, defender, exponent, expounder, lawyer, pleader, promoter, proponent, proposer, speaker, spokesman, supporter, upholder

advocate *verb.* advance, advise, bolster, boost, build up, champion, countenance, encourage, favor, further, promote, propose, push, recommend, support, tout, uphold, vindicate

affair *noun.* **1** activity, assignment, avocation, duty, employment, episode, event, happening, interest, obligation, occupation, profession, province, pursuit, responsibility, subject, topic, transaction **2** affaire, amour, carrying on, extracurricular activity, fling, goings-on, hanky-panky, intimacy, intrigue, liaison, love, matinee, playing around, relationship, rendezvous, romance, thing together, two-timing

affect *verb.* affect, alter, change, disturb, impinge, impress, induce, influence, interest, modify, move, overcome, regard, relate, stir, touch, transform, upset

affected *adjective.* **1** afflicted, changed, compassionate, concerned, distressed, excited, hurt, impressed, influenced, injured, overwhelmed, sorry, stimulated, stirred, tender, touched, troubled, upset

affected *adjective.* **2** artificial, awkward, faked, false, feigned, hollow, imitated, insincere, melodramatic, overdone, pedantic, pompous, precious, sham, stiff, stilted, superficial, unnatural

affection *noun.* case, closeness, crush, desire, emotion, friendliness, friendship, good will, inclination, itch, liking, love, mash, passion, regard, shine, tenderness, weakness

affirm *verb.* assert, certify, cinch, clinch, confirm, declare, ice, insist, lock up, maintain, okay, pronounce, ratify, repeat, set, state, swear, testify

afraid *adjective.* aghast, alarmed, anxious, aroused, daunted, discouraged, dismayed, distressed, disturbed, frightened, horrified, perturbed, shocked, startled, stunned, suspicious, terrified, upset

age *noun.* adolescence, adulthood, boyhood, childhood, dotage, elderliness, girlhood, infancy, life, lifetime, majority, maturity, middle age, milestone, old age, senility, seniority, youth

aged *adjective.* ancient, antiquated, antique, been around, creaky, elderly, getting on, gone, gray, hag, hairy, oldie, relic, rusty, shot, timeworn, venerable, worn

agency *noun.* action, activity, auspices, channel, efficiency, force, influence, instrument, instrumentality, intervention, means, mechanism, mediation, medium, operation, organ, vehicle, work

agent *noun.* ambassador, assignee, assistant, attorney, commissioner, delegate, deputy, emissary, executor, factor, lawyer, minister, operator, proctor, proxy, salesman, substitute, worker

aggregate *noun.* agglomerate, agglomeration, all, assemblage, body, bulk, combination, gross, heap, lump, mass, mixture, pile, quantity, sum, total, whole, works

aggressive *adjective.* **1** advancing, assailing, attacking, barbaric, bellicose, destructive, disruptive, disturbing, encroaching, hawkish, hostile, intruding, intrusive, invading, offensive, quarrelsome, threatening, warlike **2** bold, brassy, cocky, domineering, dynamic, energetic, enterprising, flip, forceful, fresh, imperious, masterful, militant, pushing, sassy, smart, strenuous, take-charge

agree *verb.* **1** acknowledge, acquiesce, admit, buy, check, clinch, comply, concede, concur, engage, grant, okay, permit, recognize, set, sign, subscribe, yes **2** accord, answer, blend, click, cohere, coincide, concert, concord, concur, conform, consort, correspond, equal, fit, match, parallel, square, synchronize

agreeable *adjective.* acceptable, dandy, delicious, delightful, enjoyable, fair, fine, gratifying, mild, nice, peach, pleasant, pleasurable, pleasureful, ready, spiffy, swell, welcome

agreement *noun.* **1** accommodation, accord, acknowledging, affiliation, alliance, authorizing, bargaining, compliance, complying, compromise, concession, concord, concordance, endorsing, reconciliation, similarity, union, unison **2** arrangement, bargain, bond, charter, compact, compromise, confirmation, covenant, indenture, lease, negotiation, nod, okay, pact, protocol, stipulation, transaction, writ

ahead *adverb.* advanced, ahead, along, ante, before, beforehand, earlier, first, fore, forward, leading, on, onward, onwards, precedent, preceding, previous, progressing

aid *noun.* advancement, advocacy, allowance, assist, backing, benefit, charity, cooperation, deliverance, favor, gift, leg, lift, reinforcement, relief, service, sustenance, treatment

aid *verb.* abet, alleviate, assist, bail out, befriend, encourage, favor, go with, help lighten, mitigate, promote, relieve, serve, straighten out, subsidize, support, sustain

aide *noun.* abettor, adjutant, aid, aide-de-camp, assistant, attendant, coadjutant, coadjutor, deputy, girl Friday, helper, lieutenant, man Friday, second, shop, stooge, supporter, troops

aim *noun.* ambition, aspiration, course, desideratum, design, desire, direction, end, intent, intention, mark, object, objective, plan, purpose, scheme, target, wish

aim *verb.* address, aspire, attempt, cast, covet, direct, fix, focus, level, plan, propose, purpose, slant, steer, target, train, want, wish

air *noun.* address, affectation, appearance, atmosphere, bearing, comportment, feel, flavor, impression, look, manner, mannerism, mood, pose, presence, property, quality, tone

air *verb.* broadcast, circulate, communicate, declare, disclose, display, exhibit, expose, proclaim, publish, put, reveal, speak, state, tell, utter, ventilate, voice

alarm *noun.* **1** anxiety, apprehension, consternation, dismay, distress, dread, fear, fright, horror, nervousness, panic, scare, strain, stress, tension, terror, unease, uneasiness **2** alert, bell, blast, call, caution, drum, flash, horn, nod, scramble, scream, shout, sign, siren, squeal, tip, tip off, trumpet

alcohol *noun.* booze, canned heat, cocktail, drink, ethanol, hard stuff, hootch, liquor, methanol, oil, palliative, red-eye, rotgut, sauce, smoke, spirits, tipple, toddy

alert *adjective.* active, bright, cagey, careful, circumspect, hip, intelligent, lively, looking, observant, perceptive, ready, sharp, spirited, vigilant, wary, wired, wise

alibi *noun.* account, affirmation, answer, assertion, assurance, case, cover, declaration, plea, pretext, profession, proof, reason, reply, retort, stall, statement, vindication

alien *noun.* face, floater, foreigner, guest, immigrant, incomer, interloper, intruder, invader, migrant, newcomer, outsider, refugee, settler, squatter, stranger, visitor, weed

alike *adjective.* allied, analogous, approximate, cognate, comparable, concurrent, double, duplicate, facsimile, identical, indistinguishable, kindred, like, matched, matching, parallel, related, similar

alive *adjective.* **1** animate, around, awake, breathing, conscious, dynamic, existing, extant, functioning, growing, knowing, living, mortal, operative, running, subsisting, viable, vital, working **2** active, alert, animated, awake, bustling, cheerful, dynamic, eager, energetic, lively, overflowing, ready, replete, sharp, spirited, sprightly, spry, stirring, teeming, vital, vivacious, zestful

all *noun.* accumulation, aggregate, aggregation, collection, ensemble, entirety, everything, gross, group, integer, mass, quantity, sum, total, unit, utmost, whole, works

alliance *noun.* accord, bond, coherence, collaboration, collusion, combination, communion, compact, concord, confederacy, cooperation, friendship, marriage, matrimony, membership, pact, partnership, relation

allied *adjective.* akin, amalgamated, associated, bound, cognate, combined, confederate, connected, friendly, incident, joined, joint, kindred, linked, married, related, unified, wed

allotment *noun.* allocation, allowance, apportionment, appropriation, bite, chunk, cut, end, grant, lot, part, piece, quota, ration, share, slice, split, stint

allow *verb.* accord, admit, approve, authorize, bear, brook, certify, commission, endorse, favor, let, oblige, pass, recognize, stand, support, tolerate, yes

allowance *noun.* aid, alimony, apportionment, bite, contribution, drag, gift, grant, inheritance, interest, legacy, pay, piece, prize, quota, scholarship, slice, wage

almost *adverb.* about, about to, all but, approximately, around, close to, close upon, essentially, just about, most, much, nigh, practically, pretty near, relatively, roughly, substantially, virtually

alone *adjective.* abandoned, apart, deserted, detached, forlorn, forsaken, individual, isolated, lone, lonely, only, sole, solitary, stag, unattached, unattended, unmarried, widowed

also *adverb.* additionally, again, along, along with, and, besides, conjointly, further, furthermore, including, likewise, more, moreover, plus, still, to boot, together with, too

alter *verb.* adapt, adjust, amend, change, convert, cook, develop, doctor, metamorphose, modify, reconstruct, refashion, reform, revise, shift, transform, turn, vary

altered *adjective.* adapted, adjusted, converted, cooked, corrected, diversified, fitted, fixed, modified, qualified, reformed, remodeled, renovated, reshaped, revised, spiked, turned, updated

alternate *verb.* alter, change, exchange, fluctuate, follow, interchange, intersperse, oscillate, relieve, rotate, seesaw, shift, shilly-shally, substitute, sway, vary, waver, yo-yo

amateur *noun.* am, apprentice, aspirant, beginner, bush, dabbler, dilettante, greenhorn, ham, hopeful, jackleg, layman, learner, nonprofessional, novice, probationer, putterer, recruit

ambiguity *noun.* double entendre, double meaning, doubt, doubtfulness, dubiousness, enigma, equivocacy, equivocality, equivocation, inconclusiveness, indefiniteness, indeterminateness, obscurity, puzzle, tergiversation, uncertainty, unclearness, vagueness

ambiguous *adjective.* cryptic, doubtful, dubious, enigmatic, equivocal, inconclusive, indefinite, indeterminate, inexplicit, obscure, opaque, puzzling, questionable, tenebrous, uncertain, unclear, unintelligible, vague

ambition *noun.* aspiration, craving, desire, drive, eagerness, earnestness, energy, enthusiasm, hope, itch, longing, love, passion, push, spirit, striving, vigor, zeal

ambitious *adjective.* **1** aggressive, anxious, aspiring, avid, climbing, designing, desirous, determined, driving, earnest, energetic, industrious, intent, pushing, resourceful, sharp, thirsty, vaulting **2** arduous, bold, challenging, demanding, difficult, elaborate, energetic, exacting, formidable, grandiose, hard, impressive, industrious, lofty, pretentious, severe, strenuous, visionary

ammunition *noun.* armament, ball, bomb, buckshot, bullet, cannonball, chemical, explosive, fuse, grenade, materiel, missile, rocket, round, shell, shot, shrapnel, torpedo

amount *noun.* **1** bulk, bundle, chunk, extent, flock, gang, gob, heap, hunk, load, magnitude, mass, pack, pile, pot, raft, supply, ton **2** addition, aggregate, all, body, budget, cost, damage, entirety, expense, extent, lot, outlay, output, quantum, sum, tab, tune, whole

amount *verb.* aggregate, approach, approximate, become, correspond, effect, extend, grow, match, mean, number, purport, reach, rival, sum, tally, total, touch

ample *adjective.* abounding, enough, expansive, extensive, full, great, heavy, lavish, liberal, plentiful, plenty, profuse, rich, roomy, spare, substantial, unrestricted, wide

amusing *adjective.* agreeable, ball, camp, charming, cheering, delightful, enchanting, enjoyable, entertaining, fun, gas, hoot, humorous, interesting, lively, pleasing, priceless, scream

analytical *adjective.* analytic, conclusive, diagnostic, expository, judicious, logical, penetrating, perceptive, precise, rational, reasonably, solid, sound, studious, subtle, testing, thorough, valid

analyze *verb.* **1** assay, confab, consider, estimate, evaluate, figure, hash, inspect, interpret, investigate, judge, rehash, resolve, sort out, study, talk game, test, think through **2** anatomize, breakup, cut up, decompose, decompound, determine, disintegrate, dissect, dissolve, divide, electrolyze, hydrolyzed, lay bare, parse, part, resolve, separate, x-ray

ancestry *noun.* ancestor, antecedent, breed, breeding, derivation, extraction, forerunner, heritage, house, kindred, line, lineage, origin, parentage, pedigree, race, source, stock

anchor *noun.* ballast, bower, collar, defense, fastener, grapnel, grip, hold, hook, mainstay, mooring, pillar, protection, safeguard, security, staff, stay, support

ancient *adjective.* aged, antiquated, antique, archaic, bygone, creak, early, elderly, obsolete, older, outmoded, primal, primeval, relic, remote, rusty, timeworn, venerable

anecdote *noun.* chestnut, episode, fairy tale, fish story, gag, incident, narration, narrative, old chestnut, recital, relation, reminiscence, short story, sketch, tale, tall story, tall tale, yarn

anger *noun.* animosity, antagonism, blow up, displeasure, enmity, exasperation, hatred, huff, impatience, indignation, ire, irritation, passion, rage, stew, storm, temper, violence

anger *verb.* agitate, antagonize, arouse, bait, blow up, burn, chafe, cross, exasperate, goad, incense, infuriate, madden, offend, pique, provoke, stew, tempt

angle *noun.* corner, cusp, decline, divergence, dogleg, edge, elbow, flare, fork, incline, intersection, knee, notch, point, slant, turn, turning, twist

angry *adjective.* affronted, cross, enraged, exasperated, ferocious, fierce, fiery, heated, infuriated, irate, nettled, offended, raging, storming, tumultuous, turbulent, vexed, wrathful

anguish *noun.* affliction, agony, distress, dole, grief, heartache, heartbreak, hurting, misery, pang, rue, sorrow, suffering, throe, torment, torture, woe, wretchedness

angular *adjective.* akimbo, bifurcate, cornered, crooked, crossing, crotched, divaricate, forked, intersecting, jagged, oblique, sharp-cornered, skewed, slanted, staggered, V-shaped, Y-shaped, zigzag

animal *adjective.* beastly, bestial, bodily, brute, brutish, carnal, corporeal, earthly, earthy, feral, fleshly, mammalian, muscular, natural, physical, sensual, untamed, wild

animal *noun.* beast, being, bronco, brute, bum, cob roller, creature, critter, dink, invertebrate, living thing, mutt, nigh, pet, stray, varmint, vertebrate, wild thing

announce *verb.* advertise, blast, blazon, broadcast, call, declare, disclose, drum, impart, intimate, issue, proclaim, release, report, reveal, state, tell, trumpet

announcement *noun.* advertisement, advice, briefing, broadcast, broadcasting, bulletin, dissemination, exposing, expression, narration, notice, publication, publishing, recitation, report, reporting, revelation, statement

anonymous *adjective.* bearding, incog, incognito, innominate, nameless, pseudo, pseudonymous, secret, unacknowledged, unavowed, unclaimed, uncredited, undesignated, undisclosed, unidentified, unnamed, unsigned, unspecified

answer *noun.* cooler, crack, defense, echo, elucidation, feedback, interpretation, key, plea, remark, report, resolution, result, retort, sign, solution, statement, vindication

answer *verb.* **1** acknowledge, argue, claim, deny, disprove, dispute, feedback, parry, plead, react, rebut, refute, rejoin, remark, resolve, retort, solve, top **2** conform, correlate, correspond, crack, do, dope, fill, fit, fulfill, lick, meet, pass, qualify, satisfy, serve, suffice, suit, work

antagonism *noun.* animosity, antipathy, antithesis, competition, conflict, contention, difference, disagreement, discord, dissension, enmity, friction, hatred, hostility, incongruity, rancor, resistance, rivalry

anticipate *verb.* ahead, assume, await, beyond, conjecture, divine, figure, forecast, foresee, foretell, look for, plan on, predict, see, suppose, to, visualize, wait

anticipation *noun.* apprehension, awaiting, contemplation, expectancy, foresight, foretaste, high hopes, hope, impatience, joy, outlook, preconception, premonition, preoccupation, prescience, promise, prospect, trust

anxiety *noun.* angst, creeps, disquiet, disquietude, drag, fear, fuss, jitters, jumps, misery, mistrust, needles, restlessness, shakes, suffering, suspense, sweat, trouble, uneasiness

anxious *adjective.* aghast, bugged, careful, clutched, concerned, distressed, disturbed, jittery, jumpy, restless, shaking, shaky, shivery, solicitous, troubled, unglued, wired, wrecked

apart *adverb.* aloof, aside, away, cut off, disconnected, distinct, divorced, excluded, exclusively, freely, independent, independently, individually, isolated, separated, separately, singly, special

apartment *noun.* accommodation, box, camp, cave, compartment, coop, cooperative, cubbyhole, dump, flat, flop, heap, lodging, pad, penthouse, rental, suite, turf

aperture *noun.* breach, break, chasm, cleft, crack, cut, eye, gap, gash, opening, outlet, passage, rift, rupture, slash, slot, space, vent

appalling *adjective.* astounding, bad, dire, disheartening, dreadful, formidable, frightening, frightful, ghastly, grim, gross, heavy, hideous, horrid, scaring, shocking, terrible, unnerving

apparatus *noun.* appliance, furnishings, gear, implement, jigger, machine, machinery, means, mechanism, outfit, paraphernalia, provisions, stuff, sucker, supplies, tackle, tools, utensils

apparent *adjective.* clear, conspicuous, discernible, distinct, evident, indubitable, manifest, marked, noticeable, observable, open, palpable, plain, transparent, unambiguous, understandable, unmistakable, visible

appeal *noun.* address, application, bid, call, claim, demand, invocation, overture, petition, plea, prayer, proposal, proposition, question, recourse, requisition, submission, suit

appeal *verb.* address, advance, ask, beg, beseech, bid, claim, crave, implore, plead, pray, propose, proposition, refer, require, solicit, strike, submit

appear *verb.* arise, arrive, attend, break through, check in, come, develop, emerge, expose, issue, materialize, occur, recur, rise, show, spring, surface, turn out

appearance *noun.* **1** actualization, advent, appearing, arrival, coming, debut, display, emergence, entrance, exhibition, introduction, manifestation, materialization, presence, presentation, representation, rise, unveiling **2** bearing, cast, character, dress, expression, fashion, feature, figure, form, front, mannerism, mode, outline, pose, presence, presentation, shape, stamp **3** aura, blind, countenance, dream, exterior, front, guise, idea, illusion, image, impression, likeness, look, mien, phenomenon, reflection, screen, seeming, semblance, sound, specter, vision

appetite *noun.* craving, demand, fondness, greed, inclination, itch, liking, longing, lust, passion, penchant, relish, stomach, taste, weakness, yen, zeal, zest

applause *noun.* acclaim, acclamation, accolade, approval, big hand, cheering, cheers, commendation, eulogizing, hand, hurrahs, laudation, mitt pound, ovation, plaudit(s), praise, rooting, round

applicable *adjective.* apposite, apropos, apt, associable, befitting, felicitous, fit, fitting, germane, kosher, legit, material, pertinent, relevant, usable, suitable, suited, useful

apply *verb.* address, bear down, commit, concentrate, devote, dig, direct, give, grind, hustle, persevere, plug, scratch, study, sweat, throw, try, turn

appointment *noun.* allotment, approval, assigning, authorization, certification, choice, choosing, delegation, deputation, designation, election, empowering, installation, naming, nomination, ordination, promotion, selection

appreciate *verb.* admire, adore, applaud, apprize, cherish, enjoy, esteem, extol, honor, like, love, praise, prize, regard, relish, respect, savor, treasure

appreciation *noun.* affection, appraisal, attraction, awareness, cognizance, commendation, comprehension, esteem, estimation, grasp, liking, love, perception, realization, regard, relish, sensibility, sensitivity

apprentice *noun.* amateur, beginner, boot, freshie, freshman, heel, newbie, newcomer, novice, novitiate, probationer, pupil, rook, rookie, starter, student, tenderfoot, tyro

approach *noun.* concept, course, crack, fling, idea, lick, manner, means, method, mode, offer, procedure, program, shot, technique, way, whack, wrinkle

approach *verb.* **1** advance, approximate, bear, border, buzz, catch up, come, contact, converge, equal, match, meet, near, progress, reach, resemble, surround, threaten **2** accost, address, advise, beseech, broad, confer, consult, entreat, feel, greet, implore, plead, propose, speak to, take aside, talk to, thumb, tumble

appropriate *adjective.* adapted, applicable, apropos, apt, becoming, correct, deserved, desired, due, fit, fitting, good, pertinent, proper, relevant, rightful, true, useful

appropriate *verb.* annex, borrow, clap, cop, embezzle, filch, grab, hijack, liberate, lift, pocket, secure, snatch, snitch, swipe, take over, usurp

approval *noun.* **1** acquiescence, assent, bells, blessing, compliance, concurrence, confirmation, countenance, endorsement, leave, license, mandate, ok, permission, ratification, sanction, support, validation **2** acclaim, admiration, applause, appreciation, approbation, commendation, commercial, esteem, favor, liking, praise, puff, pumping up, regard, respect, strokes, stroking, wow

approve *verb.* **1** accept, acclaim, admire, applaud, appreciate, commend, cope, countenance, esteem, face it, favor, handle, like, live with, praise, regard highly, respect, stomach **2** acquiesce, agree, authorize, boost, buy, charter, dig, encourage, endorse, establish, permit, pronounce, ratify, recommend, second, sign, support, uphold

approximately *adverb.* about, almost, around, circa, close to, closely, comparatively, generally, just about, loosely, most, much, not quite, proximately, relatively, roughly, upwards of, very close

apt *adjective.* **1** applicable, apposite, appropriate, apropos, befitting, correct, felicitous, fit, fitting, germane, happy, just, pertinent, proper, relevant, seemly, suitable, timely **2** able, adept, astute, bright, clever, expert, gifted, ingenious, intelligent, prompt, ready, savvy, sharp, skilled, skillful, smart, talented, teachable

arbitrary *adjective.* **1** approximate, capricious, discretionary, erratic, frivolous, inconsistent, irrational, irresponsible, offhand, optional, random, subjective, superficial, unaccountable, unreasonable, wayward, whimsical, willful **2** absolute, autocratic, bossy, despotic, dogmatic, domineering, downright, flat out, high-handed, imperious, magisterial, monocratic, overbearing, peremptory, straight out, summary, tyrannical, tyrannous

arch *adjective.* accomplished, champion, chief, consummate, expert, finished, first, greatest, head, highest, leading, main, major, master, premier, primary, superior, top

ardent *adjective.* avid, blazing, burning, desirous, eager, fervent, fierce, fiery, impassioned, intense, keen, lusty, passionate, spirited, thirsty, vehement, warm, zealous

area *noun.* county, division, field, locality, neighborhood, patch, precinct, quarter, sector, sphere, square, state, stretch, territory, tract, turf, ward, zone

argue *verb.* **1** battle, buck, contend, cross, disagree, dispute, feud, hammer, hammer away, hash, jump, jump on, knock around, quarrel, quibble, rehash, row, squabble **2** appeal, assert, claim, contend, demonstrate, display, establish, exhibit, explain, hold, imply, indicate, maintain, plead, reason, show, testify, vindicate

argument *noun.* **1** altercation, beef, bickering, bone, brawl, brush, debate, donnybrook, fuss, knockdown, out, quarrel, row, ruckus, scrap, spat, static, stew **2** argumentation, assertion, case, claim, contention, debate, defense, discussion, grounds, logic, plea, pleading, polemic, presentation, proof, questioning, reason, reasoning

arise *verb.* appear, begin, commence, derive, emerge, flow, follow, happen, head, issue, occur, originate, proceed, result, rise, spring, start, stem

arm *noun.* affiliation, annex, authority, block, branch, command, department, detachment, division, ell, extension, force, offshoot, power, projection, section, sector, wing

arm *verb.* appoint, array, deck, equalize, furnish, gear, gird, guard, heel, issue, load, outfit, pack, prepare, prime, protect, rig, supply

army *noun.* **1** battalion, battery, brigade, column, command, company, corps, division, formation, infantry, legion, men, outfit, platoon, soldiery, squad, troops, wing **2** array, cloud, company, crowd, division, flock, horde, host, legion, mob, multitude, outfit, pack, regiment, scores, swarm, throng, unit

arrange *verb.* **1** align, array, class, classify, dispose, file, form, group, line up, organize, police, position, range, rank, regulate, sort, spruce, tidy **2** adjust, chart, compromise, construct, contrive, devise, direct, establish, lay out, line up, manage, project, promote, resolve, schedule, scheme, tailor, work out

arrangement *noun.* **1** adjustment, agreement, compact, compromise, deal, frame-up, game plan, layout, organization, package, pecking order, plan, preparation, provision, schedule, settlement, setup, terms **2** alignment, array, classification, combination, composition, design, display, disposition, distribution, form, grouping, lineup, method, ordering, organization, ranging, sequence, system

array *noun.* arrangement, body, bunch, bundle, cluster, design, display, disposition, exhibition, formation, host, lineup, multitude, order, parade, show, supply, throng

array *verb.* attire, bedeck, clothe, deck, decorate, drape, dud, dude up, fit, garb, outfit, rag out, rag up, rig out, rig up, try on, turn out, wrap

arrest *noun.* **1** bust, captivity, capture, collar, commitment, constraint, detention, flop, jam, nail, nick, pick up, pickle, pull, restraining, rumble, snare, sweep **2** cessation, check, checking, delay, end, halt, inhibition, interruption, obstruction, prevention, restraining, restraint, stalling, stay, staying, stoppage, suppression, suspension

arrest *verb.* **1** apprehend, brace, bust, capture, collar, detain, jail, kick, nail, net, nick, pick up, pull, round up, secure, seize, snag, tag **2** can, check, delay, drop, end, freeze, halt, interrupt, obstruct, prevent, restrain, restrict, retard, scrub, shut down, stall, stay, suppress

arrival *noun.* **1** accession, advent, alighting, appearance, approach, arriving, debarkation, disembarkation, dismounting, entrance, happening, homecoming, influx, ingress, landing, meeting, occurrence, return **2** addition, caller, cargo, comer, delegate, delivery, entrant, freight, guest, mail, newcomer, parcel, passenger, representative, shipment, tourist, traveler, visitor

arrive *verb.* access, alight, appear, attain, bust in, buzz, check in, enter, get to, hit, land, pull in, reach, report, show, take place, turn up, visit

art *noun.* adroitness, aptitude, artistry, craft, craftsmanship, creativity, dexterity, expertise, facility, imagination, ingenuity, knack, knowledge, mastery, method, profession, trade, virtuosity

artery *noun.* avenue, boulevard, canal, conduit, corridor, course, duct, highway, line, passage, pathway, road, route, sewer, thoroughfare, track, tube, way

article *noun.* beat, column, commentary, composition, discourse, editorial, essay, exposition, feature, item, paper, piece, scoop, spread, story, theme, treatise, write-up

artificial *adjective.* bogus, counterfeit, ersatz, fabricated, faked, false, manufactured, mock, phony, plastic, queer, sham, simulated, specious, spurious, substitute, synthetic, unnatural

artistic *adjective.* aesthetic, creative, cultured, decorative, dramatic, elegant, exquisite, fine, grand, harmonious, musi-

cal, picturesque, pleasing, refined, rhythmical, satisfying, sublime, tasteful
ashamed *adjective.* apologetic, bashful, blushing, crestfallen, distraught, distressed, embarrassed, flustered, guilty, humiliated, meek, reluctant, repentant, shamed, shy, sorry, stammering, submissive
ask *verb.* **1** canvass, catechize, challenge, demand, direct, enjoin, examine, grill, hit, inquire, investigate, needle, pump, quiz, request, roast, strike, sweat **2** appeal, apply, beg, beseech, bite, claim, crave, hit, hustle, implore, knock, order, plead, pray, promote, request, solicit, touch
asleep *adjective.* conked, crashed, dead, dormant, dozing, dreaming, hibernating, in repose, inactive, inert, napping, out, reposing, resting, sleeping, snoozing, snoring, somnolent
aspect *noun.* angle, bearing, direction, facet, feature, outlook, perspective, phase, position, prospect, regard, scene, side, situation, slant, twist, view, vista
assault *verb.* abuse, advance, assail, beset, blast, blitz, charge, invade, jump, light into, rape, ruin, slam, storm, strike, trash, violate, zap
assemble *verb.* **1** accumulate, agglomerate, amass, bunch, call, capture, collect, flock, group, huddle, lump, meet, muster, punch, rally, round up, summon, unite **2** compile, connect, construct, contrive, erect, fabricate, fashion, fit, form, join, make, model, mold, produce, set up, shape, unite, weld
assembly *noun.* **1** aggregation, association, band, body, collection, company, conference, council, faction, flock, group, huddle, mass, meet, multitude, rally, throng, turnout **2** adjustment, attachment, building, collection, connecting, construction, erection, fabrication, fitting together, joining, manufacture, manufacturing, modeling, molding, piecing together, setting up, shaping, welding
assert *verb.* advance, affirm, allege, argue, claim, contend, declare, maintain, press, proclaim, pronounce, protest, say, state, stress, swear, uphold, vindicate
assertion *noun.* affirmation, allegation, asseveration, attestation, avowal, contention, defense, insistence, maintenance, mouthful, predication, profession, pronouncement, report, say so, statement, stressing, vindication
assign *verb.* **1** appoint, ascribe, attribute, authorize, cast, commit, delegate, designate, elect, enroll, entrust, hire, name, nominate, ordain, refer, reference, tag **2** allocate, allot, appoint, apportion, appropriate, consign, designate, detail, determine, distribute, divide, fix, give, grant, indicate, prescribe, specify, stipulate
assignment *noun.* allocation, allotment, appointment, apportionment, appropriation, assignation, authorization, choice, delegation, designation, determination, distribution, giving, grant, nomination, selection, specification, stipulation
assist *noun.* abetment, aid, assistance, backing, benefit, boost, collaboration, comfort, compensation, cooperation, furtherance, hand, helping hand, lift, reinforcement, relief, service, support
assist *verb.* aid, back, ballyhoo, benefit, boost, collaborate, cooperate, facilitate, further, puff, push, reinforce, relieve, serve, stump, support, sustain, thump
assistance *noun.* abetment, aid, assist, backing, benefit, boost, collaboration, comfort, compensation, cooperation, hand, help, lift, reinforcement, relief, service, support, sustenance
assistant *noun.* accomplice, adherent, adjunct, apprentice, auxiliary, companion, confederate, deputy, follower, friend, help, helpmate, mate, partner, secretary, slave, subordinate, supporter
associate *noun.* accomplice, aid, assistant, auxiliary, buddy, companion, compatriot, comrade, confederate, consort, fellow, friend, helper, joiner, mate, pal, partner, playmate
associate *verb.* **1** blend, bracket, combine, concord, conjoin, connect, correlate, couple, group, identify, join, league, link, mix, pair, relate, unite, yoke **2** accompany, amalgamate, bunch up, confederate, consort, fraternize, gang up, go partners,

hang out, hobnob, join, mingle, mix, pool, run around, tie up, truck with, work with

association *noun.* **1** affiliation, alliance, circle, club, combination, confederacy, congress, cooperative, corporation, gang, guild, mob, order, partnership, ring, society, syndicate, troops **2** acquaintance, affiliation, agreement, assistance, camaraderie, companionship, comradeship, conjunction, cooperation, familiarity, fellowship, friendliness, hookup, intimacy, membership, partnership, relation, relationship **3** bond, combination, concordance, connotation, correlation, identification, impression, joining, juxtaposition, linkage, linking, mixing, mixture, recollection, relation, remembrance, tie, union

assume *verb.* **1** conclude, conjecture, consider, deduce, deem, divine, estimate, expect, find, hypothesize, imagine, postulate, presume, presuppose, speculate, suppose, think, understand **2** adopt, annex, appropriate, arrogate, borrow, commandeer, expropriate, grab, hijack, liberate, moonlight requisition, preempt, seize, snatch, swipe, take over, usurp

assumed *adjective.* accepted, conjectured, connoted, counted on, expected, given, granted, hypothesized, hypothetical, inferred, postulated, presumed, presupposed, supposed, suppositional, surmised, tacit, understood

assumption *noun.* acceptance, accepting, assuming, belief, conjecture, expectation, guess, hunch, hypothesis, inference, postulate, premise, presumption, presupposition, shot, surmise, suspicion, theory

assurance *noun.* **1** affirmation, assertion, declaration, guarantee, insurance, lock, oath, pledge, profession, promise, security, shoo-in, support, sure thing, vow, warrant, warranty, word **2** aggressiveness, arrogance, audacity, boldness, bravery, certainty, conviction, coolness, courage, faith, firmness, impudence, nerve, poise, presumption, security, temerity, trust

assured *adjective.* **1** clinched, confirmed, decided, definite, dependable, fixed, guaranteed, indubitable, insured, on ice, pronounced, racked, sealed, secure, set, settled, sure, unquestionable **2** assertive, bold, brazen, certain, collected, complacent, composed, confident, cool, high, imperturbable, overconfident, poised, positive, rosy, secure, sure, upbeat

athlete *noun.* amateur, challenger, competitor, contender, contestant, games player, iron man, jock, jockey, meathead, muscle man, player, professional, shoulders, sport, sportsman, sportswoman, superjock

atmosphere *noun.* character, climate, color, feel, feeling, flavor, impression, medium, mood, place, property, quality, scene, semblance, spirit, surroundings, taste, tone

atom *noun.* bit, crumb, fragment, grain, iota, jot, minimum, mite, molecule, morsel, ounce, particle, scrap, shred, speck, spot, trace, whit

attach *verb.* **1** add, adhere, affix, annex, bind, connect, couple, fasten, fix, hitch, hook, latch, link, rivet, secure, stick, tie, unite **2** allocate, allot, appoint, ascribe, assign, associate, connect, consign, designate, detail, impute, invest with, lay, name, place, put, second, send

attack *noun.* advance, aggression, assailing, blitz, encroachment, foray, intervention, invasion, offensive, onrush, onset, push, raid, rape, storming, strike, thrust, violation

attack *verb.* assail, bean, beat, beset, besiege, blast, blister, brain, bust, club, harm, jump, kick, punch, raid, storm, strike, wallop

attain *verb.* accomplish, acquire, arrive, cop, earn, gain, get, grasp, hit, obtain, procure, promote, reach, reap, secure, snag, succeed, win

attainment *noun.* accomplishment, acquirement, acquisition, arrival, completion, feat, finish, fulfillment, gaining, getting, obtaining, procurement, reaching, realization, reaping, securing, succeeding, winning

attempt *noun.* attack, bid, crack, exertion, experiment, fling, go, lick, pursuit, shot, stab, striving, struggle, trial, undertaking, venture, whack, workout

attend *verb.* **1** appear, be at, be present, be there, bob up, catch, check in, clock in, drop in, frequent, haunt, make it, punch in, ring in, show, time in, turn up, visit **2** catch, concentrate on, follow, hear, heed, listen, listen up, look after, mark, mind, note, notice, observe, pay heed, pick up, regard, see to, watch

attendance *noun.* assemblage, assembly, audience, box office, company, congregation, crowd, draw, gate, gathering, house, observers, onlookers, patrons, public, spectators, turnout, witnesses

attendant *noun.* aide, assistant, auxiliary, chaperon, companion, custodian, follower, guide, helper, maid, nurse, orderly, secretary, servant, stewardess, usher, valet, waiter

attention *noun.* absorption, application, assiduity, consideration, contemplation, debate, deliberation, diligence, heed, heedfulness, immersion, industry, mind, scrutiny, study, thinking, thought, thoughtfulness

attitude *noun.* bent, bias, character, inclination, leaning, opinion, perspective, philosophy, posture, prejudice, reaction, sensibility, slant, stance, stand, temper, twist, view

attorney *noun.* advocate, barrister, beagle, beak, counsel, counselor, fixer, front, legal beagle, legal eagle, mouthpiece, patch, pettifogger, pleader, proxy, shyster, spieler, squeal

attract *verb.* allure, bait, beckon, bring, court, drag, entrance, interest, invite, kill, lure, pull, send, solicit, steer, tempt, vamp, wow

attraction *noun.* allure, allurement, appeal, bait, chemistry, courting, endearment, fascination, gravitation, inclination, inducement, interest, invitation, lure, magnetism, pull, seduction, temptation

attractive *adjective.* agreeable, captivating, charming, comely, enchanting, enthralling, fetching, gorgeous, handsome, hunk, inviting, luring, pleasing, provocative, taking, tantalizing, teasing, winsome

audience *noun.* admirers, assembly, congregation, devotees, fans, following, hearers, house, listeners, market, onlookers, patrons, public, spectators, theatergoers, turnout, viewers, witnesses

august *adjective.* baronial, eminent, exalted, glorious, grand, grandiose, imposing, impressive, lofty, lordly, magnificent, majestic, monumental, pompous, regal, resplendent, superb, venerable

authentic *adjective.* actual, certain, convincing, credible, creditable, dependable, faithful, genuine, legitimate, official, original, pure, reliable, sure, true, trustworthy, valid, veritable

authoritative *adjective.* **1** attested, authentic, authenticated, confirmed, dependable, faithful, learned, proven, recognized, reliable, righteous, scholarly, sound, trustworthy, truthful, validated, verified, veritable **2** assertive, authoritarian, autocratic, commanding, confident, decisive, dictatorial, doctrinaire, dogmatic, dominating, imperative, imperious, imposing, masterly, officious, peremptory, powerhouse, self-assured **3** administrative, approved, authorized, bureaucratic, canonical, departmental, ex cathedra, executive, imperial, lawful, legal, legitimate, magisterial, mandatory, ruling, sanctioned, sovereign, supreme

authority *noun.* **1** ascendancy, authorization, beef, goods, government, guts, jump, jurisdiction, might, permission, permit, prerogative, prestige, punch, ropes, steam, supremacy, weight **2** arbiter, bible, brains, connoisseur, exec, expert, feds, governor, guru, law, pro, professor, specialist, textbook, upstairs, veteran, virtuoso, whiz

automatic *adjective.* habitual, impulsive, instinctive, instinctual, intuitive, involuntary, mechanical, natural, perfunctory, reflex, routine, spontaneous, unconscious, unforced, unintentional, unmeditated, unthinking, unwilled

automobile *noun.* bug, bus, coffin, compact, crate, heap, jalopy, lemon, limousine, ride, sedan, taxi, trans, truck, tub, vehicle, wheels, wreck

available *adjective.* accessible, applicable, at hand, convenient, feasible, free, gettable, handy, obtainable, on hand, open to, possible, prepared, purchasable, reachable, serviceable, usable, vacant

avenue *noun*. access, alley, approach, boulevard, channel, course, drive, entrance, entry, exit, outlet, parkway, passage, promenade, road, route, thoroughfare, way

average *adjective*. commonplace, everyday, fair, familiar, garden, general, mainstream, mediocre, medium, moderate, ordinary, passable, plastic, standard, tolerable, typical, usual, vanilla

avoid *verb*. abstain, avert, bypass, ditch, duck, escape, eschew, evade, flee, hide, jump, recoil, shake, shun, shy, skirt, weave, withdraw

avoidance *noun*. abstention, delay, departure, dodge, dodging, elusion, escape, evasion, flight, forbearance, parry, prevention, recession, recoil, restraint, retreat, shirking, shunning

award *noun*. accolade, adjudication, allotment, bestowal, citation, cookies, decoration, decree, distinction, donation, gift, gold, grant, order, presentation, scholarship, trophy, verdict

award *verb*. accord, allocate, allot, apportion, assign, bestow, concede, confer, decree, dish out, distribute, donate, endow, gift, grant, present, render, reward

aware *adjective*. acquainted, appraised, awake, conscious, cool, enlightened, grounded, hip, into, mindful, on to, perceptive, savvy, sensible, sentient, sharp, up on, wise

awareness *noun*. acquaintance, alertness, appreciation, apprehension, attention, cognizance, comprehension, consciousness, discernment, enlightenment, experience, familiarity, information, perception, realization, recognition, sensibility, understanding

away *adjective*. abroad, absent, elsewhere, far afield, far off, gone, lacking, missing, not here, not present, not there, omitted, out, out of, out-of-pocket, remote, wanting

away *adverb*. abroad, absent, afar, apart, aside, beyond, distant, elsewhere, far off, far remote, forth, from here, hence, not present, off, out of, over

awful *adjective*. appalling, bad, deplorable, depressing, dire, disgusting, dreadful, frightful, ghastly, gross, hideous, horrifying, offensive, repulsive, shocking, tough, unpleasant, unsightly

awkward *adjective*. **1** amateurish, artless, bulky, coarse, floundering, gawky, green, incompetent, inept, inexpert, lumbering, maladroit, rude, stiff, stumbling, unfit, ungainly, unskilled **2** annoying, bulky, chancy, cramped, cumbersome, dangerous, disagreeable, discommodious, hazardous, incommodious, inconvenient, perilous, risky, troublesome, uncomfortable, unhandy, unmanageable, unwieldy

B

baby *noun*. babe, bundle, button, chick, child, crawler, deduction, dividend, kid, little angel, newborn, nursling, papoose, snooky, sugar, tad, toddler, youngster

baby *verb*. cater to, cherish, coddle, cosset, cuddle, dandle, dote on, foster, humor, indulge, nurse, overindulge, pamper, pet, please, satisfy, serve, spoil

back *verb*. advocate, ally, angel, assist, boost, champion, countenance, encourage, endorse, favor, finance, sanction, second, stake, subsidize, sustain, underwrite, uphold

background *noun*. accomplishments, actions, atmosphere, backdrop, breeding, credentials, cultivation, culture, experience, framework, grounding, history, practice, preparation, rearing, tradition, training, upbringing

backing *noun*. accompaniment, adherence, advocacy, aegis, aid, assistance, auspices, championship, encouragement, endorsement, funds, grant, help, patronage, reinforcement, sanction, sponsorship, subsidy

backward *adjective.* afraid, demure, disinclined, hesitant, hesitating, humble, indisposed, late, loath, modest, reluctant, reserved, retiring, shy, sluggish, tardy, timid, unwilling

bad *adjective.* amiss, careless, cheap, deficient, dreadful, erroneous, garbage, gross, imperfect, incorrect, inferior, lousy, off, poor, rough, sad, unacceptable, unsatisfactory

badly *adverb.* awkwardly, carelessly, clumsily, crudely, erroneously, feeble, haphazardly, imperfectly, ineffectively, ineptly, maladroitly, poorly, stupidly, unfortunately, unsuccessfully, weakly, wrong, wrongly

bag *noun.* backpack, briefcase, case, duffel, gear, handbag, kit, pack, packet, pocket, pocketbook, poke, pouch, purse, sac, sack, suitcase, tote

balance *verb.* accord, adjust, cancel, compensate, correspond, counteract, counterbalance, equate, even, level, match, neutralize, parallel, redeem, set, square, stabilize, steady

band *noun.* **1** binding, bond, cable, chain, circle, circuit, cord, harness, hoop, line, link, ring, rope, sash, string, strip, tape, tie **2** assembly, association, bevy, body, bunch, clique, club, cluster, collection, company, corps, gang, horde, menagerie, outfit, society, troop, troupe

bang *noun.* **1** blast, burst, clang, clap, crack, detonation, discharge, howl, report, roar, roll, rumble, salvo, shot, slam, sound, thud, thunder **2** bash, bat, belt, blow, box, bump, collide, crack, cuff, knock, punch, slam, smack, smash, sock, stroke, wallop, whack

bank *noun.* **1** coffer, counting house, credit union, exchequer, fund, investment firm, repository, reserve, reservoir, safe, savings, stock, store, storehouse, thrift, treasury, trust company, vault **2** beach, cliff, coast, edge, embankment, lakefront, lakeside, ledge, levee, reef, riverside, sea bank, seaboard, seafront, shore, strand, streamside, waterfront

bank *verb.* amass, deposit, heap, hill, hoard, invest, lay aside, lay away, mass, mound, pile, put by, salt away, save, sock away, speculate, squirrel, stash

bankruptcy *noun.* default, destituteness, disaster, exhaustion, failure, indebtedness, indigence, insolvency, lack, liquidation, loss, nonpayment, overdraft, pauperism, privation, repudiation, ruin, ruination

bar *noun.* **1** batten, billet, boom, lever, paling, pig, pole, rail, rib, rule, shaft, slab, spoke, stake, stick, strip, stripe, stroke **2** barricade, block, clog, deterrent, fence, hurdle, impediment, obstacle, pale, rail, railing, restraint, road block, snag, stop, stumbling block, traverse, wall **3** attorneys, barristers, bench, counsel, counselors, court, courtroom, dock, judgment, judiciary, jurists, law, law court, law practice, lawyers, legal system, solicitors, tribunal **4** barricade, block, blockade, bolt, clog, close, dam, dike, fasten, fence, jam, latch, lock, plug, seal, secure, trammel, wall

bar *verb.* boycott, deny, discourage, eliminate, enjoin, except, exile, forbid, frustrate, interfere, limit, obstruct, override, preclude, prevent, refuse, segregate, stop

bare *adjective.* **1** arid, barren, blank, bleak, clear, desert, empty, lacking, mean, open, poor, scanty, scarce, stark, vacant, vacuous, void, wanting **2** austere, bald, basic, blunt, cold, essential, hard, literal, meager, mere, modest, scant, severe, sheer, simple, spare, stark, unadorned

bargain *verb.* agree, arrange, barter, buy, compromise, confer, contract, covenant, deal, dicker, haggle, palter, promise, sell, stipulate, trade, traffic, transact

barrier *noun.* bar, barricade, blockade, bound, boundary, curtain, ditch, enclosure, fence, gully, limit, obstacle, pale, railing, rampart, roadblock, trench, wall

base *adjective.* abject, cheap, coarse, contemptible, depraved, disgraceful, foul, immoral, indelicate, menial, offensive, pitiful, plebeian, poor, servile, sordid, sorry, unworthy

base *noun.* **1** basement, basis, bed, bottom, foot, footing, ground, groundwork, pedestal, rest, root, seat, seating, stand, substratum, substructure, support, underpinning **2** authority, backbone, basis, core, essence, essential, evidence, foundation, fundamental, groundwork, heart, key, origin, principal, principle, root, source, underpinning

basic *adjective.* capital, central, chief, elemental, essential, indispensable, inherent, intrinsic, key, main, necessary, primary, primitive, principal, radical, substratal, underlying, vital

basis *noun.* antecedent, axiom, backing, base, cause, core, crux, data, essence, essential, footing, fundamental, keystone, law, nucleus, postulate, premise, reason, security, theory

bastard *adjective.* adulterated, baseborn, counterfeit, fake, false, fatherless, imperfect, inferior, irregular, misbegotten, mixed, natural, phony, sham, spurious, suppositious, unfathered, ungenuine

bat *verb.* bang, belt, bop, crack, hit, lob, loft, rap, slam, smack, sock, strike, swat, thump, thwack, wallop, whack, whop

battle *noun.* attack, barrage, brush, campaign, combat, conflict, contention, fighting, fray, havoc, onset, onslaught, scrimmage, skirmish, strife, struggle, war, warfare

bay *noun.* anchorage, arm, back harbor, basin, bayou, bight, cove, estuary, fiord, gulf, harbor, inlet, lagoon, loch, mouth, narrows, sound, strait

be *verb.* abide, act, breathe, continue, do, endure, hold, inhabit, last, move, obtain, persist, remain, rest, stand, stay, subsist, survive

beam *noun.* **1** axle, bail, bolster, brace, column, lath, pile, pillar, plank, post, rafter, reach, scaffolding, sill, strip, strut, stud, trestle **2** bar, beacon, column, finger, flicker, glare, gleam, glimmer, glitter, glow, pencil, radiation, ray, shaft, shimmer, shoot, sparkle, stream

bearing *noun.* address, aspect, attitude, behavior, carriage, comportment, demeanor, display, front, look, manner, mien, poise, port, pose, presence, set, stand

beat *noun.* cadence, flow, flutter, pound, pressure, pulsation, pulse, quake, rhyme, rhythm, ripple, shake, surge, swell, swing, thump, tick, vibration

beat *verb.* **1** break, buffet, clout, club, crush, flail, flog, hammer, maltreat, mash, pound, punch, ram, slug, smack, strike, thwack, wallop **2** be victorious, best, better, conquer, exceed, excel, outdo, outrun, outstrip, overcome, overtake, overwhelm, subdue, surpass, top, transcend, triumph, whip **3** agitate, alternate, bounce, buffet, flicker, flutter, jerk, pitch, pound, pulse, quake, quaver, ripple, shake, shiver, thump, tremble, writhe

beaten *adjective.* baffled, bested, conquered, crushed, disappointed, frustrated, humbled, licked, mastered, overcome, overpowered, overwhelmed, routed, ruined, surmounted, thwarted, undone, worsted

beautiful *adjective.* admirable, appealing, beauteous, charming, comely, dazzling, delightful, divine, exquisite, fine, gorgeous, grand, handsome, magnificent, pleasing, splendid, superb, taking

beautifully *adverb.* appealingly, attractively, bewitching, charmingly, delightfully, divinely, elegantly, excellently, exquisitely, gorgeously, gracefully, handsomely, ideally, magnificently, prettily, splendidly, superbly, wonderfully

beauty *noun.* **1** allure, allurement, artistry, attraction, bloom, class, delicacy, elegance, exquisiteness, fairness, fascination, glamour, grace, loveliness, polish, refinement, style, symmetry **2** beaut, belle, charmer, dream, enchantress, eyeful, femme fatale, goddess, good-looker, knockout, looker, lovely, ornament, seductress, siren, stunner, Venus, vision

become *verb.* **1** alter to, be reformed, be remodeled, change into, come, convert, develop into, emerge as, grow into, incline, mature, metamorphose, pass into, ripen into, shift, turn into, turn out, wax **2** accord, adorn, agree, augment, belong to, display, enrich, fit, flatter, garnish, go with, grace, harmonize, heighten, make handsome, match, ornament, suit

becoming *adjective.* acceptable, agreeable, attractive, beautiful, comely, cute, effective, enhancing, excellent, fair, graceful, handsome, neat, nice, presentable, pretty, tasteful, welcome

beer *noun.* ale, amber brew, barley pop, barley sandwich, bock, brew, brown bottle, cold coffee, head, hops, lager, malt, malt liquor, oil, porter, slops, stout, suds

before *adverb.* aforetime, ahead, ante, back, ere, fore, former, formerly, forward, gone, gone by, heretofore, in advance, past, previous, previously, since, sooner

beg *verb.* **1** advocate, ask, beseech, besiege, canvass, conjure, crave, desire, entreat, implore, plead, pray, press, requisition, solicit, sue, urge, woo **2** bite, brace, burn, chisel, fish, grub, hit, hustle, knock, make, needle, nick, promote, score, starve, tap, touch, want

begin *verb.* **1** activate, cause, do, drive, establish, eventuate, found, generate, initiate, instigate, introduce, lead, motivate, mount, open, produce, trigger, undertake **2** appear, arise, bud, commence, dawn, emerge, enter, germinate, happen, kick off, occur, rise, sail, set, spring, sprout, start, take off

beginning *noun.* **1** birth, commencement, genesis, inauguration, infancy, introduction, kickoff, opening, origin, origination, outset, preface, prelude, presentation, rise, spring, takeoff, top **2** antecedent, birth, conception, egg, embryo, font, fountain, fountainhead, generation, genesis, germ, heart, principle, resource, root, seed, stem, well

behalf *noun.* account, advantage, aid, assistance, benefit, cause, countenance, defense, favor, good, help, place, representation, sake, service, stead, support, welfare

behavior *noun.* address, code, comportment, course, deed, delivery, expression, form, habits, mode, observance, practice, presence, propriety, speech, tact, tone, way

belief *noun.* **1** admission, axiom, conclusion, confidence, conjecture, divination, faith, hypothesis, idea, intuition, judgment, opinion, persuasion, profession, reliance, suspicion, theory, thesis **2** assumption, concept, credo, creed, doctrine, faith, fundamental, gospel, hypothesis, idea, ideology, law, opinion, postulate, precept, principle, theorem, theory

believe *verb.* **1** accept, admit, affirm, buy, conclude, consider, credit, deem, have, hold, postulate, presuppose, regard, suppose, swallow, think, trust, understand **2** conjecture, consider, deem, expect, feel, guess, hold, imagine, judge, maintain, postulate, presume, reckon, speculate, suppose, take, think, understand

belly *noun.* abdomen, bay window, beer belly, breadbasket, corporation, front porch, gut, insides, intestines, paunch, pelvis, pot, pot belly, solar plexus, spare tire, tank, tummy, venter

belong *verb.* accord, agree, apply, be fitting, bear, correlate, correspond, exist, fit, match, normally, permeate, refer, regard, reside, set, suit, touch

beloved *adjective.* darling, dear, dearest, endeared, esteemed, favorite, hallowed, idolized, pet, pleasing, popular, precious, prized, respected, revered, sweet, venerated, worshiped

beloved *noun.* baby, beau, darling, dear, dearest, doll, flame, honey, idol, love, lover, prize, steady, sugar, sweet, sweetheart, tootsie, treasure

bend *noun.* angle, arc, bending, bow, corner, crook, curvature, deviation, hook, lean, loop, round, sag, shift, tack, tilt, turn, twist

bend *verb.* arch, bow, buckle, circle, crouch, curl, double, droop, incline, lean, loop, tilt, turn, twist, veer, verge, warp, wilt

beneficial *adjective.* benign, constructive, favorable, favoring, gainful, good, healthful, helpful, profitable, propitious, salubrious, salutary, serviceable, toward, useful, valuable, wholesome, worthy

benefit *noun.* aid, asset, avail, benediction, betterment, blessing, boon, cream, extras, favor, gain, godsend, good, gravy, interest, use, welfare, worth

benefit *verb.* advance, advantage, aid, assist, avail, better, build, contribute to, favor, further, improve, pay, pay off, profit, promote, relieve, serve, succor

bent *adjective.* angled, arched, contorted, crooked, drooping, hooked, humped, hunched, inclined, limp, looped, round, sinuous, slumped, stooped, twined, twisted, warped

bent *noun.* ability, aptitude, bag, disposition, facility, flair, genius, gift, groove, head, knack, leaning, penchant, predisposition, preference, set, tilt, turn

beside *adverb.* adjacent to, adjoining, alongside, aside, by, close upon, contiguous to, near, nearby, neck-and-neck, neighboring, nigh, opposite, overlooking, round, verging on, with

besides *adverb.* additionally, along with, also, beyond, else, exceeding, extra, further, furthermore, likewise, more, moreover, otherwise, plus, secondly, together with, too, yet

best *adjective.* bad, champion, choicest, cool, crowing, culminating, finest, greatest, incomparable, leading, matchless, optimum, outstanding, premium, prime, principal, tough, transcendent

best *verb.* beat, better, blank, blast, bulldoze, deck, flax, floor, overcome, shut down, surpass, total, trash, triumph, wallop, waste, wax, wipe

bet *noun.* ante, betting, hazard, long shot, lot, lottery, odds, play, pledge, plunge, pot, risk, shot, speculation, stake, uncertainty, venture, wager

bet *verb.* ante, chance, dice, game, hazard, lay down, lay odds, play for, pledge, put, risk, set, speculate, tempt fortune, toss up, trust, venture, wager

better *adjective.* bigger, choice, exceeding, exceptional, finer, greater, higher quality, improved, larger, more appropriate, preferable, preferred, prominent, sharpened, sophisticated, souped up, superior, worthier

better *verb.* advance, beat, best, cap, correct, enhance, exceed, excel, forward, further, help, promote, raise, refine, reform, surpass, top, transcend

between *preposition.* amid, amidst, among, at intervals, bounded by, centrally located, enclosed by, halfway, in, inserted, interpolated, intervening, medially, mid, midway, separating, surrounded by, within

beyond *adverb.* above, after, ahead, apart from, away from, before, behind, besides, farther, free of, moreover, outside, over, over there, past, remote, without, yonder

bias *noun.* bent, bigotry, disposition, favoritism, flash, inclination, intolerance, leaning, penchant, predisposition, preference, prejudice, proneness, standpoint, tendency, tilt, turn, viewpoint

bid *noun.* advance, amount, declaration, feeler, hit, invitation, offer, pass, price, proffer, proposal, proposition, request, submission, suggestion, sum, summons, tender

big *adjective.* **1** awash, bulky, colossal, fat, full, hulking, immense, jumbo, mammoth, monster, oversize, packed, prodigious, roomy, sizable, stuffed, vast, whopping **2** consequential, considerable, eminent, influential, leading, main, meaningful, momentous, powerful, prime, principal, prominent, serious, significant, substantial, super, valuable, weighty

bill *noun.* advertisement, affiche, agenda, bulletin, card, catalogue, flyer, handbill, handout, inventory, leaflet, listing, notice, placard, poster, program, roster, schedule

biography *noun.* adventures, autobiography, bio, close up, confessions, diary, experiences, journal, letters, life, memoir, picture, profile, record, resume, saga, sketch, vita

birth *noun.* ancestry, breeding, derivation, descent, extraction, forebears, legacy, line, lineage, nobility, parentage, pedigree, position, race, station, status, stock, strain

bit *noun.* atom, butt, excerpt, flake, grain, iota, item, mite, sample, segment, shaving, slice, specimen, speck, splinter, sprinkling, trace, trickle

bite *verb.* **1** champ, chew, crunch, crush, cut, eat, gnaw, hold, lacerate, munch, nibble, pierce, pinch, rend, seize, snap, taste, tooth **2** burn, decay, decompose, deteriorate, dissolve, eat into, engrave, erode, etch, oxidize, rot, rust, scour, sear, slash, sting, tingle, wear away

bitter *adjective.* **1** alienated, antagonistic, biting, divided, embittered, fierce, freezing, intense, irreconcilable, morose, rancorous, sardonic, severe, sore, sour, sullen, virulent, vitriolic **2** annoying, calamitous, cruel, disagreeable, disturbing, galling, grievous, hard, inclement, intense, offensive, poignant, ruthless, savage, sharp, unpleasant, vexatious, woeful

black *adjective.* **1** charcoal, clouded, coal, dingy, dusky, ebony, jet, livid, murky, obsidian, pitch, sable, shadowy, slate, somber, swart, swarthy **2** atrocious, bleak, depressing, depressive, dismal, distressing, doleful, dreary, foreboding, gloomy, horrible, mournful, ominous, oppressive, sad, sinister, somber, threatening

blame *noun.* accusation, attack, castigation, censure, chiding, complaint, criticism, denunciation, depreciation, disapprobation, disapproval, disfavor, implication, imputation, opposition, reproach, reproof, repudiation

blame *verb.* ascribe, attribute, blast, censure, chide, criticize, denounce, disapprove, finger, frame, impute, knock, rap, rebuke, reproach, roast, skin, tax

blank *adjective.* **1** bare, barren, clean, empty, fresh, new, pale, plain, spotless, unfilled, unmarked, untouched, unused, vacant, vacuous, virgin, void, white **2** dull, empty, hollow, immobile, impassive, inane, inscrutable, lifeless, masklike, meaningless, poker-faced, stiff, stupid, uncommunicative, unexpressive, vacant, vacuous, vague

blank *noun.* abyss, cavity, chasm, emptiness, gap, gulf, hole, hollow, hollowness, interval, nothingness, nullity, omission, opening, vacancy, vacuum, void, womb

blanket *noun.* afghan, carpet, coating, cover, covering, coverlet, envelope, film, layer, mat, puff, quilt, rug, sheath, sheet, strip, throw, wrapper

blast *verb.* annihilate, blight, blow up, bomb, break up, burst, damage, dash, demolish, destroy, detonate, dynamite, kill, ruin, shatter, spoil, stunt, torpedo

bleak *adjective.* **1** austere, bare, blank, blighted, bombed, burned, chilly, cold, desert, deserted, dreary, flat, gaunt, grim, open, scorched, unsheltered, wild **2** black, dark, discouraging, disheartening, dismal, drear, dreary, gloomy, grim, hard, harsh, hopeless, lonely, melancholy, oppressive, sad, somber, unpromising

bless *verb.* baptize, commend, confirm, consecrate, cross, eulogize, exalt, glorify, honor, offer, ordain, praise, pray for, pronounce holy, sacrifice, sign, sprinkle, thank

blessed *adjective.* adored, divine, enthroned, exalted, glorified, hallowed, holy, inviolable, redeemed, religious, resurrected, revered, rewarded, sacred, sacrosanct, saved, spiritual, unprofane

blessing *noun.* asset, benediction, benefit, boon, bounty, break, favor, fortune, gain, gift, godsend, good, help, kindness, miracle, service, stroke, windfall

blind *adjective.* careless, heedless, ignorant, inattentive, inconsiderate, indiscriminate, injudicious, insensitive, myopic, nearsighted, neglectful, oblivious, thoughtless, unaware, unconscious, undiscerning, unmindful, unreasoning

block *verb.* bar, barricade, blockade, check, clog, close, cut off, dam, fill, halt, hold up, interfere, prevent, stall, stop, stopper, tackle, thwart

blockade *noun.* barricade, blank wall, clog, closure, embolus, encirclement, hindrance, impediment, infarct, obstacle, obstruction, restriction, roadblock, siege, snag, stop, stoppage, wall

blonde *noun.* albino, bleached, blond, champagne, fair, flaxen, golden-haired, light, pale, platinum, sallow, sandy-haired, snowy, stramineous, straw, strawberry, yellow-haired

bloom *verb.* bear fruit, blossom, blow, bud,

burgeon, burst, develop, effloresce, flourish, fructify, germinate, grow, open, prosper, sprout, succeed, thrive, wax

blot *noun.* blemish, blotch, blur, brand, defect, discoloration, disgrace, fault, flaw, onus, patch, slur, smear, speck, spot, stain, stigma, taint

blow *noun.* **1** buffet, clump, collision, crack, jab, jolt, kick, percussion, pound, punch, slam, slug, smack, strike, swipe, thrust, thwack, wallop **2** affliction, bombshell, calamity, casualty, chagrin, debacle, disappointment, disaster, frustration, jolt, misadventure, misfortune, mishap, reverse, setback, shock, tragedy, upset

blow *verb.* breathe, buffet, drive, fan, flow, flutter, gasp, huff, inflate, pant, puff, pump, rush, stream, swell, swirl, wave, wind

bluff *adjective.* brief, candid, curt, direct, downright, forthright, frank, gruff, hearty, honest, open, outspoken, rough, short, sincere, snippy, tart, terse

bluff *noun.* bragging, bravado, deception, delusion, fake, feint, fraud, front, jiving, lie, pretence, pretext, ruse, sham, show, stall, trick

bluff *verb.* affect, beguile, betray, bull, con, counterfeit, defraud, delude, fake, fool, jive, lie, pretend, sham, simulate, trick

blunt *adjective.* abrupt, bluff, brief, candid, curt, discourteous, explicit, forthright, frank, gruff, outspoken, rude, short, snappy, snippy, tab, trenchant, uncivil

blunt *verb.* attenuate, benumb, cripple, dampen, deaden, debilitate, desensitize, disable, enfeeble, numb, obtund, sap, soften, undermine, unstrengthen, water down, weaken

boast *verb.* advertise, blow, bluster, bully, crow, exaggerate, fake, flourish, glory, grandstand, puff, shoot, shovel, sling, strut, triumph, vapor

boat *noun.* baiter, barge, bark, canoe, craft, dinghy, hulk, lifeboat, pointer, raft, sailboat, ship, skiff, sloop, steamboat, tub, vehicle, yacht

body *noun.* **1** anatomy, bod, booty, build, carcass, chassis, constitution, embodiment, figure, form, frame, make-up, protoplasm, shaft, shape, tenement, torso, trunk **2** assembly, bed, corpus, crux, essence, fuselage, gist, groundwork, hull, majority, mass, matter, pith, skeleton, substance, sum, total, whole

boil *verb.* bubble, churn, coddle, cook, decoct, effervesce, evaporate, fizz, foam, froth, parboil, poach, seethe, simmer, smolder, steam, steep, stew

bold *adjective.* **1** adventurous, assuming, aweless, bantam, courageous, daring, dauntless, enterprising, fearless, forward, gallant, heroic, intrepid, resolute, unafraid, undaunted, valiant, valorous **2** assuming, brash, brassy, confident, forward, fresh, gritty, gutsy, immodest, impudent, insolent, pert, presumptuous, rude, sassy, saucy, shameless, smart **3** clear, colorful, conspicuous, definite, evident, eye-catching, flashy, forceful, lively, loud, manifest, plain, prominent, pronounced, showy, spirited, strong, vivid

bolt *noun.* bar, brad, coupling, dowel, key, lag, latch, lock, padlock, pin, pipe, rod, screw, skewer, spike, stake, staple, stud

bolt *verb.* bound, dash, ditch, dump, escape, flee, flight, fly, jump, leap, opt out, rush, scamper, skip, spring, start, startle, take off

bond *noun.* **1** band, binding, chain, connection, cord, fastening, gunk, hookup, irons, link, linkage, manacle, network, rope, shackle, stickum, tie, wire **2** affiliation, affinity, association, attachment, connection, connective, friendship, hookup, interrelationship, liaison, link, marriage, network, obligation, relationship, restraint, tie, union **3** agreement, bargain, certificate, collateral, compact, contract, convention, covenant, guaranty, obligation, pact, pledge, promise, security, transaction, warrant, warranty, word

book *noun.* atlas, bestseller, brochure, copy, dictionary, encyclopedia, fiction, lexicon, manual, monograph, nonfiction, opus, pamphlet, periodical, portfolio, publication, reader, tract

book *verb.* bill, charter, engage, enroll, enter, hire, line up, make reservation, order, organize, pencil in, preengage, procure, program, reserve, schedule, set up, sew up

boost *verb.* add, aggrandize, amplify, augment, beef up, develop, enlarge, expand, extend, heighten, hike, jack up, jump, magnify, multiply, raise, up

boot *verb.* ax, bounce, can, chuck, discharge, dismiss, drive, dropkick, eject, evict, expel, extrude, fire, knock, punt, sack, shove, terminate

booth *noun.* berth, box, carrel, compartment, coop, corner, cote, counter, cubbyhole, dispensary, hut, hutch, nook, pen, pew, shed, stall, stand

border *noun.* bound, boundary, bounds, brim, confine, edge, end, extremity, fringe, hem, limit, line, perimeter, periphery, rim, skirt, trim, verge

border *verb.* bind, contour, decorate, encircle, flank, frame, fringe, hem, join, line, march, neighbor, outline, rim, surround, touch, trim, verge

bore *noun.* bother, creep, deadhead, deadwood, drag, drip, drone, dull person, grind, headache, lump, nudge, pain, pest, pill, stuffed shirt, wet blanket, yawn

bore *verb.* annoy, bother, burn out, cloy, discomfort, drag, exhaust, fatigue, irritate, jade, pall, pester, tire, trouble, vex, wear, wear out, worry

boredom *noun.* apathy, detachment, disgust, distaste, doldrums, dullness, fatigue, flatness, indifference, lethargy, monotony, sameness, tediousness, tedium, unconcern, weariness, world-weariness, yawn

borrow *verb.* accept loan, acquire, beg, bite, bum, chisel, hire, lift, negotiate, obtain, pawn, pledge, raise money, rent, soak, sponge, tap, touch

boss *noun.* administrator, chief, chieftain, controller, director, employer, exec, executive, foreman, head, leader, master, overseer, owner, superintendent, supervisor, taskmaster, wheel

bother *noun.* ado, difficulty, drag, exasperation, flurry, fuss, inconvenience, irritant, irritation, nudge, nuisance, pain, perplexity, pest, plague, pressure, trial, trouble

bother *verb.* cross, disconcert, dismay, disquiet, disturb, goad, grate, inconvenience, nudge, pain, perplex, pester, plague, provoke, ride, tease, torment, trouble

bottom *noun.* **1** base, basement, basis, bed, deep, depths, floor, foot, footing, groundwork, rest, seat, sole, substructure, support, underbelly, underneath, underside **2** base, basis, cause, essence, essentiality, ground, heart, mainspring, marrow, origin, pith, principle, quintessence, root, soul, source, stuff, substance

bounce *verb.* backlash, bob, boomerang, bound, buck, bump, hope, hurdle, jerk, jump, leap, rebound, recoil, ricochet, snap back, spring up, thump, vault

bound *adjective.* apprenticed, bent, certain, coerced, compelled, constrained, contracted, destined, forced, impelled, intent, made, necessitated, obligated, obliged, pledged, required, urged

bound *noun.* boundary, compass, confine, edge, end, environs, fringe, limit, limitation, line, march, pale, periphery, precinct, rim, term, termination, verge

boundary *noun.* borderline, compass, demarcation, end, extent, fringe, frontier, horizon, line, march, mark, outline, outpost, pale, perimeter, rim, terminus, verge

bounded *adjective.* belted, bordered, circumscribed, contiguous, defined, definite, determinate, edged, encircled, enclosed, encompassed, finite, flanked, fringed, hedged, restricted, rimmed, surrounded

bow *noun.* angle, arc, arch, bend, bending, bob, curtsey, curtsy, curvature, curve, genuflection, inclination, kowtow, nod, round, salaam, turn, turning

boy *noun.* buck, cadet, child, chip, fellow, gamin, guy, junior, lad, master, punk, puppy, schoolboy, sonny, sprout, squirt, youngster, youth

boycott *verb.* avoid, bar, blackball, blacklist, cut off, embargo, exclude, ice out, outlaw, pass up, prohibit, proscribe, refuse, reject, shut out, snub, spurn, strike

brace *noun.* arm, band, bar, bearing, bolster, grip, guy, lever, rafter, reinforcement, rib, shore, skid, staff, stave, stirrup, strut, vice

brace *verb.* bandage, bind, bolster, fasten, gird, hold up, prepare, prop, ready, reinforce, shove, steady, steel, strap, strengthen, support, tie, uphold

branch *noun.* annex, arm, category, chapter, classification, connection, dependency, derivative, division, extension, local, member, outpost, section, subdivision, subsection, subsidiary, wing

brave *adjective.* chivalrous, courageous, daring, dashing, fearless, foolhardy, forward, gallant, gritty, manly, militant, reckless, resolute, strong, undaunted, undismayed, valiant, venturesome

bread *noun.* aliment, brewis, cake bread, comestibles, diet, fare, feed, grub, necessities, nourishment, nurture, nutriment, provisions, shingle, subsistence, sustenance, viands, victuals

break *noun.* blow, breather, cutoff, halt, interlude, intermission, interval, lacuna, layoff, lull, pause, recess, respite, rest, suspension, ten, time off, time out

break *verb.* **1** burst, bust, crack, crush, damage, disintegrate, divide, eradicate, fracture, fragment, pull, separate, shiver, snap, splinter, split, total, trash **2** bankrupt, bust, cow, cripple, degrade, demoralize, disprove, downgrade, enervate, impair, incapacitate, rebut, reduce, refute, ruin, subdue, tame, undermine

breed *noun.* brand, character, extraction, family, feather, kind, likes, line, lineage, lot, number, pedigree, progeny, race, stamp, stock, strain, type

breed *verb.* bear, beget, bring about, bring forth, cause, create, deliver, engender, father, give birth, hatch, induce, make, multiply, originate, produce, propagate, reproduce

bridge *noun.* arch, bond, branch, catwalk, connection, extension, gangplank, link, overpass, platform, pontoon, scaffold, span, tie, transit, trestle, viaduct, wing

brief *adjective.* **1** abrupt, bluff, blunt, brusque, compendious, concise, curt, hasty, limited, little, pithy, sharp, short, skimpy, small, succinct, terse **2** concise, curtailed, ephemeral, fast, fleeting, hasty, instantaneous, little, meteoric, momentary, passing, quick, short-lived, short-term, swift, temporary, transient, transitory

brief *verb.* abridge, advise, apprise, edify, enlighten, epitomize, explain, fill in, inform, initiate, instruct, orient, prepare, prime, recapitulate, summarize, tip off, update

bright *adjective.* **1** blazing, dazzling, glistening, glittering, glossy, glowing, illuminated, illumined, incandescent, intense, irradiated, light, lighted, phosphorescent, polished, shimmering, sunny, vivid **2** acute, advanced, alert, astute, aware, brain, brainy, brilliant, clever, discerning, egghead, ingenious, inventive, keen, knowing, sharp, smart, whiz **3** airy, auspicious, benign, breezy, cheering, dexter, encouraging, excellent, favorable, golden, good, hopeful, optimistic, palmy, propitious, prosperous, rosy, white **4** alert, animated, can, gay, genial, glad, happy, jolly, joyful, joyous, keen, light-hearted, lively, merry, optimistic, spirited, sprightly, vivacious **5** brave, brilliant, clear, colored, colorful, deep, flashy, fresh, gay, hued, intense, rich, ruddy, sharp, showy, tinged, tinted, vivid

brilliant *adjective.* **1** ablaze, bright, dazzling, flashy, gleaming, glittering, glossy, glowing, incandescent, intense, luminous, lustrous, radiant, resplendent, scintillating, showy, sparkling, vivid **2** accomplished, acute, astute, brainy, bright, expert, genius, gifted, intellectual, inventive, knowledgeable, masterly, penetrating, profound, sharp, smart, talented, whiz

bring *verb.* **1** accompany, bear, buck, carry, chaperon, companion, convey, deliver, fetch, guide, hump, lead, pack, pick up, ride, take, transport, truck **2** begin, compel, contribute, convert, convince, create, dispose, engender, induce, inflict, influence, lead, make, move, occasion, produce, prompt, wreak

broad *adjective.* **1** ample, capacious, deep, expansive, extended, extensive, full, generous, immense, large, outspread, roomy, spacious, squat, thick, vast, voluminous, widespread **2** all-embracing, all-inclusive, comprehensive, encyclopedic, expansive, extended, far-flung, far-reaching, general, inclusive, nonspecific, sweeping, ubiquitous, universal, unlimited, wide, widespread **3** blue, coarse, dirty, gross, improper, indecent, indelicate, low-minded, off-color, purple, racy, risque, salty, saucy, spicy, suggestive, vulgar, wicked

broadcast *verb.* air, announce, beam, cable, circulate, colorcast, communicate, radio, radiograph, relay, send out, show, simulcast, telecast, telegraph, telephone, televise, transmit

broke *adjective.* bankrupt, beggared, bust, cleaned out, destitute, impoverished, indebted, indigent, insolvent, needy, penniless, penurious, poor, ruined, stone broke, stony, strapped, tap city

broken *adjective.* **1** burst, busted, collapsed, crippled, crumbled, demolished, dismembered, fragmented, injured, pulverized, riven, ruptured, separated, shattered, shivered, shredded, smashed, split **2** busted, disabled, down, exhausted, faulty, feeble, gone, haywire, imperfect, inoperable, out, ruined, screwed up, shot, spent, unsatisfactory, weak, wracked

brood *verb.* bleed, chafe inwardly, consider, deliberate, dream, dwell upon, fret, gloom, lament, meditate, muse, ponder, reflect, sigh, speculate, stew over, think about, worry

brown *noun.* beige, brick, bronze, chocolate, cocoa, coffee, copper, dust, ginger, khaki, ochre, rust, sepia, sorrel, tan, tawny, toast, umber

brush *noun.* bracken, brushwood, chaparral, coppice, copse, cover, dingle, fern, gorse, grove, hedge, scrub, sedge, shrubbery, spinney, thicket, undergrowth, underwood

brutality *noun.* atrocity, barbarism, barbarity, bloodthirstiness, brutishness, choke hold, cruelty, ferocity, fierceness, grossness, inhumanity, ruthlessness, sadism, savageness, savagery, unfeelingness, viciousness, violence

bubble *verb.* boil, eddy, erupt, froth, gurgle, gush, issue, moil, murmur, percolate, ripple, seep, simmer, sparkle, spume, stir, trickle, well

buck *verb.* bound, combat, contest, dispute, duel, fight, jerk, jump, kick off, leap, oppose, race, repel, start, throw, trip, vault, withstand

budget *noun.* account, aggregate, allocation, allowance, bulk, cost, estimate, finances, funds, means, plan, planned disbursement, quantity, quantum, resources, spending plan, statement, total

build *verb.* **1** assemble, carpenter, cast, compile, compose, contrive, engineer, erect, evolve, fabricate, fashion, forge, form, frame, model, produce, raise, sculpture **2** accelerate, aggrandize, amplify, augment, boost, compound, develop, enlarge, expand, extend, heighten, improve, intensify, mount, multiply, strengthen, swell, wax

bulk *noun.* aggregate, amount, amplitude, bigness, dimensions, extent, immensity, magnitude, mass, massiveness, quantity, quantum, size, substance, total, totality, volume, weight

bulky *adjective.* beefy, colossal, cumbersome, enormous, gross, heavy, high, hulking, immense, large, long, mammoth, massive, ponderous, substantial, unmanageable, voluminous, weighty

bulletin *noun.* account, break, calendar, dispatch, dope, flash, item, list, news, notice, notification, program, publication, release, report, scoop, skinny, statement

bunch *noun.* agglomeration, assortment, blob, bundle, chunk, clump, flock, gang, heap, hunk, mass, mob, multitude, pack, pile, stack, team, troop

bundle *noun.* array, assortment, box, clump, collection, crate, group, heap, lot, mass, pack, packet, pallet, parcel, pile, roll, set, stack

bunk *noun.* applesauce, balderdash, baloney, bilge, bull, flimflam, garbage, hogwash, hooey, horsefeathers, jazz, piffle, poppycock, rot, rubbish, tomfoolery, tommyrot, trash

burden *noun.* affliction, anxiety, blame, care, clog, deadweight, difficulty, duty, load, millstone, misfortune, mishap, onus, punishment, responsibility, strain, trial, trouble

burden *verb.* bother, crush, depress, dish out, hamper, handicap, load, overload, overwhelm, pile, press, snow, strain, tax, trouble, try, vex, worry

burn *verb.* **1** bake, blaze, brand, cook, cremate, flame, flare, flash, flicker, glow, light, roast, scald, sear, smoke, toast, torch, wither **2** be angry, be aroused, be inflamed, be passionate, blaze, boil, breathe fire, bristle, desire, eat up, fume, lust, rage, seethe, simmer, smolder, tingle, yearn

burning *adjective.* **1** afire, aflame, alight, fiery, flaming, flaring, gleaming, glowing, heated, ignited, illuminated, incandescent, kindled, searing, sizzling, smoking, smoldering, torrid **2** ardent, blazing, eager, earnest, fervent, fervid, feverish, frantic, frenzied, heated, hectic, impassioned, intense, passionate, red-hot, vehement, white-hot, zealous

burst *noun.* blast, break, crack, discharge, eruption, explosion, fit, gust, outpouring, round, sally, salvo, shower, spate, split, spurt, storm, surge

burst *verb.* barge, blow up, break, crack, discharge, disintegrate, erupt, explode, fracture, fragment, pierce, prick, run, shatter, shiver, splinter, split, spout

bush *noun.* backcountry, backwoods, bramble, briar, brush, creeper, forest, hedge, hinterland, jungle, plant, scrub, scrubland, shrubbery, thicket, vine, wild, woodland

busily *adverb.* agilely, briskly, carefully, diligently, eagerly, earnestly, energetically, enthusiastically, expeditiously, hurriedly, laboriously, nimbly, painstakingly, purposefully, seriously, speedily, strenuously, zealous

business *noun.* **1** bag, biz, calling, career, craft, dodge, employment, field, function, line, livelihood, occupation, pursuit, racket, specialty, trade, vocation, work **2** company, concern, corporation, establishment, factory, firm, house, market, mill, monopoly, organization, outfit, partnership, setup, shop, store, syndicate, venture **3** affairs, bargaining, buying, commercialism, contracts, deal, distribution, industrialism, manufacturing, market, merchandising, production, sales, selling, trading, traffic, transaction, undertaking **4** affair, assignment, duty, function, hanky-panky, happening, interest, issue, lookout, matter, palaver, point, problem, question, responsibility, subject, task, topic

busy *adjective.* active, assiduous, buried, diligent, employed, engaged, engrossed, full plate, hustling, industrious, occupied, on duty, overloaded, slaving, snowed, swamped, tied up, unavailable

butt *noun.* chump, derision, fool, goat, jest, joke, mark, mock, patsy, pigeon, point, sap, setup, subject, sucker, target, turkey, victim

butt *verb.* buck, buffet, bump, bunt, gore, horn, jab, knock, poke, prod, punch, push, ram, shove, smack, strike, thrust, toss

C

cabin *noun.* berth, box, camp, chalet, compartment, cot, cottage, crib, home, hovel, hut, lodge, log house, quarters, room, shack, shanty, shed

cage *verb.* close in, confine, coop up, enclose, envelop, fence in, hem, hold, immure, impound, imprison, incarcerate, jail, lock up, mew, pen, restrain, shut up

calendar *noun.* agenda, almanac, bulletin, card, chronology, diary, journal, lineup, list, log, pipeline, program, record, register, tab, table, time, timetable

caliber *noun.* ability, capability, character, constitution, dignity, distinction, essence, faculty, force, nature, power, quality, stature, strength, talent, value, virtue, worth

call *verb.* **1** announce, arouse, awaken, bellow, cry, exclaim, hail, hoot, howl, proclaim, roar, rouse, scream, screech, shout, shriek, whoop, yowl **2** appoint, ask, challenge, claim, command, declare, decree, elect, entreat, exact, ordain, order, postulate, proclaim, require, requisition, solicit, summon **3** adumbrate, approximate, augur, consider, forecast, foretell, guess, judge, place, portend, predict, presage, prognosticate, prophesy, put, reckon, regard, think

calling *noun.* art, business, career, craft, do, dodge, employment, gig, hang, line, mission, occupation, play, province, pursuit, slot, trade, work

calm *adjective.* **1** bland, civil, cool, hushed, inactive, mild, motionless, pacific, pastoral, placid, quiescent, restful, rural, serene, smooth, standstill, still, windless **2** aloof, amiable, amicable, civil, collected, detached, impassive, listless, moderate, patient, poised, relaxed, restful, sedate, serene, temperate, unemotional, unmoved

calm *noun.* calmness, doldrums, hush, impassivity, lull, patience, peace, peacefulness, quiet, quietness, repose, rest, restraint, serenity, silence, stillness, stoicism, tranquility

calm *verb.* allay, alleviate, appease, balm, compose, cool, hush, lull, mitigate, mollify, pacify, quiet, relax, relieve, soothe, steady, still, stroke

camp *noun.* bivouac, campfire, campground, camping ground, caravansary, cottage, encampment, hut, lodge, log cabin, shack, shanty, shed, summer home, tent, tent city, tilt, wigwam

campaign *verb.* agitate, attack, barnstorm, canvass, contend for, contest, electioneer, lobby, muckrake, mudsling, politick, ring doorbells, run, run for, solicit votes, stump, tour, whistle-stop

candidate *noun.* applicant, aspirant, bidder, claimant, competitor, contender, entrant, favorite son, hopeful, nominee, office-seeker, petitioner, possibility, runner, seeker, stumper, successor, suitor

cap *verb.* beat, better, can, clinch, cover, crest, crown, eclipse, exceed, excel, finish, pass, surmount, surpass, top, transcend, trump, wrap

capability *noun.* adequacy, aptitude, art, competence, craft, cunning, effectiveness, efficiency, facility, faculty, means, might, potency, potential, potentiality, power, proficiency, skill

capable *adjective.* accomplished, adapted, adept, adequate, apt, dynamite, efficient, fitted, gifted, good, intelligent, pro, proper, qualified, skillful, talented, vet, veteran

capacity *noun.* **1** accommodation, amplitude, bulk, chock full, compass, contents, dimensions, expanse, extent, full, latitude, magnitude, mass, range, reach, room, scope, sweep **2** adequacy, aptitude, bent, capability, cleverness, compass, competence, facility, gift, inclination, intelligence, knack, might, power, readiness, skill, stature, talent

cape *noun.* capote, cardinal, cloak, cope, fichu, gabardine, manteau, mantelletta, mantilla, mantle, overdress, pelerine, poncho, shawl, victorine, wrap, wrapper

capital *adjective.* **1** basic, central, controlling, dominant, first, fundamental, important, leading, main, major, outstanding, predominant, primary, prime, principal, prominent, underlying, vital **2** best, champion, choice, crack, dandy, delightful, deluxe, excellent, famous, fine, first, first-class, great, prime, splendid, superb, top, top-notch

capital *noun.* business, estate, finance, finances, financing, fortune, funds, gold, kitty, money, principal, property, resources, stake, stock, substance, treasure, wealth

captain *noun.* authority, boss, cap, chieftain, commander, director, exec, guide, head, leader, lord, master, operator, owner, pilot, skip, skipper, top

capture *noun.* abduction, bust, collar, commandeering, grasping, imprisonment, nail, obtaining, occupation, pick up, pickle, pull, seizing, seizure, snatching, sweep, taking, trapping

capture *verb.* apprehend, bust, collar, conquer, get, nab, nail, net, occupy, overwhelm, pick up, pinch, round up, secure, seize, snare, take, trap

car *noun.* automobile, bug, bus, compact, coupe, heap, jalopy, limousine, machine, motor, pickup, ride, roadster, sedan, truck, wagon, wheels, wreck

card *noun.* agenda, badge, billet, calendar, cardboard, check, identification, label, pass, poster, program, schedule, sheet, square, tally, ticket, timetable, voucher

cardinal *adjective.* basic, central, essential, first, fundamental, greatest, highest, indispensable, key, leading, main, overriding, pivotal, primary, prime, principal, ruling, vital

care *noun.* **1** anguish, anxiety, bother, dismay, disquiet, exasperation, load, nuisance, onus, perplexity, pressure, responsibility, stew, strain, stress, sweat, trouble, unhappiness **2** alertness, caution, circumspection, consideration, diligence, discrimination, effort, enthusiasm, exertion, heed, interest, management, pains, particularity, prudence, regard, thought, trouble **3** administration, aegis, auspices, charge, control, direction, guardianship, keeping, management, ministration, protection, safekeeping, superintendence, supervision, trust, tutelage, ward, wardship

care *verb.* attend, consider, foster, look after, mind, minister, mother, nurse, nurture, protect, provide for, sit, take pains, tend, treasure, wait on, watch, watch over

career *noun.* bag, calling, course, dodge, employment, field, game, job, livelihood, number, pilgrimage, profession, pursuit, racket, specialty, thing, vocation, work

carefree *adjective.* airy, blithe, breezy, buoyant, calm, careless, cheerful, cheery, cool, easy, happy, jaunty, jovial, laidback, radiant, secure, sunny, unbothered

careful *adjective.* circumspect, concerned, discreet, exacting, finicky, guarded, judicious, mindful, observant, prim, protective, scrupulous, shy, solicitous, thorough, thoughtful, vigilant, wary

carefully *adverb.* circumspectly, correctly, deliberately, delicately, discreetly, exactly, faithfully, gingerly, laboriously, meticulously, particularly, precisely, prudently, reliably, rigorously, scrupulously, thoughtfully, warily

careless *adjective.* abstracted, casual, forgetful, inadvertent, incautious, indifferent, indiscreet, indolent, lackadaisical, loose, napping, negligent, nonchalant, oblivious, offhand, reckless, thoughtless, unheeding

carnival *noun.* carny, circus, exposition, fair, feasting, festival, fete, fiesta, frolic, gala, heyday, masquerade, merrymaking, orgy, revelry, rout, side show, spree

carriage *noun.* air, appearance, aspect, attitude, bearing, behavior, cast, comportment, conduct, demeanor, gait, look, manner, mien, pace, presence, stance, step

carry *verb.* **1** backpack, bear, change, convey, convoy, displace, ferry, fetch, give, hoist, hump, move, pipe, portage, relay, remove, take, truck **2** affect, be victorious, capture, drive, effect, gain, get, impel, impress, influence, inspire, move, prevail, secure, spur, strike, sway, win

case *noun.* bin, box, caddy, chamber, chassis, chest, compact, crate, drawer, envelope, grip, holder, receptacle, safe, scabbard, tray, wrapper, wrapping

cash *noun.* buck, cabbage, coin, dough, funds, lot, pledge, principal, refund, remuneration, reserve, resources, riches, security, skins, stock, supply, treasure

cast *noun.* **1** casting, expulsion, fling, heaving, hurl, hurling, launching, lob, pitch, pitching, projection, propulsion, shooting, sling, slinging, thrust, thrusting, tossing **2** air, complexion, countenance, demeanor, embodiment, expression, face, hue, look, manner, mien, semblance, stamp, style, tint, tone, turn, visage

cast *verb.* **1** chuck, chunk, drive, drop, fire, fling, heave, hurl, launch, lob, peg, pitch, project, shed, shy, sling, thrust, toss **2** aim, bestow, deposit, diffuse, direct, distribute, give, level, point, radiate, scatter, shed, spatter, spray, spread, sprinkle, strew, train **3** allot, appoint, arrange, assign, blueprint, chart, choose, decide upon, delegate, design, designate, detail, determine, devise, name, pick, plan, project

castle *noun.* alcazar, chateau, citadel, donjon, fort, fortress, hold, keep, manor, mansion, palace, peel, safehold, seat, stronghold, tower, villa

casual *adjective.* **1** accidental, adventitious, contingent, erratic, extempore, impromptu, improvised, incidental, infrequent, irregular, occasional, odd, offhand, random, spontaneous, uncertain, unexpected, unpremeditated **2** aloof, apathetic, breezy, cool, cursory, detached, easygoing, folksy, indifferent, informal, lackadaisical, loose, mellow, offhand, perfunctory, purposeless, remote, withdrawn

cat *noun.* bobcat, cheetah, jaguar, kitten, kitty, leopard, lion, lynx, mouser, ocelot, panther, puma, puss, pussy, tabby, tiger, tomcat

catalogue *noun.* brief, bulletin, calendar, catalog, charts, classification, directory, enumeration, gazette, inventory, list, magazine, record, roll, roster, schedule, slate, specification

catastrophe *noun.* accident, adversity, blow, calamity, casualty, curtain, denouement, failure, grief, havoc, infliction, misery, misfortune, scourge, trial, trouble, upshot, wreck

catch *verb.* bust, capture, claw, clutch, collar, glove, grasp, grip, lasso, nail, net, pick, secure, seize, snag, snare, take, trap

category *noun.* class, department, division, grade, group, grouping, head, heading, kind, league, level, list, order, pigeonhole, rank, section, sort, type

catholic *adjective.* charitable, comprehensive, cosmic, cosmopolitan, diffuse, ecumenical, extensive, global, inclusive, indeterminate, liberal, planetary, receptive, tolerant, universal, whole, wide, worldly

cause *noun.* antecedent, consideration, creator, determinant, element, end, foundation, genesis, incitement, inducement, matter, object, origin, producer, purpose, source, spring, stimulation

cause *verb.* begin, bow, break in, breed, compel, evoke, generate, kickoff, let, make up, motivate, occasion, open, precipitate, produce, provoke, rev, secure

cautious *adjective.* alert, cagey, calculating, circumspect, considerate, discreet, gingerly, guarded, judicious, politic, prudent, pussyfoot, safe, shrewd, tentative, vigilant, wary, watchful

cease *verb.* break off, close, conclude, culminate, die, discontinue, drop, end, fail, finish, halt, quit, refrain, shut down, stay, surcease, terminate, wind up

celebrated *adjective.* acclaimed, distinguished, eminent, famed, glorious, great, illustrious, immortal, important, laureate, lionized, notable, outstanding, popular, prominent, renowned, revered, storied

celebration *noun.* anniversary, blast, ceremony, gaiety, gala, glorification, honoring, joviality, jubilation, magnification, merriment, merrymaking, observance, recognition, remembrance, revelry, spree, triumph

celestial *adjective.* angelic, astral, beatific, blessed, divine, empyreal, empyrean, eternal, ethereal, godlike, hallowed, holy, immortal, otherworldly, spiritual, sublime, supernatural, transcendental

cell *noun.* apartment, burrow, cavity, chamber, closet, compartment, coop, dungeon, hold, keep, lockup, pen, receptacle, recess, retreat, stall, tower, vault

cement *noun.* adhesive, binder, bond, butter, concrete, epoxy, glue, gum, gunk, lime, mortar, mucilage, mud, paste, plaster, sand, size, solder

cement *verb.* bind, blend, bond, cohere, combine, connect, fasten, fuse, glue, gum, join, merge, paste, plaster, seal, solder, stick, unite

cemetery *noun.* boneyard, boot hill, charnel, churchyard, crypt, garden, grave, graveyard, headstone, marble town, mortuary, necropolis, ossuary, potter's field, resting place, sepulcher, tomb, vault

center *noun.* **1** axis, centrality, core, essence, focus, gist, hotbed, hub, kernel, mainstream, marrow, midpoint, midst, nucleus, pith, pivot, place, seat **2** capital, city, club, crossroads, focal point, focus, heart, hub, mall, market, marketplace, mart, metropolis, plaza, polestar, social center, station, town

central *adjective.* axial, centric, dominant, essential, focal, fundamental, important, inner, key, leading, median, middle, nuclear, pivotal, predominant, prime, ruling, significant

certain *adjective.* **1** assertive, assured, believing, calm, cocksure, convinced, positive, questionless, sanguine, satisfied, secure, self-confident, sure, unconcerned, undisturbed, undoubtful, undoubting, unperturbed **2** absolute, ascertained, clear, conclusive, demonstrable, destined, determined, evident, fixed, guaranteed, incontrovertible, infallible, known, positive, safe, sound, unambiguous, undeniable **3** defined, express, individual, many, marked, numerous, one, particular, precise, regular, several, singular, some, special, specific, specified, sundry, various

certainty *noun.* belief, cinch, confidence, conviction, definiteness, dogmatism, faith, firmness, inevitability, lock, lockup, positivism, setup, steadiness, stock, store, trust, validity

challenge *verb.* arouse, assert, beard, brave, claim, cross, dare, defy, denounce, dispute, inquire, investigate, provoke, reclaim, require, summon, test, vindicate

chamber *noun.* alcove, apartment, bedchamber, bedroom, box, case, cavity, cell, chest, container, cubicle, enclosure, flat, hall, hollow, lodging, pocket, room

champion *adjective.* best, boss, chief, choice, cool, dandy, distinguished, first, greatest, head, illustrious, outstanding, premier, prime, principal, splendid, super, tops

champion *noun.* advocate, ally, challenger, champ, conqueror, defender, guardian, hero, heroine, master, paladin, partisan, patron, proponent, supporter, victor, warrior, winner

chance *adjective.* adventitious, at random, casual, contingent, fluky, fortuitous, fortunate, happy, inadvertent, incidental, lucky, odd, offhand, unforeseeable, unforeseen, unintentional, unlooked for, unplanned

chance *noun.* **1** break, contingency, indications, liability, likelihood, occasion, odds, opening, opportunity, outlook, probability, prospect, scope, shot, show, squeak, time, wager **2** accident, advantage, adventure, break, casualty, contingency, destination, doom, fluke, fortune, future, gamble, hap, happening, lot, misfortune, odds, risk

chance *verb.* arrive, befall, betide, break, bump, come, come off, fall out, go, hap, light, luck, meet, occur, stumble, transpire, tumble, turn up

change *noun.* addition, break, conversion, development, difference, distortion, diversification, innovation, remodeling, revision, revolution, shift, transformation, transition, transmutation, turn, turnover, variance

change *verb.* alter, commute, evolve, metamorphose, moderate, redo, reform, reorganize, replace, resolve, shift, substitute, temper, translate, turn, vary, veer, warp

channel *noun.* avenue, chamber, chase, course, ditch, furrow, gouge, gully, gutter, main, passage, pipe, route, runway, sewer, trough, vein, way

chaos *noun.* anarchy, ataxia, bedlam, disarray, discord, disorder, disorganization, entropy, free-for-all, holy mess, misrule, mix-up, muddle, rat's nest, snarl, tumult, turmoil, unruliness

character *noun.* **1** attribute, bent, complexion, constitution, estimation, grain, habit, mystique, personality, record, singularity, specialty, spirit, temper, tone, turn, type, vein **2** courage, fame, honor, intelligence, mind, name, place, position, rank, rectitude, rep, report, reputation, repute, standing, station, status, strength **3** crank, creepo, customer, duck, eccentric, figure, freak, nut, oddball, oddity, original, personage, personality, psycho, queer, spook, wack, wacko, zombie

characteristic *adjective.* appropriate, differentiating, discriminating, distinctive, distinguishing, essential, exclusive, individual, individualistic, innate, marked, native, normal, peculiar, singular, special, typical, unique

characteristic *noun.* attribute, bent, character, complexion, distinction, essence, essential, flavor, inclination, mannerism, mark, particularity, peculiarity, personality, property, singularity, specialty, tone

charge *noun.* care, commitment, concern, custody, deadweight, duty, millstone, must, need, obligation, onus, ought, responsibility, task, tax, trust, ward, weight

charge *verb.* choke, clog, commit, crowd, entrust, fill, heap, lade, load, pack, penetrate, permeate, pile, ram, saddle, suffuse, tax, weigh

charity *noun.* **1** alms, alms-giving, assistance, beneficence, contribution, dole, donation, endowment, fund, gift, gifting, helping hand, largesse, oblation, offering, philanthropy, relief, write-off **2** affection, altruism, amity, attachment, bounty, clemency, compassion, fellow feeling, generosity, goodness, goodwill, grace, humanity, indulgence, kindliness, love, magnanimity, mercy

charm *noun.* agreeableness, allure, allurement, appeal, attraction, beauty, charisma, chemistry, desirability, fascination, glamour, grace, lure, magic, magnetism, something, sorcery, spell

charm *verb.* allure, attract, delight, draw, entrance, fascinate, grab, hex, kill, possess, send, spell, take, transport, vamp, voodoo, win, wow

charming *adjective.* amiable, appealing, attractive, cute, delightful, electrifying, elegant, enthralling, fetching, glamorous, inviting, lovable, pleasing, provocative, sweet, tantalizing, tempting, winsome

charter *noun.* allotment, bond, code, concession, constitution, contract, deed, document, franchise, grant, indenture, license, pact, permit, prerogative, privilege, settlement, treaty

chase *verb.* bird-dog, charge, course, drive, expel, follow, go after, hound, hunt, run down, rush, seek, shag, speed, tear, track, track down, trail

cheap *adjective.* **1** bargain, budget, buy, competitive, economy, irregular, lowered, moderate, reasonable, reduced, sale, slashed, standard, steal, stingy, thrifty, tight, utility **2** bad, base, commonplace, crap, dud, flashy, garish, lemon, lousy, mediocre, meretricious, poor, rotten, tatty, tawdry, terrible, valueless, worthless

check *noun.* blow, constraint, control, curb, disappointment, frustration, harness, holdup, impediment, inhibition, limitation, rebuff, rejection, reversal, reverse, setback, stoppage, trouble

check *verb.* **1** audit, candle, case, compare, confirm, correct, count, investigate, monitor, probe, prove, quiz, read, review, study, tell, test, verify **2** baffle, bar, bit, bottleneck, counteract, delay, discourage, foil, halt, harness, hold, moderate, obstruct, pause, preclude, rebuff, repress, withhold

cheek *noun.* audacity, brashness, brass, brazenness, chutzpah, confidence, disrespect, effrontery, gall, impertinence, impudence, insolence, lip, nerve, presumption, rudeness, sauce, temerity

cheer *verb.* animate, chirk up, comfort, console, elate, encourage, enliven, gladden, help, incite, perk up, pick up, solace, steel, strengthen, uplift, upraise, warm

cheerful *adjective.* animated, bright, cheery, contented, glad, hearty, high, jaunty, jocund, jolly, lively, perky, rosy, snappy, sunny, up, vivacious, winsome

chief *adjective.* arch, central, champion, grand, head, important, key, leading, main, momentous, predominant, premier, primal, prime, ruling, star, telling, uppermost

chief *noun.* captain, chieftain, commander, dictator, duke, foreman, general, governor, head, leader, lord, monarch, overseer, president, principal, proprietor, ruler, supervisor

child *noun.* babe, baby, chick, descendant, dickens, innocent, issue, juvenile, lamb, mite, nestling, newborn, offspring, progeny, sprout, squirt, young, youth

childish *adjective.* baby, boyish, childlike, foolish, frivolous, girlish, green, imbecile, infantile, juvenile, naive, petty, primitive, simple, soft, trifling, weak, youthful

chill *adjective.* aloof, cool, depressing, discouraging, dismal, distant, formal, frigid, hostile, icy, indifferent, reserved, solitary, stony, unemotional, unhappy, unresponsive, withdrawn

chip *verb.* break, chisel, chop, crack, crumble, cut off, damage, fragment, hack, incise, nick, notch, shape, shear, slash, slice, splinter, split

choice *adjective.* best, elect, elite, exceptional, exclusive, exquisite, fine, nice, popular, precious, preferential, prime, prize, rare, special, unusual, valuable, winner

choice *noun.* appraisal, choosing, determination, discrimination, distinction, evaluation, favorite, finding, judgment, opportunity, pick, preference, rating, say, substitute, verdict, volition, weakness

choke *verb.* bar, check, clog, close, dam, die, fill, gag, gasp, gibbet, kill, noose, obstruct, retard, squeeze, stuff, throttle, wring

choose *verb.* appoint, cast, crave, elect, excerpt, favor, finger, glean, love, name, prefer, separate, tag, take, tap, want, winnow, wish

chronic *adjective.* abiding, ceaseless, confirmed, continual, continuing, enduring, habitual, inborn, incurable, obstinate, perennial, persisting, prolonged, protracted, rooted, stubborn, sustained, usual

chuck *verb.* abandon, cast, desert, ditch, eject, fire, fling, flip, hurl, junk, pitch, relinquish, scrap, shed, shy, sling, slough, toss

church *noun.* **1** abbey, bethel, cathedral, chancel, chantry, chapel, fold, god box, mission, mosque, oratory, parish, sacellum, sanctuary, shrine, synagogue, tabernacle, temple **2** affiliation, body, chapter, communion, connection, creed, cult, denomination, doctrine, faction, faith, gathering, order, persuasion, religion, schism, sect, society

circle *noun.* **1** bowl, bracelet, circuit, circus, compass, crown, ecliptic, equator, halo, horizon, parallel, perimeter, record, revolution, ring, tire, turn, wreath **2** assembly, associates, camp, clan, class, club, comrades, cronies, crush, fraternity, friends, gang, insiders, lot, mob, outfit, ring, society

circle *verb.* circuit, circulate, compass, curve, encircle, encompass, gird, loop, pivot, revolve, ring, roll, rotate, round, spiral, surround, tour, wheel

circuit *noun.* boundary, circle, circling, circulation, compass, course, cycle, gyration, line, perimeter, region, route, tour, tract, turn, way, wheel, winding

circumstance *noun.* accident, affair, cause, contingency, doom, element, episode, event, fact, fate, feature, happening, happenstance, intervention, item, lot, matter, stipulation

circumstances *noun.* affairs, chances, class, degree, dowry, income, lot, means, position, prestige, property, rating, resources, sphere, standing, state, status, substance

citizen *noun.* aborigine, burgess, burgher, civilian, commoner, dweller, freeman, householder, national, native, occupant, resident, settler, subject, taxpayer, townsman, villager, voter

city *noun.* apple, boom town, borough, burg, capital, center, downtown, dumb, hamlet, megalopolis, metropolis, metropolitan area, municipality, place, port, suburb, town, village

civil *adjective.* accommodating, affable, civilized, complaisant, cordial, courteous, courtly, cultivated, diplomatic, formal, genteel, gracious, polished, polite, politic, refined, suave, well-bred

claim *noun.* affirmation, assertion, case, declaration, due, interest, lien, plea, prerogative, pretense, privilege, profession, request, requirement, requisition, suit, title, ultimatum

claim *verb.* advance, ask, assert, believe, challenge, collect, declare, hold, insist, need, pick up, postulate, pronounce, require, reserve, solicit, take, uphold

clarity *noun.* accuracy, brightness, certainty, definition, directness, distinctness, evidence, explicitness, intelligibility, legibility, lucidity, obviousness, precision, prominence, purity, simplicity, transparency, unambiguity

class *noun.* **1** breed, caste, character, department, designation, distinction, estate, feather, grade, grain, grouping, hierarchy, mold, order, property, province, rate, value **2** ancestry, birth, breed, caste, circle, club, derivation, estate, extraction, grade, hierarchy, origin, pedigree, pigeonhole, prestige, state, stock, stratum **3** academy, colloquium, course, division, form, grade, homeroom, line, quiz group, recitation, room, section, seminar, seminary, session, study, subdivision, subject

class *verb.* appraise, assess, assign, brand, classify, consider, designate, divide, evaluate, grade, hold, identify, mark, pigeonhole, rate, reckon, regard, separate

classic *adjective.* champion, classical, consummate, definitive, distinguished, esthetic, excellent, famous, fine, finest, flawless, master, masterly, model, prime, ranking, standard, top

classical *adjective.* academic, Augustan, bookish, canonical, classic, classicistic, correct, Grecian, Greek, Hellenic, Homeric, humanistic, Latin, liberal, literary, long-hair, scholastic, vintage

classification *noun.* allotting, analysis, apportionment, assignment, categorizing, codification, denomination, department, designation, distribution, grade, grading, graduation, grouping, order, ordering, regulation, sorting

clause *noun.* article, catch, chapter, heading, item, kicker, limitation, part, passage, point, provision, proviso, requirement, section, specification, stipulation, string, ultimatum

clean *adjective.* **1** blank, bright, cleansed, clear, elegant, faultless, laundered, sanitary, shining, simple, snowy, spotless, squeaky, tidy, trim, vanilla, washed, white **2** blameless, crimeless, decent, exemplary, faultless, good, guiltless, honorable, innocent, modest, moral, respectable, sinless, unguilty, unsullied, upright, virtuous, wholesome

clean *verb.* bathe, blow, dust, erase, expunge, flush, mop, pick, pick up, polish, rasp, refine, scrape, shampoo, sterilize, vacuum, winnow, wipe

clear *adjective.* **1** audible, distinct, evident, explicit, express, incontrovertible, intelligible, lucid, palpable, perceptible, plain, precise, recognizable, sharp, simple, transparent, unambiguous, unmistakable **2** clean, cleared, discharged, dismissed, exculpated, exonerated, guiltless, immaculate, innocent, not guilty, pure, sinless, stainless, unblemished, uncensurable, undefiled, untarnished, untroubled

clear *verb.* break up, disengage, eliminate, erase, free, loosen, open, purify, refine, rid, sweep, tidy, unload, unpack, untie, vacate, void, wipe

clearly *adverb.* apparently, certainly, conspicuously, definitely, distinctly, evidently, manifestly, markedly, obviously, overtly, plainly, purely, seemingly, sharply, surely, undeniably, undoubtedly, unmistakably

clergyman *noun.* abbey, archbishop, cardinal, chaplain, clerk, dean, divine, father, missionary, pastor, preacher, priest, primate, rabbi, rector, reverend, shepherd, vicar

clerical *adjective.* apostolic, canonical, churchly, cleric, ecclesiastic, ecclesiastical, episcopal, holy, ministerial, monastic, monkish, papal, pastoral, pontifical, priestly, sacred, theocratical, theological

clerk *noun.* agent, amanuensis, auditor, cashier, company monkey, copyist, counter jumper, counterperson, employee, operator, receptionist, recorder, registrar, salesperson, secretary, seller, teller, worker

clever *adjective.* apt, canny, deep, gifted, inventive, keen, qualified, rational, resourceful, savvy, sensible, sharp, skilled, sly, talented, versatile, wise, wit

client *noun.* applicant, believer, buyer, chump, consumer, dependent, disciple, float, follower, front, habitue, head, mark, patient, patron, pigeon, shopper, sucker

climax *noun.* apex, apogee, ascendancy, crest, extremity, head, height, highlight, intensification, limit, maximum, peak, pinnacle, pitch, summit, top, utmost, zenith

clock *noun.* alarm, chronograph, chronometer, digital watch, hourglass, pendulum, stopwatch, sundial, tattler, tick-tock, ticker, time marker, timekeeper, timepiece, timer, turnip, watch

close *adjective.* **1** abutting, adjacent, adjoining, approaching, contiguous, convenient, handy, immediate, imminent, impending, nearby, nearest, nearly, neighboring, next, nigh, proximate, warm **2** circumscribed, compact, confined, confining, congested, consolidated, cropped, crowded, firm, impenetrable, narrow, packed, restricted, short, solid, substantial, thick, tight **3** attached, buddy-buddy, chummy, confidential, cozy with, dear, devoted, familiar, inseparable, loving, pally, palsy-walsy, private, related, roommates, sleeping with, thick, tight with **4** airless, breathless, confined, fusty, heavy, humid, motionless, muggy, stagnant, stale, sticky, stifling, stuffy, sultry, sweltering, thick, tight, unventilated **5** button up, clam, clam up, close-lipped, closemouthed, hidden, hush-hush, private, reserved, reticent, retired, secluded, secretive, silent, taciturn, tight-lipped, uncommunicative, unforthcoming

close *verb.* **1** bang, bar, bolt, clap, clench, clog, confine, cork, dam, fill, lock, seal, secure, shut, shutter, slam, stuff, turn off **2** cap, cease, clear, clinch, conclude, consummate, culminate, determine, discontinue, do, end, fold, halt, shut down, shutter, stop, terminate, wind up

closely *adverb.* carefully, exactly, firmly, hard, heedfully, intently, intimately, jointly, meticulously, minutely, nearly, punctiliously, scrupulously, searchingly, sharply, similarly, strictly, thoughtfully

clothing *noun.* apparel, clothes, drag, drapery, dress, ensemble, equipment, feathers, garb, garments, gear, habit, livery, rags, regalia, rigging, trappings, underclothes

cloud *noun.* darkness, film, fog, frost, gloom, haze, mist, nebula, obscurity, overcast, puff, rack, sheep, smog, smoke, steam, vapor, veil

cloud *verb.* adumbrate, becloud, befog, blur, darken, dim, eclipse, envelop, fog, gloom, mist, obfuscate, obscure, overcast, overshadow, shade, shadow, veil

club *noun.* **1** bat, baton, billy, blackjack, bludgeon, business, cudgel, hammer, hickory, mallet, quarterstaff, rosewood, sap, shill, shillelagh, staff, truncheon **2** alliance, association, brotherhood, circle, clique, company, faction, fraternity, gang, guild, lodge, mob, order, outfit, ring, set, society, union

clue *noun.* cue, evidence, giveaway, indication, key, lead, mark, notion, pointer, print, sign, solution, suggestion, suspicion, tip, trace, track, wind

cluster *noun.* array, assemblage, band, bevy, blob, body, bunch, bundle, chunk, clump, clutch, collection, crew, hunk, lot, pack, party, set

coalition *noun.* affiliation, amalgamation, association, bloc, combination, combine, compact, confederacy, consolidation, conspiracy, faction, federation, fusion, integration, merger, merging, ring, union

coarse *adjective.* **1** base, boorish, cheap, crass, crude, dirty, earthy, foul, gross, gruff, immodest, indelicate, obscene, offensive, raffish, ribald, rough, roughneck **2** coarse-grained, crude, granular, harsh, homespun, inferior, loose, lumpy, mediocre, particulate, poor quality, rough-hewn, rugged, unfinished, unpolished, unprocessed, unpurified, unrefined

coat *noun.* **1** covering, crust, ectoderm, epidermis, fell, fur, hide, husk, integument, leather, membrane, pelt, peltry, scale, scarfskin, shell, skin, wool **2** bark, blanket coat, capote, coating, crust, finish, glaze, gloss, lacquer, layer, overlay, painting, plaster, priming, roughcast, varnish, wash, whitewashing **3** cape, cloak, frock, greatcoat, jacket, mink, overcoat, pea, slicker, suit, tails, threads, topcoat, trench, tux, tuxedo, wrap

coin *noun.* bread, cash, change, chips, copper, currency, dough, gold, jack, legal tender, loonie, meter money, money, piece, scratch, silver, small change, specie

coin *verb.* compose, conceive, contrive,

counterfeit, dream up, fabricate, forge, formulate, frame, invent, make up, manufacture, mint, mold, originate, spark, stamp, strike

coincide *verb.* accompany, accord, acquiesce, agree, befall, concert, concur, correspond, equal, eventuate, harmonize, identify, jibe, match, occur simultaneously, square, synchronize, tally

cold *adjective.* **1** biting, bleak, chill, chilled, freezing, frosty, icebox, iced, icy, inclement, intense, keen, numbing, penetrating, sharp, snappy, snowy, wintry **2** apathetic, cool, dead, distant, frigid, frosty, icy, impersonal, imperturbable, indifferent, inhibited, inhospitable, lukewarm, reserved, stony, unenthusiastic, unmoved, unresponsive

cold *noun.* chill, chilliness, coldness, draft, freeze, frigidity, frost, frostbite, frostiness, frozenness, inclemency, rawness, refrigeration, shivering, snow, wintertime, wintriness

colleague *noun.* aide, ally, assistant, auxiliary, buddy, chum, collaborator, companion, compatriot, comrade, confederate, crony, fellow, friend, helper, pal, partner, teammate

collect *verb.* aggregate, amass, array, assemble, cluster, compile, congregate, congress, converge, corral, flock, group, heap, muster, rally, rendezvous, round up, save

collected *adjective.* calm, composed, confident, cool, easy, easygoing, nonchalant, peaceful, placid, poised, possessed, quiet, serene, still, sure, temperate, together, tranquil

collection *noun.* acquiring, agglomeration, anthology, assembly, assortment, clump, collation, combination, compilation, congregation, heap, mass, medley, miscellany, mobilization, pile, stack, stock

collective *adjective.* aggregate, assembled, collated, combined, concentrated, consolidated, cooperative, corporate, gathered, grouped, heaped, joint, massed, mutual, piled, shared, unified, united

colonial *adjective.* crude, dependent, dominion, emigrant, frontier, immigrant, new, outland, pilgrim, pioneer, primitive, provincial, puritan, territorial, transplanted, uncultured, unsettled, unsophisticated

color *noun.* blush, cast, coloration, coloring, complexion, glow, hue, intensity, iridescence, luminosity, paint, saturation, shade, stain, tincture, tint, value, wash

color *verb.* **1** adorn, bloom, blush, burn, chalk, enamel, flush, fresco, gild, gloss, lacquer, paint, rouge, stain, suffuse, tint, tone, wash **2** angle, cook, disguise, doctor, embroider, exaggerate, fake, falsify, fudge, garble, gloss over, overstate, pad, prejudice, slant, taint, twist, warp

colorful *adjective.* bright, chromatic, flashy, gaudy, gay, hued, intense, jazzy, loud, motley, multicolored, picturesque, rich, showy, splashy, variegated, vibrant, vivid

column *noun.* brace, colonnade, cylinder, mast, monolith, monument, obelisk, pedestal, pier, post, prop, shaft, standard, stay, support, tower, underpinning, upright

combat *noun.* action, battle royal, brush, brush-off, conflict, contest, encounter, engagement, fight, flap, fray, mix-up, run-in, service, skirmish, struggle, war, warfare

combat *verb.* battle, buck, clash, contend, contest, cope, defy, dispute, duel, engage, fight, oppose, repel, resist, strive, struggle, war, withstand

combination *noun.* **1** aggregate, amalgamation, blend, brew, combo, composite, connection, consolidation, fusion, junction, merger, order, sequence, solution, soup, stew, succession, union **2** affiliation, alliance, circle, club, coalition, combine, confederacy, connection, consolidation, conspiracy, faction, gang, guild, partnership, ring, syndicate, trust, union

combine *verb.* band, bind, blend, bond, coalesce, cooperate, fuse, incorporate, interface, join, marry, merge, mingle, network, pool, relate, unite, wed

come *verb.* **1** appear, arrive, attain, burst, check in, enter, flare, get, happen, hit, materialize, move, near, nigh, occur, reach, show, turn out **2** aggregate, amount, become, develop, expand, get, go, grow, join, mature, number, reach, run, run into, spread, stretch, total, turn

comedy *noun.* ball, burlesque, camp, chaffing, farce, fun, grins, hoopla, humor, interlude, jesting, joking, laughs, picnic, satire, slapstick, takeoff, travesty

comfort *noun.* abundance, alleviation, cheer, cheerfulness, complacency, contentment, convenience, gratification, happiness, luxury, pleasure, plenty, relief, repose, rest, satisfaction, succor, sufficiency

comfort *verb.* aid, alleviate, assist, bolster, calm, cheer, delight, encourage, reassure, refresh, relieve, remedy, soften, solace, soothe, sustain, sympathize, uphold

comfortable *adjective.* agreeable, appropriate, complacent, delightful, loose, luxurious, relaxed, restful, restored, roomy, satisfactory, satisfying, serene, sheltered, soft, strengthened, useful, warm

comforting *adjective.* abating, alleviating, analeptic, consoling, curing, encouraging, freeing, invigorating, mitigating, reassuring, refreshing, relieving, restoring, softening, soothing, sustaining, upholding, warming

comic *noun.* banana, buffoon, card, clown, comedian, droll, gag man, humorist, jester, joker, jokester, million laughs, quipster, stand-up comic, stooge, top banana, wag, wit

coming *adjective.* anticipated, aspiring, certain, due, eventual, expected, forthcoming, future, immediate, imminent, instant, marked, near, nearing, next, nigh, ordained, progressing

command *noun.* **1** canon, caveat, citation, commandment, decree, dictum, fiat, law, obligation, order, ordinance, proclamation, prohibition, regulation, request, requirement, responsibility, ultimatum **2** authorization, constraint, government, grasp, grip, hold, jurisdiction, leadership, management, might, power, prerogative, royalty, skill, sovereignty, supervision, supremacy, tyranny

command *verb.* **1** appoint, authorize, bar, beckon, bid, compel, dictate, enjoin, grant, inflict, oblige, ordain, order, proclaim, prohibit, require, summon, tell **2** coerce, compel, dictate, direct, govern, guide, head, lead, lord, manage, override, prescribe, push, reign, repress, subdue, tyrannize, wield

commander *noun.* administrator, boss, captain, chief, commandant, czar, director, don, exec, guru, head, head honcho, king, kingpin, lord, officer, ruler, skipper

commanding *adjective.* advantageous, arresting, assertive, autocratic, compelling, controlling, decisive, dictatorial, dominant, dominating, forceful, imperious, imposing, impressive, lofty, peremptory, striking, superior

comment *noun.* comeback, commentary, crack, criticism, dictum, discussion, editorial, elucidation, gloss, hearsay, illustration, input, judgment, mention, opinion, remark, report, review

comment *verb.* affirm, assert, conclude, construe, criticize, disclose, explain, express, gloss, illustrate, interpret, mention, note, observe, pronounce, remark, say, state

commentary *noun.* appreciation, comment, consideration, criticism, critique, description, discourse, exegesis, explanation, exposition, gloss, narration, notes, obiter dictum, observation, remark, review, treatise

commercial *adjective.* commissary, economic, exchange, financial, fiscal, market, marketable, merchandising, monetary, popular, profitable, retail, retailing, sales, supplying, trade, trading, wholesale

commission *noun.* **1** agency, appointment, authority, brevet, certificate, delegation, embassy, employment, errand, function, instruction, legation, mandate, mission, obligation, permit, proxy, trust **2** allowance, bite, bonus, brokerage, chunk, compensation, cut, discount, end, fee, indemnity, pay, percentage, piece, remuneration, royalty, slice, taste

commission *verb.* appoint, assign, authorize, bespeak, bid, commit, consign, constitute, contract, crown, dispatch, enroll, entrust, hire, name, ordain, order, send

commit *verb.* **1** accomplish, achieve, act, carry out, complete, do, effectuate, enact, execute, offend, perpetrate, pull, pull off, scandalize, sin, trespass, violate, wreak **2** allocate, authorize, commend, confide, consign, convey, delegate, deliver, deposit, dispatch, give, hold, ice, move, offer, ordain, remove, shift

common *adjective.* **1** bourgeois, casual, characteristic, conventional, daily, everyday, homely, informal, mediocre, monotonous, natural, prevailing, probably, standard, stock, typical, universal, wearisome **2** collective, communal, communistic, community, corporate, correspondent, general, like, mutual, popular, prevailing, reciprocal, shared, social, socialistic, united, universal, usual **3** cheap, coarse, colorless, hack, hackneyed, inferior, low, mean, nondescript, passable, pedestrian, plebeian, poor, raffish, shoddy, stale, trite, undistinguished

commonplace *adjective.* colorless, conventional, corn, garden, mainstream, mediocre, natural, normal, pedestrian, plebian, starch, stereotyped, threadbare, trite, typical, uninteresting, vanilla, widespread

commonplace *noun.* banality, bromide, chestnut, cliche, corn, inanity, motto, platitude, prosaicism, prosaism, prose, rubber stamp, shallowness, shibboleth, stereotype, triteness, triviality, truism

communicate *verb.* **1** acquaint, advertise, break, broadcast, carry, convey, correspond, disclose, discover, enlighten, interface, network, proclaim, raise, relate, signify, state, writ **2** answer, associate with, buzz, cable, chat, commune with, confabulate, confer, converse, correspond, discourse, hear from, reach, reply, talk, telephone, wire, write

communication *noun.* **1** advisement, announcing, communion, converse, delivery, dissemination, elucidation, expression, intelligence, interchange, intercourse, mention, publication, reception, revelation, talking, telling, utterance **2** bulletin, converse, dispatch, excerpt, goods, intelligence, missive, pipeline, publicity, report, revelation, skinny, speech, statement, tidings, translation, utterance, word

communion *noun.* accord, agreement, association, close relationship, closeness, communing, concord, contact, converse, fellowship, harmony, intercourse, intimacy, participation, rapport, sympathy, togetherness, unity

community *noun.* association, brotherhood, center, colony, commonwealth, company, district, hamlet, locality, nation, neighborhood, people, public, residents, society, state, territory, turf

compact *noun.* alliance, arrangement, bargain, bond, concordat, contract, convention, covenant, deal, engagement, entente, indenture, pact, settlement, stipulation, transaction, treaty, understanding

companion *noun.* accompaniment, accomplice, assistant, brother, buddy, comrade, confederate, convoy, double, fellow, governess, guide, helper, match, mate, nurse, partner, sister

company *noun.* aggregation, assembly, circle, clan, club, community, congregation, ensemble, gang, mob, order, pack, retinue, ring, team, throng, troop, turnout

comparative *adjective.* analogous, approaching, comparable, connected, corresponding, equivalent, inconclusive, like, matching, metaphorical, near, parallel, provisional, qualified, related, relative, restricted, similar

compare *verb.* **1** balance, consider, contemplate, correlate, divide, equal, examine, hang, inspect, match, parallel, ponder, rival, scan, segregate, separate, study, touch **2** allegorize, approach, approximate to, assimilate, balance, connect, correlate, equal, equate, link, match, notice similarities, paragon, parallel, put alongside, relate, resemble, tie up

comparison *noun.* allegory, analyzing, balancing, collation, connection, contrasting, correlation, discrimination, estimation, identification, illustration, likeness, paralleling, relating, relation, resemblance, similarity, testing

compartment *noun.* area, bay, berth, category, cell, chamber, corner, cubbyhole, department, division, locker, niche, piece, pigeonhole, place, slot, stall, subdivision

compass *noun.* area, bound, circle, circuit, expanse, extent, field, limitation, perimeter, precinct, range, reach, round, scope, sphere, stretch, sweep, zone

compatible *adjective.* adaptable, appropriate, congenial, congruent, consistent, consonant, cooperative, fit, fitting, good vibrations, like-minded, meet, mix, proper, reconcilable, suitable, sympathetic, togetherness

compensation *noun.* advantage, allowance, benefit, bonus, consideration, coverage, damages, gain, indemnity, pay, premium, redress, reprisal, salt, satisfaction, scale, shake, take

compete *verb.* attempt, battle, bid, challenge, clash, contend, contest, emulate, face, fence, fight, grapple, joust, rival, strive, struggle, tilt, wrestle

competence *noun.* adequacy, appropriateness, capability, capacity, competency, expertise, fitness, know-how, makings, might, moxie, proficiency, qualification, qualifiedness, savvy, skill, suitability, the goods

competent *adjective.* adapted, adequate, appropriate, crisp, dynamite, efficient, enough, fit, fool, good, pertinent, polished, qualified, satisfactory, skilled, sufficient, suitable, wicked

competition *noun.* antagonism, bout, candidacy, contention, event, fight, match, opposition, race, rodeo, run, strife, striving, struggle, tilt, tournament, trial, warfare

compilation *noun.* accumulation, aggregating, anthology, assembling, assortment, collecting, collection, collocating, combining, compiling, consolidating, garner, garnering, gathering, incorporating, joining, treasury, unifying

complain *verb.* ascribe, beef, bemoan, defy, deplore, disagree, disapprove, fuss, growl, lament, lay, moan, protest, refute, remonstrate, wail, whimper, whine

complaint *noun.* accusation, beef, clamor, criticism, disagreement, dissatisfaction, grumble, kick, lament, moan, objection, protest, rap, representation, rumble, trouble, wail, whine

complement *noun.* accompaniment, addition, aggregate, balance, completion, consummation, correlate, counterpart, enrichment, entirety, filler, pendant, quota, remainder, rest, supplement, total, wholeness

complete *adjective.* **1** all, entire, exhaustive, faultless, full, gross, intact, integrated, organic, outright, plenary, replete, thorough, thoroughgoing, unabridged, undiminished, undivided, whole **2** accomplished, achieved, attained, concluded, consummate, done, down, effected, ended, entire, executed, full, perfect, plenary, realized, sweeping, terminated, thorough **3** blank, blanket, categorical, consummate, downright, flawless, impeccable, outright, perfect, positive, sheer, thorough, thoroughgoing, total, unblemished, unqualified, utter, whole

complete *verb.* accomplish, achieve, cap, conclude, consummate, crown, discharge, do, effectuate, end, finish, furnish, halt, perform, refine, supplement, terminate, wind up

completely *adverb.* absolutely, altogether, competently, comprehensively, conclusively, exclusively, exhaustively, extensively, painstakingly, perfectly, quite, solidly, ultimately, unabridged, unanimously, unconditionally, utterly, wholly

completion *noun.* achievement, attainment, close, conclusion, consummation, culmination, curtains, dispatch, end, expiration, finish, finishing, fruition, fulfillment, hips, integration, realization, windup

complex *adjective.* **1** circuitous, complicated, composite, compound, compounded, confused, convoluted, heterogeneous, involved, knotty, manifold, mingled, miscellaneous, mosaic, motley, multiple, tortuous, variegated **2** circuitous, confused, convoluted, enigmatic, impenetrable, inscrutable, interwoven, involved, jumbled, mingled, paradoxical, puzzling, rambling, recondite, snarled, sophisticated, tortuous, winding

complicated *adjective.* arduous, convoluted, difficult, elaborate, fancy, gasser, hard, interlaced, intricate, involved, knotty, perplexing, problematic, puzzling, recondite, sophisticated, troublesome, various

composed *adjective.* calmed, cool, easygoing, icy, nonchalant, placid, poised, possessed, quieted, relaxed, repressed, sedate, sensible, serene, staid, suppressed, temperate, together

composition *noun.* **1** architecture, arrangement, balance, combination, concord, configuration, consonance, constitution, content, design, distribution, form, formation, layout, placing, proportion, relation, rhythm **2** arrangement, article, chart, fiction, manuscript, melody, music, number, opus, piece, song, stanza, study, symphony, thesis, tune, verse, writing

compound *noun.* admixture, aggregate, alloy, amalgamation, blend, combo, composite, composition, compost, conglomerate, fusion, medley, mishmash, mixture, soup, stew, synthesis, union

compound *verb.* amalgamate, associate, blend, bracket, coadunate, coalesce, commingle, concoct, connect, couple, fuse, join, link, make up, mingle, mix, synthesize, unite

comprehensive *adjective.* absolute, blanket, catholic, comprising, containing, exhaustive, expansive, extensive, full, general, global, infinite, sweeping, thorough, umbrella, whole, wide, widespread

comprise *verb.* amount to, compass, compose, comprehend, constitute, contain, cover, embody, embrace, encircle, encompass, form, hold, include, incorporate, involve, span, subsume

compromise *noun.* accommodation, accord, adjustment, arrangement, bargain, compact, composition, concession, contract, covenant, deal, happy medium, mean, middle course, pact, sellout, settlement, understanding

compromise *verb.* blight, discredit, dishonor, endanger, explode, expose, hazard, imperil, mar, menace, peril, prejudice, risk, ruin, sell out, spoil, weaken, whore

compulsion *noun.* coercion, constraint, demand, drive, driving, duress, duty, force, monkey, necessity, need, obligation, obsession, preoccupation, prepossession, pressure, urge, urgency

computer *noun.* adding machine, analog, brain, calculator, clone, compatible, data processor, digital, electronic brain, laptop, mainframe, micro, microcomputer, mini, minicomputer, number cruncher, personal computer, thinking machine

concealed *adjective.* buried, camouflaged, covert, enshrouded, guarded, inconspicuous, masked, obscure, obscured, planted, privy, recondite, screened, secret, secreted, stashed, unseen, veiled

concede *verb.* accept, accord, admit, allow, award, cede, confess, fess up, fold, grant, hand over, own, own up, quit, relinquish, surrender, waive, yield

conceive *verb.* **1** appreciate, apprehend, assume, believe, compass, comprehend, deem, dig, expect, feel, follow, grasp, imagine, perceive, realize, reckon, suppose, take **2** consider, contrive, design, develop, devise, envision, feature, form, formulate, make up, ponder, produce, project, purpose, realize, spark, speculate, visualize

concentrate *verb.* **1** apply, attend, center, contemplate, establish, examine, focus, hammer, intensify, meditate, muse, need, ponder, put, set, study, sweat, weigh **2** accumulate, agglomerate, amass, assemble, coalesce, collect, combine, compact, consolidate, contract, converge, garner, heap, integrate, localize, mass, narrow, peruse, pile, ruminate, settle, think

concentrated *adjective.* crashed, entire, fixed, lusty, potent, reduced, rich, straight, strong, stuffed, telescoped, thick, thickened, total, unadulterated, undiluted, undivided, whole

concentration *noun.* **1** absorption, assembly, centralization, clustering, combination, congregation, consolidation, debate, deliberation, fixing, flocking, focusing, heed, intensification, narrowing, need, study, unity **2** accumulation, army, array, audience, band, cluster, collection, company, concourse, convergence, flock, group, herd, horde, mass, miscellany, mob, party

concept *noun.* abstraction, apprehension, approach, conception, conceptualization, consideration, hypothesis, image, impression, notion, perception, slant, supposition, theory, thought, twist, view, wrinkle

conception *noun.* clue, comprehension, concept, consideration, considering, design, fancying, imagining, meditating, musing, notion, perception, plan, realization, representation, speculating, speculation, thought

concern *noun.* **1** affair, burden, care, company, corporation, enterprise, establishment, field, house, interest, involvement, matter, mission, occupation, organization, outfit, responsibility, transaction **2** affair, apprehension, attention, bearing, care, carefulness, consideration, disquiet, disquietude, distress, heed, matter, reference, regard, relation, relevance, solicitude, unease

conclude *verb.* **1** achieve, cease, clinch, close, close out, complete, consummate, crown, desist, end, halt, knock off, stop, terminate, top off, ultimate, wind up, wrap up **2** analyze, assume, collect, deduce, derive, draw, figure, gather, infer, intuit, judge, make, presume, reason, reckon, suppose, surmise

conclusion *noun.* cessation, close, closure, completion, consequence, culmination, denouement, development, ending, finish, issue, outcome, period, result, termination, upshot, windup, wrap

conclusive *adjective.* absolute, clear, compelling, convincing, deciding, decisive, determinant, determinative, final, incontrovertible, irrevocable, precise, revealing, settling, telling, unambiguous, undeniable, unmistakable

concord *noun.* accord, agreement, amity, calmness, concert, concordance, consonance, friendship, goodwill, peace, rapport, serenity, tranquility, tune, unanimity, understanding, unison, unity

concrete *adjective.* caked, calcified, cement, compact, compressed, congealed, conglomerated, consolidated, dried, firm, indurate, monolithic, petrified, poured, set, solid, strong, unyielding

condition *noun.* **1** case, estate, happening, mode, order, position, posture, predicament, quality, reputation, scene, shape, situation, sphere, standing, state, status, trim **2** arrangement, article, contingency, demand, essential, limitation, must, necessity, postulate, precondition, prerequisite, provision, proviso, reservation, rule, stipulation, strings, terms

condition *verb.* accustom, brainwash, build up, educate, equip, habituate, inure, make ready, modify, practice, prepare, program, ready, sharpen, tone up, train, warm up, work out

conduct *noun.* care, direction, execution, guidance, leadership, management, oversight, plan, policy, posture, regimen, regulation, rule, strategy, supervision, tactics, transaction, treatment

conduct *verb.* **1** accompany, chair, convey, direct, engineer, govern, guide, handle, head, keep, lead, manage, ordain, order, regulate, rule, shepherd, steer **2** accompany, attend, bring, carry, chaperon, companion, convoy, escort, guide, lead, move, pilot, route, send, shepherd, show, steer, transfer

conference *noun.* appointment, argument, colloquium, colloquy, congress, consultation, conversation, deliberation, discussion, forum, huddle, interchange, interview, parley, rap, seminar, symposium, ventilation

confess *verb.* acknowledge, assert, blow, concede, confide, declare, disclose, finger, grant, hose, own, post, prove, rat on, recognize, relate, sing, unload

confession *noun.* admission, affirmation, allowance, concession, enumeration, expose, exposure, proclamation, profession, publication, recitation, relation, revealing, revelation, song, statement, telling, utterance

confidence *noun.* assurance, backbone, boldness, brashness, cool, courage, daring, dash, determination, firmness, grit, impudence, pluck, presumption, reliance, resolution, spirit, tenacity

confident *adjective.* assured, brave, convinced, courageous, expectant, expecting, fearless, high, hopeful, intrepid, positive, presuming, presumptuous, racked, secure, trusting, undaunted, valiant

confined *adjective.* bedfast, bedridden, bound, chilled, circumscribed, cramp, detained, enclosed, grounded, hampered, held, iced, incarcerated, indisposed, jailed, restrained, restricted, sick

confirm *verb.* affirm, approve, authenticate, buy, certify, check, corroborate, endorse, establish, ok, prove, ratify, sign, subscribe, substantiate, support, uphold, verify

confirmed *adjective.* accepted, accustomed, chronic, clinched, deep-rooted, entrenched, firmly established, fixed, hard-shell, hardened, inured, inveterate, proved, rooted, seasoned, settled, staid, valid, worn

conflict *noun.* **1** battle, clash, collision, combat, competition, contention, contest, emulation, encounter, engagement, rivalry, set-to, strife, striving, struggle, tug-of-war, war, warfare **2** animosity, antagonism, brush, contention, dance, difference, discord, dispute, dissension, faction, friction, fuss, interference, opposition, row, ruckus, strife, variance

conflict *verb.* brawl, clash, combat, contend, contest, contrast, disagree, discord, disturb, fight, interfere, romp, scrap, slug, strive, struggle, tangle, vary

conflicting *adjective.* adverse, antagonistic, clashing, contrary, disconsonant, discrepant, dissonant, incompatible, incongruent, incongruous, inconsistent, inconsonant, opposed, opposing, paradoxical, unfavorable, unmixable

conform *verb.* accommodate, adjust, comply, coordinate, fit, follow, integrate, keep, mind, obey, observe, proportion, reconcile, square, suit, tailor, tune, yield

confront *verb.* accost, affront, beard, brave, dare, defy, encounter, face down, face with, flout, front, meet, oppose, repel, resist, scorn, tell off, withstand

confused *adjective.* **1** baffled, befuddled, bewildered, dazed, disorganized, distracted, flustered, gone, misled, perplexed, perturbed, puzzled, shook, stumped, thrown, unglued, unscrewed, upset **2** blurred, chaotic, disarranged, disordered, disorderly, disorganized, haywire, in disarray, involved, jumbled, messy, miscalculated, miscellaneous, mistaken, misunderstood, obscured, unsettled, untidy

confusion *noun.* **1** agitation, befuddling, bewilderment, commotion, confounding, demoralization, distraction, disturbing, embarrassment, lather, mixing, mystification, perplexing, perplexity, perturbation, stew, unsettling, upsetting **2** ado, difficulty, disarray, distraction, ferment, fog, hodgepodge, jumble, labyrinth, mystification, perturbation, row, stir, tangle, trouble, untidiness, upheaval, uproar

congregation *noun.* aggregation, assembly, audience, collection, company, crowd, disciples, flock, following, group, laity, meet, multitude, parish, parishioners, public, throng, turnout

congress *noun.* assembly, brotherhood, caucus, chamber, club, committee, council, delegates, delegation, diet, fraternity, government, guild, legislature, order, parliament, society, union

connection *noun.* **1** affiliation, alliance, association, attachment, bond, combination, conjunction, coupling, fastening, joining, joint, junction, link, network, partnership, seam, tie, union **2** affinity, application, association, bearing, bond, commerce, communication, correlation, correspondence, intercourse, interrelation, kinship, link, marriage, partnership, relationship, relevance, togetherness

conquest *noun.* acquisition, appropriation, conquering, coup, defeating, invasion, killing, mastery, occupation, overthrow, score, splash, subjection, subjugation, success, takeover, triumph, win

conscious *adjective.* acquainted, aesthetic, assured, awake, certain, felt, keen, known, mindful, noting, observing, on to, perceiving, remarking, seeing, sensible, sentient, vigilant

consecutive *adjective.* after, connected,

constant, continuing, ensuing, following, increasing, later, logical, numerical, progressive, running, sequential, serial, succeeding, successive, understandable, uninterrupted

consent *noun.* accord, acquiescence, allowance, approval, assent, authorization, blessing, compliance, concession, concurrence, go-ahead, leave, okay, permission, permit, sanction, understanding, yes

consent *verb.* accede, accept, acquiesce, allow, approve, assent, bless, comply, concede, concur, fold, give in, let, okay, permit, sanction, subscribe, yield

consequence *noun.* **1** aftereffect, aftermath, bottom line, chain reaction, effect, end, event, fallout, follow through, follow-up, issue, outgrowth, payback, reaction, repercussion, sequel, sequence, upshot **2** account, concern, fame, honor, import, interest, magnitude, moment, need, note, pith, portent, renown, reputation, repute, significance, value, weight

conservation *noun.* care, cherishing, conserving, control, custody, directing, economy, governing, guarding, maintenance, management, managing, protecting, protection, salvation, supervising, supervision, upkeep

conservative *adjective.* bourgeois, cautious, controlled, conventional, fearful, firm, guarded, inflexible, obstinate, orthodox, quiet, stable, steady, traditional, traditionalistic, unchangeable, unchanging, unimaginative

conservative *noun.* classicist, conventionalist, hard hat, moderate, moderatist, obstructionist, old fogy, old liner, preserver, reactionary, red-neck, right, rightist, silk-stocking, standpat, stick-in-the-mud, Tory, traditionalist

consider *verb.* **1** acknowledge, concede, contemplate, deliberate, examine, favor, grant, inspect, muse, ponder, reason, recognize, regard, revolve, scan, see, speculate, study **2** analyze, appraise, count, credit, deem, estimate, feel, hold, judge, reflect, regard, remember, respect, sense, suppose, take for, think, view

considerable *adjective.* **1** ample, astronomical, comfortable, extensive, great, huge, lavish, major, marked, much, noticeable, plentiful, reasonable, respectable, sizable, substantial, tidy, tolerable **2** big, consequential, distinguished, dynamite, essential, fat, influential, mad, meaningful, momentous, noteworthy, renowned, significant, something, substantial, super, venerable, weighty

consideration *noun.* **1** application, attention, cogitation, concentration, contemplation, debate, deliberation, discussion, examination, forethought, heed, reflection, regard, review, scrutiny, study, thinking, thought **2** development, difficulty, estate, extent, idea, incident, issue, judgment, magnitude, minutiae, particulars, perplexity, plan, proposal, scope, state, thought, trouble **3** attentiveness, awareness, concern, esteem, estimation, favor, forbearance, friendliness, heed, kindliness, kindness, mercy, mindfulness, respect, solicitude, tact, thoughtfulness, tolerance

considered *adjective.* advised, aforethought, contemplated, designed, designful, examined, express, intentional, investigated, premeditated, studied, studious, thought-about, treated, voluntary, weighed, willful, writing

consistency *noun.* **1** bendability, density, elasticity, fabric, firmness, flexibility, hardness, limberness, moldability, organization, plasticity, pliability, softness, solidity, suppleness, texture, viscidity, viscosity **2** accord, appropriateness, aptness, coherence, cohesion, concord, consonance, constancy, fitness, homogeneity, likeness, proportion, similarity, steadiness, suitability, uniformity, union, unity

consolidation *noun.* alliance, amalgamation, association, coadunation, coalition, compression, concentration, condensation, federation, fortification, fusion, incorporation, melding, merger, merging, reinforcement, strengthening, unification

conspiracy *noun.* complot, confederacy, connivance, disloyalty, fix, frame, game, hookup, intrigue, league, plot, practice, scheme, sedition, treachery, treason, trick, trickery

constant *adjective.* **1** consistent, continual, even, habitual, invariable, monophonic, monotonous, nonstop, permanent, perpetual, regular, stable, standardized, steady, together, unalterable, unchanging, uninterrupted **2** abiding, ceaseless, chronic, continual, endless, enduring, eternal, everlasting, incessant, interminable, nonstop, perpetual, persistent, persisting, sustained, uninterrupted, unrelenting, unremitting **3** allegiant, attached, dependable, determined, devoted, dogged, faithful, fast, persevering, resolute, staunch, true, trustworthy, trusty, unfailing, unflagging, unshaken, unwavering

constitute *verb.* aggregate, complement, compose, compound, construct, create, develop, embody, establish, fix, form, found, frame, incorporate, integrate, make, make up, set up

constitution *noun.* architecture, build, character, composition, content, contents, design, disposition, essence, form, formation, frame, habit, nature, physique, temper, temperament, vitality

construct *verb.* assemble, constitute, design, engineer, envision, erect, establish, fabricate, fashion, forge, form, formulate, found, frame, invent, produce, raise, shape

construction *noun.* assembly, constitution, contour, development, erecting, fabric, fabrication, form, formation, foundation, improvisation, mold, origination, outline, plan, shape, turn, type

consult *verb.* argue, ask, call in, commune, consider, debate, deliberate, discuss, examine, huddle, interview, negotiate, parley, question, regard, respect, review, treat

consultation *noun.* appointment, argument, conference, council, deliberation, dialogue, discussion, examination, flap, hearing, huddle, interview, meeting, powwow, rap, rap session, session, think-in

consumption *noun.* consuming, damage, decay, decrease, destruction, devastation, diminution, dispersion, drinking, eating, exhaustion, expenditure, loss, misuse, ruin, swallowing, utilization, waste

contain *verb.* bottle up, check, collect, compose, control, cool, cork, curb, harness, hold in, keep back, rein, repress, restrain, restrict, smother, stifle, stop

container *noun.* bin, bowl, box, canteen, chamber, chest, cistern, crate, dish, hopper, packet, pot, pouch, purse, receptacle, stein, tank, tub

contemporary *adjective.* **1** abreast, contempo, current, existent, extant, fire new, instant, latest, new, now, present, recent, red-hot, todayish, topical, ultramodern, up, up-to-the-minute **2** accompanying, associated, attendant, coetaneous, coeval, coexistent, coincident, concomitant, concurrent, connected, contemporaneous, current, linked, present, related, simultaneous, synchronic, synchronous

contempt *noun.* antipathy, aversion, condescension, defiance, derision, despite, disdain, distaste, hatred, malice, mockery, neglect, repugnance, ridicule, scorn, slight, snobbery, stubbornness

content *verb.* appease, bewitch, captivate, charm, delight, enrapture, gladden, gratify, humor, indulge, make happy, mollify, placate, reconcile, satisfy, suffice, thrill, tickle

contention *noun.* **1** altercation, argument, battle, beef, combat, conflict, difference, discord, dispute, enmity, fight, quarrel, scrap, static, strife, struggle, variance, war **2** advancement, affirmation, assertion, belief, claim, declaration, demurrer, discussion, hypothesis, idea, opinion, plea, position, profession, rumpus, stand, thesis, view

contents *noun.* constituents, details, elements, essence, freight, furnishing, gist, guts, implication, intent, load, packing, shipment, significance, subjects, substance, sum, themes

contest *noun.* altercation, battle, beef, brawl, brush, conflict, debate, discord, dispute, fray, row, rumble, scrap, static, strife, striving, struggle, warfare

contest *verb.* attack, battle, brawl, buck,

compete, conflict, contend, cross, lay out, quarrel, rival, row, scrap, scuffle, strike, struggle, tilt, withstand

continuation *noun.* assiduity, augmenting, continuance, continuing, duration, endurance, enduring, line, persisting, postscript, producing, prolongation, prolonging, sequel, succession, supplement, sustaining, tenacity

continue *verb.* abide, advance, endure, extend, last, linger, maintain, progress, project, promote, reach, remain, rest, ride, stand, survive, sustain, uphold

continuity *noun.* chain, connection, constancy, continuance, durability, duration, endurance, flow, linking, persistence, sequence, stamina, succession, survival, train, uniting, unity, whole

continuous *adjective.* connected, consecutive, continued, endless, everlasting, extended, interminable, looped, perpetual, prolonged, regular, repeated, stable, steady, unbroken, unceasing, undivided, uninterrupted

contract *noun.* arrangement, bargain, bond, commitment, compact, covenant, evidence, handshake, indenture, liability, obligation, pact, pledge, promise, record, stipulation, treaty, understanding

contract *verb.* **1** compress, confine, consume, decline, draw in, dwindle, ebb, edit, epitomize, lessen, narrow, omit, purse, recede, shrink, subside, waste, wither **2** adjust, agree, assent, bargain, bound, buy, clinch, close, commit, covenant, ink, limit, negotiate, owe, pact, pledge, promise, undertake **3** acquire, bring on, cause, decline, derange, develop, disorder, fall, get, incur, indispose, induce, obtain, sicken, sink, take, upset, weaken

contraction *noun.* abbreviation, condensation, condensing, constriction, consumption, diminishing, diminution, dwindling, evaporation, lessening, narrowing, omission, reducing, reduction, shrinkage, shrinking, tensing, withdrawal

contrary *adjective.* antithetical, contradictory, converse, diametric, dissident, hostile, inconsistent, insubordinate, negative, nonconformist, obstinate, opposed, paradoxical, refractory, restive, reverse, stubborn, unruly

contrast *noun.* adverse, antithesis, comparison, contradiction, converse, differentiation, disagreement, disparity, distinction, divergence, foil, incompatibility, inconsistency, inverse, opposition, reverse, variance, variation

contrast *verb.* balance, bracket, collate, compare, conflict, contradict, depart, deviate, differentiate, disagree, distinguish, hang, mismatch, oppose, separate, stand out, vary, weigh

contribute *verb.* **1** accord, add, assign, bequest, bestow, commit, devote, dower, enrich, furnish, give, give away, grant, sacrifice, share, subscribe, supply, tender **2** add to, advance, aid, assist, augment, be conducive, be instrumental, conduce, fortify, help, lead, redound, reinforce, strengthen, supplement, support, tend, uphold

contribution *noun.* addition, augmentation, beneficence, bestowal, charity, donation, gifting, grant, hand, handout, improvement, increase, input, offering, present, subscription, supplement, write-off

control *noun.* ascendancy, authority, clout, containment, determination, discipline, government, jurisdiction, limitation, management, might, power, predomination, regulation, ropes, supervision, supremacy, weight

control *verb.* **1** advise, bully, direct, discipline, govern, guide, handle, head, lead, manage, pilot, quarterback, regulate, rule, run, steer, subject, subjugate **2** adjust, awe, bridle, check, collect, compose, contain, cool, corner, cow, limit, master, monopolize, quell, regulate, repress, restrain, subdue

controversial *adjective.* arguable, contended, contestable, controvertible, debatable, disputable, disputatious, disputed, doubtable, doubtful, dubious, dubitable, in dispute, moot, polemical, questionable, suspect, uncertain

controversy *noun.* altercation, argument,

beef, bickering, brush, contention, difference, discussion, dispute, fuss, hurrah, polemic, quarrel, row, rumpus, scrap, strife, words

convenience *noun.* accessibility, accommodation, advantage, aid, appliance, appropriateness, avail, benefit, comforts, contribution, cooperation, facility, fitness, life, luxury, relief, satisfaction, service

convenient *adjective.* **1** acceptable, accommodating, adaptable, adapted, agreeable, aiding, appropriate, beneficial, conducive, favorable, fit, fitted, handy, helpful, ready, roomy, suitable, timely **2** accessible, adjacent, adjoining, at elbows, at fingertips, available, central, close, close-by, contiguous, handy, immediate, next, next door, nigh, on deck, on tap, within reach

conventional *adjective.* **1** accustomed, correct, everyday, expected, general, habitual, normal, orthodox, popular, predominant, prevailing, ritual, square, standard, stereotyped, traditional, typical, usual **2** bigoted, bourgeois, demure, dogmatic, inflexible, lame, literal, moderate, moral, narrow, obstinate, pedestrian, puritanical, rigid, solemn, square, stereotyped, strict

conversation *noun.* colloquy, communion, conference, consultation, converse, debate, discussion, expression, gab, intercourse, parley, questioning, rap, remark, repartee, speech, ventilation, visit

conversion *noun.* alteration, flux, growth, innovation, metamorphosis, passage, passing, progress, reconstruction, reformation, remodeling, resolution, resolving, reversal, transformation, translation, transmutation, turning

convert *verb.* **1** adapt, alter, apply, appropriate, commute, interchange, make, metamorphose, modify, remodel, reorganize, restyle, revise, switch, transform, translate, transpose, turn **2** actuate, baptize, bend, bias, bring, budge, convince, incline, lead, move, persuade, proselyte, proselytize, redeem, reform, save, sway, turn

convey *verb.* bear, carry, dispatch, ferry, fetch, forward, funnel, grant, guide, hump, lead, move, pack, pipe, ride, support, transmit, truck

conviction *noun.* confidence, creed, doctrine, dogma, eye, faith, feeling, judgment call, mind, opinion, persuasion, principle, reliance, say so, sentiment, slant, tenet, view

convincing *adjective.* acceptable, authentic, conclusive, credible, faithful, impressive, incontrovertible, possible, rational, reasonable, reliable, satisfactory, satisfying, solid, sound, swaying, telling, valid

cook *verb.* barbecue, brew, brown, burn, cremate, curry, devil, fix, grill, roast, scald, sear, spoil, steam, steep, stew, toast, warm up

cool *adjective.* **1** air-conditioned, algid, arctic, biting, chill, chilled, chilling, chilly, coldish, frigid, frore, frosty, nipping, refreshing, refrigerated, shivery, snappy, wintry **2** assured, collected, composed, coolheaded, deliberate, detached, dispassionate, impassive, imperturbable, nonchalant, philosophical, placid, quiet, relaxed, serene, stolid, together, unemotional **3** aloof, annoyed, distant, frigid, impertinent, impudent, indifferent, lukewarm, offended, offhand, reserved, solitary, uncommunicative, unenthusiastic, unfriendly, uninterested, unresponsive, withdrawn

cool *verb.* abate, allay, assuage, chill, compose, control, dampen, lessen, mitigate, moderate, quiet, reduce, rein, repress, restrain, simmer down, suppress, temper

cooperate *verb.* advance, agree, aid, band, coincide, combine, conspire, coordinate, forward, fraternize, further, help, join, participate, partner, second, succor, uphold

cooperation *noun.* aid, alliance, coalition, collaboration, combination, communion, confederacy, conspiracy, federation, fusion, partnership, service, society, teaming, teamwork, unanimity, union, unity

cooperative *adjective.* accommodating, agreeing, collective, combining, companionable, coordinated, interdependent, joining, participating, reciprocal, responsive, shared, sociable, supportive, team, united, uniting, useful

coordinate *verb.* accommodate, adjust, agree, combine, conform, correlate, harmonize, integrate, match, mesh, organize, pool, proportion, quarterback, reconcile, reconciliate, regulate, synchronize

cope *verb.* buffet, contend, deal, dispatch, encounter, endure, face, grapple, hack, handle, manage, struggle, suffer, survive, tangle, tussle, weather, wrestle

copy *noun.* carbon, facsimile, forgery, imitation, impersonation, imprint, likeness, miniature, model, parallel, portrait, print, replication, representation, reproduction, similarity, study, type

copy *verb.* **1** carbon, fake, forge, imitate, manifold, mirror, mold, paint, picture, repeat, represent, reproduce, rewrite, sculpture, sketch, stat, trace, transcribe **2** ape, do, emulate, epitomize, fake, follow, incarnate, mirror, mock, model, parrot, pirate, repeat, sham, steal, take off, travesty, typify

core *noun.* base, bulk, corpus, crux, essence, foundation, importance, middle, midpoint, midst, nucleus, origin, pith, pivot, purport, substance, thrust, upshot

corporation *noun.* association, bunch, business, clan, company, crew, crowd, enterprise, gang, hookup, jungle, outfit, partnership, ring, shell, society, syndicate, zoo

correct *adjective.* **1** actual, amen, appropriate, equitable, faithful, faultless, impeccable, nice, okay, precise, proper, regular, righteous, stone, strict, true, veracious, veridical **2** acceptable, appropriate, becoming, careful, conventional, decent, decorous, diplomatic, done, fitting, meticulous, nice, okay, right, right stuff, scrupulous, standard, suitable

correct *verb.* alter, better, change, cure, edit, help, pick up, polish, reclaim, redress, reform, regulate, remedy, reorganize, review, scrub, turn around, upgrade

correlation *noun.* alternation, analogue, complement, correspondence, correspondent, counterpart, equivalence, interaction, interchange, interconnection, interdependence, interrelation, interrelationship, match, parallel, pendant, reciprocity, relationship

correspondence *noun.* accord, analogy, coherence, coincidence, comparison, concurrence, consistency, correlation, equivalence, fitness, harmony, likeness, match, regularity, relation, resemblance, similarity, symmetry

corresponding *adjective.* akin, alike, analogous, answering, comparable, complementary, correspondent, identical, interrelated, kin, kindred, like, matching, parallel, reciprocal, similar, synonymous, undifferentiated

corrupt *adjective.* **1** base, bent, crooked, exploiting, fixed, foul, iniquitous, mercenary, open, padded, perfidious, reprobate, rotten, shady, tainted, underhanded, unfaithful, unscrupulous **2** abandoned, baneful, degenerate, degraded, deleterious, depraved, dishonored, dissolute, evil, infamous, loose, low, miscreant, monstrous, nefarious, perverse, rotten, villainous

corrupt *verb.* abuse, bribe, contaminate, decompose, disgrace, fix, harm, impair, infect, lower, lure, maltreat, mar, spoil, square, stain, violate, warp

corruption *noun.* **1** bribery, crime, demoralization, dishonesty, exploitation, fiddling, fraud, fraudulency, graft, misrepresentation, nepotism, payoff, profiteering, racket, shady deal, shuffle, skimming, squeeze **2** atrocity, decadence, degeneration, degradation, depravity, evil, immorality, impurity, infamy, looseness, lubricity, profligacy, sinfulness, turpitude, vice, viciousness, vulgarity, wickedness

cost *noun.* bite, damage, disbursement, expenditure, figure, line, outlay, payment, price, rate, setback, squeeze, tab, tariff, ticket, toll, value, worth

costly *adjective.* cher, costive, dear, excessive, executive, exorbitant, extortionate, extravagant, fancy, high, inordinate, precious, premium, pricey, steep, stiff, top, valuable

council *noun.* body, chamber, clan, committee, conference, congregation, congress, diet, directorate, gang, huddle, meet, mob, outfit, panel, parliament, ring, synod

counsel *noun.* admonition, advice, advisement, caution, consideration, consultation, deliberation, direction, forethought, information, instruction, kibitz, recommendation, steer, suggestion, tip, tip-off, warning

counsel *verb.* advocate, caution, direct, enjoin, huddle, inform, instruct, order, prescribe, prompt, recommend, steer, suggest, teach, tip off, tout, urge, warn

count *verb.* calculate, cast, cast up, cipher, compute, enumerate, estimate, figure, foot, keep tab, number, reckon, run down, score, sum, tally, tell, total

counter *adjective.* adverse, against, antagonistic, anti, antipodal, antithetical, conflicting, contradictory, contrary, contrasting, converse, diametric, hindering, obverse, opposed, opposing, polar, reverse

counter *verb.* answer, beat, buck, counteract, cross, dash, foil, frustrate, match, meet, offset, oppose, parry, pit, play off, resist, return, ruin

counterpart *noun.* analogue, complement, copy, correlate, correspondent, duplicate, equal, equivalent, fellow, like, mate, obverse, opposite, opposite number, pendant, supplement, tally, twin

countless *adjective.* endless, heap, immeasurable, incalculable, legion, limitless, load, loads, many, mess, multitudinous, peck, pile, raft, rafts, stacks, uncounted, untold

country *adjective.* agrarian, agrestic, Arcadian, bucolic, campestral, countrified, georgic, homey, out-country, outland, pastoral, provincial, rustic, uncouth, uncultured, unpolished, unrefined, unsophisticated

country *noun.* citizenry, citizens, commonwealth, community, electors, grass roots, homeland, motherland, people, public, realm, region, society, soil, state, terrain, territory, voters

couple *verb.* bracket, buckle, clasp, coalesce, cohabit, conjugate, connect, copulate, harness, hitch, hook up, link, marry, match, pair, unite, wed, yoke

courage *noun.* backbone, bravery, bravura, daring, dash, determination, endurance, gallantry, grit, guts, nerve, pluck, power, prowess, recklessness, resolution, spirit, tenacity

course *noun.* **1** advancement, chain, development, flow, line, march, order, plan, policy, polity, program, row, scheme, sequel, sequence, string, succession, way **2** canal, circuit, conduit, direction, duct, flow, groove, lap, line, passage, range, route, run, rut, scope, stream, trail, way **3** class, conference, curriculum, interest, laboratory, lecture, meeting, method, period, preparation, procedure, program, regimen, schedule, seminar, session, specialty, subject

course *verb.* career, chase, dash, follow, gallop, gush, hasten, hunt, hustle, pursue, race, run, rush, speed, spring, stream, surge, tumble

court *verb.* allure, attract, beseech, bid, chase, date, flatter, gallant, grovel, invite, pitch, praise, propose, solicit, spark, spoon, sweetheart, woo

cover *noun.* **1** bark, binding, canopy, canvas, cap, ceiling, cloak, clothing, envelope, hood, parasol, polish, pretense, smoke screen, tarpaulin, umbrella, veil, wrapper **2** asylum, camouflage, concealment, covert, defense, drop, front, guard, haven, port, protection, refuge, retreat, safety, sanctuary, screen, security, shelter

cover *verb.* **1** bury, camouflage, canopy, cap, carpet, cloak, clothe, conceal, crown, curtain, dress, hide, hood, layer, mantle, overlay, surface, veil **2** be enough, comprehend, comprise, consider, contain, deal with, embody, embrace, encompass, examine, incorporate, involve, meet, provide for, reach, refer to, suffice, survey

cow *verb.* awe, bludgeon, bluster, buffalo, bulldoze, bully, daunt, disconcert, dishearten, dismay, faze, frighten, hector, overawe, rattle, scare, subdue, terrorize

coward *noun.* alarmist, baby, big baby, chicken, craven, cur, faint-of-heart, fraidy cat, funk, milksop, milquetoast, mollycoddle, mouse, punk, rabbit, sneak, turkey, yellow

crack *adjective*. able, ace, adept, best, choice, deluxe, elite, excellent, expert, master, masterful, masterly, proficient, skilled, skillful, super, superior, talented

crack *noun*. **1** breach, chip, cleft, crevasse, crevice, cut, discontinuity, division, fissure, fracture, gap, hole, interstice, interval, rent, rift, rime, split **2** blast, blow, buffet, burst, clap, clout, cuff, explosion, report, shot, slam, slap, smack, snap, splitting, thump, thwack, wallop

crack *verb*. burst, chip, chop, crackle, crash, damage, detonate, explode, fracture, hurt, impair, pop, ring, sever, shiver, snap, splinter, split

craft *noun*. **1** ability, adeptness, adroitness, aptitude, art, artistry, cleverness, competence, cunning, dexterity, expertise, expertness, ingenuity, knack, know-how, proficiency, technique, workmanship **2** art, artfulness, artifice, cageyness, canniness, cunning, disingenuity, duplicity, guile, ruse, scheme, slyness, strategy, subterfuge, subtlety, trickery, wiles, wiliness

crash *noun*. **1** blast, boom, burst, clang, clap, clash, clatter, clattering, crack, din, peal, racket, slam, smash, smashing, sound, thunder, thunderclap **2** accident, bump, collapse, concussion, crunch, debacle, ditch, impact, jar, jolt, percussion, ram, shock, smash, thud, thump, total, wreck

crash *verb*. **1** crack up, crunch, dash, disintegrate, fender bend, fender tag, fracture, fragment, pile up, rear end, shatter, shiver, sideswipe, smash, smash up, splinter, total, wrack up **2** bump, collapse, crash-land, ditch, dive, drop, go in, lurch, meet, pitch, plunge, prang, slip, smash, sprawl, topple, tumble, upset

crazy *adjective*. **1** ape, crazed, cuckoo, demented, deranged, dingy, erratic, flaky, idiotic, insane, lunatic, nuts, psycho, screwball, touched, unbalanced, unhinged, wacky **2** balmy, cockeyed, fantastic, fatuous, foolhardy, foolish, idiotic, impracticable, inappropriate, insane, ludicrous, odd, peculiar, preposterous, quixotic, senseless, unworkable, wacky

create *verb*. constitute, construct, contrive, devise, discover, establish, fabricate, fashion, father, form, formulate, initiate, parent, perform, plan, produce, shape, start

creation *noun*. conception, constitution, establishment, formation, formulation, foundation, generation, genesis, imagination, inception, institution, making, nascency, nativity, origination, procreation, production, setting up

creative *adjective*. artistic, clever, cool, fertile, formative, gifted, hip, ingenious, innovational, innovatory, inspired, inventive, original, originative, productive, prolific, stimulating, way out

creator *noun*. architect, author, begetter, brain, deity, designer, father, founder, framer, generator, initiator, maker, mastermind, originator, patriarch, prime mover, producer, sire

creature *noun*. animal, body, brute, creation, critter, fellow, individual, living being, living thing, lower animal, man, mortal, party, person, personage, quadruped, soul, varmint

credit *noun*. **1** acclaim, acknowledgment, approval, attention, belief, commendation, confidence, distinction, faith, fame, notice, points, praise, reliance, strokes, thanks, tribute, trust **2** balance, bond, capital outlay, continuance, extension, lien, loan, mortgage, on account, on tick, plastic, respite, securities, stock, surplus cash, tab, trust, wealth

creep *verb*. edge, glide, grovel, inch, lurk, pussyfoot, scramble, skulk, slink, slither, snake, sneak, squirm, steal, tiptoe, worm, wriggle, writhe

crest *noun*. acme, apex, apogee, climax, crescendo, crown, culmination, fastigium, head, height, noon, peak, pinnacle, ridge, roof, summit, top, vertex

crew *noun*. aggregation, band, collection, congregation, faction, gang, hands, horde, lot, mob, pack, retinue, sect, squad, swarm, team, troop, troupe

crime *noun*. break, case, corruption, criminality, delinquency, dereliction, fault, felony, hit, immorality, infringement, misdemeanor, quickie, transgression, vice, violation, wrong, wrongdoing

criminal *adjective.* bent, caught, corrupt, crooked, deplorable, dirty, felonious, heavy, illegal, illegitimate, immoral, iniquitous, shady, unlawful, vicious, villainous, wildcat, wrong

criminal *noun.* blackmailer, con, convict, culprit, felon, finger, guerilla, heavy, hood, hoodlum, moll, mug, offender, racketeer, repeater, shylock, sinner, thug

crisis *noun.* catastrophe, change, climax, confrontation, contingency, crunch, crux, embarrassment, necessity, perplexity, pickle, predicament, pressure, stew, trauma, trial, trouble, urgent

criterion *noun.* basis, canon, example, exemplar, fact, foundation, law, model, norm, opinion, original, precedent, prototype, rule, scale, standard, touchstone, yardstick

critic *noun.* **1** analyzer, annotator, arbiter, authority, caricaturist, cartoonist, commentator, connoisseur, diagnostic, evaluator, expert, expositor, interpreter, judge, master, pundit, reviewer, sharpshooter **2** aristarch, attacker, belittler, carper, censor, complainant, defamer, detractor, disparager, doubter, hypercritic, Momus, nagger, nitpicker, panner, scolder, slanderer, zapper

critical *adjective.* **1** analytical, biting, captious, carping, condemning, critic, cutting, cynical, diagnostic, discriminating, exacting, finicky, lowering, nagging, penetrating, satirical, scolding, sharp **2** conclusive, deciding, decisive, desperate, determinative, grave, hairy, hazardous, momentous, perilous, pivotal, precarious, psychological, risky, significant, strategic, urgent, weighty

criticism *noun.* **1** appraisal, commentary, critique, elucidation, evaluation, examination, judgment, lemon, opinion, pan, rating, review, scorcher, slam, slap, static, study, swipe **2** blast, carping, censure, cut, cutting, denunciation, hit, knock, knocking, objection, opprobrium, pan, quibble, rap, roast, slam, swipe, vitriol

crop *verb.* chop, clip, curtail, cut, detach, disengage, lop, mow, pare, prune, reduce, shave, shear, shorten, skive, slash, snip, top

cross *adjective.* captious, cranky, crotchety, disagreeable, fractious, impatient, irritable, jumpy, petulant, put out, querulous, short, snappy, splenetic, sullen, touchy, vexed, waspish

cross *verb.* backtalk, block, bollix, buck, cramp, deny, double-cross, foil, foul up, frustrate, interfere, obstruct, oppose, resist, sell, sell out, stump, thwart

crossing *noun.* bridge, crossroad, crosswalk, crossway, exchange, grating, gridiron, interchange, intersection, junction, loop, network, overpass, passage, screen, traversal, traverse, underpass

crowd *noun.* circle, cloud, congregation, crush, deluge, drove, flock, gaggle, jam, mass, mob, multitude, pack, people, scores, stream, surge, throng

crowd *verb.* bear, bundle, congregate, crush, deluge, flock, huddle, jam, mass, pack, pile, push, shove, squash, squeeze, stream, surge, throng

crowded *adjective.* awash, brimful, busy, clean, close, compact, crammed, crushed, dense, full, huddled, loaded, massed, overflowing, packed, stuffed, teeming, thick

crown *noun.* acme, apex, climax, crest, culmination, fastigium, head, meridian, peak, perfection, pinnacle, roof, summit, tip, top, ultimate, vertex, zenith

crown *verb.* adorn, arm, authorize, commission, delegate, determine, dignify, enable, enthrone, erect, establish, exalt, fix, heighten, install, invest, raise, stabilize

crucial *adjective.* acute, central, clamorous, compelling, crucial, deciding, decisive, desperate, dire, essential, imperative, insistent, momentous, pivotal, showdown, touchy, urgent, vital

crude *adjective.* **1** awkward, barnyard, boorish, cheap, clumsy, coarse, crass, dirty, earthy, foul, gross, ignorant, indecent, indelicate, lewd, obscene, rough, savage **2** coarse, green, harsh, homemade, inexpert, makeshift, natural, outline, prentice, primitive, raw, rough, simple, thick, undeveloped, unfinished, unformed, unprepared, untrained

cruel *adjective.* depraved, excruciating, ferocious, fierce, hard, inhuman, inhumane, malevolent, monstrous, painful, pernicious, poignant, ruthless, sinful, unkind, unnatural, vicious, virulent

cruelty *noun.* brutality, callousness, coarseness, coldness, depravity, despotism, ferocity, fierceness, harshness, malice, rancor, ruthlessness, sadism, savagery, severity, spite, truculence, venom

cry *noun.* **1** bawling, blubber, blubbering, howl, howling, keening, lament, lamentation, mourning, snivel, sob, sobbing, sorrowing, tears, wailing, weep, whimpering, yowl **2** bark, chatter, clamor, fuss, hiss, hoot, outcry, pipe, ruckus, scream, screech, shout, shriek, song, uproar, wail, whine, yell

cry *verb.* **1** bemoan, bewail, blubber, break down, complain, deplore, howl, keen, lament, moan, mourn, regret, sniff, squall, wail, weep, whimper, whine **2** bark, chatter, cheer, clamor, crow, exclaim, growl, hiss, hoot, howl, pipe, roar, scream, screech, shout, shriek, whine, yell

cultural *adjective.* beneficial, broadening, constructive, developmental, edifying, educational, enlightening, enriching, expanding, helpful, humane, inspirational, learned, liberal, liberalizing, polishing, promoting, refining

culture *noun.* address, civilization, class, cultivation, delicacy, dignity, discrimination, enlightenment, experience, fashion, gentility, learning, manners, perception, polish, practice, skill, tact

cumulative *adjective.* accumulative, additive, additory, advancing, aggregate, amassed, augmenting, chain, collective, growing, heaped, heightening, increasing, intensifying, magnifying, multiplying, snowballing, summative

cup *noun.* beaker, bowl, cannikin, chalice, cupful, demitasse, draught, drink, goblet, grail, mug, pannikin, potion, stein, taster, teacup, tumbler, vessel

curb *verb.* abstain, bit, check, clog, contain, deny, hold in, ice, leash, moderate, muzzle, refrain, repress, retard, scrub, subdue, tame, withhold

cure *noun.* aid, alleviation, antidote, assistance, countermeasure, drug, fix, healing, help, medication, medicine, recovery, redress, remedy, reparation, restorative, therapeutic, treatment

cure *verb.* alleviate, attend, better, correct, dress, ease, help, improve, kick, nurse, redress, relieve, remedy, repair, restore, right, shake, treat

curiosity *noun.* **1** concern, eagerness, inquiring mind, inquisitiveness, interest, interestingness, intrusiveness, investigation, meddlesomeness, meddling, mental acquisitiveness, nosiness, officiousness, prying, questioning, regard, searching, snooping **2** anomaly, bibelot, bygone, conversation piece, curio, exoticism, freak, knickknack, marvel, monstrosity, objet d'art, oddity, peculiar object, prodigy, rarity, singular object, trinket, wonder

curious *adjective.* **1** analytical, examining, impertinent, inquiring, inquisitive, inspecting, interested, interfering, intrusive, investigative, meddling, prurient, prying, puzzled, questioning, scrutinizing, searching, tampering **2** extraordinary, marvelous, mysterious, novel, peculiar, puzzling, quaint, queer, rare, remarkable, singular, unconventional, unexpected, unique, unorthodox, unusual, weird, wonderful

currency *noun.* bill, bread, cash, coins, cold cash, color, corn, dinero, dough, folding money, lettuce, line, mint, notes, peanuts, poke, specie, wad

current *adjective.* accustomed, circulating, customary, doing, existent, extant, general, hip, in, instant, modern, popular, prevailing, rampant, ruling, swinging, topical, widespread

curse *noun.* **1** ban, bane, blasphemy, cursing, cuss word, damning, denunciation, dirty word, expletive, jinx, kibosh, malediction, oath, obloquy, obscenity, profanity, sacrilege, swearing **2** affliction, bane, burden, calamity, cancer, cross, disaster, evil, evil eye, jinx, ordeal, plague, scourge, torment, tribulation, trouble, voodoo, whammy

cursed *adjective*. **1** accursed, bedeviled, blankety-blank, blasted, blessed, blighted, confounded, doggone, doomed, excommunicate, fey, hell fire, ill-fated, star-crossed, unholy, unsanctified, villainous, voodooed **2** abominable, accursed, atrocious, damnable, detestable, devilish, disgusting, execrable, fiendish, flagitious, heinous, infamous, infernal, loathsome, odious, pernicious, pestilential, vile

curt *adjective*. blunt, brief, concise, gruff, imperious, offhand, peremptory, pithy, rude, sharp, short, snippy, succinct, summary, tart, terse, uncivil, ungracious

curtain *noun*. blind, decoration, drape, drapery, film, hanging, jalousie, oleo, portiere, rag, roller, screen, shade, shield, shroud, shutter, valance, veil

curve *noun*. arc, bow, chord, circle, circuit, compass, contour, crook, curvature, hairpin, loop, quirk, round, sweep, swerve, trajectory, turn, vault

curve *verb*. arc, arch, bow, buckle, concave, convex, curl, deviate, divert, loop, round, snake, spiral, swerve, turn, twist, veer, wind

custom *noun*. **1** addiction, characteristic, fashion, form, grind, groove, into, kick, mode, observance, practice, rule, shot, swim, trick, use, way, wont **2** canon, ceremony, character, etiquette, fashion, form, inheritance, mode, mold, mores, observance, policy, practice, precept, ritual, type, vogue, way

customary *adjective*. accustomed, chicken, chronic, confirmed, conventional, everyday, frequent, habitual, household, normal, orthodox, popular, prescriptive, regulation, standard, traditional, understood, universal

customer *noun*. chump, client, clientele, consumer, float, front, habituÈ_, head, live one, mark, patron, pigeon, prospect, purchaser, regular shopper, shopper, sucker, walk-in

cut *noun*. **1** carving, chip, chop, cleavage, furrow, graze, intersection, mark, nick, notch, opening, passage, pierce, prick, rip, sculpture, slash, trim **2** allotment, allowance, bite, chop, division, kickback, lot, member, moiety, part, partage, percentage, piece, quota, section, segment, share, slice

cut *verb*. **1** bite, carve, chisel, clip, dissect, divide, hack, hash, lacerate, lop, part, pierce, quarter, reap, rend, saber, shear, sunder **2** clip, condense, contract, crop, curtail, cut back, decrease, dock, excise, lessen, lower, pare, ration, reduce, shave, slash, slim, trim **3** disregard, ditch, duck, dump, evade, hurt, ignore, insult, neglect, pain, skip, slight, snob, snub, stay away, sting, turn aside, wound

cutting *adjective*. acid, barbed, biting, crisp, incisive, malicious, nasty, penetrating, pointed, probing, raw, sarcastic, sardonic, scathing, severe, sharp, stinging, trenchant

cycle *noun*. chain, circle, circuit, course, era, loop, orbit, period, revolution, rhythm, ring, rotation, round, sequel, sequence, series, succession, wheel

D

damage *noun*. accident, affliction, breakage, bruise, catastrophe, corruption, depreciation, deprivation, destruction, detriment, harm, illness, marring, mischief, mishap, wound, wreckage, wrecking

damage *verb*. abuse, batter, break, dirty, fade, gnaw, harm, impair, lacerate, maltreat, rust, smash, split, stab, stain, wound, wreck, wrong

damn *verb*. abuse, attack, blast, censure, criticize, curse, denounce, doom, excoriate, expel, flame, jinx, pan, proscribe, sentence, slam, swear, voodoo

damned *adjective.* bad, blasted, bloody, blooming, condemned, cursed, dang, darned, detestable, doggone, doomed, infamous, loathsome, lousy, revolting, unhappy, unwelcome

damp *adjective.* clammy, cloudy, dank, dewy, drenched, dripping, drizzly, misty, moist, muggy, saturated, soaked, soaking, sodden, soggy, sopping, sticky, wet

dance *verb.* boogie, cavort, frolic, hop, jig, jitterbug, jump, leap, rock, skip, spin, step, strut, swing, tap, tread, truck, twist

dandy *adjective.* capital, cool, exemplary, famous, fine, glorious, grand, great, keen, marvelous, model, paragon, peachy, prime, splendid, superior, swell, terrific

danger *noun.* crisis, dynamite, emergency, exposure, insecurity, instability, jeopardy, menace, peril, possibility, precipice, probability, risk, storm, threat, uncertainty, venture, vulnerability

dangerous *adjective.* alarming, bad, deadly, delicate, exposed, fatal, heavy, impending, insecure, loaded, mortal, perilous, precarious, serpentine, speculative, treacherous, ugly, unsafe

dare *verb.* **1** beard, brave, bully, confront, cope, defy, denounce, disregard, face, front, goad, insult, meet, mock, provoke, resist, scorn, threaten **2** adventure, attempt, be bold, brave, endanger, endeavor, gamble, go ahead, hazard, make bold, presume, risk, speculate, stake, take heart, try, undertake, venture

daring *adjective.* bold, brassy, brave, cocky, courageous, fearless, foolhardy, forward, game, gritty, impudent, intrepid, rash, reckless, salty, smart, valiant, venturesome

dark *adjective.* **1** black, dim, dingy, drab, dull, dusky, foggy, indistinct, lurid, murky, obscure, opaque, overcast, shaded, shadowy, shady, tenebrous, vague **2** cabalistic, complicated, concealed, cryptic, deep, Delphian, enigmatic, esoteric, hidden, intricate, knotty, mysterious, mystic, mystical, obscure, occult, puzzling, recondite

dark *noun.* darkness, dimness, dusk, duskiness, evening, gloom, midnight, murk, night, nightfall, nighttime, obscurity, opacity, semi-darkness, shade, shadows, twilight, witching hour

darkness *noun.* black, blackness, blackout, brownout, dark, dusk, duskiness, eclipse, gloom, lightlessness, murk, nightfall, obscurity, pitch darkness, shade, shadows, smokiness, twilight

darling *noun.* angel, baby, beloved, dear, dearest, dearie, flame, friend, honey, lamb, love, loved, lover, precious, princess, sugar, sweet, treasure

dash *noun.* **1** animation, energy, esprit, flair, flourish, force, intensity, life, might, power, spirit, strength, vehemence, verve, vigor, vivacity, zing, zip **2** drop, flavor, grain, hint, lick, little, part, seasoning, smack, sprinkling, squirt, streak, suggestion, suspicion, taste, touch, trace, trifle

dash *verb.* **1** beat, bludgeon, cast, charge, crash, destroy, fling, hit, hurl, lunge, plunge, shatter, shiver, slam, sling, smash, splash, splinter **2** boil, bolt, bound, career, charge, chase, course, fly, gallop, haste, hasten, lash, race, rush, shoot, speed, spring, tear **3** abash, baffle, beat, bilk, blast, blight, chagrin, chill, dampen, disappoint, discomfort, dismay, foil, frustrate, nip, ruin, spoil, thwart

data *noun.* circumstances, compilations, conclusions, details, documents, dope, evidence, facts, figures, goods, input, knowledge, materials, measurements, notes, reports, statistics, testimony

date *noun.* age, century, course, day, duration, epoch, era, generation, hour, moment, period, quarter, reign, span, spell, stage, time, year

dawn *noun.* advent, alpha, birth, commencement, dawning, emergence, foundation, genesis, head, inception, onset, opening, origin, outset, rise, source, start, unfolding

dead *adjective.* **1** bloodless, buried, cadaverous, cold, cut off, deceased, defunct, departed, erased, extinct, gone, inert, late, lifeless, liquidated, perished, stiff, wasted **2** anesthetized, apathetic, callous, cold, deadened, dull, frigid, glazed, inert, insensitive, insipid, lukewarm, numb, paralyzed, stagnant, still, torpid **3** barren, bygone, defunct, departed, exhausted, extinct, gone, inactive, inoperable, lost, obsolete, out of order, stagnant, still, unemployed, unprofitable, useless, worn, worn out

deadlock *noun.* box, catch 22, cessation, corner, dead end, dilemma, draw, gridlock, halt, hole, impasse, pause, pickle, plight, posture, predicament, standstill, tie

deadly *adjective.* baleful, baneful, bloody, cruel, deathly, destroying, destructive, fatal, grim, harmful, injurious, lethal, mortal, pernicious, pestilent, poisonous, savage, virulent

deal *verb.* **1** act, approach, behave, clear, concern, consider, control, direct, discuss, hack, handle, play, review, rid, serve, take, treat, use **2** allot, apportion, assign, bestow, deliver, distribute, divide, drop, give, impart, inflict, partake, participate, partition, render, reward, share, strike

dear *adjective.* baby, cherished, close, darling, endeared, esteemed, familiar, favorite, intimate, loved, pet, precious, prized, respected, sugar, sweetie, tootsie, treasured

death *noun.* annihilation, cessation, demise, departure, destruction, dying, ending, expiration, grave, heaven, loss, mortality, paradise, parting, passing, repose, silence, tomb

debate *noun.* agitation, altercation, argument, argumentation, bone, consideration, contention, contest, controversy, deliberation, dialectic, dispute, match, meditation, polemic, rap, reflection, words

debate *verb.* agitate, canvass, consider, contend, contest, deliberate, demonstrate, differ, disprove, dispute, hammer, hash, moot, prove, reason, rebut, refute, rehash

debris *noun.* bits, crap, dregs, dross, fragments, garbage, junk, pieces, refuse, remains, rubbish, rubble, ruins, trash, waste, wreck, wreckage

debt *noun.* arrears, baggage, bill, bite, claim, commitment, cuff, damage, deficit, due, duty, liability, manifest, obligation, receipt, reckoning, responsibility, tally

decay *noun.* consumption, corrosion, decadence, decline, decomposition, depreciation, disintegration, disrepair, dissolution, dying, extinction, fading, failing, mortification, rotting, rust, wasting, withering

decay *verb.* break up, crumble, decline, decompose, disintegrate, dissolve, dwindle, fade, fail, lessen, mildew, mold, perish, sap, sink, slump, spoil, turn

deceased *adjective.* asleep, checked out, cold, dead meat, defunct, departed, dir napping, exanimate, expired, extinct, finished, former, gone, inanimate, late, lifeless, lost, passed on

decency *noun.* appropriateness, ceremoniousness, civility, conventionality, correctness, courtesy, decorum, dignity, etiquette, fitness, formality, good manners, honesty, modesty, propriety, respectability, righteousness, virtue

decent *adjective.* **1** appropriate, becoming, befitting, comely, continent, delicate, fit, fitting, good, honest, immaculate, modest, moral, presentable, proper, right, spotless, standard **2** acceptable, adequate, ample, average, common, competent, enough, fair, good, mediocre, passable, presentable, reasonable, respectable, right, satisfactory, tolerable, unimpeachable

decide *verb.* adjudicate, agree, choose, cinch, clinch, conclude, conjecture, decree, end, figure, judge, pick, poll, resolve, rule, set, tap, will

decided *adjective.* **1** absolute, categorical, clear, clinched, determined, distinct, explicit, fated, positive, prearranged, predetermined, pronounced, settled, sure, unalterable, unambiguous, undisputed, unmistakable **2** assertive, bent, certain, decisive, determined, earnest, emphatic, firm, fixed, inflexible, intent, positive, purposeful, resolute, resolved, set, settled, sure

decision *noun.* **1** accord, adjudication, adjustment, agreement, arrangement, compromise, declaration, determination, judgment, opinion, outcome, preference, reconciliation, result, ruling, selection, sentence, settlement **2** backbone, decisiveness, determination, earnestness, firmness, fortitude, grit, perseverance, persistence, pluck, purpose, purposefulness, resoluteness, resolution, resolve, seriousness, stubbornness, volition

decisive *adjective.* absolute, certain, crisp, decided, definitive, determined, fateful, final, firm, imperious, incisive, intent, positive, resolute, set, settled, significant, trenchant

deck *verb.* adorn, appoint, array, attire, beautify, clothe, decorate, dress, dress up, garland, grace, gussy up, ornament, prettify, pretty up, slick, spiff, trim

declaration *noun.* **1** acknowledgment, admission, advertisement, broadcast, disclosure, enunciation, expression, notice, pitch, presentation, profession, remark, report, revelation, saying, statement, story, utterance **2** acclamation, bulletin, canon, charge, confirmation, constitution, credo, creed, denunciation, document, gospel, notice, plea, proclamation, profession, pronouncement, resolution, ultimatum

declare *verb.* **1** advocate, affirm, certify, claim, confess, convey, inform, maintain, pass, proclaim, profess, pronounce, reassert, render, repeat, sound, tell, validate **2** acknowledge, admit, avouch, avow, confess, convey, disclose, divulge, impart, indicate, manifest, notify, own, profess, represent, reveal, state, swear

decline *noun.* **1** diminution, dissolution, dive, downgrade, downturn, drop, dwindling, ebb, ebbing, failing, failure, fall, flop, lapse, skids, slump, waning, weakening **2** declivity, decrease, depression, downtrend, downturn, drop, falloff, hill, incline, lapse, loss, lowering, pitch, sag, slide, slip, slope, slump **3** abjure, abstain, avoid, bypass, deny, disapprove, dismiss, forgo, gainsay, not accept, not buy, refrain, refuse, reject, renounce, reprobate, repudiate, shy **4** deteriorate, droop, drop, dwindle, ebb, fade, fail, fall, lapse, lower, pine, recede, retrograde, settle, shrink, sink, slide, subside

decoration *noun.* **1** adornment, beautifying, bedecking, bedizenment, designing, elaboration, enhancement, enrichment, flourish, frill, furbelow, garnishing, illumination, improvement, ornament, ornamentation, redecorating, trimming **2** arabesque, bauble, color, design, filigree, flourish, fuss, garbage, gilt, inlay, lace, ornament, plaque, spangle, tinsel, trimming, trinket, wreath **3** accolade, award, badge, bays, chest hardware, citation, colors, cross, distinction, garter, laurels, medal, mention, order, purple heart, ribbon, ruptured duck, star

decrease *noun.* compression, condensation, constriction, contraction, cutback, decline, declining, depression, diminishing, diminution, discount, downturn, dwindling, ebb, loss, reduction, shrinkage, waning

decrease *verb.* contract, curb, deteriorate, droop, drop, dwindle, ease, ebb, evaporate, fade, lessen, lower, reduce, settle, shrink, sink, soften, subside

deduction *noun.* **1** consequence, consideration, contemplation, corollary, deliberation, derivation, finding, inference, judgment, mulling, musing, opinion, pondering, reasoning, reflection, result, speculation, thought **2** abatement, abstraction, allowance, credit, cut, decrease, decrement, depreciation, diminution, discount, dockage, excision, rebate, reduction, removal, subtraction, withdrawal, write-off

deed *noun.* **1** act, adventure, bit, cause, commission, crusade, do, doing, enterprise, exploit, fact, feat, game, plan, quest, reality, securing, stunt **2** agreement, bargain, certificate, charter, compact, conveyance, covenant, document, indenture, instrument, lease, papers, record, release, security, title, transaction, warranty

deep *adjective.* **1** abysmal, below, beneath, bottomless, broad, buried, distant, far, immersed, low, profound, rooted, submarine, submerged, sunk, underground, unfathomable, wide **2** acute, complex, complicated, concealed, discerning, heavy, hermetic, incisive, intricate, learned, mysterious, obscure, orphic, penetrating, profound, recondite, secret, wise **3** acute, artful, astute, canny, contriving, crafty, cunning, designing, insidious, intriguing, keen, plotting, scheming, sharp, shrewd, sly, tricky, wily

defeat *noun.* ambush, annihilation, beating, break, conquest, count, debacle, destruction, extermination, fall, licking, loss, massacre, rebuff, setback, subjugation, trap, whipping

defeat *verb.* **1** ambush, bear down, beat, butcher, crush, halt, lick, obliterate, overrun, repress, route, sink, subdue, surmount, trample, trash, upset, whip **2** beat, bust, deck, drop, flax, floor, lick, paste, pepper, pound, powder, skin, take, throw, trim, wallop, wax, win **3** baffle, blank, cook, cross, disconcert, disprove, foil, invalidate, neutralize, nullify, outwit, quell, reduce, refute, squash, subdue, surmount, undo

defend *verb.* **1** avert, battle, conserve, cover, fight, foster, garrison, guard, hedge, house, maintain, preserve, prevent, protect, save, secure, uphold, watch **2** advocate, aid, argue, assert, champion, endorse, express, justify, maintain, plead, rationalize, recommend, second, stand by, sustain, uphold, vent, voice

defense *noun.* **1** bastion, cover, deterrence, embankment, fort, garrison, guard, immunity, protection, resistance, safeguard, security, shelter, stronghold, wall, ward, warfare, weapons **2** answer, apologia, apology, argument, excuse, exoneration, explaining, fish, justifying, plea, rationalization, rejoinder, response, retort, return, song, story, vindication

defensive *adjective.* arresting, averting, balking, checking, conservative, defending, foiling, frustrating, guarding, interrupting, opposing, preservative, preventive, protecting, resistive, thwarting, uptight, watchful

deficiency *noun.* absence, default, defect, deficit, failing, failure, fault, flaw, imperfection, lack, loss, need, neglect, paucity, shortage, sin, want, weakness

deficit *noun.* arrears, dead horse, defalcation, default, deficiency, due bill, dues, in hock, inadequacy, insufficiency, lack, loss, paucity, red ink, scantiness, shortcoming, shortfall, underage

define *verb.* **1** ascertain, assign, characterize, construe, decide, describe, detail, entitle, exemplify, formalize, illustrate, interpret, label, name, prescribe, represent, tag, translate **2** belt, bound, compass, confine, curb, encircle, encompass, establish, fix, flank, gird, girdle, mark, rim, set, settle, surround, verge

definite *adjective.* **1** audible, categorical, clear, crisp, determined, distinct, explicit, fixed, minute, obvious, positive, ringing, sharp, specific, tangible, unambiguous, unmistakable, visible **2** assigned, assured, certain, circumscribed, convinced, decided, defined, determined, guaranteed, limited, narrow, positive, precise, prescribed, restricted, set, settled, sure

definitely *adverb.* absolutely, categorically, clearly, decidedly, doubtless, easily, explicitly, expressly, finally, obviously, plainly, positively, specifically, surely, undeniably, unequivocally, unmistakably, unquestionably

definition *noun.* characterization, clarification, clue, commentary, cue, demarcation, determination, drift, elucidation, gloss, key, rendering, rendition, representation, settling, solution, synonym, translation

degree *noun.* **1** division, height, line, mark, period, proportion, quality, range, rate, ratio, rung, scope, shade, size, stage, stair, stint, strength **2** amplitude, credentials, dignity, distinction, eminence, expanse, height, level, magnitude, proportion, quality, range, scope, sort, stage, station, strength, testimonial

delay *noun.* adjournment, bind, check, detention, filibuster, holding, impediment, interval, jam, moratorium, problem, setback, stall, stay, stoppage, surcease, suspension, wait

delay *verb.* bar, clog, confine, detain, discourage, drag, keep, linger, prevent, procrastinate, prolong, repress, retard, stall, table, tarry, temporize, withhold

delegate *noun.* agent, alternate, appointee, consul, deputy, emissary, front, member, minister, plenipotentiary, regent, rep, replacement, senator, spokesman, substitute, vicar, viceroy
delegate *verb.* appoint, assign, authorize, cast, charge, choose, commission, constitute, designate, elect, invest, license, mandate, name, nominate, ordain, select, warrant
delegation *noun.* appointment, apportioning, authorization, charge, conveyance, conveying, installation, mandate, nomination, ordination, reference, referring, relegation, submittal, submitting, transference, transferring, trust
deliberate *adjective.* advised, aforethought, careful, conscious, fixed, judged, meticulous, planned, pondered, prearranged, predetermined, projected, purposeful, reasoned, studied, studious, voluntary, willful
deliberate *verb.* argue, chaw, consider, consult, contemplate, debate, discuss, judge, muse, ponder, reason, reflect, revolve, roll, speculate, study, think, turn over
deliberately *adverb.* advisedly, consciously, designed, determinedly, emphatically, freely, independently, knowingly, meaningfully, pointedly, purposely, purposively, resolutely, studiously, voluntarily, willfully, wittingly
delicate *adjective.* **1** balmy, delightful, elegant, ethereal, exquisite, filmy, fine, flimsy, fragile, frail, gentle, pale, pastel, slight, subdued, superior, tender, weak **2** alert, careful, critical, dainty, fastidious, finical, finicking, finicky, fussy, gentle, nice, particular, prudish, pure, refined, scrupulous, sensitive, squeamish **3** accurate, adept, cautious, considerate, deft, detailed, diplomatic, discreet, expert, minute, politic, precise, proficient, prudent, skilled, tactful, tactical, wary
delight *noun.* contentment, delectation, ecstasy, enchantment, felicity, fruition, gladness, glee, gratification, happiness, hilarity, joy, mirth, pleasure, rapture, relish, satisfaction, transport
delight *verb.* allure, amuse, attract, charm, cheer, content, divert, entertain, fascinate, gladden, gratify, pleasure, rejoice, satisfy, score, send, thrill, wow
delightful *adjective.* agreeable, ambrosial, amusing, attractive, captivating, charming, cheery, congenial, delicious, enchanting, fascinating, gratifying, heavenly, ineffable, lush, pleasing, refreshing, scrumptious
deliver *verb.* **1** bear, bring, carry, cart, convey, dish out, distribute, drop, duke, gimme, give, hand, hand over, pass, put on, put out, transport, weed **2** address, broach, communicate, declare, express, give, impart, present, proclaim, pronounce, publish, read, say, state, tell, utter, vent, voice
delivery *noun.* commitment, consignment, conveyance, dispatch, distribution, drop, giving over, handing over, impartment, mailing, parcel post, portage, post, rendition, shipment, surrender, transferal, transmission
demand *noun.* appeal, bidding, charge, claim, clamor, command, interest, lien, necessity, occasion, plea, prayer, request, requisition, stipulation, ultimatum, vogue, want
demand *verb.* abuse, appeal, arrogate, beg, claim, command, compel, exact, expect, implore, knock, oblige, press, request, requisition, solicit, summon, urge
demanding *adjective.* ambitious, bothersome, clamorous, critical, exacting, exhausting, grievous, hard, imperious, insistent, oppressive, querulous, strict, taxing, tough, trying, urgent, wearing
democratic *adjective.* autonomous, bourgeois, common, communal, constitutional, equal, free, friendly, individualistic, informal, just, laissez-faire, libertarian, orderly, popular, populist, self-governing, self-ruling
demon *noun.* archfiend, beast, brute, devil, evil spirit, fiend, goblin, imp, incubus, little devil, malignant spirit, monster, rascal, rogue, Satan, vampire, villain, windigo
demonstrate *verb.* authenticate, determine, establish, evidence, evince, exhibit, expose, flaunt, indicate, make evident,

make out, manifest, prove, roll out, test, trot out, try, validate

demonstration *noun.* affirmation, confirmation, description, evidence, exhibition, exposition, expression, illustration, induction, manifestation, presentation, proof, show, substantiation, test, testimony, trial, validation

denial *noun.* abstaining, contradiction, disapproval, disclaimer, dismissal, dismissing, dissent, nay, negative, no, prohibition, rebuff, rebuttal, rejection, renunciation, repudiating, repudiation, retraction

denomination *noun.* appellation, appellative, brand, cognomen, compellation, designation, flag, handle, identification, label, moniker, nomen, slot, style, tab, tag, term, title

dense *adjective.* doltish, dull, dumb, fatheaded, half-witted, ignorant, impassive, lethargic, numskulled, obtuse, phlegmatic, simple, slow, slow-witted, sluggish, stolid, thick, torpid

deny *verb.* begrudge, curb, decline, disbelieve, disown, disprove, eschew, exclude, forbid, negative, nullify, rebuff, rebut, refute, repudiate, sacrifice, taboo, withhold

department *noun.* **1** agency, area, arena, beat, board, circuit, commission, division, parish, precinct, quarter, range, staff, station, subdivision, territory, tract, ward **2** activity, avocation, business, domain, dominion, field, function, jurisdiction, line, niche, province, realm, responsibility, specialty, sphere, spot, station, vocation

departure *noun.* **1** abandonment, desertion, emigration, exodus, flight, going, parting, passage, powder, quitting, removal, retirement, separation, stampede, vacation, walkout, withdrawal, withdrawing **2** aberration, branching out, change, declination, deflection, difference, divergence, diversion, innovation, novelty, rambling, shift, straying, turning, variance, variation, veering, wandering

dependable *adjective.* always there, certain, constant, faithful, loyal, responsible, rock, secure, stable, staunch, steadfast, steady, sure, tried, true, trustworthy, trusty, unfailing

dependence *noun.* **1** assurance, belief, credence, dependency, expectation, faith, hope, interdependence, reliance, responsibility, responsibleness, stability, stableness, steadiness, stock, trust, trustiness, trustworthiness **2** addition, attachment, contingency, dependency, habit, helplessness, hook, inability, monkey, security blanket, servility, subjection, subordination, subservience, vulnerability, weakness, yoke

dependent *adjective.* **1** abased, clinging, defenseless, humbled, immature, indigent, inferior, lesser, minor, poor, reliant, relying on, secondary, subordinate, under, unsustaining, vulnerable, weak **2** ancillary, appurtenant, conditional, controlled by, counting, depending, determined by, incidental to, provisory, reckoning, regulated by, relative, reliant, relying, subordinate, subservient, susceptible, trusting

deposit *verb.* amass, bank, commit, deliver, drop, entrust, garner, install, invest, keep, park, plank, repose, rest, save, squirrel, transfer, treasure

depot *noun.* annex, armory, base, destination, garage, haven, junction, lot, magazine, repository, station, store, storehouse, storeroom, terminal, terminus, warehouse, yard

depressed *adjective.* bad, bleeding, blue, crestfallen, crummy, despondent, destroyed, down, downcast, grim, hurting, melancholy, moody, morose, ripped, sad, unhappy, woebegone

depression *noun.* **1** abasement, abjection, blues, desperation, despondency, discouragement, distress, dole, dreariness, dullness, dumps, hopelessness, melancholy, misery, mortification, sorrow, trouble, unhappiness **2** bankruptcy, bust, crash, crisis, downturn, drop, failure, inactivity, inflation, panic, paralysis, recession, sag, slide, slowness, slump, stagnation, unemployment **3** basin, bowl, cavity, crater, dent, dip, excavation, hole, hollow, impression, pit, pocket, scoop, sink, sinkhole, vacuum, valley, void

depth *noun.* abyss, bottom, completeness,

draft, drop, expanse, extent, intensity, measure, measurement, pit, pitch, profundity, remoteness, sounding, substratum, underground

deputy *noun.* agent, aide, ambassador, appointee, commissioner, delegate, factor, legate, lieutenant, minister, proxy, regent, replacement, representative, sub, subordinate, substitute

derive *verb.* arrive, assume, collect, conclude, draw, elaborate, elicit, evolve, extract, follow, gain, glean, infer, judge, obtain, procure, trace, work out

descent *noun.* coast, crash, decline, downgrade, droop, drop, fall, grade, hill, inclination, incline, landslide, plunge, settlement, slide, slip, swoop, topple

describe *verb.* characterize, chronicle, construe, define, depict, detail, draw, illuminate, illustrate, image, impart, interpret, name, portray, recount, represent, tell, trace

description *noun.* **1** brief, characterization, chronicle, declaration, detail, fingerprint, monograph, narrative, portraiture, recital, recitation, run down, statement, story, summarization, summary, version, yarn **2** brand, breed, category, character, classification, feather, genre, genus, ilk, kidney, kind, nature, order, sort, species, stripe, type, variety

desert *verb.* beach, betray, bolt, defect, depart, ditch, duck, escape, fly, leave, light, maroon, resign, split, strand, take off, vacate, walk

deserted *adjective.* bare, barren, bereft, cast off, derelict, desolate, empty, forlorn, forsaken, godforsaken, isolated, left, lonely, neglected, relinquished, solitary, unoccupied, vacant

design *noun.* **1** architecture, arrangement, blueprint, composition, constitution, construction, drawing, dummy, form, formation, layout, makeup, map, method, plan, scheme, study, tracing **2** arrangement, configuration, construction, depiction, drawing, figure, form, illustration, motif, motive, organization, painting, pattern, picture, portrait, shape, sketch, style **3** conspiracy, enterprise, intent, meaning, objective, plan, proposition, purport, recipe, reflection, schema, scheme, story, target, undertaking, view, volition, will

design *verb.* accomplish, achieve, blueprint, construct, create, devise, draw, effect, execute, form, frame, lay out, outline, perform, plan, produce, trace, work out

designing *adjective.* artful, astute, conspiring, crafty, crooked, cunning, deceitful, devious, intriguing, observant, scheming, sharp, shrewd, sly, treacherous, tricky, unscrupulous, wily

desirable *adjective.* acceptable, advisable, agreeable, beneficial, covetable, eligible, enviable, expedient, good, grateful, gratifying, helpful, pleasing, preferable, profitable, useful, welcome, worthwhile

desire *noun.* admiration, attraction, covetousness, devotion, eagerness, fascination, fervor, fondness, inclination, libido, liking, longing, love, lust, mania, relish, will, wish

desire *verb.* aim, choose, covet, crave, crazy for, die over, enjoy, fancy, go for, hanker after, hunger for, itch for, like, pant, partial to, pine, sweet on, thirst

despair *verb.* abandon, abandon hope, be hopeless, bum out, despond, destroy, drop, flatten, give way, lose faith, lose heart, lose hope, relinquish, renounce, resign, surrender, take down, yield

desperate *adjective.* **1** bold, careless, crying, daring, determined, foolhardy, frenzied, hasty, impetuous, incautious, monstrous, precipitate, rash, risky, shocking, venturesome, violent, wild **2** acute, concentrated, critical, crucial, dire, drastic, exquisite, extreme, fierce, furious, great, intense, terrible, urgent, vehement, very grave, vicious, violent **3** dead duck, despairing, despondent, downcast, forlorn, futile, gone, inconsolable, irrecoverable, irremediable, irretrievable, no chance, no way, sad, sunk, useless, vain, wretched

destined *adjective.* **1** certain, compelled, condemned, designed, directed, doomed, impending, ineluctable, inescapable, instant, looming, meant, near, ordained, predetermined, settled, stated, unavoidable **2** appointed, appropriated, assigned, bent upon, booked, bound for, chosen, consigned, delegated, designated, determined, directed, heading, ordered to, prepared, routed, scheduled, specified

destiny *noun.* break, certainty, conclusion, cup, design, doom, expectation, finality, fortune, future, hereafter, horoscope, inevitability, intent, intention, luck, objective, ordinance

destroy *verb.* axe, butcher, consume, crush, dispatch, eradicate, erase, exterminate, extinguish, gut, impair, level, nullify, shatter, smash, suppress, trash, wreck

destruction *noun.* annihilation, crashing, crushing, disrupting, elimination, eradication, extermination, liquidation, loss, massacre, overthrow, sacking, subjugation, subversion, subverting, undoing, wreckage, wrecking

destructive *adjective.* **1** baleful, baneful, calamitous, cataclysmic, catastrophic, consumptive, cutthroat, damaging, deadly, devastating, fatal, fell, harmful, lethal, mortal, noxious, pernicious, ruinous **2** abrasive, adverse, antagonistic, cankerous, contrary, corrosive, derogatory, detrimental, discouraging, hostile, injurious, invalidating, negative, offensive, opposed, troublesome, undermining, vicious

detached *adjective.* abstract, apathetic, casual, cool, disinterested, distant, impartial, impersonal, indifferent, neutral, objective, remote, removed, reserved, uncommitted, unconcerned, uninvolved, withdrawn

detail *noun.* accessory, count, cue, design, element, fact, factor, fraction, item, part, peculiarity, plan, respect, schedule, singularity, specialty, specific, triviality

detail *verb.* catalog, depict, describe, elaborate, epitomize, exhibit, lay out, portray, produce, recapitulate, recite, recount, relate, report, show, specialize, spread, tell

detailed *adjective.* accurate, amplified, developed, disclosed, elaborate, elaborated, enumerated, exact, exhausting, exhaustive, individual, intricate, meticulous, minute, narrow, specific, specified, unfolded

detect *verb.* ascertain, disclose, distinguish, encounter, expose, find, identify, meet, note, notice, observe, recognize, reveal, scent, see, spot, track down, uncover

detective *noun.* agent, analyst, bull, constable, cop, copper, fed, ferret, fink, policeman, prosecutor, reporter, scout, sergeant, shadow, snoop, spy, tail

determination *noun.* bravery, certainty, constancy, conviction, courage, decision, dogmatism, energy, firmness, fortitude, grit, guts, nerve, persistence, pluck, resolve, stubbornness, tenacity

determine *verb.* **1** actuate, arbitrate, cinch, conclude, decide, dispose, figure, halt, incline, induce, move, persuade, regulate, resolve, rule, settle, tap, wind up **2** ascertain, be afraid, catch on, certify, check, demonstrate, detect, divine, establish, figure, hear, learn, see, tell, tumble, unearth, verify, work out **3** affect, bound, command, decide, devise, dictate, direct, impose, incline, induce, influence, invent, lead, manage, plot, regulate, rule, shape

determined *adjective.* constant, decided, decisive, dogged, firm, fixed, hardboiled, intent, pat, purposeful, resolute, resolved, set, set on, settled, solid, stubborn, tenacious

develop *verb.* **1** advance, age, enroot, establish, evolve, expand, flourish, foster, grow, maturate, mature, mellow, progress, promote, prosper, ripe, ripen, thrive **2** augment, beautify, build up, deepen, dilate, elaborate, enlarge, enrich, evolve, exploit, extend, materialize, polish, realize, spread, strengthen, stretch, widen **3** acquire, befall, betide, break, breed, commence, contract, ensue, establish, follow, form, generate, happen, invest, occur, pick up, result, start **4** acquire, disclose, disentangle, elaborate, evolve, exhibit, explain, foretell, form, materialize, produce, reach, realize, recount, state, uncover, unfold, unravel

development *noun.* addition, adulthood, augmenting, boost, buildup, developing, enlargement, evolving, flowering, growing, hike, improvement, maturity, perfecting, progress, reinforcement, reinforcing, spread

deviation *noun.* aberration, alteration, anomaly, breach, departure, difference, discrepancy, disparity, divergence, diversion, fork, inconsistency, irregularity, shift, transgression, turning, variance, variation

device *noun.* **1** accessory, agent, apparatus, appliance, arrangement, construction, creation, equipment, expedient, gadget, invention, makeshift, material, medium, outfit, resource, shift, tool **2** artifice, craft, design, dodge, expedient, fake, gambit, game, loophole, maneuver, method, plan, plot, proposition, racket, ruse, scheme, trap

devil *noun.* adversary, archfiend, beast, brute, common enemy, enfant terrible, Evil One, fiend, imp, knave, monster, rogue, Satan, scamp, scoundrel, sin, the Dickens, villain

devise *verb.* blueprint, construct, craft, create, design, discover, form, frame, imagine, improvise, make up, plan, plot, prepare, scheme, spark, vamp, work out

devote *verb.* allot, apply, apportion, appropriate, assign, bestow, bless, confide, consign, donate, entrust, give, give away, pledge, present, reserve, set apart, vow

devoted *adjective.* adherent, affectionate, ardent, caring, concerned, constant, dear, dedicated, devout, doting, faithful, fond, gone, loving, loyal, thoughtful, true, zealous

devotion *noun.* affection, ardor, attachment, consecration, constancy, deference, enthusiasm, fealty, fervor, fondness, intensity, love, observance, passion, piety, sanctity, worship, zeal

dialect *noun.* accent, argot, can, idiom, jargon, language, lingo, localism, patois, patter, pronunciation, provincialism, regionalism, slang, terminology, tongue, vernacular, vocabulary

dialogue *noun.* chat, colloquy, communication, confabulation, conference, conversation, converse, discourse, discussion, exchange, lines, parlance, parley, rap, remarks, repartee, script, sides

die *verb.* **1** be taken, cool, croak, dance, demise, depart, drop, drop off, drown, eat it, expire, finish, hang, kick off, perish, snuff, sprout wings, succumb **2** deteriorate, droop, ebb, expire, fade, fade out, fail, fall, halt, lapse, moderate, pass, recede, retrograde, sink, subside, vanish, wilt

diet *noun.* bite, chow, commons, eats, fare, goodies, grub, menu, nourishment, peckings, provisions, rations, snack, subsistence, sustenance, viands, victuals

differ *verb.* **1** alter, conflict with, contradict, contrast, depart from, deviate from, digress, disagree, diverge, diversify, jar with, lack resemblance, modify, qualify, reverse, show contrast, turn, vary **2** clash, contend, debate, disaccord, disagree, discord, dispute, dissent, divide, fight, jar, object, oppose, quarrel, squabble, take issue, vary, war

difference *noun.* **1** anomaly, antithesis, change, characteristic, departure, differentiation, discrepancy, distinction, divergence, diversity, inequality, particularity, peculiarity, separateness, separation, variance, variation, variety **2** argument, beef, brawl, clash, conflict, contention, contretemps, debate, disagreement, discord, dissent, disunity, estrangement, quarrel, row, spat, strife, variance

different *adjective.* **1** altered, colorful, contrasting, deviating, differential, disparate, distant, distinctive, divergent, diverse, incomparable, individual, offbeat, peculiar, single, unrelated, variant, various **2** another, bizarre, discrete, distinct, distinctive, diverse, express, individual, peculiar, rare, several, specialized, specific, startling, strange, unique, unusual, various **3** collected, disparate, dissonant, divergent, diverse, diversified, heterogeneous, inconsistent, manifold, many, miscellaneous, numerous, several, some, sundry, varicolored, varied, variegated

differently *adverb.* abnormally, adversely, asymmetrically, conflictingly, contradictorily, contrarily, discordantly, dissimilarly, distinctively, divergently, incompatibly, individually, negatively, nonconformably, separately, uniquely, unusually, variously

difficult *adjective.* **1** ambitious, arduous, demanding, exacting, galling, hard, heavy, intricate, irritating, labored, laborious, rigid, severe, stiff, toilsome, uphill, upstream **2** baffling, confusing, deep, enigmatic, hard, inexplicable, intricate, loose, meandering, mysterious, mystical, obscure, perplexing, profound, puzzling, rambling, unfathomable, unintelligible **3** boorish, dark, demanding, fastidious, fractious, fussy, grim, impolite, intractable, irritable, perverse, refractory, rigid, rude, tiresome, tough, troublesome, trying

difficulty *noun.* **1** awkwardness, crisis, deadlock, dilemma, distress, hazard, hitch, mess, obstacle, paradox, predicament, quagmire, scrape, snag, stew, strait, tribulation, trouble **2** bother, crisis, discouragement, distress, grievance, imbroglio, inconvenience, irritation, mess, millstone, misery, predicament, pressure, responsibility, scrape, setback, strait, trouble

dig *verb.* **1** bore, bulldoze, cat, channel, concave, deepen, grub, harvest, pierce, pit, probe, quarry, root, sap, spade, till, tunnel, turn over **2** come across, dig down, discover, expose, extricate, find, go into, inquire, probe, prospect, research, retrieve, root, search, shake down, sift, uncover, unearth

dignity *noun.* decency, distinction, elevation, eminence, grace, gravity, importance, poise, prestige, propriety, quality, regard, renown, respectability, state, station, stature, worth

dilemma *noun.* bind, box, corner, difficulty, embarrassment, fix, hole, impasse, jam, mess, perplexity, pickle, predicament, problem, puzzle, scrape, spot, strait

dim *adjective.* bleary, dingy, dreary, dull, dusky, faded, gray, indistinct, monotone, monotonous, murky, opaque, overcast, pale, shadowy, tenebrous, vague, weak

dim *verb.* becloud, bedim, befog, blear, blur, cloud, dull, eclipse, fade, fog, haze, lower, muddy, obfuscate, obscure, pale, tarnish, turn down

dimensions *noun.* amplitude, bulk, compass, depth, dimension, dimensionality, extent, height, importance, length, magnitude, measurement, proportion, reach, scale, scope, size, width

dinner *noun.* banquet, blowout, chow, collation, eats, feast, feedbag, fete, main meal, major munch, principal meal, refection, regale, repast, ribs, spread, supper, table d'hote

diplomatic *adjective.* adept, arch, artful, calculating, capable, conciliatory, courteous, cunning, deft, delicate, discreet, intriguing, scheming, sharp, sly, smooth, strategic, suave

direct *adjective.* **1** absolute, bald, blunt, candid, categorical, downright, explicit, express, forthright, frank, open, outspoken, plain, sincere, straight, straightforward, unambiguous, undisguised **2** beeline, continuous, even, horizontal, linear, nonstop, not crooked, point-blank, right, shortest, straight, straight ahead, straightaway, through, true, unbroken, uninterrupted, unswerving **3** advise, boss, dispose, dominate, govern, guide, handle, influence, keep, lead, ordain, quarterback, regulate, rule, run, shepherd, superintend, supervise **4** address, aim, cast, fix, head, incline, lay, lead, level, route, see, set, shepherd, show, steer, target, train, turn

direction *noun.* **1** aim, angle, area, bearing, inclination, line, objective, outlook, path, range, region, route, set, spot, tendency, tide, trajectory, trend **2** advice, advisement, assignment, briefing, directive, dope, guidelines, indication, notification, plan, prescription, recommendation, regulation, specification, specs, steer, summons, tip

directly *adverb.* anon, at once, contiguously, dead, due, forthwith, immediately, instantaneously, instantly, presently, promptly, pronto, quickly, right away, shortly, soon, speedily, straightaway

director *noun.* administrator, big player, boss, chairman, chief, controller, exec, executive, governor, head, kingpin, leader, man upstairs, overseer, principal, producer, skipper, supervisor

dirt *noun.* clay, crud, dreck, dregs, dust, earth, filth, filthiness, gook, ground, gunk, impurity, muck, mud, sleaze, smut, soil, stain

dirty *adjective.* **1** bedraggled, black, crummy, dusty, foul, greasy, grubby, messy, muddy, murky, nasty, smudged, spattered, stained, unkempt, unlaundered, unsightly, untidy **2** base, blue, coarse, contemptible, immoral, indecent, lewd, low, mean, nasty, pornographic, ribald, salacious, scurvy, sensual, sordid, unclean, vulgar

dirty *verb.* blur, coat, contaminate, corrupt, decay, foul, mold, muddy, rot, smear, smoke, soil, spoil, spot, stain, sweat, taint, tar

disabled *adjective.* disarmed, game, halting, helpless, impotent, incapable, lame, maimed, mangled, mutilated, paralyzed, powerless, silenced, unable, useless, weak, weakened, wounded

disagreement *noun.* **1** altercation, argument, bickering, break, conflict, debate, difference, dissent, disunion, division, feud, fight, friction, misunderstanding, quarrel, quarreling, spat, variance **2** clash, disaccord, discordance, discrepancy, disharmonism, disharmony, disparity, dissimilarity, dissimilitude, divergence, divergency, diversity, incompatibility, incongruity, incongruousness, inconsistency, unlikeness, variance

disappear *verb.* abandon, clear, depart, die, dissolve, ebb, escape, evaporate, exit, expire, fade, fly, leave, pass, perish, recede, sink, vacate

disappearance *noun.* departure, desertion, disintegration, dissolution, ebbing, eclipse, escape, evaporation, exit, exodus, fading, flight, going, loss, passing, removal, retirement, withdrawal

disappointed *adjective.* aghast, balked, beaten, complaining, defeated, depressed, despondent, discouraged, disgruntled, disillusioned, distressed, down, foiled, hopeless, objecting, unhappy, upset, worsted

disappointment *noun.* **1** blow, blunder, bust, calamity, defeat, discouragement, drag, dud, error, fiasco, lemon, miscalculation, misfortune, mishap, mistake, obstacle, setback, slip **2** adversity, blow, chagrin, defeat, despondency, discontent, discouragement, disillusion, disillusionment, dissatisfaction, distress, failure, frustration, mortification, regret, setback, unfulfillment, upset

disapproval *noun.* blame, boo, boycott, castigation, censure, denunciation, deprecation, discontent, dislike, displeasure, dissatisfaction, hiss, objection, opprobrium, ostracism, reproach, reproof, vitriol

disaster *noun.* affliction, bust, calamity, catastrophe, collision, curtains, debacle, defeat, fall, flood, grief, harm, hazard, mishap, rough, setback, undoing, upset

disastrous *adjective.* calamitous, cataclysmic, catastrophic, destructive, devastating, dire, dreadful, fatal, fateful, hapless, harmful, ruinous, terrible, tragic, unfavorable, unfortunate, unlucky, untoward

discernible *adjective.* apparent, appreciable, audible, clear, detectable, discoverable, distinct, distinguishable, noticeable, observable, obvious, palpable, perceivable, perceptible, plain, sensible, tangible, visible

discharge *verb.* **1** acquit, clear, disimprison, dismiss, emancipate, exonerate, expel, free, liberate, loose, loosen, manumit, oust, pardon, release, unchain, unimprison, unshackle **2** ax, boot, bounce, bust, can, displace, eject, excuse, expel, fire, oust, relieve, remove, replace, sack, spare, terminate **3** disembogue, dispense, ejaculate, emit, empty, erupt, excrete, exude, give off, gush, leak, ooze, pour, release, send forth, spew, void, vomit

discipline *noun.* control, cultivation, curb, development, drill, drilling, education, exercise, inculcation, limitation, method, orderliness, practice, preparation, regimen, regulation, restraint, will

disclose *verb.* acknowledge, admit, bare, broadcast, buzz, confess, display, exhibit, expose, impart, leak, mouth, open, own, publish, relate, show, tell

discount *noun.* allowance, commission, concession, cut, cut rate, decrease, deduct, deduction, depreciation, diminution, drawback, exemption, modification, percentage, premium, qualification, salvage, subtraction

discount *verb.* depreciate, derogate, disbelieve, discredit, dispraise, disregard, doubt, fail, forget, minimize, mistrust, neglect, omit, overlook, question, reject, scout, slight

discourage *verb.* **1** alarm, bother, bully, chill, damp, dampen, demoralize, dismay, distress, droop, frighten, intimidate, prostrate, repress, scare, trouble, try, warn **2** check, chill, control, curb, disfavor, dissuade, divert, frighten, interfere, obstruct, prevent, quiet, repress, restrain, scare, shake, turn off, withhold

discouraged *adjective.* beat, blue, come apart, crestfallen, dashed, daunted, depressed, dismayed, dispirited, down, downbeat, downcast, glum, lost momentum, pessimistic, psyched out, sad, unglued

discourse *noun.* address, conversation, converse, disquisition, huddle, lecture, memoir, monograph, monologue, paper, rap, sermon, speaking, speech, talk, thesis, treatise, utterance

discourse *verb.* argue, chew, comment, confer, converse, debate, develop, dispute, elaborate, enlarge, expand, explain, lecture, orate, remark, talk, treat, voice

discover *verb.* ascertain, design, detect, devise, elicit, hear, identify, learn, look up, notice, observe, perceive, pioneer, realize, recognize, see, sense, spot

discovery *noun.* **1** analysis, detection, determination, discernment, disclosure, distinction, distinguishing, encounter, experimentation, exposure, find, introduction, invention, locating, origination, perception, sensing, strike **2** algorithm, breakthrough, conclusion, coup, design, device, find, formula, godsend, innovation, law, luck, method, result, secret, theorem, treasure, way

discrepancy *noun.* alterity, difference, disagreement, disparity, dissemblance, dissimilarity, dissimilitude, distinction, divergence, divergency, error, incongruity, inconsistency, miscalculation, poles apart, split, variance, variation

discretion *noun.* attention, carefulness, concern, consideration, diplomacy, discernment, discrimination, heed, maturity, observation, precaution, providence, prudence, responsibility, sense, tact, warning, wisdom

discrimination *noun.* acumen, astuteness, clearness, decision, difference, differentiation, discernment, distinction, judgment, penetration, perception, preference, refinement, sense, separation, subtlety, taste, understanding

discuss *verb.* argue, canvass, confer, consider, contend, contest, converse, debate, deliberate, dispute, examine, explain, figure, jaw, moot, rap, review, weigh

discussion *noun.* altercation, analysis, argument, colloquy, confabulation, conference, consideration, consultation, debate, examination, excursus, huddle, interview, meet, meeting, quarrel, rap, symposium

disease *noun.* affection, attack, cancer, complaint, debility, defect, epidemic, fit, hemorrhage, illness, inflammation, misery, plague, sickness, syndrome, temperature, upset, visitation

dish *noun.* bowl, casserole, ceramic, china, container, cup, manhole cover, mug, pitcher, plate, platter, porringer, pot, pottery, salver, tray, vessel

dislike *noun.* animosity, aversion, deprecation, detestation, disapproval, disfavor, disinclination, displeasure, dissatisfaction, distaste, enmity, hate, indisposition, loathing, objection, offense, opposition, prejudice

dislike *verb.* allergic to, antipathize, avoid, condemn, deplore, despise, detest, disapprove, disfavor, disrelish, eschew, hate, mind, regret, resent, scorn, shun, turned off

dismal *adjective.* black, depressed, dim, dingy, disagreeable, doleful, dull, forlorn, frowning, ghastly, horrid, lonesome, lowering, miserable, morbid, overcast, shadowy, tenebrous

dispatch *verb.* accelerate, address, consign, dismiss, express, forward, hasten, hurry, issue, quicken, railroad, remit, route, run with, ship, speed, transmit, walk through

display *noun.* arrangement, array, blaze, bravura, demonstration, exhibit, exhibition, exposure, front, layout, pageant, panorama, presentation, sample, shine, show, splash, spread

display *verb.* bare, boast, exhibit, expand, expose, extend, feature, grandstand, illustrate, impart, lay out, manifest, model, open, perform, publish, represent, sport

disposal *noun.* **1** clearance, conveyance, demolition, destroying, destruction, dispatching, dispensation, dumping, ejection, removal, riddance, sacrifice, sale, selling, trading, transfer, transference, vending **2** arrangement, array, assignment, bestowal, conclusion, conveyance, determination, dispensation, distribution, division, end, gift, grouping, order, ordering, provision, sequence, transfer

disposition *noun.* bag, being, complexion, constitution, flash, groove, habit, humor, identity, inclination, penchant, personality, readiness, spirit, stamp, temper, tendency, tone

dispute *noun.* altercation, bickering, bone, brawl, broil, commotion, conflict, debate, disagreement, feud, fireworks, friction, fuss, hubbub, misunderstanding, quarrel, row, variance

dispute *verb.* agitate, brawl, canvass, challenge, clash, contend, contest, contradict, debate, deny, discuss, disprove, moot, negate, quarrel, quibble, rebut, refute

dissatisfaction *noun.* aversion, complaint, disapproval, discouragement, disinclination, disliking, dismay, displeasure, disquiet, distress, exasperation, hopelessness, irritation, jealousy, lamentation, regret, trouble, weariness

distance *noun.* amplitude, area, breadth, expanse, heavens, horizon, lapse, objective, orbit, outpost, range, remoteness, scope, separation, size, span, stretch, width

distant *adjective.* **1** abstracted, apart, asunder, far, further, inaccessible, isolated, obscure, outlying, piece, remote, removed, retired, secluded, secret, telescopic, ways, yonder **2** arrogant, cold, cool, cool cat, formal, haughty, modest, proud, remote, reserved, restrained, retiring, shy, solitary, stiff, unconcerned, unfriendly, withdrawn

distaste *noun.* antipathy, aversion, detestation, disfavor, disgust, disinclination, disliking, displeasure, dissatisfaction, hate, hatred, horror, indisposition, loathing, repugnance, repulsion, revolt, revulsion

distinct *adjective.* **1** audible, categorical, clear, decided, enunciated, explicit, express, incisive, lucid, manifest, marked, noticeable, obvious, sharp, specific, trenchant, unambiguous, unmistakable **2** discrete, disparate, dissimilar, distinctive, disunited, divergent, diverse, individual, offbeat, peculiar, several, single, sole, special, specific, unattached, unique, various

distinction *noun.* **1** analysis, characteristic, clearness, difference, differential, discrepancy, discrimination, divergence, division, judgment, mark, particularity, peculiarity, penetration, perception, quality, sensitivity, separation **2** accolade, account, celebrity, consequence, decoration, eminence, excellence, flair, importance, manner, prestige, prominence, quality, renown, repute, style, superiority, worth

distinctive *adjective.* characteristic, diagnostic, discrete, distinct, distinguishing, individual, offbeat, peculiar, proper, separate, single, singular, special, superior, typical, unique, unreal, wicked

distinguish *verb.* **1** ascertain, characterize, decide, diagnose, difference, divide, extricate, finger, identify, judge, know, mark, name, part, pinpoint, qualify, recognize, spot **2** beam, detect, dig, discover, flash, know, mark, notice, observe, perceive, read, recognize, remark, see, spot, spy, tell, view

distinguished *adjective.* aristocratic, arresting, conspicuous, dignified, esteemed, famed, glorious, honored, name, remarkable, reputable, royal, salient, signal, stately, striking, superior, venerable

distress *noun.* **1** ache, affliction, concern, cross, grief, heartbreak, irritation, malaise, misery, ordeal, pain, stew, torment, trial, tribulation, trouble, twinge, visitation **2** adversity, calamity, catastrophe, crunch, difficulty, disaster, drag, jam, misfortune, need, pickle, pinch, poverty, scrape, straits, trial, trouble, want

distress *verb.* bother, break, disquiet, disturb, dog, eat, harass, hound, needle, pain, pester, plague, strap, stress, torment, trouble, try, wound

distribution *noun.* allotment, allotting, apportionment, assessment, dealing, delivery, dispensation, dispersion, dissipating, division, marketing, partition, propagation, rationing, sharing, trading, transport, transportation

district *noun.* commune, community, department, locale, locality, neighborhood, parcel, parish, precinct, quarter, region, section, sector, territory, turf, vicinage, vicinity, ward

disturb *verb.* **1** agitate, alarm, arouse, astound, disrupt, distress, frighten, gall, interrupt, intrude, molest, outrage, plague, provoke, rattle, shake, tire, trouble **2** confuse, disarray, disorganize, displace, distort, foul up, interfere, jumble, mess up, mix up, move, muddle, remove, replace, shift, tamper, unsettle, upset

disturbance *noun.* agitation, bother, brawl, clamor, distraction, explosion, fray, fuss, insurrection, interruption, perturbation, quarrel, ruckus, shock, stir, storm, upheaval, violence

dive *verb.* dip, disappear, drop, duck, fall, gutter, header, jump, leap, lunge, pitch, plumb, plummet, plunge, spring, submerge, vanish, vault

diverse *adjective.* contradictory, contrary, contrasting, discrete, disparate, dissimilar, distant, distinct, divergent, diversified, incomparable, manifold, opposite, several, sundry, varied, various, varying

diversity *noun.* assortment, difference, dissimilarity, distinction, distinctiveness, divergence, diverseness, diversification, heterogeneity, medley, mixed bag, multifariousness, multiformity, multiplicity, range, variance, variegation

divide *verb.* **1** branch, break, carve, chop, cross, disengage, dissect, dissolve, divorce, loose, part, partition, quarter, rend, rupture, section, shear, sunder **2** allocate, allot, apportion, articulate, cut, deal, dispense, disperse, dole, factor, parcel, partition, prorate, quota, ration, share, shift, slice

divine *adjective.* almighty, ambrosial, celestial, eternal, exalted, glorious, heavenly, magnificent, marvelous, mystical, omniscient, religious, sacred, sanctified, spiritual, superhuman, supernatural, theistic

divine *verb.* anticipate, apprehend, conjecture, deduce, discern, forefeel, foresee, foretell, guess, infer, perceive, predict, see, suppose, surmise, suspect, understand, visualize

division *noun.* **1** analysis, autopsy, carving, concession, contrasting, demarcation, detachment, distinguishing, distribution, disunion, divorce, parting, partition, reduction, rupture, selection, separating, subdivision **2** category, chunk, concession, demarcation, department, divide, dividend, fraction, grouping, kind, lobe, member, parcel, partition, piece, section, sector, subdivision **3** breach, conflict, difficulty, disaccord, disagreement, discord, disharmony, dispute, dissension, dissent, dissidence, disunion, feud, rupture, split, trouble, variance, words

divorce *noun.* annulment, breach, break, breakup, decree nisi, detachment, dissociation, dissolution, disunion, division, divorcement, partition, rupture, separate maintenance, separation, severance, split, splitsville

do *verb.* **1** accomplish, achieve, act, cook, create, discharge, effect, execute, halt, move, perform, perk, prepare, produce, succeed, transact, wind up, work **2** act, appear, bear, carry, comport, conduct, cook, deport, fare, give, manage, operate, perform, perk, portray, produce, quit, seem

doctor *noun.* bones, butcher, croaker, doc, expert, healer, intern, MD, medic, medical man, medico, physician, professor, quack, sawbones, scientist, specialist, surgeon

doctor *verb.* add to, adulterate, alter, change, cut, deacon, debase, dilute, disguise, falsify, fudge, gloss, load, misrepresent, sophisticate, spike, tamper with, water down

doctrine *noun.* axiom, basic, belief, canon, concept, conviction, creed, declaration, fundamental, inculcation, precept, pronouncement, propaganda, proposition, regulation, rule, statement, teaching

dodge *verb.* dark, deceive, ditch, duck, escape, evade, fence, hedge, lurch, parry, shake, shift, shuffle, skirt, slide, slip, swerve, trick

dollar *noun.* ace, bank note, bill, bone, buck, certificate, clam, cucumber, currency, fish, folding money, frog, iron man, note, peso, single, skin, year

domain *noun.* area, department, dominion, estate, orbit, power, province, quarter, realm, region, rule, scope, specialty, sphere, terrain, territory, turf, walk

domestic *adjective.* calm, devoted, domesticated, family, home, home-loving, homely, indoor, pet, private, sedentary, settled, subdued, submissive, tame, trained, tranquil, wifely

dominance *noun.* ascendancy, authority, command, control, domination, dominion, government, influence, masterdom, mastery, paramountcy, power, preeminence, preponderance, prepotence, rule, sovereignty, sway

dominant *adjective.* assertive, chief, foremost, governing, imperious, leading, lordly, main, master, obtaining, powerful, predominant, presiding, prevalent, ruling, sovereign, superior, supreme

dominate *verb.* boss, command, dictate, eclipse, handle, head, influence, lead, manage, master, monopolize, overshadow, prevail, reign, rule, subject, subjugate, tyrannize

domination *noun.* ascendancy, authority, command, despotism, dictatorship, dominion, influence, jurisdiction, might, power, repression, rule, sovereignty, strings, superiority, suppression, supremacy, tyranny

dominion *noun.* command, commission, country, domain, power, prerogative, property, province, realm, regency, regiment, region, rule, sphere, terrain, territory, turf, walk

done *adjective.* completed, concluded, down, effected, effete, executed, exhausted, fixed, fulfilled, over, perfected, performed, rendered, set, succeeded, terminated, wired, wrought

doomed *adjective.* bewitched, condemned, cursed, damned, destroyed, done, fated, lost, menaced, overwhelmed, reprobate, ruined, sentenced, suppressed, threatened, unfortunate, unredeemed, wrecked

dot *noun.* atom, circle, droplet, fleck, flyspeck, grain, iota, jot, mark, mite, mote, particle, period, pin-point, point, speck, spot, tittle

double *adjective.* bifold, binary, coupled, double-barreled, doubled, dual, dualistic, duple, duplex, duplicate, duplicated, geminate, paired, repeated, second, twice, twin, twofold

double *noun.* angel, companion, coordinate, copy, counterpart, duplicate, image, lookalike, match, mate, picture, portrait, reciprocal, replica, ringer, spit, stand-in, twin

double *verb.* augment, dualize, dupe, duplicate, duplify, enlarge, fold, grow, increase, loop, magnify, multiply, pleat, plicate, redouble, repeat, replicate, supplement

doubt *noun.* ambiguity, apprehension, difficulty, dilemma, disquiet, distrust, fear, hesitancy, incredulity, indecision, mistrust, perplexity, rejection, reluctance, skepticism, suspense, suspicion, uncertainty

doubt *verb.* challenge, disbelieve, discredit, dispute, distrust, fear, have qualms, hesitate, imagine, impugn, mistrust, query, question, shilly-shally, surmise, suspect, waver, wonder at

doubtful *adjective.* **1** ambiguous, dubious, hazardous, hazy, indecisive, indistinct, insecure, open, pending, precarious, shady, sneaky, speculative, suspicious, uncertain, uneasy, unsettled, unsure **2** baffled, confused, disturbed, doubting, dubious, hesitant, hesitating, indecisive, lost, puzzled, questioning, skeptical, suspicious, tentative, uncertain, unresolved, unsettled, unsure

doubtless *adjective.* absolutely, apparently, assuredly, clearly, easily, indisputably, ostensibly, positively, precisely, presumably, probably, seemingly, supposedly, surely, truly, undoubtedly, unequivocally, unquestionably

down *adjective.* cascading, declining, depressed, descending, downgrade, downhill, downward, dropping, inferior, lower, nether, precipitating, sagging, sinking, sliding, slipping, under, underneath

downright *adjective.* absolute, blunt, categorical, certain, clear, damned, explicit, gross, honest, indubitable, open, outright, positive, simple, sincere, sure, thoroughgoing, unqualified

draft *verb.* characterize, contrive, design, devise, draw, fabricate, fashion, form, frame, invent, manufacture, outline, plan, prepare, project, rough, shape, skeleton

drag *verb.* crawl, creep, dawdle, delay, droop, hang, inch, lag, lag behind, linger, poke, procrastinate, sag, shamble, shuffle, straggle, tarry, traipse

drain *verb.* **1** bankrupt, bleed, consume, divert, exhaust, finish, lessen, milk, pump, reduce, sap, spend, strain, swallow, tap, waste, weary, withdraw **2** abate, decline, decrease, diminish, dwindle, effuse, exude, filter off, flow, flow out, leak, leave dry, ooze, reduce, run off, taper off, trickle, well

dramatic *adjective.* affecting, breathtaking, climactic, comic, electrifying, emotional, expressive, impressive, melodramatic, powerful, startling, striking, sudden, tense, theatrical, thrilling, tragic, vivid

draw *verb.* **1** attract, carry, convey, drag, elicit, evoke, extract, fetch, haul, jerk, lug, pluck, pull, pump, tap, tow, trail, tug **2** caricature, depict, describe, design, express, form, frame, graph, mark, model, outline, paint, pencil, portray, prepare, profile, trace, write **3** allure, attract, bring forth, call forth, charm, convince, elicit, enchant, engage, evoke, fascinate, get, induce, invite, lure, persuade, prompt, take

drawing *noun.* cartoon, comp, delineation, depiction, design, etching, graphics, layout, likeness, outline, painting, picture, portrayal, representation, sketch, storyboard, study, tracing

dread *noun.* affright, alarm, apprehension, aversion, awe, cold feet, consternation, creeps, dismay, fright, funk, goose bumps, horror, jitters, panic, phobia, terror

dreadful *adjective.* alarming, appalling, bad, creepy, distressing, dread, frightening, frozen, ghastly, grievous, grim, gross, monstrous, shocking, spooky, terrific, tremendous, wicked

dream *noun.* bubble, delusion, emotion, fancy, image, imagination, impression, incubus, nightmare, rainbow, reverie, romance, specter, speculation, thought, trance, vision, wraith

dream *verb.* ache, crave, create, devise, fancy, formulate, hunger, imagine, invent, long, lust, make up, picture, pine, sigh, sublimate, think, visualize

dress *noun.* bag, clothes, costume, covering, duds, ensemble, feathers, garb, garment, gown, habit, outfit, rags, robe, things, trappings, uniform, weeds

dress *verb.* adorn, apparel, array, attire, change, clothe, costume, cover, deck, decorate, dud, garb, ornament, outfit, rig, robe, trim, turn out

drift *noun.* bank, batch, bunch, bundle, clump, cluster, deposit, heap, hill, lot, mass, mound, mountain, parcel, pile, set, shock, stack

drift *verb.* accumulate, amass, coast,

dance, flicker, float, flow, flutter, linger, muck, ride, sail, slide, stray, stroll, tend, wander, wash

drill *noun.* assignment, call, conditioning, constitutional, discipline, dress, drilling, dry run, exercise, gym, instruction, maneuvers, marching, preparation, repetition, shakedown, training, workout

drink *noun.* alcohol, booze, brew, cup, glass, gulp, liquid, liquor, refreshment, shot, sip, slug, spirits, spot, swallow, swig, taste, toast

drink *verb.* absorb, belt, booze, consume, down, gargle, gulp, imbibe, indulge, irrigate, lap, nip, sip, sop, sup, swig, tipple, toast

drive *noun.* **1** commute, excursion, expedition, hitch, jaunt, joyride, lift, outing, pickup, ramble, ride, run, spin, Sunday drive, tour, trip, turn, whirl **2** ambition, clout, effort, energy, enterprise, goods, gumption, guts, impetus, impulse, momentum, motive, pressure, punch, push, steam, vigor, zip **3** arouse, bulldoze, compel, encourage, goad, hurl, induce, jawbone, kick, motivate, oblige, pound, press, pressure, prompt, propel, provoke, shove **4** bear down, bicycle, coast, cruise, cycle, drag, fly, handle, manage, mobilize, motor, move, propel, speed, start, tool, transport, travel **5** batter, beat, butt, dig, hammer, knock, plunge, pop, punch, ram, sink, stab, stick, strike, throw, thrust, thump, thwack

drop *noun.* **1** bead, bit, bubble, drip, iota, molecule, morsel, nip, ounce, particle, sip, speck, splash, spot, taste, teardrop, trace, trickle **2** cut, decline, deterioration, dip, downfall, downtrend, downturn, fall, landslide, lapse, lowering, reduction, sag, slide, slip, slump, tumble, upset

drop *verb.* **1** bead, bleed, descend, distill, drain, drip, emanate, filter, hail, leak, ooze, percolate, precipitate, seep, snow, splash, trickle, trill **2** abandon, decline, descend, fell, floor, flop, ground, knock, lower, pitch, plump, plunge, release, sink, slide, slip, topple, unload **3** adios, cancel, dismiss, disown, ditch, divorce, end, forfeit, interrupt, kick, leave, lose, repudiate, resign, sacrifice, scrub, separate, shake

drug *noun.* biologic, cure, dope, essence, medicament, medicinal, medicine, narcotic, pharmaceutic, pharmaceutical, pill, poison, potion, prescription, remedy, sedative, stimulant, tonic

drug *verb.* benumb, blunt, deaden, desensitize, dope, dope up, dose, dose up, fix, hit, medicate, narcotize, numb, poison, relax, sedate, stupefy, treat

drunk *adjective.* befuddled, buzzed, canned, drinking, gassed, glazed, groggy, jolly, lit, lush, merry, oiled, overcome, sloshed, soaked, stoned, tipsy, wasted

dry *adjective.* **1** anhydrous, arid, baked, bare, barren, dehydrated, dusty, evaporated, exhausted, hard, impoverished, parched, rainless, sapped, sear, shriveled, thirsty, torrid **2** apathetic, blah, boring, dreary, dusty, ho hum, impassive, insipid, modest, monotonous, naked, plain, simple, tedious, tiresome, trite, wearisome **3** biting, cutting, cynical, droll, harsh, humorous, ironical, keen, low-key, restrained, salty, sardonic, satirical, sharp, sly, sour, subtle, tart

dry *verb.* bake, blot, concentrate, condense, dehumidify, drain, empty, evaporate, exhaust, harden, sear, sponge, stale, swab, towel, wilt, wipe, wither

duck *verb.* avoid, bend, bow, crouch, dip, dive, dodge, double, escape, evade, fence, lower, lurch, parry, plunge, shun, shy, stoop

due *adjective.* becoming, coming, condign, deserved, earned, equitable, fair, fit, fitting, good, just, justified, merited, proper, rhadamanthine, right, rightful, suitable

due *noun.* claim, compensation, interest, lumps, need, payment, prerogative, privilege, rate, recompense, reprisal, retaliation, retribution, right, rights, satisfaction, title, vengeance

dull *adjective.* **1** backward, boring, dense, dim, dumb, ignorant, indolent, low, retarded, scatterbrained, simple, sluggish, stolid, stupid, tedious, thick, vacuous, wearisome **2** apathetic, callous, colorless, depressed, heavy, inactive, indifferent, inert, lifeless, listless, placid, regular, routine, slack, sluggish, stagnant, still, usual **3** archaic, arid, colorless, common, dreary, hackneyed, heavy, insipid, pointless, prosaic, repetitive, routine, stupid, tame, tiresome, unimaginative, usual, worn out **4** accustomed, apathetic, depressed, inactive, inert, lifeless, listless, monotonous, placid, regular, routine, slack, sluggish, stagnant, still, torpid, unresponsive, usual **5** ashen, black, cold, colorless, dim, dingy, feeble, hazy, indistinct, leaden, lifeless, muddy, murky, obscure, opaque, overcast, shadowy, subdued

dumb *adjective.* dense, dim-witted, dodo, doltish, dull, dumb bunny, dumb ox, dumbbell, dumbo, dumdum, dummy, feebleminded, foolish, moronic, numskulled, simple-minded, stupid, thick

durable *adjective.* abiding, constant, dependable, enduring, firm, fixed, impervious, permanent, persistent, reliable, resistant, sound, stable, stout, strong, substantial, tenacious, tough

dust *noun.* ashes, cinders, dirt, earth, filth, flakes, fragments, granules, grit, ground, kittens, lint, powder, refuse, sand, smut, soil, soot

duty *noun.* **1** burden, business, commission, contract, engagement, function, load, millstone, mission, must, obligation, onus, ought, province, role, trouble, trust, undertaking **2** accountability, accountableness, allegiance, answerability, burden, charge, conscience, deference, devoir, good faith, honesty, integrity, liability, loyalty, obedience, pledge, respect, reverence

dwell *verb.* bide, bunk, crash, exist, inhabit, lodge, nest, occupy, park, quarter, remain, reside, rest, roost, settle, stay, tarry, tenant

dwelling *noun.* abode, castle, commorancy, crib, cubbyhole, den, digs, domicile, dump, establishment, habitat, haunt, house, lodging, pad, quarters, residence, residency

dying *adjective.* checking out, decaying, declining, disintegrating, done for, doomed, ebbing, expiring, fading, fated, final, going, mortal, passing, perishing, sinking, vanishing, withering

dynamic *adjective.* aggressive, changing, compelling, driving, electric, energetic, energizing, enterprising, forceful, intense, lively, lusty, magnetic, potent, powerful, productive, vehement, vital

E

eager *adjective.* ambitious, ardent, avid, desiring, desirous, enthusiastic, fervent, greedy, heated, hot, intent, keen, longing, solicitous, vehement, wild, wishful, yearning

early *adjective.* **1** aboriginal, antecedent, antiquated, budding, new, preceding, premier, previous, primal, prime, primeval, primitive, prior, pristine, raw, undeveloped, virgin, young **2** advanced, anticipatory, beforehand, direct, immature, immediate, preceding, precocious, premature, previous, prompt, pronto, punctual, quick, soon, speedy, unexpected, untimely

early *adverb.* **1** before long, beforehand, briefly, directly, ere long, immediately, oversoon, prematurely, presently, previous, promptly, pronto, proximately, quick, shortly, soon, too soon, unexpectedly **2** at once, directly, first, freshly, instantaneously, instantly, newly, presto, primitively, promptly, recently, soon, straightway, summarily, thereon, thereupon, timely, without delay

earn *verb.* attain, clear, collect, cop, derive, draw, effect, gross, net, perform, pick up, pull, rate, realize, reap, secure, snag, turn

earnest *adjective.* **1** ardent, busy, devoted, diligent, eager, fervent, fervid, heartfelt, impassioned, industrious, keen, passionate, perseverant, purposeful, sincere, urgent, vehement, warm, zealous **2** constant, determined, firm, fixed, grave, important, intent, meaningful, resolute, resolved, sedate, sincere, solemn, stable, staid, steady, thoughtful, weighty

earnings *noun.* balance, gain, gate, groceries, income, melon, net, pay, payoff, proceeds, receipts, remuneration, revenue, reward, salary, salt, takings, wages

earth *noun.* **1** apple, cosmos, creation, dust, globe, macrocosm, orb, planet, real estate, spaceship Earth, sphere, star, sublunary world, terra, terrene, terrestrial sphere, universe, vale **2** clay, clod, coast, compost, deposit, dust, land, mold, muck, mud, sand, shore, sod, soil, surface, terrain, topsoil, turf

earthquake *noun.* convulsion, fault, macroseism, microseism, movement, quake, quaker, seism, seismicity, seismism, shake, shock, slip, temblor, trembler, upheaval, wiggler

earthy *adjective.* bawdy, coarse, crude, down, down-to-earth, dull, easygoing, folksy, homely, indelicate, lusty, mundane, natural, pragmatic, ribald, rough, simple, uninhibited

ease *noun.* **1** affluence, calm, calmness, comfort, content, contentment, gratification, happiness, idleness, inactivity, leisure, luxury, passivity, prosperity, repose, rest, security, serenity **2** adroitness, cinch, cleverness, dispatch, efficiency, flexibility, fluency, freedom, informality, insouciance, liberty, naturalness, poise, readiness, setup, simplicity, skillfulness, smoothness

ease *verb.* **1** aid, calm, comfort, disengage, forward, further, lessen, lift, moderate, mollify, relax, release, smooth, soften, soothe, speed, speed up, still **2** extricate, facilitate, handle, inch, induce, insert, join, loose, loosen, maneuver, relax, remove, right, slack, slide, slip, squeeze, steer

easily *adverb.* **1** calmly, comfortably, competently, conveniently, coolly, efficiently, effortlessly, evenly, fluently, freely, lightly, plainly, quickly, readily, simply, smoothly, steadily, surely **2** absolutely, actually, assuredly, certainly, clearly, decidedly, definitely, doubtless, indeed, indisputably, plainly, probably, really, surely, truly, undeniably, undoubtedly, unequivocally

easy *adjective.* **1** accessible, basic, cinch, clear, effortless, facile, inconsiderable, light, little, manifest, mere, obvious, picnic, royal, simple, slight, smooth, snap **2** calm, carefree, content, cozy, easygoing, effortless, flowing, gentle, leisurely, light, moderate, prosperous, satisfied, secure, smooth, snug, substantial, temperate **3** amenable, clement, compassionate, easygoing, forgiving, gentle, gullible, kindly, liberal, light, merciful, mild, moderate, soft, spoiling, submissive, susceptible, temperate **4** affable, amiable, carefree, casual, complaisant, easygoing, gentle, gracious, gregarious, informal, mild, natural, open, relaxed, secure, smooth, suave, tolerant

eat *verb.* **1** absorb, attack, banquet, bite, bolt, breakfast, chew, dispatch, gorge, graze, munch, nibble, pick, scarf, snack, sup, swallow, wolf **2** bite, condense, corrode, crumble, decay, decompose, disappear, disintegrate, dissolve, drain, exhaust, gnaw, nibble, rot, rust, spill, use, vanish

eccentric *adjective.* anomalous, beat, bizarre, capricious, case, curious, erratic, flaky, funny, irregular, odd, offbeat, peculiar, queer, strange, unnatural, unusual, wild

eccentric *noun.* beatnik, case, character, crackpot, creep, customer, freak, geek, heretic, maverick, nonconformist, nut, nutcake, oddity, original, rare bird, screwball, zombie

echo *noun.* answer, copy, imitation, mirror, mirror image, onomatopoeia, parallel, parroting, rebound, reflection, reiteration, repercussion, repetition, reply, reproduction, reverberation, ringing, rubber stamp

echo *verb.* ape, copy, imitate, mimic, mirror, parallel, parrot, react, recall, reflect, reiterate, reproduce, resemble, respond, ring, rubber-stamp, second, vibrate

economic *adjective.* bread-and-butter, budgetary, business, commercial, fiscal, industrial, material, mercantile, monetary, money-making, pecuniary, productive, profit-making, profitable, remunerative, solvent, trade, viable

economical *adjective.* **1** avaricious, canny, careful, circumspect, close, economizing, efficient, meager, methodical, parsimonious, penurious, practical, prudent, spare, sparing, stingy, thrifty, watchful **2** buy, cheap, cheapie, cost nothing, cut rate, dirt cheap, el cheapo, fair, low, low tariff, low-priced, marked down, moderate, modest, on sale, reasonable, sound, steal

economy *noun.* austerity, carefulness, caution, cutback, deduction, direction, discretion, frugality, husbandry, meanness, moratorium, providence, prudence, reduction, regulation, restraint, supervision, thrift

edge *noun.* bound, brim, butt, contour, crust, frame, fringe, frontier, hem, ledge, line, molding, perimeter, shore, strand, threshold, tip, verge

educated *adjective.* accomplished, civilized, developed, enlightened, expert, fitted, formed, informed, initiated, knowledgeable, literary, literate, polished, prepared, professional, shaped, tasteful, taught

education *noun.* background, breeding, catechism, civilization, direction, drilling, enlightenment, erudition, improvement, knowledge, nurture, preparation, rearing, refinement, scholarship, schooling, study, tuition

effect *noun.* **1** aftermath, backlash, conclusion, corollary, denouement, development, end, event, eventuality, fallout, issue, outcome, outgrowth, reaction, sequel, sequence, upshot, waves **2** clout, drift, effectiveness, efficacy, efficiency, fact, implementation, imprint, influence, mark, meaning, power, purport, sense, strength, validity, vigor, weight

effect *verb.* achieve, buy, cause, conclude, create, effectuate, enforce, execute, induce, perform, procure, produce, realize, render, secure, sell, turn out, yield

effective *adjective.* able, capable, compelling, competent, convincing, energetic, impressive, persuasive, powerful, practical, producing, serviceable, serving, sound, striking, trenchant, valid, wicked

effectiveness *noun.* capability, clout, effect, efficacy, efficiency, force, forcefulness, point, potency, power, punch, strength, success, use, validity, verve, vigor, weight

efficacy *noun.* ability, adequacy, capacity, competence, effect, effectiveness, efficiency, energy, influence, potency, power, strength, success, sufficiency, use, vigor, virtue, weight

efficiency *noun.* abundance, address, adequacy, capability, competence, economy, efficacy, energy, facility, faculty, power, productivity, proficiency, prowess, readiness, skill, skillfulness, talent

efficient *adjective.* able, accomplished, adept, apt, competent, deft, dynamic, economic, energetic, expert, handy, powerful, practiced, productive, proficient, profitable, qualified, valuable

effort *noun.* achievement, act, battle, energy, enterprise, exercise, exertion, intention, power, production, pull, spurt, stretch, sweat, toil, trouble, tug, undertaking

elaborate *adjective.* careful, decorated, elegant, embellished, exact, extensive, extravagant, fancy, labored, minute, ornamented, ornate, overdone, overworked, perfected, prodigious, sophisticated, studied

elaborate *verb.* clarify, complicate, deck, decorate, develop, devise, discuss, enhance, enlarge, evolve, explain, interpret, ornament, polish, produce, refine, unfold, work out

elder *noun.* ancestor, ancient, dad, firstborn, forefather, golden ager, old man, old woman, old-timer, older adult, oldest, oldster, patriarch, pop, senior, senior citizen, superior, veteran

elect *verb.* accept, admit, appoint, ballot, choose, conclude, designate, judge, mark, name, pick, prefer, receive, resolve, select, settle, take, tap

election *noun.* acclamation, alternative, appointment, ballot, choice, decision, determination, franchise, judgment, option, poll, polls, preference, primary, referendum, selection, ticket, voting

electricity *noun.* AC, current, DC, electron, galvanism, heat, ignition, juice, light, neutron, positron, proton, radioactivity, service, spark, tension, utilities, voltage

elegance *noun.* breeding, cultivation, delicacy, dignity, discernment, distinction, exquisiteness, felicity, gentility, grace, noblesse, polish, propriety, refinement, restraint, sophistication, style, taste

elegant *adjective.* affected, appropriate, apt, aristocratic, artistic, comely, courtly, dainty, exquisite, fine, neat, ornamented, ornate, overdone, polished, simple, stylized, sumptuous

element *noun.* constituent, detail, drop, fundamental, hint, material, matter, member, part, particle, piece, root, section, stem, subdivision, trace, unit, view

elementary *adjective.* basic, clear, elemental, essential, facile, fundamental, introductory, original, plain, preliminary, primary, primitive, rudimentary, simple, simplest, simplex, simplified, underlying

elevated *adjective.* animated, bright, eloquent, eminent, ethical, exalted, formal, grand, grandiloquent, heavy, lofty, moral, righteous, stately, superb, upright, upstanding, virtuous

elevation *noun.* advance, advancement, aggrandizement, apotheosis, boost, deification, eminence, exaltation, exaltedness, glorification, grandeur, loftiness, magnification, nobility, preference, preferment, raise, upgrading

eligible *adjective.* acceptable, appropriate, becoming, desirable, discretionary, fitted, licensed, nubile, preferable, privileged, proper, qualified, satisfactory, suitable, suited, trained, usable, worthy

eliminate *verb.* defeat, discharge, dismiss, disqualify, disregard, drop, eject, eradicate, erase, exclude, expel, exterminate, ignore, invalidate, kill, omit, oust, waive

elite *adjective.* aristocratic, best, choice, cool, crack, elect, exclusive, first chop, greatest, noble, pick, selected, super, tip-top, top-notch, tops, upper-class, world class

elite *noun.* aristocracy, best, celebrity, elect, establishment, fat, flower, gentility, gentry, pick, pink, pride, prime, prize, quality, society, top, u

eloquent *adjective.* ardent, articulate, expressive, fervent, glib, grandiloquent, impressive, meaningful, passionate, persuasive, poignant, powerful, revealing, significant, stirring, telling, touching, voluble

embarrassing *adjective.* awkward, compromising, confusing, delicate, disagreeable, distressing, exasperating, helpless, impossible, inconvenient, perplexing, puzzling, rattling, sticky, troubling, uneasy, unseemly, upsetting

embarrassment *noun.* awkwardness, booboo, difficulty, dilemma, distress, hitch, inhibition, mess, mistake, mortification, pickle, poverty, predicament, scrape, snag, stew, strait, tangle

embodiment *noun.* apotheosis, collection, comprehension, epitome, expression, form, formation, incarnation, inclusion, incorporation, integration, matter, organization, personification, realization, symbol, systematization, type

embrace *verb.* **1** clasp, clinch, cling, clutch, cradle, encircle, envelop, fold, grab, grasp, grip, hug, lock, nuzzle, press, seize, squeeze, wrap **2** accommodate, admit, adopt, comprehend, comprise, contain, cover, deal with, embody, encompass, grab, have, incorporate, involve, receive, seize, subsume, welcome

emerge *verb.* appear, arise, arrive, derive, develop, flow, gush, issue, loom, materialize, proceed, rise, show, spring, spurt, steam, stem, surface

emergency *noun.* accident, climax, clutch, crunch, danger, difficulty, distress, extremity, fix, hole, necessity, pass, predicament, pressure, scrape, squeeze, strait, tension

eminent *adjective.* conspicuous, distinguished, dominant, elevated, esteemed, exalted, famed, grand, lion, lofty, name, notable, noted, noteworthy, outstanding, renowned, star, superior

emotion *noun.* affect, affection, agitation, anger, ardor, commotion, despair, ecstasy, elation, empathy, fervor, grief, love, perturbation, rage, sentiment, sympathy, zeal

emotional *adjective.* ardent, disturbed, ecstatic, fanatical, fervent, fiery, heated, impetuous, irrational, nervous, poignant, responsive, roused, sentimental, stirring, tender, touching, warm

emphasis *noun.* accent, attention, force, headlined, highlighted, impressiveness, insistence, intensity, moment, power, priority, prominence, significance, strength, stress, underlined, underscoring, weight

emphasize *verb.* accent, affirm, articulate, assert, bear down, charge, dramatize, enlarge, impress, maintain, mark, pinpoint, press, pronounce, repeat, spot, spotlight, underline

employed *adjective.* active, at it, busy, employed, engaged, gainfully, hired, in collar, in harness, in place, inked, laboring, occupied, on board, on duty, operating, selected, signed

employee *noun.* agent, apprentice, assistant, attendant, clerk, craftsman, domestic, help, member, operator, plug, punk, representative, salesman, servant, slave, worker, workman

employer *noun.* businessman, chief, corporation, entrepreneur, establishment, executive, firm, kingpin, lord, manager, manufacturer, master, organization, outfit, overseer, president, proprietor, supervisor

employment *noun.* avocation, bag, biz, business, employ, enrollment, exercise, exercising, exertion, function, hiring, line, mission, number, profession, recruitment, using, work

empty *adjective.* **1** bare, barren, blank, clear, deflated, deserted, despoiled, destitute, devoid, evacuated, exhausted, hollow, lacking, vacant, vacated, vacuous, void, wanting **2** banal, barren, cheap, dumb, expressionless, fatuous, futile, idle, ineffective, insincere, insipid, meaningless, petty, purposeless, silly, unreal, vain, worthless

empty *verb.* clear, consume, discharge, drink, dump, ebb, eject, escape, exhaust, expel, gut, leak, leave, release, tap, unload, vacate, void

enable *verb.* approve, authorize, commission, empower, endow, facilitate, fit, implement, invest, let, license, permit, prepare, qualify, ready, sanction, set up, warrant

enchanting *adjective.* alluring, appealing, attractive, beguiling, captivating, charming, endearing, enthralling, exciting, fascinating, glamorous, intriguing, lovely, pleasant, pleasing, seductive, siren, winsome

encounter *noun.* argument, battle, brush, clash, collision, combat, conflict, contention, contest, dispute, engagement, fray, gin, quarrel, rumpus, scrap, skirmish, violence

encounter *verb.* alight upon, bear, bump into, close, come across, come upon, confront, detect, espy, experience, face, find, front, meet, run into, suffer, sustain, undergo

encourage *verb.* **1** animate, applaud, boost, comfort, fortify, gladden, goad, inspire, praise, prick, rally, reassure, refresh, restore, revitalize, steel, stir, strengthen **2** advocate, aid, approve, bolster, comfort, ease, endorse, forward, foster, further, reassure, reinforce, second, serve, solace, subsidize, succor, uphold

encouragement *noun.* advocacy, aid, animation, assistance, comfort, confidence, faith, firmness, helpfulness, hope, incentive, invigoration, refreshment, relieving, softening, stimulus, succor, trust

end *noun.* **1** borderline, bound, boundary, confine, deadline, extent, extreme, extremity, foot, head, heel, pole, stub, stump, tail, terminus, tip, top **2** achievement, cessation, closure, conclusion, consummation, curtain, denouement, determination, expiration, issue, omega, outcome, realization, result, retirement, target, terminus, windup

end *verb.* abolish, accomplish, achieve, break off, break up, close, conclude, crown, delay, dissolve, drop, expire, halt, interrupt, resolve, settle, shut down, wind up, wrap

ending *noun.* catastrophe, cessation, closing, closure, consummation, denouement, dissolution, epilogue, expiration, finale, lapse, omega, outcome, period, summation, terminus, upshot, windup

endless *adjective.* boundless, ceaseless, constant, continual, eternal, immeasurable, immortal, incalculable, incessant, limitless, monotonous, multitudinous, perpetual, unbroken, undivided, undying, unfathomable, untold

endurance *noun.* allowance, bearing, continuing, coolness, fortitude, grit, guts, mettle, pluck, resistance, restraint, starch, strength, submission, tenacity, tolerance, undergoing, will

endure *verb.* **1** bear, brook, eat, encounter, experience, face, feel, hang in, know, permit, stand, stick, suffer, sustain, take, undergo, weather, withstand **2** abide, be, bide, cling, exist, hold, last, linger, live, perdure, persist, prevail, remain, stand, stay, survive, sustain, wear

enemy *noun.* adversary, agent, antagonist, archenemy, betrayer, competitor, criminal, foe, guerrilla, inquisitor, invader, murderer, opponent, prosecutor, revolutionary, rival, slanderer, spy

energetic *adjective.* active, aggressive, animated, breezy, driving, dynamic, enterprising, hardy, indefatigable, kinetic, lively, lusty, powerful, snappy, strong, sturdy, tireless, unflagging

energy *noun.* **1** animation, ardor, effectiveness, efficiency, endurance, enterprise, exertion, forcefulness, fortitude, life, muscle, pluck, power, spirit, strength, toughness, vivacity, zeal **2** burn, conductivity, current, electricity, friction, gravity, horsepower, kilowatts, magnetism, potential, pressure, radioactivity, rays, reaction, service, steam, strength, voltage

enforce *verb.* compel, demand, discharge, effect, exact, execute, exert, expect, goad, impose, lash, oblige, perform, press, reinforce, urge, whip, wrest

enforcement *noun.* administration, coercion, compulsion, constraint, duress, enforcing, execution, fulfilling, implementation, imposition, lash, obligation, prescription, pressure, prosecution, reinforcement, spur, whip

engage *verb.* **1** appoint, bespeak, book, charter, commission, contract, employ, enlist, enroll, ink, lease, place, rent, reserve, retain, secure, take on, truck with **2** absorb, allure, arrest, busy, draw, employ, fascinate, grip, interest, involve, join, monopolize, partake, participate, practice, soak, tackle, undertake **3** agree, bind, catch, commit, contract, covenant, grab, guarantee, hook, obligate, oblige, pass, pledge, tie, troth, turn on, undertake, vow

engaged *adjective.* **1** affianced, asked for, betrothed, bird, bound, committed, contracted, future, going steady, hooked, intended, matched, pinned, pledged, plighted, ringed, spoken for, steady **2** committed, deep, doing, employed, engrossed, immersed, intent, interested, involved, occupied, operating, performing, practicing, preoccupied, pursuing, rapt, unavailable, working

engagement *noun.* **1** assurance, betrothal, bond, commitment, compact, contract, espousal, match, oath, obligation, pact, plight, promise, troth, undertaking, vow, word, zero hour **2** appointment, arrangement, assignation, blind date, commission, commitment, date, double date, errand, get-together, gig, heavy date, interview, invitation, meet, seeing one, stint, visit

engaging *adjective.* agreeable, appealing, attractive, captivating, enchanting, enticing, fascinating, fetching, glamorous, interesting, intriguing, inviting, lovable, magnetic, pleasing, siren, sweet, winsome

engine *noun.* agent, apparatus, appliance, barrel, cylinder, diesel, dynamo, generator, horses, instrument, mechanism, motor, piston, pot, tool, transformer, turbine, weapon

engineer *noun.* architect, bridge monkey, builder, contriver, designer, deviser, director, inventor, manager, manipulator, motorman, originator, planner, schemer, sights, surveyor, techie, technie

engineer *verb.* angle, cause, con, contrive, cook, create, doctor, effect, encompass, manage, maneuver, plan, plot, scheme, set up, superintend, swing, work

enjoy *verb.* adore, appreciate, dig, dote on, drink in, fancy, flip for, funk, go, groove on, like, love, luxuriate in, mind, relish, savor, savvy, take to

enjoyment *noun.* delectation, diversion, enjoying, fruition, fun, gladness, gratification, happiness, hedonism, indulgence, luxury, recreation, rejoicing, relish, satisfaction, thrill, triumph, zest

enormous *adjective.* blimp, colossal, excessive, gargantuan, gross, huge, immense, jumbo, mammoth, massive, monstrous, mountainous, prodigious, stupendous, titanic, tremendous, vast, whopping

enough *adjective.* abundant, acceptable, adequate, ample, comfortable, competent, complete, copious, decent, full, lavish, plentiful, replete, satisfactory, satisfying, sufficient, suitable, unlimited

enough *adverb.* abundantly, acceptably, admissibly, amply, averagely, barely, commensurately, decently, fairly, moderately, passably, proportionately, rather, reasonably, satisfactorily, so-so, sufficiently, tolerably

ensemble *noun.* band, cast, choir, chorus, composite, entirety, group, orchestra, organization, outfit, quintet, set, sum, total, totality, trio, troupe, whole

ensure *verb.* arrange, assure, certify, cinch, clinch, confirm, effect, establish, guard, ice, insure, lock up, make safe, protect, provide, safeguard, secure, warrant

enter *verb.* **1** access, arrive, break in, bust in, come, crack, crawl, creep, go in, insert, introduce, intrude, invade, pierce, probe, slip, sneak, work in **2** become member, begin, commence, enlist, enroll, inaugurate, join, join up, lead off, muster, open, participate in, set about, sign up, start, subscribe, take up, tee off

enterprise *noun.* **1** baby, business, campaign, do, effort, engagement, flier, happening, hazard, move, operation, outfit, plan, plunge, program, proposition, scheme, speculation **2** activity, alertness, ambition, audacity, courage, daring, eagerness, energy, enthusiasm, gumption, hustle, pluck, push, readiness, resource, spirit, vigor, zeal

entertain *verb.* **1** absorb, cheer, comfort, delight, distract, divert, gladden, grab, humor, indulge, inspire, interest, occupy, pique, recreate, relax, satisfy, solace **2** admit, board, chaperone, dine, feed, foster, harbor, have guests, have visitors, invite, lodge, quarter, receive, recreate, room, treat, welcome, wine

entertaining *adjective.* ball, cheering, compelling, delightful, enchanting, enthralling, fun, funny, gas, impressive, inspiring, piquant, poignant, priceless, restorative, rousing, scream, stirring

entertainment *noun.* ball, celebration, distraction, feast, frolic, fun, game, grins, laughs, merriment, merrymaking, party, pastime, recreation, relief, revelry, sport, surprise

enthusiasm *noun.* conviction, eagerness, ecstasy, emotion, energy, fervor, flame, flare, interest, life, mania, nerve, relish, spirit, transport, vivacity, zeal

enthusiastic *adjective.* animated, ardent, avid, concerned, eager, ebullient, exuberant, fanatical, fervent, hearty, intent, keen, passionate, pleased, vehement, wacky, warm, willing

entire *adjective.* absolute, all, consolidated, gross, integral, integrated, outright, plenary, sound, total, unbroken, undiminished, undivided, uninjured, unmarked, unrestricted, untouched, whole

entirely *adverb.* absolutely, alone, altogether, but, exclusively, fully, only, perfectly, plumb, quite, solely, thoroughly, totally, uniquely, utterly, well, wholly, without reservation

entity *noun.* article, being, body, creature, existence, individual, item, material, matter, organism, presence, quantity, single, something, stuff, subsistence, substance, thing

entrance *noun.* **1** access, approach, corridor,

door, doorway, entry, gate, hallway, lobby, opening, passage, passageway, path, porch, portal, portico, threshold, way **2** access, admission, approach, baptism, commencement, debut, enrollment, entry, immigration, importation, incoming, initiation, invasion, outset, passage, penetration, progress, start

entry *noun.* access, approach, avenue, door, doorway, entrance, foyer, gate, hall, ingression, inlet, lobby, opening, passage, passageway, portal, threshold, vestibule

envelope *noun.* bag, box, case, coat, coating, container, cover, covering, enclosure, hide, jacket, pocket, pouch, receptacle, sheath, shell, skin, wrapping

environment *noun.* ambiance, atmosphere, aura, background, circumstances, climate, conditions, domain, element, hood, locale, medium, milieu, scenery, terrain, territory, turf, zoo

episode *noun.* adventure, affair, business, chapter, circumstance, doings, event, experience, happening, incident, installment, interlude, matter, occasion, occurrence, part, passage, section

equal *adjective.* according, balanced, commensurate, comparable, correspondent, double, duplicate, identical, indistinguishable, invariable, level, like, matched, matching, parallel, same, tantamount, uniform

equal *noun.* brother, companion, compeer, competitor, complement, copy, counterpart, double, duplicate, equivalent, fellow, like, likeness, match, mate, parallel, rival, twin

equal *verb.* agree, approach, balance, compare, comprise, correspond, emulate, equalize, equate, level, match, meet, parallel, push, rival, tally, tie, touch

equality *noun.* balance, brotherhood, correspondence, egalitarianism, equatability, equilibrium, equivalence, evenness, fairness, fellowship, identity, impartiality, likeness, par, parallelism, sameness, tolerance, uniformity

equate *verb.* agree, associate, average, compare, consider, equalize, even, hold, level, match, pair, paragon, parallel, regard, relate, represent, square, tally

equilibrium *noun.* calm, calmness, composure, cool, coolness, counterbalance, counterpoise, equanimity, equipoise, evenness, poise, polish, rest, serenity, stability, steadiness, steadying, symmetry

equipment *noun.* accessories, accouterments, apparatus, appliances, baggage, contraptions, contrivances, fittings, fixtures, furniture, machinery, outfit, paraphernalia, setup, supply, tools, trappings, utensils

equitable *adjective.* candid, decent, due, ethical, fair, honest, impersonal, level, moral, nondiscriminatory, objective, proper, reasonable, right, rightful, square, stable, uncolored

equivalent *adjective.* alike, analogous, carbon, commensurate, comparable, copy, correspondent, duplicate, identical, indistinguishable, interchangeable, like, parallel, reciprocal, similar, substitute, synonymous, tantamount

erect *verb.* assemble, cock, construct, create, effect, form, found, frame, hoist, institute, join, lift, make up, manufacture, mount, pitch, produce, set up

erotic *adjective.* amatory, amorous, bawdy, carnal, dirty, earthy, hot, lascivious, lewd, obscene, purple, raw, rousing, salacious, suggestive, titillating, venereal, voluptuous

error *noun.* delinquency, delusion, fall, fallacy, fault, flaw, lapse, miscalculation, misconception, misstep, misunderstanding, omission, oversight, slight, stumble, transgression, untruth, wrongdoing

escape *noun.* beat, bolt, break, deliverance, departure, desertion, disappearance, ducking, fadeout, freedom, leave, liberation, out, outbreak, powder, release, rescue, withdrawal

escape *verb.* bolt, break, break away, depart, disappear, dodge, double, duck, emerge, fly, leave, pass, run away, run off, shun, skip, slip, vanish

escort *noun.* beau, bodyguard, chaperon, convoy, cortege, date, gallant, guard, guide, john, partner, protection, retinue, safeguard, shag, squire, train, warden

escort *verb.* accompany, bear, carry, chaperon, convoy, date, direct, drag, guide, lead, partner, protect, route, see, shepherd, show, squire, steer

especially *adverb.* chiefly, conspicuously, curiously, eminently, expressly, mainly, notably, oddly, particularly, remarkably, signally, specially, strangely, supremely, unaccountably, uncommonly, unusually, wonderfully

essay *noun.* aim, bid, crack, effort, endeavor, exertion, experiment, fling, lick, shot, stab, struggle, test, toil, trial, try, undertaking, work

essence *noun.* attribute, base, being, burden, constitution, core, element, entity, form, fundamentals, grain, life, meaning, nucleus, property, spirit, substance, vein

essential *adjective.* **1** capital, cardinal, chief, crucial, foremost, fundamental, imperative, important, indispensable, leading, main, necessary, needed, prerequisite, principal, required, right-hand, wanted **2** absolute, cold, congenital, constitutional, elemental, fundamental, inborn, inherent, innate, intrinsic, key, main, material, primary, prime, primitive, principal, underlying

essential *noun.* basic, brass tacks, condition, element, essence, fundamental, groceries, guts, heart, must, precondition, prerequisite, principle, quintessence, requirement, rudiment, stuff, substance

establish *verb.* **1** authorize, base, build, create, decree, erect, form, found, install, institute, lodge, put, root, secure, stabilize, start, station, stick **2** ascertain, authorize, base, certify, constitute, corroborate, decree, discover, learn, legislate, prescribe, prove, ratify, rest, show, stay, substantiate, validate

establishment *noun.* abode, building, company, concern, corporation, enterprise, factory, firm, foundation, house, institute, institution, organization, outfit, plant, quarters, setup, system

estate *noun.* **1** acreage, area, country place, domain, dominion, farm, freehold, grounds, holdings, lands, parcel, plantation, quinta, ranch, residence, rural seat, territory, villa **2** caste, category, classification, footing, form, grade, level, lot, order, period, quality, repair, shape, sphere, state, station, status, stratum

esteem *verb.* admire, appreciate, cherish, consider, honor, idolize, like, love, prize, regard, regard highly, respect, revere, reverence, treasure, value, venerate, worship

estimate *noun.* appraisal, assay, assessment, belief, conclusion, conjecture, estimation, evaluation, impression, judgment, measurement, opinion, projection, rating, reckoning, stock, survey, thought

estimate *verb.* assay, assess, budget, consider, count, deduce, evaluate, expect, figure, number, plan, rate, reason, regard, scheme, sum, suppose, think

eternal *adjective.* always, boundless, ceaseless, constant, continual, continued, everlasting, forever, immortal, immutable, incessant, indestructible, perennial, permanent, perpetual, unbroken, undying, unremitting

ethical *adjective.* clean, correct, decent, elevated, fitting, good, honest, humane, kosher, moralistic, proper, respectable, right, righteous, square, upright, upstanding, virtuous

ethics *noun.* belief, conduct, conscience, criteria, decency, ethic, goodness, honesty, imperative, integrity, morality, mores, nature, practice, principles, standard, standards, value

evaluate *verb.* appraise, assay, assess, calculate, class, classify, criticize, decide, estimate, figure, grade, peg, rate, read, reckon, size, survey, value

even *adjective.* **1** alike, balanced, constant, continual, flush, horizontal, level, matching, metrical, parallel, regular, right, smooth, steady, surfaced, true, unbroken, uniform **2** balanced, comparable, drawn, equal, equivalent, exact, identical, level, like, matching, parallel, proportional, proportionate, same, similar, square, tied, uniform

even *verb.* align, equal, equalize, flatten, flush, grade, lay, level, match, plane, regularize, roll, smooth, square, stabilize, steady, symmetrize, uniform

event *noun.* **1** accident, business, calamity, case, catastrophe, celebration, coincidence, episode, experience, function, incident, marvel, matter, mishap, phase, predicament, story, tide **2** aftermath, case, causatum, chance, conclusion, consequence, end, eventuality, hap, happenstance, issue, outcome, outgrowth, product, resultant, sequel, termination, upshot

eventual *adjective.* closing, consequent, contingent, dependent, ending, ensuing, final, hindmost, last, later, latter, overall, possible, resulting, secondary, succeeding, terminal, vicarious

ever *adverb.* anytime, at all, consistently, constantly, continually, endlessly, eternally, everlastingly, evermore, for keeps, forever, incessantly, invariably, perpetually, regularly, relentlessly, unceasingly, usually

everlasting *adjective.* abiding, boundless, ceaseless, constant, continual, endless, eternal, immortal, imperishable, incessant, indestructible, interminable, limitless, permanent, perpetual, unceasing, undying, unremitting

everyday *adjective.* accustomed, conventional, daily, dull, frequent, garden, habitual, informal, mainstream, normal, prosaic, routine, starch, stock, unimaginative, unremarkable, usual, vanilla

everything *noun.* aggregate, all, all that, all things, business, complex, each thing, fixings, lot, many things, sum, the works, total, universe, whole, whole caboodle, whole enchilada, whole shebang

evidence *noun.* affirmation, clue, confirmation, cue, data, declaration, demonstration, documentation, goods, grounds, index, indication, manifestation, mark, sign, significant, substantiation, testimonial

evidence *verb.* attest, bespeak, confirm, connote, demonstrate, designate, display, exhibit, expose, illustrate, indicate, manifest, mark, proclaim, reveal, show, signify, witness

evident *adjective.* clear, conspicuous, distinct, fact, incontestable, incontrovertible, logical, manifest, noticeable, obvious, palpable, perceptible, plain, reasonable, tangible, unambiguous, unmistakable, visible

evidently *adverb.* clearly, doubtless, doubtlessly, incontestably, indisputably, it seems, manifestly, obviously, officially, ostensibly, outwardly, patently, plainly, professedly, seemingly, undoubtedly, unmistakably, without question

evil *adjective.* bad, baneful, base, black, destructive, foul, iniquitous, injurious, loathsome, malevolent, malicious, offensive, pernicious, repugnant, revolting, sinful, unpleasant, vicious

evil *noun.* affliction, calamity, catastrophe, corruption, criminality, curse, depravity, harm, hatred, injury, looseness, meanness, mischief, misery, obscenity, outrage, sinfulness, wrongdoing

exact *adjective.* careful, clear, correct, distinct, downright, explicit, express, faultless, identical, literal, orderly, precise, right, sharp, specific, true, verbatim, very

exact *verb.* assess, bleed, claim, coerce, command, compel, extract, gouge, impose, levy, oblige, postulate, require, requisition, screw, solicit, squeeze, wrest

exactly *adverb.* altogether, correctly, explicitly, expressly, faithfully, indeed, literally, methodically, right, rigorously, severely, sharp, square, strictly, truly, truthfully, unerringly, utterly

exaggerate *verb.* boast, boost, brag, build up, caricature, color, emphasize, enlarge, expand, fabricate, falsify, hike, lie, pad, puff, romance, romanticize, stretch

exaggerated *adjective.* bouncing, embellished, exalted, excessive, extravagant, fabulous, false, farfetched, impossible, magnified, overblown, overdone, overestimated, pretentious, spectacular, strained, stylized, tall

examination *noun.* assay, audit, battery, catechism, checking, final, inquest, inquisition, investigation, observation, probe, quest, questioning, raid, study, trial, view, written

examine *verb.* assay, audit, case, consider, criticize, finger, inspect, probe, review, scope, screen, study, test, try, turn over, vet, view, winnow

example *noun.* case, citation, copy, excuse, illustration, model, paradigm, paragon, part, prototype, quotation, representation, sample, sampling, specimen, standard, stereotype, symbol

exceed *verb.* beat, best, better, cap, distance, eclipse, excel, go beyond, outdo, outreach, outrun, outstrip, overtake, pass, rise above, surmount, top, transcend

exceedingly *adverb.* awfully, enormously, especially, exceptionally, excessively, extraordinarily, extremely, greatly, highly, inordinately, powerful, really, remarkably, strikingly, terribly, unusually, vastly, vitally

excellence *noun.* arete, class, distinction, eminence, excellency, fineness, goodness, greatness, merit, perfection, preeminence, purity, quality, superbness, supremacy, transcendence, virtue, worth

excellent *adjective.* accomplished, certified, desirable, distinctive, distinguished, exceptional, exquisite, fine, good, incomparable, magnificent, peerless, premium, priceless, prime, striking, supreme, wonderful

except *verb.* ban, bar, bate, count out, debar, disallow, eliminate, exclude, exempt, inveigh, object, omit, pass over, protest, reject, remonstrate, rule out, suspend

exception *noun.* allowance, anomalism, anomaly, departure, deviation, difference, dispensation, eccentricity, exemption, freak, inconsistency, irregularity, nonconformity, oddity, peculiarity, perquisite, privilege, quirk

exceptional *adjective.* **1** anomalous, atypical, deviant, distinct, notable, noteworthy, odd, peculiar, rare, remarkable, scarce, special, strange, unimaginable, unique, unprecedented, unthinkable, unusual **2** brain, cotton, fine, good, grind, high, job, marvelous, outstanding, premium, prodigious, remarkable, singular, skull, special, splash, superior, wonderful

excess *noun.* **1** balance, enough, exuberance, fat, leavings, luxuriance, overflow, overload, overrun, overweight, redundancy, refuse, remainder, rest, spare, surfeit, surplus, waste **2** debauchery, dissipation, dissoluteness, exorbitance, extravagance, extreme, extremes, extremity, immoderacy, immoderation, indulgence, inordinateness, intemperance, overdoing, prodigality, saturnalia, self-indulgence, unrestraint

excessive *adjective.* boundless, disproportionate, dissipated, enormous, exaggerated, extra, extravagant, extreme, immoderate, limitless, more, over, redundant, stiff, super, superfluous, supernatural, unconscionable

exchange *noun.* change, conversion, dealing, interchange, interdependence, interrelation, network, replacement, revision, shuffle, substitution, supplanting, swap, switch, traffic, transaction, transfer, truck

exchange *verb.* alternate, bargain, change, commute, correspond, displace, market, network, rearrange, revise, shuffle, substitute, swap, switch, traffic, transact, transfer, truck

excited *adjective.* agitated, animated, awakened, disturbed, eager, enthusiastic, hot, hysterical, inflamed, moved, nervous, passionate, provoked, roused, ruffled, stimulated, upset, wild

excitement *noun.* agitation, animation, bother, commotion, elation, emotion, furor, fuss, hysteria, impulse, kicks, movement, perturbation, provocation, rage, stimulus, stir, urge

exciting *adjective.* appealing, arousing, arresting, astonishing, breathtaking, fine, flashy, hectic, impelling, impressive, intriguing, neat, overpowering, racy, rousing, stirring, titillating, wild

exclusive *adjective.* absolute, aristocratic, circumscribed, clannish, elegant, entire, independent, licensed, limited, narrow, peculiar, private, single, snobbish, sole, swank, undivided, unique

excuse *noun.* alibi, apology, cover, defense, expedient, fish, grounds, makeshift, plea, pretext, rationalization, routine, semblance, song, stall, story, substitute, vindication

excuse *verb.* alibi, clear, cover, defend, discharge, exonerate, extenuate, indulge, justify, liberate, overlook, pardon, pretext, rationalize, release, relieve, spare, tolerate

execution *noun.* **1** beheading, capital punishment, contract killing, crucifixion, decapitation, electrocution, gassing, guillotining, hanging, hit, impalement, lethal injection, necktie party, punishment, rub out, shooting, strangling, strangulation **2** accomplishment, achievement, administration, completion, consummation, delivery, discharge, doing, effect, enactment, enforcement, fulfilling, implementation, operation, prosecution, realization, rendering, style

executive *noun.* administrator, boss, businessman, chief, commander, entrepreneur, governor, industrialist, kingpin, leader, leadership, manager, officer, skipper, supervisor, top, tycoon, upstairs

exempt *adjective.* clear, cleared, discharged, excluded, excused, favored, free, let go, liberated, outside, privileged, released, spared, special, unbound, unchecked, unrestricted, walked

exercise *noun.* act, activity, calisthenics, constitutional, discharge, discipline, drilling, effort, examination, exercising, exertion, movement, operation, recitation, schoolwork, study, test, toil

exercise *verb.* **1** break, break in, discipline, drill, exert, fix, foster, hone, inure, maneuver, ply, practice, prepare, set, teach, train, work, work out **2** afflict, agitate, annoy, bother, bug, burden, chafe, distress, disturb, gall, irk, occupy, pain, provoke, trouble, try, upset, vex

exert *verb.* apply, dig, employ, endeavor, exercise, expend, plug, ply, push, strain, strive, struggle, throw, toil, use, utilize, wield, work

exhausted *adjective.* **1** beat, bleary, crippled, dead, debilitated, disabled, drained, effete, frazzled, limp, sapped, shot, wasted, weak, weakened, wearied, worn, worn out **2** all gone, bare, consumed, dissipated, done, drained, dry, empty, expended, finished, gone, played out, spent, squandered, used, void, washed-out, wasted

exhibit *verb.* advertise, demonstrate, disclose, display, expose, express, feature, flash, illustrate, indicate, manifest, mark, offer, parade, proclaim, reveal, show, showcase

exhibition *noun.* advertisement, carnival, display, exhibit, exposition, fair, fireworks, flash, front, manifestation, offering, pageant, performance, presentation, representation, show, sight, spectacle

exist *verb.* abide, be, breathe, continue, endure, happen, last, lie, live, move, obtain, occur, prevail, remain, stand, stay, subsist, survive

existence *noun.* actuality, animation, being, breath, continuance, continuation, duration, endurance, entity, essence, individuality, permanence, presence, reality, something, subsistence, survival, world

expand *verb.* bolster, detail, diffuse, dilate, elaborate, enlarge, fatten, grow, mount, multiply, mushroom, open, outspread, prolong, spread, stretch, upsurge, widen

expansion *noun.* breadth, development, diffusion, dilation, distance, distension, enlargement, expanse, extension, increase, inflation, magnification, maturation, multiplication, space, spread, stretch, unfolding

expect *verb.* assume, calculate, conjecture, contemplate, divine, feel, figure, foresee, hope, imagine, predict, presuppose, sense, suppose, take, think, trust, understand

expectation *noun.* apprehension, belief, calculation, confidence, conjecture, design, hope, intention, likelihood, motive, outlook, possibility, presumption, promise, reliance, suspense, trust, view

expedition *noun.* campaign, caravan, crew, cruise, crusade, enterprise, excursion, fleet, mission, party, quest, safari, squadron, swing, tour, travel, travels, undertaking

expenditure *noun.* amount, charge, consumption, cost, disbursement, expense, figure, nut, outlay, output, payoff, price, rate, spending, throw, use, value, waste

expense *noun.* bite, budget, debt, decrement, deprivation, disbursement, forfeit, loan, loss, obligation, output, overhead, payment, rate, responsibility, sacrifice, sum, worth

expensive *adjective.* costly, dear, excessive, executive, extravagant, fancy, high, holdup, immoderate, lavish, plush, rich, steep, stiff, swank, uneconomical, unreasonable, valuable

experience *noun.* acquaintance, background, caution, combat, exposure, involvement, inwardness, judgment, maturity, observation, participation, practicality, seasoning, sense, skill, sophistication, trial, wisdom

experienced *adjective.* accomplished, adept, competent, expert, master, mature, old, pistol, practical, practiced, professional, qualified, rounded, sophisticated, tested, versed, vet, wise

experiment *noun.* agreement, analysis, assay, enterprise, examination, exercise, experimentation, observation, operation, probe, procedure, search, speculation, study, test, trial, try, undertaking

experiment *verb.* analyze, assay, diagnose, examine, explore, give tryout, probe, prove, research, sample, search, speculate, study, test, try, venture, verify, weigh

experimental *adjective.* beginning, developmental, empirical, experiential, laboratory, momentary, pilot, preliminary, preparatory, primary, provisional, speculative, temporary, tentative, test, trial, under probation, unproved

expert *adjective.* able, adept, apt, crack, deft, facile, handy, master, masterful, practiced, professional, proficient, qualified, savvy, sharp, skilled, slick, virtuoso

expert *noun.* ace, adept, artist, authority, buff, connoisseur, gnome, graduate, guru, hot shot, master, pro, professional, proficient, shark, virtuoso, whiz, wizard

explain *verb.* clarify, construe, define, diagram, disclose, excuse, illustrate, interpret, justify, manifest, paraphrase, rationalize, read, render, resolve, teach, tell, translate

explanation *noun.* account, brief, demonstration, description, details, elucidation, history, illustration, meaning, reason, recital, rendition, sense, showing, statement, story, summary, talking

explicit *adjective.* absolute, accurate, categorical, certain, clear, definitive, distinct, exact, express, frank, obvious, open, outspoken, positive, stated, sure, unambiguous, unqualified

exploit *verb.* abuse, apply, beguile, bestow, bleed, employ, exercise, handle, jockey, maneuver, milk, mine, skin, soak, stick, use, utilize, work

explore *verb.* analyze, burrow, examine, hunt, inspect, probe, prospect, question, research, scout, search, seek, survey, test, tour, travel, traverse, try

explosion *noun.* access, blast, burst, clap, concussion, crack, detonation, discharge, firing, fit, gust, ignition, outbreak, percussion, pop, report, roar, salvo

explosive *adjective.* atomic, bursting, consequential, convulsive, detonating, ebullient, fiery, frenzied, hazardous, impetuous, meteoric, perilous, raging, rampant, stormy, ugly, vehement, wild

explosive *noun.* ammunition, bomb, charge, dynamite, fireworks, grease, grenade, gunpowder, mine, missile, mulligan, munition, pineapple, powder, shell, shot, soup, TNT

expose *verb.* advertise, bare, broadcast, crack, disclose, display, exhibit, feature, flash, leak, manifest, open, publish, report, show, spill, streak, unearth

exposed *adjective.* bare, caught, clear, defined, denuded, disclosed, discovered, manifest, open, peeled, revealed, shown, solved, stripped, unmasked, unsealed, unsheltered, visible

exposure *noun.* acknowledgment, danger, denunciation, disclosure, display, divulging, exhibition, expose, hazard, introduction, jeopardy, liability, nakedness, presentation, publicity, revelation, showing, susceptibility

express *adjective.* accurate, categorical, certain, clear, definitive, distinct, exact, explicit, individual, intentional, outright, set, specific, unambiguous, unmistakable, uttered, voluntary, willing

express *verb.* bespeak, convey, couch, embody, exhibit, frame, give, hint, manifest, proclaim, pronounce, put, represent, signify, suggest, tell, vent, voice

expression *noun.* **1** argument, declaration, delivery, diction, elucidation, enunciation, idiom, issue, language, mention, phrasing, rendition, statement, style, utterance, vent, voice, writ **2** air, aspect, cast, character, contortion, countenance, face, grimace, grin, look, mien, mug, pout, simper, smile, smirk, sneer, visage

extend *verb.* **1** boost, crane, dilate, draw, enhance, enlarge, expand, last, mantle, multiply, open, prolong, spread, stall, stretch, supplement, take, widen **2** accord, advance, allocate, allot, award, bestow, confer, donate, give, grant, impart, pose, present, put forward, stretch out, submit, tender, yield

extension *noun.* annex, appendix, arm, branch, broadening, compass, continuation, delay, lengthening, orbit, production, prolongation, scope, span, spread, stretch, stretching, supplement

extensive *adjective.* blanket, comprising, considerable, extended, indiscriminate, large, lengthy, pervasive, prevalent, sizable, spacious, sweeping, universal, unrestricted, vast, voluminous, wide, widespread

extent *noun.* amplitude, area, breadth, dimensions, expanse, leeway, magnitude, matter, proliferation, scope, size, span, sphere, stretch, territory, time, tract, width

exterior *adjective.* exoteric, external, extraneous, extraterrestrial, extraterritorial, extrinsic, foreign, marginal, outdoor, outer, outermost, outlying, outmost, outward, over, peripheral, superficial, surface

exterior *noun.* appearance, aspect, coating, cover, covering, exteriority, external, facade, face, finish, outside, polish, rind, shell, skin, superficies, surface, visible part

extra *adjective.* added, ancillary, another, excess, further, fuss, gravy, more, perk, plus, redundant, reserve, special, superfluous, surplus, tip, unnecessary, unneeded

extraordinary *adjective.* boss, exceptional, heavy, inconceivable, incredible, marvelous, odd, peculiar, remarkable, some, strange, surprising, unimaginable, unique, unthinkable, unusual, wicked, wonderful

extreme *adjective.* absolute, drastic, exaggerated, exceptional, excessive, extravagant, fabulous, fanatical, flagrant, immoderate, irrational, radical, remarkable, rigid, strict, uncompromising, unseemly, unusual

extreme *noun.* apogee, boundary, ceiling, climax, consummation, crest, crown, depth, end, excess, extremity, height, nadir, peak, pole, top, uttermost, zenith

extremely *adverb.* almighty, excessively, immensely, inordinately, intensely, mortally, notably, over, overly, powerful, radically, remarkably, severely, too, uncommonly, unusually, utterly, vitally

eye *noun.* appreciation, belief, conviction, discernment, discrimination, mind, opinion, perception, persuasion, recognition, scrutiny, sentiment, surveillance, tab, taste, view, viewpoint, watch

eye *verb.* check out, consider, contemplate, eyeball, gape, inspect, look at, peruse, regard, rubberneck, scan, scrutinize, size up, stare at, study, survey, view, watch

F

fabrication *noun.* bull, crap, deceit, fable, fake, falsehood, fiction, figment, forgery, invention, lie, line, myth, opus, smoke, untruth, work, yarn

face *noun.* **1** dial, exterior, front, frontage, frontal, grimace, light, makeup, map, mask, obverse, pout, presentation, semblance, showing, silhouette, top, visage **2** audacity, boldness, brass, cheek, cloak, confidence, cover, disguise, facade, front, gall, impudence, mask, nerve, presumption, semblance, show, veil

face *verb.* **1** affront, bear, beard, brook, challenge, confront, court, cross, dare, defy, encounter, endure, experience, fight, meet, resist, suffer, take **2** clad, coat, cover, decorate, dress, finish, front, level, line, overlay, plaster, polish, sheathe, side, skin, smooth, surface, veneer

facility *noun.* address, adroitness, aptitude, bent, competence, efficiency, fluency, lightness, poise, proficiency, quickness, readiness, skill, skillfulness, smoothness, tact, turn, wit

fact *noun.* **1** actuality, appearance, basis, case, certainty, dope, evidence, experience, gospel, intelligence, law, matter, permanence, scene, scripture, solidity, stability, verity **2** act, adventure, being, case, consideration, construction, creation, entity, episode, experience, feature, happening, incident, item, occurrence, organism, specific, truism

factor *noun.* agency, agent, aid, antecedent, aspect, board, cause, circumstance, consideration, constituent, element, influence, ingredient, instrument, item, means, part, point

factory *noun.* branch, co-operative, firm, forge, foundry, laboratory, machine shop, manufactory, mill, mint, plant, salt mines, shop, sweatshop, warehouse, workroom, works, workshop

facts *noun.* brass tacks, certainty, clue, cue, data, details, dope, goods, gospel, info, lowdown, numbers, reality, scoop, score, story, straight stuff, whole story

faculty *noun.* **1** adroitness, aptitude, aptness, facility, gift, instinct, peculiarity, penchant, pistol, power, property, quality, readiness, reason, sense, skill, strength, talent **2** advisers, body, clinic, college, corps, department, employees, fellows, institute, instructors, organization, personnel, professors, researchers, society, staff, tutors, workers

faded *adjective.* ashen, bedraggled, dim, dingy, dull, indistinct, murky, pale, pallid, shabby, shopworn, tattered, threadbare, tired, used, wan, wasted, worn

fail *verb.* **1** be defeated, be ruined, blunder, break down, decline, deteriorate, fall, fall short, flop, flounder, fold, founder, go astray, go downhill, miss, play into, run aground, slip **2** abort, back out, blink, desert, disappoint, discount, disregard, fault, forget, forsake, funk, go astray, ignore, neglect, omit, overlook, slight, slip **3** be ruined, become insolvent, belly up, break, bust, close, crash, default, dishonor, drop, end, finish, fold, go bust, go under, lose big, repudiate, terminate

failing *adjective.* declining, defeated, deficient, faint, feeble, inadequate, insufficient, scant, scanty, scarce, short, shy, unavailing, unprosperous, unsuccessful, unsufficient, vain, wanting

failing *noun.* blind spot, defect, deficiency, drawback, error, failure, fault, flaw, foible, frailty, imperfection, infirmity, lapse, miscarriage, misfortune, vice, weak point, weakness

failure *noun.* **1** abortion, bankruptcy, bust, defeat, deficit, dog, dud, fiasco, flop, lemon, loss, mess, misstep, rupture, stalemate, stoppage, turkey, wreck **2** bankrupt, beat, bomb, bum, derelict, disappointment, dud, flop, has-been, incompetent, loser, lumpy, might-have-been, no-good, nobody, prodigal, stiff, turkey

faint *adjective.* bleached, deep, dim, dusty, feeble, hazy, hoarse, light, moderate, padded, pale, shadowy, smooth, stifled, subdued, vague, wan, weak

fair *adjective.* **1** candid, civil, courteous, decent, frank, generous, good, honest, moderate, nonpartisan, objective, open, proper, reasonable, respectable, sincere, temperate, uncolored **2** blanched, bleached, blond, blonde, chalky, colorless, creamy, faded, light, milky, neutral, pale, pallid, pearly, sallow, silvery, snowy, white **3** adequate, average, common, commonplace, decent, indifferent, intermediate, mean, medium, moderate, okay, ordinary, passable, reasonable, respectable, satisfactory, tolerable, usual **4** attractive, beauteous, bonny, charming, chaste, comely, delicate, dishy, enchanting, exquisite, good-looking, handsome, looker, lovely, number, peach, pretty, pure

5 balmy, calm, clarion, clear, clement, dry, favorable, fine, mild, placid, pleasant, pretty, rainless, smiling, sunny, sunshiny, tranquil, unclouded

fair *noun.* bazaar, celebration, centennial, display, exhibit, exhibition, expo, exposition, fall fair, festival, fete, gala, market, observance, occasion, pageant, show, spectacle

faith *noun.* **1** acceptance, assent, assurance, belief, certainty, confidence, constancy, conviction, credulity, dependence, fealty, fidelity, hope, loyalty, reliance, stock, store, truthfulness **2** canon, church, communion, connection, conviction, credo, creed, cult, denomination, orthodoxy, persuasion, piety, profession, revelation, sect, teaching, theology, worship

faithful *adjective.* affectionate, ardent, circumspect, confiding, constant, firm, honest, incorruptible, obedient, patriotic, resolute, scrupulous, sincere, steady, sure, tried, true, truthful

fake *adjective.* affected, artificial, bogus, concocted, counterfeit, fabricated, false, fictitious, forged, invented, mock, phony, pretended, pseudo, reproduction, sham, simulated, spurious

fake *noun.* actor, bunk, cheat, deception, fabrication, faker, forgery, gyp, imitation, imposition, pretender, pretense, reproduction, sell, sham, sleight, spoof, trick

fake *verb.* act, affect, assume, bluff, copy, counterfeit, deke, disguise, dissimulate, dive, fabricate, feign, forge, put on, sham, simulate, spoof, tank

fall *noun.* **1** decline, declivity, diminution, dive, downgrade, drop, dwindling, ebb, incline, lapse, lessening, lowering, plunge, reduction, slant, slip, slump, spill **2** abasement, capitulation, collapse, death, degradation, destruction, diminution, disaster, dive, drop, failure, humiliation, loss, overthrow, resignation, ruin, surrender, tumble

fall *verb.* **1** cascade, drag, droop, drop, dwindle, ease, ebb, land, lapse, lessen, lower, plunge, recede, settle, sink, stumble, subside, topple **2** be destroyed, be lost, be taken, bend, capitulate, die, drop, give in, give up, go under, lie down, obey, perish, resign, slump, submit, succumb, yield

false *adjective.* **1** apocryphal, bogus, concocted, deceitful, deceiving, erroneous, fake, fallacious, fanciful, faulty, illusive, incorrect, invalid, lying, mendacious, unfounded, unreal, untrue **2** base, canting, crooked, deceitful, deceiving, deceptive, devious, foul, lying, malevolent, malicious, perfidious, traitorous, treacherous, treasonable, unfaithful, villainous, wicked **3** adulterated, artificial, bogus, deceptive, disguised, feigned, forged, frame, imitation, manufactured, meretricious, ostensible, pretended, queer, shady, substitute, synthetic, unreal

fame *noun.* acclaim, account, acknowledgment, dignity, distinction, elevation, eminence, heyday, luster, name, notoriety, popularity, prominence, recognition, regard, renown, repute, station

familiar *adjective.* **1** accustomed, conventional, everyday, frequent, garden, habitual, household, informal, known, native, natural, prosaic, proverbial, repeated, routine, simple, stock, usual **2** abreast, acquainted, apprised, au courant, au fait, aware, cognizant, conscious, conversant, go-go, grounded, informed, introduced, kept posted, mindful, savvy, tuned in, up **3** affable, amicable, bold, brassy, confidential, cozy, dear, flip, forward, genial, gracious, informal, intrusive, open, presumptuous, relaxed, snug, wise

familiarity *noun.* acquaintance, acquaintanceship, boldness, closeness, ease, fellowship, forwardness, freedom, freshness, friendship, informality, intimacy, liberty, naturalness, openness, presumption, sociability, unceremoniousness

family *noun.* birth, children, folk, household, inheritance, issue, kin, kindred, line, patrimony, pedigree, people, race, relations, relationship, relatives, subdivision, system

famous *adjective.* conspicuous, distinguished, elevated, exalted, foremost, glorious, grand, honored, important, memorable, mighty, noteworthy, notorious, peerless, powerful, remarkable, reputable, signal

fancy *adjective*. adorned, baroque, custom, decorative, elaborate, elegant, embellished, fanciful, florid, intricate, lavish, ornamented, ornate, resplendent, rococo, special, sumptuous, unusual

fancy *noun*. **1** bag, bee, creation, flash, groove, humor, idea, image, imagination, impression, inclination, liking, mind, thought, urge, visualization, whim, will **2** chimera, delusion, fabrication, figment, fondness, illusion, imagination, inclination, invention, itch, liking, nightmare, penchant, preference, relish, reverie, romancing, vision

fancy *verb*. **1** believe, conjecture, create, envision, fantasy, feature, image, infer, make up, phantasy, picture, realize, reckon, spark, suppose, think, vision, visualize **2** approve, care for, crave, desire, dream of, endorse, favor, go for, groove on, hanker after, itch for, like, lust after, prefer, relish, sanction, take to, wish for

fantastic *adjective*. absurd, capricious, exotic, extravagant, extreme, fanciful, illusive, imaginative, incredible, insane, irrational, nonsensical, odd, peculiar, queer, unbelievable, unreal, wacky

fantasy *noun*. apparition, bubble, delusion, dream, fabrication, fancy, fancying, figment, flight, illusion, imagining, invention, nightmare, pipe, rainbow, reverie, utopia, vision

far *adjective*. afar, bit, deep, distant, far piece, far-flung, far-off, faraway, good ways, long, miles, out-of-the-way, outlying, piece, removed, schlep, stone's throw, ways

farm *noun*. acreage, acres, claim, estate, field, garden, grassland, homestead, land, lawn, meadow, nursery, orchard, pasture, patch, plantation, soil, vineyard

farm *verb*. crop, dress, garden, graze, grow, harrow, harvest, husband, pasture, plow, reap, seed, sow, subdue, superintend, tend, till, work

farmer *noun*. breeder, feeder, gardener, grazer, grower, harvester, hillbilly, laborer, peasant, planter, producer, rancher, ranchman, rube, seed, stubble-jumper, tender, tiller

farming *noun*. agriculture, breeding, cultivation, culture, feeding, gardening, geoponics, grazing, growing, harvesting, husbandry, landscaping, operating, production, reaping, soil culture, threshing, tillage

fascinating *adjective*. alluring, appealing, attractive, bewitching, captivating, charming, compelling, delightful, enchanting, engaging, engrossing, enticing, glamorous, gripping, intriguing, irresistible, seductive, siren

fashion *noun*. **1** bandwagon, chic, configuration, craze, custom, fad, figure, form, line, mode, model, mold, rage, spinach, taste, tone, trend, vogue **2** custom, device, form, formula, manner, method, mode, observance, prevalence, procedure, style, system, technique, tendency, tone, trend, vein, vogue

fashion *verb*. adjust, build, carve, create, devise, erect, fit, form, frame, manufacture, mold, plan, plot, produce, sculpture, tailor, turn out, work

fashionable *adjective*. chic, contemporary, dashing, favored, genteel, hot, in, latest, modern, new, now, popular, prevailing, rakish, smart, spinach, swank, usual

fast *adjective*. **1** accelerated, active, agile, dashing, electric, expeditious, flashing, fleet, hasty, hot, mercurial, pronto, rapid, ready, snap, snappy, swift, winged **2** adherent, ardent, constraint, firm, fortified, held, indelible, permanent, resistant, resolute, secure, set, sound, stuck, sure, tenacious, true, wedged **3** bawdy, depraved, dissipated, extravagant, flirtatious, immoral, indecent, lascivious, lewd, libertine, light, loose, lustful, rakish, reckless, salacious, wanton, wild

fast *adverb*. chop-chop, expeditiously, flat-out, fleetly, hastily, hurriedly, in haste, like wildfire, posthaste, presto, promptly, pronto, quick, quickly, rapidly, soon, swift, swiftly

fat *adjective*. blimp, bulky, bull, burly, chunky, fleshy, heavy, husky, lard, large, meaty, oversize, paunchy, plump, portly, solid, stout, stubby

fat *noun.* blubber, bulk, cellulite, corpulence, excess, flab, flesh, grease, lard, obesity, overabundance, overflow, paunch, suet, superfluity, surfeit, surplus, tallow
fatal *adjective.* baleful, baneful, calamitous, cataclysmic, catastrophic, deathly, destructive, disastrous, fateful, final, incurable, killing, lethal, mortal, pernicious, pestilent, ruinous, virulent
fate *noun.* break, circumstance, cup, destination, destiny, doom, effect, end, ending, fortune, future, horoscope, issue, luck, outcome, providence, stars, upshot
father *noun.* **1** ancestor, begetter, dad, daddy, forebear, governor, head, pa, padre, papa, parent, pater, pop, pops, predecessor, progenitor, sire, warden **2** administrator, architect, author, creator, dean, elder, generator, initiator, inventor, leader, maker, motor, originator, patriarch, patron, promoter, publisher, supporter
father *verb.* beget, breed, engender, establish, found, generate, get, hatch, institute, invent, make, originate, parent, procreate, produce, progenerate, sire, spawn
fatigue *noun.* brain fag, burnout, debility, dullness, enervation, ennui, exhaustion, faintness, feebleness, heaviness, languor, lassitude, lethargy, listlessness, overtiredness, weakness, weariness
fatigue *verb.* bush, disable, drain, droop, drop, exhaust, flag, jade, prostrate, sag, sink, succumb, take, tucker, weaken, wear, weary, whack
fault *noun.* blunder, defect, delinquency, error, flaw, guilt, lapse, misdemeanor, mistake, offense, omission, onus, oversight, responsibility, slip, transgression, wrong, wrongdoing
faulty *adjective.* adulterated, awry, bad, erroneous, fallacious, fallible, frail, imperfect, incorrect, injured, lame, leaky, lemon, malformed, malfunctioning, unfit, unreliable, weak
favor *noun.* account, admiration, aid, assistance, benediction, benefit, boon, championship, consideration, courtesy, dispensation, encouragement, gift, good will, grace, indulgence, regard, respect
favor *verb.* **1** accommodate, advance, aid, assist, befriend, esteem, facilitate, further, gratify, humor, indulge, oblige, pamper, promote, reward, spare, spoil, value **2** advocate, appreciate, approve, champion, choose, encourage, endorse, eulogize, fancy, flash, for, groove, incline, patronize, pick, prefer, prize, value
favorable *adjective.* **1** affirmative, agreeable, amicable, benign, commending, complimentary, enthusiastic, friendly, go, inclined, kind, kindly, positive, predisposed, reassuring, sympathetic, understanding, welcoming **2** appropriate, auspicious, beneficial, cheering, fit, gratifying, healthful, helpful, lucky, pleasing, prosperous, providential, reassuring, suitable, timely, useful, welcome, white
favorably *adverb.* agreeably, approvingly, cordially, courteously, enthusiastically, fairly, generously, graciously, heartily, helpfully, kindly, positively, receptively, usefully, willingly, with approbation, with approval, without prejudice
favorite *adjective.* admired, adored, beloved, choice, darling, dear, desired, esteemed, favored, intimate, liked, main, personal, popular, precious, prized, revered, sweetheart
favorite *noun.* beloved, chalk, choice, darling, dear, evergreen, fave, ideal, idol, love, main, minion, mistress, persona grata, pet, pick, preference, shoo-in
fear *noun.* agitation, angst, aversion, concern, consternation, cowardice, despair, dismay, disquietude, distress, dread, fright, jitters, nightmare, revulsion, scare, suspicion, terror
fear *verb.* anticipate, apprehend, avoid, crouch, dread, expect, falter, foresee, fret, quaver, shrink, shudder, shun, shy, start, suspect, tremble, wilt
fearful *adjective.* **1** afraid, aghast, agitated, disturbed, hesitant, jittery, nerveless, nervous, panicky, phobic, scared, shrinking, shy, spineless, tense, uneasy, worried, yellow **2** appalling, astounding, baleful, creepy, distressing, dreadful, eerie, ghastly, gruesome, lurid, macabre, monstrous, morbid, shocking, sinister, strange, tremendous, unspeakable

feasible *adjective.* appropriate, beneficial, breeze, cinch, expedient, fit, fitting, pie, practicable, practical, probable, profitable, reasonable, snap, suitable, viable, workable, worthwhile

feature *noun.* affection, angle, attribute, constituent, detail, differential, element, gag, hallmark, item, mark, particularity, peculiarity, property, quality, slant, specialty, unit

feature *verb.* accentuate, advertise, blaze, emphasize, give prominence, headline, italicize, make conspicuous, mark, play up, point up, present, promote, set off, spotlight, star, underline, underscore

federation *noun.* alliance, amalgamation, association, bunch, coalition, combination, confederacy, crew, family, gang, mob, outfit, partnership, pool, ring, syndicate, syndication, union

fee *noun.* account, bill, bite, chunk, commission, compensation, consideration, handle, house, pay, payment, percentage, piece, recompense, remuneration, salary, slice, take

feeble *adjective.* exhausted, fragile, frail, gentle, helpless, indecisive, lame, nobody, poor, powerless, rocky, slight, tame, unconvincing, weak, weakened, weakly, zero

feed *verb.* augment, bolster, deliver, encourage, fatten, feast, find, foster, fuel, furnish, give, maintain, minister, nurture, provide, provision, strengthen, supply

feel *noun.* air, ambience, atmosphere, aura, feeling, finish, impression, mood, palpation, quality, semblance, sensation, sense, surface, tactility, taction, touch, vibes

feel *verb.* **1** caress, clutch, finger, grapple, grasp, grope, handle, paw, perceive, ply, press, sense, squeeze, test, thumb, touch, try, wield **2** appear, appreciate, encounter, endure, exhibit, have, know, meet, notice, observe, see, seem, sense, suffer, suggest, taste, undergo, welcome **3** assume, conclude, conjecture, consider, deduce, deem, esteem, guess, hold, infer, judge, know, presume, repute, sense, suppose, suspect, think

feeling *noun.* **1** activity, awareness, enjoyment, excitability, excitement, feel, pain, perceiving, perception, pleasure, reaction, reflex, responsiveness, sensation, sense, sensibility, sensitivity, touch **2** apprehension, belief, conviction, hunch, impression, inclination, instinct, mind, notion, opinion, outlook, persuasion, reaction, sense, sentiment, suspicion, thought, view **3** affection, ardor, discrimination, emotion, empathy, fervor, fondness, imagination, impression, intuition, judgment, pity, reaction, refinement, sensitivity, sentiment, spirit, taste

fell *verb.* cut, dash, down, drop, flatten, floor, gash, ground, hack, knock down, level, prostrate, sever, shoot, slash, split, sunder, tumble

fellow *noun.* **1** adolescent, apprentice, beau, boy, brother, buck, guy, hunk, individual, kid, man, master, novice, punk, scion, squirt, stallion, youth **2** assistant, associate, brother, companion, comrade, counterpart, double, duplicate, friend, instructor, lecturer, match, mate, member, partner, professor, reciprocal, twin

fellowship *noun.* acquaintance, alliance, amity, association, brotherhood, camaraderie, club, communion, companionship, company, comradeship, fraternity, friendliness, guild, kindliness, order, society, togetherness

female *adjective.* changeable, delicate, effeminate, effete, fair, feminine, fertile, gentle, girlish, ladylike, modest, reproductive, shy, soft, tender, twisty, virgin, weak

female *noun.* amazon, babe, dame, dowager, duchess, filly, frail, gal, girl, kid, madam, mama, matron, piece, she, siren, sis, ten

fence *noun.* balustrade, bar, barricade, boards, defense, guard, hedge, net, paling, pickets, posts, rail, railing, rampart, roadblock, shield, stakes, wall

fence *verb.* **1** bound, confine, coop, defend, encircle, fortify, girdle, guard, hedge, hem, mew, pen, protect, rail, secure, separate, surround, wall **2** avoid, baffle, cavil, duck, evade, feint, foil, hedge, maneuver, outwit, parry, prevaricate, quibble, shift, shirk, sidestep, stonewall, tergiversate

fertility *noun.* abundance, copiousness, fecundity, fruitfulness, generative capacity, gravidity, luxuriance, plentifulness, potency, pregnancy, productiveness, productivity, prolificacy, prolificity, puberty, richness, virility

fever *noun.* agitation, burning up, delirium, ecstasy, excitement, febrile disease, ferment, fervor, flush, frenzy, heat, intensity, passion, pyrexia, restlessness, the shakes, turmoil, unrest

few *adjective.* any, imperceptible, inconsequential, inconsiderable, lean, less, meager, minute, petty, piddling, rare, scant, scarce, slight, slim, some, stingy, straggling

fiber *noun.* cilia, cord, fabric, grain, grit, hair, quality, spirit, string, strip, substance, surface, texture, tissue, tooth, vein, warp, web

fiction *noun.* anecdote, clothesline, fable, fabrication, falsehood, fancy, imagination, invention, legend, lie, myth, narrative, potboiler, romance, smoke, story, untruth, yarn

field *noun.* **1** acreage, enclosure, farmland, garden, grassland, green, ground, mead, meadow, moorland, pasture, patch, plot, range, terrain, territory, tract, vineyard **2** area, avocation, bag, department, domain, dominion, limits, line, orbit, precinct, province, range, region, scope, specialty, terrain, territory, walk **3** amphitheater, battlefield, circuit, course, court, diamond, green, grounds, lot, park, race track, range, rink, stadium, terrain, theater, track, turf

fierce *adjective.* ape, blustery, boisterous, cruel, cutthroat, enraged, fiery, frightening, infuriated, malevolent, malign, primitive, raging, savage, stormy, strong, vehement, vicious

fight *noun.* altercation, argument, battle, brawl, combat, conflict, disagreement, fray, fuss, match, melee, quarrel, riot, round, row, ruckus, scuffle, skirmish

fight *verb.* **1** attack, battle, box, brawl, buck, clash, feud, grapple, joust, meet, protect, quarrel, scuffle, skirmish, strive, tilt, tug, wrestle **2** argue, buck, combat, defy, effect, endure, further, maintain, persist, repel, resist, row, strive, struggle, traverse, uphold, wage, withstand

fighter *noun.* aggressor, antagonist, belligerent, bully, combatant, competitor, contender, gladiator, heavy, mercenary, opponent, plug, pug, rival, slugger, soldier, tanker, wildcat

fighting *adjective.* angry, battling, belligerent, contending, determined, fencing, ferocious, hostile, militant, quarrelsome, resolute, skirmishing, sparring, tilting, truculent, under arms, warlike, warmongering, wrestling

fighting *noun.* argument, battle, beef, bout, combat, conflict, contention, donnybrook, exchange, joust, match, melee, riot, row, scuffle, spat, strife, warfare

figure *noun.* **1** anatomy, bod, body, build, chassis, configuration, constitution, development, form, frame, mass, outline, physique, pose, posture, shadow, silhouette, torso **2** cast, composition, decoration, design, device, diagram, drawing, illustration, image, model, mold, motif, motive, ornamentation, piece, portrait, representation, statue

figure *verb.* **1** add, cast, cipher, compute, count, enumerate, estimate, foot, guess, number, reckon, run down, sum, summate, tally, total, tote, work out **2** comprehend, conclude, crack, decide, discover, follow, infer, master, reason, resolve, rule, see, settle, solve, suppose, think, unravel, unscramble

file *noun.* cabinet, case, census, charts, data, directory, documents, folder, index, information, list, notebook, pigeon hole, placement, portfolio, record, register, repository

file *verb.* alphabetize, arrange, catalog, catalogue, categorize, classify, deposit, docket, document, enter, index, list, pigeonhole, place, record, register, slot, tabulate

fill *verb.* **1** charge, clog, furnish, gorge, heap, load, meet, overflow, pack, permeate, plug, ram, satiate, stock, stretch, stuff, supply, top **2** answer, assign, carry out, discharge, dispatch, distribute, elect, engage, fix, fulfill, hold, meet, name, occupy, officiate, perform, satisfy, take up

filling *noun.* bushing, cartridge, center, cylinder, fill, filler, inlay, insides, layer, liner, mixture, pack, packing, pad, padding, refill, replenishment, shim

film *noun.* blur, cloud, coat, covering, fabric, foil, gauze, haze, layer, membrane, mist, nebula, partition, sheet, skin, tissue, transparency, web

filter *verb.* clarify, clean, drain, escape, exude, leak, ooze, penetrate, permeate, purify, refine, screen, seep, sieve, soak through, strain, trickle, winnow

final *adjective.* closing, concluding, crowning, curtains, end, ending, eventual, finishing, hindmost, lag, last hurrah, last-minute, latest, latter, supreme, terminal, terminating, ultimate

finally *adverb.* assuredly, certainly, completely, conclusively, convincingly, decisively, definitely, done with, enduringly, for ever, in fine, inescapably, inexorably, irrevocably, lastly, past regret, permanently, settled

finance *verb.* angel, back, bank, bankroll, capitalize, endow, float, fund, go for, guarantee, juice, patronize, promote, sponsor, stake, subsidize, support, underwrite

find *verb.* collar, detect, discover, encounter, expose, identify, locate, meet, notice, observe, perceive, pinpoint, recognize, recover, spot, strike, track down, unearth

fine *adjective.* **1** accomplished, admirable, dandy, elegant, exceptional, expensive, exquisite, handsome, magnificent, ornate, rare, solid, striking, superior, supreme, top, unreal, wicked **2** delicate, diaphanous, ethereal, exquisite, filmy, flimsy, fragile, granular, light, lightweight, little, loose, minute, powdered, powdery, pulverized, quality, small **3** acute, clear, critical, cryptic, delicate, distinct, enigmatic, exact, keen, minute, obscure, petty, recondite, sharp, strict, subtle, tenuous, unadulterated

finish *noun.* **1** achievement, acquisition, annihilation, attainment, cessation, closing, completion, culmination, curtain, curtains, defeat, denouement, end, ending, finale, last, terminus, wrap **2** appearance, beauty, burnish, cultivation, culture, elaboration, glaze, grace, grain, luster, patina, perfection, polish, refinement, shine, smoothness, surface, texture

finish *verb.* **1** accomplish, achieve, break up, clinch, conclude, crown, discharge, do, effect, end, execute, fold, halt, round up, settle, shut down, wind up, wrap **2** annihilate, best, cool, cut off, destroy, dispatch, dispose of, do in, down, exterminate, kill, knock off, overcome, rout, ruin, slaughter, take off, worst

finished *adjective.* **1** accomplished, classic, consummate, cultured, elegant, expert, exquisite, flawless, impeccable, perfected, polished, professional, proficient, refined, skilled, smooth, suave, versatile **2** accomplished, completed, decided, discharged, done, effected, elaborated, entire, executed, final, fulfilled, lapsed, made, over, satisfied, settled, shut, stopped **3** bankrupt, consumed, devastated, done, done for, drained, empty, exhausted, gone, liquidated, lost ruined, played out, spent, through, undone, washed up, wiped out, wrecked

fire *noun.* **1** blaze, bonfire, campfire, coals, combustion, conflagration, element, flames, flare, glow, hearth, holocaust, luminosity, oxidation, pyre, searing, sparks, tinder **2** animation, ardor, eagerness, energy, enthusiasm, fervor, intensity, life, light, luster, radiance, sparkle, spirit, starch, verve, vigor, vivacity, zeal

fire *verb.* **1** cast, discharge, eject, explode, fling, heave, hurl, launch, let off, loose, pitch, pull trigger, set off, shell, shoot, throw, toss, touch off **2** animate, arouse, electrify, enliven, exalt, heighten, incite, inflame, inform, inspire, inspirit, intensify, intoxicate, provoke, quicken, rouse, stir, thrill

firm *adjective.* **1** compressed, concentrated, concrete, condensed, congealed, dense, hard, hardened, heavy, impenetrable, impervious, refractory, rigid, set, solid, stiff, sturdy, substantial **2** bolted, embedded, fixed, immovable, motionless, mounted, rooted, secure, set, settled, solid, sound, stationary, steady, strong, substantial, tenacious, unshakable **3** bound, determined, explicit, fixed, going, intent, resolute, set, settled, specific, stated, steady, strict, strong, true, unalterable, unchangeable, unshakable

firm *noun.* association, bunch, company, concern, conglomerate, corporation, crew, crowd, enterprise, gang, house, megacorp, mob, multinational, organization, outfit, partnership, ring

firmly *adverb.* **1** enduringly, fast, firm, fixedly, hard, inflexibly, rigidly, securely, solid, solidly, soundly, steadily, stiffly, strongly, substantially, thoroughly, tight, tightly **2** adamantly, constantly, doggedly, indefeasibly, intently, obdurately, perseveringly, persistently, purposefully, resolutely, staunchly, steadfastly, stolidly, strictly, stubbornly, tenaciously, unwaveringly, with decision

first *adjective.* **1** ahead, antecedent, anterior, front, fundamental, inaugural, incipient, introductory, key, least, opening, pioneer, premier, prime, primitive, pristine, rudimentary, smallest **2** advanced, arch, champion, chief, dominant, eminent, foremost, head, leading, main, outstanding, predominant, premier, prime, ranking, ruling, sovereign, supreme

fit *adjective.* able, apt, becoming, befitting, comely, competent, due, expedient, feasible, fitting, meet, practicable, preferable, prepared, proper, qualified, timely, wise

fit *noun.* access, attack, blow, bout, burst, emotion, frenzy, humor, jumps, outbreak, outburst, rage, spasm, spate, spell, turn, twitch, whim

fit *verb.* accord, agree, answer, apply, click, concur, conform, consist, correspond, dovetail, join, match, meet, parallel, relate, set, suit, tally

fitness *noun.* accordance, agreeableness, aptitude, aptness, competence, congeniality, consonance, convenience, decency, eligibility, harmony, pertinence, preparedness, propriety, qualification, relevancy, rightness, timeliness

fix *verb.* **1** affix, anchor, attach, cement, couple, glue, graft, install, lodge, pin, root, secure, set, settle, stabilize, steady, stick, tie **2** adjust, amend, correct, doctor, face lift, overhaul, patch, rebuild, recondition, reconstruct, regulate, repair, restore, retread, revamp, revise, sort, tune up

fixed *adjective.* **1** attached, firm, hitched, immovable, located, locked, rigid, rooted, secure, set, settled, situated, solid, stable, steady, stiff, still, tenacious **2** arranged, certain, circumscribed, decided, level, limited, planned, prearranged, resolute, rigged, rooted, set, settled, stated, steady, still, sure, unchangeable

flag *verb.* abate, deteriorate, die, droop, ebb, fade, fail, faint, fall, fall off, pine, sag, sink, slump, succumb, weaken, weary, wilt

flair *noun.* aptitude, aptness, bent, chic, elegance, faculty, feel, gift, glamour, head, knack, presence, shine, splash, talent, taste, turn, zip

flame *noun.* affection, ardor, baby, beau, beloved, darling, dear, desire, enthusiasm, fervor, fire, honey, love, passion, spark, steady, sweetheart, sweetie

flash *noun.* bedazzlement, dazzle, flame, flare, glance, glare, glimmer, glint, glisten, glitter, illumination, imprint, impulse, ray, reflection, shimmer, shine, twinkle

flash *verb.* **1** beam, blaze, dazzle, flame, flare, glance, glare, glimmer, glint, glisten, glitter, light, reflect, shimmer, shine, spangle, spark, twinkle **2** bolt, brandish, dart, dash, exhibit, expose, flourish, fly, parade, race, shoot, show, show off, speed, spring, streak, sweep, whistle

flat *adjective.* **1** collapsed, deflated, depressed, even, extended, fallen, flush, horizontal, leveled, planar, prone, prostrate, punctured, reclining, recumbent, smooth, supine, unbroken **2** banal, bland, bombed, colorless, dim, drab, insipid, lifeless, monotonous, muted, pointless, prosaic, tasteless, uninteresting, unsavory, vanilla, watery, weak

flavor *noun.* aroma, astringency, bitterness,

essence, extract, flavoring, odor, pungency, relish, savor, seasoning, smack, sweetness, tang, taste, wallop, zest, zing

fleet *adjective.* agile, barreling, breakneck, brisk, expeditious, fast, flying, hasty, lively, mercurial, meteoric, nimble, nimble-footed, rapid, screaming, speedy, swift, winged

flexibility *noun.* adaptability, adjustability, affability, complaisance, compliance, docility, extensibility, flaccidity, flexibleness, give, limberness, litheness, plasticity, pliability, pliancy, resilience, suppleness, tensility

flexible *adjective.* adjustable, bending, elastic, extensible, extensile, formative, limber, lithe, malleable, plastic, pliable, pliant, soft, spongy, stretch, tensile, willowy, yielding

flight *noun.* **1** aeronautics, arrival, aviation, departure, gliding, hop, journey, jump, mounting, navigation, soaring, take-off, transport, trip, volitation, voyage, winging **2** beat, break, escape, escapement, escaping, exit, exodus, fleeing, getaway, getaway car, lam, out, powder, retreat, retreating, running away, slip, spring

flock *noun.* assembly, brood, cloud, collection, colony, convoy, crush, drift, drove, flight, gaggle, group, legion, mass, multitude, pack, scores, throng

flood *noun.* abundance, bore, bounty, deluge, downpour, drift, excess, flow, multitude, outpouring, overflow, plenty, pour, stream, surge, surplus, tide, wave

flood *verb.* choke, deluge, drown, engulf, fill, flow, gush, immerse, inundate, overflow, overwhelm, rush, saturate, surge, swamp, swarm, sweep, whelm

floor *noun.* attic, basement, boards, canvas, carpet, cellar, deck, downstairs, flat, flooring, ground, landing, level, mat, nadir, stage, story, upstairs

floor *verb.* baffle, beat, bring down, conquer, defeat, disconcert, down, drop, fell, flatten, ground, knock down, level, overthrow, prostrate, puzzle, stump, throw

flow *noun.* continuation, continuity, course, discharge, draw, ebb, emanation, flood, issue, movement, outflow, river, sequence, series, spurt, tide, train, wind

flow *verb.* arise, brim, course, discharge, ebb, emit, flood, gurgle, jet, move, ooze, result, slide, spurt, squirt, surge, swirl, void

flowing *adjective.* abounding, emitting, fluid, full, issuing, liquid, overrun, prolific, rippling, rolling, running, rushing, sinuous, smooth, spouting, sweeping, teeming, unbroken

fly *verb.* **1** buzz, circle, climb, cross, drift, fleet, float, glide, hop, jet, land, maneuver, mount, speed, swoop, take off, travel, whoosh **2** barrel, bolt, breeze, career, dash, elapse, flee, glide, hasten, hurry, hustle, pass, race, roll, rush, shoot, speed, tear **3** avoid, bolt, break, decamp, disappear, flee, get away, hasten away, hide, hightail, light out, make off, run, run from, skip, steal away, take off, withdraw

flying *adjective.* aerial, aeronautical, airborne, express, flapping, fleet, floating, fluttering, hovering, mercurial, mobile, plumed, speedy, streaming, swooping, waving, winging, zooming

focus *verb.* adjust, attract, bring out, center, concentrate, converge, direct, fasten, fix, hone in, join, meet, pinpoint, put, rivet, sharpen, spotlight, sweat

fog *noun.* cloud, effluvium, film, fog-eater, gloom, grease, haze, murk, nebula, obscurity, pea soup, smog, smoke, smother, soup, steam, vapor, wisp

fog *verb.* addle, becloud, befuddle, bewilder, blind, blur, cloud, confuse, daze, dim, eclipse, mist, muddle, muddy, obfuscate, perplex, puzzle, steam up

foil *verb.* baffle, beat, buffalo, counter, cramp, curb, defeat, disconcert, ditch, dodge, duck, faze, nullify, outwit, prevent, rattle, shake, skip

fold *noun.* bend, crease, furrow, gather, gathering, groove, knife-edge, lap, lapel, layer, loop, overlap, plica, ply, ridge, tuck, turn, wrinkle

fold *verb.* bend, crease, crisp, curl, double, furrow, gather, groove, hem, knit, lap, overlap, overlay, purse, ridge, telescope, tuck, wrinkle

folk *noun.* community, confederation, family,

group, house, household, inhabitants, kin, kindred, lineage, nationality, people, population, race, settlement, society, state, stock

follow *verb.* **1** accompany, attend, chase, convoy, dog, freeze, hound, hunt, onto, pursue, run down, search, shadow, shag, tag, tail, tailgate, track **2** accord, comply, conform, copy, emulate, heed, imitate, keep, match, mind, mirror, obey, observe, reflect, regard, serve, support, watch

following *adjective.* afterwards, consequent, consequential, henceforth, later, latter, next, posterior, proximate, pursuing, resulting, sequential, serial, specified, subsequent, successive, then, when

following *noun.* adherents, audience, circle, clientele, coterie, dependents, entourage, fans, group, patronage, patrons, public, retinue, rout, suite, support, supporters, train

folly *noun.* absurdity, craziness, fatuity, foolishness, imprudence, inadvisability, inanity, irrationality, madness, obliquity, preposterousness, rashness, recklessness, stupidity, triviality, unsoundness, vice, witlessness

fond *adjective.* addicted, affectionate, amorous, attached, big, caring, devoted, doting, indulgent, loving, partial, predisposed, responsive, romantic, sentimental, sympathetic, tender, warm

food *noun.* bite, chow, cuisine, diet, eatable, fare, grit, grub, keep, meal, mess, provision, ration, refreshment, slop, snack, subsistence, table

fool *noun.* ass, bore, butt, chump, clod, clown, donkey, idiot, ignoramus, illiterate, jackass, jerk, lightweight, loon, sap, silly, simpleton, turkey

fool *verb.* bluff, cheat, chicane, con, deceive, delude, diddle, fox, gull, hoax, jive, juke, kid, outfox, pretend, snow, spoof, trifle

foolish *adjective.* absurd, asinine, dingy, fantastic, fatuous, idiotic, incautious, indiscreet, insane, irrational, jerky, ludicrous, lunatic, silly, simple, stupid, wacky, weak

force *noun.* **1** arm, brunt, clout, constraint, duress, effort, horsepower, impetus, impulse, muscle, potential, power, pressure, strength, trouble, velocity, vigor, violence **2** bite, competence, determination, duress, effect, effectiveness, efficacy, forcefulness, guts, influence, intensity, obligation, pressure, punch, requirement, validity, vehemence, vigor

force *noun.* **1** army, battalion, body, cell, corps, crew, detachment, division, horses, legion, military, regiment, servicemen, soldiers, squad, squadron, troop, unit **2** bear down, blackmail, burden, command, compel, contract, demand, drag, enforce, exact, impose, inflict, move, oblige, occasion, overcome, press, pressure

force *verb.* assault, blast, break in, burst, crack open, jimmy, propel, pry, push, rape, spoil, squeeze, thrust, twist, undo, violate, wrest, wring

forced *adjective.* affected, artificial, binding, bound, coercive, compelled, conscripted, constrained, enforced, false, insincere, labored, mandatory, rigid, slave, stiff, strained, unnatural

forceful *adjective.* bull, compelling, convincing, dominant, dynamic, electric, elemental, energetic, mighty, persuasive, puissant, punch, strong, telling, titanic, vehement, violent, virile

forecast *noun.* anticipation, budget, calculation, cast, conjecture, divination, estimate, foreknowledge, foreseeing, foresight, forethought, outlook, planning, prevision, prognosis, prognostication, projection, prophecy

forecast *verb.* anticipate, calculate, conclude, conjecture, demonstrate, determine, divine, estimate, figure, foresee, foretell, guess, infer, plan, presage, reason, surmise, telegraph

foreign *adjective.* alien, alienated, barbarian, barbaric, borrowed, derived, distant, estranged, exiled, exotic, external, far, inaccessible, overseas, remote, strange, transoceanic, unexplored

foremost *adjective.* arch, champion, chief, first, fore, front, head, heavy, highest, inaugural, initial, leading, original, premier, primary, prime, principal, supreme

forest *noun.* backwoods, brake, chase, clump, cover, covert, grove, growth, jungle, park, primeval, shelter, stand, thicket, timber, wood, woodland, woods

forever *adjective.* always, endlessly, enduringly, eternally, ever, everlastingly, evermore, for always, for keeps, forevermore, in perpetuity, infinitely, interminably, permanently, perpetually, till Doomsday, unchangingly

forge *verb.* **1** coin, copy, design, duplicate, fabricate, fake, falsify, fashion, frame, imitate, invent, make, pirate, produce, reproduce, scratch, trace, transcribe **2** beat, build, construct, contrive, create, devise, fabricate, fashion, form, frame, hammer out, invent, manufacture, mold, pound, shape, turn out, work

forgive *verb.* acquit, clear, commute, excuse, exempt, exonerate, extenuate, forget, let off, overlook, pardon, pocket, purge, release, reprieve, respite, spring

forgiveness *noun.* absolution, acquittal, charity, clemency, compassion, dispensation, exoneration, grace, immunity, impunity, indemnity, mercy, overlooking, purgation, quarter, reprieve, respite, vindication

forgotten *adjective.* abandoned, blanked out, blown over, buried, bygone, disremembered, erased, gone, lapsed, left behind, left out, lost, obliterated, omitted, past, repressed, suppressed, unrecalled

form *noun.* **1** anatomy, arrangement, configuration, construction, contour, design, die, figure, formation, mode, model, mold, plan, profile, scheme, silhouette, style, system **2** anatomy, being, build, condition, figure, fitness, frame, health, object, outline, person, phenomenon, physique, shape, silhouette, thing, torso, trim **3** canon, ceremonial, ceremony, custom, law, layout, manner, method, mode, precept, propriety, protocol, regulation, ropes, rule, setup, style, way **4** arrangement, description, design, grade, kind, manner, method, mode, order, practice, semblance, sort, species, stamp, style, system, variety, way

form *verb.* **1** assemble, build, create, design, erect, found, frame, make up, manufacture, mold, plan, plot, scheme, set, set up, trace, turn out, work **2** accumulate, acquire, appear, become visible, condense, crystallize, develop, eventuate, grow, harden, materialize, mature, rise, set, settle, shape up, show up, take shape

formal *adjective.* **1** academic, ceremonial, confirmed, conventional, directed, explicit, express, fixed, legal, orderly, proper, regular, rigid, set, solemn, stately, strict, systematic **2** affected, aloof, conventional, correct, decorous, distant, exact, nominal, polite, precise, prim, reserved, squaresville, starched, stiff, stilted, stuffy, unbending

formation *noun.* architecture, arrangement, compilation, configuration, constitution, construction, creation, crystallization, design, establishment, figure, forming, generation, grouping, makeup, manufacture, organization, production

former *adjective.* above, aforementioned, aforesaid, ancient, antecedent, anterior, bygone, departed, earlier, first, foregoing, late, old, once, past, preceding, prior, sometime

formerly *adverb.* aforetime, already, anciently, away back, back, back when, before, before now, before this, earlier, eons ago, erstwhile, heretofore, lately, long ago, of old, once, radically

formidable *adjective.* **1** appalling, awful, dangerous, daunting, dire, dismaying, dreadful, fearful, fierce, frightful, horrific, impregnable, menacing, shocking, terrible, terrific, terrifying, threatening **2** arduous, awesome, colossal, hard, impressive, indomitable, labored, laborious, mammoth, mighty, overpowering, overwhelming, powerful, puissant, rough, staggering, toilsome, tremendous

formula *noun.* blueprint, canon, code, credo, creed, custom, description, direction, equation, form, maxim, method, precept, prescription, procedure, rubric, rule, theorem

formulate *verb.* coin, contrive, couch, define, detail, develop, devise, evolve, express, forge, frame, invent, make up, prepare, put, vamp, word, work out

forthcoming *adjective*. accessible, anticipated, approaching, destined, expected, fated, future, imminent, impending, inescapable, nearing, obtainable, open, pending, predestined, ready, resulting, upcoming

fortunate *adjective*. affluent, auspicious, blessed, favored, flourishing, golden, helpful, hot, lucky, overcoming, profitable, prosperous, providential, rosy, thriving, timely, victorious, wealthy

fortune *noun*. accident, break, certainty, circumstances, contingency, destiny, expectation, experience, fluke, hazard, history, life, luck, providence, shot, stab, star, success

forward *adjective*. aggressive, assuming, bold, brazen, confident, familiar, fresh, impertinent, impudent, pert, presuming, presumptuous, pushing, rude, smart, smart-alecky, uppity, wise

forward *adverb*. ahead, alee, along, ante, antecedently, before, beforehand, fore, forth, in advance, into prominence, into view, on, onward, out, precedently, previous, vanward

forward *verb*. advance, assist, back, champion, cultivate, encourage, expedite, favor, foster, further, hasten, help, hurry, promote, serve, speed, support, uphold

foster *verb*. accommodate, assist, cherish, entertain, favor, harbor, help, house, lodge, minister to, mother, nurse, oblige, raise, rear, serve, shelter, sustain

found *verb*. constitute, construct, create, endow, erect, establish, fashion, father, fix, form, initiate, institute, launch, plant, raise, set up, settle, start

foundation *noun*. authority, ballast, base, bed, bottom, foot, footing, groceries, ground, groundwork, guts, prop, reason, root, stay, substructure, support, understructure

founder *noun*. architect, author, beginner, benefactor, builder, designer, father, forefather, framer, generator, initiator, institutor, inventor, maker, originator, patriarch, patron, planner

founder *verb*. abort, be lost, break down, collapse, fall, fall through, go down, go under, lurch, miscarry, misfire, sink, sprawl, stagger, stumble, submerge, submerse, trip

fountain *noun*. cause, fount, gush, inception, inspiration, jet, mine, origin, play, provenance, pump, reservoir, root, spout, spray, spring, stream, well

fragile *adjective*. brittle, crisp, crumbly, dainty, delicate, feeble, fine, flimsy, frail, friable, infirm, insubstantial, shatterable, shivery, slight, unsound, weak, weakly

frail *adjective*. dainty, delicate, feeble, fish, flimsy, fragile, infirm, insubstantial, puny, rocky, sad, slight, slim, tender, tenuous, vulnerable, weakly, wispy

frame *noun*. anatomy, architecture, body, build, carcass, construction, fabric, form, fringe, groundwork, hem, mount, physique, scaffold, scheme, stage, system, trim

frame *verb*. **1** assemble, constitute, construct, erect, fabricate, fashion, form, institute, lath, manufacture, mat, model, mold, mount, panel, produce, raise, set up **2** compose, conceive, contrive, design, devise, draft, form, formulate, hatch, invent, make, make up, outline, prepare, shape, sketch, vamp, write

frank *adjective*. artless, blunt, bold, brazen, candid, forthright, guileless, natural, open, outright, outspoken, real, scrupulous, sincere, truthful, uninhibited, unrestricted, upright

frantic *adjective*. agitated, deranged, distracted, distraught, frenetic, frenzied, gone, hectic, hot, insane, out, rabid, raging, unglued, violent, wicked, wild, wired

fraud *noun*. **1** artifice, blackmail, con, craft, deceit, fake, graft, guile, line, racket, sell, sham, smoke, song, sting, string, swindling, vanilla **2** bastard, charlatan, cheat, counterfeit, crook, deceiver, fake, faker, gyp, mechanic, phony, play actor, pretender, quack, racketeer, sham, shark, swindler

free *adjective*. **1** able, allowed, casual, clear, escaped, forward, frank, independent, informal, liberal, liberated, loose, open, relaxed, unattached, uncommitted, unfettered, unrestricted **2** autarchic, autonomic, autonomous, democratic, emancipated, enfranchised, freed, independent, individualistic, liberated, self-directing, self-governing, self-ruling, separate, sovereign, sui juris, unconstrained, unregimented

free *verb.* **1** clear, deliver, discharge, disengage, dismiss, extricate, loose, pardon, parole, ransom, redeem, release, rescue, save, spring, turn out, undo, untie **2** clear, deliver, discharge, disencumber, disengage, disentangle, empty, excuse, exempt, extricate, ransom, redeem, relieve, rescue, rid, undo, unload, unpack

freedom *noun.* **1** abandon, abandonment, compass, discretion, facility, flexibility, immunity, indulgence, latitude, leeway, opportunity, power, prerogative, range, right, rope, scope, swing **2** autonomy, citizenship, deliverance, delivery, discharge, emancipation, franchise, immunity, liberation, manumission, parole, prerogative, redemption, release, relief, rescue, salvation, sovereignty **3** abandon, boldness, brazenness, candor, directness, disrespect, facility, familiarity, forthrightness, frankness, informality, ingenuousness, license, overfamiliarity, presumption, readiness, spontaneity, unconstraint

freely *adjective.* advisedly, at will, candidly, deliberately, designedly, fancy-free, frankly, intentionally, openly, plainly, purposely, spontaneously, unchallenged, unreservedly, voluntarily, willingly, without hindrance, without restraint

freely *adverb.* abundantly, amply, bountifully, cleanly, copiously, effortlessly, lavishly, liberally, lightly, like water, loosely, open-handedly, readily, smoothly, unstintingly, well, without hindrance, without restraint

freezing *adjective.* arctic, biting, bitter, chill, chilled, chilly, cold, cutting, frigid, frosty, icy, numbing, penetrating, polar, raw, shivery, snappy, wintry

freight *noun.* bales, ballast, bulk, burden, carriage, contents, conveyance, fardel, haul, load, merchandise, pack, packages, shipment, shipping, transportation, wares, weight

frequency *noun.* abundance, beat, commonness, constancy, density, frequentness, iteration, number, oscillation, periodicity, persistence, prevalence, pulsation, recurrence, regularity, reiteration, repetition, rhythm

frequent *adjective.* common, constant, continual, incessant, intermittent, manifold, many, monotonous, periodic, profuse, recurrent, recurring, redundant, reiterated, successive, ubiquitous, usual, various

frequent *verb.* affect, attend, attend regularly, drop in, go to, hang about, hang around, haunt, hit, infest, overrun, patronize, play, resort, revisit, swarm over, visit, visit often

frequently *adverb.* commonly, customarily, generally, habitually, intermittently, many times, much, not seldom, oft, often, often enough, oftentimes, ordinarily, periodically, recurrently, regularly, successively, usually

fresh *adjective.* **1** cherry, comer, crisp, crude, gleaming, glistening, green, immature, late, mint, modernistic, natural, newborn, now, radical, raw, untouched, unusual **2** bracing, bright, brisk, clean, clear, colorful, cool, crisp, definite, fair, invigorating, pure, sharp, sparkling, stiff, stimulating, sweet, vivid **3** alert, blooming, bouncing, chipper, clear, dewy, florid, freshened, glowing, good, hardy, keen, refreshed, relaxed, revived, rosy, stimulated, verdant **4** bold, disrespectful, familiar, flip, flippant, forward, impertinent, impudent, insolent, nervy, pert, presumptuous, rude, saucy, smart, smart-alecky, snippy, wise

freshman *noun.* apprentice, beginner, colt, crab, dog, fish, fox, freshie, frog, frosh, newcomer, novitiate, plebe, rat, recruit, rookie, tenderfoot, tyro

friction *noun.* **1** abrasion, agitation, attrition, chafing, erosion, filing, fretting, grating, grinding, irritation, massage, rasping, resistance, scraping, soreness, traction, trituration, wearing away **2** animosity, antagonism, beef, bickering, conflict, discontent, discord, disharmony, faction, hatred, incompatibility, opposition, quarrel, resistance, row, ruckus, strife, trouble

friend *noun.* acquaintance, associate, brother, buddy, chum, classmate, colleague, companion, compatriot, comrade, countryman, fellow, mate, partner, playmate, roommate, schoolmate, sister

friendly *adjective.* affable, affectionate, amiable, attentive, auspicious, beneficial, civil, conciliatory, confiding, convivial, fond, genial, good, helpful, kind, loyal, tender, welcoming

friendship *noun.* accord, affection, alliance, association, attraction, brotherhood, closeness, concord, consideration, consonance, empathy, fondness, fusion, good will, love, rapport, regard, solidarity

frighten *verb.* agitate, alarm, astound, awe, buffalo, bulldoze, chill, daunt, demoralize, disconcert, discourage, dismay, disquiet, disturb, faze, intimidate, repel, shock

frightened *adjective.* afraid, aghast, alarmed, anxious, chicken, dismayed, fearful, frozen, jittery, jumpy, panicky, scared, shaky, shivery, startled, terrified, terrorized, yellow

fringe *noun.* binding, borderline, brim, brink, edge, edging, hem, limit, mane, march, margin, outside, outskirts, perimeter, periphery, skirt, trimming, verge

front *noun.* **1** anterior, beginning, bow, breast, brow, exterior, face, facing, fore, foreground, forehead, forepart, frontage, frontal, head, lead, obverse, top **2** bearing, coloring, countenance, cover, display, expression, exterior, face, fake, figure, manner, mask, mien, port, presence, pretext, show, veil

frustrated *adjective.* balked, bollixed up, crabbed, crimped, defeated, discontented, discouraged, embittered, foiled, irked, put away, resentful, screwed up, skinned, stonewalled, stymied, thwarted, ungratified

frustration *noun.* annoyance, bitter pill, blocking, blow, chagrin, curbing, defeat, dissatisfaction, drag, failure, foiling, grievance, impediment, irritation, obstruction, resentment, setback, thwarting

fuel *noun.* ammunition, combustible, electricity, encouragement, fodder, food, gas, go juice, incitement, juice, material, means, motion lotion, motion potion, nourishment, propellant, provocation, soup

fulfill *verb.* accomplish, achieve, conclude, conform, discharge, do, effect, effectuate, execute, finish, keep, meet, obey, observe, perform, realize, render, suit

fulfilled *adjective.* accomplished, achieved, attained, concluded, crowned, delighted, dispatched, effected, executed, finished, gratified, matured, obtained, perfected, performed, pleased, reached, satisfied

fulfillment *noun.* accomplishment, achievement, attainment, consummation, contentment, crowning, discharge, discharging, effecting, end, get off, gratification, implementation, kick, kicks, observance, perfection, realization

full *adjective.* **1** abounding, awash, burdened, bursting, crammed, entire, extravagant, imbued, impregnated, lavish, loaded, packed, padded, profuse, replete, stuffed, surfeited, weighted **2** absolute, adequate, ample, comprehensive, detailed, entire, exhaustive, extensive, generous, integral, itemized, maximum, minute, plenary, plentiful, unabridged, unlimited, whole

fully *adverb.* absolutely, all out, altogether, down, entirely, every inch, intimately, outright, perfectly, positively, quite, royal, thoroughly, through-and-through, totally, utterly, wholly, without exaggeration

fun *noun.* ball, blast, celebration, distraction, escapade, frolic, game, grins, merriment, merrymaking, nonsense, recreation, rejoicing, riot, romp, romping, solace, sport

function *noun.* business, charge, concern, employment, exercise, faculty, mark, mission, objective, operation, part, power, province, responsibility, role, target, utility, work

fund *noun.* armamentarium, capital,

endowment, foundation, inventory, kitty, mine, pool, repository, reservoir, source, stock, store, storehouse, supply, treasury, trust, vein

fundamental *adjective.* axiological, bottom, central, constitutional, elemental, essential, integral, intrinsic, key, necessary, organic, prime, primitive, radical, rudimentary, significant, supporting, underlying

fundamental *noun.* at heart, axiom, basic, basis, component, constituent, cornerstone, element, essential, factor, foundation, groceries, guts, law, principium, principle, rule, theorem

funds *noun.* assets, bread, budget, currency, dough, earnings, nut, possessions, proceeds, property, resources, securities, specie, stakes, substance, treasure, wealth, winnings

funny *adjective.* absurd, amusing, antic, capricious, comic, facetious, gas, hilarious, hysterical, jolly, ludicrous, merry, priceless, riot, riotous, silly, slapstick, whimsical

furious *adjective.* **1** crazed, demented, enraged, fierce, frenetic, frenzied, fuming, hacked, infuriated, insane, irrational, livid, maddened, rabid, raging, steamed, vehement, vicious **2** agitated, blustery, boisterous, concentrated, excessive, exquisite, extreme, fierce, flaming, impetuous, intensified, raging, rough, savage, turbulent, vehement, vicious, wild

furnish *verb.* apparel, appoint, arm, array, clothe, endow, equip, fit, fit out, gear, outfit, provide, provision, rig, stock, store, supply, turn out

furniture *noun.* appliance, appointment, bookcase, buffet, chest, cupboard, davenport, desk, dresser, effect, equipment, fittings, furnishing, goods, possession, sideboard, stove, table

further *verb.* advance, aid, assist, ballyhoo, champion, contribute, encourage, forward, foster, hasten, patronize, plug, promote, propagate, puff, push, serve, speed

fury *noun.* bluster, energy, ferocity, furor, indignation, intensity, ire, madness, power, rage, rise, savagery, sore, stew, storm, vehemence, violence, wrath

fusion *noun.* alloy, amalgamation, blend, blending, coalescence, coalition, compound, federation, integration, junction, melting, merger, merging, mixture, synthesis, union, uniting, welding

future *adjective.* approaching, booked, budgeted, destined, eventual, fated, final, forthcoming, imminent, impending, later, near, next, planned, scheduled, subsequent, unborn, unfolding,

G

gaiety *noun.* animation, brilliance, color, elation, frolic, fun, glitter, grins, joviality, merriment, merrymaking, pleasantness, radiance, revel, reveling, sparkle, sport, vivacity

gain *noun.* achievement, advantage, attainment, benefit, boost, buildup, dividend, earnings, improvement, income, proceeds, produce, progress, rise, take, velvet, winnings, yield

gain *verb.* achieve, annex, attain, bag, benefit, build up, clear, earn, enlarge, grow, have, land, progress, realize, reap, secure, snowball, succeed

gait *noun.* bearing, canter, carriage, clip, gallop, lick, march, motion, movement, pace, run, speed, step, stride, tread, trot, walk

game *adjective.* bold, courageous, dauntless, desirous, dogged, eager, fearless, gallant, hardy, heroic, inclined, interested, intrepid, prepared, resolute, unafraid, valiant, willing

game *noun.* adventure, business, distraction, enterprise, frolic, fun, jest, lark, line, merriment, merrymaking, plan, recreation, romp, scheme, sport, sports, undertaking

gang *noun.* bunch, circle, clique, club, crew, horde, mob, organization, outfit, party, ring, set, squad, syndicate, troop, troupe, workers, zoo

gap *noun.* break, chasm, clove, difference, disagreement, discontinuity, divergence, divide, division, fracture, inconsistency, intermission, interruption, opening, ravine, rest, rift, void

gate *noun.* access, bar, conduit, door, doorway, egress, entrance, exit, gateway, issue, opening, passage, port, portal, revolving door, turnstile, way, weir

gather *verb.* **1** amass, assemble, associate, choose, congregate, draw, flock, garner, group, heap, huddle, marshal, meet, pluck, rally, reunite, throng, unite **2** assume, believe, conclude, deduce, draw, expect, figure, find, hear, imagine, judge, learn, presume, reckon, suppose, take, think, understand **3** crop, cull, draw, extract, garner, glean, heap, ingather, mass, pick, pick out, pick up, pile, pluck, reap, select, stack, take in

gathering *noun.* acquisition, aggregation, assembly, caucus, collection, congress, crush, drove, flock, function, heap, huddle, meet, parley, rally, throng, turnout, union

gauge *noun.* bore, criterion, height, indicator, magnitude, mark, meter, model, rule, scope, size, span, standard, test, thickness, touchstone, width, yardstick

gauge *verb.* appraise, ascertain, assess, calculate, compute, count, dig it, evaluate, figure, judge, meter, peg, rate, reckon, scale, size, tally, value

gay *adjective.* alert, animated, brash, carefree, cheery, chipper, convivial, forward, glad, gleeful, hilarious, jolly, jovial, keen, merry, rollicking, sunny, wild

gaze *verb.* admire, beam, bore, contemplate, eyeball, glare, inspect, lamp, moon, observe, pin, pipe, regard, rubber, see, view, watch, wonder

gear *noun.* **1** accessory, apparatus, baggage, belongings, harness, instrument, luggage, machinery, material, outfit, paraphernalia, possessions, setup, stuff, supply, things, tool, trappings **2** apparel, array, attire, clothes, costume, drapery, drapes, dress, duds, feathers, garb, garments, habit, outfit, rags, threads, togs, wear

gear *verb.* adapt, adjust, appoint, arm, blend, fit, furnish, harness, match, organize, outfit, prepare, ready, regulate, rig, suit, tailor, turn out

general *adjective.* **1** accepted, accustomed, conventional, everyday, extensive, habitual, natural, normal, popular, prevailing, prevalent, regular, routine, typical, universal, usual, wide, widespread **2** blanket, collective, comprehending, diffuse, ecumenical, endless, extensive, indiscriminate, limitless, miscellaneous, panoramic, sweeping, total, ubiquitous, universal, unlimited, wide, worldwide

generally *adverb.* about, altogether, approximately, chiefly, commonly, conventionally, extensively, largely, mostly, ordinarily, popularly, practically, predominantly, roundly, thereabouts, typically, universally, widely

generous *adjective.* **1** acceptable, chivalrous, considerate, good, helpful, honest, hospitable, kind, lavish, liberal, lofty, loose, moderate, philanthropic, profuse, reasonable, tolerant, willing **2** abundant, affluent, ample, aplenty, bountiful, copious, full, handsome, large, lavish, liberal, luxuriant, no end, overflowing, plenty, rich, stink with, wealthy

genius *noun.* adept, aptitude, aptness, brain, discernment, expert, faculty, imagination, inclination, master, mature, power, precocity, prodigy, prowess, talent, virtuoso, wisdom

gentle *adjective.* **1** affable, agreeable, amiable, compassionate, disciplined, educated, genial, humane, kind, meek, merciful, moderate, placid, pliable, tame, taught, temperate, tender **2** balmy, bland, calm, clement, delicate, feeble, gradual, halcyon, imperceptible, light, moderate, placid, slight, smooth, soft, subdued, tender, tranquil **3** aristocratic, blue-blooded, courteous, cultured, elegant, genteel, gentlemanlike, gentlemanly, high-born, highbred, ladylike, noble, polished, polite, refined, upper-class, well-born, well-bred

genuine *adjective.* **1** absolute, accurate, actual, certain, certified, exact, good, hard, honest, indubitable, positive, real, sound, tested, true, unadulterated, unimpeachable, valid **2** actual, artless, candid, earnest, frank, heartfelt, known, natural, open, positive, real, reliable, righteous, sincere, true, unaffected, unimpeachable, valid

gesture *noun.* action, bow, expression, high sign, indication, intimation, kinesics, mime, nod, pantomime, reminder, salute, shrug, sign, signal, token, wave, wink

get *verb.* **1** achieve, annex, build up, clear, cop, draw, earn, elicit, evoke, grab, have, inherit, pull, realize, reap, secure, snag, take **2** amuse, arouse, bend, bias, carry, dispose, entertain, gratify, impress, influence, inspire, move, prompt, satisfy, stimulate, stir, strike, touch **3** baffle, beat, bewilder, buffalo, confound, discomfit, disconcert, distress, disturb, embarrass, mystify, nonplus, perplex, perturb, puzzle, stick, stump, upset **4** acquire, catch, comprehend, fathom, follow, gain, hear, know, learn, look at, master, memorize, notice, perceive, pick up, receive, see, work out. **5** argue into, beg, bring around, coax, compel, draw, induce, influence, persuade, press, pressure, prevail upon, prompt, provoke, sway, talk into, urge, wheedle

ghost *noun.* apparition, appearance, banshee, demon, devil, ethereal being, haunt, manes, phantom, shade, shadow, soul, specter, spirit, vision, visitor, wraith, zombie

giant *adjective.* big, blimp, colossal, enormous, gargantuan, gross, herculean, huge, hulking, immense, jumbo, mammoth, monstrous, mountainous, prodigious, titanic, vast, whaling

giant *noun.* behemoth, Brobdingnagian, bulk, colossus, cyclops, elephant, hulk, jumbo, leviathan, lump, mammoth, monster, mountain, ogre, Polyphemus, titan, whale, whopper

gift *noun.* **1** benefit, bestowal, bonus, boon, bounty, courtesy, dispensation, donation, favor, largesse, legacy, premium, presentation, provision, ration, remembrance, tip, tribute **2** ability, aptitude, aptness, attainment, attribute, bent, capability, faculty, flair, genius, head, instinct, knack, leaning, power, set, specialty, turn

gifted *adjective.* able, accomplished, adroit, brilliant, capable, class act, clever, expert, hot, hotshot, ingenious, intelligent, mad, masterly, phenom, shine in, skilled, smart

gigantic *adjective.* blimp, colossal, enormous, giant, gross, herculean, immense, jumbo, mammoth, massive, monster, monstrous, prodigious, titan, titanic, tremendous, vast, whaling

girl *noun.* babe, bird, blonde, butterfly, chick, dame, debutante, female, gal, maid, missy, nymph, piece, queen, schoolgirl, she, witch, woman

give *verb.* **1** accord, bestow, commit, confer, convey, deliver, donate, entrust, furnish, gift, lease, provide, subsidize, supply, tip, transfer, turn over, will **2** announce, carry, deliver, emit, express, furnish, impart, issue, pronounce, publish, put, read, render, state, supply, transfer, transmit, vent **3** bestow, confer, display, evidence, extend, furnish, indicate, issue, manifest, minister, offer, pose, produce, provide, render, show, tender, yield **4** bend, break, cave, concede, contract, crumble, devote, fail, fall, flex, fold, grant, open, recede, relax, sag, shrink, sink

glad *adjective.* animated, bright, cheering, cheery, contended, delightful, genial, gleeful, gratifying, hilarious, jocund, jovial, joyous, lighthearted, merry, pleased, pleasing, willing

glance *noun.* eye, eyeball, flash, gander, glimpse, glom, lamp, look, look-see, peek, peep, pike, quick look, sight, slant, squint, swivel, view

glance *verb.* **1** browse, dip into, eye, eyeball, flash, flip through, gaze, glimpse, peek, peep, peer, pipe, riffle through, run over, scan, see, thumb check, view **2** bounce, brush, careen, carom, contact, dart, graze, hit off, kiss, rebound, scrape, shave, skim, skip, slant, slide, strike, touch

glasses *noun.* bifocals, blinkers, cheaters, contact lenses, eyeglasses, four eyes, frames, goggles, grannies, lorgnette, nippers, rims, shades, specs, spectacles, trifocals, windows

glaze *verb.* buff, burnish, coat, cover, enamel, furbish, glance, glass, gloss, incrust, lacquer, make lustrous, make vitreous, overlay, polish, rub, shine, vitrify

glimpse *noun.* eye, eyeball, flash, gander, glance, glom, gun, impression, lamp, look, look-see, peep, pike, sight, sighting, slant, squint, swivel

gloom *noun.* anguish, bitterness, catatonia, despair, despondency, discouragement, distress, doldrums, dullness, dumps, grief, heaviness, malaise, misery, mourning, pessimism, unhappiness, weariness

glorious *adjective.* dazzling, delightful, distinguished, elevated, esteemed, exalted, famed, fine, heavenly, heroic, honored, immortal, magnificent, marvelous, remarkable, resplendent, venerable, wonderful

glory *noun.* **1** celebrity, dignity, distinction, eminence, exaltation, fame, grandeur, honor, immortality, magnificence, majesty, nobility, praise, prestige, renown, reputation, splendor, triumph **2** brightness, brilliance, effulgence, fineness, gorgeousness, grandeur, luster, magnificence, majesty, pageantry, pomp, preciousness, radiance, resplendence, richness, splendor, sublimity, sumptuousness

glow *noun.* bloom, blossom, blush, brilliance, flush, glare, gleam, glimmer, glitter, intensity, light, luminosity, passion, radiance, ray, splendor, vividness, warmth

glow *verb.* blaze, blush, burn, color, crimson, flame, flare, flush, gleam, glimmer, glisten, glitter, light, mantle, rose, shine, thrill, twinkle

glowing *adjective.* **1** aglow, beaming, flaming, florid, flush, flushed, gleaming, luminous, lustrous, phosphorescent, red, rich, rubicund, ruddy, suffused, vibrant, vivid, warm **2** ardent, avid, blazing, burning, complimentary, desirous, eager, ecstatic, enthusiastic, fervent, fierce, fiery, flaming, heated, impassioned, keen, passionate, zealous

go *noun.* activity, animation, bang, drive, energy, force, life, oomph, pep, potency, push, snap, starch, tuck, verve, vigor, vitality, vivacity

go *verb.* **1** approach, cruise, depart, escape, exit, fare, fly, leave, move, near, pass, proceed, progress, repair, split, take off, tool, travel **2** act, carry on, click, continue, flourish, function, maintain, make out, move, pan out, perform, persist, prosper, run, score, succeed, thrive, work **3** avail, befall, come, eventuate, fall out, fare, happen, incline, occur, persist, proceed, result, serve, tend, turn, turn out, wax, work out **4** accord, belong, blend, chime, complement, conform, correspond, dovetail, enjoy, fit, jibe, like, match, mesh, relish, set, square, suit **5** bend, break, cave, conclude, consume, crumble, decline, demise, depart, die, drop, exhaust, expire, fail, give, perish, spend, yield

god *noun.* absolute being, all powerful, almighty, creator, deity, demon, divinity, father, holiness, holy spirit, idol, lord, maker, man upstairs, power, providence, soul, spirit

golden *adjective.* **1** aureate, auric, auriferous, aurous, blond, blonde, caramel, dusty, flaxen, gold, golden, mellow yellow, ochroid, straw, tan, tawny, wheat **2** auspicious, best, blissful, bright, delightful, favorable, flourishing, glorious, joyous, precious, promising, propitious, prosperous, resplendent, rich, rosy, shining, valuable

gone *adjective.* astray, deceased, departed, displaced, dissipated, dissolved, done, elapsed, extinct, left, lost, moved, over, removed, retired, run off, vanished, withdrawn

good *adjective.* **1** acceptable, agreeable, bad, bully, exceptional, gratifying, marvelous, positive, precious, prime, reputable, satisfactory, sound, super, superior, valuable, welcome, wonderful **2** admirable, charitable, ethical, guiltless, honest, honorable, incorrupt, innocent, obedient, pure, reputable, respectable, right, righteous, sound, upright, virtuous, worthy

3 able, accomplished, adept, capable, competent, expert, proficient, proper, qualified, satisfactory, serviceable, skillful, suitable, suited, talented, thorough, useful, wicked **4** acceptable, appropriate, approving, apt, auspicious, becoming, decent, desirable, favoring, fit, fitting, healthful, helpful, meet, profitable, proper, respectable, serviceable **5** dependable, eatable, flawless, fresh, intact, loyal, normal, reliable, safe, solid, sound, stable, trustworthy, unblemished, undamaged, unhurt, unimpaired, whole **6** altruistic, approving, beneficent, benevolent, charitable, considerate, friendly, giving, gracious, humane, humanitarian, kindhearted, kindly, merciful, obliging, philanthropic, tolerant, well-disposed **7** authentic, conforming, dependable, genuine, honest, justified, legitimate, loyal, orthodox, proper, regular, reliable, sound, strict, true, trustworthy, valid, well-founded **8** adequate, ample, entire, extensive, full, immeasurable, large, long, much, paying, profitable, respectable, sizable, solid, substantial, sufficient, whole, worthwhile

good *noun*. asset, avail, behalf, benediction, benefit, boon, commonwealth, favor, gain, godsend, interest, plum, prize, prosperity, service, treasure, usefulness, worth

goodness *noun*. advantage, beneficence, benefit, excellence, generosity, good will, grace, honest, honesty, integrity, kindliness, probity, quality, rectitude, rightness, superiority, value, worth

gossip *noun*. **1** babbler, backbiter, blabbermouth, busybody, circulator, clack, informer, long-nose, magpie, old hen, parrot, prattler, scandalizer, scandalmonger, sieve, snoop, talebearer, tattler **2** account, buzz, calumny, chatter, chronicle, clothesline, conversation, grapevine, hash, hearsay, injury, jaw, meddling, report, rumble, story, talk, wire

gossip *verb*. buzz, chat, chatter, chew, dish, hint, imply, intimate, jaw, prate, rap, repeat, report, rumor, spread, suggest, talk, tattle

government *noun*. bureaucracy, command, direction, dominion, executive, influence, law, ministry, politics, power, presidency, regency, regime, restraint, rule, superiority, supervision, union

governor *noun*. administrator, boss, chief, commander, comptroller, controller, director, executive, gov, head, head honcho, leader, manager, overseer, presiding officer, ruler, superintendent, supervisor

grab *verb*. bag, capture, clutch, collar, corral, grapple, grasp, grip, hook, land, latch, nab, nail, pluck, seize, snag, snatch, take

grace *noun*. **1** adroitness, agility, breeding, consideration, cultivation, decency, dignity, ease, elegance, form, pleasantness, poise, polish, propriety, refinement, style, suppleness, tact **2** beneficence, charity, clemency, compassion, favor, forgiveness, generosity, good will, goodness, indulgence, kindliness, kindness, love, mercy, pardon, quarter, responsiveness, tenderness

grace *verb*. adorn, bedeck, crown, deck, decorate, dignify, distinguish, elevate, embellish, enhance, enrich, favor, garnish, glorify, honor, laureate, ornament, set off

graceful *adjective*. agile, artistic, becoming, comely, dainty, decorative, delicate, elastic, elegant, exquisite, fine, flowing, neat, practiced, pretty, smooth, trim, willowy

gracious *adjective*. affable, amiable, amicable, chivalrous, civil, compassionate, complaisant, considerate, courteous, courtly, gallant, genial, hospitable, merciful, pleasing, stately, suave, tender

grade *noun*. **1** category, division, estate, form, group, grouping, level, mark, notch, order, pigeonhole, quality, rung, size, stage, standard, station, step **2** ascent, bank, cant, climb, downgrade, elevation, embankment, height, hill, inclination, incline, lean, level, pitch, ramp, rise, tangent, tilt

gradually *adverb*. by degrees, by installments, constantly, continuously, deliberately, evenly, gently, imperceptibly, increasingly, moderately, perceptibly, piecemeal, progressively, regularly, serially, steadily, successively, unhurriedly

grain *noun.* atom, bit, corn, drop, grist, iota, kernel, mite, modicum, molecule, morsel, ounce, particle, piece, spark, speck, trace, whit

grand *adjective.* **1** ambitious, elevated, exalted, fine, glorious, haughty, lofty, lordly, magnificent, marvelous, monumental, pretentious, regal, stately, striking, sumptuous, super, wonderful **2** chief, dignified, elevated, exalted, grave, head, highest, leading, lofty, main, majestic, mighty, noble, preeminent, principal, regal, supreme, transcendent

grant *noun.* admission, allocation, allotment, appropriation, assistance, bequest, boon, bounty, charity, concession, contribution, dole, donation, gift, lump, privilege, reward, subsidy

grant *verb.* accord, acquiesce, admit, allot, assign, bestow, concede, confer, convey, donate, drop, give, impart, invest, own, profess, suppose, transfer

grasp *verb.* accept, appreciate, apprehend, catch, compass, comprehend, dig, fathom, follow, get, have, know, make, perceive, pick up, realize, see, take

grateful *adjective.* acceptable, agreeable, comforting, congenial, consoling, delicious, delightful, desirable, good, gratifying, refreshing, renewing, restful, restorative, restoring, satisfactory, satisfying, welcome

grave *adjective.* **1** dignified, dour, dull, earnest, gloomy, grim, heavy, jelly, leaden, meaningful, muted, sad, sage, sedate, solemn, subdued, thoughtful, unsmiling **2** acute, consequential, critical, deadly, destructive, fatal, fell, grievous, hazardous, heavy, important, momentous, ominous, perilous, severe, significant, ugly, urgent

gray *adjective.* ashen, dappled, dingy, dove, drab, dusty, heather, leaden, livid, neutral, oyster, pearly, powder, shaded, silvery, slate, smoky, stone

greasy *adjective.* anointed, creamy, daubed, fat, fatty, greased, lubricated, lubricious, oily, oleaginous, pomaded, salved, slick, slimy, slithery, smeared, swabbed, unctuous

great *adjective.* **1** bulky, colossal, considerable, decided, enormous, excessive, extended, extensive, extravagant, fat, mammoth, oversize, prodigious, pronounced, strong, tremendous, vast, voluminous **2** chief, dignified, distinguished, exalted, famed, fine, glorious, heroic, idealistic, impressive, lofty, lordly, puissant, regal, remarkable, royal, stately, superior **3** able, absolute, adept, admirable, bad, cold, exceptional, expert, fine, good, heavy, marvelous, positive, proficient, terrific, tremendous, unqualified, wonderful

greatly *adverb.* abundantly, conspicuously, eminently, enormously, extremely, glaringly, immensely, indeed, intensely, largely, mightily, much, notably, powerfully, remarkably, supremely, tremendously, vastly

greatness *noun.* **1** abundance, amplitude, bulk, enormity, force, high degree, immensity, infinity, intensity, largeness, length, magnitude, mass, might, potency, power, prodigiousness, strength **2** celebrity, chivalry, dignity, distinction, eminence, fame, generosity, glory, heroism, idealism, importance, magnanimity, majesty, morality, nobility, note, prominence, renown

green *adjective.* **1** blooming, budding, burgeoning, developing, flourishing, grassy, growing, immature, infant, juvenile, lush, pliable, raw, sprouting, tender, unripe, verdant, youthful **2** credulous, fresh, gullible, ignorant, immature, inexpert, innocent, naive, new, raw, unpolished, unpracticed, unseasoned, unsophisticated, untrained, unversed, young, youthful **3** apple, beryl, fir, forest, grass, jade, kelly, lime, moss, olive, pea, peacock, pine, sage, sap, sea, spinach, willow

grief *noun.* affliction, despair, disquiet, distress, grievance, heartbreak, lamentation, malaise, misery, mortification, mourning, pain, regret, rue, trial, tribulation, trouble, upset

grim *adjective.* crabbed, cruel, dogged, fierce, ghastly, glowering, horrid, intractable, merciless, morose, ominous, resolute, scowling, severe, shocking, sinister, sour, stubborn

grip *noun.* anchor, butt, clamping, clench, constraint, crushing, duress, enclosing, grapple, grasp, handshake, lug, musculature, purchase, restraint, squeeze, strength, vise

gross *adjective.* **1** big, bulky, bull, dense, fat, fleshy, great, heavy, hulking, lumpish, massive, obese, overweight, portly, stout, thick, unwieldy, weighty **2** boorish, breezy, callous, cheap, dull, foul, indecent, indelicate, insensitive, lewd, lustful, offensive, raw, rough, tasteless, ugly, unseemly, voluptuous **3** absolute, blatant, downright, excessive, exorbitant, extreme, flagrant, grievous, immoderate, manifest, outrageous, outright, plain, shameful, sheer, shocking, unqualified, utter

grotesque *adjective.* absurd, bizarre, eerie, extravagant, extreme, fanciful, fantastic, flamboyant, gross, ludicrous, malformed, misshapen, monstrous, odd, perverted, queer, strange, unnatural

ground *noun.* arena, dirt, dry land, dust, field, land, landscape, loam, old sod, park, real estate, sand, sod, soil, terra firma, terrain, turf

ground *verb.* base, bottom, coach, discipline, educate, found, inform, instruct, prepare, prime, qualify, rest, set, settle, stay, teach, train, tutor

grounds *noun.* **1** area, campus, country, district, domain, environs, fields, land, lot, property, realm, sphere, spot, terrace, terrain, territory, tract, zone **2** account, antecedent, argument, base, demonstration, determinant, excuse, footing, foundation, goods, motive, numbers, occasion, pretext, reason, root, test, trial

group *noun.* aggregation, assembly, association, battery, body, category, club, collection, formation, gang, mess, parcel, pool, set, suite, syndicate, troop, trust

group *verb.* **1** arrange, assemble, associate, bracket, bunch, cluster, collect, congregate, consort, crowd, fraternize, huddle, link, meet, organize, poke, punch, round up **2** arrange, assemble, associate, assort, bracket, categorize, class, dispose, file, gather, marshal, order, organize, pigeonhole, put together, range, rank, sort

grow *verb.* abound, arise, build, come, dilate, enlarge, expand, extend, issue, mature, mount, rise, spread, sprout, stem, stretch, thrive, widen

growth *noun.* aggrandizement, boost, buildup, cultivation, enlargement, flowering, growing, hike, improvement, produce, production, progress, proliferation, prosperity, rise, sprouting, surge, thickening

guarantee *noun.* agreement, bargain, certainty, charter, contract, covenant, deposit, gage, guaranty, insurance, lock, pawn, pipe, promise, security, undertaking, vow, warranty

guarantee *verb.* affirm, angel, assure, certify, endorse, ensure, guaranty, insure, maintain, promise, protect, prove, reassure, secure, stake, swear, testify, wager

guaranteed *adjective.* affirmed, approved, ascertained, assured, attested, bonded, certified, confirmed, endorsed, insured, pledged, plighted, protected, sealed, secured, sure, sure enough, warranted

guard *noun.* chaser, custodian, defender, escort, eyes, hack, lookout, picket, roller, sentinel, sentry, shields, sidewinder, stick, ward, warden, watch, watchman

guard *verb.* chaperon, convoy, cover, defend, keep, lookout, observe, police, preserve, safeguard, save, screen, secure, shelter, shotgun, superintend, supervise, watch

guardian *noun.* angel, champion, cop, curator, custodian, defender, guard, keeper, nurse, overseer, safeguard, sentinel, shepherd, sitter, superintendent, supervisor, warden, watchdog

guess *noun.* conclusion, conjecture, deduction, divination, fancy, hunch, hypothesis, inference, judgment, opinion, postulate, presumption, presupposition, reckoning, stab, suspicion, thesis, view

guess *verb.* conjecture, deduce, divine, fancy, figure, hazard, hypothesize, infer, judge, pick, predict, pretend, reason, speculate, suggest, suppose, think, work out

guest *noun.* boarder, caller, companion, company, confidant, confidante, customer, fellow, habituÈ, inmate, mate, partaker, patron, recipient, sojourner, tenant, transient, visitor

guide *noun.* **1** adviser, captain, chaperon, convoy, counselor, criterion, design, guru, lead, leader, master, model, paradigm, pioneer, rudder, scout, standard, teacher **2** beacon, bible, catalog, clue, compendium, directory, guidebook, handbook, instructions, key, landmark, manual, mark, pointer, print, sign, signal, signpost

guide *verb.* accompany, beacon, chaperon, convoy, educate, engineer, govern, handle, instruct, manage, quarterback, regulate, route, rule, see, spearhead, teach, train

guilt *noun.* criminality, delinquency, error, fault, guiltiness, lapse, misbehavior, misstep, onus, regret, remorse, responsibility, sinfulness, slip, stigma, transgression, wickedness, wrong

guilty *adjective.* ashamed, caught, condemned, criminal, damned, delinquent, doomed, felonious, indicted, iniquitous, judged, liable, offending, remorseful, responsible, sentenced, sinful, wicked

gun *noun.* cannon, difference, handgun, hardware, heavy ordnance, insurance, magnum, mortar, musket, ordnance, peashooter, piece, pistol, revolver, rifle, rod, shotgun, toy

guts *noun.* audacity, backbone, balls, boldness, courage, daring, dauntlessness, effrontery, forcefulness, fortitude, grit, heart, mettle, pluck, resolution, sand, spirit, spunk

H

habit *noun.* addiction, constitution, custom, dependence, gravitation, groove, inclination, manner, mode, penchant, persuasion, routine, rule, set, style, susceptibility, tendency, wont

habitat *noun.* abode, accommodations, digs, dwelling, element, haven, home, house, housing, lodging, nest, quarters, range, roost, settlement, terrain, territory, turf

hail *verb.* accost, address, flag, flag down, greet, hello, holler, salute, shoulder, shout, signal, sing out, speak to, wave down, welcome, whistle down, yell, yoohoo

hair *noun.* beard, bristle, coiffure, down, eyebrow, fiber, fluff, fringe, fur, grass, lock, mop, moustache, shock, strand, thread, wig, wool

halfway *adjective.* center, centermost, central, equidistant, imperfect, incomplete, intermediate, medial, median, mid, middle, middlemost, midway, moderate, part, part-way, partial, smack dab

halfway *adverb.* comparatively, compromising, conciliatory, imperfectly, in part, incomplete, insufficiently, medially, middling, midway, moderately, nearly, partially, partly, pretty, rather, restrictedly, unsatisfactory

hall *noun.* amphitheater, arena, armory, auditorium, ballroom, casino, chamber, church, gallery, gym, gymnasium, lounge, mart, meeting place, refectory, salon, stateroom, theater

halt *noun.* arrest, break, break-off, close, cutoff, end, freeze, grinding halt, impasse, interruption, letup, pause, screaming halt, screeching halt, stand, standstill, stop, termination

halt *verb.* arrest, bar, break off, check, curb, end, frustrate, interrupt, obstruct, pause, rest, stall, stand still, stay, stem, suspend, terminate, wait

hammer *verb.* bang, batter, bear down, beat, clobber, defeat, drive, fashion, forge, form, knock, make, pound, shape, strike, tap, wallop, whack

hand *noun.* 1 duke, extremity, fin, fist, grabber, grappler, grasp, grip, ham, hold, hook, knuckles, manus, metacarpus, palm, paw, phalanges, shaker **2** ability, agency, aid, assistance, control, direction, guidance, influence, instruction, knack, lift, part, participation, relief, share, skill, succor, support

handle *verb.* bestow, command, discuss, dominate, employ, exercise, exploit, govern, guide, maneuver, ply, serve, steer, supervise, swing, take, wield, work

handsome *adjective.* **1** admirable, aristocratic, becoming, comely, dapper, elegant, fair, fine, hunk, impressive, majestic, muscular, sharp, slick, smooth, stately, strong, virile **2** ample, bounteous, bountiful, considerable, extensive, full, generous, gracious, large, lavish, liberal, magnanimous, munificent, openhanded, plentiful, princely, sizable, unsparing

handy *adjective.* adaptable, advantageous, available, beneficial, central, convenient, functional, gainful, helpful, manageable, neat, practicable, practical, profitable, ready, serviceable, useful, utile

hang *verb.* adhere, attach, cover, dangle, deck, depend, droop, drop, float, furnish, incline, lop, lower, remain, rest, stick, swing, wave

happen *verb.* appear, arise, befall, betide, fall, follow, issue, light, luck, materialize, meet, pass, proceed, result, shake, smoke, stumble, turn out

happily *verb.* blissfully, blithely, brightly, contentedly, delightfully, enthusiastically, freely, gaily, gleefully, graciously, hilariously, joyfully, lightly, lovingly, merrily, peacefully, pleasantly, sincerely

happiness *noun.* content, contentment, delectation, delight, delirium, ecstasy, elation, euphoria, felicity, joviality, jubilation, laughter, merriment, paradise, prosperity, rejoicing, sanctity, vivacity

happy *adjective.* **1** blessed, blest, captivated, chipper, content, convivial, ecstatic, glad, gleeful, intoxicated, jolly, joyous, laughing, light, merry, pleased, satisfied, sunny, thrilled, tickled, tickled pink, up, upbeat **2** appropriate, apt, auspicious, befitting, casual, correct, efficacious, enviable, fitting, lucky, meet, proper, propitious, providential, right, satisfactory, suitable, timely

harbor *noun.* anchorage, arm, bay, breakwater, chuck, cove, destination, dock, embankment, gulf, haven, inlet, landing, mooring, pier, port, road, wharf

harbor *verb.* board, bunk, conceal, defend, domicile, entertain, guard, house, lodge, nurture, protect, quarter, safeguard, screen, secure, shelter, suppress, withhold

hard *adjective.* **1** callous, compact, compressed, concentrated, consolidated, dense, firm, hardened, impenetrable, iron, packed, rigid, rocky, set, solid, stiff, strong, tough **2** arduous, demanding, distressing, exacting, heavy, intricate, irksome, labored, laborious, merciless, rough, scabrous, severe, slavish, sticky, tiring, toilsome, wearing **3** austere, callous, cold, disagreeable, distressing, dour, exacting, grim, inclement, intolerable, perverse, rancorous, resentful, severe, strict, stubborn, unkind, unpleasant

hard *adverb.* **1** briskly, earnestly, energetically, ferociously, forcibly, heavily, intensely, keenly, painfully, powerfully, relentlessly, rigorously, savagely, severely, sharply, strongly, uproariously, vigorously **2** closely, diligently, doggedly, earnestly, exhaustively, industriously, intensely, intensively, intently, painstakingly, persistently, searchingly, sharply, steadily, strenuously, thoroughly, unremittingly, untiringly **3** agonizingly, arduously, awkwardly, badly, carefully, exhaustingly, gruelingly, hardly, harshly, inconveniently, laboriously, painfully, ponderously, roughly, severely, strenuously, tiredly, vigorously

hardened *adjective.* accustomed, blasphemous, callous, contemptuous, cruel, disdainful, heartless, impenetrable, impious, inaccessible, inured, irreverent, lost, prepared, resistant, seasoned, steeled, unemotional

hardly *adverb.* barely, comparatively, faintly, gradually, imperceptibly, infrequently, just, little, noticeably, only, perceptibly, practically, rarely, seldom, simply, slightly, somewhat, sparsely

hardship *noun.* accident, affliction, austerity, calamity, case, catastrophe, curse, danger, distress, grief, grievance, hazard, injury, misery, toil, torment, trouble, want

hardy *adjective.* able, acclimatized, burly, capable, firm, fit, hale, hearty, mighty, muscular, powerful, resistant, solid, sound, stout, substantial, tenacious, unflagging

harm *noun.* abuse, detriment, immorality, infliction, loss, marring, mischief, misfortune, misuse, outrage, prejudice, sabotage, sinfulness, vandalism, vice, violence, wickedness, wrong

harm *verb.* abuse, bruise, crush, impair, inconvenience, maltreat, misuse, molest, nick, outrage, sap, shatter, shock, stab, trample, wound, wreck, wrong

harmony *noun.* **1** accord, affinity, amity, concord, consistency, cooperation, correspondence, empathy, friendship, good will, kinship, peace, rapport, sympathy, tranquility, unanimity, understanding, unity **2** accord, agreement, balance, concord, concordance, consonance, fitness, form, integration, integrity, oneness, order, parallelism, proportion, regularity, togetherness, tune, unity **3** accord, accordance, arrangement, blend, blending, chord, chorus, composition, concert, concurrence, consonance, melody, music, piece, richness, triad, tune, unison

harness *verb.* channel, collar, couple, curb, employ, exploit, furnish, govern, leash, mobilize, muzzle, outfit, rein, secure, strap, tame, tie, yoke

harry *verb.* annoy, attack, devastate, disturb, fret, gnaw, harass, molest, pester, pillage, plague, plunder, sack, tease, torment, trouble, upset, vex

harsh *adjective.* **1** cracked, craggy, croaking, crude, dissonant, grating, grim, hard, hoarse, jagged, jangling, raucous, rigid, rusty, severe, sharp, sour, uneven **2** austere, cruel, discourteous, dour, grim, gruff, hairy, hard, punitive, ruthless, severe, sharp, stern, tough, ungracious, unkind, unpleasant, wicked

harvest *noun.* autumn, consequence, cropping, effect, fall, fruition, harvesting, intake, output, produce, reaping, result, return, season, storing, summer, yield, yielding

harvest *verb.* accumulate, acquire, amass, bin, cache, collect, crop, cut, garner, get, glean, harrow, pick, plow, pluck, reap, squirrel, strip

haste *noun.* alacrity, briskness, bustle, carelessness, celerity, dash, dispatch, flurry, hustle, impatience, pace, press, quickness, rapidity, recklessness, scramble, swiftness, velocity

hastily *adverb.* agilely, carelessly, expeditiously, fast, hurriedly, impetuously, nimbly, prematurely, promptly, quickly, rapidly, rashly, recklessly, speedily, straightaway, suddenly, swiftly, thoughtlessly

hat *noun.* beaver, boater, bonnet, bucket, chimney, cow's breakfast, fedora, headpiece, helmet, lid, millinery, plug, rim, roof, sailor, sky, stove pipe, straw

hate *noun.* animosity, bother, destination, detestation, enmity, frost, grievance, hatred, objection, pain, rancor, repugnance, repulsion, revulsion, scorn, spite, trouble, venom

hate *verb.* abhor, allergic to, can't stand, curse, deprecate, despise, detest, disapprove, disdain, disfavor, dislike, down on, nauseate, object to, scorn, shudder at, shun, spit upon

hatred *noun.* animosity, aversion, bitterness, coldness, detestation, displeasure, enmity, grudge, hate, loathing, rancor, repugnance, repulsion, revulsion, scorn, spite, spleen, venom

have *verb.* **1** admit, annex, bear, carry, compass, enjoy, gain, hog, keep, land, obtain, occupy, own, pick up, procure, receive, secure, take **2** bear, consider, enjoy, entertain, experience, feel, know, leave, let, must, need, ought, permit, see, suffer, sustain, tolerate, undergo

hazard *noun.* accident, adventure, coincidence, dynamite, fluke, go at, long shot, luck, luck into, misfortune, mishap, outside chance, possibility, risk, snowball chance, stab, venture, wager

hazard *verb.* adventure, chance, conjecture, dare, endanger, gamble, guess, imperil, jeopardize, presume, speculate, stake, submit, suppose, try, venture, volunteer, wager

head *noun.* **1** attic, bean, belfry, biscuit, brain, coconut, crown, dome, nob, nut, pate, poll, pumpkin, scalp, skull, thinker, upstairs, wig **2** boss, captain, chief, chieftain, commander, commanding officer, director, dominator, executive, headmaster, lead-off man, manager, master, officer, president, principal, superintendent, supervisor **3** ability, aptitude, aptness, bent, brains, bump, faculty, flair, genius, gift, intellect, knack, mentality, mind, talent, thought, turn, understanding

head *verb.* address, be first, command, control, direct, dominate, go first, govern, guide, lead, oversee, pioneer, precede, rule, run, supervise, train, zero in

health *noun.* bloom, complexion, constitution, energy, euphoria, fitness, form, pink, prime, robustness, shape, soundness, stamina, state, strength, tone, vigor, wholeness

healthy *adjective.* **1** aiding, aseptic, beneficial, compensatory, conducive, desirable, harmless, healing, healthful, helpful, nourishing, nutritive, profitable, restorative, sanitary, tonic, unadulterated, useful **2** blooming, chipper, firm, fit, flourishing, hale, hardy, healthful, hearty, husky, muscular, normal, sound, stout, strong, trim, virile, you

heap *noun.* abundance, agglomeration, aggregation, bank, bunch, cargo, collection, concentration, harvest, haul, jumble, load, million, mound, much, shock, sum, thousand

heap *verb.* accumulate, add, amass, augment, bank, bunch, deposit, dump, fill, group, load, lump, mass, mound, pack, pile, stack, swell

hear *verb.* **1** apprehend, attend, auscultate, catch, descry, devour, eavesdrop, get, give attention, give ears, hark, heed, listen, make out, perceive, pick up, read, strain **2** apperceive, ascertain, be informed, catch, catch on, descry, determine, discover, find out, gather, glean, learn, pick up, receive, see, tumble, understand, unearth

hearing *noun.* **1** audition, auditory, auditory range, detecting, distinguishing, ear, earshot, effect, extent, faculty, hearing distance, listening, perception, range, reach, recording, sense, sound **2** attendance, attention, audience, audit, conference, congress, consultation, interview, investigation, meeting, negotiation, notice, parley, presentation, reception, review, test, trial

heart *noun.* **1** affection, character, compassion, concern, emotion, humanity, inclination, love, palate, pity, relish, sensitivity, sentiment, soul, sympathy, tenderness, understanding, zest **2** boldness, bravery, dauntlessness, fortitude, gallantry, guts, mettle, mind, moxie, nerve, pluck, purpose, resolution, resolve, soul, spirit, spunk, will **3** basic, bosom, center, core, crux, focus, gist, groceries, hub, kernel, marrow, middle, nucleus, pith, quick, root, seat, soul

heat *noun.* calefaction, dog days, fever, fieriness, hot spell, hot weather, hotness, incalescence, incandescence, sultriness, swelter, temperature, torridity, torridness, warmness, warmth, wave

heat *verb.* blaze, chafe, char, fire, flame, flush, fry, glow, roast, scald, sear, smelt, steam, sun, thaw, toast, warm, warm up

heated *adjective.* **1** ardent, avid, excited, fervent, fierce, fiery, frenzied, furious, hectic, impassioned, intense, irate, passionate, raging, stormy, vehement, violent, wrathful **2** baked, baking, boiling, broiled, broiling, burned, burning, burnt, cooked, fiery, fired, friend, hot, parched, scalding, scorched, sizzling, toasted

heaven *noun.* atmosphere, beyond, ecstasy, eternity, felicity, happiness, harmony, heights, hereafter, immortality, nirvana, paradise, rapture, sky, transport, upstairs, utopia, wonderland

heavenly *adjective.* ambrosial, beatific, blessed, blissful, celestial, delicious, delightful, divine, exquisite, extraterrestrial, glorious, immortal, lush, scrumptious, superhuman, supernatural, sweet, wonderful

heavy *adjective.* **1** bulky, chunky, considerable, excessive, expecting, fat, fatso, fleshy, gravid, large, loaded, massive, oppressed, overweight, portly, stout, substantial, weighted **2** arduous, boisterous, confused, grave, grievous, hard, intolerable, labored, laborious, profound, recondite, rough, severe, stormy, toilsome, turbulent, vexatious, wild **3** crestfallen, damp, despondent, dismal, downcast, dull, gloomy, grieving, leaden, lowering, melancholy, oppressive, overcast, sad, sodden, soggy, stifling, wet

heed *noun.* attention, caution, cognizance, concentration, concern, consideration, debate, ear, interest, mark, notice, observance, observation, regard, respect, spotlight, study, thought

heed *verb.* attend, consider, dig, follow, hark, hear, listen, mark, mind, note, obey, observe, pick up, regard, see, sit, spot, watch

height *noun.* **1** apogee, crest, crown, elevation, extent, highness, hill, peak, pitch, prominence, rise, solstice, stature, summit, tip, top, vertex, zenith **2** crest, crisis, culmination, dignity, eminence, end, exaltation, extremity, grandeur, heyday, high point, importance, limit, maximum, prominence, top, ultimate, uttermost

hell *noun.* abyss, affliction, agony, anguish, difficulty, emergency, grave, limbo, martyrdom, misery, nightmare, ordeal, pit, suffering, torment, trial, underworld, wretchedness

help *noun.* **1** aid, assist, avail, balm, benefit, comfort, cooperation, cure, guidance, lift, relief, remedy, service, succor, support, sustenance, use, utility **2** aide, ally, assistant, attendant, auxiliary, collaborator, colleague, deputy, domestic, helper, helpmate, mate, partner, representative, servant, subsidiary, supporter, worker

help *verb.* **1** advocate, aid, ballyhoo, benefit, bolster, encourage, endorse, further, intercede, maintain, patronize, puff, save, second, serve, stand by, succor, uphold **2** alleviate, amend, attend, better, cure, doctor, ease, facilitate, heal, meliorate, mitigate, nourish, palliate, relieve, remedy, restore, revive, treat

helpful *adjective.* accessible, applicable, bettering, constructive, cooperative, important, instrumental, kind, practical, pragmatic, productive, profitable, serviceable, significant, supportive, timely, usable, valuable

helpless *adjective.* dependent, destitute, exposed, feeble, forlorn, impotent, incapable, inexpert, invalid, paralyzed, pinned, powerless, prostrate, shiftless, unable, unfit, vulnerable, weak

herald *verb.* advertise, announce, ballyhoo, broadcast, declare, forerun, harbinger, indicate, portend, precede, preindicate, presage, proclaim, promise, publish, show, tout, trumpet

herd *noun.* brood, collection, crush, drift, drove, flight, flock, gaggle, horde, mass, mob, multitude, nest, pack, people, press, school, throng

herd *verb.* assemble, associate, collect, congregate, drive, flock, goad, guide, huddle, lead, muster, poke, punch, rally, round up, run, shepherd, spur

heritage *noun.* ancestry, bequest, birthright, convention, culture, custom, dowry, endowment, estate, fashion, inheritance, legacy, lot, patrimony, portion, right, share, tradition

hero *noun.* celebrity, champion, combatant, diva, gallant, god, goddess, heavy, heroine, idol, lead, lion, martyr, master, model, protagonist, saint, star

heroic *adjective.* bold, champion, courageous, daring, dauntless, elevated, epic, exaggerated, fearless, gallant, grand, gritty, inflated, intrepid, mythological, unafraid, undaunted, valiant

hesitate *verb.* alternate, balance, debate, defer, delay, falter, flounder, hang, hedge, linger, pause, ponder, shift, shrink, stop, stumble, swerve, waffle

hidden *adjective.* buried, clandestine, covered, cryptic, disguised, eclipsed, invisible, masked, mysterious, mystical, private, recondite, screened, shadowy, surreptitious, underground, undetected, undisclosed

hide *verb.* cache, cloak, cover, curtain, ditch, eclipse, mask, obscure, protect, reserve, screen, shadow, shelter, smuggle, squirrel, suppress, veil, with

hideous *adjective.* appalling, beast, dreadful, ghastly, gruesome, hateful, horrid, loathsome, macabre, monstrous, morbid, offensive, repugnant, revolting, shocking, terrifying, ugly, unsightly

high *adjective.* **1** aerial, colossal, elevated, eminent, formidable, giant, grand, great, hovering, huge, immense, lanky, large, lofty, long, steep, tremendous, upraised **2** costly, dear, excessive, expensive, extravagant, grand, great, intensified, lavish, luxurious, precious, rich, sharp, special, steep, stiff, strong, unusual **3** arch, chief, consequential, crucial, distinguished, eminent, essential, exalted, extreme, grave, leading, necessary, noble, powerful, prominent, ruling, significant, superior **4** delirious, doped, drugged, drunk, euphoric, hopped-up, hyped-up, inebriated, potted, spaced out, stoned, tipsy, tripped-out, tripping, tuned-in, turned-on, wasted, zonked

highly *adverb.* bloody, deeply, eminently, extremely, greatly, immensely, jolly, mighty, much, notably, powerful, real, really, remarkably, right, supremely, tremendously, vastly

highway *noun.* artery, avenue, boulevard, bricks, drag, freeway, interstate, parking lot, parkway, path, pike, roadway, skyway, street, thoroughfare, toll road, track, turnpike

hill *noun.* ascent, butte, climb, dune, elevation, eminence, heap, highland, inclination, incline, mesa, mount, prominence, protuberance, range, ridge, rise, shock

hint *noun.* allusion, implication, impression, iota, mention, notice, observation, omen, print, sign, suggestion, taste, tip, trace, warning, whiff, wink, wrinkle

hint *verb.* angle, coax, cue, drop, expose, fish, impart, imply, infer, inform, leak, mention, press, prompt, signify, solicit, suggest, wink

hire *verb.* appoint, authorize, carry, charter, delegate, employ, exploit, ink, lease, let, obtain, occupy, pact, pledge, procure, promise, secure, sublease

history *noun.* account, annals, autobiography, biography, diary, epic, journal, memoirs, narration, narrative, recapitulation, recital, record, relation, report, saga, story, version

hit *noun.* box, buffet, butt, chop, clash, clip, clout, collision, glance, knock, lick, pat, rap, roundhouse, shock, slap, smash, swing

hit *verb.* **1** beat, blast, box, brain, buffet, clap, clout, club, flail, flax, kick, knock, pound, slap, stone, thump, thwack, trash **2** buffet, butt, clash, crash, glance, jostle, knock, light, meet, pat, rap, run into, scrape, smash, stumble, tap, thud, thump

hold *noun.* authority, clench, clinch, clout, clutch, control, dominion, grasp, grip, influence, occupancy, occupation, ownership, pull, purchase, retention, tenacity, tenure

hold *verb.* **1** adhere, carry, clench, confine, detain, handle, keep, maintain, occupy, own, secure, squeeze, stick, take, trammel, vise, wield, withhold **2** assume, buy, consider, credit, deem, entertain, esteem, feel, judge, lap up, maintain, OK, presume, reckon, regard, sense, think, view **3** apply, be valid, continue, exist, have bearing, hold good, hold true, last, operate, persevere, persist, remain, remain true, resist, stand up, stay, stay staunch, wear

hole *noun.* aperture, break, cavity, chamber, chasm, crater, excavation, fracture, leak, mouth, nest, niche, outlet, passage, pit, shaft, vent, void

holiday *noun.* anniversary, break, celebration, feast, festival, fete, fiesta, gala, holy day, jubilee, layoff, leave, liberty, long weekend, recess, red-letter day, saint's day, vacation

hollow *adjective.* **1** alveolate, arched, cavernous, cleft, concave, cupped, curved, deep-set, depressed, infundibular, not solid, notched, sunken, troughlike, unfilled, vacant, vaulted, void **2** dull, echoing, flat, ghostly, low, muffled, mute, muted, resonant, resounding, ringing, roaring, rumbling, sounding, thunderous, toneless, vibrant, vibrating

hollow *noun.* basin, bottom, cave, cavity, chamber, channel, crater, dale, den, dish, excavation, groove, hole, notch, pit, pocket, sinkhole, void

hollow *verb.* channel, chase, dent, dig, dish, ditch, furrow, gorge, groove, indent, notch, pit, rabbet, remove, rut, scoop, shovel, trench

holy *adjective.* believing, blessed, dedicated, devotional, devout, divine, faultless, glorified, good, immaculate, moral, pious, prayerful, reverent, sanctified, spiritual, spotless, venerable

home *noun.* **1** abode, cabin, cottage, digs, domicile, dwelling, farm, house, joint, mansion, nest, orphanage, palace, roost, shanty, trailer, turf, villa **2** abode, country, element, family, farm, haunt, haven, hills, homeland, household, land, locality, motherland, neighborhood, range, site, soil, territory

homely *adjective.* cozy, domestic, everyday, familiar, friendly, gross, informal, modest, natural, pig, plain, simple, snug, ugly, unaffected, unpretentious, welcoming

honest *adjective.* authentic, candid, decent, ethical, forthright, frank, impartial, open, outright, proper, real, reputable, scrupulous, sincere, true, truthful, upright, virtuous

honesty *noun.* bluntness, confidence, equity, fairness, fidelity, goodness, incorruptibility, integrity, justness, morality, probity, rectitude, responsibility, right, sincerity, soundness, truthfulness, veracity

honor *noun.* **1** aggrandizement, apotheosis, celebration, confidence, consideration, deference, dignity, distinction, elevation, faith, glorification, notice, popularity, recognition, repute, tribute, trust, wreath **2** character, chastity, courage, decency, fairness, goodness, honesty, innocence, modesty, morality, morals, principles, probity, rectitude, righteousness, truthfulness, virginity, virtue **3** acclaim, accolade, badge, commendation, compliment, decoration, deference, distinction, favor, homage, laurels, pleasure, privilege, recognition, regard, respect, tribute, veneration

honor *verb.* acclaim, appreciate, celebrate, commemorate, commend, compliment, dignify, erect, esteem, glorify, keep, observe, praise, prize, respect, revere, value, worship

hope *noun.* achievement, ambition, anticipation, buoyancy, concern, confidence, dependence, endurance, expectation, faith, fancy, fortune, longing, promise, reverie, security, utopia, wish

hope *verb.* anticipate, aspire, assume, believe, cherish, contemplate, desire, expect, foresee, hang in, hold, pray, presume, suppose, suspect, sweat, trust, wish

hopeful *adjective.* **1** assured, buoyant, calm, confident, content, eager, enthusiastic, expectant, expecting, faithful, hoping, lighthearted, reassured, rosy, satisfied, serene, trustful, unflagging **2** arousing, auspicious, cheering, expeditious, fine, fit, good, heartening, helpful, inspiring, lucky, providential, reasonable, rosy, rousing, stirring, sunny, timely

hopeless *adjective.* bad, cynical, despairing, forlorn, futile, gone, helpless, impossible, incurable, irredeemable, irreparable, irreversible, irrevocable, lost, sinister, unfortunate, useless, woebegone

horrible *adjective.* appalling, cruel, disagreeable, dreadful, eerie, fairy, ghastly, grim, gruesome, horrid, loathsome, lurid, nasty, offensive, revolting, shocking, terrifying, unkind

horror *noun.* alarm, antipathy, apprehension, aversion, awe, consternation, detestation, dislike, dismay, dread, fright, hate, hatred, loathing, monstrosity, repugnance, revulsion, terror

hostile *adjective.* alien, belligerent, chill, cold, competitive, dour, hateful, inhospitable, malevolent, malicious, nasty, ornery, rancorous, sour, unfavorable, unfriendly, unkind, virulent

hot *adjective.* **1** ardent, blazing, fevered, fiery, flaming, heated, incandescent, piping, scalding, sizzling, smoking, steaming, sweltering, torrid, tropic, tropical, warm, white **2** animated, ardent, distracted, eager, enthusiastic, excited, fervent, fierce, fiery, impassioned, impetuous, inflamed, intense, lustful, raging, stormy, vehement, violent **3** approved, cool, dandy, favored, fresh, glorious, groovy, in demand, keen, latest, marvelous, neat, new, nifty, peachy, popular, recent, super

hotel *noun.* auberge, caravansary, dump, fleabag, flop box, hospice, hostel, house, inn, lodging, motel, motor inn, resort, roadhouse, rooming house, scratch crib, spa, tavern

house *noun.* abode, apartment, box, cave, den, digs, domicile, dwelling, edifice, home, joint, layout, mansion, roost, setup, shack, shanty, turf

huge *adjective.* bulky, colossal, enormous, extensive, giant, magnificent, mammoth, massive, mighty, monstrous, monumental, mountainous, oversize, prodigious, titanic, tremendous, vast, walloping

hull *noun.* bark, body, case, casing, cast, covering, frame, framework, husk, mold, peel, peeling, pod, rind, shell, shuck, skin, structure

human *adjective.* animal, anthropological, anthropomorphic, biped, bipedal, civilized, creatural, fallible, forgivable, hominid, hominine, humanistic, individual, manmade, mortal, of man, personal, vulnerable

human *noun.* being, biped, body, character, child, creature, Homo sapiens, human being, individual, life, mortal, naked ape, party, person, personage, soul, wight, woman

humble *adjective.* **1** blushing, content, courteous, demure, gentle, hesitant, modest, obsequious, respectful, retiring, sedate, servile, shy, simple, submissive, subservient, tentative, withdrawn **2** base, common, contemptible, insignificant, meager, menial, miserable, modest, petty, pitiful, rough, severe, simple, small, underprivileged, unfit, unimportant, wretched

humble *verb.* break, chagrin, chasten, confuse, crush, degrade, deny, discredit, disgrace, hide, lower, overcome, reduce, silence, sink, squash, subdue, upset

humidity *noun.* damp, dampness, dankness, dew, dewiness, evaporation, heaviness, liquidity, moistness, moisture, sogginess, steam, sweatiness, swelter, thickness, vaporization, wet, wetness

humor *noun.* **1** amusement, badinage, banter, clowning, fun, gag, gaiety, happiness, jest, jesting, joke, joking, kidding, levity, lightness, raillery, salt, wit **2** bee, bent, bias, character, complexion, fancy, makeup, mind, notion, personality, quirk, spirits, strain, temper, temperament, tone, vein, whim

humorous *adjective.* amusing, camp, comic, entertaining, facetious, hilarious, jocose, jocular, laughable, ludicrous, merry, playful, pleasant, priceless, ribald, screaming, whimsical, witty

hunger *noun.* ache, craving, desire, emptiness, famine, famishment, greed, itch, longing, lust, mania, panting, starvation, vacancy, void, want, yearning, yen

hungry *adjective.* avid, carnivorous, covetous, craving, desirous, eager, empty, famished, famishing, greedy, hollow, insatiate, keen, ravenous, starved, starving, unfilled, yearning

hunt *noun.* coursing, game, hunting, inquest, inquisition, investigation, probe, prosecution, prying, pursuing, quest, race, raid, seeking, sifting, snooping, study, tracing

hunt *verb.* **1** capture, course, dog, drag, fish, follow, hawk, heel, hound, kill, press, pursue, ride, shadow, shoot, snare, start, trail **2** drag, examine, forage, grope, inquire, investigate, look, probe, prowl, quest, question, ransack, run down, scour, seek, trace, trail, winnow

hurried *adjective.* abrupt, breakneck, brief, cursory, fast, hasty, headlong, hectic, impetuous, perfunctory, precipitate, quick, rushing, short, speedy, sudden, superficial, swift

hurry *noun.* bustle, celerity, commotion, dash, dispatch, drive, expedition, expeditiousness, flurry, haste, push, quickness, rush, rustle, scurry, speediness, swiftness, urgency

hurry *verb.* accelerate, barrel, bullet, bustle, fly, fog, goad, haste, move, nip, quicken, race, rocket, smoke, speed, speed up, tool, urge

hurt *adjective.* aching, bruised, burned, crushed, disturbed, mutilated, nicked, offended, pained, resentful, scarred, scraped, screwed up, sore, struck, tender, tortured, wounded

hurt *noun.* ache, bruise, chop, detriment, disadvantage, distress, gash, harm, loss, mark, mischief, misfortune, nick, outrage, pain, sore, soreness, wound

hurt *verb.* **1** abuse, bite, cramp, flail, harm, impair, kick, lacerate, maltreat, pierce, prick, slap, slug, squeeze, sting, torment, trouble, whip **2** abuse, annoy, burn, chafe, distress, faze, martyr, pain, prejudice, punish, put out, sting, torment, torture, try, upset, wound, zing

husband *noun.* benedict, bridegroom, buffalo, consort, cuckold, groom, head, helpmate, hubby, man, mate, mister, monogamist, monogynist, old man, other half, polygamist, spouse

hut *noun.* box, bungalow, cabana, cabin, camp, cottage, crib, den, dugout, dump, hovel, lodge, pigeonhole, refuge, shack, shanty, shed, shelter

hymn *noun.* canticle, carol, chant, choral, chorale, descant, ditty, evensong, hosanna, laud, lay, lied, litany, ode, oratorio, paean, psalm, shout

hypothesis *noun.* antecedent, axiom, conclusion, deduction, demonstration, derivation, foundation, ground, layout, plan, presupposition, proposition, reason, scheme, speculation, suggestion, system, theorem

hypothetical *adjective.* academic, casual, concocted, contingent, debatable, doubtful, imaginary, indefinite, indeterminate, postulated, presupposed, pretending, questionable, speculative, stochastic, supposed, uncertain, vague

hysterical *adjective.* agitated, blazing, convulsive, crazed, fiery, frenzied, fuming, impetuous, maddened, nervous, passionate, possessed, raging, rampant, turbulent, uncontrollable, vehement, wild

I

ice *noun.* chunk, clamper, crystal, diamonds, dry ice, floe, glacier, glare crust, glaze, glitter, hail, hailstone, ice cube, iceberg, icicle, permafrost, sleet

icy *adjective.* arctic, biting, bitter, chill, chilling, chilly, cold, freezing, frigid, frosty, glaring, iced, polar, raw, refrigerated, shivering, shivery, slippery

idea *noun.* abstraction, conclusion, conviction, design, form, hint, impression, intention, judgment, meaning, objective, perception, plan, reason, scheme, solution, suggestion, view

ideal *adjective.* **1** absolute, archetypal, classic, classical, complete, consummate, excellent, exemplary, fitting, flawless, indefectible, model, optimal, paradigmatic, perfect, prototypical, representative, supreme, very **2** abstract, dreamlike, extravagant, fanciful, fictitious, hypothetical, imaginary, impractical, intellectual, mental, mercurial, quixotic, theoretical, transcendent, transcendental, unattainable, unearthly, unreal

ideal *noun.* archetype, criterion, epitome, example, exemplar, goal, jewel, last word, mirror, nonesuch, nonpareil, paradigm, paragon, pattern, perfection, phoenix, prototype, standard

identical *adjective.* corresponding, double, duplicate, equal, equivalent, exact, identic, indistinguishable, interchangeable, like, look-alike, matching, same, same difference, tantamount, twin, very, very same

identification *noun.* assimilation, badge, bracelet, classifying, credentials, description, dog tag, establishment, ID, ID bracelet, identification bracelet, identity bracelet, naming, papers, passport, recognition, tag, testimony

identify *verb.* card, catalog, classify, describe, determinate, diagnose, establish, find, finger, name, peg, pinpoint, place, recognize, separate, spot, tab, tag

identity *noun.* **1** character, circumstances, coherence, distinctiveness, existence, identification, integrity, name, oneness, parentage, particularity, personality, self, selfness, singleness, singularity, status, uniqueness **2** accord, agreement, congruence, correspondence, empathy, equality, equivalence, likeness, oneness, rapport, resemblance, sameness, selfsameness, semblance, similitude, unanimity, uniformity, unity

idiom *noun.* argot, colloquialism, dialect, expression, jargon, jive, language, lingo, parlance, phrase, provincialism, style, talk, tongue, usage, vernacular, weasel words, word

idle *adjective.* **1** barren, deserted, down, dusty, inactive, inert, jobless, motionless, redundant, resting, rusty, sleepy, stationary, still, unemployed, untouched, vacant, void **2** abortive, empty, frivolous, fruitless, futile, groundless, hollow, insignificant, irrelevant, pointless, rambling, superficial, unnecessary, unproductive, unsuccessful, useless, vain, worthless

idol *noun.* beloved, dad, darling, dear, deity, desire, favorite, fetish, god, goddess, Head Knock, hero, image, inamorata, pagan symbol, pet, pin-up, true-love

ignorance *noun.* benightedness, bewilderment, blindness, crudeness, disregard, dumbness, fog, greenness, half-knowledge, incapacity, incomprehension, innocence, insensitivity, oblivion, shallowness, simplicity, unawareness, vagueness

ignorant *adjective.* apprenticed, benighted, dense, green, illiterate, inexperienced, innocent, mindless, naive, oblivious, shallow, thick, unconscious, uneducated, uninitiated, unmindful, untrained, unwitting

ignore *verb.* avoid, blink, cut, dial out, discount, disdain, evade, fail, forget, high hat, ice, neglect, omit, overlook, pooh-pooh, reject, scorn, slight

ill *adjective.* **1** afflicted, ailing, bum, diseased, down, green, indisposed, infirm, peaked, poorly, punk, ratty, rocky, rotten, run down, runs, unhealthy, upchucking **2** damaging, foul, harmful, hateful, hostile, iniquitous, injurious, malevolent, malicious, ominous, ruinous, sinister, unfavorable, unfortunate, unfriendly, unkind,unwholesome, wicked

ill *noun.* abuse, affection, affliction, ailment, complaint, depravity, destruction, disease, harm, illness, injury, malaise, mischief, misery, sickness, syndrome, trouble, unpleasantness

illegal *adjective.* banned, contraband, crooked, extralegal, felonious, forbidden, heavy, irregular, lawless, outlawed, shady, smuggled, unconstitutional, unlawful, unlicensed, unwarranted, violating, wrongful

illiterate *adjective.* benighted, catachrestic, dumb, ignorant, inerudite, know-nothing, solecistic, uncultured, uneducated, unenlightened, ungrammatical, uninstructed, unlearned, unlettered, unread, unschooled, untaught, untutored

illness *noun.* affliction, ailing, ailment, attack, bug, complaint, confinement, convalescence, disability, disorder, dose, fit, indisposition, infirmity, malady, malaise, seizure, sickness

illusion *noun.* apparition, bubble, chimera, deception, delusion, error, fallacy, fancy, fantasy, ghost, image, invention, misconception, mockery, myth, rainbow, seeming, semblance

illustrate *verb.* clarify, clear, embody, exhibit, expose, illuminate, imitate, instance, interpret, lay out, manifest, mark, mirror, portray, proclaim, represent, spotlight, typify

illustration *noun.* adornment, artwork, cartoon, decoration, depiction, design, engraving, etching, figure, halftone, image, line drawing, painting, photo, picture, plate, sketch, vignette

image *noun.* copy, counterpart, double, drawing, facsimile, figure, form, icon, idol, illustration, likeness, match, model, photograph, reflection, replica, reproduction, spit, statue

imaginary *adjective.* apocryphal, deceptive, dreamlike, dreamy, fabulous, fancied, fanciful, fantastic, fictional, illusive, imaginative, mythological, nonexistent, quixotic, shadowy, spectral, supposed, unreal

imagination *noun.* artistry, awareness, creation, enterprise, fancy, illusion, image, imagery, ingenuity, insight, invention, realization, thought, unreality, verve, vision, visualization, wit

imaginative *adjective.* artistic, dreamy, enterprising, extravagant, fanciful, fantastic, fertile, fictive, flaky, ingenious, inventive, offbeat, productive, quixotic, romantic, utopian, vivid, whimsical

imagine *verb.* **1** create, devise, dream, fancy, feature, figure, form, frame, image, make up, nurture, perceive, plan, realize, scheme, spark, vision, visualize **2** apprehend, believe, conjecture, deduce, deem, expect, fancy, gather, guess, infer, presume, realize, reckon, suppose, surmise, suspect, think, understand

imitation *noun.* counterpart, duplication, fake, forgery, impression, match, matching, mockery, parallel, paralleling, parroting, reflection, replica, representing, reproduction, semblance, substitution, takeoff

immediate *adjective.* actual, at once, critical, current, existing, extant, first, hair-trigger, instant, live, next, now, on hand, paramount, present, pressing, prompt, urgent

immediately *adverb.* away, directly, forthwith, instantaneously, instantly, now, promptly, pronto, rapidly, right now, shortly, soon, straight away, thereupon, this instant, unhesitatingly, urgently, without delay

immense *adjective.* colossal, endless, enormous, eternal, extensive, giant, gross, limitless, mammoth, massive, mighty, monstrous, monumental, prodigious, super, titanic, tremendous, vast

impact *noun.* bounce, brunt, buffet, concussion, crunch, crush, kick, knock, percussion, pound, ram, rap, shake, shock, slap, smash, strike, thump

impartial *adjective.* candid, detached, disinterested, dispassionate, equal, equitable, even-steven, fair-minded, impersonal, just, neutral, nondiscriminatory, nonpartisan, objective, open-minded, unbiased, uncolored, without favor

impassioned *adjective.* animated, blazing, deep, fervent, fierce, fiery, flaming, heated, inflamed, passionate, powerful, profound, rousing, sentimental, stirring, stoned, vehement, warm

impatience *noun.* agitation, anger, ants, anxiety, avidity, disquietude, eagerness, excitement, haste, intolerance, irritability, nervousness, restlessness, shortness, suspense, uneasiness, vehemence, violence

impatient *adjective.* abrupt, anxious, ardent, avid, chafing, curt, demanding, eager, edgy, hasty, impetuous, keen, ripe, snappy, straining, sudden, vehement, violent

imperative *adjective.* **1** acute, burning, clamorous, compulsory, critical, crucial, crying, essential, immediate, important, indispensable, inescapable, insistent, instant, obligatory, pressing, urgent, vital **2** aggressive, autocratic, bidding, commanding, dictatorial, dominant, domineering, harsh, imperial, imperious, lordly, magisterial, masterful, ordering, overbearing, peremptory, powerful, stern

impersonal *adjective.* abstract, candid, cold, colorless, cool, detached, disinterested, fair, formal, impartial, indifferent, inhuman, neutral, nondiscriminatory, objective, remote, straight, uncolored

implication *noun.* association, assumption, conclusion, connection, entanglement, guess, hint, hypothesis, indication, inference, innuendo, involvement, link, meaning, presumption, reference, significance, union

implicit *adjective.* absolute, accurate, certain, constant, constructive, contained, entire, firm, fixed, implied, inferential, inferred, latent, practical, unqualified, unshakable, unspoken, virtual

implied *adjective.* constructive, implicit, inferential, inferred, involved, latent, lurking, meant, parallel, perceptible, potential, signified, suggested, symbolized, understood, unsaid, unspoken, unuttered

imply *verb.* betoken, connote, denote, designate, entail, evidence, hint, import, include, intend, intimate, involve, mean, mention, presuppose, refer, signify, suggest

import *noun.* **1** bearing, construction, drift, gist, heart, implication, intention, interpretation, meat, message, point, purport, score, sense, significance, stuff, thrust, understanding **2** consequence, design, emphasis, importance, intent, magnitude, moment, momentousness, object, objective, pith, purpose, signification, stress, substance, value, weight, worth

importance *noun.* **1** accent, attention, bearing, concern, distinction, effect, gist, gravity, influence, interest, moment, precedence, preponderance, purport, relevance, sense, substance, usefulness **2** consequence, conspicuousness, distinction, eminence, esteem, fame, greatness, influence, mark, note, noteworthiness, prominence, rank, reputation, salience, status, usefulness, worth

important *adjective.* **1** chief, considerable, conspicuous, exceptional, extensive, foremost, grave, heavy, large, material, meaningful, necessary, relevant, salient, signal, significant, smash, something **2** aristocratic, distinctive, distinguished, esteemed, foremost, heavy, honored, incomparable, majestic, notable, noteworthy, powerful, remarkable, seminal, signal, solid, superior, talented

impose *verb.* appoint, burden, command, compel, decree, demand, enforce, exact, inflict, institute, intrude, levy, oblige, put, set, visit, wish, wreck

impossible *adjective.* absurd, beyond, futile, impassable, impervious, impracticable, inaccessible, inconceivable, insurmountable, irreparable, preposterous, unachievable, unattainable, unimaginable, unrecoverable, unthinkable, unworkable, useless

impression *noun.* **1** apprehension, concept, conjecture, conviction, fancy, hunch, idea, image, memory, opinion, perception, recollection, sensation, sense, suspicion, theory, thought, view **2** brand, cast, dent, depression, fingerprint, form, hollow, impress, imprint, mark, matrix, mold, outline, print, sign, stamp, trace, vestige

impressive *adjective.* arresting, consequential, deep, eloquent, exciting, important, inspiring, lavish, massive, monumental, profound, remarkable, rousing, stately, stirring, striking, sumptuous, touching

improve *verb.* augment, better, boost, edit, enhance, lift, look up, pick up, polish, progress, rally, recover, reform, revise, rise, take off, update, upgrade

improvement *noun.* amendment, change, civilization, correction, cultivation, elevation, enrichment, gain, preferment, progress, promotion, rally, recovery, renovation, revision, rise, upgrade, upswing

impulse *noun.* **1** appeal, bent, fancy, flash, goad, hunch, inclination, influence, instinct, lash, lust, motive, passion, resolve, thought, urge, whim, wish **2** beat, catalyst, drive, impetus, lash, momentum, movement, pressure, propulsion, pulsation, pulse, push, shock, shove, stimulus, surge, thrust, vibration

inability *noun.* disability, disqualification, failure, impotence, inadequacy, inaptitude, incapability, incapacity, incompetence, ineffectiveness, inefficiency, ineptitude, ineptness, lack, necessity, powerlessness, unfitness, weakness

inadequate *adjective.* bare, barren, faulty, feeble, imperfect, impotent, inapt, incapable, incompetent, lame, lemon, meager, parsimonious, poor, scarce, small, unproductive, weak

incapable *adjective.* disqualified, feeble, impotent, incompetent, ineffective, ineligible, inept, inexperienced, inexpert, muff, poor, powerless, turkey, unable, unfit, unqualified, unskilled, weak

incentive *noun.* bait, consideration, determinant, encouragement, excuse, goad, ground, impetus, impulse, influence, motive, persuasion, provocation, reason, stimulus, temptation, urge, whip

inclination *noun*. **1** affection, aptitude, aptness, attachment, attraction, fondness, groove, impulse, liking, movement, penchant, persuasion, preference, susceptibility, taste, trend, will, wish **2** bank, bend, bevel, bowing, cant, declivity, deviation, direction, downgrade, grade, hill, incline, lean, list, pitch, ramp, slant, tilt

include *verb*. admit, bear, build, build in, carry, combine, comprise, constitute, count, cover, embody, encircle, encompass, enter, have, insert, number, work in

income *noun*. assets, commission, compensation, drawings, earnings, gains, gate, handle, harvest, interest, net, pay, proceeds, royalty, salary, take, takings, velvet

incomplete *adjective*. abridged, crude, defective, deficient, fractional, fragmentary, garbled, immature, imperfect, incoherent, lacking, meager, part, partial, rough, rudimentary, undeveloped, wanting

increase *noun*. access, aggrandizement, boost, breakthrough, burgeoning, enlargement, hike, incorporation, inflation, intensification, multiplication, rise, spread, surge, upgrade, upsurge, upturn, wax

increase *verb*. annex, build up, deepen, dilate, double, enhance, enlarge, exaggerate, extend, further, grow, mount, progress, prolong, reinforce, rise, supplement, widen

incredible *adjective*. absurd, farfetched, flimsy, impossible, improbable, inconceivable, outlandish, preposterous, questionable, suspect, thick, thin, unbelievable, unconvincing, unimaginable, untenable, unthinkable, weak

indebted *adjective*. accountable, answerable for, appreciative, beholden, bound, chargeable, grateful, hooked, in debt, in hock, into, liable, obligated, obliged, owe, owing, responsible, thankful

indefinite *adjective*. confused, doubtful, dubious, imprecise, indistinct, intangible, loose, obscure, shadowy, uncertain, unclear, undefined, undependable, undetermined, unsettled, unsure, vague, wide

independent *adjective*. absolute, autonomous, individualistic, liberated, nonaligned, nonpartisan, self-contained, self-determining, self-governing, self-reliant, self-ruling, separate, separated, sovereign, unaided, unconnected, uncontrolled, unregimented

index *noun*. basis, clue, evidence, formula, guide, indication, indicator, mark, model, needle, pointer, ratio, rule, sign, significant, symbol, symptom, token

indicate *verb*. argue, bespeak, display, express, finger, hint, illustrate, imply, manifest, mark, name, peg, pinpoint, sign, signal, signify, suggest, testify

indication *noun*. clue, cue, expression, gesture, hint, implication, index, mark, omen, pledge, sign, signal, significant, suggestion, trace, warning, wind, wink

indifference *noun*. apathy, callousness, carelessness, coldness, coolness, detachment, disdain, disinterest, disregard, equity, immunity, impartiality, insouciance, lethargy, objectivity, stoicism, torpor, unconcern

indifferent *adjective*. apathetic, callous, cold, distant, haughty, heartless, impervious, inattentive, listless, neutral, nonpartisan, objective, scornful, supercilious, superior, unconcerned, unemotional, unmoved

indignant *adjective*. annoyed, bent, bugged, disgruntled, displeased, exasperated, fuming, heated, incensed, irate, livid, provoked, resentful, scornful, sore, steamed, upset, wrathful

indignation *noun*. boiling point, danger, displeasure, exasperation, fury, huff, ire, mad, miff, pique, rage, resentment, rise, scorn, slow burn, sore, stew, wrath

indirect *adjective*. ancillary, circular, contingent, crooked, devious, erratic, implied, meandering, obscure, rambling, secondary, serpentine, sinister, sneaking, sneaky, subsidiary, unintended, vagrant

individual *adjective*. alone, characteristic, diagnostic, discrete, distinct, express, indivisible, odd, own, peculiar, proper, several, single, sole, solitary, specific, unique, unusual

individual *noun.* being, body, cat, child, entity, guy, man, material, matter, mortal, number, party, self, somebody, something, substance, unit, woman

induce *verb.* activate, breed, bulldoze, coax, convince, draw, draw in, effect, influence, motivate, move, occasion, persuade, press, produce, prompt, squeeze, urge

indulge *verb.* allow, baby, cater, delight, entertain, favor, foster, gratify, humor, mollycoddle, oblige, pamper, pet, please, satiate, satisfy, spoil, yield

indulgence *noun.* allowance, attention, courtesy, endurance, excess, favor, favoring, fondness, good will, gratifying, hedonism, intemperance, petting, placating, pleasing, spoiling, tolerance, understand

industry *noun.* **1** bunch, business, commerce, corporation, crew, crowd, gang, management, manufactory, megacorp, mob, monopoly, multinational, outfit, production, ring, trade, traffic **2** activity, application, assiduity, attention, care, determination, diligence, effort, energy, enterprise, labor, pains, patience, perseverance, persistence, toil, vigor, zeal

inevitable *adjective.* binding, cold, decided, decreed, determined, doomed, fated, fateful, fixed, imminent, ineluctable, inescapable, irresistible, irrevocable, pat, settled, sure, unalterable

infant *adjective.* baby, childish, childlike, developing, emergent, green, growing, immature, infantile, juvenile, kid, naive, nascent, newborn, tender, unripe, weak, youthful

infectious *adjective.* communicable, contagious, contaminating, corrupting, diseased, epidemic, infective, miasmic, noxious, pestilent, poisoning, polluting, spreading, taking, toxic, transferable, transmittable, virulent

infinite *adjective.* absolute, bottomless, boundless, enduring, enormous, eternal, everlasting, immeasurable, immense, incalculable, incessant, perpetual, supreme, total, uncounted, untold, vast, wide

influence *noun.* clout, drag, grease, importance, imprint, leadership, mark, moment, monopoly, notoriety, power, prerogative, pressure, prominence, pull, ropes, rule, string

influence *verb.* affect, arouse, bribe, change, channel, compel, count, form, impress, incline, induce, mold, move, prompt, regulate, rule, train, urge

influential *adjective.* controlling, dominant, governing, guiding, important, impressive, inspiring, instrumental, leading, meaningful, momentous, name, persuasive, significant, strong, substantial, telling, touching

informal *adjective.* breezy, colloquial, congenial, democratic, easygoing, everyday, folksy, frank, inconspicuous, loose, mixed, motley, natural, open, relaxed, simple, spontaneous, unofficial

information *noun.* ammo, break, confidence, cue, enlightenment, erudition, hash, illumination, knowledge, leak, lore, material, notice, pipeline, propaganda, tidings, tip, wisdom

informed *adjective.* abreast, acquainted, briefed, enlightened, erudite, expert, familiar, hip, into, knowledgeable, learned, posted, primed, reliable, savvy, up, versed, with in

ingenious *adjective.* able, artistic, bright, canny, crafty, creative, cunning, fertile, gifted, imaginative, intelligent, inventive, ready, resourceful, shrewd, skillful, sly, subtle

inherent *adjective.* characteristic, congenital, constitutional, distinctive, fixed, fundamental, immanent, implicit, inborn, indigenous, individual, inner, integral, internal, intrinsic, inward, native, unalienable

inhibit *verb.* arrest, avert, bar, bit, cramp, curb, discourage, enjoin, forbid, hold in, obstruct, prevent, prohibit, repress, suppress, taboo, ward, withhold

initial *adjective.* antecedent, basic, earliest, early, first, foremost, fundamental, germinal, inaugural, incipient, infant, introductory, leading, nascent, opening, pioneer, primary, virgin

initiative *noun.* action, ambition, drive,

dynamism, energy, enterprise, enthusiasm, gumption, inventiveness, leadership, originality, punch, push, resource, resourcefulness, spunk, steam, vigor

injury *noun.* abuse, bad, bite, bruise, chop, cramp, detriment, distress, fracture, harm, lesion, loss, mischief, misery, shock, sore, sting, trauma

injustice *noun.* abuse, damage, discrimination, encroachment, favoritism, grievance, inequality, infraction, infringement, mischief, negligence, offense, outrage, prejudice, transgression, violation, wrong, wrongdoing

inn *noun.* auberge, B and B, bed and breakfast, flophouse, hospice, hostel, hostelry, hotel, last house, lodge, motel, public house, resort, roadhouse, saloon, scratch crib, stopping house, tavern

inner *adjective.* central, concealed, emotional, essential, focal, gut, individual, innate, internal, intrinsic, intuitive, inward, private, psychological, secret, spiritual, subconscious, visceral

innocence *noun.* chastity, credulousness, forthrightness, frankness, freshness, gullibility, harmlessness, ignorance, inexperience, innoxiousness, lack, plainness, purity, simplicity, sincerity, unawareness, virginity, virtue

innocent *adjective.* **1** clean, clear, faultless, good, guiltless, honest, immaculate, impeccable, legal, pristine, righteous, safe, sinless, spotless, stainless, unblemished, uncorrupt, unimpeachable, upright, virgin, virtuous **2** artless, childlike, credulous, frank, green, guileless, gullible, ignorant, inexperienced, open, raw, safe, simple, soft, square, unacquainted, unmalicious, youthful

inquiry *noun.* analysis, audit, disquisition, examination, inquest, inquisition, investigation, poll, probe, probing, pursuit, quest, questioning, request, scrutiny, search, study, third

insane *adjective.* crazed, cuckoo, demented, deranged, fatuous, frenzied, gone, irrational, lunatic, nuts, paranoid, raging, schizophrenic, stupid, touched, unglued, unsettled, wild

insert *verb.* admit, drag in, enter, implant, include, inject, inlay, interlope, introduce, intrude, lug in, place, root, set, squeeze in, stick, work in, worm in

inside *noun.* belly, bowels, breast, center, contents, gut, guts, heart, innards, inner portion, innermost, interior, inward, lining, soul, stuffing, within, womb

insight *noun.* acumen, awareness, click, comprehension, discernment, divination, drift, intuition, judgment, observation, penetration, perception, sagacity, savvy, understanding, vision, wavelength, wisdom

insist *verb.* assert, be firm, contend, demand, expect, hold, importune, maintain, order, persist, press, reiterate, repeat, request, require, swear, urge, vow

insistent *adjective.* assertive, clamorous, crying, dire, dogged, emphatic, forceful, imperative, imperious, incessant, obstinate, peremptory, persistent, pressing, resolute, resounding, unrelenting, urgent

inspect *verb.* audit, case, catechize, flash, lamp, notice, observe, probe, review, scope, scout, search, study, superintend, supervise, vet, view, watch

inspection *noun.* analysis, flash, inquest, inquisition, inventory, investigation, maneuvers, pageant, probe, read, research, review, scan, scrutiny, search, supervision, surveillance, view

inspiration *noun.* approach, arousal, awakening, elevation, encouragement, enthusiasm, fancy, hunch, illumination, impulse, incentive, influence, insight, motive, muse, stimulus, thought, vision

install *verb.* build in, establish, fix, furnish, inaugurate, induct, institute, introduce, invest, lay, line, lodge, place, plant, position, put in, settle, station

instance *noun.* detail, example, exemplification, ground, illustration, item, occasion, occurrence, particular, precedent, proof, reason, representative, sample, sampling, situation, specimen, time

instant *adjective.* burning, contemporary, crying, current, dire, direct, existent, extant, fast, hair-trigger, imperative, insistent, instantaneous, present, pressing, prompt, quick, urgent

instant *noun.* breath, breathing, crack, flash, jiffy, minute, mo, occasion, point, sec, second, shake, tick, time, twinkle, twinkling, while, wink

instantly *adverb.* at once, away, directly, double time, first off, forthwith, immediately, instantaneously, instanter, like now, now, PDQ, pronto, right, right away, spontaneously, straight away, without delay

instinct *noun.* aptitude, faculty, feeling, gift, hang, hunch, idea, impulse, inclination, intuition, knack, predisposition, savvy, sense, sentiment, talent, tendency, urge

institute *noun.* custom, decree, doctrine, edit, establishment, fixture, habit, maxim, ordinance, practice, precedent, precept, regulation, rite, ritual, rule, statute, tradition

institute *verb.* appoint, break in, constitute, create, fix, found, initiate, install, invest, kick off, launch, make up, open, pioneer, rev, set up, settle, start

institution *noun.* academy, association, asylum, business, clinic, college, establishment, fixture, foundation, guild, institute, institution, orphanage, school, seminar, seminary, society, system

instruction *noun.* apprenticeship, chalk talk, coaching, direction, discipline, drilling, edification, enlightenment, grounding, guidance, information, lesson, preparation, schooling, skull session, teaching, training, tuition

instructor *noun.* adviser, babysitter, coach, demonstrator, guide, lecturer, master, mentor, pedagogue, preceptor, prof, professor, schoolmaster, slave driver, teach, teacher, trainer, tutor

instrument *noun.* apparatus, appliance, contraption, contrivance, device, doodad, equipment, gadget, gear, implement, machine, machinery, mechanism, paraphernalia, tackle, thingamabob, thingamajig, utensil

intact *adjective.* complete, entire, flawless, maiden, perfect, sound, together, unblemished, unbroken, uncut, undeflowered, unhurt, unimpaired, uninjured, unscathed, untouched, virgin, whole

intellectual *adjective.* bookish, cerebral, conscious, creative, highbrow, intellective, intelligent, inventive, learned, mental, psychic, psychological, rational, scholarly, studious, subjective, thoughtful, unconscious

intellectual *noun.* academic, beard, bluestocking, brain, conehead, doctor, egghead, genius, highbrow, intelligentsia, philosopher, pointy-head, scholar, skull, thinker, whiz, wig, wizard

intelligence *noun.* **1** agility, alertness, aptitude, brilliance, cleverness, comprehension, discernment, intellect, judgment, luminosity, penetration, perception, precocity, reason, sense, skill, subtlety, wit *noun.* **2** advice, clue, data, dirt, disclosure, facts, findings, knowledge, leak, lowdown, news, notice, notification, picture, report, rumor, tidings, word

intelligent *adjective.* able, acute, alert, alive, apt, comprehending, deep, discerning, exceptional, ingenious, keen, knowledgeable, profound, rational, reasonable, responsible, sharp, wise

intend *verb.* aim, appoint, contemplate, decree, design, devote, endeavor, expect, plan, plot, propose, resolve, scheme, signify, spell, strive, think, try

Intended *adjective.* advised, affianced, aforethought, contracted, designed, destined, expected, future, intentional, meant, pinned, planned, prearranged, predetermined, proposed, set, setup, steady

intense *adjective.* agonizing, biting, concentrated, deep, exaggerated, excessive, exquisite, fanatical, fierce, heightened, intensified, intensive, keen, profound, sharp, strained, strong, vehement

intensity *noun.* ardor, concentration, emotion, energy, excess, extreme, extremity, ferment, ferocity, fervor, forcefulness, magnitude, might, power, strength, vehemence, vigor, violence

intent *adjective.* alert, attentive, bound, committed, concentrated, concentrating, decided, deep, eager, engrossed, firm, fixed, occupied, preoccupied, resolute, set, settled, steady

intent *noun.* aim, design, drift, end, goal, hope, idea, intention, meaning, objective, plan, purport, scheme, sense, target, volition, will, wish

intercourse *noun.* **1** association, commerce, communion, connection, contact, converse, correspondence, dealings, give-and-take, interchange, intercommunication, mesh, team play, teamwork, trade, traffic, transactions, truck **2** action, carnal knowledge, coition, coitus, congress, copulation, fooling around, fornication, intimacy, relations, sex, sexual relations

interest *noun.* **1** affection, bag, case, concern, curiosity, enthusiasm, hobby, importance, into, lookout, matter, moment, notice, racket, recreation, regard, relevance, sympathy **2** bonus, claim, commitment, discount, drag, due, earnings, gain, influence, involvement, participation, percentage, piece, points, premium, right, stake, title

interest *verb.* affect, amuse, appeal, arouse, attract, concern, divert, engage, entertain, fascinate, grab, lure, move, pique, pull, snare, tempt, touch

interested *adjective.* affected, awakened, caught, concerned, engrossed, gone, impressed, intent, keen, lured, occupied, open, prejudiced, roused, stimulated, struck, taken, touched

interesting *adjective.* amusing, arresting, compelling, delightful, elegant, enchanting, enthralling, exceptional, fine, gripping, impressive, intriguing, inviting, magnetic, refreshing, stirring, suspicious, unusual

interfere *verb.* baffle, conflict, foil, frustrate, handicap, hold up, inconvenience, intercede, intermediate, intervene, intrude, jam, obstruct, prevent, suspend, tamper, trammel, trouble

interference *noun.* arrest, back-seat driving, background, barring, blocking, buckshot, checking, choking, clogging, conflict, interposition, intervention, intrusion, opposition, prying, resistance, retardation, tampering

interim *noun.* breach, break, breather, coffee break, cutoff, five, freeze, gap, hiatus, interlude, interregnum, interruption, meantime, meanwhile, pause, ten, time, time-out

interior *adjective.* central, domestic, endogenous, gut, home, inland, inner, inner space, innermost, internal, intimate, inward, private, remote, secret, visceral, within

interior *noun.* belly, bosom, center, contents, heart, heartland, inner parts, inside, intrinsicality, lining, marrow, midst, pith, pulp, soul, substance, upcountry, within

intermediate *adjective.* average, center, central, common, compromising, fair, halfway, indifferent, interposed, intervening, median, mediocre, medium, midway, moderate, neutral, standard, transitional

internal *adjective.* centralized, circumscribed, civic, constitutional, enclosed, gut, home, indigenous, innate, inner, intestine, intrinsic, inward, municipal, national, native, private, visceral

interpret *verb.* clarify, construe, depict, describe, gloss, illustrate, image, improvise, paraphrase, perform, portray, read, render, represent, take, translate, understand, view

interruption *noun.* abeyance, blackout, break, cessation, cutoff, delay, division, halt, hitch, interim, intermission, obstacle, rift, rupture, separation, shortstop, stoppage, suspension

interval *noun.* comma, delay, distance, interim, interlude, intermission, interregnum, interruption, meantime, opening, period, rest, season, spell, spurt, ten, time, wait

interview *noun.* account, audience, call, cattle call, communication, conference, consultation, conversation, dialogue, evaluation, examination, hearing, meeting, oral, parley, record, statement, talk

intimate *adjective.* **1** affectionate, bosom, close, confidential, cozy, dear, faithful, fond, loving, near, nearest, next, regular, roommates, snug, thick, warm, white **2** confidential, deep, elemental, essential, exhaustive, guarded, gut, inborn, innate, innermost, internal, intrinsic, privy, profound, secret, special, trusted, visceral

intimate *noun.* acquaintance, amigo, associate, bosom buddy, brother, buddy, chum, close friend, companion, comrade, confidant, confidante, familiar, family, lover, mate, pal, sister

intimate *verb.* affirm, announce, assert, connote, declare, expose, express, hint, impart, imply, infer, leak, profess, spring, state, vent, voice, warn

intricate *adjective.* baroque, Byzantine, complex, convoluted, daedal, difficult, elaborate, entangled, fancy, hard, involved, knotty, obscure, perplexing, rococo, sophisticated, tortuous, tricky

introduce *verb.* **1** acquaint, advance, announce, boot, broach, herald, kick off, knock down, moot, offer, open, precede, preface, propose, recommend, submit, suggest, usher **2** admit, commence, enter, establish, found, initiate, innovate, install, institute, invent, kick off, launch, organize, pioneer, plan, preface, set up, start **3** carry, enter, fill in, freight, import, include, inject, inlay, inlet, insert, inset, interpose, put in, send, ship, throw in, transport, work in

introduction *noun.* addition, awakening, baptism, commencement, debut, establishment, inauguration, initiation, insertion, installation, institution, interpolation, launch, lead, opening, preface, prelude, presentation

intuition *noun.* clairvoyance, discernment, divination, ESP, feeling, foreknowledge, funny feeling, hunch, innate knowledge, inspiration, instinct, nose, penetration, perception, perceptivity, premonition, presentiment, sixth sense

invalid *adjective.* bad, baseless, fallacious, false, ill-founded, illogical, inoperative, irrational, mad, not binding, null, unfounded, unreasonable, unscientific, unsound, untrue, void, wrong

invasion *noun.* aggression, assault, breach, encroachment, foray, forced entrance, incursion, infiltration, infraction, infringement, intrusion, offense, offensive, onslaught, overstepping, raid, transgression, violation

invent *verb.* **1** author, bear, coin, design, devise, discover, execute, fake, find, form, frame, imagine, improvise, make up, mint, plan, produce, turn out **2** concoct, conjure up, cook up, fake, falsify, feign, forge, lie, make believe, make up, misrepresent, misstate, pretend, prevaricate, simulate, tell untruth, trump up, vamp

invention *noun.* apparatus, creativeness, creativity, design, development, device, discovery, gadget, genius, imagination, ingenuity, innovation, inspiration, novelty, opus, original, originality, resourcefulness

inventory *noun.* account, backlog, catalogue, file, fund, index, itemization, list, record, reserve, reservoir, roll, roster, schedule, summary, supply, table, tabulation

investigate *verb.* buzz, case, consider, dig, explore, inquire, inspect, listen in, probe, pry, read, review, run down, scout, search, spy, study, tap

investigation *noun.* analysis, case, examination, gander, hustle, inquest, inquisition, observation, observing, pike, probe, probing, quest, review, scrutiny, search, study, surveying

investment *noun.* asset, financing, flyer, grease, hunch, interests, investing, loan, nut, piece, plunge, property, purchase, spec, speculation, stab, stake, transaction

invisible *adjective.* concealed, deceptive, disguised, ethereal, gaseous, ghostly, imperceptible, inconspicuous, intangible, masked, microscopic, obliterated, screened, supernatural, undisclosed, unreal, unseen, veiled

invitation *noun.* appeal, asking, attraction, bidding, compliments, dating, encouragement, paper, pass, pressure, proposition, provocation, reason, request, suggestion, summons, temptation, urge

invite *verb.* beg, command, court, draw, encourage, insist, issue, persuade, ply, press, provoke, request, solicit, suggest, summon, urge, welcome, woo

inviting *adjective.* agreeable, appealing, attractive, beguiling, captivating, charming, delightful, enticing, fascinating, intriguing, magnetic, open, persuasive, pleasing, tempting, warm, welcoming, winsome

involve *verb.* absorb, affect, associate, catch up, commit, comprise, compromise, concern, cover, draw in, imply, necessitate, number, presuppose, require, suggest, tangle, touch

involved *adjective.* affected, caught, concerned, embarrassed, embroiled, enmeshed, entangled, heavily into, hooked into, incriminated, interested, into, occupied, participating, really into, sucked into, taking part, tangled

iron *adjective.* adamant, cruel, dense, firm, heavy, immovable, implacable, indomitable, inexorable, inflexible, rigid, steel, steely, strong, stubborn, thick, touch, unyielding

ironic *adjective.* alert, biting, contradictory, cutting, cynical, exaggerated, incisive, ironical, keen, pungent, sardonic, satiric, satirical, scathing, scoffing, sharp, trenchant, wry

irony *noun.* banter, burlesque, contempt, criticism, derision, humor, incongruity, mockery, mordancy, paradox, raillery, repartee, reproach, ridicule, satire, taunt, twist, wit

irrational *adjective.* absurd, demented, disconnected, disjointed, fallacious, flaky, foolish, incoherent, insane, invalid, mindless, nonsensical, preposterous, silly, stupid, wacky, wild, wrong

irregular *adjective.* **1** capricious, casual, desultory, disconnected, erratic, fluctuating, fragmentary, indiscriminate, intermittent, purposeless, recurrent, shifting, uncertain, unmethodical, unreliable, unsettled, variable, weaving **2** anomalous, atypical, capricious, deviant, disorderly, divergent, exceptional, immoderate, odd, overt, peculiar, queer, strange, unique, unnatural, unofficial, unorthodox, unusual

irrelevant *adjective.* extraneous, foreign, garbage, immaterial, impertinent, inapplicable, inappropriate, inapt, inconsequential, insignificant, outside, pointless, remote, trivial, unapt, unconnected, unimportant, unrelated

irresistible *adjective.* beckoning, charming, enchanting, fascinating, glamorous, indomitable, ineluctable, inescapable, lovable, overpowering, overwhelming, powerful, scrumptious, sexy, stone, stunning, tempting, urgent

irresponsible *adjective.* capricious, carefree, fickle, giddy, immature, immoral, incautious, loose, rash, reckless, scatterbrained, shiftless, thoughtless, undependable, unpredictable, unreliable, unstable, wild

isolate *verb.* abstract, block off, confine, detach, disengage, divide, divorce, garrison, insulate, island, part, quarantine, remove, seclude, segregate, separate, sever, sunder

isolated *adjective.* alone, anomalous, apart, exceptional, lonesome, outlying, remote, retired, screened, segregated, single, solitary, special, stranded, unique, unrelated, unusual, withdrawn

issue *verb.* **1** allot, announce, assign, bring out, broadcast, circulate, consign, declare, deliver, dispatch, dispense, emit, publish, put out, release, send, send out, transmit **2** appear, arise, birth, emanate, emerge, exude, flow, ooze, originate, proceed, release, rise, send forth, spring, spurt, stem, vent, well

item *noun.* account, bit, bulletin, column, consideration, detail, dispatch, element, entry, feature, matter, notice, novelty, paragraph, part, piece, specific, story

J

jail *noun.* brig, bucket, can, cooler, coop, dungeon, freezer, joint, jug, keep, limbo, mill, pen, pound, reformatory, solitary, stir, tank

jail *verb.* book, cage, can, confine, constrain, cool, detain, hold, impound, imprison, jug, lock up, prison, quad, railroad, sentence, settle, slough

jam *verb.* bear, bind, clog, crush, halt, jostle, obstruct, pack, press, push, ram, squash, squeeze, stall, stick, stuff, tamp, throng

jar *noun.* basin, beaker, bottle, can, chalice, crock, cruet, decanter, ewer, flagon, flask, jug, pitcher, pot, urn, vase, vat, vessel

jar *verb.* **1** agitate, bounce, clash, crash, disturb, grate, jerk, jolt, offend, quake, rasp, rattle, shake, shock, slam, thump, wiggle, wobble **2** annoy, bicker, clash, contend, disaccord, disagree, discord, grate, grind, interfere, irk, mismatch, nettle, oppose, outrage, quarrel, shock, wrangle

job *noun.* **1** appointment, billet, business, career, engagement, faculty, function, line, niche, opening, operation, post, profession, racket, spot, stint, vocation, work **2** act, burden, business, commission, effort, enterprise, function, kick, matter, mission, obligation, operation, province, responsibility, role, stint, undertaking, work

join *verb.* **1** accompany, adhere, annex, assemble, attach, blend, cement, clip, coalesce, concrete, fuse, grapple, leash, mate, span, touch, wed, yoke **2** align, associate with, be in, come aboard, consort, cooperate, enlist, enroll, enter, follow, fraternize, go to, mingle with, pair with, plug into, side with, sign on, sign up **3** adjoin, border, bound, butt, communicate, conjoin, extend, fringe, hem, line, march, meet, neighbor, open into, parallel, reach, rim, skirt

joint *noun.* articulation, bend, bond, bracket, bridge, connection, coupling, crux, hinge, junction, knot, link, meeting, seam, swivel, tangency, tie, union

jointly *adverb.* accordingly, agreeably, alike, collectively, combined, concomitantly, concurrently, connectedly, cooperatively, harmoniously, in common, intimately, mutually, similarly, simultaneously, synchronically, together, unitedly

joke *noun.* escapade, frolic, gag, game, humor, jest, lark, mischief, parody, prank, pun, quirk, raillery, repartee, revel, sport, spree, yarn

joke *verb.* banter, deceive, frolic, fun, jest, jolly, mock, needle, pun, rag, revel, rib, ride, ridicule, roast, spoof, sport, tease

journal *noun.* account, annals, annual, calendar, daily, gazette, memento, memoir, minutes, monthly, newspaper, observation, organ, paper, periodical, review, statement, weekly

journalist *noun.* announcer, columnist, commentator, contributor, correspondent, editor, hack, ink slinger, news hen, newsman, newspaperman, pen pusher, publicist, reporter, scribe, scrivener, stringer, writer

journey *noun.* beat, campaign, circuit, constitutional, course, crossing, passage, pilgrimage, quest, range, roaming, round, route, stroll, tour, transit, travel, visit

journey *verb.* circuit, cruise, fare, fly, hop, jet, pass, proceed, process, ramble, range, repair, rove, safari, tour, traverse, trek, wander

joy *noun.* alleviation, animation, comfort, delectation, ecstasy, elation, exultation, felicity, fruition, gratification, humor, indulgence, merriment, refreshment, rejoicing, solace, transport, treasure

judge *noun.* arbiter, assessor, authority, bench, conciliator, court, critic, expert, inspector, interpreter, judiciary, justice, magistrate, marshal, moderator, quarterback, warden, wig

judge *verb.* adjudicate, appreciate, arbitrate, ascertain, assess, consider, criticize, decree, derive, draw, evaluate, find, put, rate, rule, sit, suppose, try

judgment *noun.* **1** apprehension, discernment,

discrimination, experience, incisiveness, intuition, knowledge, penetration, perception, prudence, range, reason, reasoning, sophistication, soundness, taste, wisdom, wit **2** analysis, appraisal, assaying, conclusion, contemplation, conviction, decree, determination, examination, inquest, inquisition, quest, regard, result, ruling, sifting, summary, view

judicial *adjective.* administrative, authoritative, constitutional, discriminating, distinguished, equitable, forensic, impartial, judgelike, judiciary, juridical, jurisdictional, lawful, official, pontifical, principled, regular, statutory

juice *noun.* abstract, alcohol, booze, distillation, drink, essence, extract, fluid, liquor, milk, nectar, oil, sap, sauce, secretion, serum, spirit, water

jump *noun.* bounce, bound, buck, canter, dance, drop, fall, hop, jerk, jolt, leaping, plunge, rise, shock, skip, start, twitch, upsurge

jump *verb.* bounce, bound, buck, canter, clear, drop, fall, hop, jerk, lop, lunge, rattle, shake, skip, surge, take, top, wobble

junction *noun.* alliance, attachment, combination, combine, conjugation, crossing, crossroads, interface, intersection, joining, joint, knee, meeting, miter, pivot, reunion, seam, union

jurisdiction *noun.* area, circuit, commission, dominion, inquisition, limits, orbit, power, prerogative, province, range, rule, scope, sphere, supervision, territory, turf, zone

just *adjective.* **1** aloof, decent, due, ethical, good, honest, impartial, nondiscriminatory, objective, right, righteous, rigid, scrupulous, strict, tried, true, uncolored, virtuous **2** cogent, correct, exact, faithful, good, justified, normal, precise, proper, regular, right, sound, strict, true, undistorted, veracious, veridical, well-founded **3** appropriate, apt, befitting, condign, deserved, due, felicitous, fit, fitting, happy, justified, legitimate, meet, merited, proper, reasonable, right, rightful

justice *noun.* appeal, charter, code, compensation, consideration, correction, credo, creed, decree, equity, integrity, justness, law, penalty, recompense, rectitude, right, rule

justification *noun.* absolution, account, advocacy, apologia, apology, argument, confirmation, exoneration, grounds, palliative, plea, pretext, rationalization, rebuttal, redemption, salvation, story, validation

justify *verb.* advocate, alibi, approve, assert, brief, claim, clear, crawl, defend, excuse, favor, maintain, pardon, plead, rationalize, rebut, uphold, validate

juvenile *adjective.* adolescent, blooming, boyish, budding, childlike, developing, girlish, green, growing, immature, infant, infantile, junior, teenage, tender, undeveloped, vernal, younger

K

keen *adjective.* **1** alert, animate, animated, anxious, ardent, avid, eager, ebullient, fervent, fierce, intense, intent, interested, lively, thirsty, vehement, vivacious, warm **2** acid, acute, cutting, edged, extreme, fine, incisive, intense, observant, penetrating, perceptive, piercing, pointed, sardonic, satirical, strong, tart, trenchant **3** astute, bright, brilliant, canny, clever, discerning, discriminating, Einstein, perceptive, perspicacious, quick, sagacious, sapient, sensitive, sharp, shrewd, whiz, wise

keep *verb.* **1** amass, cache, carry, conserve, detain, garner, grasp, have, heap, maintain, manage, own, preserve, put, reserve, save, season, withhold **2** board, command, continue, defend, endure, foster, guard, maintain, manage, mind, nurture, ordain, protect, provision, safeguard, shelter, subsidize, sustain **3** arrest, avert, block, check, control, curb, delay, detain, deter, hamper, inhibit, limit, obstruct, restrain, retard, stall, stop, withhold **4** adhere to, bless, celebrate, comply with, consecrate, fulfill, hold, honor, laud, obey, observe, perform, praise, regard, respect, ritualize, sanctify, solemnize

key *noun.* blueprint, clue, code, core, crux, cue, guide, index, indicator, lead, lever, nucleus, passport, pivot, root, sign, solution, translation

kick *noun.* backlash, blow, boot, force, intensity, jar, jolt, pep, punch, pungency, snap, sparkle, strength, tang, verve, vitality, zest, zing

kick *verb.* combat, criticize, curse, except, fight, fuss, grumble, inveigh, mumble, object, oppose, protest, rebel, remonstrate, resist, wail, whine, withstand

kid *noun.* baby, bairn, boy, calf, child, daughter, girl, infant, juvenile, lad, lamb, little one, nipper, son, teenager, tot, youngster, youth

kid *verb.* banter, bother, cozen, delude, fun, gull, jest, joke, jolly, mock, pretend, rag, rib, ridicule, roast, spoof, tease, trick

kill *verb.* **1** butcher, chill, croak, dispatch, do in, drown, eradicate, erase, execute, exterminate, massacre, neutralize, obliterate, off, poison, sacrifice, take, waste **2** cease, counteract, defeat, extinguish, forbid, halt, negative, neutralize, nullify, prohibit, quell, refuse, ruin, scotch, stifle, still, suppress, turn out

kind *adjective.* affectionate, amiable, amicable, clement, compassionate, congenial, considerate, courteous, generous, gentle, gracious, humane, humanitarian, kindly, philanthropic, propitious, thoughtful, tolerant

kind *noun.* complexion, denomination, description, feather, fiber, gender, kidney, likes, manner, mold, number, persuasion, set, stamp, stripe, style, tendency, variety

kindly *adjective.* attentive, beneficial, benevolent, cordial, generous, genial, gentle, good, gracious, hearty, helpful, humane, kind, merciful, mild, polite, thoughtful, warm

kindly *adverb.* affectionately, agreeably, carefully, charitably, compassionately, considerately, courteously, delicately, generously, graciously, helpfully, humanely, politely, sympathetically, tenderly, thoughtfully, understandingly, well

king *noun.* baron, caesar, caliph, czar, emperor, kaiser, khan, magnate, majesty, monarch, pasha, prince, rajah, rex, shah, sovereign, sultan, tycoon

kingdom *noun.* commonwealth, country, county, crown, division, domain, dominion, empire, lands, possessions, province, realm, rule, sphere, suzerainty, territory, throne, tract

kiss *noun.* buss, butterfly, caress, embrace, endearment, kissy-face, mouth music, mouth-to-mouth, mush, muzzle, osculation, peck, salutation, salute, smack, sugar, touch, X

kiss *verb.* blow, brush, buss, butterfly, buzz, caress, glance, graze, greet, muzzle, neck, peck, salute, smack, smash, spark, sugar, touch

knife *noun.* bait chopper, bayonet, blade, bolo, cutlass, cutter, edge, lance, point, saber, scimitar, shank, skewer, steel, stiletto, switchblade, sword

knife *verb.* brand, carve, clip, cut, hurt, jag, kill, lacerate, lance, pierce, shank, shiv, slash, slice, spit, stick, thrust, wound

knit *verb.* affix, bind, cable, connect, contract, heal, join, link, loop, net, repair, secure, sew, spin, tie, unite, weave, web

knock *noun.* beating, blow, box, clip, conk, cuff, hammering, hit, injury, lick, rap, slap, smack, striking, swat, swipe, thump, whack

knock *verb.* **1** abuse, batter, beat, bruise, buffet, clap, clout, deck, flatten, floor, level, maltreat, pound, rap, slap, thump, thwack, wound **2** abuse, blame, carp, cavil, censure, condemn, denounce, denunciate, deprecate, disparage, find fault, lambaste, rap, reprehend, reprobate, run down, skin, slam

knot *noun.* **1** bond, bow, bunch, coil, connection, entanglement, hitch, joint, ligament, mat, perplexity, screw, snag, tangle, tie, twist, warp, yoke **2** aggregation, assortment, band, bunch, circle, clique, clump, collection, crew, gang, group, heap, mass, mob, pack, pile, set, squad

know *verb.* appreciate, apprehend, comprehend, differentiate, distinguish, experience, fathom, grasp, have, ken, learn, notice, perceive, prize, realize, recognize, see, undergo

knowing *adjective.* alive, awake, aware, canny, competent, conscious, discerning, expert, intentional, into, knowledgeable, observant, qualified, sensible, sharp, sophisticated, watchful, wise

knowledge *noun.* accomplishments, acquaintance, education, enlightenment, erudition, facts, goods, insight, judgment, light, principles, proficiency, recognition, scholarship, schooling, substance, tuition, wisdom

known *adjective.* accepted, acknowledged, admitted, certified, common, confessed, conscious, hackneyed, manifest, noted, notorious, obvious, plain, popular, proverbial, published, received, recognized

L

label *noun.* **1** characterization, classification, company, description, design, epithet, hallmark, identification, mark, marker, number, price mark, stamp, sticker, tag, tally, ticket, trademark **2** characterization, classification, company, description, design, epithet, hallmark, identification, mark, marker, number, price mark, stamp, sticker, tag, tally, ticket, trademark

labor *noun.* **1** activity, diligence, effort, employment, endeavor, energy, exercise, exertion, grind, job, operation, pains, pull, stress, struggle, sweat, toil, undertaking **2** apprentice, breadwinner, doormat, employee, floater, hack, hand, help, helper, instrument, laborer, operative, prentice, proletariat, robot, slave, worker, workmen

labor *verb.* bear down, cultivate, dog it, drive, endeavor, grind, moil, plod, plug away, scratch, slave, strain, strive, struggle, sweat, tend, toil, tug

lack *noun.* absence, default, defect, deficit, deprivation, distress, inferiority, loss, miss, necessity, need, paucity, poverty, reduction, shortage, shrinking, stint, want

lady *noun.* adult, babe, bag, baroness, bitch, butterfly, dame, duchess, female, gal, girl, mama, mare, matron, mistress, queen, rib, squaw

land *noun.* acreage, area, beach, continent, estate, expanse, homeland, parcel, province, quarry, realty, region, shore, soil, stretch, terrain, territory, tract

land *verb.* alight, berth, check in, come down, come in, debark, ditch, dock, drop anchor, ground, make three-pointer, pilot, put in, set down, settle, steer, thump, touchdown

language *noun.* accent, cant, dialect, diction, dictionary, idiom, jargon, lexicon, parlance, prose, signal, sound, style, talk, utterance, vocabulary, voice, wording

large *adjective.* blimp, booming, bulky, colossal, considerable, enormous, excessive, extensive, extravagant, massive, monumental, mountainous, sizable, substantial, sweeping, tidy, vast, wide

largely *adverb.* abundantly, chiefly, comprehensively, considerably, copiously, extensively, generally, generously, grandly, lavishly, liberally, magnificently, mainly, mostly, predominantly, principally, prodigally, widely

last *adjective.* climactic, closing, conclusive, crowning, curtains, definitive, determinative, end, ending, extreme, far, farthest, finishing, hindmost, least, newest, supreme, uttermost

lasting *adjective.* constant, continual, continuing, durable, endless, eternal, everlasting, forever, incessant, indelible, lifelong, old, perennial, permanent, perpetual, persisting, undying, unremitting

late *adjective.* **1** backward, behind, belated, blown, delayed, eleventh hour, gone, held up, hung up, jammed, lagging, last-minute, overdue, postponed, remiss, stayed, strapped, tardy **2** asleep, bygone, cold, deceased, defunct, departed, exanimate, extinct, former, inanimate, lifeless, old, once, onetime, past, preceding, previous, sometime

latent *adjective.* contained, idle, immature, inert, inferential, intrinsic, invisible, possible, potential, quiescent, rudimentary, secret, sleeping, smoldering, suppressed, suspended, undeveloped, unseen

laugh *verb.* beam, break up, burst, chuckle, crow, die, fracture, giggle, grin, howl, roar, scream, shout, shriek, smile, split, titter, whoop

laughter *noun.* chortling, chuckle, crow, crowing, fit, gesture, giggle, giggling, glee, merriment, peal, rejoicing, roar, roaring, shout, shouting, shriek, sound

launch *verb.* barrage, cast, discharge, dispatch, drive, eject, fire, fling, heave, hurl, lance, pitch, project, propel, shoot, sling, throw, toss

law *noun.* **1** bidding, canon, case, caveat, charter, code, constitution, decree, divestiture, enactment, equity, jurisprudence, notice, ordinance, precept, ruling, statute, writ **2** axiom, base, canon, criterion, formula, foundation, fundamental, ground, maxim, postulate, precept, proposal, proposition, reason, regulation, rule, source, theorem

lawyer *noun.* advocate, ambulance chaser, attorney, attorney-at-law, beagle, counsel, counselor, defender, jurist, legal adviser, legal eagle, legist, mouthpiece, pettifogger, pleader, practitioner, proctor, solicitor

lay *verb.* **1** arrange, deposit, dispose, establish, fix, leave, locate, order, organize, place, plant, position, repose, rest, set, settle, spread, stick **2** address, aim, allocate, allot, ascribe, assess, assign, attribute, burden, cast, charge, direct, impose, incline, level, refer, train, turn **3** allay, alleviate, appease, assuage, calm, even, flatten, flush, iron, level, plane, press, quiet, relieve, smooth, steam, still, suppress

layer *noun.* blanket, coat, course, cover, covering, film, floor, lap, mantle, overlap, panel, ply, row, seam, slab, story, stripe, zone

lazy *adjective.* apathetic, drowsy, dull, idle, inattentive, indifferent, indolent, inert, lackadaisical, lifeless, shiftless, slack, sleepy, somnolent, tardy, torpid, unconcerned, unready

lead *noun.* advance, advantage, ahead, direction, guidance, head, heavy, leadership, model, over, precedence, primacy, priority, protagonist, spark, star, start, top

lead *verb.* **1** accompany, coerce, compel, convey, convoy, guard, induce, manage, persuade, prevail, protect, route, safeguard, see, show in, span, squire, traverse **2** affect, command, contribute, draw, govern, incline, induce, manage, motivate, move, persuade, prevail, produce, prompt, quarterback, serve, spearhead, supervise

leader *noun.* baton, boss, captain, chief, chieftain, commander, eminence, forerunner, kingpin, lion, maestro, manager, master, pioneer, president, rector, skipper, superior

leadership *noun.* administration, authority, command, conduction, control, conveyance, direction, directorship, domination, foresight, hegemony, influence, management, power, primacy, skill, superiority, supremacy

leading *adjective.* arch, best, champion, chief, dominant, dominating, foremost, governing, inaugural, main, notorious, outstanding, popular, premier, primary, principal, ruling, stellar

league *noun.* alliance, brotherhood, bunch, circuit, club, conference, crew, fellowship, gang, group, guild, loop, mob, organization, outfit, pool, union, unit

lean *adjective.* angular, bare, barren, emaciated, gaunt, lanky, meager, pitiful, poor, rangy, sinewy, slim, stick, svelte, unproductive, wasted, wiry, worn

lean *verb.* angle, cant, cock, decline, divert, droop, heel, incline, list, pitch, prop, repose, rest, roll, sink, tilt, tip, turn

leaning *noun.* aptitude, bag, bent, bias,

disposition, drift, favor, favoritism, groove, inclination, liking, lurch, penchant, predisposition, proneness, sentiment, taste, weakness

leap *verb.* advance, arise, ascend, bounce, bound, caper, cavort, clear, hop, increase, lop, mount, rise, rocket, skip, spring, surge, vault

learn *verb.* **1** apprentice, attain, con, enroll, gain, get, grasp, grind, imbibe, master, matriculate, memorize, pick up, prepare, read, receive, review, study **2** ascertain, catch on, detect, determine, dig up, discern, find out, gain, gather, hear, see, smoke out, stumble upon, trip over, tumble, uncover, understand, unearth

learned *adjective.* accomplished, bookish, brain, deep, educated, expert, grave, grounded, literary, literate, omniscient, posted, recondite, sharp, solid, sound, studious, versed

least *adjective.* atomic, bottom, gutter, last, lowest, microscopic, minimal, minimum, minute, molecular, nadir, piddling, poorest, second, smallest, third, tiniest, unimportant

leave *verb.* **1** abandon, blow, break away, defect, disappear, ditch, embark, exit, fly, issue, migrate, move, part, start, take off, vacate, vanish, walk out **2** abandon, back out, cease, desert, drop, drop out, evacuate, forsake, give up, quit, refrain, relinquish, resign, stop, surrender, terminate, waive, yield **3** allot, apportion, assign, bequest, cede, commit, confide, consign, demise, devise, entrust, give, hand down, leave behind, legate, refer, transmit, will

leg *noun.* brace, column, lap, limb, member, part, pile, pole, post, prop, section, segment, shank, stage, stake, stretch, stump, upright

legal *adjective.* allowed, authorized, constitutional, contractual, decreed, due, enforced, judged, judicial, justified, legalized, proper, right, sanctioned, sound, statutory, valid, warranted

legion *noun.* army, body, brigade, cloud, company, division, drove, flock, group, horde, host, multitude, myriad, number, phalanx, scores, throng, troop

legitimate *adjective.* accredited, admissible, appropriate, authorized, certain, normal, proper, real, reasonable, received, regular, sanctioned, sensible, sound, statutory, true, usual, valid

leisure *noun.* convenience, ease, freedom, holiday, intermission, liberty, opportunity, pause, range, recreation, repose, respite, rest, retirement, scope, time, unemployment, vacation

lend *verb.* afford, bestow, confer, contribute, entrust, extend, furnish, give, grant, impart, let, oblige, permit, provide, shark, stake, supply, trust

length *noun.* breadth, expanse, height, longitude, magnitude, orbit, panorama, period, piece, range, realm, remoteness, season, section, span, stretch, unit, width

lengthy *adjective.* diffuse, dragging, elongated, interminable, lengthened, long, long-winded, longish, padded, prolonged, protracted, tedious, tiresome, verbose, very long, wearisome, windy, wordy

less *adjective.* beneath, declined, deficient, depressed, excepting, inferior, lacking, lesser, limited, lower, minor, negative, reduced, secondary, shortened, shorter, subordinate, subtracting

lesser *adjective.* bottom, bush, bush-league, inferior, insignificant, low, low man, lower, minor, minor-league, nether, second fiddle, slighter, small, small-fry, subordinate, third string, under

lesson *noun.* assignment, class, drill, education, exercise, instruction, lecture, period, practice, quiz, reading, recitation, schooling, study, task, teaching, test, tutoring

let *verb.* approve, authorize, cause, certify, commission, concede, enable, endorse, grant, have, leave, license, make, permit, sanction, suffer, tolerate, warrant

letter *noun.* acknowledgment, answer, billet, cannonball, dispatch, kite, line, memo, memorandum, message, missive, note, postcard, reply, report, scratch, tab, tag

level *adjective.* alike, calm, common, constant, exact, flush, horizontal, matching, parallel, planed, polished, regular, rolled, smooth, steady, trim, trimmed, unbroken

level *verb.* **1** bulldoze, equalize, equate, even, even out, flatten, flush, grade, lay, make equal, make flat, plane, press, roll, smooth, smoothen, straighten, surface **2** bulldoze, demolish, devastate, down, drop, equalize, fell, flatten, floor, ground, knock down, knock over, pull down, ruin, smooth, tear down, waste, wreck

levy *verb.* call, call up, charge, collect, demand, exact, extort, gather, impose, lay on, place, put on, raise, set, summon, tax, wrest, wring

liability *noun.* **1** accountability, accountableness, amenability, amenableness, arrearage, blame, burden, compulsion, culpability, debt, duty, indebtedness, obligation, onus, owing, responsibility, subjection, susceptibility **2** accident, baggage, bite, burden, contract, drag, due, inconvenience, involvement, lease, loan, millstone, obligation, onus, pledge, possibility, remainder, responsibility

liberal *adjective.* **1** advanced, detached, enlightened, general, humanistic, humanitarian, impartial, intelligent, interested, left, loose, permissive, pink, radical, rational, reasonable, tolerant, unorthodox **2** benevolent, big, bighearted, casual, charitable, exuberant, free, generous, handsome, kind, lavish, loose, openhanded, philanthropic, prince, prodigal, profuse, unselfish

liberty *noun.* autonomy, convenience, decision, deliverance, delivery, dispensation, emancipation, enlightenment, franchise, immunity, leave, liberation, opportunity, prerogative, release, rest, right, suffrage

license *noun.* **1** authorization, certificate, charter, consent, dispensation, freedom, grant, immunity, independence, latitude, leave, liberty, permission, permit, privilege, right, ticket, warrant **2** abandon, anarchy, arrogance, audacity, boldness, complacency, debauchery, disorder, excess, impropriety, irresponsibility, looseness, profligacy, relaxation, sensuality, temerity, unruliness, wildness

lie *noun.* calumny, deceit, deception, dishonesty, distortion, fable, fabrication, falsehood, fiction, forgery, guile, hyperbole, inaccuracy, invention, libel, misrepresentation, myth, perjury

lie *verb.* **1** beguile, bull, con, deceive, delude, distort, exaggerate, fabricate, fake, falsify, frame, invent, jazz, malign, plant, promote, queer, victimize **2** be prone, be supine, couch, laze, lie down, loll, lounge, nap, prostrate, recline, repose, rest, retire, siesta, sleep, sprawl, stretch out, turn in **3** be, be buried, be even, be found, be interred, be on, be seated, be set, be smooth, belong, exist, extend, occupy, prevail, reach, remain, spread, stretch

life *noun.* **1** activity, being, energy, enthusiasm, entity, esprit, essence, impulse, lifeblood, liveliness, soul, sparkle, spirit, verve, viability, vigor, vivacity, zest **2** being, career, course, cycle, days, decade, endurance, generation, history, length, lifetime, orbit, period, pilgrimage, season, span, survival, time **3** animation, body, creature, endurance, entity, human, individual, living, man, mortal, organism, presence, reproduction, soul, subsistence, survival, viability, wildlife **4** attainment, circumstances, conduct, development, dread, enlightenment, frustration, growth, happiness, knowledge, participation, personality, reaction, realization, retardation, suffering, vicissitudes, world

lift *verb.* **1** arise, ascend, aspire, boost, build up, climb, disappear, erect, goose, hike, hoist, mount, pick up, raise, rise, up, uphold, vanish **2** abstract, appropriate, cop, copy, crib, filch, hook, nip, pilfer, pinch, pirate, plagiarize, pocket, purloin, snitch, swipe, take, thieve

light *adjective.* **1** bright, burnished, clear, cloudless, flashing, fluorescent, glassy, glossy, glowing, luminous, phosphorescent, polished, resplendent, rich, shining, shiny, sunny, vivid **2** agile, buoyant, dainty, ethereal, featherweight, filmy, flimsy, floating, fluffy, friable, inconsequential, lightweight, loose, meager, petty, slight, small, spongy **3** casual, fragmentary, gentle, inconsequential, inconsiderable, indistinct, insignificant, minor, minute, moderate, modest, puny, shoestring, slight, soft, tiny, unimportant, weak **4** amusing, animated, carefree, cheery, chipper, entertaining, fickle, frivolous, humorous, lively, merry, perky, pleasing, sunny, superficial, swimming, trifling, up

light *noun.* **1** beacon, bulb, daylight, emanation, flare, glare, glimmer, glint, glitter, illumination, lamp, luminosity, ray, shine, sun, sunshine, taper, torch **2** angle, approach, awareness, comprehension, context, education, elucidation, enlightenment, exemplar, illustration, insight, interpretation, knowledge, model, paragon, slant, standing, viewpoint

light *verb.* **1** animate, brighten, cast, fire, flood, floodlight, highlight, ignite, illumine, inflame, irradiate, kindle, limelight, make visible, put on, shine, spot, spotlight **2** alight, arrive, come down, debus, detrain, disembark, drop, fly down, perch, rest, roost, set down, settle, settle down, sit, sit down, stop, touch down

lightly *adverb.* agilely, airily, carelessly, casually, daintily, faintly, freely, moderately, quietly, readily, simply, smoothly, softly, sparsely, subtly, tenderly, tenuously, thoughtlessly

like *adjective.* alike, allied, analogous, cognate, commensurate, comparable, compatible, consonant, double, identical, matching, near, parallel, related, such, twin, undifferentiated, uniform

like *verb.* admire, adore, appreciate, approve, care for, cherish, dig, esteem, exclaim, fancy, find appealing, go for, love, luxuriate in, prize, relish, savor, take

likelihood *noun.* coin flip, direction, even break, fair shake, fifty-fifty, liability, likeliness, long shot, outside chance, possibility, presumption, probability, prospect, shot at, strong possibility, tendency, toss-up, trend

likely *adjective.* acceptable, anticipated, apt, assuring, conceivable, credible, expected, feasible, inclined, liable, ostensible, plausible, possible, practicable, predisposed, rational, reasonable, true

liking *noun.* affection, appetite, appreciation, attachment, attraction, devotion, fancy, inclination, love, palate, penchant, preference, relish, sympathy, taste, tendency, tooth, will

limit *noun.* absolute, ape, bound, brim, cap, ceiling, conclusion, confinement, confines, curb, deadline, destination, end, extremity, fence, finality, restraint, verge

limit *verb.* appoint, assign, bar, bound, cap, confine, contract, cork, cramp, curb, define, fix, lessen, narrow, prescribe, ration, reduce, set

limitation *noun.* bar, check, circumspection, constraint, control, cramp, curb, definition, disadvantage, drawback, impediment, inhibition, injunction, qualification, reservation, snag, stint, taboo

limited *adjective.* **1** bound, bounded, checked, circumscribed, constrained, defined, determinate, finite, fixed, hampered, local, modified, narrow, precise, qualified, reserved, restrained, sectional **2** borne, cramped, diminished, faulty, ineffectual, insufficient, little, mean, minimal, narrow, paltry, poor, reduced, restricted, set, short, small, unsatisfactory

limp *adjective.* debilitated, drooping, exhausted, feeble, flimsy, floppy, formative, infirm, limber, listless, loose, plastic, pliable, relaxed, slack, soft, weakened, worn out

limp *verb.* clump, falter, flag, gimp, halt, hitch, hobble, hop, lag, scuff, shamble, shuffle, stagger, stumble, teeter, totter, waddle, walk lamely

line *noun.* **1** bar, boundary, channel, configuration, contour, demarcation, figure, frontier, groove, outline, profile, rule, silhouette, streak, stripe, tracing, underline, wrinkle **2** arrangement, channel, course, direction, division, file, formation, groove, lane, list, mark, ridge, route, row, sequence, series, string, train **3** activity, area, business, department, employment, field, forte, interest, job, occupation, profession, province, pursuit, racket, specialization, trade, vocation, work

line *verb.* align, array, bound, draw, follow,

fringe, group, join, mark, marshal, neighbor, outline, range, rule, touch, trace, underline, verge

linger *verb.* crawl, delay, idle, muck, potter, procrastinate, putter, remain, shuffle, slouch, stagger, stay, stroll, tarry, tool, trail, trifle, wait

link *noun.* association, attachment, channel, connective, constituent, coupler, division, element, hitch, joint, loop, member, piece, relationship, seam, section, tie, yoke

link *verb.* associate, attach, bind, bracket, combine, conjugate, couple, fasten, group, identify, incorporate, interface, join, network, relate, tie, unite, yoke

liquid *adjective.* aqueous, damp, dissolved, dulcet, flowing, juicy, luscious, melted, melting, molten, running, smooth, soft, solvent, thawed, viscous, watery, wet

liquid *noun.* aqua, aqueous material, broth, elixir, extract, flow, flux, goo, goop, juice, liquor, melted material, nectar, sap, secretion, slop, solution, swill

liquor *noun.* booze, broth, drinkable, extract, fluid, gravy, infusion, joy juice, juice, liquid, poison, sauce, solvent, spirits, stock, varnish, water, whiskey

list *noun.* agenda, arrangement, calendar, canon, catalog, contents, dictionary, enumeration, file, gazette, loop, poll, program, row, schedule, statistics, table, timetable

list *verb.* bill, chronicle, classify, detail, file, index, insert, inventory, manifest, peg, poll, post, record, run down, schedule, specialize, tabulate, tally

listen *verb.* accept, admit, adopt, attend, audit, catch, concentrate, entertain, get, hark, mind, monitor, obey, observe, pay attention, pick up, receive, welcome

literal *adjective.* accurate, actual, authentic, close, critical, faithful, gospel, methodical, natural, plain, real, scrupulous, simple, strict, true, usual, verbatim, written

literally *adverb.* actually, completely, correctly, direct, directly, faithfully, indisputably, plainly, really, rightly, rigorously, sic, simply, strictly, truly, unerringly, unmistakably, verbatim

literature *noun.* books, brochure, classics, composition, critique, disquisition, findings, history, lit, lore, observation, pamphlet, paper, story, summary, thesis, tract, treatise

little *adjective.* **1** brief, hasty, imperceptible, junior, light, limited, meager, miniature, minute, peanut, petite, shrimp, slight, stubby, tiny, toy, truncated, undeveloped **2** base, bigoted, borne, cheap, contemptible, hidebound, ineffectual, limited, mean, narrow, petty, provincial, self-centered, selfish, set, small, vulgar, wicked

live *adjective.* active, alert, controversial, dynamic, earnest, effectual, efficacious, efficient, functioning, hot, lively, pertinent, prevalent, running, topical, unsettled, vital, vivid

live *verb.* **1** abide, be, breathe, continue, endure, get along, have life, last, lead, maintain, make it, move, pass, persist, prevail, remain, subsist, survive **2** abide, bide, bunk, crash, dwell, hang out, hole up, locate, lodge, nest, occupy, park, perch, reside, roost, settle, shack up, squat

lively *adjective.* agile, alert, animate, animated, bright, buoyant, chipper, dashing, driving, enterprising, jocund, jumping, keen, merry, refreshing, rousing, snappy, stirring

living *adjective.* active, alert, alive, animated, around, awake, contemporary, continuing, developing, dynamic, extant, live, lively, persisting, strong, ticking, vital, warm

living *noun.* bread, existence, income, job, keep, livelihood, maintenance, means, mode, occupation, salt, subsistence, support, sustainment, sustenance, sustentation, way, work

load *noun.* **1** amount, bale, bundle, capacity, charge, contents, freight, goods, haul, incubus, jag, mass, pack, parcel, part, shipment, shot, weight **2** affliction, care, charge, deadweight, drag, drain, duty, incubus, liability, millstone, obligation, onus, pressure, responsibility, tax, trouble, trust, weight

load *verb.* ballast, bear, carry, charge, flood, freight, gorge, heap, lumber, mass, pack, pile, place, stack, stuff, surfeit, top, weight

lobby *verb.* affect, ballyhoo, build up, change, further, induce, influence, jawbone, plug, press, pressure, puff, request, solicit, splash, spot, thump, urge

local *adjective.* bounded, civic, divisional, geographical, historical, limited, narrow, neighborhood, parish, parochial, provincial, regional, restricted, sectarian, sectional, territorial, town, vernacular

locate *verb.* come upon, detect, determine, discover, establish, hook, pinpoint, place, position, read, smell out, smoke out, spot, station, strike, track down, uncover, unearth

location *noun.* area, fix, hole, locale, locality, locus, neighborhood, part, post, region, section, site, spot, station, tract, turf, where, whereabouts

lock *noun.* bar, bolt, bond, catch, clamp, clasp, clinch, connection, fastening, fixture, grapple, grip, hasp, hook, junction, latch, link, padlock

lock *verb.* bar, bolt, clench, close, clutch, embrace, encircle, grapple, grasp, join, link, mesh, press, seal, secure, shut, slough, unite

lodge *noun.* abode, box, cabin, cottage, couch, den, dwelling, home, hospice, hotel, house, motel, roadhouse, shack, shanty, shelter, stopover, villa

lodge *verb.* bestow, board, bunk, crash, domicile, dwell, house, locate, nest, park, perch, quarter, reside, roost, shelter, sojourn, station, stay

logic *noun.* argumentation, coherence, connection, deduction, dialectic, induction, inference, linkage, philosophy, ratiocination, rationale, relationship, sanity, sense, sound judgment, syllogism, syllogistics, thesis

logical *adjective.* analytic, analytical, clear, compelling, congruent, consequent, convincing, discriminating, fly, inferential, obvious, pertinent, rational, relevant, sensible, sound, valid, wise

lone *adjective.* abandoned, alone, deserted, forsaken, isolated, lonely, lonesome, one, secluded, separate, separated, single, singular, sole, solitary, solo, stag, unique

lonely *adjective.* **1** alone, apart, deserted, destitute, down, estranged, forsaken, isolated, left, lone, lonesome, outcast, rejected, secluded, single, solitary, unattended, withdrawn **2** alone, deserted, desolate, devious, godforsaken, isolated, obscure, private, quiet, remote, removed, retired, secluded, secret, sequestered, solitary, unfrequented, uninhabited

long *adjective.* **1** continued, deep, distant, elongated, enlarged, extensive, lanky, lengthened, lengthy, lofty, rangy, remote, running, stretch, stretched, stretching, sustained, tall **2** boundless, delayed, diffuse, dragging, excessive, for ages, late, lengthy, limitless, lingering, prolonged, protracted, slow, sustained, tardy, unending, verbose, wordy

long *verb.* ache, aim, aspire, covet, crave, cream for, dream of, hanker, hunger, itch, lust, miss, pine, sigh, thirst, want, wish, yearn

longing *noun.* ambition, aspiration, coveting, craving, hankering, hots, hunger, hungering, itch, lech, pining, sweet tooth, thirst, urge, wish, yearning, yen

look *noun.* **1** case, contemplation, eyeful, gander, gaze, glance, introspection, lamp, marking, observation, pike, regard, review, scrutiny, speculation, squint, surveillance, view **2** bearing, cast, complexion, countenance, demeanor, effect, expression, face, fashion, guise, manner, mien, mug, physiognomy, presence, seeming, semblance, visage

look *verb.* behold, beware, consider, contemplate, gaze, glance, goggle, inspect, lamp, mark, notice, regard, scout, see, spy, study, view, watch

loop *noun.* bend, circuit, circumference, coil, convolution, curl, curve, hoop, kink, knot, loophole, noose, ring, spiral, twirl, twist, whorl, wreath

loop *verb.* arc, arch, bend, beset, coil, compass, curl, curve, encircle, encompass, fold, gird, girdle, join, roll, surround, turn, twist

loose *adjective.* **1** apart, baggy, clear, disconnected, floating, hanging, insecure, limp, movable, relaxed, slack, unattached, unbound, unfastened, unhinged, unlocked, unrestricted, wobbly **2** capricious, careless, disreputable, dissipated, immoral, lewd, libertine, light, negligent, operating, playboy, rash, reckless, speeding, swinging, thoughtless, unmindful, wanton

lord *noun.* baron, captain, commandant, commander, count, dad, duke, governor, leader, magnate, marquis, monarch, nobleman, prince, royalty, sovereign, superior, viscount

lore *noun.* belief, custom, enlightenment, erudition, experience, fable, folklore, knowledge, learning, legend, mythology, saga, saying, scholarship, superstition, teaching, tradition, wisdom

lose *verb.* consume, default, displace, divest, drain, drop, exhaust, fail, forfeit, forget, lavish, miss, oust, rob, sacrifice, suffer, waste, yield

loss *noun.* accident, calamity, catastrophe, debt, defeat, deprivation, destruction, disappearance, fall, harm, injury, losing, mishap, sacrifice, trouble, undoing, want, wreckage

lost *adjective.* **1** absent, adrift, astray, disappeared, disoriented, forfeit, gone, invisible, irrevocable, lacking, misplaced, missed, obscured, strayed, unredeemed, vanished, wandering, wayward **2** abolished, bygone, dead, demolished, destroyed, devastated, dissipated, forgotten, gone, lapsed, obliterated, obsolete, past, perished, ruined, squandered, wasted, wrecked **3** absent, absorbed, abstracted, bemused, bewildered, distracted, dreamy, engrossed, entranced, feeble, ignorant, musing, perplexed, preoccupied, rapt, spellbound, unconscious, wasted

lot *noun.* **1** acreage, allotment, apportionment, area, block, bush, clearing, division, field, frontage, parcel, part, patch, percentage, piece, plot, property, tract **2** abundance, aggregation, amplitude, barrel, body, collection, group, heap, load, loads, mess, much, number, numbers, reams, requisition, scores, set **3** accident, beads, break, breaks, cards, chance, circumstance, decree, destiny, doom, foreordination, fortune, hazard, karma, plight, portion, predestination, weird

loud *adjective.* **1** blaring, blatant, boisterous, booming, clamorous, crashing, deep, emphatic, heavy, powerful, raucous, resonant, ringing, roaring, sonorous, strong, turbulent, vehement **2** brash, brassy, brazen, coarse, crass, crude, flamboyant, flashy, garish, gaudy, lurid, meretricious, obnoxious, ostentatious, raucous, tasteless, tawdry, vulgar

lounge *noun.* bar, barroom, candy store, club room, cocktail lounge, dive, drinkery, hideaway, juice joint, lobby, mezzanine, parlor, pub, reception, saloon, spot, tap, water hole

lounge *verb.* bum, dawdle, fritter away, goldbrick, goof off, idle, kill time, laze, loaf, loiter, loll, pass time, potter, recline, relax, repose, saunter, sprawl

lousy *adjective.* base, contemptible, dirty, disliked, faulty, harmful, hateful, horrible, inferior, low, miserable, outrageous, poor, rotten, terrible, unpopular, unwelcome, vicious

love *noun.* **1** affection, attachment, case, cherishing, crush, devotion, emotion, fervor, flame, fondness, idolatry, inclination, involvement, liking, regard, relish, taste, zeal **2** admirer, angel, beau, beloved, darling, dear, dearest, flame, honey, inamorata, lover, passion, spark, squire, suitor, sweet, sweetheart, valentine

love *verb.* **1** admire, adulate, care for, cherish, choose, dote on, esteem, exalt, fancy, glorify, go for, hold high, idolize, like, prefer, prize, treasure, worship **2** canoodle, caress, court, embrace, feel, grass, hold, hug, kiss, lick, neck, pet, press, shine, soothe, spoon, stroke, woo

lovely *adjective.* admirable, agreeable, amiable, attractive, captivating, charming, comely, dainty, delicate, delightful, enchanting, exquisite, gratifying, handsome, pretty, rare, scrumptious, stunning

lover *noun.* admirer, beau, beloved, darling, dear, dearest, flame, mama, master, mistress, papa, petitioner, solicitor, squeeze, steady, suitor, sweetheart, valentine

loving *adjective.* admiring, affectionate, amiable, amorous, ardent, attentive, concerned, dear, expressive, fervent, fond, kind, liking, passionate, respecting, sentimental, tender, warm

low *adjective.* **1** below, beneath, bottom, crouched, deep, depressed, inferior, junior, lesser, level, little, lowering, minor, nether, profound, prostrate, small, sunken **2** cheap, gentle, inexpensive, insignificant, little, meager, mediocre, moderate, modest, nominal, poor, puny, reasonable, scant, small, soft, subdued, worthless **3** base, common, contemptible, creepy, disgraceful, disreputable, gross, menial, miserable, nasty, obscene, offensive, raw, rough, scurvy, unworthy, woebegone, wretched **4** bad, blue, crestfallen, despondent, down, downcast, downhearted, dragged, fed up, forlorn, gloomy, glum, low-down, miserable, moody, morose, sad, unhappy **5** ailing, debilitated, dizzy, dying, exhausted, faint, feeble, frail, ill, indisposed, poorly, prostrate, reduced, sick, sickly, sinking, stricken, weak

lower *adjective.* curtailed, decreased, diminished, inferior, junior, lessened, lesser, low, low man, minor, nether, reduced, second fiddle, second-class, secondary, smaller, subordinate, under

lower *verb.* **1** bring low, cast down, couch, demit, depress, descend, detrude, droop, drop, fall, ground, let down, push down, reduce, set down, sink, submerge, take down **2** abate, clip, curtail, cut, cut back, decrease, decry, diminish, downgrade, lessen, minimize, moderate, pare, prune, shave, slash, soften, undervalue

loyal *adjective.* ardent, attached, believing, constant, dependable, devoted, dutiful, firm, patriotic, resolute, staunch, steadfast, steady, true, trustworthy, trusty, unfailing, unswerving

loyalty *noun.* ardor, attachment, constancy, devotion, faith, fealty, homage, honesty, incorruptibility, integrity, inviolability, patriotism, probity, reliability, submission, tie, truthfulness, zeal

luck *noun.* advantage, blessing, break, fluke, godsend, happiness, health, occasion, opportunity, prosperity, smile, stroke, success, triumph, victory, wealth, win, windfall

lucky *adjective.* adventitious, auspicious, beneficial, benign, blessed, charmed, favored, felicitous, golden, hopeful, hot, promising, propitious, prosperous, providential, successful, timely, well

luminous *adjective.* beaming, bright, brilliant, clear, crystal, illuminated, incandescent, lighted, lit, lucid, luminescent, lustrous, radiant, resplendent, shining, translucent, transparent, vivid

lump *noun.* agglomeration, ball, bit, bunch, chunk, group, handful, hunk, morsel, much, part, piece, protrusion, protuberance, section, solid, spot, tumor

lure *noun.* allurement, ambush, appeal, attraction, bribe, delusion, draw, fake, illusion, incentive, inducement, magnet, pull, seduction, snare, temptation, tout, trap

lure *verb.* allure, bag, bait, beckon, beguile, capture, drag, draw, fascinate, grab, haul, invite, pull, rope, steer, tempt, train, vamp

luxury *noun.* affluence, bliss, comfort, delight, enjoyment, exorbitance, extra, frill, gratification, hedonism, intemperance, leisure, rarity, richness, satisfaction, splendor, sumptuousness, treat

lying *adjective.* deceitful, deceptive, dissembling, false, falsifying, fibbing, inventing, mendacious, misleading, misrepresenting, perfidious, prevaricating, roguish, shifty, treacherous, tricky, unreliable, wrong

M

machine *noun.* apparatus, appliance, automaton, automobile, computer, contraption, contrivance, engine, gadget, implement, instrument, job, mechanism, motor, robot, thingamabob, tool, vehicle

machinery *noun.* agency, agent, apparatus, appliance, channel, engine, equipment, gadget, instrument, medium, method, motor, organ, outfit, paraphernalia, system, tool, vehicle

mad *adjective.* **1** absurd, bananas, crazed, cuckoo, demented, deranged, distracted, foolhardy, frenetic, frenzied, illogical, irrational, lunatic, nonsensical, nuts, rabid, unsafe, wacky **2** agitated, distracted, distraught, enraged, exasperated, excited, frenetic, fuming, furious, incensed, infuriated, irritated, livid, provoked, raging, resentful, wild, wrathful

madden *verb.* anger, bother, craze, distract, enrage, exasperate, frenzy, incense, inflame, infuriate, ire, pester, possess, provoke, shatter, unbalance, upset, vex

magazine *noun.* annual, booklet, brochure, circular, gazette, glossy, joint, journal, manual, monthly, newsletter, newspaper, organ, paper, periodical, quarterly, sheet, weekly

magic *noun.* alchemy, allurement, divination, enchantment, fascination, foreboding, illusion, incantation, magnetism, power, prediction, presage, prophecy, sorcery, spell, superstition, taboo, voodoo

magical *adjective.* bewitched, clairvoyant, eerie, enchanted, enchanting, fascinating, ghostly, haunted, magic, magnetic, marvelous, miraculous, mysterious, necromantic, spectral, spooky, unusual, wonderful

magnetic *adjective.* alluring, appealing, arresting, attractive, bewitching, captivating, charismatic, charming, drawing, enchanting, entrancing, fascinating, hypnotic, inviting, irresistible, mesmerizing, pulling, seductive

magnetism *noun.* allure, appeal, attraction, attractiveness, captivation, charisma, draw, enchantment, fascination, glamour, hypnotism, influence, lure, magic, power, pull, spell, witchcraft

magnificent *adjective.* arresting, elegant, elevated, exalted, fine, imperial, impressive, lavish, lofty, lordly, proud, regal, resplendent, royal, stately, striking, sumptuous, swanky

magnitude *noun.* amount, amplitude, breadth, bulk, compass, dimension, dimensions, enormity, expanse, extent, immensity, intensity, mass, measurement, proportion, range, reach, strength

maid *noun.* au pair, biddy, chambermaid, cleaning lady, cleaning woman, damsel, domestic, factotum, girl, handmaiden, help, hired girl, housemaid, live-in, maidservant, miss, nursemaid, woman

main *adjective.* central, chief, controlling, critical, essential, foremost, fundamental, head, leading, necessary, predominant, premier, prevailing, prime, special, star, stellar, supreme

maintain *verb.* **1** cache, conserve, guard, husband, keep, manage, nurture, perpetuate, preserve, prolong, protect, provide, renew, repair, save, supply, sustain, uphold **2** advocate, affirm, champion, claim, correct, defend, emphasize, insist, justify, persist, profess, protest, report, right, stand by, state, stress, uphold

maintenance *noun.* allowance, bread, carrying, conservation, continuation, food, keep, living, nurture, perpetuation, preservation, prolongation, provision, repairs, resources, salt, subsistence, supply

majestic *adjective.* awesome, courtly, dignified, elevated, exalted, imperial, lofty, magnificent, marvelous, monumental, pompous, regal, royal, sovereign, stately, stunning, sumptuous, superb

major *adjective.* **1** better, chief, considerable, dominant, elder, exceeding, extensive, extreme, large, larger, leading, main, over, sizable, superior, supreme, ultra, uppermost **2** chief, critical, dangerous, grave, great, grievous, main, meaningful, notable, outstanding, principal, radical, significant, star, stellar, top, vital, weighty

make *verb.* **1** accomplish, adjust, assemble, beget, brew, build, constitute, cook, effect, form, frame, manufacture, mold, occasion, prepare, produce, secure, whip **2** begin, bring about, cause, coerce, compel, drive, effect, force, initiate, interfere, meddle, oblige, press, require, secure, shotgun, start, tamper **3** act, conduct, declare, decree, do, effect, establish, execute, fix, form, formulate, frame, legislate, pass, perform, practice, prepare, wage **4** amount to, come to, compose, compound, comprise, construct, embody, equal, fabricate, form, make up, mix, organize, put together, represent, structure, synthesize, texture **5** acquire, clear, cop, gain, get, harvest, hustle, knock down, net, obtain, pull, rate, realize, reap, receive, secure, turn, win **6** advance, arrive at, attain, bear, break for, catch, get to, go, head, light out, meet, move, proceed, progress, reach, set out, strike out, take off

malaise *noun.* angst, anxiety, debility, depression, despair, discomfort, disquiet, distress, doldrums, enervation, illness, infirmity, infirmness, melancholy, pain, unease, uneasiness, weakness

male *noun.* ape, boy, buck, bull, chap, father, fellow, gentleman, guy, he, hunk, jock, john, papa, stud, tiger, tom, wolf

man *noun.* **1** being, body, character, creature, flesh, folk, human, humanity, individual, mankind, mortal, mortality, person, personage, populace, somebody, soul, species **2** ape, beau, bloke, boy, cat, fellow, guy, hunk, husband, lord, master, mister, papa, partner, pops, sir, spouse, stud

manage *verb.* **1** advocate, captain, concert, dominate, engineer, govern, handle, influence, instruct, maintain, minister, ply, regulate, request, rule, train, watch, wield **2** achieve, arrange, bring about, con, contrive, cook, doctor, effect, engineer, execute, fix, jockey, plant, put over, rig, succeed, swing, work

management *noun.* **1** administration, authority, board, bosses, brass, directorate, directors, employers, execs, executive, executives, front office, head, mainframe, man upstairs, management, micro management, top brass **2** administration, care, charge, command, conduct, control, direction, governance, government, guidance, handling, intendance, manipulation, operation, oversight, rule, superintendence, supervision

manager *noun.* administrator, boss, comptroller, conductor, digger, director, exec, executive, foreman, governor, head, impresario, officer, official, overseer, producer, proprietor, supervisor

mandate *noun.* authorization, behest, bidding, charge, command, commission, decree, dictate, directive, fiat, imperative, injunction, instruction, order, precept, sanction, warrant, word

manifest *adjective.* bold, clear, conspicuous, disclosed, distinct, evidenced, evident, noticeable, open, palpable, plain, prominent, revealed, shown, told, unambiguous, unmistakable, visible

manifest *verb.* display, embody, expose, express, flash, illustrate, mark, materialize, proclaim, prove, show, showcase, signify, sport, strut, suggest, vent, voice

manifold *adjective.* assorted, complex, copious, different, diverse, diversified, diversiform, many, multifarious, multifold, multiform, multiple, multiplied, multitudinous, numerous, varied, various

manner *noun.* **1** address, affectation, air, appearance, aspect, bearing, comportment, conduct, demeanor, look, mannerism, mien, peculiarity, presence, style, tone, turn, way **2** approach, custom, form, habit, line, mode, modus, practice, procedure, routine, style, system, technique, tone, vein, way, wise, wont

manners *noun.* bearing, breeding, ceremony, comportment, courtesy, culture, dignity, elegance, etiquette, formalities, mien, mores, polish, propriety, protocol, refinement, sophistication, taste

manufacture *verb.* accomplish, assemble, carve, construct, create, execute, fabricate, fashion, form, frame, make up, mill, mold, process, produce, shape, tool, turn out

manufacturing *noun.* assembling, assembly, casting, completion, composing, composition, construction, creation, doing, erection, fabrication, finishing, forging, formation, making, manufacture, preparing, produce

many *adjective.* abounding, frequent, innumerable, legion, manifold, multiplied, multitudinous, myriad, numerous, plentiful, prevalent, profuse, several, sundry, teeming, uncounted, varied, various

many *noun.* bags, heaps, horde, jillion, lots, mass, mess, multitude, oodles, piles, plenty, rafts, scads, scores, thousands, tons, umpteen, whole slew

map *noun.* atlas, delineation, design, diagram, draft, drawing, elevation, globe, graph, outline, picture, plan, plat, portrayal, print, projection, sketch, tracing

mar *verb.* blemish, blight, blot, break, bruise, damage, detract, harm, impair, queer, ruin, scar, scratch, spoil, stain, taint, warp, wreck

march *verb.* advance, boot, drill, file, mount, move, pace, parade, pound, proceed, progress, range, space, step, stride, strut, tramp, tread

margin *noun.* allowance, bound, boundary, brim, compass, confine, extra, frame, hem, latitude, leeway, perimeter, scope, shore, side, surplus, trimming, verge

marine *adjective.* coastal, hydrographic, littoral, maritime, nautical, naval, navigational, Neptunian, ocean-going, oceanic, oceanographic, pelagic, saltwater, sea, seafaring, seashore, seaside, shore

mark *noun.* **1** blaze, bruise, cross, dot, impression, imprint, ink, line, nick, record, sign, spot, stain, stamp, streak, symbol, trace, trademark **2** affection, attribute, device, distinction, hallmark, image, impression, marking, particularity, peculiarity, print, property, quality, seal, sign, significant, stamp, symbol **3** blaze, bruise, dot, impress, imprint, ink, letter, nick, pinpoint, print, seal, sign, stain, stamp, streak, trace, underline, write **4** bespeak, brand, demonstrate, designate, exemplify, exhibit, feature, identify, illustrate, indicate, label, manifest, proclaim, qualify, remark, show, signify, stamp **5** attend, behold, chronicle, discern, distinguish, eye, mind, note, notice, observe, pay attention, perceive, regard, register, remark, view, watch, write down

marked *adjective.* arresting, clear, considerable, conspicuous, decided, distinct, evident, manifest, notable, noted, noticeable, outstanding, pointed, pronounced, remarkable, salient, signal, striking

market *noun.* bazaar, booth, drugstore, emporium, exchange, fair, mall, mart, outlet, shop, showroom, square, stall, store, supermarket, truck, variety store, warehouse

marriage *noun.* alliance, amalgamation, association, bells, confederation, coupling, espousal, link, match, mating, matrimony, merger, monogamy, sacrament, shotgun, tie, wedding, wedlock

marry *verb.* associate, bond, combine, conjugate, contract, couple, join, land, match, mate, one, pledge, promise, relate, tie, unite, wed, yoke

marshal *verb.* align, arrange, array, assemble, collect, conduct, direct, dispose, distribute, group, guide, lead, line up, mobilize, order, rally, shepherd, usher

marvelous *adjective.* **1** astounding, awesome, fabulous, inconceivable, incredible, miraculous, prodigious, remarkable, spectacular, staggering, striking, supernatural, surprising, unbelievable, unimaginable, unusual, wonderful, wondrous **2** agreeable, astonishing, bad, boss, colossal, divine, dreamy, fabulous, glorious, keen, magnificent, neat, prime, rewarding, solid, spectacular, super, wonderful

masculine *adjective.* adult, ape, bold, courageous, gallant, hairy, hardy, hunk, male, manly, muscular, powerful, resolute, stallion, strapping, strong, stud, virile

mask *noun.* affectation, beard, camouflage, cloak, concealment, dissembling, dissimulation, front, hood, pose, posture, pretense, pretext, screen, semblance, show, veil, veneer

mask *verb.* beard, camouflage, cloak, conceal, cover, cover up, defend, dissimulate, front, guard, hide, obscure, protect, safeguard, screen, secrete, shield, veil

mass *noun.* chunk, collection, core, group, heap, horde, hunk, load, majority, mob, much, number, piece, preponderance, shock, sum, throng, troop

massive *adjective.* blimp, bulky, colossal, enormous, extensive, heavy, impressive, mammoth, mighty, monumental, mountainous, prodigious, solid, stately, substantial, tremendous, vast, walloping

master *adjective.* ascendant, chief, controlling, foremost, grand, great, leading, main, major, overbearing, paramount, predominant, predominate, prevalent, prime, principal, sovereign, supreme

master *noun.* **1** administrator, boss, captain, chief, chieftain, commandant, commander, husband, instructor, judge, lord, manager, overseer, schoolmaster, skipper, supervisor, teacher, tutor **2** adept, authority, champion, connoisseur, doctor, expert, guru, maestro, pro, professional, proficient, protagonist, sage, scientist, shark, virtuoso, whiz, winner **3** acquire, blow away, bone up, comprehend, cram, excel in, gain mastery, get, get down, grasp, grind, pick up, plug, study, swamp, understand, win out **4** break, bust, command, curb, defeat, dominate, gentle, govern, lick, manage, overcome, regulate, rule, subdue, suppress, surmount, tame, throw

mastery *noun.* **1** adroitness, attainment, cleverness, command, comprehension, cunning, deftness, grasp, grip, ken, knack, knowledge, power, proficiency, prowess, skill, understanding, virtuosity **2** ascendancy, authority, command, conquest, control, dominion, government, jurisdiction, might, power, rule, sovereignty, superiority, supremacy, sway, swing, triumph, victory

match *noun.* adversary, analogue, antagonist, companion, competitor, copy, counterpart, double, duplicate, equivalent, fellow, like, mate, opponent, parallel, replica, rival, twin

mate *noun.* acquaintance, associate, bride, buddy, chum, colleague, counterpart, double, friend, helpmate, husband, match, playmate, reciprocal, roommate, spouse, subordinate, twin

mate *verb.* cohabit, copulate, couple, crossbreed, generate, get hitched, hitch, join, land, match, merge, pair, procreate, serve, splice, tie, wed, yoke

material *adjective.* **1** actual, appreciable, carnal, concrete, corporeal, earthly, incarnate, objective, palpable, perceptible, physical, real, sensible, sensual, substantial, tangible, true, worldly **2** applicable, apropos, consequential, considerable, essential, fundamental, grave, intrinsic, key, meaningful, momentous, pertinent, primary, relevant, significant, substantial, vital, weighty

material *noun.* apparatus, being, body, bolt, cloth, constituent, crop, element, entity, equipment, goods, individual, machinery, matter, outfit, paraphernalia, substance, supply

matter *noun.* **1** amount, being, body, constituents, corporeality, corporeity, element, entity, individual, material, object, phenomenon, physical world, protoplasm, quantity, stuff, sum, thing **2** affair, bag, business, circumstance, concern, episode, event, incident, job, lookout, occurrence, proceeding, question, situation, subject, topic, transaction, undertaking **3** amount, body, burden, content, core, gist, importance, magnitude, moment, order, pith, range, sense, substance, text, tune, upshot, weight

mature *adjective.* cultivated, cultured, developed, fit, grown, manly, matured, mellowed, perfected, prepared, prime, ready, ripe, ripened, seasoned, settled, sophisticated, womanly

mature *verb.* advance, age, arrive, bloom, blossom, culminate, develop, evolve, flower, grow, mellow, mushroom, perfect, prime, progress, round, season, snowball

maturity *noun.* advancement, capability, civilization, completion, cultivation, culture, development, experience, fitness, fullness, majority, manhood, maturation, mentality, prime, readiness, sophistication, wisdom

maximum *noun.* apex, apogee, ceiling, climax, crest, culmination, extremity, height, limit, most, peak, pinnacle, record, summit, supremacy, top, uttermost, zenith

meal *noun.* bag, board, breakfast, chow, collation, dessert, dinner, fare, feast, grub, mess, nosebag, refreshment, snack, spread, supper, table, tea

mean *adjective.* **1** callous, contemptible, dirty, disagreeable, hard, infamous, malicious, malign, perfidious, rough, scurrilous, sour, touch, ugly, unfriendly, unpleasant, vexatious, vicious **2** base, common, contemptible, hack, inferior, insignificant, limited, mediocre, menial, miserable, modest, narrow, obscure, petty, pitiful, servile, tawdry, wretched **3** argue, connote, convey, designate, express, foretell, imply, indicate, intimate, name, presage, promise, purport, represent, spell, suggest, symbolize, talking **4** aim, anticipate, aspire, contemplate, design, desire, direct, expect, fate, fit, match, plan, propose, purpose, resolve, suit, want, wish

meaning *noun.* allusion, bearing, content, drift, effect, gist, hint, implication, pith, purport, sense, spirit, subject, substance, suggestion, thrust, upshot, worth

meaningful *adjective.* clear, concise, consequential, considerable, deep, eloquent, exact, explicit, expressive, heavy, important, intelligible, material, purposeful, relevant, substantial, valid, worthwhile

meaningless *adjective.* absurd, aimless, blank, futile, hollow, inconsequential, insignificant, nonsensical, nutmeg, pointless, purposeless, unimportant, useless, vacant, vague, vain, valueless, worthless

means *noun.* **1** agency, aid, apparatus, channel, course, equipment, expedient, machinery, manner, medium, mode, organization, paraphernalia, power, route, system, technique, vehicle **2** assets, budget, dough, estate, fortune, funds, income, intangibles, nut, pocket, possessions, property, purse, reserves, resources, riches, securities, substance

measure *noun.* **1** allotment, amplitude, area, breadth, distance, magnitude, part, proportion, quantum, range, ratio, ration, scope, size, slug, span, strength, sum **2** canon, criterion, example, gauge, meter, method, model, norm, pattern, quintal, rule, scale, system, test, touchstone, trial, type, yardstick **3** act, agency, course, deed, device, effort, expedient, makeshift, maneuver, moderation, move, procedure, proposal, proposition, resource, restraint, step, temperance **4** accent, cadence, cadency, division, foot, melody, meter, rhyme, rhythm, step, stress, stroke, swing, tempo, time, tune, verse, vibration

measure *verb.* adjust, align, assess, beat, blend, bound, choose, figure, fit, level, line, mark, rate, rhyme, shade, sound, tailor, time

measurement *noun.* amplitude, analysis, appraisal, area, assessment, density, determination, distance, height, judgment, length, magnitude, range, scope, size, thickness, time, width

meat *noun.* aliment, back bacon, brawn, chow, comestible, eats, edible, fare, food, grub, muscle, nourishment, pemmican, provision, ration, subsistence, sustenance, victual

mechanical *adjective.* automated, automatic, cold, cursory, fixed, habitual, impersonal, involuntary, lifeless, monotonous, perfunctory, programmed, routine, standardized, stereotyped, unchanging, unconscious, useful

mechanism *noun.* apparatus, appliance, black box, components, contrivance, device, doohickey, gears, innards, instrument, machinery, motor, structure, system, tool, workings, works

medicine *noun.* antidote, antiseptic, balm, dose, drug, injection, inoculation, liniment, medication, pharmaceutical, pill, prescription, remedy, salve, sedative, tablet, tonic, vaccine

medium *adjective.* average, common, commonplace, fair, intermediate, mean, median, mediocre, middle, moderate, neutral, normal, ordinary, par, passable, popular, standard, tolerable

medium *noun.* **1** agency, agent, avenue, channel, clairvoyant, factor, form, instrument, intermediate, measure, mechanism, ministry, mode, organ, psychic, tool, vehicle, way **2** art, delineation, evidence, gesture, interpretation, manifestation, mark, media, music, painting, revelation, sculpture, sign, speech, statement, symbol, token, writing

meek *adjective.* docile, gentle, mild, modest, orderly, passive, patient, plain, resigned, serene, soft, spineless, subdued, submissive, tame, tolerant, weak, zero

meet *adjective.* accommodated, applicable, appropriate, apt, conformed, equitable, expedient, fair, felicitous, fit, good, happy, just, proper, reconciled, right, suitable, timely

meet *verb.* **1** affront, clash, confront, contact, cross, encounter, experience, face, find, front, grapple, hit, light, luck, salute, strike, stumble, wrestle **2** answer, approach, carry out, comply, discharge, equal, execute, fit, fulfill, gratify, handle, match, measure up, rival, satisfy, suffice, tie, touch **3** appear, assemble, be presented, collect, congregate, converge, enter in, flock, foregather, gather, join, make acquaintance, muster, open, rally, rendezvous, show, sit

meeting *noun.* assembly, bunch, conclave, conference, conflict, congress, convocation, date, engagement, gang, huddle, introduction, meet, parley, rally, rendezvous, session, turnout

melancholy *adjective.* crummy, despondent, destroyed, dismal, doleful, down, downcast, gloomy, grim, mirthless, miserable, moody, mournful, sad, sorry, wistful, woebegone, woeful

melancholy *noun.* blues, boredom, dejection, despair, desperation, despondency, dumps, funk, gloom, grief, misery, sadness, sorrow, tedium, unhappiness, wistfulness, woe, wretchedness

melody *noun.* assonance, concord, consonance, inflection, lay, lyric, measure, music, musicality, refrain, resonance, run, song, strain, theme, tune, tunefulness, unison

member *noun.* associate, branch, brother, chapter, comrade, constituent, cut, division, fellow, joiner, parcel, piece, post, representative, section, segment, sister, unit

memorable *adjective.* catchy, distinguished, heavy, historic, hot, important, impressive, indelible, meaningful, monumental, observable, remarkable, rubric, signal, something, striking, super, terrific

memorial *noun.* ceremony, column, mausoleum, memento, obelisk, plaque, record, relic, remembrance, reminder, shaft, slab, souvenir, statue, tablet, testimonial, tombstone, trophy

memory *noun.* anamnesis, awareness, camera-eye, cognizance, consciousness, flashback, memorization, mind, recall, recapture, recognition, recollection, reflection, remembrance, reminiscence, retention, retentiveness, thought

menace *verb.* alarm, bother, bully, chill, compromise, endanger, hazard, imperil, intimidate, jeopardy, loom, lower, overhang, peril, risk, scare, threaten, torment

mental *adjective.* cerebral, clairvoyant, deep, heavy, ideological, imaginative, inner, intellectual, mysterious, psychic, psychical, rational, reasoning, savvy, spiritual, subconscious, thoughtful, unreal

mention *verb.* acknowledge, acquaint, detail, disclose, discuss, impart, infer, instance, name, notice, observe, quote, recount, remark, report, state, suggest, tell

merchant *noun.* big wheel, broker, businessman, consigner, dealer, exporter, handler, operator, retailer, salesman, seller, shipper, shopkeeper, storekeeper, trader, tradesman, tycoon, vendor

mercy *noun.* boon, charity, clemency, favor, forgiveness, generosity, gentleness, godsend, goodwill, grace, humanity, kindliness, luck, pity, quarter, relief, sympathy, tolerance

mere *adjective.* bare, blunt, common, entire, insignificant, little, minor, plain, poor, pure, sheer, simple, small, stark, unadorned, unadulterated, unmixed, very

merge *verb.* absorb, blend, cement, coalesce, combine, compound, consolidate, converge, fuse, interface, join, meet, meld, mingle, network, pool, tag, unite

merger *noun.* alliance, amalgamation, cahoots, coadunation, coalition, combination, fusion, hookup, incorporation, lineup, mergence, merging, organization, pool, takeover, tie-up, unification, union

merit *noun.* asset, benefit, caliber, credit, desert, dignity, excellence, good, goodness, honor, integrity, quality, stature, talent, value, virtue, worth

merry *adjective.* amusing, boisterous, boon, carefree, convivial, facetious, funny, glad, gleeful, hilarious, jolly, joyous, riotous, rocking, rollicking, sunny, wild, winsome

mess *noun.* blend, chaos, combination, compound, disarray, disorganization, fright, hash, hectic, hodgepodge, jumble, mayhem, monstrosity, sight, turmoil, untidiness, wreck, wreckage

message *noun.* bulletin, cannonball, directive, dispatch, dope, information, intelligence, letter, memo, memorandum, missive, news, note, notice, paper, report, tidings, word

messenger *noun.* agent, ambassador, angel, boy, carrier, courier, delegate, detachment, detail, emissary, forerunner, herald, minister, post, prophet, runner, speed, trumpeter

metaphysical *adjective.* abstract, deep, eternal, fundamental, insubstantial, intangible, intellectual, mystical, numinous, philosophical, profound, recondite, spiritual, superhuman, superior, supernatural, universal, unreal

method *noun.* arrangement, course, form, formula, line, mode, plan, program, receipt, recipe, rubric, schema, scheme, shortcut, system, tactics, wise, wrinkle

middle *adjective.* average, between, center, centermost, equidistant, halfway, inner, inside, intermediate, intervening, mainstream, mean, median, medium, mezzo, mid, midmost, straddle fence

might *noun.* arm, beef, clout, command, competence, efficacy, efficiency, energy, forcefulness, jurisdiction, muscle, power, prowess, punch, qualification, steam, strength, vigor

mighty *adjective.* **1** boss, doughty, hardy, indomitable, lusty, manful, muscular, omnipotent, potent, powerful, powerhouse, puissant, stalwart, stout, strapping, strong, sturdy, vigorous **2** bulky, colossal, considerable, dynamic, enormous, extensive, heroic, impressive, irresistible, large, magnificent, massive, monumental, notable, prodigious, titanic, tremendous, vast

mild *adjective.* **1** balmy, calm, clear, clement, dainty, exquisite, fine, genial, light, lukewarm, medium, moderate, placid, smooth, sunny, temperate, warm, weak **2** amiable, calm, clement, dull, feeble, forgiving, humane, insipid, meek, merciful, moderate, patient, smooth, subdued, subservient, temperate, tender, warm

militant *adjective.* active, aggressive, assertive, belligerent, combating, contending, contentious, embattled, fighting, militaristic, military, offensive, quarrelsome, truculent, vigorous, warlike, warring

milk *noun.* bovine extract, buttermilk, certified, chalk, condensed, cow juice, cream, dried, evaporated, formula, goat, half-and-half, moo juice, powdered, raw, skim, two-percent, whole

milk *verb.* bleed, drain, draw off, elicit, empty, evince, evoke, exhaust, express, extract, fleece, impose on, press, pump, suck, tap, use, wring

mind *noun.* **1** brain, cognizance, function, instinct, intellectual, intellectuality, intuition, judgment, perception, power, psyche, reason, regard, soundness, spirit, talent, thinker, wisdom **2** conviction, determination, fancy, humor, impulse, inclination, intention, judgment, liking, outlook, persuasion, sentiment, temper, tone, vein, view, will, wish **3** adhere to, attend, behave, follow, follow orders, heed, keep, listen, mark, note, notice, obey, observe, pay attention, regard, respect, take heed, watch **4** attend, behold, dig, discipline, ensure, govern, guard, look, mark, notice, observe, perceive, regard, see, sit, superintend, supervise, watch

mine *noun*. abundance, bed, bonanza, deposit, ditch, excavation, field, fountain, pit, quarry, reserve, shaft, source, spring, stock, treasury, vein, wealth

miniature *adjective*. baby, diminutive, dwarf, dwarfish, itty-bitty, Lilliputian, little, minute, mite, model, petite, pocket, reduced, scaled-down, small, teensy, toy, wee

minimize *verb*. curtail, decrease, decry, derogate, detract, diminish, discount, dwarf, knock, knock down, lessen, pan, play down, prune, reduce, run down, shrink, underestimate

minimum *noun*. atom, bottom, depth, dot, gleam, grain, hair, iota, least, modicum, molecule, nadir, particle, shadow, smallest, spark, speck, trifle

minister *noun*. **1** abbot, chaplain, clergyman, clerical, clerk, deacon, diocesan, divine, lecturer, missionary, monk, parson, preacher, priest, rector, reverend, shepherd, vicar **2** administrator, agent, aide, ambassador, assistant, consul, delegate, diplomat, envoy, executive, legate, liaison, lieutenant, official, plenipotentiary, premier, secretary, statesman

minister *verb*. accommodate, administer, aid, answer, attend, cure, doctor, foster, heal, mother, nurse, pander to, remedy, serve, succor, tend, treat, watch over

minor *adjective*. accessory, casual, dependent, inconsequential, junior, lesser, light, petty, piddling, secondary, shoestring, slight, small, smaller, subordinate, subsidiary, unimportant, younger

minor *noun*. adolescent, baby, boy, child, girl, infant, jailbait, junior, juvenile, lad, little one, punk, schoolboy, schoolgirl, teenager, underage, youngster, youth

mint *verb*. cast, coin, construct, devise, fabricate, fashion, forge, invent, issue, make, make up, mold, monetize, produce, provide, punch, stamp, strike

minute *adjective*. **1** atomic, diminutive, exact, fine, inconsiderable, insignificant, invisible, little, microscopic, miniature, minimal, molecular, piddling, precise, pulverized, puny, teensy, tiny **2** careful, circumstantial, clocklike, close, critical, detailed, elaborate, exhaustive, full, itemized, meticulous, painstaking, particular, particularized, precise, scrupulous, specialized, thorough

minute *noun*. breath, breathing, crack, flash, instant, jiffy, min, mo, moment, nothing flat, sec, second, shake, short time, split second, tick, trice, twinkling

mirror *verb*. copy, depict, double, echo, embody, emulate, epitomize, exemplify, follow, glass, illustrate, image, imitate, represent, show, simulate, take off, typify

miscellaneous *adjective*. confused, disordered, disparate, divergent, diverse, heterogeneous, indiscriminate, jumbled, many, mixed, motley, odd, scrambled, sundry, unmatched, varied, variegated, various

miserable *adjective*. **1** afflicted, anguished, depressed, despairing, destroyed, doleful, downcast, forlorn, injured, mournful, pained, pitiable, strained, tormented, tortured, woebegone, wounded, wretched **2** abject, bad, contemptible, deplorable, destitute, disgraceful, impoverished, indigent, inferior, meager, needy, penniless, piteous, pitiable, poor, scurvy, worthless, wretched

misery *noun*. **1** ache, agony, anguish, depression, despair, despondency, distress, grief, hardship, hurting, melancholy, passion, stew, suffering, torment, twinge, unhappiness, wretchedness **2** adversity, affliction, burden, calamity, catastrophe, curse, difficulty, disaster, grief, load, misfortune, need, ordeal, penury, poverty, trial, tribulation, want

misfortune *noun*. accident, affliction, burden, calamity, catastrophe, contretemps, crunch, debacle, disadvantage, harm, inconvenience, loss, misery, mishap, setback, tribulation, trouble, unpleasantness

misleading *adjective*. ambiguous, beguiling, catchy, confounding, confusing, deceitful, deceiving, deluding, evasive, fallacious, false, inaccurate, perplexing, puzzling, specious, spurious, tricky, wrong

miss *verb*. blow, blunder, disregard, drop,

err, forget, fumble, ignore, lose, mistake, muff, neglect, omit, overlook, skip, slight, slip, trip

missile *noun.* ammunition, arrow, bat bomb, beast, bird, bolt, bullet, cartridge, cruise, dart, dingbat, egg, pellet, projectile, rocket, shot, stealth, trajectile

mission *noun.* aim, assignment, business, charge, commission, errand, job, objective, operation, profession, pursuit, quest, responsibility, sortie, trust, undertaking, vocation, work

missionary *noun.* apostle, clergyman, converter, evangelist, herald, Holy Joe, messenger, minister, missioner, padre, pastor, preacher, preacher man, promoter, propagandist, revivalist, sin hound, teacher

mist *verb.* becloud, befog, blur, dim, drizzle, film, fog, haze, mizzle, murk, obscure, overcast, overcloud, rain, shower, sprinkle, steam, steam up

mistake *noun.* aberration, blunder, delusion, fault, fluff, illusion, inaccuracy, lapse, miscalculation, misconception, misinterpretation, misstep, misunderstanding, omission, overestimation, oversight, slight, slip

mistake *verb.* addle, blunder, confuse, err, fail, jumble, lapse, miscount, misinterpret, miss, misunderstand, omit, overestimate, overlook, slip, slip up, tangle, underestimate

mistaken *adjective.* confused, duped, erroneous, fallacious, false, faulty, fooled, illogical, incorrect, misconstrued, misguided, misled, misunderstanding, tricked, unfounded, unreal, untrue, warranted

misunderstanding *noun.* beef, blowup, break, clash, conflict, debate, difference, difficulty, disagreement, discord, fight, fuss, quarrel, rift, rupture, spat, variance, words

mix *verb.* alloy, associate, blend, coalesce, compound, cross, embody, fuse, join, jumble, knead, make up, mingle, stir, suffuse, tangle, unite, work in

mixed *adjective.* amalgamated, brewed, composite, compound, disordered, diverse, diversified, embodied, heterogeneous, hybrid, incorporated, interdenominational, joint, married, merged, motley, tied, varied

mixture *noun.* alloy, association, blend, brew, compound, crossing, dough, fusion, hodgepodge, infiltration, jumble, miscellany, mosaic, saturation, soup, stew, union, variety

mob *noun.* body, camp, circle, clique, collection, crew, crush, drove, flock, gang, horde, mass, multitude, press, riot, set, throng, troop

mobile *adjective.* adaptable, ambulatory, changeable, fluid, free, itinerant, liquid, locomotive, loose, migrant, migratory, moving, portable, unsettled, unstable, unsteady, versatile, wandering

mock *adjective.* bogus, dummy, fake, faked, false, feigned, forged, imitation, imitative, phony, pretended, pseudo, quasi, sham, simulated, spurious, substitute, unreal

mock *verb.* **1** buffoon, burlesque, caricature, hoot, insult, jive, kid, needle, parody, rally, rib, scoff, scorn, scout, sneer, taunt, tease, travesty **2** affect, ape, assume, burlesque, caricature, counterfeit, do, fake, feign, hoke, imitate, lampoon, mirror, parody, send up, simulate, take off, travesty **3** beguile, belie, betray, challenge, cheat, defeat, defy, delude, disappoint, double-cross, dupe, elude, foil, fool, frustrate, mislead, sell out, thwart

mode *noun.* **1** approach, course, custom, form, method, modus, plan, posture, procedure, quality, rule, style, system, technique, tone, vein, wise, wrinkle **2** chic, convention, craze, cry, fad, fashion, furor, in-thing, last word, latest wrinkle, look, mainstream, mod, now, rage, spinach, style, vogue

model *adjective.* classic, classical, commendable, copy, dummy, exemplary, facsimile, flawless, illustrative, imitation, miniature, paradigmatic, perfect, prototypical, representative, standard, typical, very

model *noun.* **1** cartoon, copy, dummy, facsimile, figure, illustration, image, layout, miniature, photograph, pocket, print, relief, replica, setup, statue, statuette, tracing **2** apotheosis, criterion, design, embodiment, epitome, exemplar, hero, mirror, mold, original, paradigm, paragon, prototype, saint, standard, symbol, touchstone, type

moderate *adjective.* **1** balanced, calm, careful, compromising, conservative, disciplined, gentle, inexpensive, limited, measured, modest, neutral, nonpartisan, reasonable, steady, tame, tolerant, tranquil **2** average, bland, fairish, inconsequential, inconsiderable, indifferent, intermediate, mean, mediocre, medium, middling, ordinary, paltry, passable, piddling, trifling, trivial, unexceptional

moderate *verb.* alleviate, calm, coast, curb, decline, fall, lessen, mollify, qualify, reduce, regulate, relieve, repress, soften, subdue, subside, tame, temper

modern *adjective.* concurrent, contemporary, current, fresh, late, latest, modernistic, modernized, modish, novel, now, present, prevailing, prevalent, recent, stylish, today, twentieth-century

modest *adjective.* **1** bashful, blushing, demure, discreet, meek, moderate, nice, proper, prudent, quiet, reserved, resigned, retiring, silent, simple, temperate, unobtrusive, withdrawing **2** average, cheap, discreet, economical, fair, humble, inexpensive, moderate, natural, ordinary, plain, reasonable, simple, small, unadorned, unaffected, unobtrusive, unpretentious

moist *adjective.* clammy, damp, dampish, dank, dewy, dripping, drippy, drizzly, humid, irriguous, muggy, not dry, oozy, rainy, soggy, teary, watery, wettish

mold *noun.* cavity, character, class, description, design, die, form, frame, image, impression, kind, matrix, model, shape, sort, stamp, type, womb

mold *verb.* build, construct, devise, erect, fashion, forge, form, frame, make, pat, plan, plant, plot, put together, round, scheme, shape, whittle

moment *noun.* **1** bit, breathing, crack, date, flash, hour, instant, jiffy, minute, mo, occasion, second, shake, stage, tick, time, twinkle, twinkling **2** advantage, avail, concern, consequence, gravity, import, magnitude, note, pith, profit, seriousness, significance, signification, substance, use, value, weight, worth

momentous *adjective.* consequential, considerable, critical, decisive, fateful, grave, heavy, historic, material, meaningful, memorable, notable, outstanding, pivotal, significant, substantial, vital, weighty

money *noun.* beans, bread, cabbage, chips, coin, dough, funds, green, loot, payment, property, resources, riches, salary, silver, skin, treasure, wealth

monotonous *adjective.* colorless, dreary, dull, monotone, pedestrian, plodding, prosaic, recurrent, reiterated, repetitive, tiresome, toneless, treadmill, unchanged, uniform, uninteresting, unrelieved, wearisome

monotony *noun.* boredom, continuance, continuity, dreariness, dryness, dullness, equability, evenness, flatness, humdrum, invariability, likeness, monotone, oneness, routine, similarity, tedium, uniformity

monstrous *adjective.* **1** cruel, diabolical, disgraceful, dreadful, foul, gruesome, horrible, infamous, inhuman, intolerable, loathsome, macabre, morbid, obscene, ominous, unusual, vicious, villainous **2** colossal, cracking, enormous, fantastic, giant, grandiose, immense, impressive, magnificent, mammoth, massive, monumental, mortal, prodigious, stupendous, titanic, tremendous, vast

monument *noun.* column, erection, gravestone, masterpiece, memento, obelisk, pile, record, remembrance, reminder, slab, statue, stone, tablet, tomb, tombstone, tower, tribute

mood *noun.* affection, atmosphere, aura, bag, bit, color, cue, doldrums, emotion, fancy, humor, inclination, spirit, temper, tendency, timbre, vein, wish

moral *adjective.* courteous, decent, elevated, good, honest, immaculate, incorruptible, meet, meritorious, modest, proper, respectable, right, scrupulous, square, truthful, upstanding

moral *noun.* adage, axiom, dictum, gnome, maxim, meaning, message, moralism, motto, point, precept, proverb, rule, saw, saying, sermon, significance, truism

morale *noun.* assurance, attitude, confidence, disposition, drive, esprit, heart, humor, mettle, mood, outlook, resolve, self-possession, spirit, temper, temperament, turn, vigor

morality *noun.* chastity, decency, gentleness, goodness, habits, honesty, incorruptibility, integrity, manners, mores, philosophy, principles, probity, rectitude, righteousness, rightness, saintliness, standards

more *adjective.* added, also, and, another, augmented, besides, deeper, exceeding, extended, extra, further, heavier, increased, innumerable, larger, massed, new, wider

morning *noun.* AM, ante meridiem, aurora, bright, cockcrow, dawn, daybreak, daylight, dayspring, first blush, light, morrow, peep, prime, sun-up, sunrise, wee hours

mortal *adjective.* **1** deathly, destructive, ending, extreme, fatal, grave, grievous, grim, intense, last, lethal, merciless, monstrous, pestilent, poisonous, ruthless, severe, terrible **2** bipedal, corporeal, creatural, earthly, ephemeral, evanescent, fading, finite, frail, impermanent, momentary, passing, perishable, precarious, temporal, transient, weak, worldly

most *adverb.* about, all but, almost, approximately, close, eminently, exceedingly, mightily, much, nearly, nigh, practically, remarkably, super, surpassingly, too, very, well-nigh

mostly *adverb.* above all, almost entirely, chiefly, customarily, essentially, frequently, largely, mainly, many times, most often, often, overall, particularly, predominantly, primarily, principally, regularly, usually

mother *verb.* baby, bear, bring forth, cherish, fuss over, indulge, minister to, nurse, nurture, pamper, produce, protect, raise, rear, serve, spoil, tend, wait on

motion *noun.* act, agitation, change, changing, direction, flow, gesture, inclination, move, passage, passing, progress, sign, stir, stirring, tendency, travel, wave

motionless *adjective.* becalmed, deathly, firm, fixed, frozen, inert, lifeless, numb, paralyzed, quiescent, spellbound, stagnant, stalled, static, stationary, still, torpid, unmoved

motivation *noun.* angle, encouragement, impetus, impulse, incentive, incitement, inclination, inducement, interest, kick, motive, persuasion, provocation, push, reason, stimulus, suggestion, wish

motive *noun.* aim, antecedent, cause, consideration, design, determinant, emotion, grounds, impulse, incentive, influence, intent, intention, occasion, passion, root, spring, stimulus

mount *verb.* **1** arise, ascend, back, bestride, clamber up, climb onto, escalade, escalate, get astride, go up, jump on, lift, rise, scale, soar, tower, up, vault **2** accumulate, aggravate, augment, build, deepen, enhance, enlarge, expand, grow, heighten, intensify, multiply, pile up, rise, rouse, swell, upsurge, wax

mountain *noun.* abundance, bank, bluff, butte, dome, elevation, eminence, glob, heap, height, mesa, mound, mount, peak, pike, range, ridge, shock

mouth *noun.* aperture, box, buss, cavity, chops, clam, crevice, delta, door, entrance, funnel, gate, gob, jaws, lips, portal, rim, trap

movable *adjective.* adaptable, adjustable, ambulatory, detachable, loose, mobile, moving, not fastened, on wheels, portable, removable, separable, shiftable, transferable, turnable, unattached, unfastened, unsteady

move *noun.* act, alteration, change, deed, maneuver, measure, modification, motion, movement, procedure, proceeding, shift, step, stir, stirring, stroke, turn, variation

move *verb.* **1** budge, bustle, carry, change, climb, crawl, disturb, flow, fly, leave, migrate, ship, shove, stir, take off, transport, travel, walk **2** activate, advocate, affect, agitate, budge, carry, impress, induce, prompt, propel, propose, quicken, recommend, shove, start, stir, strike, touch

movement *noun.* **1** act, agitation, change, changing, evolving, flow, gesture, move, operation, passage, regression, steps, stir, stirring, transfer, transit, undertaking, velocity **2** campaign, change, crusade, demonstration, flight, flow, front, group, grouping, march, organization, party, swing, tendency, transfer, transition, trend, withdrawal

movie *noun.* cine, cinema, cinematograph, feature, film, flick, flicker, motion picture, moving picture, photoplay, picture, screenplay, show, silver screen, talkie, talking picture, videotape

moving *adjective.* **1** arousing, awakening, dynamic, expressive, gripping, impelling, impressive, inspirational, inspiring, meaningful, motivating, poignant, rallying, rousing, significant, something, stirring, touching **2** advancing, changing, climbing, evolving, flying, going, jumping, movable, portage, progressing, running, shifting, traversing, unfixed, unstable, unsteadfast, unsteady, walking

much *adjective.* considerable, endless, enough, extravagant, full, generous, heaps, immeasurable, lavish, loads, many, plentiful, profuse, satisfying, sizeable, substantial, sufficient, voluminous

much *adverb.* considerably, decidedly, eminently, exceedingly, exceptionally, extremely, frequently, highly, hugely, indeed, notably, oft, often, regularly, repeatedly, surpassingly, very, very much

much *noun.* abundance, amplitude, barrel, breadth, excess, exuberance, fullness, heaps, loads, lots, mass, mess, multiplicity, overage, pile, riches, sufficiency, wealth

muddy *adjective.* black, caked, confused, dingy, dirty, dull, foul, gloomy, greasy, grubby, hazy, indistinct, obscure, opaque, smoky, sodden, unclean, unclear

multiple *adjective.* collective, different, diverse, heterogeneous, indiscriminate, legion, manifold, many, mixed, motley, multitudinous, numerous, several, sundry, varied, variegated, various, voluminous

multiply *verb.* augment, boost, breed, build up, compound, cube, double, enlarge, expand, extend, manifold, mount, populate, produce, repeat, rise, spread, square

municipal *adjective.* borough, burghal, city, civic, civil, community, corporate, domestic, home, incorporated, internal, local, metropolitan, native, public, self-governing, town, urban

murder *noun.* annihilation, assassination, bloodshed, butchery, crime, destruction, dispatching, felony, hit, homicide, liquidation, manslaughter, massacre, off, offing, shooting, slaying, wasting

murder *verb.* abolish, butcher, chill, defeat, dispatch, do in, eliminate, eradicate, execute, exterminate, extinguish, knife, mar, massacre, misuse, off, shoot, waste

muscular *adjective.* bruising, burly, fibrous, herculean, hulk, hunk, husky, mighty, muscle, powerful, sinewy, stout, strapping, strong, sturdy, tiger, wicked, wiry

music *noun.* bebop, bop, classical, folk, harmony, jazz, melody, modern, piece, popular, rap, refrain, rock, song, soul, strain, swing, tune

musical *adjective.* agreeable, blending, choral, consonant, dulcet, harmonious, lilting, lyrical, melodic, melodious, orchestral, pleasing, silvery, songful, sweet, tuned, tuneful, vocal

must *noun.* charge, commitment, committal, condition, devoir, duty, essential, fundamental, imperative, necessary, need, obligation, ought, precondition, prerequisite, requirement, requisite, right

must *verb.* be compelled, be destined, be directed, be doomed, be driven, be made, be necessitated, be obliged, be ordered, be required, got to, have, have to, must needs, need, should, should want, want

mutual *adjective.* alternate, associated, bilateral, collective, common, communal, connected, dependent, interchangeable, interdependent, joint, participated, public, reciprocal, related, respective, returned, united

muzzle *verb.* check, choke, curb, gag, hush, ice, prevent, repress, restrain, restrict, shut down, silence, squash, stifle, still, stop, suppress, trammel

myriad *adjective.* countless, endless, heap, immeasurable, incalculable, infinite, loads, mint, multiple, multitudinous, numberless, oodles, raft, scads, stacks, uncounted, untold, variable

myriad *noun.* army, flood, heap, horde, host, loads, million, millions, mint, mountain, multitude, raft, scores, sea, stacks, swarm, thousand, thousands

mysterious *adjective.* baffling, cryptic, curious, enigmatic, impenetrable, inexplicable, insoluble, magical, mystical, necromantic, obscure, perplexing, puzzling, recondite, spiritual, strange, unfathomable, unnatural

mystery *noun.* crux, difficulty, enigma, inscrutability, mystification, oracle, perplexity, problem, puzzle, puzzlement, question, riddle, secrecy, sphinx, stickler, subtlety, twister, why

myth *noun.* allegory, creation, delusion, fable, fabrication, fancy, fantasy, fiction, figment, illusion, imagination, invention, legend, lore, parable, saga, superstition, tradition

N

naive *adjective.* artless, candid, confiding, credulous, forthright, frank, green, guileless, gullible, harmless, lamb, natural, open, simple, sincere, spontaneous, square, virgin

naked *adjective.* **1** bald, bare, barren, defenseless, denuded, exposed, helpless, natural, nude, open, peeled, raw, stripped, threadbare, uncovered, unprotected, unveiled, vulnerable **2** artless, blatant, disclosed, discovered, manifest, obvious, open, overt, palpable, plain, revealed, sheer, simple, stark, unadorned, undisguised, unmistakable, unqualified

name *noun.* agnomen, alias, autograph, denomination, designation, epithet, flag, handle, head, heading, label, pseudonym, rubric, sign, signature, style, surname, tag

name *verb.* **1** baptize, call, characterize, classify, define, denominate, designate, entitle, identify, label, nickname, nomenclature, style, tag, term, ticket, title **2** appoint, commission, connote, delegate, finger, identify, index, instance, list, mark, mention, nominate, peg, recognize, signify, suggest, tag, tap

narrative *noun.* account, anecdote, chronicle, chronology, clothesline, description, detail, fiction, history, line, narration, potboiler, recount, report, statement, tale, version, yarn

narrow *adjective.* circumscribed, compressed, constricted, contracted, fine, fixed, limited, linear, meager, precarious, set, shrunken, slim, small, strait, taper, tapered, tapering

nation *noun.* colony, commonwealth, community, democracy, domain, dominion, empire, kingdom, land, people, population, public, race, realm, society, sovereignty, state, tribe

national *adjective.* civic, civil, communal, countrywide, federal, home, imperial, inland, internal, municipal, nationwide, native, politic, political, royal, sovereign, sweeping, widespread

native *adjective.* **1** congenital, constitutional, essential, fundamental, genuine, hereditary, implanted, inborn, indigenous, inherent, inherited, intrinsic, inveterate, natal, natural, original, real, wild **2** aboriginal, belonging, from, homemade, indigenous, inland, internal, local, mother, municipal, national, original, primary, primeval, primitive, regional, related, vernacular

native *noun.* aboriginal, aborigine, Amerindian, ancient, autochthon, citizen, countryman, dweller, indigene, inhabitant, landsman, local, local yokel, national, paisano, resident

natural *adjective.* **1** anticipated, characteristic, common, congenital, constant, inborn, indigenous, intuitive, natal, native, prevalent, probable, reasonable, regular, spontaneous, uniform, universal, usual **2** artless, candid, childlike, credulous, direct, folksy, forthright, frank, ignorant, naive, open, plain, primitive, provincial, real, simple, sincere, spontaneous

naturally *adverb.* candidly, casually, characteristically, commonly, consistently, easily, freely, generally, informally, instinctively, natch, normally, ordinarily, readily, simply, typically, uniformly, usually

nature *noun.* **1** attributes, bag, being, complexion, constitution, description, drift, essence, humor, like, outlook, personality, quality, stuff, temper, texture, traits, type **2** anatomy, brand, cast, category, character, color, description, figure, framework, kidney, kind, shape, sort, species, stripe, style, variety, way **3** cosmos, country, countryside, earth, environment, forest, generation, landscape, macrocosm, natural history, outdoors, scenery, seascape, setting, universe, view, world

near *adjective.* abreast, adjacent, adjoining, around, beside, bordering, contiguous, handy, hot, nearby, neighboring, nigh, practically, proximal, proximate, ready, touching, warm

nearly *adverb.* about, all but, approaching, approximately, circa, closely, most, much, nigh, practically, pretty near, roughly, round, roundly, some, something like, somewhere, virtually

neat *adjective.* **1** accurate, chipper, dainty, elegant, exact, finicky, immaculate, natty, orderly, prim, proper, regular, slick, spotless, systematic, tidy, trig, trim **2** able, adept, adroit, agile, apt, artful, deft, efficient, effortless, elegant, expert, finished, handy, precise, proficient, ready, skillful, stylish

necessarily *adverb.* accordingly, automatically, by definition, consequently, fundamentally, ineluctably, inescapably, inevitably, inexorably, irresistibly, naturally, of necessity, perforce, positively, significantly, undoubtedly, unquestionably, vitally

necessary *adjective.* binding, chief, cold, compelling, decisive, expedient, fundamental, mandatory, momentous, name, prime, required, significant, specified, unavoidable, urgent, vital, wanted

necessity *noun.* cause, claim, compulsion, demand, duress, essence, essential, fundamental, godsend, imperative, inevitability, must, necessary, obligation, precondition, requirement, stress, want

need *noun.* **1** charge, commitment, compulsion, demand, duty, essential, extremity, itch, longing, must, obligation, occasion, ought, requirement, right, use, weakness, wish **2** deprivation, destitution, distress, extremity, impecuniousness, impoverishment, inadequacy, indigence, insufficiency, lack, neediness, paucity, pennilessness, penury, poorness, privation, shortage, want

need *verb.* be short, claim, covet, crave, demand, desire, die for, exact, hunger, lack, long, miss, necessitate, pine, require, thirst, wish, yearn

needle *verb.* aggravate, bait, bother, dun, examine, gnaw, goad, harass, hector, pester, plague, prick, prod, provoke, quiz, ride, spur, sting

negative *adjective.* antagonistic, bad, colorless, con, contrary, cynical, denying, detrimental, dissenting, gloomy, opposing, removed, repugnant, resistive, unenthusiastic, unfavorable, uninterested, weak

neglect *noun.* **1** carelessness, coolness, delinquency, disdain, disrespect, heedlessness, inadvertence, inattention, inconsideration, indifference, laxity, laxness, oversight, scorn, slight, thoughtlessness, unconcern **2** carelessness, chaos, default, delay, delinquency, dereliction, dilapidation, forgetfulness, lapse, laxness, limbo, negligence, omission, oversight, pretermission, remissness, slackness, slovenliness **3** affront, depreciate, despise, detest, discount, disdain, dismiss, ignore, let go, overlook, pass up, rebuff, reject, scant, scorn, shake off, slight, underestimate **4** be remiss, bypass, defer, discard, dismiss, disregard, elide, evade, forget, let go, miss, omit, overlook, postpone, procrastinate, skip, suspend, trifle

negotiate *verb.* adjudicate, adjust, agree, arbitrate, concert, confer, consult, contract, debate, discuss, drop, handle, intercede, manage, moderate, parley, swap, transact

neighborhood *noun.* area, closeness, confines, environs, parish, part, precinct, quarter, region, section, slum, suburb, territory, tract, turf, ward, zone, zoo

nerve *noun.* bravery, cheek, confidence, crust, determination, endurance, energy, face, firmness, gall, grit, mettle, pluck, presumption, spirit, starch, vigor, will

nervous *adjective.* afraid, agitated, concerned, disturbed, edgy, hesitant, jittery, querulous, ruffled, tense, troubled, uneasy, unstrung, upset, waspish, weak, wired, worried

network *noun.* arrangement, artery, chain, circuitry, connections, fabric, fiber, grill, grillwork, labyrinth, mesh, net, organization, screening, system, tracks, web, wiring

neurotic *adjective.* abnormal, anxious, choked, compulsive, deviant, disordered, distraught, disturbed, erratic, nervous, screwed up, shot, sick, unhealthy, unstable, upset, wired, wreck

neutral *adjective.* aloof, calm, clinical, collected, detached, disinterested, impersonal, inactive, indifferent, inert, nonchalant, noncombatant, noncommittal, nonpartisan, pacifistic, relaxed, uncommitted, unconcerned

new *adjective.* advanced, contemporary, dewy, dissimilar, distinct, inexperienced, late, modernistic, now, strange, ultramodern, unique, unskilled, untouched, untrained, unusual, virgin, youthful

newcomer *noun.* alien, arrival, beginner, colt, fish, foreigner, freshman, immigrant, latecomer, maverick, novice, novitiate, outsider, rookie, settler, stranger, tenderfoot, turkey

news *noun.* account, bulletin, cable, cognizance, description, discovery, dispatch, enlightenment, expose, headlines, itemization, knowledge, recital, recognition, rumor, statement, story, tidings

newspaper *noun.* community, daily, extra, gazette, journal, magazine, metropolitan, organ, paper, periodical, press, rag, record, review, sheet, tabloid, trade, weekly

next *adjective.* adjacent, adjoining, after, attached, beside, close, closest, consequent, ensuing, following, later, meeting, nearest, neighboring, proximate, subsequent, succeeding, touching

nice *adjective.* **1** admirable, agreeable, amiable, becoming, charming, considerate, courteous, delightful, genial, gentle, good, helpful, ingratiating, inviting, kind, superior, welcome, winsome **2** becoming, befitting, careful, dainty, decent, discriminating, distinguishing, exact, exacting, fine, meticulous, minute, neat, proper, respectable, strict, tidy, trim

night *noun.* after dark, after hours, bedtime, black, blackness, dark, darkness, dim, duskiness, evening, eventide, gloom, midnight, nightfall, nighttime, obscurity, twilight, witching hour

noble *adjective.* courtly, dignified, distinguished, elevated, generous, gracious, humane, impressive, liberal, lofty, lordly, magnificent, meritorious, remarkable, reputable, stately, supreme, tolerant

noble *noun.* archduchess, blue blood, bluestocking, count, countess, gentleman, gentlewoman, lace curtain, lady, lord, nobleman, noblewoman, patrician, peer, prince, princess, royalty, upper-crust

nobody *noun.* cipher, insignificancy, lightweight, little guy, menial, nix, nonentity, nothing, nullity, parvenu, small potato, squirt, upstart, wimp, zero, zilch, zip

nod *verb.* acknowledge, acquiesce, agree, approve, assent, beck, beckon, bend, bow, consent, dip, duck, greet, indicate, recognize, salute, sign, signal

noise *noun.* bedlam, bellow, blast, boom, clamor, clang, commotion, detonation, disquiet, explosion, fireworks, fuss, hubbub, racket, roar, row, shouting, squawk

nominal *adjective.* alleged, apparent, formal, given, honorary, mentioned, named, ostensible, pretended, professed, puppet, purported, seeming, simple, stated, suggested, theoretical, titular

nonsense *noun.* bananas, bull, bunk, folly, foolishness, fun, gab, gas, giddiness, irrationality, jest, ludicrousness, madness, pretense, rubbish, stupidity, trash, tripe

normal *adjective.* accustomed, acknowledged, average, conventional, general, habitual, median, methodical, natural, orderly, popular, prevalent, regular, routine, standard, traditional, typical, usual

nose *noun.* adenoids, banana, bill, bow, bugle, horn, muzzle, nares, nostrils, nozzle, prow, schnoz, snout, snuffer, stem, trunk, whiffer

nostalgia *noun.* goo, homesickness, loneliness, longing, mush, pining, regret, regretfulness, reminiscence, remorse, schmaltz, sentimentality, slop, slush, sob story, tear-jerker, wistfulness, yearning

notable *adjective.* conspicuous, distinguished, famed, heavy, important, manifest, marked, memorable, momentous, noteworthy, noticeable, observable, pronounced, rare, remarkable, rubric, striking, unusual

notable *noun.* baron, chief, eminence, executive, figure, heavy, kingpin, leader, light, lion, magnate, name, personage, personality, power, prince, somebody, star

notably *adverb.* conspicuously, distinctly, exceedingly, exceptionally, extremely, greatly, highly, hugely, markedly, noticeably, outstandingly, particularly, prominently, remarkably, signally, strikingly, uncommonly, very

note *noun.* **1** agenda, commentary, dispatch, entry, gloss, jotting, journal, letter, line, mark, memorandum, minute, missive, observation, record, remark, reminder, summary **2** character, degree, figure, flat, football, indication, interval, key, lick, mark, natural, pitch, representation, scale, sharp, sign, step, tone

note *verb.* designate, dig, discover, distinguish, enter, heed, indicate, mark, mention, notice, perceive, record, remark, see, spot, transcribe, view, write

noted *adjective.* acclaimed, celebrated, conspicuous, distinguished, eminent, face, illustrious, leading, lion, name, notable, notorious, popular, prominent, recognized, renowned, somebody, star

noteworthy *adjective.* boss, conspicuous, exceptional, heavy, hot, manifest, meaningful, memorable, noticeable, observable, remarkable, rubric, significant, splash, terrific, underlined, unique, unusual

nothing *noun.* annihilation, blank, cipher, crumb, extinction, naught, no thing, nobody, nothingness, nullity, obliteration, oblivion, scratch, trifle, void, wind, zero, zip

notice *noun.* **1** apprehension, attention, care, civility, cognizance, concern, consideration, ear, grasp, heed, mark, mind, observance, regard, remark, respect, thought, understanding **2** advertisement, caution, caveat, circular, comments, critique, cue, declaration, enlightenment, goods, know, memorandum, proclamation, review, sign, story, tip, warning

notice *verb.* acknowledge, clock, detect, dig, discern, distinguish, heed, mark, mind, note, perceive, recognize, refer, regard, remark, see, spot, tumble

noticeable *adjective.* arresting, clear, distinct, manifest, marked, notable, noteworthy, observable, obvious, outstanding, perceptible, pointed, remarkable, salient, signal, spectacular, striking, unmistakable

notify *verb.* alert, brief, cable, convey, cue, give, hint, mention, proclaim, radio, spread, suggest, teach, telephone, tell, vent, warn, wire

notion *noun.* consideration, cue, discernment, hint, imagination, impression, inclination, insight, intuition, judgment, knowledge, penetration, perception, sentiment, suggestion, view, wind, wrinkle

notorious *adjective.* blatant, candy, crying, disreputable, flagrant, infamous, leading, noted, obvious, open, overt, popular, prominent, questionable, shady, undisputed, wanted, wicked

novel *adjective.* atypical, avant-garde, different, fresh, modernistic, new, now, odd, offbeat, peculiar, rare, recent, singular, strange, uncommon, unfamiliar, unique, unusual

now *adverb.* any more, at once, away, directly, forthwith, immediately, instantly, just now, momentarily, nowadays, PDQ, promptly, pronto, right now, soon, straightaway, these days, today

nucleus *noun.* basis, bud, center, crux,

embryo, focus, foundation, germ, heart, hub, kernel, matter, nub, pivot, premise, principle, seed, spark

nude *adjective.* bald, bare, bare-skinned, buff-bare, dishabille, exposed, garmentless, naked, nudie, peeled, raw, skin, stark, stripped, unclad, unclothed, uncovered, undressed

null *adjective.* absent, bad, barren, imaginary, ineffective, ineffectual, inoperative, invalid, negative, nonexistent, nothing, powerless, unavailing, unreal, useless, vain, void, worthless

number *noun.* **1** cardinal, character, cipher, count, decimal, digit, figure, folio, fraction, integer, numeral, prime, representation, sign, sum, symbol, total, whole number **2** abundance, amount, bunch, collection, company, crowd, estimate, flock, horde, lot, many, multitude, plenty, sum, throng, total, totality, whole

number *verb.* account, add, aggregate, amount, calculate, come, computer, estimate, include, reckon, run, run down, sum, tale, tally, tell, total, tote

numerous *adjective.* abundant, big, copious, diverse, great, heaps, infinite, large, legion, multitudinous, plentiful, populous, profuse, several, sundry, thick, various, voluminous

nurse *verb.* aid, cherish, encourage, father, forward, foster, further, humor, indulge, nurture, pamper, preserve, promote, serve, sit, succor, support, tend

nut *noun.* bug, crackpot, crank, cuckoo, dement, eccentric, fanatic, fiend, freak, harebrain, kook, loony, lunatic, madman, maniac, nutcase, screwball, zealot

O

obedience *noun.* accordance, acquiescence, agreement, compliance, conformity, deference, dutifulness, duty, meekness, observance, orderliness, quietness, respect, reverence, submission, submissiveness, subservience, willingness

obey *verb.* accord, acquiesce, agree, assent, comply, concur, discharge, embrace, execute, follow, heed, keep, mind, observe, perform, serve, submit, surrender

object *noun.* **1** article, body, bulk, commodity, doohickey, entity, fact, gadget, item, mass, matter, phenomenon, reality, something, substance, thing, volume **2** aim, design, duty, end, function, goal, idea, intent, intention, mark, mission, motive, objective, reason, target, use, view, wish

object *verb.* argue, beef, buck, challenge, complain, criticize, cross, disapprove, dissent, frown, inveigh, kick, rail, remonstrate, squawk, storm, tangle

objection *noun.* argument, beef, censure, challenge, difficulty, disapproval, discontent, disinclination, dislike, displeasure, dissatisfaction, grievance, kick, rejection, reluctance, shrinking, squawk

objective *adjective.* cold, cool, detached, disinterested, dispassionate, equitable, impartial, impersonal, judicial, just, nondiscriminatory, open-minded, straight, unbiased, uncolored, unemotional, uninvolved, unprepossessing

obligation *noun.* agreement, burden, business, conscience, constraint, contract, debt, engagement, must, necessity, occasion, onus, ought, part, promise, restraint, right, trust

obscure *adjective.* **1** ambiguous, confusing, cryptic, deep, dim, doubtful, enigmatic, hazy, illogical, indecisive, inexplicable, intricate, mysterious, opaque, recondite, unbelievable, unintelligible, vague **2** blurred, clouded, dark, dense, dim, dusk, dusky, faint, gloomy, indistinct, murky, shadowy, shady, somber, somber, tenebrous, umbrageous, veiled **3** covered, cryptic, deep, devious, distant, enigmatic, far, inaccessible, inconspicuous, irrelevant, lonesome, minor, mysterious, odd, recondite, solitary, undisclosed, unimportant

obscure *verb.* blur, cloak, con, conceal, cover, dim, eclipse, fuzz, gray, haze, mask, mist, muddy, overcast, overshadow, screen, shade, wrap

observation *noun.* **1** cognizance, conclusion, consideration, detection, examination, experience, mark, measurement, monitoring, notice, perception, probe, recognizing, regard, study, supervision, surveillance, view **2** catch phrase, comeback, commentary, crack, finding, mention, mouthful, note, obiter dictum, opinion, pronouncement, reflection, remark, say so, saying, thought, utterance, wisecrack

observe *verb.* beam, behold, contemplate, detect, dig, inspect, lamp, mark, perceive, read, recognize, regard, see, spot, spy, study, view, watch

obstacle *noun.* bar, barrier, block, bump, check, clog, difficulty, hamper, handicap, hardship, hitch, hurdle, interference, interruption, mountain, rub, snag, traverse

obtain *verb.* access, achieve, annex, cop, earn, effect, grab, have, inherit, invade, occupy, realize, reap, recover, save, secure, snag, take

obtainable *adjective.* achievable, at hand, available, cherry pie, derivable, duck soup, gettable, in stock, no problem, no sweat, on deck, on offer, on tap, procurable, purchasable, pushover, ready, securable

obvious *adjective.* accessible, clear, conclusive, conspicuous, discernible, distinct, explicit, exposed, lucid, manifest, noticeable, observable, open, overt, perceptible, pronounced, unmistakable, visible

occasion *noun.* **1** break, convenience, demand, excuse, incident, instant, moment, need, occurrence, opening, opportunity, possibility, season, shot, show, squeak, time, use **2** antecedent, basis, cause, circumstance, determinant, excuse, foundation, ground, grounds, incident, inducement, influence, motive, necessity, obligation, provocation, purpose, right **3** affair, celebration, circumstance, episode, experience, go, goings-on, hap, happening, incident, instant, milestone, moment, occurrence, scene, thing, time, while

occasion *verb.* breed, cause, create, do, effect, elicit, engender, evoke, generate, induce, influence, inspire, move, muster, persuade, produce, prompt, provoke

occasional *adjective.* casual, desultory, exceptional, exclusive, few, infrequent, intermittent, odd, particular, random, rare, scarce, seldom, special, specific, sporadic, uncommon, unusual

occupation *noun.* activity, bag, biz, business, do, dodge, employment, game, grindstone, job, lick, line, number, post, racket, setup, vocation, work

occupy *verb.* **1** absorb, amuse, attend, busy, divert, employ, engage, entertain, fill, hold attention, immerse, interest, involve, monopolize, soak, take up, tie up, utilize **2** cover, dwell, establish, fill, hold, inhabit, keep, maintain, own, people, permeate, populate, possess, remain, sit, stay, tenant, utilize

occur *verb.* appear, arise, befall, betide, cook, ensue, eventuate, exist, follow, hap, manifest, materialize, obtain, result, shake, show, smoke, turn out

occurrence *noun.* accident, adventure, bit, contingency, episode, event, hap, incidence, incident, instance, occasion, pass, piece, routine, spot, state, transaction, transpiration

ocean *noun.* blue, bounding main, brine, briny, deep, drink, great sea, high seas, main, pond, puddle, salt water, sea, seaway, Seven Seas, sink, splash, tide

odd *adjective.* **1** atypical, bizarre, curious, deviant, erratic, exceptional, fantastic, flaky, funny, irregular, offbeat, peculiar, queer, rare, remarkable, strange, unique, unusual **2** accidental, casual, chance, contingent, different, fluky, fortuitous, fragmentary, incidental, irregular, occasional, odd-lot, periodic, random, seasonal, sundry, varied, various **3** additional, alone, exceeding, individual, irregular, left, lone, lonely, over, remaining, single, singular, sole, solitary, spare, surplus, unmatched, unpaired

odor *noun.* air, aroma, bouquet, effluvium, emanation, essence, exhalation, flavor, fragrance, perfume, pungency, smell, stench, stink, tang, tincture, trail, whiff

off *adverb.* above, absent, afar, ahead, aside, away, behind, below, beneath, beside, disappearing, divergent, elsewhere, far, out, over, removed, vanishing

offense *noun.* **1** affront, aggression, attack, battery, blitz, displeasure, harm, indignation, injury, injustice, offensive, onset, onslaught, outrage, push, rap, slam, slight **2** annoyance, conniption, displeasure, explosion, fit, hard feelings, huff, indignation, ire, miff, needle, outburst, pique, resentment, scene, tantrum, wounded feelings, wrath

offensive *adjective.* annoying, biting, cutting, disagreeable, discourteous, distasteful, dreadful, embarrassing, foul, ghastly, horrid, insolent, irritating, objectionable, offending, repugnant, revolting, shocking

offer *verb.* accord, afford, bid, donate, exhibit, extend, furnish, give, move, ply, pose, press, propose, provide, sacrifice, suggest, tender, volunteer

office *noun.* **1** appointment, billet, business, charge, commission, duty, employment, function, job, obligation, occupation, post, province, role, spot, station, trust, work **2** agency, building, bureau, cave, center, department, facility, factory, foundry, front office, room, salt mines, setup, shop, store, suite, warehouse, workstation

officer *noun.* administrator, agent, appointee, bureaucrat, chief, deputy, dignitary, director, executive, functionary, head, leader, magistrate, manager, officeholder, official, president, representative

official *adjective.* accredited, authentic, authenticated, authorized, cathedral, certified, cleared, decided, fitting, formal, licensed, ordered, positive, proper, real, sanctioned, true, valid

official *noun.* administrator, agent, boss, comptroller, executive, governor, incumbent, kingpin, leader, manager, marshal, minister, officer, premier, president, secretary, top, treasurer

offset *verb.* account, allow for, balance, be equivalent, charge, compensate, counteract, counterpoise, equal, equalize, equipoise, negate, neutralize, outweigh, recompense, redeem, requite, set off

offspring *noun.* baby, brood, children, descendant, family, generation, heir, issue, kid, lineage, posterity, produce, progeny, pup, scion, seed, sprout, succession

oily *adjective.* **1** buttery, creamy, fatty, lubricant, lustrous, oiled, polished, rich, saponaceous, sleek, slippery, smeary, smooth, soapy, soothing, swimming, unctuous, waxy **2** bland, cajoling, coaxing, compliant, glib, hypocritical, ingratiating, insinuating, obsequious, plausible, servile, slick, smarmy, smooth, soapy, suave, unctuous

old *adjective.* **1** aged, deficient, elderly, exhausted, geriatric, gray, impaired, inactive, mature, matured, patriarchal, seasoned, senile, skilled, venerable, versed, veteran, wasted **2** archaic, bygone, dated, decayed, done, former, hackneyed, late, onetime, outdated, primitive, pristine, relic, remote, rusty, sometime, traditional, venerable **3** constant, continuing, enduring, familiar, firm, hardened, inveterate, lifelong, perennial, perpetual, practiced, skilled, solid, staying, steady, versed, veteran, vintage

ominous *adjective.* baleful, baneful, doomed, fateful, forbidding, gloomy, grim, haunting, hostile, impending, inhospitable, lowering, malign, perilous, prophetic, sinister, unfriendly, unpromising

on *adverb.* above, adjacent, against, approaching, at, beside, covering, forth, forward, held, near, next, onward, over, touching, toward, upon, with

once *adverb.* already, away back, back, back when, before, bygone, earlier, erstwhile, formerly, heretofore, late, long ago, old, once only, one, previously, sometime, whilom

one *adjective.* alone, definite, different, lone, odd, only, particular, peculiar, precise, separate, single, singular, sole, solitary, special, specific, uncommon, unique

only *adjective.* alone, apart, exclusive, individual, isolated, lone, matchless, one, particular, peerless, single, sole, solitary, solo, unaccompanied, unequaled, unique, unparalleled

only *adverb.* alone, at most, barely, but, entirely, hardly, just, merely, nothing but, particularly, plainly, purely, simply, solely, totally, uniquely, utterly, wholly

onset *noun.* access, aggression, attack, birth, charge, commencement, encounter, incipience, offense, offensive, onrush, onslaught, opening, origin, outbreak, outset, seizure, start

open *adjective.* **1** accessible, bare, clear, expansive, extended, extensive, navigable, peeled, revealed, rolling, stripped, unburdened, unfurled, unlocked, unsealed, vacated, wide, yawning **2** admissible, agreeable, allowable, appropriate, fit, free, general, nondiscriminatory, obtainable, practicable, proper, public, suitable, unqualified, unrestricted, usable, vacant, welcoming **3** apparent, avowed, barefaced, blatant, conspicuous, downright, evident, flagrant, frank, manifest, noticeable, obvious, overt, plain, unconcealed, undisguised, visible, well-known **4** artless, candid, disinterested, fair, frank, free, guileless, impartial, innocent, natural, objective, plain, receptive, sincere, transparent, uncommitted, undisguised, vanilla

open *verb.* bare, bust in, display, disrupt, expand, expose, hole, lacerate, lance, pierce, pop, release, rupture, slit, spread, unlock, untie, vent

opening *noun.* **1** aperture, break, cavity, cleft, crack, crevice, discontinuity, door, gap, mouth, outlet, recess, rift, rupture, slit, split, spout, vent **2** availability, break, connection, cut, fling, go, occasion, opportunity, place, possibility, run, scope, shot, show, squeak, time, vacancy, whack

openly *adverb.* brazenly, candidly, flagrantly, forthrightly, frankly, fully, honestly, naively, naturally, plainly, publicly, readily, simply, straight, unashamedly, unhesitatingly, unreservedly, willingly

operate *verb.* **1** achieve, act, benefit, compel, convey, cook, do, exert, influence, keep, lift, move, perform, progress, revolve, serve, take, transport **2** administer, command, conduct, drive, handle, keep, manage, maneuver, manipulate, ordain, pilot, play, ply, run, steer, use, wield, work

operation *noun.* act, agency, course, effort, employment, engagement, enterprise, exercising, exertion, handiwork, happening, influence, motion, procedure, progress, transference, undertaking, workmanship

operative *adjective.* accessible, alive, dynamic, efficient, functional, functioning, important, key, live, open, operational, practicable, relevant, running, serviceable, significant, standing, usable

opinion *noun.* assessment, conclusion, fancy, impression, inclination, judgment, persuasion, presumption, presupposition, reaction, sentiment, speculation, take, theorem, thesis, think, thought, view

opponent *noun.* adversary, antagonist, anti, aspirant, assailant, bidder, candidate, challenger, competitor, con, enemy, entrant, foe, litigant, match, opposition, player, rival

opportunity *noun.* break, contingency, convenience, excuse, freedom, hap, happening, hope, hour, moment, occasion, opening, pass, prayer, relief, scope, stab, time

oppose *verb.* assail, attack, bar, battle, combat, confront, counter, counterattack, debate, defy, deny, disagree, disapprove, encounter, expose, face, neutralize, prevent

opposed *adjective.* against, antithetical, battling, combating, contrary, counter, crossing, defending, defensive, disputed, enemy, exposing, facing, hostile, objecting, opposing, rival, warring

opposite *adjective.* antagonistic, antithetical, contradictory, counter, crosswise, diametric, dissimilar, diverse, facing, hostile, independent, inverse, obverse, ornery, repugnant, retrograde, unconnected, unrelated

opposite *noun.* adverse, antipole, antithesis, contra, contradiction, contrary, contrast, converse, counterpart, foil, inverse, obverse, opposition, other extreme, other side, paradox, reverse, vice versa

opposition *noun.* antithesis, clash, combat, con, conflict, contention, contradistinction, counterattack, encounter, engagement, fray, grapple, negativism, repugnance, repulsion, resistance, skirmish, warfare

optimism *noun.* anticipation, assurance, brightness, buoyancy, calmness, certainty, cheer, cheerfulness, confidence, elation, encouragement, enthusiasm, expectation, happiness, idealism, mysticism, positivism, trust

optimistic *adjective.* assured, bright, buoyant, cheerful, cheering, confident, encouraged, expectant, high, hopeful, hoping, idealistic, merry, positive, promising, rosy, sunny, trusting

optimum *adjective.* ace, capital, choice, choicest, excellent, flawless, greatest, highest, ideal, matchless, maximum, most favorable, optimal, peak, peerless, perfect, select, superlative

oral *adjective.* articulate, lingual, narrated, phonated, phonetic, phonic, recounted, related, said, sonant, sounded, told, uttered, verbal, viva voce, vocal, voiced, word-of-mouth

orbit *noun.* area, arena, boundary, career, circumference, compass, course, department, domain, dominion, jurisdiction, pilgrimage, precinct, province, range, realm, scope, sphere

order *noun.* **1** array, codification, distribution, form, grouping, layout, line, orderliness, placement, plan, propriety, regularity, rule, scheme, sequence, series, system, uniformity **2** calm, control, decorousness, decorum, discipline, goodness, integrity, law, orderliness, peace, probity, properness, propriety, quiet, rectitude, rightness, suitability, tranquility **3** branch, breed, caste, description, estate, family, feather, genus, grade, hierarchy, kidney, kind, line, set, sort, species, station, stripe **4** authorization, bidding, charge, commandment, decree, dictate, direction, injunction, instruction, law, mandate, ordinance, permission, precept, regulation, rule, stipulation, word **5** authorize, bid, buy, charge, decree, dictate, enjoin, hire, instruct, obtain, ordain, prescribe, request, require, reserve, secure, tell, warn **6** adjust, align, array, assign, distribute, file, furnish, group, lay out, line, manage, marshal, plan, range, regulate, routine, tabulate, tidy

orderly *adjective.* alike, arranged, careful, conventional, correct, exact, fixed, formal, neat, regular, regulated, set up, slick, systematic, systematized, tidy, trim, uniform

ordinance *noun.* authorization, canon, code, command, decree, dictum, direction, enactment, fiat, mandate, order, precept, prescript, reg, regulation, rule, ruling, statute

ordinary *adjective.* **1** accustomed, everyday, frequent, general, habitual, natural, normal, popular, prevailing, public, regular, routine, settled, standard, stock, traditional, typical, usual **2** common, conventional, dull, garden, household, indifferent, inferior, mediocre, modest, normal, pedestrian, plastic, prosaic, routine, simple, unremarkable, usual, vanilla

organ *noun.* agency, agent, channel, device, element, forum, instrument, journal, medium, member, ministry, newspaper, paper, part, periodical, unit, vehicle, voice

organic *adjective.* animate, biological, cellular, constitutional, elemental, essential, fundamental, innate, integral, live, living, natural, necessary, nuclear, prime, primitive, principal, vital

organization *noun.* **1** arranging, assembling, assembly, chemistry, composition, configuration, constitution, design, formation, forming, grouping, making, method, organizing, plan, planning, structuring, system **2** aggregation, alliance, body, brotherhood, business, club, concord, cooperative, corporation, guild, lodge, monopoly, outfit, profession, squad, syndicate, trust, union

organize *verb.* adjust, constitute, construct, create, dispose, fit, form, frame, group, marshal, mold, range, regulate, set up, settle, straighten, tabulate, tailor

origin *noun.* **1** antecedent, author, base, derivation, determinant, egg, element, embryo, generator, germ, impulse, influence, nucleus, occasion, producer, root, seed, source **2** alpha, birth, commencement, creation, entry, forging, foundation, genesis, inauguration, initiation, introduction, launch, opener, origination, outbreak, outset, rise, start

original *adjective.* **1** aboriginal, authentic, beginning, commencing, early, first, infant, introductory, master, opening, pioneer, primary, prime, primeval, primitive, pristine, rudimentary, starting **2** causal, causative, cherry, creative, devising, fertile, formative, imaginative, ingenious, inspiring, inventive, new, productive, ready, resourceful, seminal, unprecedented, unusual

orthodox *adjective.* accepted, conformist, conservative, conventional, devout, doctrinal, pious, proper, received, religious, right, sanctioned, sound, square, standard, traditional, traditionalistic, true

out *adjective.* absent, antiquated, away, cold, dated, dead, doused, ended, exhausted, expired, extinguished, finished, impossible, outmoded, outside, ruled out, unacceptable, used up

outcome *noun.* aftereffect, aftermath, causatum, chain reaction, conclusion, consequence, end, end result, event, fallout, issue, payback, payoff, reaction, result, score, sequel, upshot

outdoor *adjective.* alfresco, casual, free, garden, healthful, hilltop, informal, invigorating, mountain, natural, nature-loving, outside, patio, picnic, rustic, unrestricted, woods, yard

outer *adjective.* alien, beyond, exoteric, exposed, exterior, extraneous, extrinsic, outermost, outlying, outmost, outside, outward, over, peripheral, remote, superficial, surface, without

outfit *noun.* **1** accouterments, apparatus, appliances, clothing, costume, ensemble, equipment, garb, gear, machinery, materiel, paraphernalia, rigging, suit, supplies, tackle, togs, trappings **2** band, clique, concern, corporation, corps, crew, enterprise, establishment, firm, house, organization, party, set, squad, team, troop, troupe, unit

outfit *verb.* appoint, arm, deck, drape, dud, equip, furnish, gear, kit out, prepare, provide, provision, rag out, rig, rig up, stock, supply, turn out

outgoing *adjective.* approachable, civil, communicative, cordial, easy, expansive, extrovert, friendly, genial, gregarious, informal, kind, open, sociable, sympathetic, unconstrained, unreserved, warm

outlet *noun.* aperture, avenue, break, channel, crack, duct, egress, escape, exit, hole, nozzle, opening, porthole, release, safety valve, spout, tear, vent

outline *noun.* blueprint, diagram, draft, drawing, floor plan, frame, framework, layout, recapitulation, resume, rough draft, rough idea, rundown, skeleton, sketch, summary, thumbnail sketch, tracing

outline *verb.* adumbrate, block out, characterize, chart, delineate, describe, draft, lay out, paint, plot, recapitulate, rough out, skeleton, skeletonize, sketch out, summarize, tell about, trace

outright *adjective.* absolute, all, consummate, definite, direct, downright, entire, flat, gross, positive, pure, thorough, thoroughgoing, total, undeniable, unqualified, whole, wholesale

outside *adjective.* alfresco, alien, away from, exterior, external, extramural, extraneous, extreme, farther, farthest, foreign, out, outdoor, outer, outermost, outward, over, surface

outstanding *adjective.* bad, boss, chief, crack, distinguished, dominant, exceptional, important, impressive, magnificent, meritorious, momentous, predominant, special, stellar, super, superior, ten

over *adverb.* beyond, ever, excessively, extra, extremely, immensely, inordinately, left over, more, overfull, overly, overmuch, remaining, superfluous, surplus, too, unduly, unused

overcast *adjective.* clouded, clouded over, dark, darkened, dismal, dreary, dull, gray, hazy, leaden, lowering, murky, nebulous, not clear, not fair, oppressive, somber, threatening

overcome *verb.* crush, defeat, drown, helpless, kick, lick, master, overthrow, prevail, prostrate, reduce, render, shock, subdue, surmount, survive, throw, weather

owner *noun.* buyer, governor, heir, heiress, holder, keeper, landlord, legatee, lord, master, mistress, partner, possessor, proprietor, proprietrix, purchaser, saw, squire

ownership *noun.* buying, claim, deed, dominion, end, having, holding, occupancy, partnership, piece, property, proprietorship, purchase, purchasing, slice, tenancy, tenure, title

P

pace *noun.* beat, bounce, celerity, clip, downbeat, lick, momentum, motion, movement, progress, quickness, rapidity, rapidness, rate, swiftness, tempo, time, velocity

pack *noun.* barrel, bunch, bundle, collection, crew, deck, drove, flock, gang, heap, horde, mess, mob, much, number, press, set, troop

pack *verb.* **1** bind, charge, compact, compress, condense, contract, heap, insert, jam, load, mob, pile, press, push, ram, squeeze, stuff, tamp **2** bear, buck, carry, convey, ferry, freight, gun, haul, heel, hump, jag, journey, lug, ride, shoulder, tote, trek, truck

package *noun.* bag, baggage, bale, bottle, box, bunch, burden, can, combination, crate, entity, load, luggage, packet, parcel, suitcase, tin, unit

packed *adjective.* arranged, awash, brimful, bundled, compact, compressed, congested, consigned, crammed, crowded, jammed, loaded, overflowing, overloaded, prepared, stuffed, swarming, wrapped

pad *verb.* amplify, augment, bulk, embroider, enlarge, exaggerate, expand, fill out, flesh out, fudge, increase, inflate, lengthen, magnify, overdraw, protract, spin, stretch

pain *noun.* **1** ache, affliction, cramp, distress, illness, injury, irritation, malady, misery, prick, sickness, soreness, spasm, sting, torment, trouble, twinge, wound **2** affliction, agony, anguish, anxiety, bitterness, despondency, distress, grief, hurt, malaise, martyrdom, misery, rack, shock, suffering, torment, tribulation, wretchedness

pain *verb.* ache, bite, chafe, disquiet, distress, exasperate, gall, harass, harm, harrow, nick, prick, sting, suffer, torment, trouble, upset, wound

painful *adjective.* aching, agonizing, arduous, biting, disagreeable, distressing, dreadful, excruciating, hard, inflamed, irritated, laborious, sharp, sore, tender, tormenting, unpleasant, vexatious

paint *noun.* acrylic, color, coloring, cosmetic, covering, emulsion, enamel, flat, gloss, latex, oil, overlay, pigment, rouge, stain, varnish, veneer, wax

paint *verb.* brush, coat, color, cover, decorate, depict, design, draw, figure, fresco, ornament, outline, portray, represent, shade, sketch, tint, wash

pair *noun.* brace, combination, combine, combo, couple, deuce, doublet, duality, duo, dyad, match, mates, span, team, twins, two, twosome, yoke

pale *adjective.* anemic, ashen, bleached, bloodless, colorless, dim, dull, feeble, ghastly, gray, ineffective, livid, lurid, pallid, poor, spectral, wan, weak

panic *noun.* agitation, alarm, bust, consternation, crash, crush, depression, dismay, dread, fear, frenzy, fright, hysteria, jam, scare, slump, stampede, terror

panic *verb.* alarm, be terror-stricken, become hysterical, chicken out, clutch, come apart, crap out, have kittens, lose it, lose nerve, overreact, pucker, run scared, scare, stampede, startle, terrify, unnerve

pants *noun.* bell bottoms, bells, breeches, briefs, britches, chaps, cords, corduroys, drawers, dungarees, jeans, longies, overalls, panties, pegs, shorts, slacks, trousers

papers *noun.* bill, citation, contract, credentials, data, deed, diaries, documentation, file, grant, instrument, order, passport, plea, record, summons, visa, will

par *noun.* balance, coequality, criterion, equal footing, equality, equatability, equilibrium, equivalence, equivalency, level, mean, median, model, norm, sameness, standard, usual

parade *noun.* array, ceremony, column, demonstration, display, exhibition, fanfare, flaunting, line, march, pomp, procession, review, ritual, shine, show, spectacle, train

parade *verb.* advertise, air, boast, brag, declare, demonstrate, disclose, display, divulge, exhibit, expose, flash, march, prance, proclaim, publish, reveal, strut

paradise *noun.* bliss, cloud nine, delight, divine abode, Eden, fairyland, fat city, felicity, heaven, heavenly kingdom, hog heaven, kingdom come, promised land, up there, upstairs, utopia, wonderland, Zion

parallel *noun.* analogue, analogy, comparison, corollary, correspondence, correspondent, counterpart, double, duplicate, duplication, equivalent, kin, likeness, match, parallelism, resemblance, similarity, twin

parallel *verb.* agree, assimilate, chime, collocate, compare, complement, conform, copy, correlate, correspond, equal, equate, imitate, keep pace, liken, match, paragon, parallelize

paramount *adjective.* chief, controlling, crowning, dominant, eminent, foremost, leading, main, master, outstanding, predominant, premier, prevalent, primary, prime, sovereign, superior, supreme

pardon *noun.* absolution, acquittal, allowance, anchor, commute, discharge, excuse, exoneration, freeing, grace, indemnity, indulgence, kindness, lifeboat, mercy, release, reprieve, vindication

pardon *verb.* accept, acquit, clear, discharge, excuse, exonerate, free, justify, let off, liberate, lifeboat, overlook, release, reprieve, rescue, spring, suspend charges, tolerate

parent *noun.* ancestor, architect, author, begetter, cause, creator, father, folks, forerunner, fountainhead, guardian, mother, origin, originator, progenitor, prototype, root, wellspring

park *noun.* esplanade, estate, forest, garden, grass, green, grounds, lawn, lot, meadow, place, playground, plaza, pleasure garden, recreation area, square, tract, woodland

parochial *adjective.* biased, bigoted, cathedral, conservative, conventional, insular, limited, local, narrow, petty, prejudiced, provincial, regional, restricted, sectarian, sectional, shallow, small-town

part *noun.* **1** allotment, bite, chunk, department, division, element, extra, fraction, hunk, member, molecule, particle, partition, piece, section, sector, splinter, subdivision **2** behalf, bit, business, cause, charge, concern, duty, faction, function, involvement, party, place, responsibility, role, say, share, side, work **3** articulate, break, break up, detach, divide, factor, partition, portion, rend, section, segment, separate, sever, slice, split, strip, sunder, tear **4** blow off, break, break off, break up, cut out, depart, ease out, go, kiss off, leave flat, push off, quit, say goodbye, separate, ship out, shove off, split, withdraw

partial *adjective.* colored, discriminatory, disposed, favorably inclined, influenced, interested, jaundiced, minded, one-sided, partisan, predisposed, prejudiced, prepossessed, tendentious, unfair, unjust, warped

participate *verb.* aid, be into, be participant, chip in, come in, compete, concur, cooperate, engage, go into, join in, latch on, partake, perform, play, share, strive, tune in

particle *noun.* atom, bit, dot, drop, fleck, grain, hoot, iota, mite, modicum, molecule, morsel, ounce, ray, seed, speck, spot, whit

particular *adjective.* **1** accurate, appropriate, distinct, exact, express, full, individual, intrinsic, itemized, limited, local, meticulous, minute, peculiar, scrupulous, singular, special, thorough **2** exceptional, exclusive, marked, notable, noteworthy, odd, one, only, peculiar, remarkable, respective, separate, single, singular, sole, solitary, unique, unusual **3** careful, choosy, crab, critical, dainty, demanding, discriminating, exacting, fastidious, finical, fussbudget, fussy, meticulous, nice, rough, stickler, tough

particular *noun.* article, case, circumstance, clue, cue, element, fact, feature, goods, gospel, item, know, numbers, rundown, skinny, specific, specification, story

particularly *adverb.* decidedly, distinctly, especially, exceptionally, explicitly, expressly, in particular, individually, markedly, notably, outstandingly, peculiarly, principally, singularly, specially, surprisingly, uncommonly, unusually

partisan *adjective.* accessory, adhering, biased, blind, colored, conspiratorial, denominational, devoted, die-hard, exclusive, partial, prejudiced, sectarian, sympathetic, unjust, unreasoning, warped, zealous

partisan *noun.* accessory, adherent, backer, champion, cohort, defender, devotee, disciple, follower, henchman, satellite, stalwart, supporter, sycophant, sympathizer, upholder, votary, zealot

partly *adverb.* at best, at most, by degrees, carelessly, halfway, inadequately, incompletely, insufficiently, measurably, not fully, notably, noticeably, partially, piecemeal, relatively, slightly, somewhat, within limits

partner *noun.* accomplice, associate, buddy, chum, collaborator, colleague, comrade, confederate, date, friend, helper, helpmate, husband, mate, participant, playmate, spouse, teammate

partnership *noun.* association, body, brotherhood, business, clique, club, companionship, conjunction, cooperative, corporation, gang, house, interest, lodge, mob, organization, ownership, union

party *noun.* **1** ball, bust, celebration, cocktails, crush, dinner, do, feast, fun, function, gala, hop, jig, orgy, reception, riot, tea, time **2** assembly, band, body, bunch, company, corps, crew, crowd, detachment, gang, mob, multitude, outfit, squad, team, troop, troupe, unit **3** alliance, association, bloc, body, clique, coalition, combination, combine, confederacy, electorate, faction, grouping, junta, ring, sect, set, side, union

pass *noun.* admission, chit, comp, free ride, freebie, furlough, identification, license, order, paper, passport, permission, permit, pigeon, right, ticket, visa, warrant

pass *verb.* **1** befall, crawl, cruise, drag, fare, flow, fly, give, hap, happen, lapse, leave, linger, move, occur, progress, rise, travel **2** close, demise, depart, die, disappear, discontinue, dissolve, drop, dwindle, ebb, end, evaporate, expire, fade, perish, succumb, terminate, vanish **3** accept, adopt, approve, authorize, become ratified, become valid, carry, decree, enact, engage, establish, ordain, pledge, promise, ratify, sanction, undertake, validate **4** decline, discount, disregard, duke, fail, forget, ignore, masquerade, miss, neglect, not heed, omit, overlook, pass up, refuse, skip, slight, weed

passage *noun.* **1** access, channel, corridor, course, doorway, exit, gap, hallway, lane, line, lobby, opening, passageway, route, shaft, subway, tunnel, way **2** change, conversion, crossing, flow, motion, movement, passing, progress, progression, tour, transfer, transference, transit, transition, transmission, traverse, trek, voyage

passing *adjective.* casual, cursory, ephemeral, evanescent, fleeting, fugitive, glancing, hasty, impermanent, momentary, quick, shallow, short, short-lived, slight, superficial, temporary, transient

passion *noun.* **1** affection, animation, devotion, distress, eagerness, ecstasy, fervor, fit, indignation, misery, outbreak, rage, spirit, storm, temper, transport, wrath, zeal **2** affection, appetite, ardor, attachment, case, craving, crush, desire, excitement, fondness, infatuation, itch, keenness, lust, mash, urge, weakness, yen

passionate *adjective.* **1** amorous, ardent, aroused, desirous, erotic, heavy, hot, lascivious, loving, lustful, prurient, romantic, sexy, stimulated, sultry, turned on, wanton, wistful **2** animated, blazing, deep, eager, expressive, fierce, fiery, flaming, frenzied, heated, impetuous, inspiring, poignant, stimulated, stirring, strong, vehement, warm **3** crabby, fall apart, fiery, frantic, hot-headed, hot-tempered, inflamed, irascible, irritable, mean, peppery, quick-tempered, shook, stormy, testy, touchy, vehement, violent

passive *adjective.* apathetic, asleep, bearing, docile, enduring, idle, inactive, indifferent, inert, latent, motionless, nonviolent, patient, quiescent, resigned, sleepy, static, submissive

past *adjective.* **1** accomplished, ago, antecedent, anterior, completed, elapsed, ended, extinct, finished, foregoing, forgotten, former, gone, over, precedent, preceding, previous, prior **2** ages ago, ancient, bygone, earlier, early, foregoing, late, latter, old, olden, once, over, preceding, previous, prior, recent, retired, sometime

patch *noun.* area, bit, blob, chunk, fix, ground, hunk, land, lot, plot, reinforcement, scrap, scrape, shred, spot, stretch, strip, tract

patent *adjective.* blatant, clear, controlled, distinct, downright, evident, exclusive, flagrant, gross, limited, manifest, obvious, open, palpable, plain, prominent, transparent, unmistakable

path *noun.* aisle, beat, boulevard, direction, drag, footpath, groove, lane, line, pass, passage, procedure, rail, route, shortcut, stroll, terrace, walk

pathetic *adjective.* crummy, deplorable, distressing, feeble, heartbreaking, meager, miserable, petty, pitiable, pitiful, plaintive, poignant, poor, tender, touching, useless, worthless, wretched

patience *noun.* bearing, constancy, diligence, endurance, fortitude, grit, guts, humility, moderation, passivity, poise, resignation, restraint, serenity, starch, stoicism, submission, tolerance

patient *adjective.* accommodating, calm, composed, enduring, forgiving, gentle, indulgent, meek, mild, persistent, philosophic, philosophical, resigned, serene, submissive, tolerant, tranquil, understanding

patrol *noun.* convoying, defending, escorting, garrison, guarding, lookout, patrolman, policing, protecting, protection, rounds, scouting, sentinel, spy, vigilance, watch, watching, watchman

patronage *noun.* advocacy, aegis, aid, assistance, auspices, backing, championship, encouragement, financing, grant, guardianship, help, promotion, protection, recommendation, sponsorship, subsidy, support

pattern *noun.* **1** arrangement, decoration, device, diagram, figure, guide, impression, instruction, markings, mold, motif, motive, ornament, plan, stencil, template, trim **2** archetype, beau ideal, copy, criterion, cynosure, ensample, exemplar, guide, mirror, model, norm, original, paradigm, paragon, prototype, sample, specimen, standard

pause *noun.* abeyance, break, breather, cessation, comma, cutoff, delay, freeze, halt, hitch, intermission, interregnum, interruption, lapse, rest, stoppage, suspension, ten

pause *verb.* break, call time, cease, delay, deliberate, discontinue, drop, halt, hesitate, hold back, interrupt, pigeonhole, reflect, rest, shake, sideline, suspend, waver

pay *noun.* allowance, bread, commission, compensation, consideration, fee, income, indemnity, payment, proceeds, reckoning, recompense, redress, remuneration, salary, settlement, takings, wages

pay *verb.* adjust, bestow, clear, confer, defray, discharge, extend, foot, grant, handle, meet, offer, recompense, refund, reimburse, render, settle, stake

payment *noun.* amount, bounty, disbursement, discharge, down, fee, part, premium, reckoning, recompense, redress, remuneration, restitution, retaliation, salary, settlement, sum, wage

peace *noun.* **1** accord, agreement, amity, armistice, brotherhood, cessation, concord, friendship, love, neutrality, order, pacification, pacifism, reconciliation, treaty, unanimity, union, unity **2** amity, calmness, composure, concord, congeniality, contentment, equanimity, harmony, hush, lull, quiet, repose, reserve, rest, serenity, silence, stillness, sympathy

peaceful *adjective.* amicable, bloodless, calm, collected, constant, gentle, halcyon, level, neutral, neutralist, nonviolent, peaceable, placid, restful, smooth, steady, still, tranquil

peak *noun.* aiguille, alp, apex, brow, bump, cope, crest, crown, hill, mount, mountain, pinnacle, point, roof, spike, summit, tip, vertex

peculiar *adjective.* **1** abnormal, beat, bent, character, creep, curious, exceptional, flaky, funny, idiosyncratic, odd, offbeat, outlandish, queer, singular, strange, unusual, wonderful **2** appropriate, diagnostic, distinct, distinctive, distinguishing, exclusive, idiosyncratic, individual, intrinsic, local, personal, private, proper, restricted, special, specific, typical, unique

peer *verb.* beam, bore, eagle eye, eye, eyeball, focus, gaze, glare, inspect, look, peep, pin, pry, rubber, snoop, spy, squint, stare

penalty *noun.* amends, amercement, cost, damages, disadvantage, discipline, fall, fine, forfeit, forfeiture, handicap, mortification, mulct, pay dues, price, rap, retribution, rip

penetrate *verb.* **1** access, bore, break in, bust in, charge, come, diffuse, insert, invade, jab, knife, permeate, prick, probe, seep, spear, stab, thrust **2** ace in, affect, become clear, come across, comprehend, discern, fathom, figure out, get over, get through, grasp, impress, perceive, put over, sink in, touch, unravel, work out

penetrating *adjective.* **1** biting, carrying, crisp, cutting, edged, entering, forcing, harsh, infiltrating, intrusive, pervasive, pointed, puncturing, pungent, sharp, shrill, strong, trenchant **2** acute, astute, critical, discerning, discriminating, incisive, keen, penetrative, perceptive, perspicacious, profound, quick, quick-witted, sagacious, searching, sharp, sharp-witted, shrewd

people *noun.* cats, citizens, community, family, folk, folks, heads, horde, humanity, humans, inhabitants, mankind, mob, mortals, multitude, nationality, population, race

perceive *verb.* **1** behold, dig, divine, grasp, identify, lamp, mark, observe, realize, recognize, regard, remark, see, seize, sense, spot, spy, take **2** appreciate, apprehend, comprehend, conclude, copy, deduce, dig, feature, feel, grasp, know, learn, pin, read, realize, recognize, see, sense

percentage *noun.* allotment, bite, bonus, chunk, commission, division, fee, interest, per cent, piece, proportion, rate, ratio, section, shake, squeeze, taste, winnings

perception *noun.* apprehension, approach, attention, awareness, discernment, image, impression, insight, judgment, knowledge, observation, plan, recognition, sensation, sense, study, taste, thought

perfect *adjective.* **1** absolute, completed, downright, entire, finished, flawless, full, gross, integral, outright, positive, simple, sound, unadulterated, unalloyed, unbroken, unmixed, unqualified **2** absolute, accomplished, adept, classical, culminating, expert, faultless, immaculate, masterful, matchless, peerless, skilled, sound, spotless, superb, supreme, ten, unequaled **3** accurate, appropriate, certain, distinct, exact, express, fit, model, precise, proper, required, right, sharp, strict, suitable, textbook, true, very

perfect *verb.* accomplish, consummate, crown, cultivate, develop, effect, elaborate, finish, fulfill, hone, improve, perform, polish, realize, refine, round, slick, smooth

perfection *noun.* achievement, completion, consummation, crown, ending, exquisiteness, finishing, idealism, integrity, maturity, paragon, phoenix, precision, quality, realization, superiority, supremacy, wholeness

perform *verb.* **1** accomplish, achieve, act, discharge, do, effect, enforce, execute, function, meet, move, observe, perk, realize, take, transact, wind up, work **2** be on, discourse, display, dramatize, enact, execute, exhibit, give, ham, offer, personate, play, present, produce, render, represent, show, stage

performance *noun.* **1** achievement, act, administration, attainment, completion, conduct, consummation, discharge, doing, enforcement, execution, exploit, feat, fruition, fulfillment, pursuance, realization, work **2** act, business, ceremony, concert, custom, display, exhibition, gig, pageant, presentation, production, recital, representation, review, set, show, special, spectacle

perilous *adjective.* delicate, dynamite, exposed, hairy, hazardous, hot, insecure, loaded, precarious, risky, treacherous, uncertain, unhealthy, unsafe, unsure, vulnerable, wicked, zoo

period *noun.* age, course, cycle, date, days, duration, epoch, era, generation, interval, season, span, spell, stage, stretch, term, time, years

periodic *adjective.* alternate, annual, cyclical, daily, fluctuating, hourly, monthly, orbital, perennial, periodical, recurrent, recurring, regular, routine, seasonal, serial, weekly, yearly

permanent *adjective.* abiding, constant, continual, durable, enduring, everlasting, fixed, forever, immutable, imperishable, indestructible, invariable, perennial, perpetual, persistent, set, stable, unchanging

permission *noun.* acknowledgment, admission, agreement, allowance, concession, concurrence, consent, dispensation, endorsement, freedom, imprimatur, indulgence, leave, nod, permit, promise, recognition, tolerance

permit *noun.* allowance, charter, concession, consent, empowering, favor, franchise, grant, indulgence, leave, liberty, pass, passport, permission, privilege, toleration, visa, warrant

permit *verb.* acquiesce, admit, agree, authorize, buy, charter, concede, enable, endorse, endure, franchise, have, humor, indulge, leave, pass, sign, suffer

perpetual *adjective.* ceaseless, constant, continued, endless, eternal, everlasting, immortal, incessant, intermittent, perennial, permanent, recurrent, repeated, repeating, returning, undying, unfailing, unremitting

persistent *adjective.* bound, constant, continual, dogged, endless, firm, fixed, immovable, insistent, resolute, steady, sticky, stubborn, tenacious, tireless, unflagging, unremitting, unshakable

person *noun.* being, bird, body, cat, guy, human, identity, individual, lad, life, man, mortal, party, personality, self, somebody, spirit, unit

personality *noun.* **1** big cheese, brass, chief, cynosure, dignitary, distinguished person, eminence, face, hot shot, individual, monster, name, notable, personage, prince, somebody, star, worthy **2** attraction, charisma, charm, complexion, disposition, emotions, humor, identity, individuality, magnetism, nature, pleasantness, psyche, selfdom, singularity, temper, temperament, traits

perspective *noun.* angle, aspect, attitude, broad view, context, headset, mindset, objectivity, outlook, panorama, proportion, prospect, relation, relativity, scape, scene, viewpoint, vista

persuade *verb.* actuate, affect, allure, assure, coax, draw, impress, incline, induce, influence, lead, move, prompt, reason, sell, touch, urge, woo

persuasion *noun.* **1** alignment, alluring, brainwashing, con, conversion, force, goose, hard sell, hook, inducement, juice, potency, power, promote, pull, seduction, sell, squeeze **2** bias, camp, church, communion, conviction, credo, creed, denomination, faith, mind, opinion, party, prejudice, school, sect, sentiment, side, view

pertinent *adjective.* ad rem, admissible, applicable, appropriate, apropos, apt, connected, fit, fitting, germane, kosher, material, opportune, pat, pertaining, proper, related, suitable

pet *verb.* baby, caress, chuck, dandle, embrace, grab, hug, love, make out, mollycoddle, neck, pamper, pat, perch, spoil, spoon, stroke, touch

petty *adjective.* base, casual, cheap, contemptible, insignificant, irrelevant, junior, lesser, light, lower, peanut, picayune, piddling, secondary, slight, small, subordinate, unimportant

phenomenon *noun.* actuality, anomaly, curiosity, episode, event, experience, fact, happening, incident, marvel, miracle, paradox, peculiarity, prodigy, reality, sensation, spectacle, uniqueness

philosophy *noun.* aesthetics, axiom, beliefs, convictions, ideology, knowledge, logic, outlook, rationalism, reason, reasoning, system, theory, thought, values, view, viewpoint, wisdom

photograph *noun.* blowup, image, Kodak, likeness, microfilm, mug, negative, photo, picture, pinup, pix, portrait, positive, print, shot, slide, snap, transparency

photograph *verb.* can, capture, copy, film, get, illustrate, lens, microfilm, mug, photo, print, record, reproduce, roll, shoot, snap, take, turn

phrase *noun.* byword, diction, expression, idiom, maxim, motto, parlance, phraseology, phrasing, remark, saying, shibboleth, slogan, styling, tag, terminology, utterance, wording

pick *noun.* aces, bag, best, choice, choosing, cream, decision, elect, elite, fat, flower, preference, pride, prime, prize, selection, top, weakness

pick *verb.* cull, elect, finger, hand-pick, mark, name, prefer, select, separate, settle on, single out, slot, sort out, tab, tag, take, tap, winnow

pick up *verb.* acquire, annex, buy, compass, extract, find, gain, garner, get, glean, have, learn, master, procure, purchase, score, secure, take

picnic *noun.* breeze, cakewalk, child's play, cinch, duck soup, good time, joy ride, kid stuff, lark, light work, party, pie, pushover, setup, smooth sailing, snap, sure thing, walkover

picture *noun.* account, art, blueprint, canvas, description, double, drawing, figure, impression, panorama, photo, piece, portraiture, print, replica, statue, tableau, twin

piece *noun.* **1** allotment, bit, bite, case, chunk, division, fraction, hunk, instance, interest, item, length, member, morsel, parcel, percentage, section, snack **2** arrangement, bit, composition, creation, item, junk, lines, paper, part, production, sketch, song, study, thesis, treatise, treatment, vignette, work

pile *noun.* aggregation, assortment, bank, barrel, buildup, chunk, collection, drift, gob, hill, hunk, jumble, mass, mound, much, ocean, shock, stack

pile *verb.* accumulate, amass, assemble, bank, bunch, charge, collect, crush, flock, heap, hill, jam, load, mass, mound, pack, stack, stream

pilot *noun.* ace, aviator, captain, conductor, dean, director, eagle, flier, fly-boy, flyer, guide, helmsman, jockey, lead, leader, navigator, scout, wheelman

pinch *noun.* box, clutch, contingency, crisis, crossroads, crunch, difficulty, emergency, hardship, juncture, necessity, oppression, pass, plight, pressure, strait, stress, turning point

pine *verb.* ache, agonize, brood, covet, crave, desire, dream, fret, grieve, hunger for, itch for, lust after, mope, mourn, sigh, want, wish, yearn

pioneer *noun.* colonist, colonizer, developer, explorer, founder, founding father, frontiersman, guide, homesteader, immigrant, innovator, leader, pathfinder, pilgrim, scout, settler, squatter, trailblazer

pioneer *verb.* begin, colonize, create, develop, discover, establish, explore, found, initiate, instigate, institute, launch, map out, originate, prepare, spearhead, start, trailblaze

pious *adjective.* clerical, devoted, devout, divine, ecclesiastical, godly, hallowed, holy, knee bender, orthodox, prayerful, priestly, religious, reverent, righteous, sacred, sanctimonious, spiritual

pipe *verb.* blubber, cheep, cry, play, say, shout, sing, sob, sound, speak, talk, toot, trill, tweet, wail, warble, weep, whistle

pit *noun.* abyss, chasm, crater, dent, depression, excavation, grave, gulf, hell, hole, hollow, indentation, mine, pothole, shaft, tomb, trench, well

pitch *verb.* bend, descend, drop, fall, lean, lunge, plunge, rise, rock, roll, slope, slump, stagger, tilt, topple, toss, vault, welter

pity *noun.* charity, clemency, comfort, distress, empathy, favor, goodness, grace, humanity, identification, kindliness, melancholy, quarter, rue, solace, sympathy, tenderness, yearning

pity *verb.* ache, comfort, commiserate, compassion, compassionate, condole, console, feel with, forgive, have compassion, pardon, reprieve, show sympathy, solace, soothe, spare, sympathize, understand

place *noun.* abode, area, distance, dwelling, home, joint, latitude, longitude, niche, property, quarter, region, section, stead, suburb, village, void, zone

place *verb.* **1** allot, assign, distribute, finger, install, lodge, park, peg, plank, put, quarter, repose, rest, set, settle, spot, station, stick **2** appoint, approximate, assign, charge, classify, commission, constitute, delegate, entrust, fix, give, grade, group, judge, name, nominate, put, sort

plain *adjective.* **1** apparent, audible, broad, clear, definite, distinct, evident, lucid, manifest, open, palpable, patent, talk turkey, transparent, unambiguous, understandable, unmistakable, visible **2** abrupt, artless, blunt, candid, direct, downright, forthright, frank, guileless, honest, open, outspoken, rude, sincere, straightforward, unconcealed, undisguised, unvarnished **3** average, common, commonplace, conventional, dull, everyday, homely, modest, ordinary, plain Jane, routine, simple, traditional, unaffected, unpretentious, unremarkable, usual, vanilla **4** austere, bare, basic, clean, discreet, dry, modest, muted, pure, restrained, severe, simple, stark, unadorned, undecorated, unpretentious, unvarnished, vanilla

plan *noun.* **1** arrangement, design, expedient, intent, intention, layout, meaning, method, orderliness, platform, procedure, program, proposition, scheme, suggestion, system, tactics, undertaking **2** agenda, agendum, blueprint, chart, delineation, diagram, draft, drawing, form, illustration, layout, map, projection, representation, road map, scale drawing, sketch, view

plan *verb.* blueprint, contemplate, craft, design, devise, engineer, form, frame, map, outline, plot, prepare, quarterback, represent, scheme, steer, trace, work out

plastic *adjective.* **1** amenable, bending, compliant, docile, flexible, giving, impressionable, malleable, manageable, moldable, pliable, pliant, receptive, responsive, suggestible, susceptible, tractable, yielding **2** artificial, bending, cast, cellulose, chemical, elastic, fictile, molded, pliable, pliant, pseudo, resilient, shapeable, soft, substitute, superficial, synthetic, workable

plate *verb.* bronze, chrome, cover, electroplate, enamel, encrust, face, flake, foil, gild, laminate, layer, nickel, overlay, platinize, scale, silver, stratify

platoon *noun.* army, array, batch, battery, bunch, clump, cluster, company, detachment, lot, outfit, parcel, patrol, set, squad, squadron, team, unit

play *noun.* **1** comedy, drama, entertainment, farce, flop, hit, legit, mask, musical, opera, performance, potboiler, show, smash, smash hit, theatrical, tragedy, turkey **2** delectation, diversion, frolic, fun, gambling, game, gaming, happiness, humor, jest, lark, match, pastime, prank, recreation, romp, sport, teasing

play *verb.* caper, cavort, clown, dance, divert, entertain, frolic, gambol, joke, jump, let go, rejoice, revel, romp, skip, sport, toy, trifle

player *noun.* **1** amateur, animal, ape, athlete, champ, competitor, contestant, jock, meathead, member, opponent, participant, pro, professional, rookie, sportsman, sweat, team player **2** actor, actress, bit player, entertainer, ham, impersonator, lead, mime, mimic, performer, play actor, scene stealer, spear carrier, stand-in, star, thespian, trouper

plea *noun.* alibi, apology, argument, cause, claim, defense, explanation, justification, mitigation, out, pleading, pretext, rationalization, right, song, story, suit, vindication

pleasant *adjective.* affable, agreeable, amiable, amusing, cheering, cheery, civil, convivial, delightful, enchanting, fine, fun, genial, gratifying, jolly, jovial, refreshing, welcome

please *verb.* amuse, cheer, content, delight, entertain, gladden, grab, gratify, humor, indulge, kill, pleasure, rejoice, satisfy, score, sell, suit, wow

pleasing *adjective.* agreeable, amiable, amusing, attractive, charming, congenial, delicious, delightful, enchanting, good, gratifying, luscious, satisfactory, satisfying, savory, suitable, sweet, welcome

pleasure *noun.* buzz, comfort, contentment, delectation, ease, felicity, fruition, gratification, hobby, indulgence, kick, kicks, recreation, relish, seasoning, solace, thrill, velvet

plentiful *adjective.* abounding, bumper, competent, excessive, extravagant, exuberant, flowing, flush, generous, large, lavish, liberal, lush, productive, profuse, replete, superfluous, swimming

plenty *noun.* affluence, bunch, cornucopia, deluge, fertility, flood, fruitfulness, heaps, loads, lots, mass, mountains, much, piles, prosperity, stacks, sufficiency, wealth

plight *noun.* box, case, circumstances, corner, difficulty, extremity, fix, hole, jam, perplexity, pickle, pinch, predicament, scrape, spot, state, straits, trouble

plot *noun.* **1** artifice, collusion, complicity, connivance, conspiracy, design, device, fix, frame, game, intrigue, little game, maneuver, practice, ruse, scheme, setup, trick **2** buildup, climax, denouement, design, development, enactment, events, movement, narrative, outline, progress, scenario, scheme, story line, subject, suspense, theme, thread

plot *verb.* angle, brew, conspire, contrive, design, devise, frame, hatch, imagine, lay, maneuver, operate, outline, project, promote, scheme, set up, sketch

plow *verb.* break, bulldoze, farm, furrow, harrow, harvest, list, push, rake, reap, ridge, rush, shove, smash, till, trench, turn, turn over

plug *verb.* block, choke, clog, close, congest, cork, cover, drive in, fill, obstruct, pack, ram, seal, secure, stop, stopper, stopple, stuff

pocket *adjective.* abridged, canned, capsule, compact, concise, condensed, diminutive, dwarfish, epitomized, little, miniature, minute, peewee, portable, potted, tiny, wee, weeny

poet *noun.* artist, author, balladist, bard, dilettante, dramatist, librettist, lyricist, lyrist, maker, metrist, odist, parodist, poetaster, rhapsodist, rhymer, writer

poetic *adjective.* anapestic, beautiful, dramatic, elegiac, epic, epical, iambic, idyllic, imaginative, lyric, lyrical, melodious, metrical, odic, rhythmical, romantic, songlike, tuneful

point *noun.* **1** bit, count, dot, fleck, flyspeck, full stop, iota, mark, minim, mite, mote, notch, particle, period, scrap, stop, tittle, trace **2** bill, cape, claw, end, head, headland, jag, pin point, prick, snag, spike, stiletto, summit, sword, thorn, tip, tooth, top **3** brink, condition, date, degree, duration, edge, extent, instant, juncture, limit, moment, period, position, stage, threshold, time, verge, very minute **4** aim, appeal, attraction, design, effectiveness, end, fascination, intent, intention, interest, motive, object, objective, punch, reason, usefulness, utility, validity **5** argument, burden, core, crux, drift, essence, gist, head, matter, motif, motive, pith, proposition, subject, text, thrust, tip, topic **6** attribute, case, circumstance, constituent, detail, element, facet, feature, instance, item, material, part, peculiarity, property, quality, respect, side, trait

point *verb.* bespeak, button down, denote, designate, direct, finger, hint, imply, indicate, lead, make, name, offer, peg, signify, suggest, tab, tag

pointed *adjective.* **1** acicular, aciculate, acuminate, acuminous, acute, barbed, cornered, cuspidate, edged, fine, keen, mucronate, peaked, piked, pointy, pronged, sharp, spiked **2** accurate, acid, acute, barbed, biting, cutting, incisive, insinuating, keen, kosher, meaty, pertinent, pregnant, sarcastic, sharp, tart, telling, trenchant

poison *noun.* adulteration, bacteria, bane, blight, cancer, contagion, contamination, corruption, germ, infection, malignancy, miasma, toxicant, toxin, toxoid, venin, venom, virus

poison *verb.* adulterate, corrupt, debase, defile, deprave, destroy, fester, harm, infect, kill, make ill, murder, pollute, stain, subvert, taint, undermine, warp

pole *noun.* bar, beam, extremity, flagpole, leg, mast, pile, plank, rod, shaft, spar, staff, stake, standard, stave, stick, stud, terminus

police *noun.* badge, bear, blue, bobby, bull, constable, cop, copper, corps, detective, fed, fuzz, law, man, officers, patrolman, pig, police

policy *noun.* approach, arrangement, code, course, custom, design, line, method, order, organization, plan, polity, practice, procedure, program, protocol, rule, scheme

polish *verb.* amend, better, brush up, correct, cultivate, emend, enhance, finish, furbish, mature, mend, perfect, refine, round, sleek, slick, smooth, touch up

polite *adjective.* affable, amenable, amiable, attentive, civil, civilized, complaisant, concerned, conciliatory, considerate, courteous, courtly, elegant, gentle, polished, politic, respectful, smooth

politician *noun.* boss, chieftain, congressman, flesh presser, glad-hander, hack, leader, legislator, officeholder, orator, partisan, party member, pol, politico, speaker, statesman, warhorse, whistle-stopper

politics *noun.* backroom, bossism, campaigning, civics, domestic affairs, foreign affairs, government, government policy, internal affairs, jungle, legislature, political science, polity, smoke-filled room, statecraft, statesmanship, stumping, zoo

poor *adjective.* **1** bankrupt, broke, destitute, flat, impoverished, indigent, low, meager, needy, penniless, penurious, pinched, reduced, scanty, strapped, suffering, tapped, underprivileged **2** base, common, contemptible, diminutive, feeble, imperfect, insignificant, meager, mediocre, miserable, modest, pitiable, pitiful, reduced, slight, subnormal, weak, worth **3** bare, barren, exhausted, feeble, fruitless, impaired, imperfect, impoverished, indisposed, infertile, infirm, puny, sick, sterile, unfertile, unfruitful, unproductive, worthless

pop *verb.* appear, blow, crack, explode, hit, insert, jump, leap, push, put, report, rise, shove, snap, stick, strike, thrust, whack

popular *adjective.* **1** accepted, attractive, beloved, favored, hip, in, liked, lovable, notorious, now, okay, pleasing, praised, selling, societal, sought, spinach, suitable **2** accepted, accessible, conventional, current, demanded, embraced, general, ordinary, prevailing, prevalent, public, rampant, ruling, standard, stock, ubiquitous, universal, widespread

popularity *noun.* acceptance, acclaim, celebrity, currency, demand, esteem, fame, fashion, favor, following, heyday, prevalence, regard, renown, reputation, repute, universality, vogue

porter *noun.* bearer, bellboy, bellhop, boy, caretaker, carrier, concierge, doorkeeper, doorman, gatekeeper, hop, janitor, pack rat, punk, sky cap, transporter, watchman

portion *noun.* allotment, chunk, division, drag, fraction, glob, helping, hunk, member, morsel, parcel, piece, quantum, ration, section, serving, slug, taste

portion *verb.* administer, allocate, allot, apportion, assign, deal, dispense, distribute, parcel, part, partition, piece, prorate, quota, ration, section, share, shift

portrait *noun.* account, characterization, depiction, description, figure, image, like-

ness, model, painting, photograph, picture, portraiture, portrayal, profile, silhouette, simulacrum, sketch, vignette
pose *noun.* affectation, air, attitude, bearing, carriage, facade, fake, front, guise, mannerism, masquerade, mien, posture, pretense, pretension, role, stance, stand
pose *verb.* **1** act, affect, attitudinize, fake, feign, grandstand, impersonate, make believe, masquerade, pass off, peacock, playact, posture, profess, purport, put on, sham, show off **2** advance, ask, extend, give, prefer, present, propone, propose, proposition, put, put forward, query, question, set, state, submit, suggest, tender
position *noun.* **1** area, fix, geography, ground, locale, locality, location, locus, post, region, seat, setting, site, spot, stand, station, tract, whereabouts **2** arrangement, bearing, circumstances, disposition, form, habit, manner, mien, pass, port, pose, posture, predicament, spot, stand, state, status, strait **3** cachet, capacity, caste, character, consequence, dignity, footing, importance, place, prestige, rank, reputation, situation, sphere, standing, station, stature, status **4** bag, berth, billet, connection, do, dodge, duty, employment, function, gig, job, occupation, place, post, profession, role, slot, spot
positive *adjective.* absolute, actual, affirmative, categorical, certain, clear, cold, concrete, decided, explicit, hard, incontrovertible, outright, real, specific, thoroughgoing, unambiguous, unmistakable
positively *adverb.* absolutely, amen, assuredly, categorically, certainly, doubtless, easily, emphatically, firmly, flat, flat out, sure, surely, undeniably, undoubtedly, unequivocally, unmistakably, unquestionably
possess *verb.* acquire, bear, carry, control, corner, dominate, enjoy, grab, hog, hold, lock up, maintain, occupy, own, retain, seize, take over, take possession
possessed *adjective.* consumed, crazed, cursed, demented, enchanted, fiendish, frenetic, frenzied, gone, haunted, hooked, insane, into, mad, obsessed, raving, really into, violent
possession *noun.* accessories, appointments, assets, baggage, chattels, equipment, estate, fixtures, furniture, goods, paraphernalia, province, settlement, territory, things, trappings, tricks, wealth
possibility *noun.* break, contingency, fluke, hap, happening, hazard, hope, incident, instance, liability, occasion, occurrence, opportunity, potentiality, practicability, prayer, shot, stab
possible *adjective.* accessible, adventitious, conceivable, dependent, desirable, dormant, earthly, expedient, feasible, mortal, obtainable, on, potential, practicable, setup, uncertain, viable, welcome
post *noun.* column, leg, mast, newel, pale, panel, pedestal, picket, pile, pole, prop, rail, shaft, stake, standard, stock, stud, upright
posture *noun.* aspect, attitude, bearing, brace, carriage, circumstance, demeanor, disposition, mien, mode, phase, port, pose, position, presence, set, situation, state
potent *adjective.* almighty, compelling, convincing, dominant, dynamic, impressive, lusty, mighty, persuasive, powerful, puissant, stiff, strong, sturdy, telling, trenchant, useful, virile
potential *adjective.* abeyant, budding, conceivable, dormant, embryonic, future, hidden, implied, inherent, latent, likely, lurking, plausible, possible, probable, quiescent, undeveloped, unrealized
pound *verb.* batter, bruise, buffet, clobber, crush, hammer, hit, malleate, pestle, powder, pulse, pummel, strike, thrash, thump, tramp, triturate, wallop
pour *verb.* cascade, course, discharge, emit, flood, flow, issue, jet, proceed, rain, roll, sheet, sluice, splash, spring, surge, throng, void
poverty *noun.* abjection, bankruptcy, beggary, debt, deficit, distress, emptiness, famine, hardship, necessity, pass, penury, reduction, shortage, starvation, straits, vacancy, want
powder *verb.* cover, crumble, crunch, dust,

file, flour, granulate, grate, grind, pestle, pound, rasp, reduce, scatter, scrape, smash, sprinkle, triturate

power *noun.* **1** ability, aptitude, bent, capability, capacity, effectiveness, efficacy, faculty, function, gift, influence, potential, potentiality, qualification, skill, talent, turn, virtue **2** arm, beef, energy, forcefulness, horsepower, intensity, might, muscle, omnipotence, potency, potential, powder, stream, strength, vigor, virtue, voltage, weight **3** beef, clout, command, direction, dominion, hegemony, influence, jurisdiction, law, leadership, omnipotence, prerogative, regency, right, rule, strength, superiority, wire

powerful *adjective.* able, almighty, authoritarian, compelling, competent, controlling, convincing, dominant, dynamic, energetic, impressive, mighty, persuasive, puissant, ruling, sovereign, strapping, wicked

practical *adjective.* **1** applied, constructive, empirical, feasible, handy, implicit, orderly, possible, practicable, pragmatic, rational, reasonable, sensible, serviceable, solid, sound, usable, virtual **2** accomplished, cosmopolitan, effective, efficient, old, old-time, proficient, qualified, seasoned, skilled, sophisticated, trained, versed, vet, veteran, working, worldly, worldly-wise

practice *noun.* **1** custom, fashion, form, habit, manner, method, mode, procedure, proceeding, process, rule, system, tradition, trick, usefulness, utility, way, wont **2** action, assignment, background, discipline, drill, drilling, effect, experience, operation, preparation, recitation, recounting, rehearsal, relating, seasoning, study, training, use

practice *verb.* build up, discipline, dress, drill, exercise, habituate, hone, polish, prepare, recite, rehearse, shakedown, sharpen, study, train, warm up, work at, work out

praise *noun.* acclaim, accolade, applause, appreciation, boost, celebration, cheering, citation, commendation, devotion, flattery, glorification, homage, puff, recognition, regard, thanks, tribute

praise *verb.* acclaim, advocate, appreciate, approve, bless, boost, build up, celebrate, clap, dignify, endorse, eulogize, flatter, proclaim, puff, recommend, root, tout

pray *verb.* adjure, appeal, ask, beseech, brace, crave, entreat, implore, importune, invocate, invoke, petition, recite, request, say, solicit, sue, urge

prayer *noun.* appeal, application, begging, benediction, communion, devotion, grace, imploring, invocation, orison, petition, plea, pleading, request, rogation, service, suit, worship

preacher *noun.* churchman, clergyman, cleric, clerical, divine, ecclesiastic, evangelist, Holy Joe, minister, missionary, padre, parson, pulpiter, reverend, revivalist, sermonizer, sky pilot

precarious *adjective.* ambiguous, contingent, delicate, dubious, hazardous, hot, indecisive, insecure, loaded, open, perilous, rocky, slippery, uncertain, unreliable, unsafe, unsettled, unsure

precaution *noun.* anticipation, canniness, care, caution, circumspection, discreetness, discretion, foresight, forethought, insurance, protection, providence, provision, prudence, regard, safeguard, safety measure, wariness

preceding *adjective.* aforementioned, aforesaid, antecedent, anterior, before, foregoing, former, forward, front, introductory, lead, one time, past, pioneer, preliminary, previous, prior, supra

precious *adjective.* affected, artful, artificial, choosy, dainty, delicate, fastidious, finicky, fragile, fussy, nice, ostentatious, particular, pretentious, refined, showy, sophisticated, studied

precise *adjective.* **1** absolute, accurate, actual, categorical, circumscribed, explicit, express, fixed, individual, limited, literal, narrow, proper, restricted, right, rigid, specific, strict **2** careful, choosy, exact, fastidious, finicky, formal, fussy, genteel, inflexible, nice, prim, puritanical, rigid, scrupulous, stiff, strict, stuffy, uncompromising

precisely *adverb.* absolutely, accurately, bang, correctly, definitely, even, expressly, literally, plumb, right, sharp, smack, specifically, square, squarely, strictly, sure, yes

predict *verb.* conclude, conjecture, croak, divine, envision, figure, forecast, foresee, foretell, infer, judge, omen, presage, presume, read, suppose, telegraph, think

prediction *noun.* anticipation, cast, conjecture, divination, dope, forecast, forecasting, foresight, horoscope, hunch, indicator, omen, presage, prevision, prognosis, prognostication, prophecy, tip

prefer *verb.* choose, elect, fancy, finger, incline, mark, pick, pose, promote, proposition, put, raise, suggest, tag, take, tap, upgrade, wish

preference *noun.* alternative, bag, choice, desire, election, favorite, flash, groove, inclination, option, pick, predilection, prepossession, say, say so, selection, top, weakness

preferred *adjective.* adopted, advantageous, approved, chosen, elected, endorsed, fancied, favored, handpicked, liked, named, picked, popular, sanctioned, selected, set apart, taken, well-liked

pregnant *adjective.* **1** abundant, anticipating, bumped, expectant, fecund, fertile, fragrant, fruitful, full, gone, gravid, heavy, hopeful, productive, prolific, replete, rich, teeming **2** charged, consequential, creative, eloquent, expressive, imaginative, important, inventive, loaded, momentous, original, pointed, rich, seminal, significant, suggestive, telling, weighty

prejudice *noun.* animosity, apartheid, aversion, belief, bias, detriment, discrimination, dislike, displeasure, enmity, injustice, repugnance, revulsion, slant, spleen, tilt, twist, warp

prejudice *verb.* angle, bend, bias, blemish, color, damage, dispose, distort, harm, hurt, impair, incline, mar, poison, slant, spoil, twist, warp

preliminary *adjective.* basic, elemental, elementary, first, fundamental, initial, opening, pilot, preceding, preparatory, preparing, primal, primary, prior, qualifying, readying, test, trial

premises *noun.* campus, digs, establishment, hole, home, house, joint, land, lay, layout, limits, pad, property, site, spot, terrace, turf, zone

premium *noun.* appreciation, boon, bounty, carrot, dividend, extra, fee, gravy, percentage, perk, plum, prize, recompense, regard, remuneration, reward, stock, value

preoccupied *adjective.* abstracted, bugged, daydreaming, deep, distracted, engaged, engrossed, fascinated, forgetful, immersed, intent, lost, oblivious, obsessed, rapt, removed, spellbound, wrapped

preparation *noun.* alertness, anticipation, arrangement, background, base, construction, education, establishment, expectation, fitting, formation, foundation, plan, precaution, preparedness, provision, schoolwork, study

prepare *verb.* adjust, appoint, assemble, build up, cook, fit, form, furnish, gird, make up, outfit, plan, prime, qualify, steel, supply, train, turn out

prepared *adjective.* able, arranged, bagged, fit, fixed, handy, inclined, minded, packed, pat, planned, primed, qualified, rigged, set, stacked, willing, wired

presence *noun.* **1** address, air, aspect, aura, bearing, behavior, carriage, comportment, demeanor, ease, look, mien, personality, poise, port, seeming, self-assurance, set **2** acumen, alertness, aplomb, calmness, cool, coolness, imperturbability, level-headedness, quickness, sang-froid, self-assurance, self-command, self-composure, self-possession, sensibility, sobriety, watchfulness, wits

present *adjective.* **1** already, begun, being, commenced, contemporary, current, existent, extant, going on, immediate, instant, just now, modern, nowadays, prompt, started, today, topical **2** accounted for, attendant, available, check, existent, here, in attendance, in view, near, on board, on deck, on hand, on-the-spot, ready, show, show up, there, within reach

present *noun.* benefaction, benevolence, boon, bounty, compliment, donation, endowment, favor, giveaway, goodie, grant, gratuity, handout, largess, lump, offering, stake, write-off

present *verb.* do, exhibit, expose, extend, give, imply, infer, manifest, mount, offer, perform, pose, produce, proposition, recount, stage, suggest, tender

presentation *noun.* act, arrangement, bestowal, delivering, delivery, demonstration, display, donation, exhibition, introduction, launch, production, proposition, reception, remembrance, rendition, staging, submission

preservation *noun.* canning, care, conservation, curing, defense, evaporation, freezing, guard, perpetuation, refrigeration, safeguard, salvation, security, shield, storage, support, upholding, ward

preserve *verb.* bottle, can, conserve, defend, evaporate, freeze, guard, keep, perpetuate, pickle, protect, safeguard, save, season, secure, shelter, sustain, uphold

press *verb.* **1** bear down, bulldoze, condense, crush, express, flatten, iron, level, mass, move, pile, ram, reduce, shove, smooth, squash, squeeze, thrust **2** assail, beg, beset, besiege, compel, demand, disquiet, enjoin, harass, implore, plague, plead, pressure, push, sell, squeeze, torment, urge

pressing *adjective.* acute, claiming, clamorous, compelling, critical, crying, demanding, distressing, exacting, forcing, immediate, imperative, important, insistent, instant, requiring, urgent, vital

pressure *noun.* burden, clout, constraint, crunch, demand, distress, drag, duress, load, necessity, obligation, persuasion, power, press, pull, ropes, string, trouble

prestige *noun.* authority, celebrity, consequence, dignity, distinction, eminence, esteem, importance, influence, power, prominence, regard, renown, repute, state, stature, status, weight

pretend *verb.* act, affect, assume, bluff, cheat, claim, copy, cozen, deceive, delude, falsify, fish, imitate, profess, purport, sham, simulate, sucker

pretended *adjective.* affected, alleged, artificial, bogus, cheating, covered, fake, false, feigned, lying, masked, ostensible, pretend, professed, purported, quack, sham, supposed

pretty *adjective.* appealing, boss, charming, comely, dainty, delicate, delightful, dreamboat, elegant, eyeful, fine, handsome, lulu, neat, number, pleasing, ten, trim

pretty *adverb.* a little, ample, fairly, kind of, large, moderately, much, notable, pretty much, quite, rather, reasonably, sizeable, some, something, somewhat, sort of, tolerably

prevail *verb.* abound, beat, best, carry, command, conquer, dominate, gain, get there, master, obtain, overcome, prove, reign, succeed, take off, triumph, win

prevailing *adjective.* chicken, common, ecumenical, main, popular, predominant, preponderating, prevalent, rampant, regular, ruling, set, steady, sweeping, universal, usual, widespread, worldwide

prevent *verb.* arrest, avert, baffle, bar, chill, cork, counter, counteract, foil, forbid, forestall, halt, interrupt, obstruct, preclude, prohibit, repress, retard

previously *adverb.* ahead, already, ante, away back, back, back when, before, beforehand, erstwhile, fore, formerly, forward, heretofore, hitherto, long ago, once, previous, then

prey *noun.* casualty, chase, dupe, fall guy, game, kill, loot, mark, martyr, mug, pillage, quarry, quest, raven, spoil, sufferer, underdog, victim

prey *verb.* blackmail, bleed, bully, burden, consume, devour, distress, eat, exploit, haunt, hunt, intimidate, load, plunder, raid, seize, trouble, weigh

price *noun.* appraisal, bite, compensation, consideration, demand, disbursement, fare, fee, figure, output, premium, quotation, ransom, rate, reckoning, tune, wages, worth

pride *noun.* **1** amour propre, delight, dignity, ego, egotism, face, gratification, happiness, honor, joy, pleasure, satisfaction, self-glorification, self-love, self-regard, self-respect, self-satisfaction, sufficiency **2** airs, assumption, condescension, disdain, disdainfulness, egotism, haughtiness, hubris, huff, immodesty, insolence, morgue, patronage, pragmatism, presumption, pretension, snobbery, vanity

pride *verb.* be proud, boast, brag, cavalier, congratulate, crow, felicitate, flatter oneself, huff, overbear, pique, plume, prance, presume, puff up, strut, swagger, swell

priest *noun.* churchman, clergyman, cleric, divine, ecclesiastic, elder, father, friar, Holy Joe, holy man, monk, padre, pontiff, preacher, rabbi, rector, sky pilot, vicar

primary *adjective.* **1** bad, cardinal, chief, dominant, excellent, first, greatest, heavy, highest, hot, leading, main, prime, principal, stellar, ten, top, tough **2** basic, beginning, bottom, central, elemental, elementary, essential, first, introductory, original, prime, primitive, principal, radical, rudimentary, simple, ultimate, underlying

prime *noun.* **1** bloom, choice, cream, elite, fat, flower, flowering, maturity, peak, perfection, pink, prize, spring, springtime, top, virility, vitality, zenith **2** adolescence, aurora, dawn, daybreak, dew, greenness, morn, morning, opening, puberty, spring, springtime, start, sunrise, tender years, vitality, youth, youthfulness

prime *verb.* break in, brief, clue, coach, cram, excite, fill in, fit, groom, inform, motivate, move, notify, prep, provoke, stimulate, tell, train

primitive *adjective.* **1** archaic, basic, earliest, early, elementary, essential, first, fundamental, old, original, primal, primary, primeval, pristine, substratal, underivative, underlying, undeveloped **2** austere, barbarian, childlike, crude, fierce, green, ignorant, naive, natural, preliterate, raw, rough, rudimentary, savage, simple, undeveloped, untrained, wild

principal *adjective.* arch, chief, controlling, dominant, essential, foremost, head, incomparable, key, peerless, predominant, premier, prime, sovereign, stellar, superior, supreme, unequaled

principal *noun.* administrator, boss, bread, chief, dean, director, exec, guru, head, headmaster, lead, leader, master, protagonist, rector, ruler, star, superintendent

principally *adverb.* chiefly, dominantly, eminently, especially, essentially, fundamentally, generally, importantly, largely, materially, mostly, notably, particularly, peculiarly, predominantly, supremely, universally, vitally

principle *noun.* **1** axiom, canon, criterion, dictum, form, formula, foundation, fundamental, ground, maxim, postulate, precept, proposition, rule, source, standard, theorem, verity **2** belief, character, code, conscience, credo, ethic, ethics, faith, ideals, integrity, morality, opinion, policy, principles, probity, rectitude, system, teaching

print *noun.* characters, composition, copy, edition, face, impress, impression, imprint, issue, lithograph, newspaper, periodical, photograph, publication, stamp, type, typescript, writing

print *verb.* compose, disseminate, impress, imprint, indent, issue, let roll, letter, mark, offset, publish, reissue, reprint, run off, set, set type, stamp, strike off

priority *noun.* antecedence, arrangement, crash project, greatest importance, lead, on line, order, ordering, pre-eminence, precedence, preference, prerogative, previousness, rank, seniority, superiority, supremacy, transcendence

prison *noun.* big house, big joint, campus, can, confinement, cooler, dungeon, guardhouse, jail, joint, keep, lockup, pen, penitentiary, reformatory, slam, stockade

prisoner *noun.* captive, chain gang, con, convict, culprit, defendant, detainee, escapee, hostage, internee, jailbird, lag, lifer, loser, punk, rat, tough, yard bird

private *adjective.* clandestine, closet, confidential, discreet, exclusive, hushed, independent, individual, inside, own, particular, personal, privy, reserved, secret, separate, special, unofficial

privilege *noun.* advantage, allowance, appanage, authorization, benefit, boon, charter, claim, concession, due, favor, franchise, freedom, immunity, liberty, opportunity, prerogative, right

privileged *adjective.* authorized, chartered, eligible, empowered, entitled, excused, exempt, franchised, free, furnished, granted, kosher, legit, licensed, qualified, sanctioned, special, vested
prize *noun.* acquisition, bonus, booty, bounty, crown, decoration, dividend, haul, loot, possession, premium, purse, recompense, scholarship, stakes, strokes, title, trophy
probability *noun.* anticipation, chance, chances, conceivability, contingency, credibility, expectation, feasibility, hazard, liability, odds, possibility, practicability, prayer, presumption, promise, prospect, shot
probably *adverb.* apparently, assumably, believably, doubtless, expediently, feasibly, imaginably, like enough, maybe, no doubt, perchance, perhaps, plausibly, possibly, practicably, presumably, reasonably, seemingly
problem *noun.* **1** box, complication, count, crunch, dilemma, disagreement, dispute, doubt, hitch, issue, mess, nut, obstacle, pickle, predicament, scrape, squeeze, trouble **2** bugaboo, bugbear, conundrum, enigma, example, grabber, illustration, intricacy, mind-boggler, mystery, puzzler, query, question, riddle, stickler, stumper, teaser, twister
procedure *noun.* agenda, course, custom, form, formula, layout, line, method, mode, move, operation, plan, program, routine, scheme, setup, style, system
proceed *verb.* advance, continue, fare, get, go ahead, go on, hie, journey, march, move on, move out, pass, press on, progress, push on, repair, travel, wend
proceeding *noun.* act, adventure, casualty, course, deed, exercise, experiment, hap, happening, incident, maneuver, move, movement, occurrence, operation, procedure, step, transaction
proceeds *noun.* gain, gate, handle, income, interest, produce, product, profit, receipts, result, returns, revenue, reward, split, take, takings, till, yield
process *noun.* case, course, formation, manner, mode, movement, operation, outgrowth, procedure, progress, routine, rule, stage, system, technique, trial, way, wise
proclaim *verb.* affirm, blast, blaze, blazon, broadcast, circulate, drum, enunciate, exhibit, illustrate, manifest, mark, profess, publish, show, trumpet, vent, voice
produce *noun.* aftermath, amount, consequence, crop, effect, fruitage, gain, goods, harvest, outcome, outgrowth, product, production, profit, realization, result, return, yield
produce *verb.* **1** assemble, author, beget, contribute, create, deliver, design, effectuate, erect, form, frame, furnish, give, imagine, render, reproduce, supply, turn out **2** beget, breed, bring about, draw on, effect, engender, generate, hatch, induce, make, make for, muster, occasion, provoke, result in, secure, set off, work up
product *noun.* blend, brew, commodity, compound, effect, goods, handiwork, invention, issue, legacy, line, outcome, outgrowth, output, preparation, production, synthetic, work
production *noun.* assembly, bearing, construction, creation, direction, generation, lengthening, making, manufacture, origination, preparation, presentation, producing, prolongation, provision, rendering, reproduction, result
productive *adjective.* beneficial, constructive, creative, dynamic, energetic, fertile, gainful, gratifying, inventive, plentiful, producing, profitable, prolific, rewarding, teeming, useful, valuable, worthwhile
profession *noun.* art, avocation, bag, billet, biz, business, career, concern, dodge, employment, engagement, game, line, role, specialty, sphere, undertaking, vocation
professional *adjective.* able, acknowledged, adept, competent, crack, efficient, expert, finished, known, learned, licensed, polished, practiced, proficient, qualified, sharp, skillful, slick
professional *noun.* adept, artist, authority, brain, egghead, expert, hotshot, maestro, master, old war-horse, pro, proficient, shark, specialist, star, virtuoso, whiz, wizard

professor *noun.* assistant, brain, don, educator, egghead, fellow, guru, instructor, ivory dome, lecturer, pedagogue, principal, prof, sage, savant, schoolmaster, teach, tutor

profit *noun.* acquisition, aggrandizement, avail, benefit, earnings, gate, good, income, interest, output, percentage, proceeds, receipt, remuneration, take, takings, turnout, velvet

profit *verb.* aid, avail, benefit, better, clear, contribute, earn, exploit, help, pay, promote, prosper, realize, recover, serve, thrive, use, utilize

profitable *adjective.* assisting, beneficial, conducive, effectual, going, good, instrumental, paying, practical, pragmatic, productive, remunerative, rewarding, serviceable, sweet, useful, valuable, worthwhile

profound *adjective.* **1** deep, discerning, enlightened, heavy, informed, intellectual, intelligent, knowledgeable, learned, mysterious, recondite, sage, secret, shrewd, skilled, subtle, thoughtful, wise **2** abject, absolute, acute, buried, deep, emotional, exhaustive, extensive, extreme, hard, heartfelt, hearty, intense, keen, pronounced, sincere, thorough, total

program *noun.* affairs, appointments, arrangements, bulletin, business, calendar, catalog, curriculum, details, index, list, meetings, memoranda, plan, plans, schedule, slate, timetable

program *verb.* bill, budget, compile, computer, design, edit, figure, instruct, lay out, list, poll, process, schedule, set, set up, slate, supply, work out

progress *noun.* break, breakthrough, buildup, course, flowering, impetus, improvement, lunge, motion, movement, pace, passage, proficiency, promotion, rate, rise, tour, way

progress *verb.* advance, come on, continue, dash, edge, forge ahead, gain ground, get along, get on, go forward, lunge, make headway, make strides, move on, proceed, shoot, speed, travel

progressive *adjective.* accelerating, advanced, continuing, developing, dynamic, enlightened, enterprising, gradual, graduated, growing, intensifying, left, modern, onward, radical, revolutionary, tolerant, wide

prohibited *adjective.* banned, barred, contraband, crooked, heavy, illegal, no-no, not allowed, not approved, off limits, proscribed, refused, restricted, shady, taboo, verboten, vetoed, wildcat

prohibition *noun.* bar, bleeper, constraint, don't, embargo, exclusion, injunction, interdict, negation, obstruction, prevention, proscription, refusal, repudiation, restriction, taboo, temperance, veto

project *noun.* adventure, aim, baby, bag, blueprint, business, concern, design, enterprise, intention, job, matter, plan, program, proposition, scheme, setup, work

project *verb.* **1** blueprint, contemplate, design, devise, diagram, extrapolate, feature, frame, image, imagine, outline, predict, propose, scheme, see, think, vision, visualize **2** be conspicuous, be prominent, beetle, extend, hang out, hang over, jut, lengthen, overhang, poke, pop out, pout, prolong, protrude, protuberate, push out, stand out, stretch out

projection *noun.* bump, bunch, extension, hook, knob, ledge, overhang, prolongation, prominence, protrusion, protuberance, ridge, rim, shelf, sill, spine, spur, step

prominent *adjective.* **1** arresting, candy, embossed, extended, flashy, jutting, marked, noticeable, obvious, pronounced, protruding, raised, remarkable, rough, salient, signal, striking, unmistakable **2** chief, distinguished, eminent, famed, famous, foremost, great, leading, main, notable, noted, notorious, outstanding, popular, renowned, respected, top, underlined

promise *noun.* agreement, consent, contract, covenant, engagement, espousal, obligation, parole, pawn, pledge, profession, security, stipulation, swear, swearing, undertaking, vow, warranty

promise *verb.* **1** affirm, agree, bargain, commit, consent, contract, covenant, ensure, insure, pass, pawn, pledge, profess, secure, subscribe, swear, underwrite, vow **2** augur, bespeak, betoken, denote, encourage, forebode, foreshadow, give hope, hint, hold probability, indicate, like, look, omen, portend, presage, seem likely, suggest

promote *verb.* **1** aid, avail, ballyhoo, benefit, bolster, build up, encourage, endorse, forward, foster, further, nurture, patronize, puff, recommend, serve, succor, uphold **2** advance, aggrandize, ascend, better, deadhead, dignify, elevate, exalt, favor, graduate, honor, increase, kick upstairs, magnify, prefer, raise, up, upgrade

promotion *noun.* **1** advocacy, aggrandizement, boom, boost, break, breakthrough, buildup, elevation, encouragement, favoring, hike, improvement, lift, preference, preferment, progress, rise, upgrading **2** advertising, advertising campaign, ballyhoo, buildup, hard sell, hoopla, notice, pitch, plug, plugging, PR, press, propaganda, public relations, publicity, puff, pushing, spread

prompt *adjective.* alert, apt, eager, early, efficient, expeditious, immediate, instant, instantaneous, precise, rapid, ready, responsive, smart, swift, vigilant, watchful, willing

prompt *verb.* aid, arouse, convince, cue, evoke, goad, hint, imply, mention, motivate, move, occasion, prick, propel, propose, provoke, refresh, sic

promptly *adverb.* at once, directly, expeditiously, fast, fleetly, hastily, instantly, PDQ, posthaste, pronto, punctually, quickly, rapidly, sharp, speedily, straightaway, swiftly, unhesitatingly

prone *adjective.* apt, bent, devoted, disposed, exposed, fain, given, inclined, likely, minded, open, predisposed, ready, sensitive, subject, susceptible, tending, willing

proof *noun.* argument, case, confirmation, credentials, criterion, cue, demonstration, documents, establishment, exhibit, facts, goods, ground, reason, reasons, substantiation, trace, validation

prop *verb.* bear up, bolster, brace, buoy, carry, lean, maintain, rest, set, shore, stand, stay, strengthen, support, sustain, truss, underprop, uphold

propaganda *noun.* advertising, agitprop, announcement, ballyhoo, brainwashing, disinformation, doctrine, evangelism, handout, hogwash, implantation, inculcation, indoctrination, newspeak, promotion, proselytism, publication, publicity

proper *adjective.* **1** able, applicable, appropriate, apt, becoming, befitting, capable, competent, decent, desired, fit, fitting, good, meet, qualified, right, suited, true **2** becoming, befitting, comely, correct, decent, demure, genteel, gentlemanly, kosher, ladylike, moral, prim, puritanical, respectable, right, solid, square, stone **3** absolute, accepted, accurate, complete, consummate, correct, customary, decorous, established, exact, formal, orthodox, out-and-out, precise, right, unmistaken, usual, utter

property *noun.* acreage, chattels, claim, dominion, equity, estate, farm, goods, home, inheritance, realty, resources, riches, substance, title, tract, wealth, worth

proportion *noun.* amplitude, apportionment, breadth, dimension, distribution, division, equation, expanse, fraction, magnitude, measurement, part, percentage, rate, ratio, relationship, scope, segment

proportionate *adjective.* commensurate, comparable, comparative, compatible, consistent, contingent, correspondent, corresponding, dependent, equal, equitable, equivalent, even, proportional, reciprocal, relative, symmetrical, uniform

proposal *noun.* angle, bid, design, idea, layout, motion, offer, outline, pass, pitch, plan, presentation, program, proposition, scenario, scheme, setup, tender

propose *verb.* affirm, ask, assert, invite, name, nominate, offer, pose, prefer, press, proposition, recommend, request, solicit, state, tender, urge, volunteer

propriety *noun.* **1** accordance, advisability, agreeableness, appropriateness, aptness, concord, consonance, convenience, fitness, harmony, justice, morality, order, pleasantness, rectitude, respectability, rightness, suitability **2** breeding, civilities, correctness, courtesy, decency, decorum, delicacy, dignity, good form, etiquette, manners, modesty, mores, niceties, politeness, protocol, rectitude, refinement, respectability

prospect *noun.* anticipation, calculation, contemplation, expectancy, expectation, forecast, future, hope, likelihood, odds, opening, plan, possibility, presumption, probability, promise, proposal, thought

prospective *adjective.* approaching, awaited, coming, considered, destined, eventual, expected, forthcoming, future, imminent, impending, intended, likely, planned, possible, potential, promised, proposed

prosperity *noun.* abundance, advantage, affluence, benefit, boom, clover, do, ease, fortune, good, inflation, interest, riches, success, thriving, velvet, victory, wealth

prosperous *adjective.* **1** affluent, blooming, booming, comfortable, easy, flourishing, halcyon, lucky, moneyed, opulent, prospering, rich, roaring, snug, substantial, thriving, wealthy, well **2** advantageous, appropriate, auspicious, bright, convenient, desirable, favorable, felicitous, fortunate, good, happy, lucky, opportune, profitable, propitious, seasonable, timely, well-timed

protect *verb.* chaperon, conserve, cover, cushion, defend, foster, hedge, keep, preserve, safeguard, save, screen, secure, sentinel, shade, shelter, shotgun, watch

protection *noun.* armament, buffer, certainty, charge, conservation, cover, guard, guarding, preservation, refuge, safeguard, salvation, screen, security, stability, strength, umbrella, ward

protective *adjective.* careful, conservative, covering, custodial, defensive, emergency, fatherly, guardian, insulating, maternal, motherly, possessive, protecting, securing, shielding, vigilant, warm, watchful

protest *noun.* beef, challenge, clamor, complaint, declaration, demonstration, dissent, grievance, kick, knock, march, moratorium, objection, rally, revolt, riot, squawk

protest *verb.* affirm, assert, blast, buck, combat, complain, disagree, fight, insist, kick, maintain, profess, remonstrate, revolt, squawk, testify, vow

proud *adjective.* **1** appreciative, content, dignified, fiery, fine, glad, glorious, gorgeous, gratifying, honored, impressive, magnificent, memorable, pleasing, rewarding, satisfied, stately, valiant **2** bloated, cocky, conceited, disdainful, haughty, imperious, insolent, lofty, lordly, masterful, pompous, presumptuous, pretentious, scornful, snobbish, supercilious, superior, vain

prove *verb.* affirm, ascertain, assay, certify, convince, experiment, find, justify, manifest, result, settle, test, testify, trial, try, turn out, uphold, validate

provide *verb.* bestow, contribute, feather, fit, furnish, give, heel, impart, keep, line, maintain, minister, outfit, render, serve, supply, transfer, turn out

province *noun.* business, colony, county, department, division, domain, employment, function, line, region, role, rule, section, sphere, territory, tract, walk, zone

provincial *adjective.* bigoted, bucolic, country, hidebound, limited, local, narrow, parochial, pastoral, petty, rude, rural, rustic, sectarian, small-town, uninformed, unpolished, unsophisticated

provision *noun.* **1** arrangement, catering, emergency, equipping, fitting out, foundation, furnishing, groundwork, outline, plan, prearrangement, precaution, preparation, procurement, providing, stock, store, supplying **2** agreement, catch, clause, demand, kicker, limitation, prerequisite, proviso, qualification, requirement, reservation, restriction, rider, specification, stipulation, strings, term, terms

provisional *adjective.* conditional, dependent, ephemeral, experimental, interim, limited, makeshift, passing, pro tem, provisionary, provisory, qualified, stopgap, temporary, tentative, test, transient, transitional

provocative *adjective.* annoying, challenging, disturbing, exciting, galling, heady, inciting, influential, inspirational, insulting, intoxicating, offensive, outrageous, provoking, pushing, spurring, stimulant, stimulating

pseudo *adjective.* bogus, counterfeit, ersatz, fake, false, imitation, mock, not kosher, phony, pirate, pretend, pretended, quasi, queer, sham, simulated, spurious, wrong

public *adjective.* **1** accessible, civic, civil, common, communal, country, federal, governmental, metropolitan, municipal, mutual, national, open, popular, state, universal, unrestricted, widespread **2** acknowledged, exposed, general, notorious, obvious, open, overt, patent, plain, popular, prevalent, published, recognized, social, societal, usual, vulgar, widespread

public *noun.* buyers, cats, citizens, clientele, community, country, electorate, followers, following, heads, men, mob, multitude, patrons, people, population, suite, supporters

publication *noun.* advertisement, appearance, ballyhoo, broadcast, broadcasting, declaration, disclosure, discovery, dissemination, issuance, issuing, proclamation, publicity, reporting, revelation, statement, ventilation, writing

publicity *noun.* advertising, announcing, attention, ballyhoo, billing, broadcasting, clout, currency, distribution, ink, notoriety, plug, press, propaganda, puff, release, spotlight, spread

pull *verb.* drag, extract, haul, jerk, lug, paddle, pick, pluck, remove, rend, row, stretch, tow, trail, truck, tug, twitch, weed

pump *verb.* blow up, dilate, distend, draft, drain, draw, drive, empty, force, force out, inflate, inject, pour, push, send, supply, swell, tap

punch *verb.* belt, box, buffet, clip, clout, dig, knock, plug, prod, rap, slap, slug, smack, smash, strike, thrust, thump, wallop

punishment *noun.* abuse, beating, castigation, chastisement, correction, deprivation, discipline, forfeit, galleys, lumps, mortification, ostracism, pain, penance, retribution, rod, trial, unhappiness

pupil *noun.* adherent, attendant, beginner, bone, brain, dig, disciple, follower, grind, novice, satellite, scholar, schoolboy, schoolgirl, skull, student, tool, undergraduate

purchase *verb.* achieve, acquire, attain, cop, earn, gain, invest, market, obtain, patronize, pick up, procure, realize, redeem, secure, take, truck, win

pure *adjective.* **1** authentic, bright, clear, flawless, kosher, limpid, lucid, natural, neat, plenary, real, simple, total, true, unadulterated, unalloyed, undiluted, unmixed **2** germ-free, immaculate, pristine, purified, refined, sanitary, snowy, spotless, stainless, sterile, sterilized, unadulterated, unblemished, unpolluted, unstained, unsullied, untarnished, wholesome **3** cherry, clean, continent, decent, good, guileless, honest, immaculate, kid, modest, righteous, sinless, spotless, true, unstained, upright, virgin, virtuous

purely *adverb.* absolutely, all, altogether, barely, entirely, essentially, exactly, exclusively, just, merely, only, plainly, quite, simply, solely, totally, utterly, wholly

purpose *noun.* **1** determination, direction, expectation, function, hope, intent, meaning, mecca, mission, objective, plan, proposition, reason, scheme, scope, target, view, wish **2** advantage, avail, benefit, duty, effect, function, gain, goal, good, mark, mission, object, objective, outcome, profit, result, target, utility

purpose *verb.* aim, aspire, commit, conclude, consider, contemplate, decide, design, determine, intend, mean, meditate, mind, plan, ponder, propose, pursue, resolve

purse *noun.* bag, billfold, bursa, carryall, clutch, frame, handbag, hide, leather, lizard, moneybag, pocket, pocketbook, poke, pouch, receptacle, sack, wallet

pursue *verb.* **1** accompany, bait, dog, fish, follow, harass, haunt, hound, persist, plague, ride, run down, shadow, tag, tail, trace, track down, trail **2** adhere, apply oneself, conduct, continue, cultivate, engage in, keep on, maintain, perform, persevere, ply, practice, proceed, prosecute, see through, tackle, wage, work at

pursuit *noun.* accomplishing, activity, bag, biz, business, career, do, dodge, employment, game, hobby, interest, job, line, racket, undertaking, vocation, work

push *noun.* **1** attack, bearing, butt, charge, driving, effort, energy, exertion, forcing, jolt, lean, offensive, onset, prod, propulsion, shove, straining, thrust **2** ambition, bang, drive, dynamism, energy, enterprise, get-up-and-go, go, gumption, guts, initiative, pep, punch, snap, spunk, starch, vigor, vitality **3** accelerate, bear down, budge, bulldoze, butt, dig, exert, launch, move, muscle, pressure, propel, ram, shoulder, shove, squash, squeeze, stir **4** bear down, bulldoze, encourage, goad, influence, inspire, jolly, kid, motivate, oblige, persuade, press, pressure, prod, speed, speed up, squeeze, urge

put *verb.* **1** deposit, establish, fix, insert, install, invest, lay, nail, park, peg, plank, quarter, repose, rest, seat, set, settle, stick **2** couch, express, formulate, forward, give, offer, pose, prefer, proposition, render, set, state, suggest, tender, translate, turn, vent, word **3** assign, condemn, consign, constrain, doom, employ, enjoin, force, impose, induce, inflict, levy, make, oblige, require, set, subject, subject to

puzzle *verb.* addle, baffle, beat, buffalo, complicate, disconcert, disturb, floor, foil, lick, obscure, perplex, pose, rattle, stir, stumble, stump, throw

puzzled *adjective.* baffled, beaten, bewildered, doubtful, floured, foggy, hung, lost, mystified, perplexed, rattled, screwed up, shook, stuck, stumped, thrown, unglued, unscrewed

puzzling *adjective.* ambiguous, baffling, bewildering, beyond one, difficult, enigmatic, hard, incomprehensible, inexplicable, involved, knotty, misleading, mystifying, obscure, perplexing, unaccountable, unclear, unfathomable

Q

quack *noun.* actor, bum, cheat, counterfeit, fake, faker, fraud, phony, pretender, pseudo, rogue, sham, shark, sharp, sharpie, slicker, whip

quaint *adjective.* **1** bizarre, curious, erratic, fanciful, fantastic, funny, idiosyncratic, odd, offbeat, original, outlandish, peculiar, queer, singular, special, unusual, weird, whimsical **2** affected, antiquated, antique, archaic, artful, baroque, captivating, charming, colonial, curious, cute, enchanting, fanciful, gothic, ingenious, picturesque, pleasing, whimsical

qualification *noun.* **1** accomplishment, adequacy, aptitude, attainment, attribute, capability, capacity, competence, eligibility, experience, fitness, goods, makings, might, quality, skill, stuff, suitability **2** allowance, caveat, contingency, criterion, essential, exception, exemption, limitation, modification, need, objection, postulate, prerequisite, provision, proviso, reservation, restriction, stipulation

qualified *adjective.* able, accomplished, adept, capable, certified, competent, disciplined, examined, expert, fit, good, knowledgeable, practiced, proficient, proper, tested, vet, wicked

qualify *verb.* **1** authorize, certify, commission, empower, enable, endow, entitle, fit, ground, meet, pass, permit, prepare, ready, score, suffice, suit, train **2** abate, adapt, alter, change, diminish, ease, lessen, limit, mitigate, moderate, modify, reduce, regulate, restrain, soften, temper, vary, weaken

quality *noun.* **1** affection, affirmation, attribute, character, constitution, description, element, essence, factor, feature, kind, mark, parameter, peculiarity, property, savor, sort, virtue **2** character, class, distinction, excellence, excellency, footing, grade, group, kind, repute, state, station, stature, step, superiority, value, variety, worth

quantity *noun.* abundance, allotment, amount, amplitude, body, budget, expanse, extent, figure, length, load, magnitude, mass, multitude, part, size, sum, variety

quarrel *noun.* altercation, argument, bickering, brawl, combat, commotion, complaint, difference, dust, feud, fight, fray, fuss, misunderstanding, objection, row, ruckus, spat

quarrel *verb.* argue, battle, brawl, charge, clash, complain, differ, disapprove, dissent, divide, feud, fight, row, spat, strive, struggle, tangle, vary

quarter *noun.* bearing, direction, division, domain, part, precinct, province, region, section, sector, side, slum, spot, station, territory, turf, zone, zoo

quarter *verb.* accommodate, billet, board, bunk, domicile, domiciliate, entertain, establish, harbor, house, install, lodge, place, post, put up, settle, shelter, station

quarters *noun.* abode, billet, cabin, chambers, coop, cottage, digs, domicile, dwelling, home, house, lodge, lodging, post, roost, shelter, sorority, station

quest *noun.* adventure, chase, crusade, delving, enterprise, examination, inquest, inquisition, investigation, mission, pilgrimage, prey, probe, probing, pursuit, quarry, research, seeking

question *noun.* argument, challenge, confusion, contention, controversy, debate, difficulty, dispute, enigma, mystery, objection, problem, protest, puzzle, query, remonstrance, remonstration, uncertainty

question *verb.* catechize, challenge, cook, examine, grill, hit, inquire, interview, investigate, knock, probe, pry, pump, quest, quiz, roast, search, solicit

questionable *adjective.* ambiguous, apocryphal, contingent, cryptic, dubious, enigmatic, indecisive, moot, mysterious, obscure, provisional, shady, suspicious, uncertain, undefined, unreliable, unsettled, vague

quick *adjective.* **1** abrupt, agile, alert, animated, brief, curt, energetic, expeditious, hasty, impetuous, instantaneous, keen, mercurial, perfunctory, prompt, rapid, snappy, winged **2** able, acute, adept, apt, bright, canny, capable, competent, deft, discerning, effectual, keen, prompt, savvy, sharp, slick, wired, wise

quiet *adjective.* **1** close, dumb, hushed, iced, inaudible, low, muffled, mute, muted, noiseless, quiescent, quieted, reserved, soft, speechless, still, uncommunicative, unuttered **2** collected, fixed, gentle, halcyon, inactive, isolated, level, meek, motionless, placid, private, retired, secret, sedate, smooth, stagnant, still, tranquil

quiet *noun.* calm, cessation, ease, hush, lull, peace, quietness, relaxation, repose, rest, serenity, silence, speechlessness, still, stillness, stop, termination, tranquility

quiet *verb.* calm, gag, inactivate, lull, moderate, mollify, muzzle, reconcile, relax, settle, silence, slack, smooth, soften, soothe, squash, still, subdue

quit *verb.* **1** blow, book, chuck, depart, desert, drop, evacuate, exit, forsake, go, leave, relinquish, resign, surrender, take off, vacate, withdraw, yield **2** abandon, break off, cease, conclude, discontinue, drop, end, halt, knock off, leave, resign, retire, secede, surcease, suspend, terminate, wind up, withdraw

quite *adverb.* absolutely, actually, all, altogether, considerably, entirely, just, largely, perfectly, positively, precisely, purely, really, thoroughly, truly, utterly, well, wholly

R

race *noun.* **1** chase, clash, clip, competition, contention, course, dash, engagement, event, marathon, match, meet, pursuit, relay, rivalry, run, speed, spurt **2** breed, color, culture, family, folk, house, issue, kin, kind, kindred, line, nationality, offspring, people, seed, species, stock, variety

race *verb.* bolt, bustle, career, chase, compete, course, fling, fly, gallop, haste, lash, post, pursue, scramble, shoot, speed, spurt, swoop

rack *verb.* afflict, agonize, distress, force, harass, harrow, martyr, oppress, pain, pull, shake, strain, stress, stretch, tear, torment, try, wring

radiant *adjective.* beaming, brilliant, effulgent, gleaming, glittering, glorious, glowing, incandescent, lambent, lucent, luminous, lustrous, radiating, refulgent, resplendent, shining, sparkling, sunny

radical *adjective.* **1** basic, bottom, cardinal, constitutional, essential, inherent, innate, intrinsic, native, natural, organic, original, primary, primitive, profound, thoroughgoing, underlying, vital **2** advanced, communistic, entire, excessive, fanatical, forward, gone, immoderate, insubordinate, lawless, refractory, revolutionary, riotous, seditious, severe, sweeping, uncompromising, unruly

radical *noun.* agitator, anarchist, communist, crusader, individualist, leftist, militant, nazi, nihilist, nonconformist, objector, pacifist, rebel, red, revolutionary, secessionist, socialist, subversive

rage *noun.* **1** agitation, bitterness, bluster, explosion, ferocity, fireworks, furor, hemorrhage, huff, indignation, irritation, madness, mania, storm, temper, upset, violence, wrath **2** chic, craze, cry, enthusiasm, fad, fancy, fashion, freak, happening, in, latest, mania, mode, now, passion, style, vogue, whim

rage *verb.* be uncontrollable, blow up, bristle, chafe, erupt, fret, fulminate, go berserk, overflow, rail at, rampage, roar, scream, steam, storm, surge, tear, yell

ragged *adjective.* contemptible, desultory, dilapidated, dingy, disorganized, fragmented, frayed, irregular, notched, patched, poor, rough, shaggy, shredded, tattered, torn, unfinished, unkempt

raid *noun.* arrest, assault, bust, capture, descent, foray, forced entrance, incursion, invasion, onset, onslaught, pull, reconnaissance, roundup, sally, seizure, sortie, sweep

raid *verb.* assail, blockade, break in, charge, foray, harass, invade, loot, overrun, pirate, rifle, sally, slough, storm, strafe, strike, swoop, waste

rail *verb.* abuse, attack, blast, castigate, censure, chew out, complain, fulminate, inveigh, jaw, objurgate, rant, rate, revile, scold, thunder, upbraid, whip

rain *noun.* cloudburst, condensation, deluge, drizzle, fall, flood, flurry, mist, monsoon, pour, pouring, raindrops, rainfall, rainstorm, shower, spit, sprinkling, stream

raise *noun.* accession, accretion, addition, advance, boost, bump, hike, hike upstairs, hold up, increment, jump, jump up, leg, leg up, promotion, raising, rise, step up

raise *verb.* **1** boost, build, build up, construct, erect, establish, exalt, heave, hoist, hold up, lever, lift, mount, promote, pry, set up, shove, uplift **2** assemble, build up, congregate, congress, dignify, enhance, enlarge, exaggerate, form, levy, look up, mobilize, mushroom, rally, reinforce, rendezvous, snowball, strengthen **3** activate, advance, arouse, awaken, broach, cause, evoke, excite, foster, incite, instigate, introduce, moot, motivate, provoke, set, set on, suggest **4** breed, care for, cultivate, develop, drag up, foster, group, grow, nurse, plant, produce, propagate, provide, rear, sow, support, train, wean

rake *noun.* Casanova, chaser, debauchee, lecher, libertine, make-out artist, philanderer, playboy, player, rascal, roué, seducer, sensualist, sport, tomcat, voluptuary, wolf, womanizer

rake *verb.* break up, clear, collect, comb, examine, grade, graze, grub, harrow, rasp, remove, scan, scrape, scratch, search, smooth, sweep, weed

rally *verb.* **1** arouse, assemble, awaken, challenge, charge, counterattack, encourage, marshal, mobilize, refresh, renew, restore, round up, summon, surge, unite, urge, wake **2** bounce back, brace up, come along, enliven, get better, grow stronger, improve, invigorate, perk up, pick up, pull through, recover, recuperate, refresh, regain strength, shape up, surge, turn around

random *adjective.* accidental, adventitious, aimless, arbitrary, casual, chance, contingent, designless, desultory, hit-or-miss, incidental, indiscriminate, irregular, odd, purposeless, spot, stray, unpremeditated

range *noun.* **1** amplitude, area, dimensions, distance, expanse, ken, latitude, leeway, magnitude, matter, province, scope, span, spectrum, sphere, stretch, territory, width **2** assortment, chain, class, collection, file, gamut, kind, line, lot, order, rank, row, selection, sequence, sort, string, tier, variety **3** align, arrange, array, bias, bracket, catalogue, categorize, class, classify, dispose, file, grade, group, incline, line, line up, order, pigeonhole **4** cover, cross, cruise, drift, encompass, explore, float, ply, ramble, rove, search, spread, straggle, stroll, tramp, travel, traverse, trek

rank *adjective.* **1** coarse, dense, excessive, extreme, exuberant, fertile, flourishing, grown, lavish, lush, luxurious, productive, profuse, prolific, rampant, rich, tropical, wild **2** blatant, conspicuous, consummate, downright, excessive, extravagant, flagrant, gross, noticeable, outright, outstanding, positive, rampant, sheer, thorough, total, undisguised, utter **3** bad, dank, disagreeable, fetid, foul, fusty, gross, loathsome, nasty, off, offensive, pungent, repulsive, revolting, sour, strong, tainted, turned

rank *noun.* birth, caste, dignity, distinction, division, estate, family, footing, grade, level, pedigree, primacy, quality, sort, sphere, station, stature, stratum

rank *verb.* align, array, assign, dispose, evaluate, grade, judge, list, locate, marshal, order, peg, put, range, rate, regard, settle, sort

rapid *adjective.* accelerated, active, agile, brisk, expeditious, express, fleet, hasty, hurried, lively, mercurial, precipitate, prompt, quickened, ready, screaming, swift, winged

rare *adjective.* **1** deficient, exceptional, few, flimsy, inconceivable, isolated, light, limited, occasional, scarce, singular, strange, subtle, tenuous, unimaginable, unique, unthinkable, unusual **2** admirable, choice, dainty, delicate, elegant, excellent, exquisite, extreme, fine, great, incomparable, matchless, peerless, priceless, rich, select, superb, unique

rarely *adverb.* barely, exceptionally, extra, extraordinarily, extremely, finely, hardly, hardly ever, infrequently, little, notably, not often, remarkably, seldom, singularly, uncommon, uncommonly, unfrequently, unusually

rate *verb.* assay, assess, calculate, consider, count, esteem, evaluate, fix, grade, judge, peg, pigeonhole, price, reckon, regard, respect, tag, value

rather *adverb.* a bit, a little, averagely, comparatively, enough, fairly, kind of, passably, pretty, quite, reasonably, relatively, slightly, some, something, somewhat, sort of

ration *noun.* allowance, apportionment, assignment, bit, cut, distribution, division, dole, drag, food, helping, part, provision, quantum, quota, share, store, supply

ration *verb.* allocate, allot, apportion, assign, budget, conserve, control, deal, distribute, issue, limit, parcel, proportion, prorate, quota, restrict, save, share

rational *adjective.* analytical, balanced, calm, cerebral, circumspect, cognitive, collected, discriminating, intellectual, normal, objective, philosophic, reasonable, reasoning, sensible, sound, synthetic, wise

raucous *adjective.* acute, blaring, blatant, braying, dissonant, grating, grinding, gruff, harsh, hoarse, husky, inharmonious, loud, rasping, rough, sharp, thick, unharmonious

raw *adjective.* **1** basic, bloody, coarse, crude, fibrous, green, hard, immature, native, natural, organic, rough, unformed, unprepared, unripe, unstained, untreated, virgin **2** blistered, bruised, cut, dressed, exposed, galled, grazed, naked, nude, open, peeled, scraped, scratched, sensitive, skinned, sore, uncovered, wounded **3** coarse, crass, crude, dirty, filthy, foul, gross, indecent, low, mean, nasty, obscene, pornographic, rank, rough, rude, smutty, unscrupulous

ray *noun.* bar, beam, blaze, blink, emanation, flicker, gleam, glimmer, glint, glitter, hint, patch, radiance, shaft, shine, spark, streak, trace

reach *noun.* command, compass, distance, grasp, horizon, influence, jurisdiction, ken, latitude, magnitude, orbit, power, range, scope, spread, stretch, sweep, swing

reach *verb.* **1** arrive, attain, buzz, check in, come, come to, enter, gain on, get to, hit, land, make, make it, overtake, ring in, roll in, show, sky in **2** approach, attain, buck, encompass, give, grasp, join, lead, lunge, pass, seize, span, spread, stand, strike, touch, transfer, turn over

react *verb.* acknowledge, act, answer, behave, boomerang, counter, echo, feel, function, operate, perform, proceed, rebound, reciprocate, recoil, recur, take, work

reaction *noun.* acknowledgment, backlash, boomerang, compensation, cooler, echo, feedback, kick, opinion, rebound, reception, recoil, reflection, rejoinder, retort, reverberation, revulsion, take

reactionary *noun.* bitter-ender, counterrevolutionary, diehard, fogy, hard hat, intransigent, lunatic fringe, mossback, obscurantist, radical, radical right, reactionary, reactionist, red-neck, rightwinger, rightist, royalist, standpatter, ultraconservative

read *verb.* **1** comprehend, construe, discover, express, glance, interpret, know, learn, paraphrase, perceive, put, render, see, study, translate, understand, unravel, view **2** affirm, announce, assert, declaim, deliver, display, hold, indicate, mark, pronounce, recite, record, register, say, show, speak, state, utter

readily *adverb.* at once, cheerfully, eagerly, easily, effortlessly, freely, gladly, immediately, lightly, promptly, smoothly, speedily, straight away, unhesitatingly, well, willingly, without delay, without difficulty

readiness *noun.* address, adroitness, alacrity, aptness, deftness, dispatch, eagerness, ease, eloquence, facility, fluency, good will, inclination, maturity, preparation, preparedness, prowess, sleight

reading *noun.* account, commentary, construction, education, erudition, examination, grasp, impression, knowledge, paraphrase, perusal, rendering, rendition, review, scholarship, scrutiny, study, version

ready *adjective.* **1** accessible, apt, arranged, available, bagged, completed, covered, expectant, fit, handy, near, organized, primed, qualified, ripe, set, waiting, wired **2** agreeable, apt, ardent, bagged, disposed, eager, enthusiastic, fain, game, glad, inclined, keen, minded, predisposed, prompt, prone, wired, zealous **3** active, acute, adept, alert, apt, bright, deft, dynamic, expert, handy, keen, live, proficient, prompt, rapid, resourceful, sharp, skilled

ready *verb.* arrange, brace, brief, fit, fix, fortify, get, gird, make, make up, order, organize, post, prep, provide, set, strengthen, warm up

real *adjective.* absolute, actual, authentic, bodily, certain, concrete, intrinsic, perceptible, positive, sensible, sincere, solid, sound, substantial, substantive, tangible, true, valid

realistic *adjective.* astute, down-to-earth, earthy, hard, hard-boiled, practical, pragmatic, prudent, rational, real, reasonable, sane, sensible, shrewd, sober, sound, unromantic, utilitarian

reality *noun.* absoluteness, actuality, being, certainty, concrete, corporeality, deed, entity, facts, matter, presence, realism, realness, sensibility, substance, substantive, validity, verity

realize *verb.* **1** apprehend, comprehend, dig, envision, fancy, feature, get, grasp, image, imagine, know, pick up, recognize, think, tumble, understand, vision, visualize **2** actualize, bring about, bring off, carry out, carry through, complete, consummate, do, effect, effectuate, fulfill, make concrete, make good, materialize, perfect, perform, reify **3** accomplish, achieve, acquire, attain, clear, gain, get, go for, make, net, obtain, produce, rack up, reach, receive, score, sell for, win

really *adjective.* absolutely, actually, admittedly, amen, assuredly, authentically, categorically, certainly, easily, honestly, indeed, legitimately, literally, surely, truly, undoubtedly, unmistakably, you

realm *noun.* branch, country, department, domain, dominion, empire, expanse, ground, land, orbit, province, range, region, scope, sphere, territory, turf, zone

rear *adjective.* aft, after, astern, back, backward, behind, dorsal, following, hind, hindmost, last, posterior, postern, rearward, retral, reverse, stern, tail

rear *noun.* back, backside, behind, bottom, butt, buttocks, end, fanny, heel, hind, hindquarters, posterior, rear guard, reverse, rump, seat, stern, tail

rear *verb.* hoist, hold up, jump, leap, loom, pick up, raise, rise, set upright, soar, spring up, support, take up, tower, turn up, uphold, uplift, upraise

reason *noun.* **1** apprehension, brain, deduction, discernment, intellect, judgment, limits, logic, moderation, propriety, rationalism, rationalization, reasoning, sense, soundness, speculation, wisdom, wit **2** aim, antecedent, argument, cause, consideration, design, determinant, end, goal, grounds, impetus, incentive, inducement, motive, occasion, root, spring, target **3** account, apologia, apology, argument, case, cover, defense, excuse, exposition, ground, justification, proof, rationale, rationalization, stall, vindication, wherefore, why **4** conclude, contemplate, decide, deduce, deliberate, examine, gather, generalize, infer, rationalize, reflect, resolve, solve, speculate, study, suppose, think, work out **5** bring around, contend, debate, demonstrate, discourse, discuss, dispute, dissuade, establish, justify, move, persuade, prevail upon, prove, remonstrate, talk into, trace, urge

reasonable *adjective.* **1** acceptable, analytical, cheap, circumspect, conservative, discreet, feasible, fit, humane, inexpensive, modest, objective, proper, rational, sensible, sound, temperate, valid **2** cerebral, cognitive, conscious, consequent, credible, judicious, justifiable, perceiving, plausible, practical, rational, reasoned, reasoning, sane, sensible, sound, tolerant, wise

reasoning *noun.* acumen, analysis, argument, case, corollary, deduction, exposition, hypothesis, induction, inference, interpretation, logistics, premise, proof, proposition, reason, thinking, thought

rebel *noun.* agitator, anarchist, antagonist, dissenter, experimenter, guerrilla, independent, individualist, insurgent, mutineer, nihilist, nonconformist, opponent, resistance, revolutionary, secessionist, traitor, underground

rebel *verb.* boycott, censure, combat, criticize, defy, denounce, dissent, fight, mutiny, oppose, overthrow, remonstrate, resist, revolt, riot, secede, strike, upset

recall *verb.* **1** arouse, awaken, cite, elicit, evoke, extract, flash, mind, recollect, reestablish, remind, renew, retain, retrospect, revive, rouse, stir, summon **2** abjure, call back, call in, cancel, discharge, dismiss, disqualify, forswear, lift, nullify, palinode, repeal, rescind, reverse, suspend, take back, unsay, withdraw

receipts *noun.* cash flow, comings in, earnings, gain, gate, get, handle, income, melon, net, proceeds, profit, return, revenue, royalty, take, taking, velvet

receive *verb.* **1** admit, appropriate, arrogate, assume, cop, derive, draw, earn, grab, hear, inherit, pocket, pull, reap, redeem, secure, snag, take **2** accept, accommodate, admit, entertain, greet, host, induct, initiate, install, introduce, invite, let in, let through, meet, permit, shake hands, show in, welcome

recent *adjective.* contempo, contemporary, fresh, just out, late, latter, latter-day, modern, modernistic, neoteric, new, newborn, novel, present-day, the latest, today, up-to-date, young

reception *noun.* acknowledgment, acquisition, admission, disposition, encounter, gathering, greeting, induction, introduction, meeting, reaction, receipt, receiving, recognition, response, salutation, treatment, welcome

recession *noun.* bad times, bankruptcy, big trouble, bust, collapse, decline, deflation, depression, downturn, hard times, inflation, rainy days, return, shakeout, slide, slump, stagnation, unemployment

reciprocal *adjective.* alternate, changeable, companion, complementary, convertible, coordinate, corresponding, dependent, double, duplicate, equivalent, fellow, interchangeable, interdependent, matching, mutual, reciprocative, twin

recital *noun.* account, concert, description, enumeration, fable, musicale, narrative, portrayal, presentation, reading, recapitulation, recitation, relation, rendering, report, statement, story, telling

reckless *adjective.* brash, carefree, careless, daring, desperate, foolhardy, hasty, hopeless, inattentive, incautious, indiscreet, mindless, negligent, precipitate, rash, thoughtless, venturesome, wild

reckon *verb.* **1** account, approximate, compute, consider, count, evaluate, figure, foot, judge, number, put, rate, regard, run down, square, sum, tally, view **2** assume, bargain for, believe, conjecture, depend on, expect, fancy, gather, guess, imagine, plan on, rely on, surmise, suspect, take, think, trust in, understand

recognition *noun.* **1** acknowledgment, allowance, appreciation, awareness, cognizance, concession, detection, discovery, notice, perceiving, perception, realization, recalling, recollection, recurrence, remembrance, respect, salute **2** acceptance, acknowledgment, approval, attention, credit, esteem, gratitude, greeting, honor, notice, plum, PR, puff, rave, regard, renown, salute, strokes

recognize *verb.* **1** admit, diagnose, finger, know, lamp, nail, notice, observe, peg, perceive, pinpoint, place, recollect, remark, remember, see, spot, tag **2** admit, agree, appreciate, approve, assent, comprehend, concede, confess, grant, greet, make, own, perceive, realize, respect, salute, see, understand

recommend *verb.* acclaim, advocate, applaud, approve, celebrate, endorse, eulogize, favor, hold up, justify, plug, prescribe, propose, second, stand by, suggest, uphold, urge

recommendation *noun.* advocacy, charge, commendation, direction, endorsement, esteem, judgment, order, pass, plug, praise, proposal, proposition, steer, suggestion, testimonial, tip, tribute

record *noun.* **1** annals, chronicle, document, documentation, entry, file, history, jacket, journal, manuscript, memoir, memorandum, minutes, remembrance, story, trace, transcript, transcription **2** album, canned music, compact disk, cut, cylinder, disc, disk, LP, manhole cover, platter, pressing, recording, release, side, single, take, transcription, wax

record *verb.* can, catalog, chronicle, copy, document, enroll, enter, file, insert, list, mark, post, preserve, report, tabulate, transcribe, video, wax

recover *verb.* **1** balance, bring back, catch up, compensate, make good, offset, recapture, reclaim, recruit, redeem, rediscover, regain, repair, rescue, restore, resume, retrieve, salvage **2** better, gain, get over, grow, heal, increase, mend, overcome, pick up, rally, reach, realize, rebound, refresh, renew, restore, revive, snap back

recreation *noun.* avocation, ball, distraction, ease, exercise, frolic, fun, game, grins, hobby, holiday, laughs, pastime, refreshment, relief, repose, sport, vacation

recruit *noun.* apprentice, boot, chicken, draftee, fledgling, freshman, helper, initiate, jeep, john, new man, newcomer, novice, novitiate, sailor, soldier, tenderfoot, volunteer

recruit *verb.* augment, better, build up, deliver, impress, levy, mobilize, obtain, recover, refresh, reinforce, renew, repair, restore, retrieve, round up, strengthen, supply

red *noun.* bittersweet, bloodshot, blush, brick, burgundy, carmine, cerise, cherry, crimson, flaming, inflamed, maroon, rose, rosy, rust, titian, vermeil, wine

reduce *verb.* **1** bankrupt, break, chop, clip, contract, cut back, diet, dwindle, impair, lessen, lower, moderate, nutshell, pare, recede, slim, taper, trim **2** bear down, break, bring, conquer, cripple, crush, disable, drive, enfeeble, force, master, overcome, overpower, ruin, subdue, subjugate, undermine, weaken

refer *verb.* **1** ascribe, assign, associate, attribute, charge, excerpt, exemplify, extract, glance, hint, indicate, insert, instance, introduce, lay, name, notice, quote **2** answer, apply, belong, comprise, connect, cover, deal with, encompass, have reference, hold, include, incorporate, involve, pertain, point, regard, relate, touch

reference *noun.* allusion, associating, attributing, citation, commercial, connecting, hint, implication, indicating, innuendo, mention, mentioning, plug, quotation, relating, resource, source, stating

reflect *verb.* **1** cast, catch, copy, echo, emulate, flash, follow, imitate, match, mirror, rebound, repeat, reply, reproduce, return, reverse, revert, shine **2** cerebrate, chew, cogitate, consider, contemplate, deliberate, head trip, meditate, mull over, muse, ponder, reason, speculate, stew, study, think, weigh, wonder

reflection *noun.* absorption, brainwork, cogitation, consideration, contemplation, deliberation, idea, imagination, impression, meditation, musing, observation, opinion, pondering, speculation, study, thought, view

reform *verb.* better, convert, correct, cure, rearrange, rebuild, reclaim, redeem, refashion, remake, remedy, renew, reorganize, repair, resolve, restore, revise, transform

refrain *verb.* abstain, arrest, avoid, cease, check, curb, eschew, forgo, halt, inhibit, interrupt, keep, pass, quit, resist, restrain, stop, withhold

refuge *noun.* ambush, anchorage, cover, den, expedient, haven, hole, home, immunity, makeshift, opening, outlet, preserve, protection, resource, sanctuary, security, stronghold

refugee *noun.* alien, boat person, derelict, DP, emigrant, evacuee, exile, foreigner, foundling, fugitive, homeless person, maroon, outcast, outlaw, pariah, prodigal, renegade, runaway

refund *noun.* acquittance, allowance, compensation, consolation, discharge, discount, give up, kickback, payment, rebate, reimbursement, remuneration, repayment, restitution, retribution, return, satisfaction, settlement

refund *verb.* adjust, balance, compensate, give back, indemnify, make good, make repayment, recompense, recoup, redeem, redress, reimburse, relinquish, remunerate, repay, restore, reward, settle

refusal *noun.* disapproval, disclaimer, disfavor, dissent, forbidding, no, noncompliance, pass, prohibition, proscription, rebuff, regrets, rejection, renunciation, repudiation, repulsion, withholding, writ

refuse *noun.* debris, dregs, dross, dump, dust, junk, leavings, muck, offal, remains, residue, rubbish, scraps, sediment, slop, sweepings, trash, waste

refuse *verb.* corn, decline, disapprove, dissent, dodge, evade, ignore, protest, rebuff, regret, reject, repel, reprobate, repudiate, say no, shun, withdraw, withhold

regard *noun.* **1** attention, carefulness, cognizance, concern, curiosity, gaze, glance, heed, interest, mark, mind, notice, observance, observation, remark, scrutiny, stare, view **2** account, affection, appreciation, attachment, cherishing, concern, consideration, curiosity, deference, devotion, fondness, homage, interest, liking, love, repute, respect, sympathy **3** beam, behold, contemplate, dig, gaze, heed, lamp, mark, notice, observe, overlook, pipe, rap, respect, see, spy, view, watch **4** account, admire, assay, assess, consider, deem, esteem, judge, rate, reckon, respect, revere, see, suppose, think, treat, value, view

regardless *adjective.* careless, crude, delinquent, derelict, disregarding, inadvertent, inattentive, insensitive, listless, mindless, negligent, rash, reckless, slack, unconcerned, unheeding, uninterested, unmindful

region *noun.* clearing, division, environs, expanse, precinct, province, quarter, range, scope, section, sector, sphere, territory, tract, turf, walk, ward, zone

register *noun.* annals, archives, book, catalog, catalogue, chronicle, diary, entry, file, ledger, list, log, memorandum, registry, roll, roster, schedule, scroll

register *verb.* catalogue, check in, chronicle, enlist, enroll, enter, file, inscribe, join, list, note, record, schedule, set down, sign up, subscribe, take down, weigh in

regret *noun.* affliction, anguish, apologies, apology, bitterness, care, concern, conscience, disappointment, dissatisfaction, grief, heartbreak, lamentation, nostalgia, remorse, repentance, ruefulness, uneasiness

regret *verb.* apologize, bemoan, bewail, cry over, deplore, deprecate, disapprove, feel sorry, feel uneasy, have compunctions, have qualms, lament, miss, moan, mourn, repent, rue, weep

regular *adjective.* **1** common, correct, daily, everyday, formal, natural, normal, official, orthodox, prevailing, prevalent, proper, routine, sanctioned, standard, traditional, typical, usual **2** arranged, exact, fixed, formal, invariable, level, measured, mechanical, ordered, rational, recurrent, regulated, serial, set, smooth, stated, steady, successive

regulation *noun.* **1** adjustment, arrangement, classification, codification, coordination, direction, governing, government, management, moderation, modulation, organizing, reconciliation, reorganization, settlement, supervision, systematization, tuning **2** bible, book, canon, code, commandment, decree, dictate, direction, Hoyle, law, no-no, numbers, order, ordinance, precept, principle, procedure, statute

reign *verb.* administer, boss, command, dominate, domineer, govern, helm, hold sway, influence, manage, obtain, occupy, predominate, preponderate, rule, run things, sit, superabound

reinforce *verb.* augment, bolster, boost, build up, carry, emphasize, enlarge, fortify, harden, multiply, pick up, pillar, prop, stress, supplement, support, sustain, underline

reject *verb.* adios, decline, deny, disbelieve, disdain, dismiss, eliminate, exclude, kill, rebuff, refuse, repel, reprobate, repudiate, scorn, scout, second, slough

rejection *noun.* bounce, cold shoulder, cut, denial, ding, dismissal, elimination, exclusion, gate, go-by, kick, no dice, no way, pass, rebuff, renunciation, repudiation, veto

relate *verb.* **1** chronicle, depict, describe, detail, disclose, express, impart, picture, recite, recount, report, retell, reveal, run down, sling, spill, state, tell **2** affect, apply, ascribe, assign, associate, combine, compare, concern, connect, coordinate, correlate, couple, join, orient, refer, touch, unite, yoke

related *adjective.* accompanying, affiliated, alike, allied, cognate, complementary, correspondent, dependent, enmeshed, incident, interconnected, interwoven, joint, linked, mutual, parallel, pertinent, relevant

relationship *noun.* accord, alliance, analogy, association, conjunction, dependence, homogeneity, interrelation, liaison, parallel, pertinence, proportion, rapport, ratio, relativity, relevance, similarity, tie

relative *adjective.* about, allied, analogous, approximate, associated, comparative, concerning, contingent, corresponding, dependent, near, parallel, proportionate, reciprocal, referring, related, reliant, respective

relax *verb.* **1** abate, diminish, ease, ease off, ebb, lax, loose, loosen, lower, mitigate, moderate, modify, reduce, relieve, slack, slacken, slow, weaken **2** breathe easy, calm, collect oneself, compose oneself, cool off, ease off, hang loose, knock off, laze, lie down, loosen up, repose, rest, settle back, sit back, soften, stop work, unwind

relaxation *noun.* alleviation, amusement, assuagement, diversion, enjoyment, fun, leisure, loosening, mitigation, pleasure, quiescence, reclining, recovering, recreation, refreshment, relief, repose, rest

release *noun.* **1** absolution, charge, commute, deliverance, discharge, dispensation, emancipation, exoneration, floater, freedom, liberation, liberty, lifeboat, manumission, relief, spring, turnout, walkout **2** announcement, dope, flash, handout, issue, leak, news, notice, offering, poop, proclamation, propaganda, publicity, scoop, skinny, song, story, the goods

release *verb.* clear, commute, deliver, discharge, disengage, drop, excuse, extricate, issue, leak, liberate, loose, spring, turn out, undo, untie, vent, yield

relevant *adjective.* allowable, applicable, apt, becoming, cognate, compatible, concerning, congruent, correspondent, fit, fitting, important, pat, pertinent, proper, related, relative, significant

reliable *adjective.* candid, careful, certain, decent, determined, good, positive, regular, respectable, responsible, sincere, solid, sound, steady, strong, sure, true, unfailing

relief *noun.* aid, alleviation, assistance, balm, break, breather, comforting, contentment, deliverance, ease, lift, palliative, refreshment, release, rest, softening, solace, succor

relieve *verb.* **1** break, calm, comfort, divert, dull, ease, interrupt, moderate, mollify, qualify, relax, salve, soften, solace, soothe, subdue, temper, vary **2** absolve, deliver, discharge, disembarrass, disencumber, dismiss, dispense, excuse, exempt, free, let off, privilege, pull, release, spare, throw out, unburden, yank

religion *noun.* ceremonial, church, creed, denomination, devotion, myth, mythology, observance, orthodoxy, persuasion, pietism, prayer, preference, religiosity, sacrifice, standards, theology, veneration

religious *adjective.* believing, churchgoing, churchly, devotional, devout, doctrinal, ecclesiastical, goody, honest, moral, prayerful, reverent, sacred, sectarian, spiritual, supernatural, theistic, theological

relish *noun.* appetite, bias, delectation, diversion, enjoying, fancy, flair, flavor, fondness, liking, love, palate, penchant, prejudice, smack, tang, taste, zest

reluctant *adjective.* afraid, calculating, cautious, circumspect, discouraged, hesitant, hesitating, involuntary, loath, opposed, recalcitrant, shy, slack, squeamish, tardy, uncertain, unwilling, wary

rely *verb.* await, bank, believe in, bet, build, calculate, commit, confide, count, depend, entrust, expect, gamble on, hope, lean, look, reckon, trust

remain *verb.* bide, bivouac, bunk, delay, dwell, endure, freeze, halt, inhabit, last, linger, lodge, nest, rest, roost, survive, tarry, visit

remainder *noun.* butt, dregs, excess, hangover, heel, leavings, obverse, refuse, relic, remains, remnant, rest, ruins, surplus, trace, vestige, wreck, wreckage

remark *noun.* acknowledgment, attention, cognizance, conclusion, consideration, declaration, elucidation, illustration, mention, notice, observance, observation, recognition, reflection, regard, saying, statement, utterance

remark *verb.* behold, crack, declare, heed, mark, mention, note, notice, observe, perceive, reflect, regard, say, see, speak, spot, state, utter

remarkable *adjective.* arresting, distinguished, exceptional, fat, important, impressive, noticeable, odd, peculiar, significant, solid, striking, surprising, ten, unique, unusual, wicked, wonderful

remedy *noun.* antidote, assistance, biologic, drug, fix, improvement, medicine, pharmaceutical, pill, quick fix, redress, relief, restorative, solution, support, therapy, treatment

remedy *verb.* aid, change, correct, doctor, ease, heal, launder, pick up, redress, reform, renew, repair, restore, revise, right, soothe, square, upgrade

remember *verb.* cite, commemorate, elicit, extract, flash, get, learn, master, memorize, mind, recognize, recollect, relive, remind, retain, retrospect, revive, treasure

remind *verb.* advise, caution, cite, emphasize, hint, imply, intimate, mention, prod, prompt, recollect, remember, retain, retrospect, revive, stress, suggest, warn

reminder *noun.* admonition, expression, gesture, hint, indication, memento, memo, memorandum, note, notice, relic, remembrance, sign, souvenir, suggestion, token, trinket, trophy

remote *adjective.* **1** alien, beyond, devious, distant, far, foreign, frontier, inaccessible, isolated, lonesome, obscure, outlandish, outlying, private, removed, secluded, secret, unsettled **2** abstracted, alien, alone, apart, detached, exclusive, extraneous, farfetched, foreign, immaterial, inappropriate, obscure, outside, pointless, removed, strange, unconnected, unrelated **3** abstracted, aloof, casual, cold, cool, disinterested, distant, indifferent, introspective, introverted, removed, reserved, stuck up, uncommunicative, unconcerned, uninterested, uninvolved, withdrawn

remove *verb.* **1** abolish, depose, discharge, dislodge, dismiss, displace, disturb, eject, eliminate, erase, expel, expunge, extract, oust, ship, transfer, transport, unload **2** do in, drag, drag down, eliminate, eradicate, erase, exclude, execute, expunge, exterminate, knock off, murder, obliterate, off, purge, scratch, sterilize, waste

render *verb.* **1** deliver, distribute, exchange, furnish, give, impart, minister, pay, provide, repay, restore, show, submit, supply, swap, tender, turn over, yield **2** act, administer, depict, display, do, execute, exhibit, give, govern, image, interpret, manifest, perform, picture, play, portray, present, represent

rent *noun.* break, cleavage, crack, discord, dissension, division, faction, flaw, fracture, gash, hole, rift, rip, rupture, slash, slit, split, tear

repair *verb.* **1** correct, doctor, heal, overhaul, patch, rebuild, recover, redress, reform, refresh, remedy, renew, restore, retrieve, revive, right, settle, square **2** apply, fare, go, journey, move, pass, proceed, process, recur, refer, remove, resort, retire, run, travel, turn, wend, withdraw

repay *verb.* accord, award, balance, compensate, indemnify, make restitution, offset, pay back, recompense, refund, reimburse, remunerate, requite, restore, return, reward, settle up, square

repeal *verb.* abolish, abrogate, back out, back water, blow, cancel, invalidate, kill, lift, nullify, opt out, recall, rescind, reverse, scrub, vacate, void, withdraw

repeat *verb.* duplicate, echo, imitate, play back, quote, reappear, recapitulate, recur, redo, reform, rehash, reissue, relate, remake, renew, reproduce, retell, revolve

repel *verb.* buck, confront, cool, decline, dismiss, disown, dispute, duel, fight, kick, knock down, parry, rebuff, rebut, refuse, resist, traverse, withstand

repetition *noun.* alliteration, copy, echo, paraphrase, practice, reappearance, recapitulation, recital, recurrence, redundancy, rehearsal, relation, repeat, replication, report, reproduction, restatement, rhythm

replace *verb.* alter, change, displace, follow, oust, patch, recover, redeem, redress, reestablish, refund, reimburse, restore, retrieve, stand in, substitute, succeed, supply

reply *noun.* acknowledgment, antiphon, comeback, cooler, counter, echo, feedback, lip, reaction, rejoinder, respond, response, retaliation, retort, return, riposte, vibes, wisecrack

reply *verb.* acknowledge, come back, come in, counter, crack, echo, feedback, react, reciprocate, rejoin, respond, retaliate, retort, return, riposte, shoot back, top, write back

report *noun.* **1** brief, cable, chronicle, declaration, description, dispatch, history, narrative, paper, piece, recital, release, statement, story, summary, tidings, version, wire **2** advice, buzz, chatter, conversation, dirt, grapevine, hash, hearsay, intelligence, murmur, rumble, rumor, scandal, speech, talk, tattle, tidings, word

report *verb.* cable, circulate, cover, detail, document, impart, inform, list, mention, proclaim, publish, radio, recount, relay, spread, telephone, tell, wire

reporter *noun.* anchorman, announcer, columnist, correspondent, editor, goat, hack, ink slinger, interviewer, journalist, news hen, newspaperman, pen pusher, pencil driver, scribe, scrivener, star, writer

represent *verb.* **1** be, body, copy, embody, epitomize, equate, exhibit, express, imitate, perform, produce, reproduce, serve, show, stage, steward, substitute, typify **2** design, display, evoke, exhibit, express, hint, illustrate, interpret, mirror, outline, portray, realize, relate, render, reproduce, run down, show, suggest

representative *adjective.* adumbrative, archetypal, classic, classical, depictive, emblematic, evocative, exemplary, ideal, illustrative, model, presentational, prototypal, prototypical, rep, symbolic, symbolical, typical

representative *noun.* attorney, commissioner, congressman, congresswoman, councilman, councilwoman, counselor, delegate, deputy, lawyer, legislator, member, messenger, proxy, rep, salesman, senator, spokesman

reproduce *verb.* **1** echo, follow, imitate, manifold, match, mirror, parallel, photograph, portray, print, recount, redo, reflect, relive, remake, repeat, represent, stereotype **2** bear, beget, breed, engender, father, fecundate, generate, hatch, impregnate, multiply, procreate, produce young, proliferate, propagate, repopulate, sire, spawn

reputable *adjective.* acclaimed, constant, distinguished, eminent, esteemed, famed, favored, good, honest, honored, notable, popular, renowned, respectable, righteous, sincere, truthful, upright

reputation *noun.* acceptability, account, distinction, eminence, favor, influence, mark, name, notoriety, prestige, prominence, regard, reliability, renown, rep, repute, respectability, stature

request *noun.* appeal, application, asking, begging, call, commercial, demand, desire, entreaty, inquiry, invitation, offer, petition, prayer, recourse, requisition, suit, supplication

request *verb.* appeal, beg, beseech, bespeak, bite, burn, demand, desire, hit, hustle, inquire, knock, nick, pray, promote, requisition, solicit, touch

require *verb.* beg, beseech, bid, challenge, claim, command, compel, crave, demand, exact, expect, instruct, oblige, postulate, request, requisition, solicit, take

required *adjective.* appropriate, demanded, deserved, due, enforced, essential, imperative, imperious, mandatory, needed, prescribed, recommended, right, rightful, set, suitable, unavoidable, vital

requirement *noun.* claim, concern, demand, element, extremity, fundamental, must, need, obligation, obsession, preliminary, preoccupation, prescription, provision, proviso, qualification, stipulation, want

rescue *noun.* accomplishment, deed, deliverance, delivery, emancipation, exploit, feet, heroics, liberation, ransom, recovering, recovery, redemption, release, relief, salvage, salvation, saving

rescue *verb.* buy, conserve, deliver, extricate, free, keep, liberate, preserve, protect, ransom, recapture, recover, redeem, regain, release, retrieve, safeguard, spring

resemblance *noun.* affinity, analogy, carbon, closeness, coincidence, comparison, correspondence, counterpart, double, facsimile, image, kinship, likeness, parallel, sameness, semblance, simile, similitude

resemble *verb.* appear like, approximate, coincide, double, duplicate, echo, favor, feature, follow, match, mirror, parallel, pass for, relate, seem like, simulate, sound like, take after

resentment *noun.* bitterness, cynicism, displeasure, exacerbation, exasperation, fog, grudge, hate, huff, indignation, irritation, offense, outrage, perturbation, rage, rise, spite, wrath

reservation *noun.* catch, circumscription, demur, doubt, fine print, hesitancy, joker, kicker, provision, proviso, qualification, restriction, scruple, skepticism, stipulation, string, strings, terms

reserve *noun.* **1** assets, backlog, cache, capital, drop, fund, hoard, insurance, inventory, nest egg, plant, provisions, reservoir, resources, savings, stock, store, wealth **2** aloofness, calmness, caution, coldness, constraint, coyness, diffidence, formality, inhibition, modesty, quietness, reluctance, repression, reservation, restraint, secretiveness, silence, suppression

reserve *verb.* bespeak, contract, defer, delay, ditch, duck, have, hold, husband, keep, maintain, possess, preserve, save, schedule, secure, squirrel, withhold

reserved *adjective.* **1** aloof, cold, collected, conventional, demure, distant, formal, gentle, icy, modest, noncommittal, placid, prim, retiring, sedate, shy, solitary, withdrawn **2** appropriated, arrogated, booked, claimed, engaged, kept, laid away, limited, pre-empted, private, qualified, restricted, retained, roped off, set apart, set aside, spoken for, taken

reservoir *noun.* backlog, basin, cistern, fund, holder, lake, pond, pool, receptacle, repository, reserve, source, spring, stock, storage, store, supply, tank

residence *noun.* abode, box, cave, digs, domicile, dwelling, headquarters, hole, home, house, household, inhabitation, lodging, mansion, palace, roost, settlement, villa

resident *noun.* citizen, cliff dweller, denizen, dweller, habitant, householder, indweller, inmate, liver, local, lodger, native, occupant, resider, squatter, suburbanite, tenant, townie

residue *noun.* balance, debris, dregs, excess, extra, heel, junk, leavings, parings, remainder, remains, remnant, residual, rest, scraps, shavings, surplus, trash

resignation *noun.* acceptance, acquiescence, compliance, conformity, deference, fortitude, humbleness, humility, longanimity, meekness, modesty, nonresistance, passivity, patience, resignedness, submission, submissiveness, sufferance

resigned *adjective.* accommodated, agreeable, amenable, calm, genial, gentle, obedient, patient, quiescent, reconciled, relinquishing, renouncing, satisfied, subdued, subservient, tame, tolerant, willing

resist *verb.* assail, battle, buck, combat, confront, curb, defy, die hard, endure, maintain, persist, prevent, remain, repel, stay, suffer, traverse, weather

resistance *noun.* battle, combat, contention, cover, detention, fight, fighting, friction, halting, impediment, intransigence, protecting, protection, rebuff, refusal, safeguard, screen, watch

resolution *noun.* **1** aim, constancy, decision, declaration, determination, energy, firmness, fortitude, intent, intention, judgment, mettle, pluck, settlement, spirit, stubbornness, tenacity, will **2** analysis, conclusion, decision, declaration, determination, elucidation, judgment, motion, outcome, presentation, proposal, proposition, recitation, resolve, settlement, solution, solving, upshot

resolve *noun.* boldness, conclusion, courage, design, determination, earnestness, firmness, fixed purpose, intention, objective, project, purpose, purposefulness, resoluteness, resolution, steadfastness, undertaking, will

resolve *verb.* agree, break, chill, choose, conclude, crack, decide, decree, design, dissect, dissolve, figure, lick, propose, rule, settle, will, work

resort *noun.* **1** bath, camp, den, haunt, haven, hideaway, hideout, hotel, inn, lodge, motel, nest, park, refuge, rendezvous, retreat, spot, spring **2** chance, course, device, expediency, expedient, hope, makeshift, opportunity, possibility, recourse, reference, refuge, relief, resource, shift, stopgap, substitute, surrogate

resort *verb*. address, affect, apply, devote, direct, employ, exercise, frequent, go, haunt, recur, repair, run, try, turn, use, utilize, visit

resource *noun*. appliance, course, device, expedient, fortune, makeshift, method, mode, property, refuge, riches, source, string, substance, system, talent, wealth, worth

resources *noun*. assets, backing, basics, belongings, budget, funds, holdings, income, kitty, means, nut, property, reserves, revenue, riches, stuff, supplies, wealth

respect *noun*. account, appreciation, awe, consideration, courtesy, deference, dignity, esteem, estimation, favor, homage, recognition, regard, repute, testimonial, tribute, veneration, worship

respect *verb*. adore, appreciate, attend, awe, esteem, follow, heed, note, notice, obey, observe, of, recognize, regard, revere, spare, uphold, value

respectable *adjective*. admirable, appropriate, becoming, befitting, comely, decent, dignified, done, honest, mediocre, moderate, modest, presentable, proper, reputable, reputed, satisfactory, venerable

respond *verb*. acknowledge, answer, answer back, behave, come back, come in, counter, feedback, feel for, have heart, have vibes, react, reciprocate, rejoin, reply, retort, return, talk back

response *noun*. acknowledgment, antiphon, comeback, cooler, counter, echo, feedback, hit, lip, reaction, rejoinder, reply, respond, retort, return, reverberation, riposte, vibes

responsibility *noun*. **1** blame, burden, can, charge, constraint, contract, engagement, fault, guilt, importance, incubus, obligation, onus, pledge, power, rap, restraint, trust **2** ability, capableness, capacity, competency, conscientiousness, dependableness, efficiency, firmness, honesty, loyalty, maturity, rationality, reliability, sensibleness, stability, steadfastness, trustiness, uprightness

responsible *adjective*. **1** amenable, answerable, bound, chargeable, compelled, constrained, contracted, executive, exposed, guilty, hampered, held, important, liable, obligated, open, subject, tied **2** able, adult, capable, competent, efficient, faithful, firm, loyal, mature, qualified, rational, reliable, sensible, sound, stable, steady, tried, upright

rest *noun*. **1** break, breather, calm, cessation, cutoff, ease, halt, idleness, interlude, intermission, peace, recreation, refreshment, repose, siesta, silence, stay, stillness **2** basis, bed, bottom, footing, foundation, ground, groundwork, holder, pedestal, pillar, prop, seat, seating, shelf, stand, stay, support, trestle **3** breathe, dream, idle, laze, lean, lie still, loaf, lounge, nap, nod, refresh oneself, relax, repose, slack, sleep, slumber, spell, stretch out **4** base, be contingent, be dependent, be founded, be supported, be upheld, bottom, count, establish, found, ground, hang, hinge, lie, rely, reside, stay, turn

restaurant *noun*. bar, cafe, cafeteria, canteen, chuck wagon, diner, drive-in, eating house, grill, hash house, heaven, hideaway, inn, joint, lunchroom, night club, outlet, saloon

restless *adjective*. active, agitated, anxious, bustling, changeable, disturbed, edgy, intermittent, nervous, roving, sleepless, troubled, turbulent, uneasy, unquiet, unruly, unsettled, worried

restore *verb*. build up, cure, heal, improve, modernize, rebuild, recover, redeem, refresh, renew, repair, replace, rescue, return, revitalize, revive, strengthen, update

restrain *verb*. arrest, confine, cork, curb, detain, gag, govern, guide, harness, keep, kill, muzzle, prescribe, prevent, repress, stay, subdue, suppress

restrained *adjective*. aseptic, chilled, conservative, discreet, hip, mild, moderate, muted, reasonable, retiring, shrinking, soft, square, steady, subdued, tasteful, temperate, withdrawn

restraint *noun*. **1** caution, coercion, command, compulsion, confines, constraint, coolness, economy, grip, hold, inhibition, limitation, moderation, prevention, repression, reserve, silence, withholding **2** bar, bondage, captivity, command, constraint, cramp, curb, deprivation, detention, deterrence, obstacle, prohibition, reduction, rope, stoppage, string, taboo, violence

restrict *verb.* bind, bound, contain, contract, cramp, curb, define, encircle, moderate, narrow, qualify, reduce, regulate, shorten, shrink, surround, temper, tie

restriction *noun.* brake, confinement, constraint, contraction, cramp, curb, custody, demarcation, inhibition, lock, qualification, regulation, reservation, restraint, rule, stint, stipulation, string

result *noun.* aftermath, arrangement, conclusion, consummation, corollary, decision, denouement, determination, emanation, fruition, issue, outcome, outgrowth, proceeds, production, reaction, sequel, sequence

result *verb.* appear, arise, derive, effect, ensue, flow, follow, grow, happen, issue, occur, proceed, produce, rise, spring, stem, turn out, wind up

resume *noun.* abstract, bio, biography, curriculum vitae, CV, digest, epitome, précis, recapitulation, review, rundown, sum, summary, summation, summing-up, synopsis, vita, work history

resume *verb.* come back, continue, go on, keep on, occupy again, pick up, proceed, reassume, recapitulate, recommence, recoup, regain, reopen, repossess, retake, return to, take back, take up

retain *verb.* absorb, clutch, detain, grasp, have, husband, keep, maintain, memorize, own, preserve, recognize, recollect, remember, reserve, retrospect, save, withhold

retarded *adjective.* backward, defective, dim, dull, dumbbell, dummy, exceptional, imbecile, opaque, pinhead, sappy, simple, simple-minded, slow, stupid, subnormal, touched, weak

retire *verb.* depart, ebb, exit, get away, part, recede, relinquish, remove, repeal, rescind, resign, retreat, secede, separate, surrender, take off, withdraw, yield

retiring *adjective.* backward, bashful, coy, demure, diffident, humble, meek, modest, quiet, reserved, restrained, shrinking, timid, timorous, unaffable, undemonstrative, withdrawing, withdrawn

retreat *noun.* asylum, convent, cover, defense, den, haunt, haven, hideaway, hole, port, privacy, refuge, retirement, sanctuary, seclusion, security, shelter, solitude

retreat *verb.* abandon, depart, disengage, ebb, escape, evade, fold, hide, leave, recede, recoil, resign, retrograde, reverse, run, shrink, vacate, withdraw

return *noun.* **1** acknowledgment, entrance, entry, homecoming, occurrence, reaction, reappearance, rebound, recoil, recompense, recovery, recurrence, rejoinder, replacement, restitution, restoration, restoring, retreat **2** advantage, avail, benefit, compensation, gain, gate, income, interest, proceeds, recompense, reimbursement, reparation, repayment, retaliation, revenue, take, takings, yield **3** bounce back, come back, go again, react, reappear, rebound, recoil, reconsider, recur, repair, repeat, retire, retrace steps, retreat, revert, revolve, rotate, turn **4** bestow, convey, give, make restitution, react, reciprocate, recompense, refund, reimburse, render, repay, replace, requite, restore, retaliate, send, take back, transmit **5** announce, arrive at, bring in, come back, come in, come to, communicate, declare, deliver, pass, rejoin, render, reply, report, respond, retort, state, submit

reveal *verb.* acknowledge, admit, affirm, broadcast, concede, confess, declare, disclose, impart, inform, leak, proclaim, publish, rat, report, stool, talk, tell

revelation *noun.* beat, break, broadcasting, clue, cue, disclosure, discovery, display, divination, exhibition, expose, exposure, leak, proclamation, showing, sign, tip, vision

revenge *noun.* attack, avenging, counterinsurgency, counterplay, fight, getting even, ill will, malevolence, rancor, repayment, reprisal, retribution, return, ruthlessness, satisfaction, sortie, vengeance, vindictiveness

revenge *verb.* avenge, defend, fight back, fix, get, justify, match, pay off, punish, reciprocate, redress, repay, requite, retort, return, score, square, vindicate

revenue *noun.* dividend, earnings, gate, handle, interest, net, pay, proceeds, receipt, resources, salary, strength, take, taking, velvet, wages, wealth, yield

reverse *noun.* **1** about-face, antithesis, back, contradiction, contradictory, contrary, converse, counter, inverse, overturning, rear, regression, reversal, reversion, turn, turn around, turning, underside **2** adversity, affliction, bath, blow, catastrophe, check, conquering, defeat, disappointment, failure, hardship, misadventure, misfortune, mishap, reversal, setback, trial, turnabout **3** back, capsize, double back, exchange, flip flop, go backwards, interchange, inverse, invert, move backwards, rearrange, retreat, revert, shift, transfer, turn around, turn over, upset **4** alter, change, convert, double back, invalidate, lift, modify, negate, nullify, overset, overthrow, recall, repeal, rescind, set aside, turn around, undo, upset

review *noun.* **1** analysis, audit, column, display, drill, file, procession, recapitulation, reconsideration, reflection, report, rethink, retrospect, revision, scan, scrutiny, study, view **2** analysis, appraisal, assessment, investigation, journal, judgment, mention, monograph, notice, organ, outline, pan, periodical, recapitulation, study, summary, thesis, treatise **3** analyze, chew over, cop, debrief, hammer, kick around, reassess, recall, recapitulate, recollect, reconsider, reflect on, rehash, remember, rethink, revise, revisit, summon up **4** assess, boo, correct, discuss, evaluate, examine, inspect, judge, knock, lay out, needle, pan, rap, revise, rip, slam, study, trash

revision *noun.* alteration, amendment, correction, editing, improvement, modification, overhauling, polish, re-examination, reconsideration, redaction, retrospect, retrospection, review, revisal, revise, rewriting, updating

revival *noun.* awakening, cheering, consolation, enkindling, freshening, invigoration, quickening, recovery, recrudescence, regeneration, renaissance, renewal, restoration, resurgence, resurrection, revitalization, revivification, risorgimento

revive *verb.* animate, arouse, awaken, cheer, comfort, encourage, gladden, overcome, quicken, rally, recover, refresh, renew, repair, restore, revitalize, solace, strengthen

revolt *verb.* arise, boycott, break, defect, defy, drop out, make waves, mutiny, oppose, opt out, overthrow, rebel, renounce, resist, riot, rise up, strike, turn against

revolution *noun.* **1** coup, debacle, destruction, mutiny, outbreak, overthrow, plot, rebellion, revolt, row, strike, subversion, transformation, turnover, upheaval, uproar, upset, violence **2** circle, cycle, gyration, lap, orbit, pirouette, reel, revolve, revolving, roll, rotation, round, spin, swirl, turn, turning, wheel, whirl

reward *noun.* benefit, bonus, bounty, compensation, crown, cue, dividend, garland, grease, perk, premium, recompense, remuneration, salve, strokes, subway, tip, wages

rhythm *noun.* accent, bounce, cadence, flow, lilt, measure, meter, meter, movement, pattern, periodicity, pulse, regularity, rhyme, swing, tempo, time, uniformity

rich *adjective.* **1** affluent, bloated, comfortable, easy, fat, flush, gilded, independent, loaded, moneyed, opulent, plush, prosperous, rolling, stinking rich, swimming, uptown, wealthy **2** abounding, costly, elegant, embellished, expensive, exquisite, extravagant, fine, lavish, magnificent, precious, priceless, productive, snazzy, sumptuous, swank, swanky, valuable **3** creamy, delicious, fatty, full-bodied, heavy, highly-flavored, juicy, luscious, nourishing, nutritious, oily, satisfying, savory, spicy, succulent, sustaining, sweet, tasty **4** bright, canorous, deep, dulcet, eloquent, expressive, gay, intense, mellow, resonant, rotund, significant, silvery, sonorous, strong, vibrant, vivid, warm **5** absurd, amusing, diverting, entertaining, foolish, hilarious, humorous, incongruous, laughable, ludicrous, odd, preposterous, queer, ridiculous, risible, slaying, splitting, strange

rid *verb.* abolish, adios, bounce, can, chill, clear, deliver, disabuse, ditch, eject, eliminate, eradicate, exterminate, extinguish, liberate, release, remove, unload

ride *noun.* commute, drive, excursion, expedition, hitch, jaunt, joyride, lift, outing, pick up, run, spin, Sunday drive, tour, transportation, trip, turn, whirl

ride *verb.* **1** cruise, curb, direct, drift, float, guide, handle, hitch, manage, motor, move, post, progress, roll, sit, tour, travel, wash **2** annoy, bait, be autocratic, enslave, grip, harass, harry, haunt, hector, hound, override, rate, reproach, revile, torment, torture, tyrannize, upbraid

ridge *noun.* backbone, crease, elevation, fold, furrow, hill, moraine, parapet, plica, pole, range, rib, rim, seam, spine, upland, windrow, wrinkle

ridiculous *adjective.* antic, bizarre, comic, contemptible, fantastic, foolish, funny, hilarious, impossible, incredible, jerky, ludicrous, nonsensical, preposterous, silly, stupid, unbelievable, wacky

rifle *verb.* go through, grab, gut, knock off, knock over, loot, pillage, plunder, rip, rip off, rob, rummage, sack, strip, take, tip over, trash, waste

right *adjective.* **1** appropriate, due, ethical, fitting, fly, good, hold up, honest, justifiable, legal, moral, proper, righteous, rightful, scrupulous, suitable, true, virtuous **2** absolute, admissible, amen, authentic, exact, immaculate, indubitable, infallible, proper, real, satisfactory, sound, strict, sure, thoroughgoing, true, valid, veridical **3** acceptable, becoming, befitting, comely, common, correct, decent, desirable, done, due, fit, fitting, good, proper, propitious, satisfactory, suitable, tolerable **4** balanced, circumspect, discerning, discreet, enlightened, fine, fit, hale, judicious, lucid, normal, penetrating, rational, reasonable, sane, sound, unimpaired, wise **5** absolutely, altogether, bang, clear, completely, correctly, entirely, exactly, perfectly, precisely, quite, sharp, slap, square, squarely, truly, utterly, wholly **6** decently, dispassionately, equitably, ethically, evenly, honestly, honorably, impartially, justly, lawfully, legitimately, morally, objectively, properly, reliably, sincerely, squarely, without prejudice **7** at once, away, dead, direct, due, forthwith, immediately, instanter, instantly, now, promptly, quickly, right away, straight, straightaway, straightly, undeviatingly, without delay **8** advantage, appanage, benefit, business, claim, due, favor, franchise, freedom, immunity, interest, liberty, lumps, power, preference, prerogative, priority, title

right *noun.* emancipation, equity, freedom, good, goodness, honor, independence, integrity, justice, liberty, morality, propriety, reason, rectitude, righteousness, rightness, straight, virtue

right *verb.* adjust, balance, correct, doctor, launder, overhaul, patch, pick up, recompense, redress, repair, restore, scrub, settle, square, straighten, turn around, vindicate

rigid *adjective.* austere, chiseled, determined, exact, firm, fixed, hard, inexorable, invariable, set, severe, solid, static, stern, strict, unalterable, unbreakable, uncompromising

rigorous *adjective.* accurate, ascetic, austere, dogmatic, exact, exacting, hard, inclement, meticulous, oppressive, proper, right, rigid, scrupulous, severe, stiff, strict, uncompromising

rim *noun.* band, brim, brow, circumference, confine, curb, end, fringe, hem, ledge, line, outline, perimeter, ring, strip, terminus, top, verge

ring *noun.* association, bloc, bunch, clique, crew, gang, mob, monopoly, organization, outfit, party, pool, racket, string, syndicate, troop, troupe, trust

ring *verb.* **1** begird, belt, circle, circumscribe, compass, confine, enclose, encompass, gird, girdle, hem in, inclose, loop, move around, rim, round, seal off, surround **2** bang, beat, bong, buzz, clang, clap, jingle, peal, play, pull, punch, resonate, reverberate, sound, strike, tinkle, toll, vibrate

riot *noun.* **1** brawl, burst, commotion, donnybrook, fray, fuss, protest, quarrel, racket, row, ruckus, rumble, shower, stir, storm, strife, trouble, uproar **2** confusion, excess, flourish, frolic, howl, lark, merrymaking, panic, revelry, romp, scream, sensation, show, skylark, smash, splash, uproar, wow

ripe *adjective.* accomplished, adult, completed, conditioned, fit, increased, informed, learned, mature, overdue, plump, prepared, prime, sound, timely, usable, versed, wise

rise *noun.* **1** acceleration, aggrandizement, ascent, boost, breakthrough, climb, doubling, enlargement, improvement, inflation, intensification, intensifying, progress, promotion, surge, upsurge, upswing, upturn **2** acclivity, ascension, ascent, climb, elevation, eminence, highland, hillock, incline, lift, mount, rising, rising ground, soaring, surge, towering, upland, upsurge **3** arise, arouse, aspire, awake, climb, grow, lift, mount, push up, rocket, scale, sprout, surface, surge, surmount, tower, turn out, up **4** accelerate, aggravate, arise, build, climb, deepen, double, enhance, enlarge, expand, grow, lift, mount, multiply, speed up, spread, take off, upsurge **5** appear, arise, befall, betide, come, derive, emerge, fall out, flow, happen, head, issue, loom, occur, proceed, spring, stem, surface

risk *noun.* accident, contingency, danger, exposure, flier, flyer, fortune, gamble, hazard, jeopardy, liability, luck, opportunity, plunge, possibility, speculation, stab, wager

risk *verb.* adventure, beard, compromise, confront, dare, defy, encounter, endanger, face, gamble, hazard, imperil, jeopardy, meet, menace, plunge, speculate, wager

rite *noun.* act, celebration, ceremonial, communion, custom, form, formality, liturgy, observance, occasion, ordinance, practice, procedure, ritual, sacrament, service, solemnity, tradition

ritual *noun.* act, ceremonial, communion, custom, form, habit, observance, ordinance, practice, prescription, procedure, protocol, routine, sacrament, service, solemnity, stereotype, tradition

rival *noun.* adversary, antagonist, bandit, buddy, challenger, competition, competitor, contender, entrant, equal, equivalent, fellow, match, meat, opponent, opposite number, peer

rival *verb.* amount, approach, approximate, compare with, compete, contend, contest, correspond, emulate, equal, go for, match, meet, near, partake, resemble, tie, touch

road *noun.* asphalt, boulevard, cobblestone, concrete, course, direction, drag, expressway, lane, line, parkway, passage, pavement, pike, route, subway, terrace, thruway

roar *noun.* barrage, bay, bellow, blast, bluster, boom, clamor, clash, crash, detonation, drum, explosion, growl, reverberation, shout, thunder, uproar, yell

roar *verb.* bark, bay, bellow, blast, bluster, boom, brawl, clamor, crash, drum, explode, growl, rebound, roll, shout, sound, thunder, yell

rob *verb.* appropriate, boost, buzz, con, cop, divest, embezzle, liberate, lift, loot, lose, oust, raid, requisition, rifle, strip, take, withhold

rock *noun.* bedrock, boulder, cobblestone, crust, earth, gravel, lava, lodge, mass, metal, mineral, ore, pebble, quarry, reef, rubble, shelf, slab

rock *verb.* agitate, falter, heave, jolt, lurch, move, pitch, quake, quaver, reel, roll, shake, shock, stagger, swing, toss, tremble, wobble

rocky *adjective.* **1** adamant, bloodless, firm, flinty, hard, impassible, insensate, insensible, insensitive, obdurate, pitiless, rocklike, rough, rugged, solid, steady, tough, unyielding **2** dizzy, ill, rickety, shaky, sick, sickly, staggering, ticklish, tottering, tricky, uncertain, undependable, unreliable, unstable, unsteady, unwell, weak, wobbly

rod *noun.* baton, billet, birch, cane, cylinder, dowel, ingot, pin, pole, shaft, slab, spike, staff, stave, stick, strip, switch, wand

role *noun.* **1** act, banana, bit, clothing, extra, face, hero, heroine, lead, part, personification, piece, presentation, semblance, show, stint, super, title **2** act, bit, business, capacity, execution, function, game, guise, job, part, piece, pose, position, post, posture, province, stint, task

roll *noun.* **1** ball, barrel, cartouche, coil, cone, convolution, cornucopia, cylinder, fold, reel, rundle, scroll, shell, spiral, spool, trundle, wheel, whorl **2** barrage, boom, booming, clatter, drone, drumbeat, drumming, echoing, grumble, quaver, racket, rat-a-tat, rattle, resonance, roar, rumble, rumbling, thunder **3** alternate, arch, bend, coil, elapse, flow, follow, pass, pirouette, pivot, propel, rotate, succeed, swirl, trundle, turn, wind, wrap **4** boom, cannonade, clatter, drum, echo, growl, grumble, hum, pattern, quaver, rattle, re-echo, roar, rumble, rustle, sound, thunder, trill **5** drift, flow, glide, incline, lean, lurch, pitch, ramble, range, roam, rove, stagger, surge, swing, toss, wallow, wave, welter

romance *noun.* affair, attachment, carrying on, courtship, enchantment, fairy tale, fascination, fling, flirtation, goings-on, hanky-panky, intrigue, liaison, love, love affair, love story, passion, relationship, thing together

romantic *adjective.* amorous, colorful, daring, dreamy, enchanting, exotic, extravagant, fond, glamorous, idealistic, idyllic, imaginative, mysterious, passionate, picturesque, quixotic, tender, wild

room *noun.* **1** allowance, area, clearance, compass, expanse, extent, latitude, leeway, occasion, opening, opportunity, range, reach, rein, rope, scope, sweep, territory **2** accommodation, apartment, box, cabin, cave, chamber, cubbyhole, den, flat, flop, joint, lodging, niche, pad, setup, suite, turf, vault

root *noun.* beginnings, bottom, core, derivation, footing, foundation, fountain, fountainhead, fundamental, germ, ground, nucleus, occasion, reason, seed, source, stem, substance

rosy *adjective.* aflush, blooming, blushing, colored, coral, deep pink, fresh, glowing, healthy-looking, high-colored, pale red, peach, red, red-complexioned, reddish, roseate, rubicund, ruddy

rot *noun.* balderdash, bilge, bull, bunk, bunkum, claptrap, crap, drivel, foolishness, guff, hogwash, hooey, moonshine, nonsense, poppycock, rubbish, silliness, tommyrot

rot *verb.* corrupt, crumble, decay, decline, decompose, demoralize, descend, deteriorate, disintegrate, perish, retrograde, sink, spoil, stain, taint, turn, warp, wither

rough *adjective.* **1** bearded, coarse, craggy, fuzzy, hairy, jagged, knobby, nodular, rocky, ruffled, scabrous, shaggy, sharp, tousled, uneven, unfinished, unshaven, woolly **2** agitated, blustery, boisterous, choppy, coarse, furious, grating, gruff, hoarse, husky, inclement, inharmonious, raging, rasping, raucous, tumultuous, turbulent, wild **3** bluff, blunt, boisterous, boorish, brief, cruel, curt, discourteous, drastic, extreme, hairy, hard, indelicate, nasty, raw, severe, sharp, unpleasant **4** austere, crude, cursory, hard, imperfect, incomplete, raw, rough-hewn, rudimentary, shapeless, sketchy, Spartan, uncompleted, uncut, undressed, unfinished, unformed, unpolished

round *adjective.* arced, arched, bent, bowed, circular, coiled, curled, curved, cylindrical, discoid, elliptical, looped, oval, ringed, rotund, rounded, spherical, spiral

round *noun.* **1** arc, arch, band, bend, bow, circle, curvature, curve, disc, disk, equator, hoop, loop, orb, orbit, ring, sphere, wheel **2** beat, bout, circuit, course, cycle, division, gyration, lap, level, period, revolution, rotation, routine, schedule, sequence, series, session, tour **3** bypass, circle, circulate, compass, encompass, flank, gird, girdle, hem, pivot, revolve, ring, roll, rotate, spin, surround, turn, wheel **4** arch, bend, bow, coil, crook, curl, curve, form, loop, mold, perfect, polish, refine, shape, sleek, slick, smooth, whorl

route *noun.* beat, circuit, course, direction, divergence, layout, line, map, meandering, passage, pike, plans, plot, program, rambling, range, round, short cut

route *verb.* address, conduct, consign, convey, direct, dispatch, escort, forward, guide, lead, pilot, see, send, shepherd, ship, show, steer, transmit

routine *adjective.* accepted, accustomed, chronic, conventional, everyday, familiar, general, methodical, normal, ordinary, periodic, plain, regular, seasonal, standard, typical, unremarkable, usual

routine *noun.* act, bit, custom, cycle, formula, groove, line, method, pace, piece, procedure, program, round, system, technique, treadmill, way, wont

row *noun.* **1** bank, chain, column, consecution, echelon, file, line, order, progression, queue, range, rank, sequel, series, string, succession, tier, train **2** altercation, beef, bickering, brawl, broil, castigation, commotion, fray, fuss, lecture, melee, quarrel, racket, reproof, riot, ruckus, trouble, uproar

row *verb.* argue, bawl out, berate, bicker, brawl, carpet, chew out, dispute, jaw, quarrel, ream, scold, scrap, spat, squabble, tiff, tongue-lash, wrangle

royal *adjective.* aristocratic, baronial, dignified, elevated, grand, imperial, impressive, lofty, magnificent, majestic, regal, resplendent, ruling, sovereign, stately, superb, superior, supreme

rugged *adjective.* **1** broken, coarse, craggy, difficult, furrowed, harsh, irregular, jagged, leathery, mountainous, ragged, rocky, rough, scabrous, stark, uneven, worn, wrinkled **2** arduous, demanding, exacting, formidable, hairy, hard, heavy, laborious, murder, rough, stern, strenuous, taxing, tough, trying, uncompromising, uphill **3** beefy, big, brawny, burly, energetic, hale, hardy, healthy, husky, indefatigable, lusty, muscular, robust, sturdy, tough, unflagging, vigorous, well-built

ruin *noun.* bankruptcy, bath, crash, defeat, demolition, destruction, disintegration, disrepair, downgrade, fall, havoc, loss, overthrow, skids, subversion, undoing, wreck, wreckage

ruin *verb.* bankrupt, beggar, break, bust, crush, defeat, deplore, do in, exhaust, mar, overthrow, overwhelm, reduce, shatter, smash, total, wrack, wreck

rule *noun.* **1** axiom, canon, command, criterion, decree, dictum, direction, formula, fundamental, keystone, maxim, moral, ordinance, precept, propriety, ruling, statute, truism **2** administration, ascendancy, authority, command, control, direction, domination, dominion, empire, government, influence, jurisdiction, mastery, power, regime, reign, sovereignty, supremacy **3** command, conduct, control, curb, decree, dictate, direct, dominate, guide, lead, manage, order, preside, prevail, regulate, reign, restrain, run **4** adjudicate, conclude, decide, decree, deduce, determine, establish, figure, find, fix, gather, hold, infer, postulate, prescribe, pronounce, resolve, settle

rumor *noun.* buzz, clothesline, dispatch, fabrication, falsehood, fiction, gossip, grapevine, innuendo, invention, lie, notoriety, repute, story, suggestion, tattle, tidings, wire

run *noun.* **1** bound, break, canter, dash, drop, escape, fall, flight, flow, gallop, lope, pace, race, rush, spring, spurt, tear, trot **2** bearing, continuation, course, cycle, endurance, flow, line, passage, period, prolongation, round, route, season, series, stretch, string, tide, trend **3** barrel, bolt, bound, bustle, canter, career, course, fly, gallop, pace, race, shag, smoke, speed, spurt, take off, travel, trot **4** bleed, cascade, course, discharge, dissolve, drop, fall, flow, fuse, glide, issue, leak, pass, pour, proceed, roll, slide, spread **5** act, bear, carry, command, convey, drive, govern, handle, manage, maneuver, move, perform, ply, propel, tick, transport, use, work **6** administer, boss, conduct, control, coordinate, direct, head, helm, keep, lead, look after, mastermind, operate, ordain, own, regulate, superintend, supervise **7** be current, circulate, cover, encompass, extend, go, go around, go on, last, lie, persevere, proceed, range, reach, spread, stretch, trail, vary

running *adjective.* active, alive, constant, dynamic, effortless, executing, flowing, functioning, going, in action, incessant, live, operating, perpetual, proceeding, producing, smooth, unbroken

running *noun.* administration, care, charge, conduct, control, coordination, direction, functioning, handling, leadership, maintenance, operation, organization, oversight, performance, regulation, supervision, working

rural *adjective.* agrarian, agricultural, Arcadian, backwoods, bucolic, farm, georgic, idyllic, natural, pastoral, provincial, ranch, rustic, simple, small-town, suburban, sylvan, unsophisticated

rush *noun.* blitz, charge, dash, dispatch, expedition, flood, flow, flux, haste, hurriedness, precipitation, race, scramble, speed, stream, surge, swiftness, urgency

rush *verb.* accelerate, barrel, bolt, break, career, charge, course, dispatch, fly, haste, press, quicken, race, roll, speed, speed up, streak, surge

ruthless *adjective.* callous, cold, cruel, cutthroat, fierce, grim, hard, heartless, inhuman, killer, malevolent, merciless, mortal, rancorous, savage, severe, vicious, vindictive

S

sack *verb.* demolish, desolate, destroy, devastate, devour, fleece, gut, lay waste, loot, maraud, pillage, plunder, rifle, rob, ruin, spoil, strip, waste

sacred *adjective.* angelic, blessed, cherished, consecrated, divine, enshrined, godly, hallowed, numinous, pious, pure, religious, revered, sanctified, solemn, spiritual, venerable

sacrifice *verb.* cede, drop, endure, eschew, forfeit, forgo, immolate, kiss goodbye, let go, lose, offer, offer up, renounce, spare, suffer, surrender, waive, yield

sad *adjective.* **1** depressed, despairing, despondent, doleful, down, downcast, forlorn, gloomy, hurting, melancholy, morbid, morose, mournful, sorry, troubled, weeping, wistful, woebegone **2** bad, calamitous, deplorable, depressing, discouraging, dreary, grave, grievous, hapless, miserable, oppressive, pitiable, pitiful, poignant, sorry, unfortunate, upsetting, wretched

safe *adjective.* **1** fostered, guarded, impervious, intact, invulnerable, maintained, preserved, secure, sheltered, shielded, snug, tended, unhurt, uninjured, unmolested, unscathed, vindicated, watched **2** certain, checked, clear, competent, dependable, harmless, healthy, innocent, neutralized, nonpoisonous, pure, reliable, risk-free, secure, sound, tame, trustworthy, wholesome **3** calculating, careful, chary, circumspect, competent, conservative, considerate, dependable, discreet, gingerly, guarded, prudent, realistic, reliable, sure, trustworthy, unadventurous, wary

sail *verb.* captain, cross, cruise, drift, embark, float, fly, leave, navigate, pilot, shoot, skipper, skirr, steer, sweep, travel, voyage, wing

sale *noun.* auction, business, buying, clearance, deal, demand, dumping, enterprise, exchange, marketing, negotiation, purchase, purchasing, reduction, selling, transaction, unloading, vending

saloon *noun.* alehouse, bar, barroom, beverage room, bucket shop, dive, drinkery, gin mill, hangout, joint, juice joint, night club, place, pub, rum room, shebang, tavern, watering hole

salvation *noun.* conservancy, conservation, deliverance, emancipation, escape, exemption, extrication, keeping, liberation, pardon, preserve, preservation, redemption, release, reprieve, rescue, restoration, safekeeping

same *adjective.* aforementioned, aforesaid, carbon, comparable, compatible, double, duplicate, identical, indistinguishable, interchangeable, like, related, similar, similarly, synonymous, tantamount, twin, very

sample *noun.* bit, bite, case, constituent, element, illustration, indication, individual, instance, model, morsel, part, piece, sampling, segment, sign, specimen, unit

sanction *noun.* allowance, approval, assent, authority, backing, confirmation, consent, countenance, encouragement, endorsement, fiat, leave, nod, permission, permit, ratification, support, word

sanction *verb.* accredit, allow, approve, back, bless, certify, commission, confirm, countenance, empower, endorse, go for, license, permit, ratify, support, vouch for, warrant

sanctuary *noun.* asylum, convent, cover, covert, defense, den, haven, hideaway, hideout, hole, port, protection, refuge, resort, retreat, screen, shelter, shield

sane *adjective.* balanced, discerning, fit, healthy, intelligent, judicious, logical, lucid, moderate, normal, oriented, rational, right, sage, sensible, sound, steady, wise

satire *noun.* banter, burlesque, caricature, chaffing, irony, lampoon, mockery, parody, pasquinade, persiflage, raillery, sarcasm, send-up, skit, spoof, takeoff, travesty, wit

satisfaction *noun.* achievement, comfort, compensation, complacency, contentment, ease, gratification, happiness, indulgence, prosperity, recompense, redress, refreshment, relief, satiety, serenity, settlement, vindication

satisfactory *adjective.* adequate, appeasing, average, competent, decent, enough, fair, fulfilling, good, gratifying, pleasing, satisfying, solid, sound, sufficient, suitable, tolerable, valid

satisfy *verb.* **1** amuse, animate, capture, cheer, comfort, content, delight, entertain, flatter, gladden, gorge, humor, indulge, mollify, satiate, sell, suit, surfeit **2** accomplish, appease, assure, avail, convince, do, fill, furnish, induce, meet, observe, perform, provide, qualify, reassure, sell, serve, suffice **3** answer, atone, compensate, disburse, discharge, indemnify, make good, make reparation, meet, pay off, quit, recompense, remunerate, repay, requite, reward, settle, square

savage *adjective.* **1** archaic, barbarian, barbaric, bestial, brute, earliest, fierce, fundamental, native, natural, primitive, pristine, rough, simple, turbulent, unbroken, unmodified, vicious **2** bestial, bloody, crazed, destructive, diabolical, fell, ferocious, fierce, grim, heartless, inhuman, malevolent, malicious, merciless, rabid, raging, vicious, violent

save *verb.* amass, cache, collect, conserve, deposit, economize, gather, hide away, hold, husband, keep, maintain, manage, reserve, spare, squirrel, store, treasure

savings *noun.* accumulation, cache, fund, funds, harvest, investment, kitty, means, property, provision, provisions, reserve, reserves, resources, riches, sock, stake, store

say *verb.* affirm, claim, convey, deliver, do, imagine, imply, jaw, maintain, mention, orate, perform, pronounce, rap, render, repeat, rumor, tell

scale *noun.* computation, degrees, extent, hierarchy, proportion, range, ranking, rate, ratio, rule, scope, sequence, series, spectrum, spread, steps, system, way

scandal *noun.* calumny, depreciation, disgrace, disrepute, dynamite, gossip, hearsay, mud, offense, opprobrium, reproach, rumor, scorcher, shame, sin, skeleton, talk, wrongdoing

scar *verb.* beat, blemish, brand, cut, damage, deface, disfigure, flaw, hurt, injure, maim, mar, pinch, score, scratch, slash, stab, traumatize

scene *noun.* arena, background, blackout, display, exhibition, flats, locale, locality, outlook, pageant, scenery, set, site, spot, stage, tableau, theater, view

scenery *noun.* backdrop, decor, flat, flats, furnishings, furniture, landscape, neighborhood, properties, props, prospect, set, setting, spectacle, sphere, terrain, view, vista

schedule *noun.* agenda, appointments, calendar, car, catalog, catalogue, chart, inventory, itinerary, lineup, list, program, record, registry, roll, roster, table, timetable

schedule *verb.* appoint, arrange, be due, book, card, catalogue, engage, line up, list, organize, pencil in, program, record, register, reserve, set up, slate, time

scheme *noun.* **1** arrangement, blueprint, codification, design, device, expedient, layout, ordering, outline, plan, presentation, program, proposition, schedule, schema, suggestion, system, tactics **2** angle, bit, child, conspiracy, dodge, frame, game, layout, maneuver, pitch, practice, proposition, ruse, setup, slant, story, switch, tactics

scholar *noun.* academic, brain, critic, disciple, doctor, gnome, grind, intellectual, philosopher, professor, pupil, sage, schoolboy, schoolgirl, scientist, student, teacher, wig

school *noun.* academy, alma mater, blackboard jungle, college, department, discipline, establishment, faculty, hall, institute, institution, jail, knowledge box, schoolhouse, seminary, system, university

school *verb.* advance, coach, control, direct, discipline, drill, educate, guide, inform, instruct, lead, manage, prepare, prime, show, train, tutor, verse

scope *noun.* amplitude, area, breadth, compass, confines, field, freedom, fullness, latitude, leeway, liberty, opportunity, orbit, outlook, range, reach, span, sphere

score *noun.* **1** account, addition, amount, average, count, grade, mark, number, outcome, points, rate, reckoning, record, result, sum, summary, summation, tally **2** army, cloud, crowd, drove, flock, host, hundred, legion, lot, mass, million, multitude, myriad, rout, scores, swarm, throng, very many **3** accomplish, amass, arrive, attain, click, gain, get, impress, notch, procure, prosper, reach, realize, secure, succeed, thrive, triumph, win **4** cleave, crosshatch, deface, furrow, gash, gouge, graze, groove, indent, line, mark, mill, nick, notch, scrape, scratch, slash, slit

scout *noun.* advance, adventurer, detective, escort, explorer, guard, investigator, lookout, outpost, outrider, patrol, picket, pioneer, recruiter, runner, sleuth, spy, vanguard

scout *verb.* case, examine, explore, eyeball, ferret out, hunt, inspect, observe, probe, reconnoiter, search, seek, spot, spy, stake out, survey, track down, watch

scrap *noun.* bite, butt, chunk, cutting, glob, grain, hunk, iota, leaving, mite, modicum, morsel, part, particle, piece, remains, speck, trace

scrap *verb.* abandon, adios, break up, cast, chuck, discard, dismiss, dispense with, ditch, drop, forsake, junk, kiss off, reject, retire, shed, slough, throw away

scream *verb.* bellow, blare, caterwaul, holler, howl, jar, roar, screak, screech, shout, shriek, shrill, squeal, voice, wail, yell, yip, yowl

screen *noun.* canopy, cloak, concealment, cover, covering, curtain, divider, envelope, guard, hedge, mantle, mask, net, partition, security, shade, shelter, veil

screen *verb.* **1** cache, camouflage, cloak, conceal, cover, defend, guard, mask, obscure, obstruct, protect, safeguard, seclude, secure, shade, shadow, shelter, veil **2** choose, cull, eliminate, evaluate, examine, extract, filter, gauge, grade, pick out, process, riddle, scan, separate, sieve, sift, sort, winnow

screw *verb.* bilk, bleed, cheat, chisel, coerce, constrain, defraud, do, exact, extract, force, gyp, oppress, pinch, shake down, squeeze, wrest, wring

scrutiny *noun.* analysis, audit, eagle eye, exploration, inquiry, inspection, investigation, look-see, perusal, review, scan, search, sifting, study, surveillance, survey, tab, view

sea *noun.* abundance, blue, bounding main, deep, drink, expanse, main, multitude, number, ocean, pond, profusion, sheet, sink, splash, surf, swell, waves

seal *verb.* close, cork, enclose, fasten, gum, isolate, make airtight, paste, plaster, plug, quarantine, secure, segregate, shut, stop, stop up, stopper, waterproof

search *noun.* chase, examination, exploration, frisking, going-over, hunt, inquest, inquiry, inspection, investigation, pursuing, pursuit, quest, research, scrutiny, shakedown

search *verb.* beat, comb, examine, explore, ferret, grope, grub, inquire, inspect, probe, pry, quest, root, run down, scan, scout, study, track down

seat *noun.* abode, axis, center, cradle, headquarters, heart, house, hub, location, mansion, place, post, residence, site, situation, source, spot, station

seat *verb.* accommodate, deposit, establish, fix, hold, install, locate, lounge, nestle, perch, plant, put, roost, set, settle, sit, squat, take

second *adjective.* another, double, duplicate, extra, following, further, inferior, lesser, lower, next, other, repeated, reproduction, secondary, subsequent, supporting, twin, unimportant

secondary *adjective.* **1** accessory, alternate, consequential, contingent, dependent, extra, insignificant, lesser, lower, minor, petty, second, small, subject, subservient, subsidiary, supporting, unimportant **2** auxiliary, borrowed, consequent, dependent, derivate, derivational, derived, developed, eventual, indirect, proximate, resultant, resulting, secondhand, subordinate, subsequent, subsidiary, vicarious

secrecy *noun.* clandestineness, confidence, confidentiality, dark, darkness, hiding, hush, isolation, mystery, privacy, retirement, seclusion, secretiveness, silence, solitude, stealth, suppression, surreptitiousness

secret *adjective.* **1** ambiguous, closet, covered, cryptic, deep, disguised, mysterious, mystical, obscure, private, recondite, retired, strange, underground, undisclosed, unintelligible, unpublished, unseen **2** backstairs, camouflaged, clandestine, classified, close, confidential, covert, cryptic, discreet, disguised, inside, restricted, sly, sneak, sneaky, surreptitious, unacknowledged, underhanded

section *noun.* area, bite, category, chunk, department, drag, hunk, member, passage, piece, quarter, region, sector, sphere, subdivision, territory, tract, zone

secure *adjective.* **1** adjusted, bound, firm, fixed, fortified, immovable, iron, locked, set, solid, sound, stable, staunch, steady, strong, sure, tenacious, tight **2** able, absolute, assured, balanced, carefree, cinch, conclusive, confident, determined, firm, reassured, resolute, settled, solid, sound, steady, strong, sure **3** access, achieve, annex, bag, buy, capture, cinch, ensure, gain, grasp, have, insure, land, lock, pick up, procure, take, win **4** adjust, anchor, bind, bolt, cement, chain, clinch, close, fix, lash, lock, lock up, nail, padlock, settle, slough, tie, tighten

security *noun.* agreement, armament, contract, cover, freedom, guard, immunity, pledge, precaution, preservation, promise, protection, refuge, safeguard, salvation, sanctuary, surveillance, ward

see *verb.* **1** behold, contemplate, detect, gaze, glare, identify, inspect, mark, notice, peg, pierce, recognize, regard, scope, spot, spy, view, watch **2** ascertain, behold, experience, fancy, follow, have, imagine, know, learn, mark, notice, realize, recognize, study, think, undergo, view, visualize **3** attend, call, date, direct, encounter, guide, lead, look up, meet, pilot, receive, route, shepherd, show, steer, usher, visit, walk

seed *noun.* berry, bud, core, corn, earn, egg, embryo, germ, grain, image, impression, kernel, nucleus, nut, particle, source, spark, start

seek *verb.* chase, comb, dragnet, explore, fan, fish, follow, hunt, inquire, investigate, mouse, prowl, pursue, quest, root, scout, scratch, track down

select *adjective.* boss, chosen, dainty, delicate, discriminating, eclectic, elegant, exquisite, favored, limited, preferable, prime, rare, screened, superior, top, weeded, winner

select *verb.* button down, choose, decide, elect, finger, make, mark, name, peg, pick, prefer, slot, sort out, tab, tag, take, tap, winnow

selfish *adjective.* egocentric, egoistic, egoistical, egomaniacal, egotistic, greedy, hog, mean, mercenary, narcissistic, narrow, parsimonious, prejudiced, self-centered, self-indulgent, self-seeking, stingy, ungenerous

sell *verb.* **1** auction, ballyhoo, bargain, boost, contract, dispose, drum, exchange, handle, market, merchandise, move, peddle, persuade, plug, puff, traffic, unload **2** beguile, break faith, bunk, cross, deceive, deliver up, delude, disappoint, fail, four-flush, give away, give up, mislead, play false, rat on, sell out, surrender, violate

send *verb.* accelerate, assign, commit, convey, deliver, dispatch, drop, emit, forward, freight, hurl, impart, issue, propel, relay, route, ship, transfer

senior *noun.* ancient, dean, elder, elderly person, first born, granny, head, master, old folks, old geezer, oldster, patriarch, pensioner, pops, relic, retired person, senior citizen, superior

sensation *noun.* agitation, bomb, commotion, excitement, flash, furor, hit, marvel, miracle, phenomenon, portent, prodigy, scandal, stir, surprise, thrill, wonder, wow

sense *noun.* **1** atmosphere, cognizance, discrimination, imagination, impression, insight, intellect, intuition, judgment, perception, premonition, prudence, reason, reasoning, recognition, spirit, wisdom, wit **2** advantage, burden, core, drift, gist, good, implication, logic, matter, nuance, purport, reason, stuff, substance, thrust, upshot, value, worth

sense *verb.* appreciate, believe, consider, dig, divine, feel, grasp, hold, know, notice, observe, perceive, pick up, read, realize, savvy, think, understand

sensibility *noun.* affection, appreciation, awareness, discernment, emotion, feeling, heart, insight, intuition, judgment, perceptiveness, sensation, sense, sensitivity, sentiment, susceptibility, taste, vibes

sensible *adjective.* alive, attentive, aware, canny, conscious, consequent, discerning, discreet, discriminating, informed, judicious, practical, rational, reasonable, sane, sentient, sound, wise

sensitive *adjective.* acute, conscious, delicate, emotional, fine, keen, nervous, perceiving, precarious, psychic, responsive, seeing, sensory, sentient, supersensitive, susceptible, tense, wired

sensory *adjective.* acoustic, audible, aural, clear, conscious, discernible, distinct, lingual, neural, neurological, ocular, ophthalmic, perceptible, phonic, sensible, sonic, tactile, visual

sentence *noun.* censure, decision, determination, dictum, fall, hitch, icebox, jolt, judgment, knock, order, penalty, rap, ruling, stretch, time, vacation, verdict

sentence *verb.* adjudicate, blame, condemn, confine, convict, damn, denounce, devote, doom, ice, jail, judge, ordain, proscribe, punish, railroad, rule, settle

sentiment *noun.* affect, bias, conviction, emotionalism, inclination, judgment, opinion, passion, penchant, persuasion, posture, romanticism, saying, sensibility, slant, tendency, thought, view

sentimental *adjective.* affected, affectionate, dreamy, effusive, idealistic, insipid, maudlin, passionate, pathetic, schoolgirlish, silly, sloppy, soapy, soft, sweet, syrupy, tender, touching

separate *adjective.* **1** abstracted, apart, apportioned, discrete, disjointed, distant, disunited, divergent, divided, divorced, independent, isolated, loose, marked, removed, severed, sovereign, unattached **2** alone, apart, autonomous, different, discrete, distinct, distinctive, diverse, independent, one, only, peculiar, several, single, sole, solitary, unique, various **3** break, break off, cleave, detach, dichotomize, disentangle, disjoin, dissect, distribute, divide, intersect, part, rupture, sever, split, sunder, uncouple, undo **4** assign, break up, classify, comb, compartment, cut off, discriminate, distribute, group, insulate, interval, intervene, island, order, seclude, segregate, sort, winnow **5** alienate, bifurcate, break off, break up, depart, discontinue, disunify, diverge, divorce, drop, go away, kiss off, leave, part, split up, uncouple, unlink

separation *noun.* break, departure, detachment, dissociation, dissolution, disunion, division, divorce, estrangement, farewell, gap, parting, partition, rift, rupture, segregation, split

sequence *noun.* arrangement, array, chain, continuity, course, cycle, distribution, flow, graduation, grouping, order, ordering, placement, row, sequel, streak, string, train

serene *adjective.* clear, collected, composed, content, easygoing, halcyon, limpid, patient, placid, poised, quiescent, reconciled, resting, satisfied, sedate, smooth, still, tranquil

series *noun.* arrangement, array, category, continuity, course, file, group, line, list, range, row, sequel, sequence, set, streak, string, suite, train

serious *adjective.* **1** austere, bound, determined, grave, grim, honest, intent, meditative, resolute, resolved, sedate, set, severe, sincere, solemn, steady, thoughtful, unsmiling **2** arduous, deep, fateful, fell, grave, grievous, grim, hard, heavy, important, laborious, meaningful, momentous, severe, significant, smoking, ugly, urgent

seriously *adverb.* **1** actively, determinedly, down, earnestly, fervently, gravely, intently, passionately, purposefully, resolutely, sedately, sincerely, soberly, solemnly, sternly, thoughtfully, vigorously, zealously **2** acutely, badly, dangerously, decidedly, deplorably, gravely, grievously, harmfully, intensely, menacingly, perilously, precariously, quite, regrettably, severely, sorely, threateningly, very

sermon *noun.* address, advice, angel food, discourse, doctrine, dressing-down, exhortation, harangue, homily, lecture, lesson, moralism, pastoral, preach, preaching, preachment, talking-to, tirade

servant *noun.* assistant, attendant, boy, cleaning lady, dependent, domestic, girl, help, helper, maid, man, menial, peon, retainer, serf, servitor, slave, woman

serve *verb.* **1** aid, arrange, assist, deal, deliver, distribute, give, handle, hit, mother, nurse, oblige, play, present, provide, provision, succor, supply **2** accept, agree, attend, complete, discharge, do, follow, fulfill, function, go through, labor, obey, observe, officiate, pass, perform, toil, work **3** advantage, answer, apply, avail, be acceptable, be adequate, benefit, content, do, fit, function, make, profit, satisfy, service, suit, work, work for

service *noun.* account, aid, assistance, avail, benefit, business, courtesy, dispensation, employ, employment, favor, indulgence, relevance, servicing, supply, usefulness, utility, work

session *noun.* affair, assembly, bull session, clambake, concourse, confab, conference, discussion, gathering, hearing, huddle, jam session, meet, period, rap session, showdown, sitting, term

set *adjective.* **1** appointed, arranged, certain, determined, entrenched, fixed, immovable, intent, pat, prearranged, resolute, rigid, rooted, scheduled, settled, specified, stubborn, usual **2** entrenched, firm, fixed, hidebound, immovable, inflexible, located, placed, positioned, rigid, settled, situated, solid, stable, stiff, strict, stubborn, unyielding

set *noun.* **1** array, body, bunch, bundle, camp, circle, clique, clump, clutch, collection, compendium, crew, gaggle, gang, mob, organization, outfit, series **2** aim, anchor, bestow, insert, install, level, lodge, mount, park, plank, prepare, put, rest, settle, spread, station, stick, train **3** allot, appoint, assign, conclude, decree, establish, fix, impose, instruct, name, ordain, prescribe, rate, regulate, resolve, schedule, settle, value

set up *verb.* assemble, build, build up, constitute, construct, create, erect, found, initiate, inspire, install, institute, launch, open, prepare, raise, strengthen, subsidize

setting *noun.* backdrop, background, context, distance, environment, frame, framework, horizon, locale, location, mounting, perspective, set, shade, shadow, site, surroundings, zoo

settle *verb.* **1** achieve, adjudicate, adjust, appoint, choose, clear, concert, discharge, dispose, figure, judge, pay, reconcile, regulate, resolve, rule, seal, square **2** decline, descend, flop, land, lay, light, lodge, perch, place, plunge, put, repose, roost, seat, sink, sit, subside, touch down

settlement *noun.* adjustment, agreement, arrangement, clearance, compact, compensation, completion, conclusion, confirmation, contract, covenant, determination, discharge, establishment, liquidation, pay, payment, remuneration

several *adjective.* any, certain, considerable, disparate, distinct, diverse, handful, individual, manifold, many, rare, scant, scarce, single, some, specific, sundry, various

severe *adjective.* **1** austere, biting, cold, cruel, cutting, dour, firm, grave, grim, hard, resolute, rigid, satirical, scathing, stiff, strict, unalterable, unsmiling **2** acute, arduous, consequential, dear, demanding, distressing, drastic, exacting, fierce, grave, hard, heavy, inclement, punishing, sharp, toilsome, unpleasant, wicked

severely *adverb.* acutely, badly, critically, dangerously, extremely, gravely, hard, hardly, intensely, markedly, painfully, rigorously, roughly, seriously, sharply, sorely, sternly, strictly

sex *noun.* affinity, appeal, attraction, coition, copulation, courtship, desire, fornication, generation, intimacy, libido, love, lovemaking, magnetism, relations, reproduction, sensuality, sexuality

sexual *adjective.* animal, animalistic, bestial, carnal, erotic, generative, genital, intimate, loving, passionate, procreative, reproductive, sensual, sex, sharing, venereal, voluptuous, wanton

shade *noun.* amount, cast, dash, degree, distinction, gradation, hint, nuance, proposal, semblance, spice, streak, suggestion, suspicion, tincture, trace, variation, variety

shade *verb.* cloud, conceal, cover, deepen, dim, eclipse, gray, hide, mute, obscure, overshadow, protect, screen, shadow, shelter, shield, shutter, veil

shadow *verb.* adumbrate, becloud, bedim, cloud, dim, gray, haze, obscure, overcast, overcloud, overhang, overshadow, screen, shade, shelter, shield, veil

shake *verb.* **1** agitate, chatter, disquiet, disturb, flicker, jerk, move, quake, rattle, shimmer, shiver, shudder, stagger, swing, upset, wave, whip, wobble **2** bother, daunt, dismay, distress, disturb, frighten, impair, intimidate, jar, make waves, move, rattle, throw, undermine, unstring, upset, weaken, worry

shallow *adjective.* cursory, flimsy, foolish, frivolous, hollow, idle, ignorant, lightweight, meaningless, petty, piddling, simple, slight, superficial, surface, trifling, uncritical, vain

shame *noun.* blot, contempt, contrition, degradation, derision, disrepute, embarrassment, guilt, humiliation, infamy, irritation, mortification, opprobrium, remorse, reproach, scandal, smear, stigma

shame *verb.* abash, blot, confound, debase, defile, degrade, disconcert, discredit, dishonor, embarrass, humble, humiliate, reproach, ridicule, shoot down, smear, stain, take down

shape *noun.* architecture, bod, build, configuration, constitution, construction, contour, figure, frame, likeness, model, mold, outline, profile, semblance, shadow, silhouette, stamp

shape *verb.* **1** assemble, build, carve, chisel, construct, create, crystallize, embody, frame, knead, mint, model, mold, pat, produce, sculpture, stamp, trim **2** accommodate, adapt, become, define, develop, devise, form, frame, grow, guide, modify, prepare, regulate, remodel, tailor, take form, throw together, work up

share *noun.* allotment, bite, chunk, claim, divide, dividend, division, drag, due, fraction, heritage, interest, parcel, percentage, piece, proportion, serving, taste

share *verb.* accord, allot, assign, bestow, distribute, divide, experience, part, partake, participate, partition, quota, ration, receive, shift, slice, split, yield

sharp *adjective.* **1** acute, barbed, cutting, edged, fine, horned, jagged, keen, peaked, pointed, salient, splintery, stinging, tapered, tapering, thorny, tipped, whetted **2** acute, alert, apt, astute, bright, canny, critical, discerning, discriminating, ingenious, intelligent, keen, observant, resourceful, savvy, slick, subtle, wise **3** artful, bent, crafty, cunning, deceitful, designing, ornery, salty, shady, shrewd, slick, slippery, sly, smart, snake, underhand, unscrupulous, wily **4** acute, agonizing, biting, cutting, distinct, distressing, drilling, excruciating, fierce, intense, keen, knifelike, painful, penetrating, shooting, sore, stinging, violent **5** barbed, biting, cutting, incisive, penetrating, peppery, pungent, sarcastic, sardonic, scathing, severe, stinging, tart, thoughtless, trenchant, ungracious, virulent, vitriolic **6** acid, acrid, active, astringent, austere, bitter, brisk, burning, harsh, hot, lively, piquant, pungent, sour, suffocating, tart, vigorous, vinegary

shed *verb.* afford, beam, cast, diffuse, drop, emit, give, junk, radiate, scrap, shower, slip, slough, spill, sprinkle, take off, throw, yield

sheer *adjective.* **1** altogether, blasted, blessed, downright, gross, outright, pure, quite, ran, simple, single, thoroughgoing, total, unadulterated, unalloyed, undiluted, unmixed, unqualified **2** clear, delicate, diaphanous, filmy, fine, flimsy, fragile, gossamer, lacy, limpid, lucid, pure, slight, smooth, soft, thin, translucent, transparent

sheet *noun.* area, blanket, coat, covering, expanse, film, foil, layer, membrane, page, pane, panel, piece, ply, slab, stretch, surface, veneer

shell *noun.* carapace, case, chassis, crust, frame, framework, hull, husk, integument, nut, pericarp, pod, scale, shard, shuck, skeleton, skin, structure

shelter *noun.* cover, digs, dwelling, guard, haven, hide, housing, lodging, pen, preserve, refuge, retirement, roost, security, shade, tower, turf, umbrella

shelter *verb.* chamber, conceal, cover, defend, guard, haven, hide, house, lodge, preserve, protect, roof, safeguard, screen, secure, shield, surround, ward

shield *noun.* absorber, aegis, armament, armor, buffer, bulwark, bumper, cover, defense, escutcheon, guard, mail, rampart, safeguard, screen, security, shelter, ward

shield *verb.* bulwark, chamber, conceal, cover, defend, give cover, give shelter, guard, harbor, haven, house, roof, safeguard, screen, secure, shelter, shotgun, stonewall

shift *noun.* **1** bend, change, conversion, deviation, double, fault, move, passage, removal, shifting, substitution, switch, transfer, transference, transformation, transit, variation, veering **2** artifice, craft, device, dodge, evasion, expediency, expedient, gambit, makeshift, maneuver, move, recourse, refuge, resort, resource, ruse, strategy, substitute

shift *verb.* budge, change, cook, deviate, displace, disturb, exchange, fault, move, rearrange, remove, ship, shuffle, stir, substitute, transfer, vary, waffle

ship *verb.* address, consign, direct, dispatch, drop, embark, export, forward, freight, haul, move, route, shift, ship out, smuggle, transfer, transmit, transport

shock *noun.* clash, collision, concussion, consternation, crash, distress, earthquake, encounter, hysteria, injury, jolt, percussion, ram, scare, start, trauma, upset, wreck

shock *verb.* agitate, anger, astound, dismay, disquiet, disturb, flood, floor, jolt, numb, offend, outrage, overcome, paralyze, revolt, rock, shake, stagger

shoot *verb.* **1** bag, barrage, blast, dispatch, emit, execute, expel, explode, fling, hurl, kill, launch, loose, pick off, plug, pop, propel, pump **2** bolt, charge, chase, flash, fling, fly, gallop, highball, lash, pass, race, reach, run, speed, spring, spurt, streak, whiz

shore *noun.* bank, beach, border, brim, brink, coast, embankment, littoral, margin, riverbank, riverside, sand, sands, seaboard, seacoast, seashore, strand, waterfront

short *adjective.* **1** bare, brief, compressed,

concise, condensed, curtailed, epigrammatic, lessened, little, momentary, pointed, precise, shortened, succinct, summarized, summary, terse, undersized **2** chunky, compact, diminutive, dwarf, dwarfed, little, low, petite, pocket, skimpy, slight, small, squat, stocky, stubby, thick, tiny, undersized **3** deficient, failing, inadequate, lacking, limited, meager, needing, poor, scant, scanty, scarce, shy, skimpy, slender, slim, sparse, tight, wanting **4** bluff, blunt, brief, curt, direct, discourteous, gruff, offhand, rude, sharp, snappy, snippy, straight, terse, thoughtless, unceremonious, uncivil, ungracious

shortage *noun.* curtailment, dearth, defalcation, deficit, failure, inadequacy, lack, lapse, leanness, paucity, pinch, poverty, scarcity, shortfall, tightness, underage, want, weakness

shot *noun.* attempt, break, conjecture, crack, effort, endeavor, fling, occasion, opening, opportunity, pop, show, slap, stab, time, try, turn, whack

shout *noun.* bark, bellow, call, cheer, clamor, cry, howl, hue, roar, salvo, scream, screech, shriek, squall, squawk, tallyho, whoop, yell

shout *verb.* bay, bellow, call out, cheer, clamor, exclaim, holler, roar, scream, screech, shriek, squall, squawk, vociferate, whoop, yammer, yap, yell

show *noun.* **1** array, display, fair, fireworks, flash, manifestation, occurrence, pageant, pageantry, pomp, presentation, program, representation, shine, showing, spectacle, splash, view **2** act, appearance, burlesque, carnival, cinema, comedy, drama, entertainment, film, flick, movie, pageant, picture, play, presentation, production, showing, spectacle **3** display, effect, face, flash, front, illusion, impression, likeness, pose, pretense, pretext, profession, seeming, semblance, sham, shine, showing, splash **4** appear, arrive, assert, clarify, come, disclose, discover, display, emerge, illustrate, instruct, lay out, loom, manifest, mark, materialize, proclaim, teach **5** afford, bare, blazon, display, exhibit, expose, flash, lay out, mount, offer, produce, sell, showcase, sport, spread, stage, streak, supply

shrewd *adjective.* acute, artful, brain, calculating, canny, cunning, deep, discerning, discriminating, ingenious, keen, profound, sensible, sharp, slippery, sly, smooth, wise

shrill *adjective.* acute, blaring, blatant, clangorous, ear-splitting, harsh, high, metallic, noisy, penetrating, piercing, piping, raucous, screeching, sharp, thin, treble

shut *verb.* bar, cage, close down, close up, confine, draw, enclose, exclude, fasten, fold, imprison, lock, push, seal, secure, shut down, slam, wall off

shy *adjective.* afraid, bashful, cautious, circumspect, conscious, demure, hesitant, introverted, loath, modest, nervous, reluctant, reserved, retiring, shrinking, suspicious, unresponsive, wary

sick *adjective.* defective, delicate, diseased, disordered, feeble, frail, funny, green, impaired, imperfect, incurable, infected, nauseated, peaked, rocky, run down, weak, wobbly

side *adjective.* ancillary, flanking, incidental, indirect, lateral, lesser, marginal, oblique, roundabout, secondary, sidelong, sideward, sideways, sidewise, skirting, subordinate, subsidiary, superficial

side *noun.* bottom, direction, division, elevation, face, flank, front, lee, loin, part, perimeter, posture, quarter, sector, stance, top, verge, view

sigh *verb.* blow, complain, cry, gasp, groan, howl, lament, moan, murmur, pant, respire, roar, sorrow, sough, wheeze, whine, whisper, whistle

sign *noun.* **1** beacon, divination, foreknowledge, gesture, hint, light, mark, omen, premonition, presage, signal, suggestion, symbol, trace, warning, wave, whistle, wink **2** badge, board, character, cipher, crest, device, document, ensign, guidepost, mark, notice, proof, representation, signboard, signpost, token, type, warning

signal *adjective.* arresting, characteristic, conspicuous, distinctive, distinguished, exceptional, individual, marked, memorable, momentous, noteworthy, noticeable, peculiar, pronounced, remarkable, salient, significant, striking

signal *noun.* alarm, alert, authorization, beacon, cue, flag, flare, gesture, go-ahead, high sign, indicator, mark, movement, nod, omen, sign, token, wink

significance *noun.* **1** acceptation, connotation, drift, force, heart, implication, import, kicker, meat, message, nub, point, punch line, purport, score, sense, stuff, understanding **2** authority, consequence, consideration, credit, excellence, gravity, import, influence, magnitude, matter, merit, moment, perfection, pith, prestige, relevance, virtue, weight

significant *adjective.* compelling, convincing, denoting, eloquent, expressing, expressive, forceful, heavy, important, meaning, momentous, powerful, pregnant, sound, suggestive, telling, valid, weighty

silence *noun.* blackout, calm, censorship, death, hush, inarticulateness, iron curtain, lull, muteness, peace, quiet, quietness, reserve, saturninity, secrecy, sleep, speechlessness, still

silence *verb.* clam, close up, cut off, dampen, dull, dumb, extinguish, gag, hush, ice, lull, mute, muzzle, quell, squash, still, subdue, suppress

silent *adjective.* bashful, checked, dumb, hushed, iced, incoherent, indistinct, mute, muted, noiseless, reserved, shy, speechless, still, unclear, uncommunicative, unheard, zipped

silly *adjective.* asinine, balmy, childish, fatuous, foolhardy, foolish, idiotic, illogical, immature, irrational, ludicrous, meaningless, nonsensical, pointless, preposterous, simple, stupid, vacuous

similar *adjective.* allied, analogous, companion, comparable, complementary, congruent, consonant, homogeneous, identical, kin, kindred, like, matching, parallel, reciprocal, related, twin, uniform

similarity *noun.* agreement, analogy, association, closeness, coincidence, collation, comparison, concordance, concurrence, harmony, homogeneity, identity, interrelation, parallel, proportion, relationship, sameness, semblance

simple *adjective.* **1** clean, effortless, facile, intelligible, light, lucid, mild, picnic, plain, quiet, royal, smooth, snap, transparent, understandable, uninvolved, unmistakable, vanilla **2** absolute, austere, clean, discreet, folksy, homely, mere, modest, natural, single, unadorned, unadulterated, unaffected, unalloyed, undecorated, unmixed, unqualified, vanilla **3** amateur, artless, basic, childish, direct, frank, green, guileless, honest, innocent, naive, natural, plain, sincere, square, stark, unaffected, undeniable **4** amateur, asinine, credulous, dense, dull, dumb, fatuous, feeble, foolish, green, idiotic, illiterate, inexpert, mindless, retarded, silly, soft, stupid

simplicity *noun.* candor, chastity, clarity, clearness, directness, ease, homogeneity, innocence, integrity, modesty, monotony, naturalness, obviousness, restraint, severity, singleness, uniformity, unity

simplify *verb.* analyze, break down, chasten, clarify, cut down, disentangle, disinvolve, explain, facilitate, interpret, lay out, make clear, make plain, nutshell, order, reduce, shorten, unscramble

simply *adverb.* artlessly, candidly, clearly, commonly, directly, easily, frankly, guilelessly, honestly, ingenuously, modestly, naturally, openly, ordinarily, quietly, sincerely, straightforwardly, unpretentiously

sin *noun.* anger, covetousness, damnation, debt, error, fault, guilt, immorality, imperfection, lust, offense, sinfulness, transgression, vice, violation, wickedness, wrong, wrongdoing

sin *verb.* backslide, break commandment, break law, cheat, commit crime, deviate, do wrong, err, fall, go astray, lapse, misbehave, misconduct, offend, sleep around, stray, trespass, wander

sincere *adjective.* actual, artless, candid, dear, devout, forthright, frank, guileless, heartfelt, honest, natural, open, outspoken, real, regular, righteous, square, true

sincerity *noun.* candor, earnestness, frankness, good faith, goodwill, heart, honor, impartiality, innocence, justice, probity, reliability, seriousness, singleness, truth, truthfulness, veracity, wholeheartedness

sing *verb.* buzz, carol, choir, duet, groan, hum, lullaby, pipe, roar, shout, solo, trill, tune, vocalize, wait, whine, whistle, yodel

singer *noun.* accompanist, artist, canary, chanter, chanteuse, choralist, chorister, crooner, diva, minstrel, musician, nightingale, soloist, songbird, vocalist, voice, warbler, yodeler

single *adjective.* **1** distinct, distinguished, exceptional, individual, indivisible, odd, one, peerless, private, simple, sole, solitary, specific, strange, undivided, unique, unmixed, unusual **2** bachelor, celibate, divorced, eligible, fancy-free, free, living alone, maiden, separated, sole, solo, spouseless, unattached, unfettered, unmarried, unwed, virgin

singular *adjective.* bizarre, conspicuous, curious, exceptional, noteworthy, odd, peculiar, prodigious, puzzling, queer, rare, remarkable, special, strange, unimaginable, unprecedented, unthinkable, unusual

sinister *adjective.* bad, baleful, baneful, disquieting, harmful, injurious, lowering, malevolent, malign, mischievous, obnoxious, ominous, pernicious, perverse, poisonous, unfavorable, unfortunate, woeful

sink *verb.* **1** bore, couch, descend, dig, droop, drop, ebb, fall, lower, plunge, ram, set, shipwreck, stab, stick, stoop, subside, wreck **2** decay, decline, decrease, descend, deteriorate, die, diminish, disintegrate, dwindle, fade, fail, flag, lessen, retrograde, rot, spoil, waste, weaken

sit *verb.* be seated, cover, ensconce, hunker, install, lie, park, perch, plop down, pose, posture, relax, remain, rest, seat, seat oneself, settle, squat

site *noun.* armpit, fix, ground, haunt, home, lay, layout, locale, locality, location, locus, plot, post, range, section, spot, station, where

situation *noun.* **1** direction, footing, latitude, locale, locality, location, locus, longitude, position, post, seat, setting, site, spot, stage, station, where, whereabouts **2** bargain, case, character, footing, hap, mode, picture, place, position, posture, scene, sphere, stage, standing, standpoint, state, station, status

sizable *adjective.* burly, considerable, decent, extensive, good, gross, husky, jumbo, massive, respectable, sensible, spacious, strapping, substantial, thumping, tidy, voluminous, whopping

size *noun.* amplitude, area, body, breadth, content, dimensions, enormity, highness, immensity, magnitude, measurement, proportion, range, scope, stature, stretch, substance, width

skeptical *adjective.* agnostic, cynical, dissenting, doubtful, doubting, dubious, from Missouri, hesitating, incredulous, leery, questioning, quizzical, scoffing, show-me, suspicious, unbelieving, unconvinced

sketch *noun.* account, blueprint, cartoon, compendium, configuration, description, design, figure, form, illustration, likeness, monograph, outline, piece, plan, rough, summary, version

sketch *verb.* blueprint, chalk, characterize, depict, describe, design, detail, diagram, lay out, line, outline, paint, plan, plot, portray, represent, skeleton, trace

skill *noun.* adroitness, aptitude, artistry, clout, command, competence, cunning, deftness, experience, goods, line, makings, profession, proficiency, prowess, skillfulness, talent, technique

skillful *adjective.* accomplished, adept, apt, brain, expert, good, handy, into, learned, old, practical, practiced, prepared, primed, sharp, smooth, versed, vet

skin *noun.* bark, case, crust, fell, film, fur, hide, hull, jacket, membrane, outside, parchment, peel, sheath, sheathing, slough, surface, vellum

skin *verb.* bare, bark, cast, cut off, excoriate, gall, graze, hull, pare, peel, remove, scale, scalp, scrape, shed, slough, strip, trim

skinny *adjective.* angular, bony, emaciated, gaunt, lank, lanky, lean, malnourished, rawboned, scraggy, scrawny, skeletal, skin-and-bone, slender, spare, twiggy, undernourished, weedy

slab *noun.* bar, billet, bit, board, boulder, chip, cutting, hunk, lump, muck, piece, plate, rod, slice, stave, stick, stone, strip

slack *adjective.* **1** baggy, dull, feeble, flexible, flimsy, inactive, inert, infirm, leisurely, limp, passive, quiet, relaxed, sloppy, sluggish, soft, supine, weak **2** careless, delinquent, derelict, dormant, dull, idle, inactive, inattentive, indolent, inert, lackadaisical, negligent, permissive, quiescent, quiet, sluggish, stagnant, tardy

slack *verb.* decrease, diminish, dodge, dog, dwindle, ease, featherbed, flag, idle, lessen, loose, moderate, neglect, reduce, relax, release, taper, tire

slaughter *verb.* butcher, crush, defeat, destroy, do in, exterminate, finish, maim, massacre, murder, overwhelm, rout, stick, thrash, torture, total, trounce, waste

slave *noun.* bondsman, captive, chattel, drudge, help, laborer, menial, peon, retainer, serf, servant, subservient, toiler, vassal, victim, worker, workhorse

slavery *noun.* captivity, chains, constraint, drudgery, enslavement, feudalism, grind, helotry, indenture, labor, menial labor, moil, peonage, restraint, serfhood, subjugation, toil, work

sleep *noun.* beddy-bye, blanket drill, coma, down, dream, dullness, lethargy, nap, nod, pad duty, repose, rest, sandman, siesta, slumber, torpidity, torpor, trance

sleep *verb.* bunk, crash, dream, drop off, fall out, flag, flop, hibernate, nap, nod, relax, repose, rest, retire, sack out, sack up, slumber, yawn

sleepy *adjective.* asleep, blah, drowsy, dull, heavy, hypnotic, inactive, lethargic, listless, out, quiet, sleeping, slow, sluggish, somnolent, soporific, torpid, yawning

slender *adjective.* **1** beanstalk, fine, insubstantial, lean, lithe, narrow, reedy, skeleton, skinny, slight, slim, spare, stick, svelte, tenuous, trim, twiggy, willowy **2** bare, feeble, flimsy, fragile, inconsiderable, little, meager, poor, remote, scant, scarce, shy, slight, slim, small, tenuous, wanting, weak

slice *verb.* carve, cut, dissect, divide, gash, hack, incise, pierce, segment, sever, shave, shred, slash, slit, split, strip, sunder, whack

slick *adjective.* adroit, cagey, canny, clever, deft, dexterous, glib, knowing, meretricious, plausible, professional, sharp, shrewd, skillful, sly, smooth, sophisticated, wise

slide *verb.* accelerate, coast, drift, drop, fall, flow, glide, launch, move, propel, sag, shove, skid, slip, slump, stream, thrust, veer

slight *adjective.* **1** fat, feeble, inconsiderable, insubstantial, meager, minor, modest, negligible, off, outside, petty, piddling, remote, slim, small, superficial, unimportant, weak **2** broomstick, dainty, delicate, feeble, flimsy, fragile, frail, light, reedy, shadow, skeleton, skinny, slender, slim, small, spare, stick, twiggy

slight *noun.* affront, brush-off, call-down, cold shoulder, contempt, cut, discourtesy, disdain, disregard, disrespect, inattention, indifference, kick, neglect, put-down, rebuff, rejection, snub

slight *verb.* affront, chill, cool, cut, despise, discount, disdain, disregard, fail, forget, ignore, insult, neglect, omit, overlook, reject, scorn, skip

slip *noun.* blooper, blunder, bobble, failure, fault, flap, flub, fluff, howler, lapse, misdeed, misstep, mistake, muff, omission, oversight, slip-up, trip

slope *noun.* abruptness, bank, bend, bevel, cant, declivity, deviation, diagonal, downgrade, hill, inclination, incline, lean, pitch, ramp, rise, tilt, tip

slope *verb.* angle, ascend, bank, bevel, cant, descend, dip, drop, fall, heel, incline, lean, list, pitch, rake, rise, tilt, tip

slow *adjective.* **1** creeping, dreamy, heavy, idle, imperceptible, indolent, lackadaisical, leaden, leisurely, listless, measured, moderate, negligent, plodding, reluctant, slack, sluggish, stagnant **2** belated, conservative, down, gradual, inactive, late, moderate, off, overdue, reduced, slack, sleepy, sluggish, stagnant, stiff, tame, tardy, unproductive

slow *verb.* brake, curb, cut back, decelerate, detain, hold up, lessen, moderate, procrastinate, qualify, reduce, reef, regulate, relax, retard, set back, stall, temper

slump *noun.* bust, crash, depreciation, depression, downtrend, downturn, drop, dumps, failure, fall, falloff, funk, reverse, rut, sag, slide, slip, trough

slump *verb.* bend, blight, crash, decay, deteriorate, droop, drop, fall, fall off, hunch, pitch, plunge, sag, sink, slide, slip, slouch, topple

small *adjective.* **1** baby, inconsequential, limited, meager, miniature, minute, modest, monkey, petite, petty, picayune, piddling, pitiful, poor, shrimp, slight, teensy, toy **2** bush, inconsiderable, ineffectual, inferior, insignificant, lesser, light, limited, lower, minor, minute, narrow, negligible, petty, secondary, set, trifling, trivial

smart *adjective.* **1** acute, adept, agile, alert, apt, astute, bold, brain, bright, canny, good, ingenious, keen, resourceful, sharp, skull, slick, wise **2** chic, dapper, dashing, elegant, exclusive, fashionable, fine, last word, latest thing, modish, natty, neat, snappy, spruce, swank, trendy, trim, well turned-out **3** active, bold, brazen, cracking, energetic, forward, good, jaunty, lively, nervy, pert, quick, saucy, scintillating, spanking, spirited, sprightly, vigorous

smell *noun.* aroma, bouquet, emanation, essence, flavor, fragrance, incense, perfume, redolence, savor, scent, spice, stench, stink, tang, trace, trail, whiff

smooth *adjective.* **1** creamy, effortless, flowing, flush, gentle, glossy, horizontal, invariable, polished, regular, shiny, soft, steady, still, tranquil, unbroken, uniform, velvety **2** agreeable, bland, civilized, courteous, courtly, dapper, facile, genial, glib, ingratiating, mellow, mild, persuasive, pleasant, polite, slick, smarmy, unctuous **3** clear, even, flatten, flush, gloss, grade, iron, lay, level, plane, polish, press, refine, round, sand, sleek, slick, varnish **4** allay, alleviate, appease, assuage, calm, comfort, cool, ease, extenuate, facilitate, iron out, mellow, mitigate, mollify, palliate, pat, soften, stroke

soak *verb.* absorb, assimilate, bathe, damp, dip, drink, drown, dunk, flood, merge, moisten, penetrate, permeate, soften, sop, steep, wash, water

sober *adjective.* **1** abstaining, abstinent, ascetic, calm, clear-headed, cold sober, continent, controlled, dry, moderate, nonindulgent, not drunk, restrained, sedate, self-possessed, serious, steady, temperate **2** calm, cold, collected, constrained, disciplined, drab, dull, grave, lucid, practical, rational, reasonable, sedate, severe, soft, sound, steady, subdued

social *adjective.* amusing, civil, collective, common, communal, communicative, community, convivial, cordial, gracious, gregarious, group, hospitable, organized, polished, polite, popular, societal

society *noun.* **1** association, camaraderie, civilization, commonwealth, community, companionship, company, comradeship, culture, fellowship, friendship, humanity, jungle, nation, people, population, public, world **2** alliance, association, brotherhood, clique, club, companionship, comradeship, corporation, fellowship, gang, group, guild, institute, institution, mob, outfit, syndicate, union **3** aristocracy, beautiful people, country set, elite, flower, gentry, glitterati, haut monde, high life, high society, main line, patriciate, quality, smart set, the 400, top drawer, upper crust, who's who

soft *adjective.* **1** cozy, creamy, delicate, elastic, fine, fleshy, flimsy, flowing, fluffy, limp, malleable, plastic, pliable, rounded, smooth, snug, spongy, velvety **2** balmy, diffuse, dim, dull, gentle, hazy, light, murmured, pale, pallid, pastel, smooth, subdued, temperate, tinted, twilight, understated, wan **3** affectionate, amiable, benign, courteous, effortless, gentle, gracious, indulgent, kind, kindly, liberal, permissive, pitying, sentimental, simple, spineless, tender, weak

soil *verb.* besmirch, contaminate, crumb, degrade, dirty, disgrace, foul, mess, muck, muddy, shame, smear, spatter, spoil, spot, stain, taint, tar

soldier *noun.* commando, conscript,

draftee, fighter, guerrilla, gunner, infantryman, marine, mercenary, officer, pilot, private, recruit, scout, trooper, veteran, volunteer, warrior

sole *adjective.* ace, exclusive, individual, lone, one, only, only one, particular, remaining, separate, single, singular, solitary, solo, spouseless, unique, unmarried, unwed

solemn *adjective.* **1** austere, deliberate, dignified, earnest, glum, grave, heavy, intense, moody, portentous, reflective, sedate, sober, somber, staid, stern, thoughtful, weighty **2** ceremonial, conventional, devotional, dignified, divine, formal, grand, grave, impressive, magnificent, majestic, momentous, overwhelming, plenary, religious, sanctified, stately, venerable

solid *adjective.* **1** concentrated, concrete, consolidated, dense, dimensional, firm, fixed, heavy, hulk, hunk, massed, rooted, secure, set, sound, strong, substantial, unshakable **2** constant, decent, genuine, good, pure, real, reliable, satisfactory, satisfying, sensible, sober, sound, stalwart, trustworthy, upright, upstanding, valid, worthy

solitary *adjective.* aloof, deserted, distant, individual, introverted, isolated, lonesome, only, remote, retired, secluded, single, singular, sole, solo, unattended, unique, withdrawn

solve *verb.* break, chill, clarify, construe, crack, decide, divine, do, enlighten, illuminate, interpret, lick, ravel, reason, resolve, settle, unlock, work

somebody *noun.* anybody, big shot, big wheel, bigwig, celebrity, dignitary, heavyweight, household name, name, notable, one, personage, public figure, so-and-so, some person, someone, star, whoever

somewhat *adverb.* a little, adequately, considerably, fairly, far, incompletely, insignificantly, kind of, moderately, partially, pretty, quite, rather, significantly, slightly, some, something, well

song *noun.* anthem, ballad, canticle, carol, chorale, chorus, expression, lyric, melody, number, piece, poem, psalm, rock, round, shanty, tune, vocal

soon *adverb.* before long, directly, early, ere long, expeditiously, fast, fleetly, hastily, instantly, posthaste, presently, promptly, pronto, quick, quickly, rapidly, shortly, speedily

sophisticated *adjective.* adult, bored, cynical, hip, into, jaded, mature, on to, practical, practiced, seasoned, sharp, skeptical, smooth, studied, suave, svelte, swinging

sore *adjective.* **1** aching, acute, afflicted, annoying, bruised, burned, distressing, extreme, inflamed, irritated, pained, reddened, severe, sharp, tender, ulcerated, unpleasant, vexatious **2** afflicted, aggrieved, annoyed, annoying, critical, distressing, grieving, indignant, irritated, pained, pressing, resentful, stung, troubled, upset, urgent, vexed, weighty

sorrow *noun.* affliction, blow, catastrophe, distress, hardship, heartbreak, misery, misfortune, mourning, pain, rain, regret, repentance, rue, trial, tribulation, trouble, upset

sorry *adjective.* abject, base, cheap, contemptible, deplorable, disgraceful, distressing, insignificant, miserable, piteous, pitiable, pitiful, poor, scurvy, small, unimportant, worthless, wretched

sort *noun.* array, battery, body, category, denomination, description, family, group, kind, likes, number, parcel, quality, race, set, stamp, suite, variety

sort *verb.* catalogue, choose, class, classify, comb, distribute, divide, file, grade, group, order, peg, pick, pigeonhole, riddle, screen, separate, winnow

sound *adjective.* **1** effectual, entire, firm, fit, flawless, hale, hearty, right, safe, sane, solid, sturdy, substantial, total, uninjured, vibrant, virile, whole **2** consequent, convincing, deep, exact, faultless, flawless, intellectual, profound, proper, rational, reasonable, responsible, satisfactory, sensible, solid, true, valid, wise **3** fly, hold up, kosher, legal, loyal, orthodox, proper, proven, received, reputable, safe, sanctioned, secure, signify, solid, solvent, true, valid

sound *noun.* accent, din, harmony, intonation, modulation, music, pitch, racket, report, resonance, reverberation, ringing, softness, sonority, static, tone, vibration, voice

sound *verb.* boom, chatter, clang, clap, echo, emit, explode, murmur, patter, rattle, roar, shout, shriek, smash, squawk, thump, thunder, whine

source *noun.* antecedent, author, birthplace, commencement, derivation, determinant, expert, fountain, fountainhead, informant, onset, opening, origination, rise, root, specialist, start, supply

sovereign *adjective.* absolute, autonomous, chief, directing, effectual, efficacious, guiding, imperial, independent, majestic, master, predominant, prevalent, regal, royal, ruling, supreme, unlimited

space *noun.* amplitude, area, arena, breadth, distance, expanse, headroom, leeway, omission, range, scope, sphere, spot, stretch, territory, tract, turf, zone

spacious *adjective.* ample, boundless, endless, enormous, expansive, extended, generous, great, immense, infinite, large, limitless, roomy, sizable, vast, voluminous, wide, widespread

spare *adjective.* **1** additional, backup, emergency, free, in reserve, in store, leftover, odd, option, over, reserve, supererogatory, superfluous, supernumerary, surplus, unoccupied, unused, unwanted **2** angular, bony, gaunt, lanky, lean, meager, modest, poor, rangy, scant, shadow, skinny, slight, slim, sparse, stick, stingy, wiry **3** accommodate with, afford, allow, bestow, dispense with, do without, give, grant, lay aside, let have, pinch, relinquish, salt away, save, scrape, scrimp, short, stint **4** absolve, bail out, be merciful, discharge, dispense, excuse, exempt, leave, let go, let off, pardon, pity, privilege from, refrain from, release, relent, save bacon, spring

spark *noun.* atom, beam, fire, flare, flicker, gleam, glint, glitter, glow, hint, jot, nucleus, ray, scrap, sparkle, spit, trace, vestige

speak *verb.* **1** articulate, assert, bull, chew, convey, deliver, gab, gas, jaw, mouth, murmur, pronounce, rap, shout, sound, tell, vocalize, voice **2** argue, back channel, declaim, descant, discourse, get across, give lecture, harangue, hold forth, pitch, plead, prelect, recite, sermonize, spiel, spout, stump, talk

special *adjective.* appropriate, certain, characteristic, chief, distinctive, exceptional, gala, important, individual, limited, peculiar, proper, set, significant, specialized, specific, unique, unusual

specialist *noun.* ace, adept, authority, connoisseur, consultant, devotee, doctor, guru, high priest, master, pro, professional, sage, savant, scholar, technician, veteran, virtuoso

specific *adjective.* categorical, characteristic, definitive, distinct, distinguishing, exact, explicit, express, individual, limited, outright, peculiar, restricted, set, sole, specialized, unambiguous, unique

specifically *adverb.* accurately, categorically, characteristically, clearly, concretely, correctly, definitely, distinctively, especially, exactly, explicitly, expressly, individually, minutely, peculiarly, pointedly, respectively, specially

specify *verb.* blueprint, decide, define, detail, establish, finger, fix, instance, inventory, lay out, list, mention, name, peg, set, settle, specialize, tag

specimen *noun.* case, copy, embodiment, exemplar, exhibit, illustration, individual, instance, model, part, representation, sample, sampling, sort, species, type, unit, variety

speck *noun.* atom, defect, dot, fault, flaw, fleck, grain, iota, mark, mite, modicum, molecule, particle, shred, spot, stain, trace, whit

spectacle *noun.* comedy, curiosity, demonstration, display, event, marvel, movie, pageant, parade, production, representation, scene, show, sight, spectacular, tableau, view, wonder

spectacular *adjective.* astonishing, astounding, breathtaking, daring, dazzling, fabulous, impressive, magnificent, marked, marvelous, miraculous, prodigious, remarkable, staggering, striking, stunning, theatrical, wondrous

spectator *noun.* beholder, bystander, deadhead, eyewitness, fan, gazer, looker, moviegoer, observer, onlooker, perceiver, seer, showgoer, stander-by, theatergoer, viewer, watcher, witness

speculate *verb.* conjecture, consider, contemplate, deliberate, dope, figure, guess, hypothesize, muse, read, reason, reflect, review, scheme, study, suppose, weigh, wonder

speech *noun.* **1** accent, dialect, dialogue, diction, enunciation, expressing, gab, gas, idiom, intercourse, jargon, language, parlance, prose, tone, tongue, utterance, voice **2** appeal, commentary, debate, disquisition, invocation, keynote, lecture, opus, oration, oratory, paper, parlance, parley, pitch, recitation, salutation, sermon, stump

speed *noun.* acceleration, activity, agility, alacrity, briskness, celerity, clip, dispatch, eagerness, gait, haste, lick, pace, rapidity, readiness, rustle, ton, velocity

speed *verb.* advance, aid, assist, barrel, belt, boost, career, dispatch, flash, fly, further, gallop, hasten, promote, quicken, race, spring, urge

spell *noun.* **1** bit, bout, course, hitch, interlude, intermission, patch, period, relay, season, shift, stint, streak, stretch, time, tour, trick, turn **2** allure, amulet, bewitching, charm, enchanting, enchantment, fascination, glamour, hex, incantation, jinx, magic, mumbo-jumbo, rune, sorcery, trance, voodoo, whack

spend *verb.* **1** absorb, allocate, bestow, blow, confer, consume, contribute, defray, donate, drop, employ, exhaust, give, invest, lavish, lay out, settle, waste **2** consume, drift, employ, fill, fool around, fritter away, go, idle, kill, laze, let pass, misuse, occupy, pass, put in, squander, waste, while away

spent *adjective.* bleary, blown, dissipated, done, exhausted, gone, hacked, limp, lost, prostrate, shattered, shot, used, wasted, weakened, weary, whacked, worn out

sphere *noun.* department, domain, dominion, employment, function, level, orbit, pale, precinct, province, range, realm, scope, station, terrain, territory, turf, zone

spice *noun.* aroma, color, excitement, fragrance, gusto, guts, kick, pep, piquancy, relish, salt, savor, scent, seasoning, tang, zap, zest, zip

spiral *adjective.* circling, circular, circumvolutory, cochlear, coiled, corkscrew, curled, helical, radial, rolled, screw-shaped, scrolled, tortile, voluted, whorled, winding, wound

spirit *noun.* animation, ardor, complexion, energy, enterprise, enthusiasm, grit, humor, life, mettle, nerve, outlook, psyche, quality, substance, temper, vigor, will

spirited *adjective.* alert, animated, avid, chipper, courageous, dauntless, eager, energetic, fiery, intrepid, keen, mettlesome, passionate, resolute, rocking, sharp, snappy, valiant

spiritual *adjective.* airy, devotional, discarnate, disembodied, divine, ethereal, ghostly, holy, immaterial, incorporeal, intangible, metaphysical, nonphysical, otherworldly, platonic, pure, refined, sacred

spite *noun.* animosity, antipathy, contempt, despite, enmity, gall, grudge, hate, hatred, malevolence, malice, pique, rancor, resentment, revenge, spleen, vengeance, venom

spite *verb.* annoy, begrudge, beset, crab, cramp style, gall, get even, grudge, harass, harm, hurt, needle, nettle, persecute, pique, provoke, put out, vex

splendid *adjective.* **1** baroque, costly, dazzling, elegant, expensive, fat, flamboyant, glowing, gorgeous, impressive, lavish, magnificent, marvelous, ornate, resplendent, sumptuous, superb, swanky **2** distinguished, divine, exceptional, exquisite, fine, glorious, heroic, impressive, magnificent, marvelous, premium, proud, remarkable, resplendent, royal, supreme, unsurpassed, wonderful

splendor *noun.* brightness, brilliance, ceremony, dazzle, display, effulgence, grandeur, luster, magnificence, majesty, pageant, pomp, radiance, renown, richness, show, solemnity, spectacle

split *noun.* **1** breach, chasm, cleavage,

cleft, crack, damage, division, gap, rent, rift, rip, rupture, separation, slash, slit, tear **2** alienation, breach, break, break-up, difference, discord, disruption, dissension, divergence, division, estrangement, fissure, fracture, partition, rent, rift, rupture, schism **3** branch, break, burst, crack, disjoin, divide, divorce, fork, hack, isolate, open, part, rend, rip, separate, sever, splinter, sunder **4** allocate, allot, apportion, carve up, distribute, divide, divvy, divvy up, dole out, go even-steven, go fifty-fifty, go halvesies, halve, parcel out, partition, share, slice, slice up

spoken *adjective.* announced, articulate, communicated, expressed, lingual, mentioned, oral, phonetic, phonic, said, sonant, told, traditional, unwritten, uttered, verbal, viva voce, voiced

sponsor *noun.* adherent, advocate, angel, benefactor, fairy godmother, godparent, grubstaker, guarantor, lady bountiful, mainstay, patron, promoter, Santa Claus, sugar daddy, supporter, surety, sustainer, underwriter

spontaneous *adjective.* automatic, casual, down, free, impetuous, impromptu, improvised, involuntary, irresistible, natural, offhand, simple, unavoidable, unconscious, unpremeditated, unsophisticated, voluntary, willing

sporadic *adjective.* desultory, few, fitful, hit-or-miss, infrequent, intermittent, irregular, isolated, occasional, on-again-off-again, random, rare, scarce, scattered, seldom, semioccasional, spotty, uncommon

sport *noun.* **1** amusement, athletics, ball, diversion, exercise, frolic, fun, gaiety, game, games, grins, hoopla, laughs, pastime, picnic, play, pleasure, recreation **2** antics, badinage, banter, derision, escapade, frolic, fun, jest, jesting, laughter, merriment, mirth, mockery, nonsense, raillery, scorn, teasing, trifling

sporting *adjective.* antic, considerate, fair, game, gay, generous, gentlemanly, jaunty, joyous, kittenish, lively, merry, mischievous, reasonable, rollicking, sprightly, square, wild

spot *noun.* **1** atom, blemish, blot, dram, drop, flaw, iota, jot, mite, molecule, nip, particle, pinch, shot, speck, stain, taint, whit **2** digs, dump, hole, joint, layout, locality, locus, pad, place, position, post, roof, seat, section, sector, site, station, where **3** besmirch, blot, dapple, dirty, dot, fleck, marble, mottle, pepper, soil, spatter, speck, splash, stain, streak, stripe, stud, taint **4** detect, determinate, diagnose, discern, discover, distinguish, encounter, find, finger, identify, locate, observe, pinpoint, place, recognize, sight, trace, track

spread *noun.* advance, advancement, compass, development, diffusion, dispersion, dissemination, enlargement, extent, period, proliferation, radiation, range, reach, scope, span, stretch, transmission

spread *verb.* **1** array, coat, cover, diffuse, dilate, enlarge, extend, flatten, flow, level, lie, mushroom, open, prepare, set, spray, stretch, widen **2** abroad, advertise, blazon, broadcast, cast, circulate, declare, diffuse, distribute, make known, proclaim, propagate, publish, radiate, scatter, shed, sow, transmit

spring *verb.* appear, arise, arrive, birth, come, derive, descend, emerge, flow, grow, head, issue, loom, mushroom, proceed, rise, start, stem

sprinkle *verb.* baptize, dampen, dot, dust, mist, moisten, pepper, powder, rain, shake, shower, smear, speck, spit, spot, spray, squirt, stud

sprinkling *noun.* admixture, dash, dust, dusting, few, handful, lick, mixture, powdering, scattering, several, smattering, sprinkle, strain, taste, tinge, touch, trace

spur *noun.* activation, catalyst, goad, goose, impetus, impulse, incentive, incitation, inducement, motivation, motive, needle, prick, stimulant, stimulus, trigger, turn-on, urge

spur *verb.* animate, arouse, awaken, favor, goad, instigate, press, prick, prod, prompt, propel, push, rally, sic, spark, stir, trigger, urge

spy *noun.* agent, beagle, detective, emissary, investigator, lookout, mole, observer, operative, patrol, picket, plant, scout, secret service, sleeper, sleuth, snoop, spook

spy *verb.* case, discover, eyeball, heel, hound, notice, observe, pry, scout, search, shadow, snoop, spot, stag, tail, trail, view, watch

square *adjective.* decent, equal, equitable, ethical, even, fair, genuine, impartial, impersonal, just, nonpartisan, objective, sporting, straight, straightforward, unbiased, unprejudiced, upright

square *verb.* balance, bribe, buy, buy off, clear, clear up, corrupt, discharge, fix, have, liquidate, pay, pay up, quit, rig, satisfy, settle, tamper with

squeeze *verb.* bear, clip, clutch, compress, contract, crush, grip, jam, jostle, nip, pack, press, ram, squash, stuff, throttle, thrust, wring

stability *noun.* assurance, balance, constancy, determination, durability, endurance, establishment, firmness, immobility, maturity, permanence, rock, security, soundness, steadiness, strength, support, toughness

stable *adjective.* balanced, calm, fixed, invariable, permanent, resistant, resolute, secure, set, solid, sound, stationary, steady, strong, substantial, sure, unalterable, unchangeable

staff *noun.* agents, assistants, cadre, cast, crew, deputies, faculty, force, help, officers, organization, personnel, savages, shop, slaves, teachers, team, workers

stage *noun.* **1** date, degree, division, footing, grade, lap, leg, length, moment, notch, period, phase, plane, point, rung, standing, status, step **2** arena, boards, dais, drama, frame, limelight, play, scaffold, scaffolding, scene, scenery, set, setting, show business, spotlight, staging, theater, wings

stake *verb.* back, capitalize, chance, finance, gamble, game, hazard, imperil, jeopardize, lay, play, pledge, put, put on, risk, set, venture, wager

stall *verb.* arrest, brake, check, die, fence, filibuster, halt, hedge, interrupt, quibble, shut down, stand, stand still, stay, still, suspend, tarry, temporize

stamp *verb.* brand, cast, drive, engrave, etch, fix, grave, hammer, impress, infix, inscribe, letter, mark, mold, offset, pound, press on, print

stand *noun.* base, board, booth, bracket, counter, dais, frame, gantry, grandstand, place, platform, rack, rank, staging, stall, station, support, table

stand *verb.* **1** be located, be valid, belong, continue, endure, fill, halt, hold, last, obtain, occupy, pause, prevail, remain, rest, stay, stop, take up **2** abide, bear, brook, cope, experience, handle, hang in, hold, last, suffer, support, sustain, swallow, take, tolerate, undergo, weather, withstand

standard *adjective.* accepted, average, basic, common, definitive, everyday, general, normal, official, orthodox, popular, prevailing, regulation, set, stock, typical, usual, vanilla

standard *noun.* average, axiom, canon, code, criterion, fundamental, grade, law, median, mirror, model, paradigm, requirement, rule, sample, test, touchstone, yardstick

standing *noun.* character, consequence, credit, dignity, eminence, estimation, footing, place, prestige, reputation, repute, situation, slot, state, station, stature, status, term

star *noun.* box office, celeb, celebrity, draw, face, favorite, headliner, hero, idol, lead, leading lady, leading man, luminary, monster, name, starlet, superstar

stare *verb.* beam, bore, eagle eye, eye, eyeball, fix, focus, gaze, glare, goggle, gun, look, peer, pin, pipe, rivet, rubber, watch

stark *adjective.* **1** abrupt, bare, blasted, blessed, blunt, consummate, downright, entire, firm, flagrant, gross, palpable, pure, severe, sheer, simple, stiff, unalloyed **2** austere, barren, bleak, clear, cold, depressing, dreary, forsaken, grim, nude, raw, severe, solitary, stripped, unadorned, vacant, vacuous, void

start *noun.* alpha, birth, bow, commencement, derivation, exit, foundation, inauguration, initiation, kickoff, leaving, onset, opening, origin, outset, source, spring, takeoff

start *verb.* **1** activate, appear, arise, arouse, create, depart, embark, found, institute, issue, kick off, launch, leave, light, open, pioneer, rise, set up **2** blanch, blench, bolt, bounce, bound, buck, dart, draw back, jerk, jump, leap, recoil, shrink, shy, spring, startle, twitch, wince

state *noun.* case, category, element, estate, eventuality, footing, form, humor, occasion, outlook, pass, phase, posture, predicament, proviso, station, stipulation, time

state *verb.* affirm, articulate, assert, deliver, describe, enunciate, express, give, interpret, pitch, pronounce, put, recount, relate, speak, tell, vent, voice

statement *noun.* account, acknowledgment, aside, charge, description, dictum, mention, narrative, observation, presentation, proclamation, profession, recital, recitation, rundown, utterance, vent, voice

static *adjective.* constant, fixed, immovable, inactive, inert, latent, passive, rigid, stable, stagnant, stalled, stationary, sticky, still, stopped, stuck, unchanging, unvarying

station *noun.* **1** base, depot, house, location, locus, main office, outpost, place, position, post, seat, site, situation, spot, stop, terminal, where, whereabouts **2** business, calling, caste, character, class, duty, employment, estate, footing, grade, level, occupation, order, post, service, sphere, state, stratum

statue *noun.* bronze, bust, cast, effigy, figure, icon, image, ivory, likeness, marble, memorial, piece, representation, sculpture, simulacrum, statuary, statuette, torso

stature *noun.* competence, consequence, development, dignity, elevation, eminence, position, prestige, prominence, qualification, quality, size, state, station, status, value, virtue, worth

status *noun.* character, consequence, degree, dignity, distinction, eminence, footing, grade, mode, prestige, prominence, quality, renown, stage, state, station, stature, worth

stay *verb.* **1** bide, bunk, delay, endure, halt, hang in, last, linger, nest, pause, procrastinate, remain, reside, respite, roost, settle, sweat, tarry **2** arrest, check, curb, defer, delay, detain, discontinue, halt, hold, interrupt, obstruct, postpone, prevent, prorogue, shelve, stall, stop, suspend

steady *adjective.* **1** abiding, certain, constant, durable, enduring, firm, fixed, immovable, regular, safe, set, solid, substantial, sure, unchangeable, unchanging, uniform, unqualified **2** ceaseless, confirmed, consistent, constant, eternal, even, faithful, habitual, incessant, nonstop, persistent, regular, stable, unbroken, uniform, uninterrupted, unremitting, unvarying **3** ardent, balanced, calm, constant, cool, dependable, intense, loyal, poised, reliable, reserved, resolute, sedate, sensible, serene, settle, staid, staunch

steel *verb.* animate, brace, buck up, cheer, embolden, encourage, fortify, gird, grit teeth, harden, hearten, inspirit, nerve, prepare, rally, ready, reinforce, strengthen

steep *adjective.* abrupt, arduous, breakneck, declivitous, elevated, erect, headlong, high, lifted, lofty, perpendicular, precipitate, precipitous, raised, sharp, sheer, sideling

steep *verb.* bathe, damp, drench, fill, imbue, impregnate, ingrain, invest, marinate, moisten, permeate, saturate, soak, sodden, sop, submerge, suffuse, waterlog

steer *verb.* beacon, captain, conduct, control, direct, drive, govern, helm, lead, pilot, point, route, run, see, shepherd, show, skipper, take over

step *noun.* act, advancement, deed, expedient, grade, level, maneuver, motion, move, notch, phase, procedure, proceeding, process, remove, rung, stage, start

step *verb.* advance, ascend, dance, descend, go forward, hoof, mince, move backward, pace, prance, skip, stride, tiptoe, traipse, tread, trip, troop, walk

sterile *adjective.* antiseptic, arid, aseptic, bare, barren, bleak, clean, effete, fallow, fruitless, futile, gaunt, impotent, sanitary, septic, sterilized, unprofitable, vain

stern *adjective.* ascetic, austere, authoritarian, cruel, disciplinary, forbidding, frowning, grim, hard, hard shell, mule, rigid, rough, severe, steely, stiff, strict, stubborn

stick *noun.* bar, baton, billet, birch, board, branch, cane, club, rod, rule, slab, staff, stake, stave, stem, strip, switch, wand

stick *verb.* **1** affix, attach, cement, clog, cohere, fix, fuse, glue, join, linger, lodge, paste, persist, remain, snag, solder, stay, unite **2** dig, drive, gore, impale, insert, jab, penetrate, pierce, pin, plunge, prod, ram, run, sink, spear, stab, thrust, transfix

sticky *adjective.* awkward, delicate, embarrassing, formidable, hairy, hard, heavy, knotty, laborious, nasty, operose, painful, rough, rugged, strenuous, thorny, tricky, unpleasant

stiff *adjective.* **1** chilled, contracted, firm, fixed, frozen, hardened, mechanical, refractory, resistant, rheumatic, rigid, set, solid, starched, starchy, steely, tense, thickened **2** artificial, austere, chilly, cold, constrained, intractable, labored, mannered, obstinate, pompous, prim, starchy, stilted, strong, stubborn, uneasy, ungainly, unnatural **3** austere, cruel, drastic, exact, excessive, extravagant, hard, heavy, immoderate, inexorable, oppressive, powerful, severe, sharp, steep, strict, strong, unconscionable

still *adjective.* deathly, fixed, halcyon, hushed, iced, inert, lifeless, motionless, noiseless, pacific, placid, restful, serene, smooth, stagnant, static, stationary, tranquil

still *verb.* alleviate, arrest, balm, calm, cork, fix, gag, lull, muzzle, settle, shut down, silence, slack, smooth, soothe, squash, stall, subdue

stimulus *noun.* boost, cause, charge, encouragement, fillip, fireworks, flash, goad, impetus, impulse, incentive, inducement, kick, motive, needle, stimulation, sting, whip

stir *noun.* activity, ado, agitation, bustle, din, disorder, disquiet, excitement, ferment, flurry, fuss, hoopla, hubbub, movement, racket, row, uproar, whirlwind

stir *verb.* affect, agitate, arouse, awaken, craze, inspire, motivate, move, prompt, provoke, quicken, rally, set, spark, thrill, touch, urge, wake

stock *adjective.* banal, basic, common, conventional, dull, formal, hackneyed, normal, ordinary, regular, routine, set, standard, stereotyped, traditional, trite, typical, usual

stock *noun.* **1** array, articles, assets, assortment, backlog, cache, choice, commodities, fund, goods, inventory, produce, range, reserve, selection, supply, variety, wares **2** background, breed, clan, extraction, family, folk, forebears, house, kin, kindred, line, lineage, pedigree, race, species, strain, type, variety

stock *verb.* accumulate, amass, carry, equip, fill, furnish, gather, handle, have, keep, lay in, provide, provision, put away, reserve, save, sell, store

stomach *noun.* abdomen, bag, balcony, basement, basket, bay, corporation, gut, inside, insides, keg, kitchen, maw, pail, pantry, paunch, pot, tank

stomach *verb.* abide, bear, bear with, brook, digest, go, hang in, hang on, live with, reconcile oneself, resign oneself, stand, submit to, suffer, swallow, sweat it, take, tolerate

stop *noun.* bar, blockade, break, break off, cessation, closing, conclusion, cutoff, ending, freeze, halt, impediment, lull, plug, roadblock, stay, stoppage, wall

stop *verb.* **1** break, break off, conclude, drop, end, finish, halt, hold, kill, pause, run down, scrub, shut down, stall, stand, stay, tarry, wind up **2** bar, break, can, clog, cut off, disrupt, gag, interrupt, muzzle, plug, repress, seal, silence, stall, stay, stem, still, suspend

store *noun.* **1** abundance, backlog, cache, fountain, fund, inventory, lot, mine, plenty, provision, reserve, reservoir, spring, stock, supply, treasure, wares, wealth **2** arsenal, bank, barn, box, cache, conservatory, depot, magazine, pantry, repository, reservoir, stable, storehouse, storeroom, tank, treasury, vault, warehouse **3** boutique, chain store, discount house, discount store, drugstore, emporium, five-

and-dime, grocery store, market, mart, outlet, repository, shop, showroom, stand, storehouse, super, supermarket

store *verb.* amass, bank, bin, bottle, cache, can, cumulate, freeze, garner, hide, husband, keep, park, put, save, squirrel, treasure, warehouse

storm *noun.* **1** blast, blizzard, blow, cloudburst, disturbance, downpour, gale, gust, hurricane, monsoon, sheep storm, snowstorm, squall, tempest, tornado, twister, whirlwind, windstorm **2** agitation, attack, barrage, bustle, clamor, furor, hysteria, offensive, onset, onslaught, perturbation, rage, roar, row, stir, temper, upheaval, violence

storm *verb.* assail, beset, bluster, charge, complain, drizzle, drop, fly, howl, pour, rage, rain, rip, roar, spit, strike, tear, thunder

stormy *adjective.* blustery, boisterous, cold, damp, dirty, foul, frigid, murky, pouring, raging, roaring, savage, torrid, turbulent, violent, wet, wild, windy

story *noun.* allegory, anecdote, beat, chronicle, clothesline, description, fable, fiction, gag, history, myth, narrative, recital, romance, sequel, serial, version, yarn

straight *adjective.* **1** erect, horizontal, invariable, level, lineal, linear, plumb, rectilinear, right, running, smooth, solid, square, successive, true, unbent, unbroken, unrelieved **2** accurate, authentic, blunt, candid, categorical, decent, fair, forthright, frank, good, moral, outright, plain, reliable, respectable, summary, unqualified, upright

straight *adverb.* at once, away, dead, direct, directly, due, exactly, forthwith, instantly, lineally, now, point-blank, right, right away, straightaway, straightforwardly, straightly, undeviatingly

straighten *verb.* align, arrange, compose, correct, even, level, make straight, neaten, order, put perpendicular, put straight, put upright, smarten up, tidy, uncurl, unfold, unravel, untwist

straightforward *adjective.* **1** candid, direct, forthright, frank, guileless, honorable, level, mellow, open, outspoken, plain, sincere, straight, truthful, undisguised, upright, upstanding, veracious **2** apparent, clear, direct, distinct, easy, elementary, evident, manifest, palpable, patent, plain, routine, straight, through, unambiguous, uncomplicated, undemanding, uninterrupted

strain *noun.* **1** ache, anxiety, bruise, brunt, burden, constriction, effort, endeavor, exertion, injury, jerk, pressure, pull, stress, stretch, struggle, tension, twist **2** hint, humor, manner, mind, shade, spirit, streak, style, suspicion, temper, tendency, tinge, tone, touch, trace, trait, vein, way **3** distend, distort, draw tight, drive, exert, extend, fatigue, pull, push, rack, task, tax, tear, tighten, tire, twist, weaken, wrench **4** bear down, dig, endeavor, exert, grind, hump, hustle, labor, moil, plug, push, scratch, strive, struggle, sweat, toll, try, tug

strained *adjective.* artificial, awkward, choked, constrained, embarrassed, false, farfetched, labored, pretended, stiff, taut, tense, tight, uneasy, unglued, unnatural, wired, wreck

strange *adjective.* **1** astonishing, astounding, bizarre, exceptional, fantastic, funny, irregular, marvelous, odd, off, offbeat, peculiar, perplexing, queer, rare, remarkable, unusual, wonderful **2** alien, apart, awkward, detached, external, foreign, irrelevant, isolated, lost, new, novel, outside, remote, romantic, unexplored, unknown, unrelated, without

stranger *noun.* foreigner, guest, immigrant, incomer, intruder, itinerant person, migrant, new arrival, new girl, newcomer, outsider, squatter, transient, unknown, visitor, wanderer, wetback

strategy *noun.* angle, blueprint, cunning, design, layout, maneuvering, method, plan, planning, procedure, program, proposition, racket, scheme, story, subtlety, system, tactics

stray *verb.* be abandoned, be lost, deviate, drift, err, gad, get lost, go amiss, go astray, ramble, range, roam, rove, straggle, swerve, traipse, turn, wander off

streak *noun.* bar, beam, element, hint, layer, line, ray, ridge, rule, shade, slash, stream, strip, stripe, suggestion, suspicion, touch, trace

stream *noun.* beck, branch, brook, burn, course, creek, current, drift, flood, flow, race, rill, run, rush, spate, surge, tide, torrent

stream *verb.* cascade, continue, course, emerge, emit, flood, glide, gush, issue, pour, roll, run, shed, sluice, spill, spout, spurt, surge

street *noun.* boulevard, bricks, court, cove, drag, groove, lane, parkway, passage, pavement, route, row, stroll, terrace, thoroughfare, trail, turf, way

strength *noun.* **1** body, clout, durability, energy, firmness, fortitude, health, kick, muscle, nerve, physique, power, security, soundness, substance, tenacity, toughness, vigor **2** beef, clout, concentration, depth, effectiveness, efficacy, energy, extremity, fervor, kick, potency, power, resolution, sock, spirit, vehemence, vigor, virtue **3** anchor, asset, body, burden, connection, core, gist, guts, in, license, pith, purport, security, sense, substance, succor, weight, wire

strengthen *verb.* **1** animate, bloom, brace, cheer, consolidate, flower, fortify, gird, nerve, prepare, prosper, rally, refresh, restore, steel, temper, thrive, uphold **2** bolster, build up, enhance, enlarge, extend, fortify, justify, mount, multiply, reinforce, renew, restore, rise, set up, steel, temper, tone, wax

strenuous *adjective.* **1** arduous, demanding, effortful, energy-consuming, exhausting, hard, herculean, laborious, mean, operose, taxing, toilful, toilsome, tough, tough going, uphill, uphill battle, wicked **2** active, aggressive, ardent, bold, determined, dynamic, eager, earnest, lusty, persistent, red-blooded, resolute, spirited, strong, tireless, vigorous, vital, zealous

stress *noun.* affliction, alarm, burden, clutch, crunch, disquiet, draw, dread, ferment, hardship, impatience, intensity, passion, pull, spring, stretch, trauma, trial

stress *verb.* accent, accentuate, belabor, dwell on, feature, harp on, headline, italicize, limelight, make emphatic, play up, point up, repeat, rub in, spot, spotlight, underline, underscore

stretch *noun.* amplitude, area, branch, breadth, compass, dimension, distance, extent, length, orbit, proliferation, range, reach, region, scope, span, spread, tract

stretch *verb.* cover, crane, draw, expand, grow, open, overlap, pad, prolong, pull, rack, range, repose, span, spread, strain, tighten, widen

strict *adjective.* **1** austere, disciplinary, dour, exacting, firm, forbidding, grim, hard, oppressive, puritanical, rigid, scrupulous, set, severe, square, stern, stuffy, tough **2** absolute, close, complete, exact, faithful, just, meticulous, particular, perfect, precise, religious, right, scrupulous, total, true, utter, veracious, veridical

strike *verb.* **1** beat, box, buffet, clash, clip, clout, crash, cuff, knock, pop, pound, slap, slug, smack, thrust, thump, touch, wallop **2** affect, be plausible, carry, come to, dawn on, get, have semblance, hit, impress, influence, inspire, look, move, reach, register, seem, sway, touch **3** achieve, arrive at, attain, catch, chance upon, come across, come upon, dig up, discover, effect, encounter, light upon, reach, seize, stumble across, take, uncover, unearth **4** affect, afflict, assail, assault, attack, beset, harrow, hit, invade, martyr, rack, set upon, smite, storm, torment, torture, try, wring **5** arbitrate, boycott, hold out, mediate, mutiny, negotiate, picket, quiet, resist, revolt, sick in, sick out, sit down, sit in, slow down, stick out, stop, tie up

striking *adjective.* arresting, boss, compelling, conspicuous, dazzling, distinguished, impressive, jazzy, lofty, noticeable, powerful, remarkable, staggering, startling, surprising, unusual, wonderful, wondrous

strip *noun.* band, banding, bar, belt, billet, bit, layer, ribbon, rod, section, segment, shred, slab, slip, stick, stripe, tape, tongue

strip *verb.* displace, disrobe, divest, expose, gut, lift, peel, plunder, remove, rob, scale, shed, skin, spoil, take off, tear, uncover, withdraw

strive *verb.* aim, assay, attempt, bear down, compete, contend, endeavor, fight, offer, push, scramble, strain, struggle, sweat, tackle, toil, tug, work

strong *adjective.* **1** able, energetic, firm, fixed, hale, hearty, heavy, mighty, muscular, powerful, secure, sinewy, solid, sound, steady, substantial, tenacious, virile **2** aggressive, clear, courageous, dedicated, deep, eager, fervent, fierce, firm, handful, independent, keen, resolute, severe, tenacious, uncompromising, vehement, wicked **3** clear, compelling, convincing, firm, hard, marked, mighty, overpowering, persuasive, powerful, secure, sharp, sound, stiff, telling, trenchant, unmistakable, urgent **4** biting, bold, bright, concentrated, dazzling, fetid, hard, heady, high, hot, intoxicating, piquant, powerful, pungent, sharp, stark, undiluted, unmixed

structure *noun.* anatomy, architecture, arrangement, build, configuration, construction, design, fabric, form, formation, frame, interrelation, morphology, network, order, organization, system, texture

struggle *noun.* battle, clash, combat, conflict, donnybrook, effort, encounter, endeavor, exertion, grindstone, row, ruckus, skirmish, stew, toil, try, undertaking, work

struggle *verb.* **1** assay, attempt, cope, dig, endeavor, grind, hustle, offer, plug, slave, strain, strive, sweat, tackle, toil, try, undertake, work **2** battle, brawl, buck, compete, contend, contest, grapple, hassle, romp, roughhouse, row, scrap, scuffle, shuffle, slug, smack, tangle, wrestle

stubborn *adjective.* determined, dogged, firm, fixed, inexorable, insubordinate, intractable, ornery, perverse, recalcitrant, refractory, rigid, tenacious, tough, unmanageable, unshakable, untoward, willful

student *noun.* apprentice, coed, disciple, docent, grad, graduate, grind, novice, observer, pupil, rat, registrant, scholar, schoolboy, skill, tool, undergrad, undergraduate

studied *adjective.* advised, affected, aforethought, conscious, considered, deliberate, designed, examined, planned, plotted, prepared, purposeful, reviewed, studious, thoughtful, voluntary, willful, willing

study *noun.* abstraction, analysis, analyzing, comparison, consideration, contemplation, course, debate, examination, investigation, memorizing, muse, musing, pondering, questioning, reflection, subject, trance

study *verb.* **1** bone, coach, consider, contemplate, dig, examine, grind, inquire, meditate, mind, plug, plunge, ponder, read, refresh, think, tutor, weigh **2** analyze, canvass, case, check over, check up, compare, deliberate, eagle eye, figure, inspect, investigate, peg, peruse, read, research, scope, survey, view

stuff *noun.* being, cloth, entity, equipment, fabric, gear, goods, individual, junk, luggage, material, objects, paraphernalia, possessions, substance, tackle, things, trappings

stuff *verb.* compress, cram, crowd, fill, force, gobble, gorge, guzzle, jam, overfill, pack, pad, push, ram, satiate, shove, squeeze, wedge

stupid *adjective.* dense, dim, dull, dumb, dummy, foolish, futile, gullible, idiotic, indiscreet, irrelevant, meaningless, mindless, nonsensical, pointless, rash, simple, sluggish

sturdy *adjective.* bulky, bull, determined, firm, flourishing, hearty, hulk, hunk, muscular, powerful, resolute, secure, solid, sound, stiff, strong, substantial, tenacious

style *noun.* **1** bearing, characteristic, custom, description, design, form, groove, kind, mode, number, peculiarity, rage, spirit, technique, tone, trend, vein, vogue **2** chic, comfort, cosmopolitanism, craze, delicacy, ease, elegance, fad, flair, grace, luxury, mode, polish, rage, refinement, sophistication, taste, vogue

subdued *adjective.* controlled, crestfallen, dim, downcast, grave, hushed, muted, neutral, repentant, restrained, sad, shaded, soft, solemn, submissive, subtle, tasteful, tempered

subject *adjective.* apt, captive, contingent, dependent, exposed, governed, liable, obedient, open, ruled, satellite, secondary, slavish, submissive, subordinate, subservient, tentative, vulnerable

subject *noun.* argument, business, case, chapter, core, course, gist, material, matter, motif, motion, motive, study, substance, text, theorem, thought, topic

submit *verb.* **1** abide, acknowledge, acquiesce, agree, bend, bow, buckle, cave, concede, endure, fold, humor, indulge, obey, stoop, tolerate, withstand, yield **2** affirm, argue, assert, claim, commit, contend, move, offer, propose, proposition, put, refer, state, suggest, table, tender, urge, volunteer

subsequent *adjective.* consecutive, consequent, consequential, ensuing, following, later, next, posterior, proximate, resultant, resulting, sequent, sequential, serial, succeeding, successive

subsidiary *adjective.* accessory, aiding, ancillary, assistant, assisting, auxiliary, branch, contributory, cooperative, helpful, lesser, minor, serviceable, subject, subordinate, subservient, supplementary, useful

subsistence *noun.* bread, competence, earnings, fortune, income, keep, legacy, living, nurture, property, provision, ration, resources, riches, salary, substance, wages, wealth

substance *noun.* **1** actuality, being, body, bulk, chunk, core, corpus, element, fabric, gob, hunk, individual, item, mass, material, matter, something, texture **2** amount, body, bottom, burden, core, effect, gist, guts, kernel, matter, meaning, pith, purport, sense, soul, strength, subject, thrust

substantial *adjective.* **1** bulky, consequential, considerable, firm, heavy, key, massive, meaningful, significant, sizable, solid, sound, steady, strong, tidy, valuable, vast, worthwhile **2** actual, concrete, corporeal, existent, gross, material, objective, phenomenal, physical, positive, righteous, sensible, solid, tangible, true, valid, visible, weighty

substitute *adjective.* acting, alternate, another, artificial, dummy, false, imitation, makeshift, near, other, provisional, replacement, reserve, second, sham, temporary, tentative, vicarious

substitute *noun.* agent, alternate, deputy, double, dummy, expedient, ghost, makeshift, recourse, refuge, relay, relief, replacement, resource, supply, symbol, temporary, vicar

substitute *verb.* alternate, back up, change, commute, displace, palm off, proxy, relieve, replace, ring, ring in, spell, sub, supersede, supplant, swap, switch, take over

subtle *adjective.* **1** deep, delicate, discriminating, ethereal, exquisite, fine, illusive, implied, inconspicuous, indistinct, inferred, ingenious, profound, slight, sophisticated, suggestive, tenuous, understated **2** analytic, analytical, artful, astute, cunning, deep, designing, devious, exacting, insidious, intriguing, keen, penetrating, perceptive, scheming, shrewd, skillful, sly

suburb *noun.* bedroom community, country, countryside, environs, fringe, hamlet, hinterland, outpost, outskirts, precinct, purlieu, residential area, spread city, sticks, suburbia, village

succeed *verb.* **1** achieve, avail, benefit, distance, earn, master, outwit, overcome, prevail, realize, reap, recover, retrieve, secure, surmount, thrive, turn out, work **2** accede, assume, be subsequent, come into, come next, displace, ensue, enter upon, follow, follow after, go next, inherit, postdate, replace, result, supersede, supplant, take over

success *noun.* achievement, attainment, benefit, boom, clover, consummation, do, eminence, fortune, fruition, progress, prosperity, realization, sensation, strike, triumph, velvet, victory

successful *adjective.* auspicious, blooming, booming, crowned, flourishing, lucky, notable, noteworthy, prosperous, rewarding, rolling, smash, strong, thriving, top, triumphant, victorious, wealthy

successive *adjective.* alternating, consecutive, ensuing, following after, in line, next, next off, next up, rotating, sequent, sequential, serial, seriate, subsequent, succedent, succeeding, successional

sudden *adjective.* abrupt, accelerated, acute, expeditious, flash, fleet, hasty, immediate, impetuous, impromptu, precipitate, quickened, rapid, rash, rushing, speeded, unforeseen, unusual

sue *verb.* accuse, appeal, beg, beseech, charge, claim, contest, demand, entreat, file, follow up, have up, indict, petition, plead, prosecute, solicit, summon

suffer *verb.* **1** ache, agonize, be affected, be racked, brave, deteriorate, droop, endure, experience, fall off, flag, get, hurt, look green, pain, smart, undergo, writhe **2** acquiesce, admit, bear, bleed, brook, concede, encounter, experience, have, indulge, know, let, see, stand, sweat, take, undergo, yield

sufficient *adjective.* acceptable, adequate, agreeable, ample, appreciate, comfortable, commensurate, common, competent, copious, decent, due, pleasing, plentiful, plenty, proportionate, satisfactory, tolerable

suggest *verb.* **1** advance, advocate, commend, conjecture, move, offer, plug, pose, prefer, propose, proposition, put, recommend, steer, submit, tip, tip off, tout **2** advert, connote, denote, evoke, hint, indicate, infer, insinuate, intimate, occur, point, promise, refer, represent, shadow, signify, symbolize, typify

suggestion *noun.* **1** angle, approach, bid, bit, charge, commendation, lead, motion, plan, presentation, proposition, scheme, setup, submission, tender, testimonial, thesis, tip **2** allusion, association, clue, cue, implication, indication, innuendo, reminder, shade, smack, strain, suspicion, symbol, symbolism, thought, trace, vein, wind

suggestive *adjective.* bawdy, blue, erotic, immodest, indecent, indelicate, obscene, provocative, purple, racy, ribald, salty, sexy, shady, tempting, titillating, unseemly, wicked

suit *noun.* address, application, asking, attention, court, courtship, entreaty, imprecation, invocation, petition, plea, prayer, request, requesting, solicitation, soliciting, supplication, wooing

suit *verb.* **1** accord, agree, benefit, check, conform, correspond, do, enhance, fit, flatter, fulfill, gratify, match, satisfy, serve, square, suffice, tally **2** accommodate, adjust, amuse, change, conform, entertain, fashion, fill, fit, gratify, modify, proportion, readjust, reconcile, revise, satisfy, square, tailor

suitable *adjective.* acceptable, applicable, apt, becoming, befitting, due, expedient, fit, fitting, good, handy, meet, pertinent, proper, reasonable, relevant, satisfactory, suited

suite *noun.* array, attendants, batch, body, clutch, cortege, court, escort, faculty, followers, group, lot, retainers, retinue, servants, set, staff, train

sullen *adjective.* black, crabbed, cynical, dour, dull, frowning, glowering, heavy, malevolent, malicious, malign, moody, morose, petulant, sour, stubborn, tenebrous, upset

sum *noun.* all, amount, body, bulk, entity, epitome, gross, integral, mass, reckoning, summary, summation, system, tally, totality, value, whole, worth

summary *adjective.* arbitrary, boiled down, brief, compact, compacted, compendious, condensed, cursory, curt, hasty, perfunctory, pithy, rehashed, run-through, short, succinct, terse

summary *noun.* abridgment, analysis, brief, capitulation, case, compendium, condensation, core, epitome, extract, inventory, nutshell, recapitulation, reduction, rehash, sense, substance, version

summit *noun.* apex, apogee, capstone, climax, crest, crown, culmination, head, height, max, meridian, most, peak, pinnacle, roof, up there, vertex, zenith

super *adjective.* cool, divine, glorious, great, hot, incomparable, keen, magnificent, marvelous, matchless, neat, outstanding, peerless, smashing, superb, terrific, topnotch, wonderful

superb *adjective.* elegant, elevated, exalted, exquisite, fine, glorious, lofty, magnificent, marvelous, optimal, optimum, prime, proud, resplendent, solid, stunning, super, superior

superficial *adjective.* casual, desultory, exterior, external, flimsy, glib, hasty, inattentive, lightweight, ostensible, passing, perfunctory, peripheral, silly, slight, summary, surface, uncritical

superintendent *noun.* administrator, boss, caretaker, chief, conductor, controller, curator, custodian, director, foreman, governor, head, inspector, manager, overseer, sitter, super, supervisor

superior *adjective.* **1** admirable, dandy, distinguished, exceeding, exceptional, expert, fine, finer, good, grander, noteworthy, over, overlying, predominant, preferable, premium, remarkable, superhuman **2** airy, cocky, condescending, cool, disdainful, haughty, high hat, insolent, lofty, lordly, overbearing, patronizing, pretentious, proud, sniffy, snobbish, supercilious, uppity

superior *noun.* better, boss, boss man, brass, chief, chieftain, czar, director, elder, exec, guru, head, leader, manager, principal, ruler, senior, supervisor

superiority *noun.* ahead, ascendancy, better, eminence, excellence, influence, lead, over, power, predomination, preponderance, prestige, prevalence, pull, spark, supremacy, top, victory

supernatural *adjective.* celestial, fabulous, fairy, ghostly, heavenly, invisible, miraculous, mythological, obscure, paranormal, rare, secret, spectral, superhuman, superior, unfathomable, unintelligible, unusual

supplement *noun.* added feature, addendum, addition, additive, appendix, bell, codicil, complement, continuation, extra, insert, option, postscript, pull-out, rider, sequel, spin-off, subsidiary

supplement *verb.* augment, beef up, build up, bump, complement, complete, enhance, enrich, extend, fortify, improve, increase, pad, reinforce, strengthen, subsidize, supply, top

supply *verb.* afford, contribute, deliver, drop, endow, find, give, heel, minister, outfit, produce, provide, provision, stake, stock, transfer, turn over, yield

support *noun.* **1** agency, base, bed, cornerstone, device, footing, foundation, lining, medium, platform, pole, post, prop, reinforcement, rest, rod, shore, stay **2** aid, approval, assist, assistance, backing, blessing, championship, comfort, encouragement, friendship, hand, lift, loyalty, patronage, protection, relief, succor, sustenance **3** alimony, allowance, bread, care, keep, livelihood, living, payment, provision, relief, responsibility, salt, stock, stores, subsistence, sustenance, upkeep, victuals **4** adherent, advocate, angel, apologist, champion, confederate, defender, disciple, follower, friend, partisan, patron, prop, proponent, satellite, second, stay, supporter **5** base, bear, bed, bolster, bottom, carry, crutch, found, ground, poise, prop, reinforce, shore, shoulder, stand, stay, strut, uphold **6** chaperon, encourage, finance, fortify, foster, guard, keep, maintain, prop, raise, set up, stake, strengthen, subsidize, succor, sustain, underwrite, uphold **7** advocate, aid, approve, assist, bolster, boost, carry, comfort, endorse, forward, foster, justify, maintain, promote, second, stay, sustain, uphold **8** abide, bear, brook, continue, countenance, go, handle, hang in, maintain, stand, stick, stomach, submit, suffer, swallow, take, tolerate, undergo

suppose *verb.* **1** admit, calculate, conjecture, divine, expect, figure, hypothesize, imagine, infer, judge, make up, presuppose, pretend, spark, speculate, take, think, understand **2** assume, conclude, conjecture, consider, dream, expect, fancy, feel, hypothesize, imagine, judge, postulate, pretend, regard, take, think, understand, view

supreme *adjective.* absolute, chief, closing, extreme, final, foremost, incomparable, last, marvelous, master, peerless, predominant, prime, sovereign, top, unequaled, unmatched, unsurpassed

sure *adjective.* clear, convincing, decided, doubtless, firm, fixed, incontrovertible, indubitable, positive, real, satisfied, set, steady, unchangeable, uncompromising, unfailing, unshakable, valid

surely *adverb.* admittedly, assuredly, certainly, clearly, decidedly, definitely, distinctly, evidently, explicitly, indeed, inevitably, inexorably, manifestly, plainly, undoubtedly, unequivocally, unerringly, unmistakably

surface *noun.* area, cover, covering, expanse, exterior, face, facet, level, obverse, outside, peel, plane, side, skin, stretch, superficiality, top, veneer

surge *verb.* arise, climb, deluge, eddy, flow, grow, gush, heave, mount, pour, ripple, rise, roll, sluice, stream, swell, swirl, tower

surplus *noun.* balance, excess, overage, overflow, overkill, overmuch, overrun, overstock, oversupply, plus, remainder, residue, something extra, superabundance, superfluity, surfeit, the limit, too much

surprise *noun.* abruptness, amazement, attack, consternation, curiosity, fortune, incredulity, jolt, kick, marvel, miracle, miscalculation, prodigy, shock, start, suddenness, unforeseen, wonder

surprise *verb.* **1** amaze, astound, awe, confuse, dazzle, disconcert, dismay, floor, jar, jolt, leave aghast, overwhelm, perplex, rattle, rock, shock, stagger, startle **2** ambush, bushwhack, capture, catch, catch napping, catch off-guard, catch redhanded, catch unawares, discover, grab, grasp, lay for, nab, seize, spring on, startle, take, waylay

surrender *verb.* abandon, commit, concede, consign, entrust, fall, fold, forego, go under, knuckle, leave, quit, relinquish, resign, submit, succumb, waive, yield

survey *noun.* analysis, audit, check, compendium, critique, digest, examination, inquiry, inspection, outline, perusal, précis, review, sample, scan, sketch, study, view

survey *verb.* assay, assess, case, contemplate, evaluate, inspect, observe, overlook, plan, plot, quarterback, rate, scope, size, study, superintend, supervise, view

survive *verb.* bear, endure, exist, handle, keep, last, live, lump, persevere, persist, recover, remain, revive, subsist, suffer, sustain, weather, withstand

suspect *adjective.* doubtable, dubious, incredible, open, problematic, pseudo, questionable, ridiculous, shaky, suspected, suspicious, thick, thin, unbelievable, uncertain, unclear, unlikely, unsure

suspect *verb.* assume, believe, conclude, conjecture, consider, disbelieve, expect, feel, hold, imagine, mistrust, presume, reckon, speculate, suppose, think, understand, wonder

suspension *noun.* abeyance, adjournment, break, breather, cessation, conclusion, cutoff, ending, freeze, halt, intermission, interruption, moratorium, period, stay, stoppage, suspense, ten

suspicion *noun.* conjecture, cynicism, distrust, guess, guesswork, hunch, idea, impression, incredulity, jealousy, mistrust, nonbelief, notion, skepticism, surmise, uncertainty, wariness, wonder

suspicious *adjective.* **1** cagey, careful, cautious, doubtful, incredulous, jealous, jelly, questioning, quizzical, skeptical, suspect, suspecting, unbelieving, uptight, wary, watchful, without faith, wondering **2** debatable, different, doubtful, dubious, farfetched, funny, irregular, open, overt, peculiar, queer, questionable, reaching, shady, shaky, uncertain, unsure, unusual

sustain *verb.* **1** aid, approve, bolster, carry, convey, defend, endorse, foster, lug, nurture, preserve, save, stand by, supply, transfer, transport, uphold, validate **2** abide, bear, brook, encounter, experience, feel, go, hang in, have, know, lump, see, stand, stomach, suffer, tolerate, undergo, withstand

swallow *verb.* absorb, belt, bolt, devour, dispatch, dispose, down, drink, drop, eat, gulp, imbibe, sip, swig, swill, take, toss, wolf

swear *verb.* affirm, assert, attest, covenant, depend on, depose, give witness, maintain, plight, promise, rely on, say so, state, testify, trust, vouch, vow, warrant

sweat *verb.* abide, agonize, bear, brook, chafe, endure, exert, fret, go, labor, lump, stand, stomach, suffer, take, toil, tolerate, torture

sweeping *adjective.* blanket, broad, comprehensive, exaggerated, exhaustive, extensive, full, general, global, inclusive, indiscriminate, overall, radical, thorough, unqualified, vast, wholesale, wide

sweet *adjective.* **1** affectionate, agreeable, amiable, appealing, beloved, considerate, dear, delightful, generous, gentle, heavenly, kind, patient, precious, reasonable, taking, tender, winsome **2** dulcet, euphonic, euphonious, harmonious, mellow, melodic, melodious, musical, orotund, rich, rotund, silvery, smooth, soft, sonorous, soothing, sweet-sounding, tuneful

sweetheart *noun.* admirer, baby, beau, beloved, chick, companion, dear, dreamboat, flame, honey, love, lover, squeeze, steady, stud, sweet, treasure, valentine

swell *adjective.* cool, dandy, deluxe, desirable, excellent, exclusive, fashionable, fine, grand, keen, marvelous, neat, plush, posh, smart, stylish, super, terrific

swell *verb.* aggravate, augment, bloat, dilate, enhance, enlarge, expand, extend, fatten, grow, intensity, mount, plump, pouch, pout, puff, rise, surge

swelling *noun.* blister, boil, bruise, bump, corn, dilation, enlargement, growth, hump, increase, inflammation, injury, knob, protuberance, puff, ridge, sore, tumor

swift *adjective.* abrupt, cracking, expeditious, express, fleet, hasty, hurried, precipitate, prompt, pronto, rapid, ready, screaming, short, snappy, sudden, supersonic, winged

swim *verb.* bathe, breast-stroke, crawl, dive, dog paddle, float, freestyle, glide, go wading, high-dive, move, paddle, practice, race, slip, stroke, submerge, wade

swing *verb.* avert, dangle, divert, pitch, pivot, revolve, rock, roll, rotate, shunt, suspend, swivel, turn, vary, veer, wave, wiggle, wobble

switch *verb.* change course, convert, deflect, deviate, divert, exchange, interchange, rearrange, replace, shift, shunt, substitute, swap, trade, turn, turn aside, turnabout, veer

symbol *noun.* attribute, badge, design, device, figure, image, indication, letter, mark, motif, note, pattern, regalia, representation, sign, stamp, token, type

symbolize *verb.* betoken, body forth, connote, denote, emblematize, embody, epitomize, exemplify, express, illustrate, indicate, mean, mirror, show, signify, suggest, symbol, typify

symmetry *noun.* agreement, arrangement, balance, centrality, conformity, correspondence, equality, equilibrium, equivalence, evenness, finish, form, harmony, order, proportionality, regularity, rhythm, similarity

sympathetic *adjective.* **1** affectionate, appreciating, caring, compassionate, comprehending, concerned, considerate, interested, kind, kindly, pitying, responsive, supportive, sympathizing, tender, thoughtful, vicarious, warm **2** amenable, appreciative, approving, companionable, compatible, congenial, consistent, consonant, cool, down, encouraging, friendly, hip, open, pro, receptive, responsive, vicarious

sympathize *verb.* ache, agree, appreciate, be compassionate, comfort, commiserate, compassionate, comprehend, condole, empathize, have compassion, identify with, love, pity, show kindliness, show tenderness, tune in, understand

sympathy *noun.* accord, affinity, agreement, alliance, attraction, concord, congeniality, connection, empathy, feelings, harmony, kindliness, rapport, responsiveness, sensitivity, tenderness, union, unity

synthesis *noun.* amalgamation, blend, coalescence, combination, composite, compound, constructing, construction, entirety, forming, fusion, integration, organism, organization, union, unit, welding, whole

system *noun.* **1** arrangement, classification, combination, entity, ideology, integral, integrate, order, orderliness, organization, philosophy, regularity, rule, scheme, setup, sum, theory, totality **2** arrangement, custom, manner, method, methodology, mode, modus, operation, orderliness, procedure, regularity, routine, scheme, systematization, tactics, technique, way, wise

T

table *noun.* **1** bar, bench, board, buffet, bureau, console, counter, desk, dining table, dinner table, dresser, lectern, pulpit, sideboard, sink, slab, stand, wagon **2** agenda, appendix, canon, catalogue, chart, compendium, graph, illustration, index, inventory, list, plan, record, roll, schedule, statistics, summary, tabulation

table *verb.* cool, defer, delay, enter, hang, hang fire, hang up, hold off, hold up, move, pigeonhole, propose, put aside, put forward, put off, shelve, submit, suggest

tackle *verb.* **1** accept, apply oneself, attack, attempt, begin, deal with, dig in, embark upon, essay, launch, pitch into, plunge into, set about, take on, take up, try, turn to, undertake **2** attack, block, catch, challenge, clutch, confront, down, grapple, grasp, halt, nail, sack, seize, smear, stop, take, throw, upset

tactics *noun.* approach, campaign, course, defense, device, line, maneuver, maneuvering, method, move, plan, policy, procedure, scheme, system, technique, trick, way

tail *noun.* behind, butt, buttocks, caudal appendage, conclusion, end, extremity, fag end, posterior, rear, rear end, reverse, rudder, rump, stub, tag, tag end, train

take *verb.* **1** arrest, attain, bag, capture, clutch, collar, collect, earn, grab, grasp, handle, have, pick up, reap, secure, seize, snag, strike **2** abstract, annex, appropriate, arrogate, bag, boost, borrow, cop, liberate, lift, nip, pick up, pluck, pocket, seize, snag, snare, swipe **3** borrow, buy, charter, choose, derive, draw, elect, gain, get, hire, lease, mark, obtain, pick, prefer, procure, purchase, rent **4** abide, bear, brave, brook, contain, hack, hang in, hold, receive, stand, stomach, suffer, swallow, tolerate, undergo, weather, welcome, withstand **5** admit, appropriate, assume, do, effect, execute, exercise, exert, experience, function, have, observe, perform, relish, sense, serve, welcome, work **6** assume, compass, comprehend, consider, expect, experience, follow, grasp, imagine, know, observe, perceive, receive, regard, see, sense, suppose, think **7** accompany, bear, buck, carry, convey, convoy, ferry, haul, heel, jag, lead, lug, move, ride, shoulder, tour, truck, user

tale *noun.* **1** account, anecdote, fable, fairy tale, fiction, folk tale, legend, myth, narration, narrative, novel, relation, report, romance, saga, short story, yarn **2** canard, chestnut, clothesline, cock-and-bull story, defamation, detraction, exaggeration, fabrication, falsehood, falsity, fiction, lie, misrepresentation, prevarication, rumor, scandal, untruth, yarn

talent *noun.* aptitude, aptness, art, bent, bit, capability, craft, facility, faculty, flair, gift, head, knack, power, savvy, set, skill, turn

talk *noun.* **1** allocution, chalk talk, declamation, descant, discourse, disquisition, dissertation, epilogue, exhortation, expatiation, harangue, lecture, monologue, oration, peroration, recitation, sermon, speech **2** allusion, banter, bull, bunk, buzz, cant, chatter, chaw, gas, hint, jaw, nonsense, prose, racket, rap, rumor, trash, yarn **3** argument, colloquy, conclave, confabulation, conference, consultation, dialogue, encounter, huddle, interview, meeting, negotiation, parlance, parley, rapping, seminar, symposium, visit **4** articulate, chatter, chaw, confess, express, gab, gossip, influence, inform, parley, patter, persuade, pronounce, rap, sing, speak, tell, voice **5** argue, chew, commune, confer, confide, consult, deliberate, dialogue, exchange, huddle, interface, interview, network, parley, reason, relate, touch, visit **6** accost, discourse, give speech, harangue, hold forth, induce, influence, jawbone, lecture, orate, persuade, pitch, sermonize, soapbox, speak, spout, stump, sway

tan *noun.* beige, biscuit, bronze, brown,

brownish, buff, coffee, cream, drab, gold, khaki, natural, olive, sand, suntan, tawny, umber, yellow

tangible *adjective.* actual, concrete, discernible, distinct, embodied, gross, manifest, material, objective, observable, obvious, perceptible, positive, sensible, solid, substantial, tactile, visible

tangle *noun.* coil, complication, confusion, entanglement, jam, jungle, labyrinth, mass, mat, maze, mesh, mess, morass, skein, snag, snarl, twist, web

tangle *verb.* catch, coil, complicate, confuse, hamper, interweave, involve, jam, mat, mesh, muck, obstruct, perplex, ravel, trap, twist, unbalance, upset

tap *verb.* bleed, bore, broach, drain, draw, drill, empty, lance, milk, mine, open, pump, riddle, spear, spike, stab, use, utilize

tart *adjective.* acid, acidulous, barbed, biting, bitter, cutting, harsh, nasty, piquant, pungent, scathing, sharp, short, snappy, snippy, tangy, trenchant, wounding

task *noun.* bother, burden, business, deadweight, effort, employment, function, grindstone, load, millstone, mission, onus, province, responsibility, stint, toil, trouble, undertaking

taste *noun.* **1** aroma, drive, ginger, jolt, kick, punch, relish, salt, savor, smack, sour, suggestion, sweet, tang, wallop, zest, zing, zip **2** bit, bite, chaw, delicacy, drop, gob, hint, morsel, nip, sampling, sip, sprinkling, suggestion, tidbit, touch, trifle, whiff, wink **3** affection, appetite, attachment, bag, bent, comprehension, fancy, flash, fondness, leaning, liking, palate, penchant, preference, relish, tendency, type, zest **4** appreciation, cultivation, delicacy, discernment, discretion, discrimination, distinction, elegance, grace, penetration, perception, polish, propriety, refinement, restraint, style, susceptibility, tact

taste *verb.* assay, bite, chew, criticize, differentiate, eat, judge, lick, nibble, partake, perceive, relish, sample, sense, sip, test, touch, try

tax *noun.* assessment, bite, brokerage, contribution, cost, custom, duty, excise, expense, fine, imposition, levy, nick, obligation, price, rate, tariff, tribute

tax *verb.* charge, drain, exhaust, load, overburden, pressure, push, saddle, sap, strain, stress, stretch, task, tire, try, weary, weigh, weight

taxing *adjective.* demanding, difficult, disturbing, enervating, exacting, grievous, heavy, oppressive, punishing, sapping stressful, tedious, tiring, tough, troublesome, trying, wearing, wearisome, weighty

teach *verb.* brief, catechize, coach, exercise, fit, form, ground, illustrate, impart, inform, instruct, interpret, lecture, nurture, prepare, profess, school, train

teacher *noun.* advisor, coach, educator, governess, grind, guide, instructor, lecturer, maestro, master, mistress, professor, scholar, schoolmaster, schoolteacher, supervisor, teach, tutor

team *noun.* aggregation, body, bunch, club, foursome, gang, organization, outfit, partners, set, span, squad, string, tandem, trio, troop, troupe, yoke

tear *noun.* crying, discharge, distress, drops, grieving, lamentation, moisture, mourning, pain, regret, sobbing, teardrop, wailing, water, weep, weeping, whimpering, woe

tear *verb.* **1** break, divide, extract, fray, gash, grab, impair, lacerate, pluck, pull, rend, rift, rupture, seize, slash, slit, sunder, wrest **2** boil, bolt, career, charge, chase, course, dash, fling, fly, gallop, hurry, lash, race, run, rush, shoot, speed, spring

technique *noun.* approach, art, artistry, course, delivery, manner, mode, modus, procedure, proficiency, routine, skill, style, system, tactics, touch, way, wise

tell *verb.* **1** acquaint, authorize, bid, command, communicate, confess, express, impart, inform, instruct, leak, level, mention, proclaim, represent, require, speak, state, summon **2** ascertain, be sure, clinch, comprehend, deduce, describe, determine, differentiate, discern, discover, discriminate, distinguish, divine, identify, know, learn, perceive, recognize, see

telling *adjective.* considerable, conspicuous, convincing, decisive, devastating, effectual, important, impressive, marked, powerful, satisfactory, satisfying, significant, solid, sound, striking, trenchant, valid

temper *noun.* **1** atmosphere, attribute, climate, complexion, constitution, humor, makeup, outlook, peculiarity, posture, property, quality, spirit, style, timbre, tone, trend, vein **2** anger, excitability, fit, furor, impatience, ire, irritability, irritation, outburst, passion, petulance, rage, resentment, sensitivity, stew, tantrum, tear, wax **3** adjust, allay, alleviate, cool, curb, dilute, ease, lessen, mitigate, moderate, mollify, pacify, relieve, restrain, soften, soothe, switch, weaken **4** anneal, bake, braze, cement, chill, congeal, dry, indurate, mold, petrify, set, solidify, starch, steel, stiffen, strengthen, toughen, toughen up

temperament *noun.* complexion, constitution, humor, inclination, intellect, kind, mettle, outlook, peculiarity, personality, quality, soul, spirit, stamp, susceptibility, temper, tendency, way

temporary *adjective.* acting, alternate, brief, changeable, interim, limited, makeshift, momentary, mortal, overnight, passing, perishable, provisional, shifting, substitute, summary, supply, unstable

temptation *noun.* allurement, appeal, attraction, bait, coaxing, come-on, draw, fancy, fascination, inducement, invitation, provocation, pull, seduction, snare, tantalization, trap, yen

tend *verb.* **1** aim, bear, bend, contribute, dispose, drift, favor, go, head, incline, influence, lead, lean, look, move, point, trend, turn **2** accomplish, defend, do, foster, guard, handle, keep, maintain, manage, nurture, perform, protect, safeguard, serve, sit, superintend, supervise, watch

tendency *noun.* **1** addiction, affection, bag, custom, drift, flash, groove, habit, impulse, liability, penchant, readiness, set, susceptibility, temper, trend, turn, way **2** aim, bearing, bent, bias, course, curve, drift, heading, inclination, leaning, movement, purport, shift, tenor, trend, turn, turning, way

tender *adjective.* amorous, caring, compassionate, considerate, emotional, fond, forgiving, gentle, humane, kind, merciful, poignant, responsive, sentimental, soft, tolerant, touching, warm

tense *adjective.* agitated, anxious, bugged, choked, concerned, edgy, jittery, moved, nervous, shaky, shot, strained, stressful, uneasy, unquiet, wired, worried, wreck

tension *noun.* agitation, ants, anxiety, apprehension, brunt, concern, disquiet, jitters, jumps, nerves, nervousness, pressure, restlessness, shakes, strain, suspense, unease, uneasiness

tentative *adjective.* acting, conjectural, contingent, dependent, experimental, indefinite, makeshift, not final, on trial, probationary, provisional, provisory, speculative, temporary, test, trial, unconfirmed, unsettled

tenure *noun.* administration, clench, clinch, clutch, dynasty, grasp, grip, hold, holding, occupancy, occupation, ownership, possession, proprietorship, regime, reign, security, tenancy

term *noun.* **1** appellation, article, caption, denomination, designation, expression, head, indication, language, locution, moniker, name, nomenclature, phrase, style, terminology, title, word **2** course, cycle, duration, hitch, interval, phase, quarter, season, semester, session, space, span, spell, standing, stretch, time, tour, turn

terminal *adjective.* bounding, closing, curtains, deadly, eventual, extreme, fatal, hindmost, incurable, killing, lag, last, latest, latter, lethal, mortal, period, utmost

terminate *verb.* abolish, achieve, boot, bounce, bound, confine, cut off, discharge, dissolve, drop, eliminate, extinguish, halt, issue, lapse, result, wind up, wrap

termination *noun.* abortion, cease, cessation, close, completion, conclusion, consequence, curtains, effect, ending, finale, finish, issue, outcome, period, result, terminus, thirty

terms *noun.* agreement, charge, circumstances,

conclusion, details, fee, particulars, payment, points, premise, provision, proviso, qualifications, rate, reservation, specifications, stipulation, treaty

terrain *noun.* area, contour, country, domain, dominion, field, form, ground, land, profile, province, region, shape, soil, sphere, territory, topography, turf

terrible *adjective.* appalling, awesome, bad, dread, dreadful, extreme, ghastly, horrid, inconvenient, loathsome, monstrous, offensive, poor, revolting, severe, shocking, unfortunate, unpleasant

terribly *adverb.* decidedly, desperately, disturbingly, drastically, exceedingly, extremely, gravely, greatly, horribly, intensely, mightily, much, notoriously, remarkably, staggeringly, unbelievably, unfortunately, unhappily

territory *noun.* area, colony, country, dominion, expanse, mandate, province, quarter, region, section, sector, sphere, terrain, township, tract, turf, walk, zone

test *noun.* analysis, assessment, catechism, confirmation, criterion, elimination, final, inquest, investigation, lick, ordeal, probing, shibboleth, stab, substantiation, touchstone, try, yardstick

test *verb.* analyze, assay, assess, check, confirm, demonstrate, experiment, hang, inquire, investigate, prove, question, quiz, shake down, substantiate, try, validate, verify

testify *verb.* affirm, announce, argue, assert, bespeak, certify, corroborate, declare, demonstrate, depose, indicate, mount, prove, rat on, show, sing, state, swear

testimony *noun.* affirmation, confirmation, data, demonstration, deposition, documentation, evidence, facts, grounds, illustration, indication, manifestation, profession, statement, submission, substantiation, support, verification

text *noun.* argument, body, consideration, content, contents, extract, fundamentals, issue, line, matter, motive, paragraph, passage, quotation, subject, topic, vocabulary, wording

texture *noun.* arrangement, being, composition, constitution, fabric, fineness, flexibility, form, grain, makeup, organization, quality, scheme, stiffness, taste, tissue, touch, web

theater *noun.* amphitheater, arena, auditorium, barn, boards, cinema, coliseum, deck, hall, hippodrome, house, locale, movie, oak, room, scene, site, theatre

theatrical *adjective.* affected, amateur, artificial, comic, exaggerated, ham, mannered, melodramatic, meretricious, operatic, pompous, show, stilted, superficial, tragic, unnatural, unreal, vaudeville

theft *noun.* appropriation, boost, cheating, deprivation, embezzlement, grab, holdup, job, lift, pilfering, racket, robbery, steal, swindling, swiping, thieving, touch, vandalism

theme *noun.* affair, argument, burden, business, case, head, keynote, line, matter, motif, motive, proposition, stuff, subject, text, thesis, thought, topic

theoretical *adjective.* academic, analytical, codified, contingent, ideational, ideological, imaginative, intellectual, logical, open, pedantic, postulated, presumed, quixotic, speculative, tentative, unproved, vague

theory *noun.* argument, base, code, codification, conditions, foundation, hunch, ideology, impression, method, plan, plea, presumption, scheme, speculation, suppose, system, theorem

therefore *adverb.* accordingly, and so, consequently, ergo, for, forasmuch as, hence, in consequence, inasmuch as, since, so, then, thence, therefrom, thereupon, thus, whence, wherefore

thesis *noun.* assumption, contention, hypothesis, idea, line, opinion, position, postulate, premise, presumption, presupposition, proposal, proposition, sentiment, statement, surmise, theory, view

thick *adjective.* **1** bulky, burly, chunky, concrete, consolidated, deep, fat, firm, hard, heavy, husky, massive, solid, stocky, stubby, stumpy, substantial, wide **2** caked, compressed, concrete, condensed, consolidated, deep, dense, firm, fixed, heavy, impervious, opaque, set, solid, stiff, syrupy, thickened, viscous **3** bursting, compressed, concentrated, condensed, considerable, covered, crammed, dense, frequent, heaped, impenetrable, impervious, multitudinous, packed, profuse, replete, several, solid

thief *noun.* booster, burglar, cheat, clip, crasher, criminal, crook, dip, highwayman, lifter, nip, owl, pirate, punk, robber, sniper, spider, stealer

thin *adjective.* **1** emaciated, ethereal, featherweight, fine, fragile, gaunt, lightweight, meager, peaked, pole, rangy, reedy, slight, slim, small, starved, stick, wan **2** attenuated, delicate, diaphanous, filmy, fine, flimsy, gossamer, paper-thin, permeable, rare, refined, sheer, slight, slim, subtle, tenuous, translucent, wispy **3** diluted, feeble, flimsy, improbable, inconceivable, incredible, lame, meager, poor, questionable, scant, scarce, slight, stretched, unbelievable, unconvincing, untenable, weak

thin *verb.* cook, cut, cut back, decrease, diminish, doctor, edit, expand, extenuate, irrigate, lace, needle, reduce, refine, shave, spike, trim, water

thing *noun.* **1** apparatus, being, body, business, commodity, configuration, corporeality, element, entity, figure, form, goods, individual, matter, piece, subject, substance, tool **2** circumstance, deed, doing, duty, episode, event, eventuality, exploit, feat, happening, incident, job, movement, obligation, occasion, occurrence, proceeding, work **3** apparel, attire, baggage, belongings, chattels, clothes, clothing, duds, equipment, gear, goods, luggage, paraphernalia, property, stuff, things, trappings, tricks

think *verb.* **1** assume, consider, expect, fancy, feature, foresee, image, imagine, judge, realize, regard, see, sense, suppose, take, understand, vision, visualize **2** appreciate, brood, chew, consider, deduce, evaluate, imagine, infer, judge, muse, rationalize, reason, reflect, resolve, revolve, stew, study, turn over

thorough *adjective.* **1** absolute, careful, comprehensive, detailed, efficient, exact, full, intensive, itemized, meticulous, minute, particular, plenty, royal, scrupulous, sweeping, thoroughgoing, tough **2** arrant, complete, consummate, downright, entire, gross, out-and-out, outright, perfect, pure, rank, sheer, straight-out, thoroughgoing, total, unmitigated, unqualified, utter

thoroughly *adverb.* all, carefully, comprehensively, earnestly, efficiently, extremely, hard, intensely, intensively, meticulously, notably, painstakingly, remarkably, scrupulously, smack, sweepingly, throughout, very

thought *noun.* **1** anticipation, attention, consideration, contemplation, hope, inducing, introspection, intuition, judging, logic, musing, perceiving, rationalization, reasoning, reflection, regard, speculation, study **2** aim, assessment, concern, conclusion, conviction, design, expectation, fancy, hope, image, intention, intuition, judgment, knowledge, plan, regard, sympathy, view

thoughtful *adjective.* **1** attentive, aware, canny, careful, circumspect, civil, concerned, considerate, cooperative, courteous, discreet, gallant, helpful, kind, mindful, observant, observing, responsive **2** analytical, cerebral, deep, engrossed, grave, intellectual, intent, keen, musing, pondering, preoccupied, rational, reasonable, reasoning, reflecting, retrospective, studious, wise

threat *noun.* blackmail, bluff, else, fix, foreboding, foreshadowing, fulmination, hazard, intimidation, menace, omen, or else, peril, portent, presage, risk, thunder, warning

threaten *verb.* **1** advance, approach, be brewing, be dangerous, be gathering, come on, forebode, foreshadow, frighten, hang over, impend, imperil, jeopardize, loom, overhang, portend, presage, warn **2** abuse, blackmail, bluster, bulldoze, bully, caution, chill, cow, enforce, fulminate, growl, intimidate, menace, presage, pressure, scare, terrorize, torment

threatening *adjective.* aggressive, alarming, baleful, baneful, black, fateful, grim, imminent, impending, looming, lowering, ominous, scowling, sinister, terrorizing, ugly, unsafe, warning

threshold *noun.* beginning, brink, dawn, door, doorstep, doorway, edge, entrance, gate, inception, origin, outset, point, sill, start, starting point, verge, vestibule

throw *verb.* barrage, buck, butt, deliver, discharge, flick, flip, floor, hurl, lift, pepper, put, shove, spray, start, stone, toss, upset

thrust *noun.* advance, blitz, boost, drive, impetus, jump, lunge, momentum, onset, onslaught, pressure, prod, propulsion, punch, push, shove, stab, whack

thrust *verb.* assail, attack, bear down, buck, bulldoze, butt, chunk, clout, dig, lunge, pierce, plunge, put, ram, shoulder, shove, sink, stick

thunder *noun.* barrage, blast, boom, booming, clap, cracking, crash, crashing, detonation, discharge, explosion, outburst, peal, roar, rumble, rumbling, thunderbolt, uproar

ticket *noun.* admission, board, card, coupon, document, invite, key, notice, paper, pass, passage, passport, permit, receipt, record, slip, stub, tag

tide *noun.* course, direction, drag, drift, ebb, flood, flow, movement, race, sluice, spate, stream, tendency, trend, undercurrent, undertow, wave, whirlpool

tie *noun.* attachment, band, bond, brace, connection, cord, gang, joint, ligament, link, network, outfit, rope, strap, string, tackle, yoke, zipper

tie *verb.* anchor, attach, band, bind, cinch, clinch, fasten, gird, join, knot, lash, link, marry, rope, secure, tighten, unite, wed

tight *adjective.* **1** bound, constricted, contracted, dense, firm, fixed, rigid, secure, set, snug, solid, steady, stiff, strained, stretched, strong, tenacious, tense **2** blocked, bolted, crushing, cutting, fastened, firm, fixed, impenetrable, impervious, locked, padlocked, pinching, secure, shrunken, shut, snapped, sound, tied **3** arduous, critical, distressing, disturbing, even, exacting, hazardous, near, perilous, precarious, punishing, rough, sticky, tense, tough, trying, upsetting, worrisome

till *verb.* dig, dress, farm, grow, harrow, hoe, labor, mulch, plant, plough, plow, prepare, raise crops, sow, tend, turn, turn over, work

timber *noun.* beam, board, boom, club, forest, frame, grove, log, mast, plank, pole, rafter, rib, stake, stumpage, wood, woodland, woods

time *noun.* date, day, hour, instance, instant, life, moment, month, pace, season, second, span, stage, stint, stretch, ticks, tide, tour

timely *adjective.* appropriate, auspicious, convenient, favorable, fit, fitting, judicious, likely, meet, modern, now, pat, promising, prompt, proper, propitious, prosperous, suitable

tiny *adjective.* diminutive, dwarf, dwarfish, infinitesimal, insignificant, little, microscopic, miniature, minute, negligible, petite, pocket, puny, slight, teensy, trifling, wee, weeny

tip *noun.* **1** baksheesh, bird, bus ride, chip, compensation, cue, fee, gift, grease, lagniappe, money, one way, palm oil, perk, reward, something, subway, turkey **2** bang, bug, buzz, clue, cue, dope, forecast, hint, in, information, inkling, knowledge, pointer, prompt, steer, suggestion, warning, word

tip *verb.* bend, cant, dump, heel, incline, lean, list, pour, shift, slant, slope, spill, tilt, topple, turn over, unload, upset, upturn

tire *verb.* bore, crawl, distress, droop, drop, exasperate, fail, flag, fold, harass, overburden, pain, prostrate, sap, sink, strain, weary, wilt

tired *adjective.* beat, bored, distressed, drooping, drowsy, exasperated, fatigued, haggard, irritated, jaded, overtaxed, overworked, sleepy, wasted, weary, whacked, worn, worn out

title *noun.* **1** appellation, banner, caption, close, description, excellency, head, headline, inscription, label, legend, name, rubric, salutation, sign, streamer, style, subtitle **2** appellation, appellative, brand, denomination, designation, epithet, front name, handle, honorific, label, moniker, nomen, pseudonym, sobriquet, style, tab, tag, term **3** authority, championship, claim, commission, crest, crown, decoration, deed, degree, due, holding, medal, ownership, power, prerogative, pretense, privilege, right

together *adverb.* all together, closely, coincidentally, collectively, combined, commonly, concomitantly, concurrently, conjointly, contemporaneously, en masse, in concert, jointly, mutually, simultaneously, synchronically, unanimously, unitedly

token *noun.* demonstration, favor, gift, index, mark, memento, omen, pawn, pledge, presage, relic, remembrance, security, sign, significant, symbol, trophy, warning

tolerance *noun.* altruism, charity, clemency, concession, endurance, freedom, good will, grace, humanity, indulgence, liberalism, magnanimity, mercy, permission, sensitivity, sympathy, toleration, understanding

tolerant *adjective.* advanced, benevolent, charitable, clement, complaisant, fair, forgiving, humane, indulgent, liberal, merciful, patient, permissive, radical, soft, sophisticated, understanding, wide

tone *noun.* approach, character, drift, effect, expression, frame, grain, habit, humor, manner, mode, movement, quality, spirit, style, temper, trend, vein

too *adverb.* awfully, beyond, ever, exceptionally, extremely, greatly, highly, immensely, inordinately, notably, over, overly, remarkably, strikingly, unconscionably, unduly, unreasonably, very

tool *noun.* **1** apparatus, appliance, bucksaw, contraption, contrivance, device, engine, gadget, gizmo, implement, job, machine, means, mechanism, utensil, weapon **2** accessory, accomplice, agent, auxiliary, cat's-paw, chump, creature, idiot, intermediary, jackal, mark, medium, messenger, patsy, pawn, puppet, sucker, vehicle

top *adjective.* chief, crack, culminating, dominant, elite, fine, foremost, head, lead, maximal, outside, prime, ruling, sovereign, superior, supreme, topmost, uppermost

top *noun.* apogee, cap, ceiling, climax, cork, cover, crest, crown, face, finial, head, height, peak, summit, surface, tip, vertex, zenith

top *verb.* **1** ascend, cap, climb, cloak, clothe, cover, crest, crown, face, finish, piggyback, protect, reinforce, roof, scale, superimpose, surmount, tip **2** beat, best, better, bury, clobber, cream, eclipse, exceed, excel, fox, goose, outdo, outfox, overrun, swamp, total, transcend, trash **3** amputate, cream, crop, curtail, cut off, detruncate, dock, file off, lop off, pare, prune, ream, shave off, shear, shorten, skim, trim, truncate

topic *noun.* affair, argument, business, case, division, field, head, issue, material, matter, motif, motion, motive, proposition, subject, text, theorem, thesis

torn *adjective.* broken, burst, cleaved, cracked, divided, fractured, impaired, mangled, ragged, rent, ripped, ruptured, severed, sliced, slit, snapped, split, wrenched

toss *verb.* agitate, buffet, disturb, flounder, jolt, labor, lurch, pitch, rock, roll, shake, stir, swing, tumble, wallow, wave, wobble, writhe

total *adjective.* absolute, entire, every, full, gross, integral, outright, plenary, positive, sweeping, thoroughgoing, totalitarian, undisputed, undivided, unlimited, unqualified, unrestricted, whole

total *noun.* aggregate, all, amount, body, budget, bulk, entirety, flat out, gross, mass, quantity, quantum, result, sum, tale, totality, whole enchilada, whole shebang

total *verb.* add, aggregate, calculate, cast, come, come to, comprise, equal, figure, foot, number, reach, reckon, ring up, run into, summate, tote, yield

totally *adverb.* absolutely, all, altogether, comprehensively, consummately, entirely, exactly, exclusively, flat out, fully, just, perfectly, quite, thoroughly, unconditionally, utterly, wholeheartedly, wholly

touch *noun.* **1** blow, caress, collision, crash, graze, grope, junction, licking, manipulation, pat, perception, percussion, petting, shock, stroking, tap, taste, touching **2** dash, detail, drop, hint, inkling, jot, pinch, shade, smack, speck, spot, streak, suggestion, suspicion, taste, tincture, trace, whiff **3** acquaintance, adroitness, art, artistry, characteristic, command, deftness, direction, effect, handiwork, influence, manner, method, skill, style, talent, technique, trademark **4** caress, finger, glance, grope, handle, inspect, join, lick, line, meet, partake, pat, probe, smooth, strike, taste, tip, verge **5** affect, arouse, carry, disturb, get, grab, impress, influence, inspire, mark, move, quicken, soften, stimulate, stir, strike, stroke, upset **6** affect, bear on, bear upon, belong to, center upon, concern, consume, deal with, drink, eat, handle, interest, involve, partake of, pertain to, refer to, use, utilize

touched *adjective.* barmy, bizarre, bonkers, cuckoo, eccentric, fanatic, flighty, insane, neurotic, not right, nuts, obsessed, odd, peculiar, pixilated, queer, screwy, unhinged

touching *adjective.* affecting, compassionate, grabbed by, heart-breaking, impressive, melting, pathetic, piteous, pitiable, pitiful, poignant, responsive, sad, stirring, stunning, sympathetic, tear-jerking, tender

tough *adjective.* **1** conditioned, dense, fibrous, firm, fit, hard, hardy, indigestible, mighty, resistant, rigid, sinewy, solid, steeled, stiff, stout, strapping, tenacious **2** arbitrary, callous, cruel, drastic, exacting, fierce, fixed, hard, refractory, resolute, rough, savage, stiff, strict, stubborn, unalterable, uncompromising, vicious **3** arduous, baffling, demanding, exacting, handful, hard, heavy, intractable, intricate, irksome, labored, laborious, perplexing, puzzling, severe, stiff, toilsome, wicked

tour *noun.* bout, circuit, course, cruise, excursion, hitch, hop, overnight, progress, round, roundabout, spell, stint, stretch, swing, time, travel, turn

tour *verb.* barnstorm, cruise, do wherever, explore, globe-trot, holiday, hop, jaunt, jet, journey, junket, peregrinate, sightsee, stump, swing, travel, vacation, voyage

toward *preposition.* against, almost, approaching, close to, en route, facing, for, fronting, just before, moving, nearing, nearly, proceeding, shortly before, to, towards, via, vis-à-vis

tower *noun.* belfry, castle, citadel, column, fort, fortress, keep, lookout, mast, monolith, obelisk, pillar, refuge, skyscraper, spire, steeple, stronghold, turret

towering *adjective.* colossal, elevated, excessive, extravagant, extreme, immoderate, imperial, impressive, lofty, magnificent, massive, mighty, monumental, prodigious, stately, superior, tall, tremendous

trace *noun.* drop, element, hint, iota, mark, memento, minimum, particle, relic, remains, remnant, shade, sign, spot, suggestion, survival, taste, touch

trace *verb.* ascertain, detect, determine, discern, discover, find, follow, hunt, perceive, pursue, run down, shadow, smell out, spoor, spot, track, trail, unearth

track *noun.* **1** clue, footstep, groove, impress, impression, imprint, path, print, record, remains, remnant, sign, step, symbol, trace, tract, trail, wake **2** boulevard, clearing, course, drag, footpath, lane, line, orbit, passage, rail, rails, route, street, thoroughfare, trail, trajectory, walk, way

track *verb.* capture, chase, cover, discover, do, dog, expose, find, follow, run down, scout, shadow, tail, trace, track down, trail, travel, traverse

tract *noun.* amplitude, belt, estate, expanse, extent, field, parcel, part, piece, plot, preserve, quarter, region, section, sector, spread, stretch, zone

trade *noun.* **1** business, clientele, contract, custom, customers, deal, dealing, enterprise, exchange, interchange, market, patronage, public, sales, swap, traffic, transaction, truck **2** art, avocation, bag, biz, business, calling, craft, dodge, employment, game, gig, job, line, occupation, pursuit, skill, vocation, work

tradition *noun.* conclusion, culture, custom, fable, form, habit, heritage, inheritance, institution, law, legend, lore, mores, myth, mythology, opinion, practice, wisdom

traditional *adjective*. acceptable, ancestral, classical, common, conventional, doctrinal, fixed, folk, historic, old, oral, popular, regular, rooted, sanctioned, transmitted, universal, widespread

traffic *noun*. **1** cartage, flux, freight, influx, jam, movement, parking lot, passage, passengers, service, shipment, transfer, transit, transport, transportation, travel, truckage, vehicles **2** business, closeness, communion, connection, custom, dealing, dealings, doings, exchange, interchange, intercourse, intimacy, patronage, relations, relationship, soliciting, transactions, truck

traffic *verb*. bargain, contact, deal, exchange, fence, handle, interface, market, negotiate, network, peddle, push, relate, shove, swap, touch, truck, work out

tragedy *noun*. adversity, affliction, blow, calamity, catastrophe, contretemps, curse, curtains, doom, failure, hardship, humiliation, misfortune, mishap, reverse, shock, struggle, wreck

tragic *adjective*. anguished, appalling, bad, crushing, deathly, destructive, doleful, dreadful, forlorn, hapless, heartbreaking, miserable, mournful, pitiable, pitiful, ruinous, shocking, unfortunate

trail *noun*. aisle, footpath, footsteps, groove, mark, marks, road, route, rut, scent, stream, stroll, tail, trace, track, train, wake, way

trail *verb*. dangle, delay, dog, drag, draw, droop, extend, halt, haul, linger, procrastinate, pull, pursue, shag, straggle, tarry, tow, trace

train *noun*. caravan, convoy, cortege, course, court, file, line, order, retinue, row, sequel, sequence, set, string, suite, tail, trail, wake

train *verb*. coach, discipline, educate, exercise, ground, hone, instruct, inure, mold, prime, qualify, school, season, study, tame, teach, tutor, update

training *noun*. background, basics, cultivation, discipline, drill, education, exercise, foundation, grounding, groundwork, practice, preparation, principles, schooling, seasoning, sharpening, tuition, workout

transfer *noun*. alteration, assignment, conduction, convection, deportation, displacement, move, relegation, relocation, removal, shift, substitution, transference, translation, transmission, transmittal, transposition, variation

transfer *verb*. assign, carry, change, convey, deliver, dispatch, displace, disturb, forward, give, haul, metamorphose, move, ship, supply, translate, transport, turn over

transform *verb*. alter, commute, convert, cook, denature, do up, doctor, metamorphose, mold, mutate, reconstruct, renew, revamp, shift gears, switch, transfer, translate, turn around

transit *noun*. alteration, carrying, conveyance, crossing, infiltration, motion, movement, passage, penetration, portage, shift, shipment, transfer, transference, transport, transporting, travel, traverse

transition *noun*. alteration, conversion, development, evolution, flux, growth, metamorphosis, passage, passing, progress, progression, shift, transformation, transit, transmutation, turn, turning point, upheaval

translate *verb*. construe, convert, decode, do into, elucidate, explain, explicate, gloss, make clear, metaphrase, paraphrase, put, render, reword, simplify, transcribe, transpose, turn

translation *noun*. adaptation, construction, crib, decoding, elucidation, explanation, gloss, interpretation, key, metaphrase, paraphrase, reading, rendering, rendition, restatement, simplification, transcription, version

transparent *adjective*. **1** cellophane, clear, crystalline, diaphanous, filmy, gauzy, glassy, gossamer, hyaline, limpid, lucid, permeable, plain, sheer, thin, translucent, transpicuous, vitreous **2** articulate, artless, candid, direct, distinct, evident, explicit, forthright, frank, guileless, honest, manifest, open, sincere, unambiguous, undisguised, unmistakable, visible

transport *noun.* carrier, carrying, conveyance, conveying, conveyor, hauling, lift, movement, passage, removal, shipment, shipping, transfer, transference, transferring, transit, transportation, vehicle

transport *verb.* **1** bear, carry, convey, ferry, fetch, haul, heel, hump, jag, lug, pack, remove, ride, ship, shoulder, take, transfer, truck **2** agitate, carry away, delight, enchant, entrance, excite, inflame, move, provoke, quicken, ravish, send, slay, stimulate, stir, thrill, trance, wow

trap *noun.* ambush, bait, conspiracy, deception, device, gambit, lure, maneuver, net, noose, pit, plot, prank, quagmire, ruse, snag, snare, temptation

trap *verb.* ambuscade, ambush, bag, collar, corner, deceive, fool, grab, land, nail, net, overtake, snag, snare, surprise, take, tangle, trammel

travel *noun.* driving, excursion, hop, movement, overnight, passage, ramble, ride, riding, seafaring, swing, tour, touring, transit, travel, trek, walk, weekend

travel *verb.* carry, cover, cruise, fly, jet, migrate, motor, move, overnight, proceed, progress, ramble, rove, tour, vacation, visit, walk, wander

traveler *noun.* barnstormer, commuter, explorer, floater, globetrotter, gypsy, itinerant, migrant, peddler, pilgrim, rover, sailor, tourist, tramp, truant, vagabond, vagrant, voyager

treasury *noun.* bank, bursar, bursary, cache, chest, depository, exchange, exchequer, gallery, museum, register, repository, safe, storage, store, storehouse, strongbox, vault

treat *noun.* banquet, celebration, dainty, delicacy, delight, entertainment, feast, fun, gift, goody, gratification, party, refreshment, satisfaction, surprise, sweet, thrill, tidbit

treat *verb.* **1** account, appraise, consider, employ, estimate, evaluate, handle, hold, manage, negotiate, rate, regard, respect, serve, take, use, value, wield **2** amuse, blow, divert, entertain, escort, feast, give, indulge, play host, pop, pop for, provide, satisfy, set up, shot, spring for, stake, stand **3** advise, approach, confer, consider, consult, contain, criticize, deliberate, discuss, explain, huddle, interpret, parley, reason, review, study, tackle, think

treatment *noun.* angle, approach, custom, dealing, employment, habit, line, management, manipulation, manner, method, mode, practice, procedure, proceeding, reception, strategy, way

treaty *noun.* accord, alliance, arrangement, bargain, bond, charter, compact, concord, contract, convention, covenant, deal, negotiation, pact, reconciliation, sanction, settlement, understanding

tremendous *adjective.* appalling, astounding, awesome, blimp, colossal, dreadful, enormous, exceptional, fabulous, incredible, mammoth, marvelous, massive, monstrous, monumental, prodigious, vast, wonderful

trend *noun.* aim, bearing, bent, bias, course, current, direction, drift, inclination, leaning, movement, orientation, progression, run, swing, tendency, tenor, wind

trial *noun.* **1** analysis, assay, attempt, effort, endeavor, examination, experience, experiment, experimentation, investigation, lick, shot, showcase, stab, struggle, testing, try, undertaking **2** action, case, citation, claim, contest, counterclaim, court action, cross-examination, hearing, indictment, lawsuit, litigation, prosecution, rap, seizure, suit, tribunal, try **3** affliction, bother, burden, distress, drag, grief, inconvenience, irritation, load, misery, nightmare, ordeal, pest, plague, thorn, tribulation, visitation

tribute *noun.* accolade, acknowledgment, applause, appreciation, citation, commendation, compliment, esteem, gift, honor, memorial, offering, praise, recognition, recommendation, respect, salutation, salvo

trick *noun.* **1** ambush, bluff, con, concealment, conspiracy, cover, delusion, distortion, dodge, fake, forgery, illusion, invention, perjury, pretense, ruse, snare, trap **2** accomplishment, antic, caper, catch, device, dido, escapade, feat, frolic, gag, gambol, jape, jest, lark, prank, sport, stunt, tomfoolery

trick *verb.* catch, cheat, con, deceive, defraud, delude, fool, gull, have, hoax, jive, outwit, screw, set up, shaft, throw, trap, victimize

trifle *noun.* beans, bit, drop, fraction, hint, little, particle, picayune, piece, shade, smack, speck, spice, spot, suggestion, suspicion, touch, trace

trifle *verb.* dabble, dawdle, flirt, fool, fool with, fribble, idle, lounge, misuse, monkey, philander, play, play with, potter, putter, toy, wanton, waste

trim *adjective.* apple-pie order, clean, clean-cut, compact, dapper, fit, natty, nice, orderly, shipshape, slick, smart, snug, spruce, streamlined, symmetrical, tidy, uncluttered

trim *verb.* **1** barber, bob, clip, crop, curtail, cut, cut back, cut down, dock, lop, pare, plane, prune, shave, shear, shorten, slice off, tidy **2** adorn, array, beautify, bedeck, deck, deck out, dress, dress up, embroider, gussy up, ornament, prank, pretty up, prink, spangle, spruce up, trick out

trip *noun.* cruise, errand, excursion, expedition, foray, hop, jaunt, outing, overnight, peregrination, ramble, run, swing, tour, travel, trek, voyage, weekend

trip *verb.* buck, canter, disconcert, err, fall, frolic, hop, lapse, misstep, pitch, plunge, skip, slide, slip, sprawl, spring, stumble, topple

triumph *noun.* , ascendancy, attainment, cinch, conquest, coup, gain, kill, riot, sell, sensation, slam, smash, splash, success, victory, win, wow

triumph *verb.* best, conquer, dominate, flourish, master, overcome, overwhelm, prevail, prosper, sink, skunk, subdue, succeed, sweep, thrive, trounce, vanquish, win

trivial *adjective.* atomic, diminutive, flimsy, inconsequential, insignificant, irrelevant, little, meager, meaningless, minor, minute, petty, piddling, slight, small, unimportant, vanishing, worthless

troop *noun.* assembly, body, collection, corps, drove, flock, forces, gang, horde, men, military, multitude, number, outfit, squad, throng, troops, troupe

trophy *noun.* booty, citation, cookies, crown, cup, decoration, gold, laurels, medal, memento, memorial, palm, prize, reminder, ribbon, souvenir, spoils, token

trouble *noun.* **1** agitation, bother, commotion, danger, dilemma, discontent, disquiet, dissatisfaction, distress, grief, inconvenience, irritation, mess, pest, predicament, row, scrape, torment **2** ado, attention, bother, bustle, concern, difficulty, effort, exertion, flurry, fuss, hardship, inconvenience, pains, stress, struggle, thought, trial, work

trouble *verb.* agitate, burden, concern, craze, disconcert, disquiet, distress, disturb, fret, harass, inconvenience, pain, pester, plague, stress, torment, try, upset

troublesome *adjective.* annoying, arduous, demanding, disquieting, harassing, hard, heavy, intractable, irksome, irritating, laborious, messy, refractory, rough, tiresome, ugly, unruly, vexatious

truck *noun.* **1** barter, business, commodities, communication, communion, connection, contact, dealings, exchange, goods, intercourse, merchandise, relations, stock, stuff, trade, traffic, wares **2** boat, buggy, car, carryall, crate, dump, eighteen-wheeler, four-wheel drive, freight box, horse, jeep, lorry, pickup, rig, semi, van, wagon, wheels

true *adjective.* **1** accurate, actual, appropriate, authentic, exact, fitting, honest, indubitable, legal, natural, normal, proper, regular, right, sincere, truthful, typical, valid **2** ardent, confirmed, constant, dedicated, firm, honest, resolute, right, scrupulous, sincere, square, steady, strict, sure, unaffected, upright, veridical, worthy

truly *adverb.* accurately, actually, authentically, correctly, definitely, exactly, faithfully, honestly, honorably, legitimately, reliably, rightly, sincerely, steadily, surely, truthfully, unequivocally, very

trust *noun.* **1** assurance, certainty, certitude, confidence, conviction, credence, credit, dependence, entrustment, expectation, faith, gospel truth, hope, positiveness, reliance, stock, store, sureness **2** bunch, business, chain, combine, corporation, crew, crowd, gang, group, institution, mob, monopoly, multinational, organization, outfit, pool, ring, syndicate **3** accredit, assume, bank on, be convinced, bet on, confide in, depend on, expect, hope, imagine, lean on, presume, reckon on, rely upon, suppose, surmise, take, think likely **4** advance, aid, assign, command, commission, commit, confer, confide, consign, delegate, entrust, grant, lend, let, loan, patronize, transfer, turn over

truth *noun.* **1** accuracy, actuality, axiom, case, certainty, fact, facts, law, maxim, precision, rectitude, rightness, truism, truthfulness, validity, veracity, verisimilitude, verity **2** authenticity, candor, constancy, dedication, devotion, dutifulness, faith, fidelity, frankness, honesty, integrity, openness, realism, revelation, sincerity, uprightness, veridicality, verity

try *noun.* bid, crack, effort, endeavor, essay, fling, go, jab, pop, shot, slap, stab, striving, struggle, trial, undertaking, whack, whirl

try *verb.* **1** aim, aspire, attack, bear down, compete, contend, contest, endeavor, labor, propose, risk, speculate, strive, struggle, tackle, undertake, venture, work **2** annoy, distress, harass, inconvenience, martyr, pain, plague, rack, strain, stress, tax, tire, torment, trouble, upset, vex, weary, wring

trying *adjective.* annoying, arduous, demanding, exacting, exasperating, hard, irksome, irritating, oppressive, pestilent, rough, severe, sticky, taxing, tiresome, upsetting, vexing, wearisome

tune *noun.* air, carol, chorus, composition, concert, consonance, descant, ditty, harmony, jingle, lay, measure, motif, number, piece, song, strain, theme

turmoil *noun.* agitation, ailment, bedlam, bustle, commotion, disquiet, distress, fuss, hectic, hubbub, riot, row, ruckus, stew, stir, trouble, uproar, violence

turn *noun.* **1** angle, bend, branch, change, circuit, cycle, departure, direction, gyration, pirouette, pivot, rotation, round, swing, tendency, trend, turning, wind **2** alteration, bend, branch, crotch, deflection, departure, detour, deviation, distortion, double, fork, modification, shift, tack, twist, variation, warp, yaw **3** act, bit, bout, crack, deed, favor, fling, gesture, move, period, round, routine, shot, spell, stint, time, tour, try **4** ability, affinity, aptness, bent, bias, bump, disposition, faculty, flair, genius, gift, head, inclination, knack, leaning, predisposition, propensity, talent **5** arc, bend, circulate, curve, ground, incline, loop, orbit, pass, pirouette, pivot, revolve, roll, rotate, round, swing, swivel, wind **6** aim, alternate, change, deviate, incline, inverse, loop, move, pivot, recoil, retrace, shunt, swing, swirl, transform, upset, vary, whip **7** alter, change, come, divert, fashion, fit, form, metamorphose, mold, put, refashion, remake, render, shape, transform, translate, vary, wax **8** address, appeal, approach, bend, devote, direct, employ, favor, give, incline, look, prefer, recur, repair, tend, throw, undertake, utilize

turn *verb.* bring round, change sides, defect, desert, go over, influence, persuade, prejudice, prevail upon, rat, rat on, renege, renounce, repudiate, retract, talk into, tergiversate

twin *adjective.* accompanying, copied, corresponding, coupled, double, dual, identical, joint, like, matched, matching, paired, parallel, same, second, self-same, similar, twofold

twist *noun.* aberration, bent, change, characteristic, confusion, eccentricity, entanglement, knot, mess, peculiarity, quirk, revelation, slant, surprise, tangle, trait, turn, variation

twist *verb.* coil, corkscrew, encircle, screw, spin, spiral, swivel, turn, turn around, twine, warp, weave, wiggle, wind, wrap, wring, writhe

type *noun.* category, description, feather,

form, group, kidney, kind, likes, mold, number, persuasion, rubric, sort, species, stamp, stripe, subdivision, variety

typical *adjective.* average, characteristic, classical, common, conventional, essential, expected, illustrative, model, natural, normal, orthodox, paradigmatic, prevalent, regular, standard, standardized, stock

tyranny *noun.* absolutism, authoritarianism, autocracy, coercion, cruelty, despotism, domination, fascism, high-handedness, imperiousness, monocracy, oppression, peremptoriness, severity, terrorism, totalitarianism, totality, unreasonableness

U

ugly *adjective.* **1** appalling, beast, dog, foul, frightful, gross, hideous, homely, horrid, loathsome, misshapen, monstrous, plug, repugnant, repulsive, revolting, unseemly, unsightly **2** base, dirty, distasteful, foul, horrid, messy, monstrous, nasty, objectionable, offensive, repugnant, revolting, shocking, sickening, unpleasant, vexatious, wicked, wretched **3** black, crabbed, disagreeable, dour, fell, grave, grievous, malevolent, morose, nasty, ominous, quarrelsome, rough, scowling, sinister, treacherous, vicious, wicked

ultimate *adjective.* **1** closing, concluding, conclusive, curtains, decisive, end, eventual, extreme, farthest, furthest, hindmost, lag, last, latest, latter, most distant, payoff, terminal **2** extreme, greatest, highest, incomparable, max, maximum, most significant, paramount, pre-eminent, superlative, supreme, the most, topmost, towering, transcendent, utmost

unable *adjective.* clumsy, helpless, impotent, impuissant, inadequate, incapable, incapacitated, incompetent, ineffectual, inefficient, inept, no good, not able, powerless, unfit, unqualified, unskilled, weak

unaware *adjective.* blind, careless, daydreaming, deaf, doped, forgetful, heedless, ignorant, inattentive, negligent, oblivious, stoned, unacquainted, unconcerned, unconscious, unknowing, unmindful, unwitting

unbroken *adjective.* ceaseless, constant, deep, endless, entire, even, incessant, intact, perpetual, profound, regular, solid, sound, successive, total, uninterrupted, unremitting, whole

uncertain *adjective.* ambiguous, ambivalent, dubious, hazy, hesitant, indistinct, insecure, irregular, precarious, questionable, speculative, undetermined, unreliable, unresolved, unsettled, unsure, vague, variable

uncertainty *noun.* ambiguity, bewilderment, concern, conjecture, contingency, dilemma, disquiet, distrust, indecision, mystification, perplexity, reserve, salt, suspicion, trouble, unpredictability, vagueness, wonder

uncomfortable *adjective.* **1** agonizing, annoying, awkward, bitter, difficult, disagreeable, distressing, excruciating, galling, grievous, hard, harsh, irritating, rough, thorny, troublesome, vexatious, wearisome **2** aching, anguished, confused, disturbed, exhausted, fatigued, galled, miserable, nervous, pained, sore, stiff, strained, uneasy, vexed, weary, wracked, wretched

uncommon *adjective.* **1** anomalous, bizarre, exceptional, exotic, extreme, irregular, nondescript, odd, peculiar, prodigious, queer, remarkable, scarce, startling, strange, surprising, unique, unusual **2** distinctive, exceptional, extraordinary, incomparable, notable, noteworthy, outstanding, rare, remarkable, singular, special, superior, unimaginable, unique, unparalleled, unprecedented, unthinkable, unwonted

unconcerned *adjective.* apathetic, callous, cold, distant, forgetful, hardened, inattentive, indifferent, insensitive, lackadaisical, lukewarm, negligent, neutral, nonchalant, oblivious, relaxed, uninterested, unmoved

unconscious *adjective.* **1** bombed, cold, drowsy, entranced, flattened, inanimate, inert, numb, out, paralyzed, put away, raving, senseless, spacey, stoned, stunned, torpid, zonked out **2** automatic, gut, ignorant, inadvertent, inattentive, innate, involuntary, latent, lost, reflex, repressed, subconscious, suppressed, unheeding, unintended, unmindful, unpremeditated, unwitting

under *adverb.* amenable, consequent, corollary, dependent, directed, following, governed, inferior, junior, lesser, lower, obedient, subject, subordinate, subsequent, subservient, subsidiary, subsumed

undergo *verb.* abide, bear, bow, encounter, endure, experience, feel, have, know, see, stand, suffer, support, sustain, tolerate, weather, withstand, yield

underground *adjective.* alternative, avant-garde, clandestine, concealed, covert, experimental, hidden, private, radical, resistant, resistive, revolutionary, subversive, surreptitious, unconventional, under wraps, undercover, unusual

underlying *adjective.* basic, bottom, concealed, critical, crucial, elemental, essential, intrinsic, latent, lurking, necessary, primary, prime, primitive, radical, root, veiled, vital

undermine *verb.* blunt, corrode, dig, disable, foil, frustrate, hurt, impair, mine, ruin, sabotage, sap, soften, threaten, thwart, tunnel, undercut, wreck

understand *verb.* **1** appreciate, deduce, dig, follow, grasp, infer, interpret, ken, know, learn, master, perceive, read, realize, recognize, see, seize, sense **2** accept, assume, concede, conclude, conjecture, consider, deduce, expect, fancy, guess, hear, imagine, infer, learn, presume, reckon, suppose, think

understanding *noun.* **1** appreciation, apprehension, awareness, discernment, discrimination, insight, intellect, intuition, judgment, ken, knowledge, penetration, perception, realization, reason, recognition, sense, wit **2** conclusion, estimation, idea, impression, inkling, interpretation, judgment, knowledge, meaning, notion, opinion, perception, purport, sense, significance, sympathy, view, viewpoint

understood *adjective.* accepted, appreciated, axiomatic, dug, implicit, implied, inferential, inferred, known, on to, pat, pegged, presumed, roger, tacit, undeclared, unsaid, unspoken

undertake *verb.* agree, bargain, commit, contract, covenant, devote, embark, endeavor, hazard, launch, move, offer, pledge, promise, shoulder, stake, try, volunteer

undesirable *adjective.* annoying, defective, disagreeable, distasteful, dreaded, inconvenient, loathsome, objectionable, offensive, repellent, repugnant, scorned, shunned, unacceptable, unpopular, unsavory, unwanted, useless

undue *adjective.* exceeding, extravagant, extreme, forbidden, illegal, immoderate, inapt, inept, sinister, unconscionable, undeserved, unfitting, unjustifiable, unnecessary, unseasonable, unseemly, untimely, unwarranted

uneasy *adjective.* agitated, alarmed, anguished, constrained, dismayed, disturbed, edgy, harassed, insecure, jittery, precarious, shaken, strained, suspicious, tormented, unsettled, upset, vexed

unexpected *adjective.* abrupt, accidental, amazing, astonishing, chance, electrifying, impetuous, impulsive, instantaneous, prodigious, staggering, startling, stunning, sudden, swift, unforeseen, unpredictable, wonderful

unfair *adjective.* arbitrary, bad, base, bigoted, criminal, crooked, cruel, discriminatory, foul, illegal, iniquitous, injurious, petty, unlawful, unwarranted, vicious, wicked, wrongful

unfamiliar *adjective.* **1** alien, anomalous, bizarre, curious, exotic, fantastic, foreign, new, obscure, outlandish, peculiar, recondite, remarkable, remote, strange, unexplored, unknown, unusual **2** ignorant, incognizant, nonconversant, not associated, oblivious, unaccustomed, unacquainted, unaware, uninformed, uninitiated, uninstructed, unknowing, unknown, unpracticed, unskilled, unversed, unwitting

unfortunate *adjective.* afflicted, burdened, calamitous, cursed, damaging, deplorable, destitute, doomed, hapless, pained, poor, ruined, ruinous, shattered, troubled, unfavorable, untoward, wretched

unhappy *adjective.* black, crestfallen, crummy, depressed, despondent, destroyed, down, downcast, dreary, grim, hurting, mirthless, miserable, mournful, oppressive, ripped, sorry, troubled

unification *noun.* affinity, alliance, amalgamation, coalition, combination, concurrence, confederation, connection, consolidation, coupling, federation, fusion, interlocking, linkage, merger, merging, union, uniting

uniform *adjective.* **1** compatible, fated, fixed, homogeneous, invariable, irreversible, level, monolithic, normal, ordered, orderly, regular, rigid, smooth, steady, true, unalterable, unbroken **2** akin, analogous, carbon, comparable, consistent, consonant, correspondent, double, equal, identical, like, mated, monotonous, parallel, same, similar, treadmill, undifferentiated

uniform *noun.* attire, bag, costume, dress, garb, gown, habit, khaki, livery, monkey clothes, monkey suit, OD, olive drab, regalia, regimentals, robe, stripes, suit

unimportant *adjective.* beans, casual, inconsequential, indifferent, insignificant, irrelevant, little, minor, minute, petty, picayune, piddling, shoestring, slight, unnecessary, useless, worthless, zero

union *noun.* **1** accord, agglutination, agreement, blend, centralization, compound, concord, concurrence, conjunction, fusion, harmony, intercourse, joint, meeting, seam, unanimity, unison, uniting **2** alliance, association, brotherhood, club, coalition, confederacy, confederation, congress, employees, federation, guild, labor union, league, local, order, society, syndicate, trade union

unique *adjective.* **1** different, exclusive, individual, lone, one, only, particular, rare, separate, single, singular, solitary, solo, sui generis, uncommon, unexampled, unrepeated **2** anomalous, best, exceptional, incomparable, matchless, most, only, peerless, rare, singular, special, strange, unequalled, unimaginable, unmatched, unprecedented, unreal, utmost

unit *noun.* **1** assemblage, assembly, bunch, crew, crowd, detachment, entirety, entity, gang, group, mob, one, outfit, ring, section, system, total, totality **2** arm, constituent, detachment, detail, digit, element, feature, fraction, integer, item, joint, layer, length, member, piece, section, segment, square

unite *verb.* associate, band, blend, coalesce, confederate, consolidate, cooperate, couple, embody, fuse, join, marry, meet, merge, pool, relate, strengthen, wed

united *adjective.* affiliated, allied, amalgamated, assembled, banded, cognate, collective, congruent, consolidated, cooperative, corporate, federal, homogeneous, incorporated, integrated, linked, one, undivided

unity *noun.* accord, agreement, alliance, concord, consonance, entity, harmony, homogeneity, integral, integrity, oneness, peace, rapport, solidarity, unanimity, uniformity, union, unison

universal *adjective.* accepted, all, astronomical, celestial, common, cosmopolitan, diffuse, earthly, entire, extensive, prevalent, regular, sweeping, ubiquitous, undisputed, unrestricted, usual, widespread

unknown *adjective.* alien, distant, exotic, far, mysterious, new, remote, secret, strange, uncharted, unexplained, unexplored, unidentified, unnamed, unperceived, unrecognized, unsung, untold

unlike *adjective.* contradictory, contrary, contrasted, disparate, dissimilar, dissonant, distant, distinct, divergent, diverse, heterogeneous, hostile, inconsistent, offbeat, opposite, unrelated, variant, various

unlikely *adjective.* absurd, contrary, doubtful, dubious, faint, improbable, inconceivable, incredible, outside chance, questionable, rare, remote, slight, strange, unbelievable, unconvincing, unimaginable, untoward

unlimited *adjective.* absolute, boundless, endless, full, immeasurable, immense, incalculable, indefinite, interminable, limitless, total, totalitarian, unfettered, universal, unqualified, unrestricted, untold, vast

unload *verb.* break bulk, cast, discharge, discommode, disencumber, disgorge, dump, jettison, lighten, off-load, relieve, remove, rid, slough, take off, unlade, unpack, void

unmistakable *adjective.* apparent, clear, conspicuous, decided, definite, distinct, evident, explicit, glaring, manifest, obvious, palpable, plain, positive, pronounced, sure, transparent, unambiguous

unnatural *adjective.* affected, feigned, imitation, incredible, insincere, irregular, labored, odd, perverse, perverted, queer, stiff, strained, studied, supernatural, synthetic, unusual, wonderful

unnecessary *adjective.* casual, excess, expendable, futile, irrelevant, lavish, needless, optional, profuse, redundant, superfluous, surplus, uncritical, undesirable, unneeded, useless, wanton, worthless

unpleasant *adjective.* abhorrent, disagreeable, distasteful, fierce, gross, irksome, lousy, nasty, objectionable, obnoxious, poison, repulsive, rotten, sour, unacceptable, undesirable, unhappy, unlovely

unprecedented *adjective.* abnormal, anomalous, bizarre, exotic, fantastic, idiosyncratic, marvelous, miraculous, modern, new, odd, outlandish, prodigious, remarkable, signal, singular, unique, unusual

unrelated *adjective.* different, dissimilar, extraneous, inapplicable, inappropriate, irrelative, irrelevant, mismatched, nongermane, not germane, not kin, not kindred, not related, separate, unassociated, unattached, unconnected, unlike

unsatisfactory *adjective.* bad, deficient, disquieting, distressing, lame, mediocre, offensive, poor, punk, rotten, second, unacceptable, undesirable, unworthy, upsetting, vexing, weak, wrong

unstable *adjective.* ambiguous, capricious, dubious, fluctuating, insecure, irrational, mercurial, mobile, movable, precarious, rocky, slippery, uncertain, unsettled, variable, weak, weaving, wobbly

untouched *adjective.* clear, entire, flawless, good, immaculate, indifferent, sanitary, secure, shipshape, sound, spotless, unbroken, unconcerned, uninjured, unmoved, unscathed, unstained, virgin

unusual *adjective.* astonishing, awesome, bizarre, conspicuous, distinguished, exceptional, important, inconceivable, incredible, odd, prodigious, queer, refreshing, remarkable, significant, strange, surprising, unique

unusually *adverb.* almighty, curiously, extra, extraordinarily, mighty, oddly, plenty, powerful, rarely, real, really, remarkably, right, so, strangely, surprisingly, uncommonly, very

unwilling *adjective.* afraid, against, compelled, contrary, evasive, hesitating, involuntary, loath, opposed, recalcitrant, refractory, reluctant, resistant, shrinking, shy, slack, uncooperative, unready

uphold *verb.* advocate, aid, assist, bolster, boost, carry, defend, encourage, endorse, hoist, justify, pick up, promote, prop, raise, second, stand by, sustain

upright *adjective.* circumspect, correct, ethical, fair, faithful, good, honest, impartial, incorruptible, kosher, moral, right, righteous, square, straight, true, unimpeachable, virtuous

upset *adjective.* agitated, amazed, chaotic, confused, dismayed, disordered, distressed, disturbed, ill, jittery, ruffled, shocked, thrown, toppled, troubled, unglued, unsettled, worried

upset *noun.* agitation, bother, complaint, defeat, destruction, disquiet, distress, illness, malady, overthrow, queasiness, reverse, shock, sickness, stew, subversion, surprise, trouble

upset *verb.* **1** capsize, change, disarray, disorganize, disturb, invert, jumble, mess up, muddle, pitch, reverse, spill, spoil, tilt, topple, tumble, turn, upturn **2** agitate, bug, cramp, craze, disconcert, dismay, disquiet, distract, distress, disturb, fire up, flip, floor, flurry, get to, rattle, trouble, turn

urge *noun.* appetite, compulsion, craving, fancy, goad, impetus, impulse, incentive, itch, longing, lust, motive, passion, pressure, stimulus, weakness, wish, yearning

urge *verb.* advocate, compel, conjure, encourage, endorse, further, goad, implore, move, plead, press, prompt, propel, propose, rationalize, recommend, request, solicit

urgent *adjective.* chief, clamorous, compelling, crying, demanded, demanding, driving, foremost, heavy, impelling, important, insistent, instant, necessary, persuasive, required, salient, wanted

usable *adjective.* accessible, applicable, beneficial, expendable, fit, function, good, helpful, instrumental, open, practicable, practical, profitable, running, serviceable, subservient, valid, valuable

usage *noun.* currency, custom, form, formula, management, method, mode, operation, practice, procedure, regime, regulation, routine, rule, running, treatment, way, wont

use *noun.* adoption, appliance, avail, benefit, convenience, custom, employment, exertion, good, helpfulness, kick, necessity, occasion, operation, reason, usefulness, utility, worth

use *verb.* bestow, consume, employ, exercise, exert, exhaust, exploit, govern, handle, manage, ply, practice, regulate, relate, spend, waste, wield, work

useful *adjective.* applied, appropriate, beneficial, fit, good, handy, helpful, instrumental, meet, practicable, practical, pragmatic, profitable, proper, serviceable, subsidiary, suited, worthwhile

useless *adjective.* expendable, fruitless, futile, idle, incompetent, ineffective, inept, meaningless, pointless, purposeless, stupid, unavailable, unproductive, unprofitable, unworkable, vain, weak, worthless

usual *adjective.* accepted, average, chronic, constant, conventional, fixed, frequent, grind, groove, natural, normal, plastic, prevalent, regular, routine, standard, typical, unremarkable

utility *noun.* account, adequacy, advantage, applicability, appropriateness, avail, benefit, convenience, efficacy, efficiency, favor, fitness, function, practicality, relevance, service, use, usefulness

utmost *adjective.* absolute, chief, entire, exhaustive, farthest, final, last, plenary, supreme, ten, thoroughgoing, top, topmost, ultra, undiminished, unqualified, uttermost, whole

utopian *adjective.* abstract, ambitious, dream, fanciful, fantasy, grandiose, hopeful, idealist, idealistic, ideological, illusory, imaginary, impossible, lofty, otherworldly, pretentious, quixotic, romantic

utter *adjective.* absolute, blasted, blessed, blooming, complete, confounded, consummate, downright, entire, perfect, pure, sheer, stark, thorough, thoroughgoing, total, unmitigated, unqualified

utter *verb.* affirm, articulate, assert, deliver, enunciate, exclaim, express, jaw, mouth, proclaim, pronounce, publish, shout, speak, state, talk, vocalize, voice

V

vacant *adjective.* **1** abandoned, available, bare, clear, deserted, devoid, free, idle, stark, tenantless, unemployed, unengaged, unfilled, unlived in, unoccupied, untenanted, unused, void **2** abstracted, blank, daydreaming, dreaming, dreamy, empty-headed, expressionless, foolish, idle, inane, incurious, silly, stupid, thoughtless, unthinking, vacuous, vapid, witless

vague *adjective.* ambiguous, bleary, dim, doubtful, dubious, enigmatic, hazy, inexplicable, loose, muddy, perplexing, puzzling, shadowy, tenebrous, uncertain, undetermined, unsettled, unsure

vain *adjective.* **1** arrogant, big-headed, cocky, conceited, egocentric, egoistic, haughty, high-and-mighty, inflated, narcissistic, ostentatious, overweening, proud, puffed up, self-important, swaggering, swollen-headed, vainglorious **2** abortive, barren, frivolous, fruitless, hollow, idle, insignificant, petty, pointless, puny, slight, unimportant, unproductive, unprofitable, useless, valueless, void, worthless

valid *adjective.* attested, authentic, binding, compelling, convincing, determinative, good, legal, persuasive, powerful, proven, solid, sound, strong, substantial, tested, true, unadulterated

validity *noun.* authority, effectiveness, efficacy, force, foundation, gravity, grounds, legality, legitimacy, point, potency, power, punch, right, soundness, strength, substance, weight

valuable *adjective.* admired, appreciated, beneficial, costly, dear, esteemed, expensive, helpful, hot, important, precious, profitable, relevant, scarce, serviceable, useful, valued, worthwhile

value *noun.* bearing, benefit, content, distinction, eminence, goodness, implication, importance, mark, meaning, power, preference, regard, repute, stature, substance, usefulness, worth

vanity *noun.* affected way, affection, airs, arrogance, conceitedness, display, ego trip, egotism, ostentation, pretension, pride, self-admiration, self-love, self-worship, show, showing off, smugness, vainglory

variable *adjective.* capricious, changeable, fickle, fitful, flexible, fluctuating, fluid, irregular, mercurial, mobile, shifting, shifty, slippery, uncertain, unsettled, unstable, unsteady, volatile

variation *noun.* aberration, adaptation, bend, break, change, contradistinction, curve, departure, deviation, discrepancy, distinction, divergence, diversity, inequality, innovation, novelty, turn, variety

variety *noun.* **1** array, change, collection, departure, discrepancy, diversification, diversity, incongruity, medley, miscellany, mixture, multiplicity, potpourri, range, soup, stew, variance, variation **2** assortment, breed, category, character, description, division, family, genus, grade, kidney, kind, order, quality, race, sort, species, strain, stripe

various *adjective.* changeable, changing, discrete, disparate, distinct, distinctive, diverse, diversified, individual, manifold, many, multitudinous, peculiar, several, sundry, variant, varied, variegated

vary *verb.* alter, alternate, convert, depart, deviate, differ, disagree, displace, dissent, divide, interchange, modify, part, range, separate, swerve, transform, turn

vast *adjective.* astronomical, colossal, endless, enormous, eternal, extensive, giant, limitless, mammoth, massive, monstrous, monumental, prodigious, spacious, sweeping, tremendous, voluminous, widespread

vehicle *noun.* agent, automobile, bicycle, buckboard, buggy, cab, carrier, chariot, conveyance, crate, jalopy, jeep, taxi, transport, truck, vector, wagon, wheels

veil *verb.* beard, blanket, camouflage, cloak, conceal, cover, curtain, dim, disguise, enclose, invest, launder, mantle, mask, obscure, screen, shield, wrap

vein *noun*. characteristic, complexion, faculty, hint, humor, line, manner, mode, spirit, streak, style, suggestion, temper, tone, touch, trace, wave, way

velocity *noun*. acceleration, celerity, dispatch, expedition, fleetness, gait, haste, headway, hurry, impetus, momentum, pace, quickness, rapidity, rapidness, rate, swiftness, tempo

vent *verb*. air, assert, declare, discharge, emit, empty, express, give, give out, issue, loose, put, release, state, unleash, utter, ventilate, voice

venture *noun*. baby, bag, dare, endeavor, enterprise, experiment, flyer, hazard, jeopardy, plunge, proposition, setup, spec, speculation, stab, test, trial, undertaking

venture *verb*. assay, attempt, bet, challenge, dare, defy, endanger, experiment, expose, front, gamble, grope, hazard, imperil, speculate, stake, try, volunteer

version *noun*. adaptation, chronicle, clarification, condensation, construction, exercise, form, history, narrative, paraphrase, reading, rendering, rendition, restatement, side, statement, story, transcription

vertex *noun*. apex, apogee, cap, cope, crest, crown, culmination, extremity, fastigium, height, peak, pinnacle, roof, summit, tip, tip-top, upper extremity, zenith

very *adjective*. actual, appropriate, authentic, bare, correct, exact, express, identical, indubitable, mere, model, precise, right, same, simple, special, true, unqualified

very *adverb*. considerably, cruel, deeply, eminently, excessively, extremely, largely, notably, particularly, powerfully, pretty, really, remarkably, surprisingly, uncommonly, unusually, vastly, wonderfully

veteran *adjective*. adept, disciplined, exercised, expert, hardened, hip, inured, old, practical, practiced, proficient, seasoned, sophisticated, steady, versed, vet, wise, worldly

veteran *noun*. expert, hep cat, master, old dog, old guard, old hand, old pro, old salt, oldster, past master, past mistress, pro, shellback, sourdough, sport, trouper, vet, warhorse

veto *verb*. adios, ban, burn, chuck, cut, decline, defeat, deny, disapprove, forbid, kill, negate, negative, pass, prohibit, refuse, reject, zing

vice *noun*. carnality, corruption, debauchery, decay, depravity, evil, ill, immorality, looseness, lust, offense, profligacy, rot, sensuality, sin, transgression, wickedness, wrong

vicious *adjective*. **1** bad, base, cruel, diabolical, foul, indecent, infamous, iniquitous, insubordinate, lewd, miscreant, monstrous, perverse, savage, sinful, villainous, wicked, worthless **2** cruel, dirty, fierce, frightful, hateful, horrid, malevolent, malicious, malign, ornery, poison, rancorous, rough, savage, slanderous, vehement, vindictive, wicked

victim *noun*. butt, casualty, chump, clown, fatality, forfeit, gambit, game, hunted, mark, pawn, pigeon, prey, quarry, sacrifice, tool, tourist, turkey

victor *noun*. champ, champion, conquering hero, conqueror, defeater, first, gold medalist, greatest, hero, king, master, medalist, number one, subjugator, title holder, top, vanquisher, winner

victory *noun*. achievement, advantage, ascendancy, conquest, defeat, destruction, dominion, gain, killing, overthrow, prize, slam, subjugation, success, superiority, supremacy, triumph, upset

view *noun*. **1** composition, contour, design, illustration, look, opening, outline, outlook, panorama, perspective, representation, show, spectacle, stretch, tableau, vision, vista, way **2** analysis, audit, check, contemplation, display, flash, gander, lamp, look, pike, review, scan, scrutiny, sight, slant, squint, survey, viewing **3** attitude, belief, concept, consideration, conviction, deduction, feeling, impression, inference, judgment, mind, notion, opinion, persuasion, sentiment, slant, thought, twist

view *verb*. beam, behold, consider, contemplate, dig, gaze, inspect, mark, notice, observe, pipe, read, regard, scope, see, spot, spy, watch

viewpoint *noun*. angle, aspect, direction,

estimation, ground, light, outlook, perspective, position, posture, respect, side, slant, stance, stand, standpoint, twist, view

vigor *noun.* agility, alertness, beef, bounce, endurance, enterprise, exercise, intensity, kick, manliness, motion, muscle, pith, power, soundness, starch, strength, vehemence

vigorous *adjective.* bouncing, driving, dynamic, enterprising, exuberant, flourishing, hale, hardy, hearty, masterful, mettlesome, persuasive, powerful, snappy, sound, strapping, strong, virile

violate *verb.* breach, contaminate, defy, disregard, disrupt, encroach, err, infringe, meddle, offend, oppose, outrage, profane, resist, sacrilege, sin, trespass, withstand

violation *noun.* **1** abuse, break, breaking, encroachment, illegality, infraction, infringement, misbehavior, misdemeanor, negligence, nonobservance, offense, rupture, transgressing, transgression, trespass, violating, wrong **2** assault, blasphemy, defacing, degradation, desecration, destruction, devastation, dishonor, invasion, mistreatment, outrage, pollution, profanation, rape, ravishment, ruin, sacrilege, spoliation

violence *noun.* abandon, attack, clash, constraint, duress, ferocity, fervor, fighting, fuss, onslaught, power, raging, rampage, ruckus, savagery, storm, uproar, vehemence

violent *adjective.* **1** agitated, ape, cruel, disturbed, enraged, fierce, fiery, fuming, impetuous, maddened, mighty, raging, riotous, rough, savage, strong, vehement, vicious **2** acute, agonizing, biting, blustery, concentrated, excruciating, exquisite, extreme, immoderate, mighty, powerful, raging, rough, ruinous, sharp, strong, turbulent, wild

virgin *adjective.* first, idle, immaculate, innocent, intact, modest, natural, new, primeval, pristine, pure, single, snowy, spotless, unmarried, untouched, unwed, white

virtue *noun.* asset, chastity, consideration, excellence, faith, fineness, generosity, goodness, hope, incorruptibility, integrity, love, prudence, quality, rectitude, respectability, temper, worth

visible *adjective.* arresting, bold, clear, conspicuous, discernible, in sight, inescapable, noticeable, observable, obvious, ocular, open, perceptible, pronounced, revealed, signal, striking, unmistakable

vision *noun.* **1** angle, concept, discernment, divination, dream, fancy, foreknowledge, imagination, insight, intuition, muse, nightmare, outlook, penetration, perspective, retrospect, slant, view **2** apocalypse, chimera, delusion, ecstasy, fantasy, ghost, haunt, illusion, nightmare, oracle, phantom, presence, prophecy, revelation, specter, spirit, trance, wraith

visit *verb.* call, chat, come by, converse, crash, drop in, dwell, frequent, hit, inspect, look up, play, reside, see, sojourn, talk, tarry, tour

vital *adjective.* basic, critical, crucial, decisive, fundamental, heavy, imperative, important, integral, key, meaningful, name, necessary, needed, required, significant, underlined, urgent

vitality *noun.* animation, ardor, audacity, being, bounce, clout, continuity, endurance, fervor, life, power, pulse, spirit, starch, strength, verve, vigor, vivacity

vivid *adjective.* animated, clear, colorful, distinct, dynamic, eloquent, energetic, expressive, lifelike, meaningful, picturesque, powerful, resplendent, sharp, stirring, striking, strong, theatrical

vocal *adjective.* **1** articulate, articulated, choral, expressed, lyric, modulated, operatic, oral, phonetic, phonic, pronounced, said, singing, sung, uttered, vocalic, voiced, vowel **2** articulate, blunt, clamorous, eloquent, expressive, facile, fluent, forthright, frank, free, glib, noisy, outspoken, plain-spoken, round, smooth-spoken, stentorian, vociferous

voice *noun.* **1** articulation, delivery, intonation, language, modulation, murmur, mutter, roar, shout, song, sound, speech, statement, tone, tongue, utterance, vent, yell **2** approval, choice, decision, expression, option, part, participation, preference, representation, say, say-so, suffrage, vent, view, vote, vox populi, will, wish

voice *verb.* announce, articulate, assert, cry, declare, deliver, emphasize, enunciate, proclaim, pronounce, put, recount, say, sound, speak, talk, tell, vocalize

void *adjective.* **1** abandoned, bare, barren, bereft, clear, deprived, destitute, devoid, drained, emptied, free, lacking, scant, short, shy, vacant, vacuous, without **2** avoided, bad, dead, fruitless, ineffective, ineffectual, inoperative, invalid, meaningless, negated, not viable, null, sterile, unsuccessful, useless, vain, voided, worthless **3** clear, deplete, discharge, dispose, drain, dump, eject, eliminate, emit, evacuate, flow, give off, go, pour, relieve, remove, throw out, vacate **4** black out, cut, discharge, dissolve, drop, gut, invalidate, kill, launder, nullify, queer, rescind, rub, squash, sterilize, trim, vacate, zing

voluntary *adjective.* autonomous, chosen, deliberate, elected, freely, gratuitous, independent, intended, intentional, opted, optional, spontaneous, unasked, unpaid, volitional, volunteer, willed, willful

volunteer *verb.* advance, bring forward, chip in, come forward, enlist, go in, offer services, present, propose, put forward, sign up, speak up, stand up, step forward, submit oneself, suggest, take initiative, tender

vote *verb.* ballot, cast vote, choose, confer, declare, determine, effect, elect, enact, establish, grant, judge, pronounce, propose, recommend, return, second, suggest

vulgar *adjective.* base, boorish, cheap, common, contemptible, dirty, indecent, indelicate, malicious, nasty, obscene, raw, rough, slippery, tasteless, tawdry, unworthy, villainous

vulnerable *adjective.* accessible, assailable, defenseless, exposed, liable, naked, pigeon, ready, sensitive, sitting duck, sucker, susceptible, tender, thin-skinned, unprotected, unsafe, weak, wide open

W

wage *noun.* allowance, bacon, bill, bread, compensation, cut, fee, hire, pay, payment, price, recompense, remuneration, returns, salary, share, take, wages

wait *verb.* abide, ambush, anticipate, await, bide, delay, expect, foresee, hang, linger, pray for, remain, rest, save it, stall, stand by, stay, tarry

wake *verb.* **1** awake, awaken, be roused, bestir, call, come to, nudge, pile out, prod, rise, roll out, rouse, shake, stir, stretch, turn out, wake up, waken **2** activate, animate, arouse, awaken, challenge, fire, fire up, freshen, grasp, notice, provoke, quicken, rally, renew, rouse, see, stimulate, understand

walk *noun.* **1** carriage, circuit, constitutional, gait, hike, march, pace, parade, promenade, ramble, step, stretch, stride, stroll, tour, tramp, tread, turn **2** aisle, avenue, boulevard, bricks, course, court, crossing, footpath, lane, mall, passage, path, pavement, pier, platform, sidewalk, street, trail **3** area, arena, bailiwick, calling, career, course, domain, dominion, field, line, métier, profession, province, sphere, terrain, territory, trade, vocation

walk *verb.* accompany, ankle, boot, canter, exercise, file, leg, pace, race, rove, scuff, shuffle, stroll, tour, tramp, traverse, troop, wander

wall *noun.* bank, bar, barricade, blockade, curb, divider, embankment, fence, impediment, limitation, panel, parapet, partition, rampart, roadblock, screen, side, surface

wander *verb.* cruise, deviate, drift, float, hike, hopscotch, ramble, range, roam, roll, rove, straggle, stray, stroll, trail, tramp, trek, vagabond

want *noun.* absence, dearth, default, defect, deficiency, famine, impecuniousness, impoverishment, inadequacy, meagerness, neediness, paucity, penury, poverty, privation, scarcity, shortage, skimpiness

want *verb.* ache, aspire, choose, covet, crave, die over, fancy, hunger, itch for, long, lust, need, pine, prefer, require, thirst, wish, yearn

wanting *adjective.* bankrupt, bereft, cut off, defective, destitute, devoid, faulty, gone, imperfect, incomplete, inferior, less, omitted, poor, scant, scarce, shy, unfulfilled

war *verb.* attack, attempt, battle, challenge, clash, combat, contend, differ, disagree, endeavor, kill, meet, murder, shell, shoot, strive, struggle, tug

ward *noun.* adopted child, care, charge, child, client, dependant, foster child, guardianship, keeping, minor, orphan, pensioner, protection, protégé, pupil, safekeeping, trust

wardrobe *noun.* apparel, buffet, chest, closet, clothing, costumes, cupboard, drapes, dresser, duds, garments, locker, rags, suits, togs, trunk, vestments, weeds

warfare *noun.* armed struggle, arms, battle, blows, campaigning, clash, combat, competition, contest, discord, fighting, hostilities, rivalry, strategy, strife, striving, struggle, war

warm *adjective.* **1** balmy, clement, flushed, glowing, heated, hot, lukewarm, perspiring, sizzling, snug, sunny, sweating, sweaty, sweltering, temperate, tepid, thermal, warmish **2** affable, affectionate, amiable, amorous, ardent, compassionate, cordial, fervent, genial, gracious, heartfelt, hearty, hospitable, kind, kindly, responsive, sincere, tender **3** amorous, animated, ardent, earnest, effusive, emotional, fervent, glowing, heated, hot, intense, keen, lively, passionate, spirited, stormy, vehement, violent

warn *verb.* advocate, alert, caution, forbid, hint, inform, instruct, predict, prepare, prompt, recommend, remonstrate, signal, suggest, summon, tell, tip, urge

warning *noun.* admonition, alarm, alert, caution, caveat, hint, lesson, look out, omen, premonition, presage, sign, signal, suggestion, threat, tip, wink, word

warrant *noun.* accreditation, authentication, commission, credentials, foundation, pass, passport, pawn, permission, permit, pledge, right, security, summons, tag, testimonial, warranty, word

warrant *verb.* affirm, approve, authorize, certify, claim, commission, defend, demand, endorse, entitle, guaranty, justify, maintain, pledge, promise, secure, uphold, vow

wary *adjective.* alert, attentive, cagey, calculating, canny, cautious, circumspect, considerate, discreet, doubting, guarded, safe, sly, sparing, suspicious, thrifty, vigilant, watchful

wash *verb.* bath, bathe, bubble, float, hose, lap, launder, moisten, rinse, scrub, shampoo, shine, shower, soak, starch, tub, wet, wipe

waste *noun.* **1** decay, desolation, destruction, devastation, disuse, exhaustion, expenditure, extravagance, havoc, lavishness, loss, misapplication, misuse, overdoing, prodigality, ruin, wastage, wastefulness **2** badlands, barren, bog, brush, brushland, bush, desert, dust bowl, jungle, marsh, moor, quagmire, solitude, swamp, void, wasteland, wild, wilderness **3** debris, dreck, dregs, dross, excess, junk, leavings, litter, offal, refuse, rubbish, rubble, ruins, scrap, slop, sweepings, swill, trash

waste *verb.* blow, consume, crumble, decline, disable, disappear, divert, droop, ebb, fade, gnaw, lavish, lose, misuse, perish, sap, sink, wilt

wasteful *adjective.* careless, cavalier, destructive, extravagant, immoderate, lavish, liberal, overdone, overgenerous, prodigal, profuse, reckless, ruinous, thriftless, uneconomical, unthrifty, wanton, wild

watch *noun.* alertness, attention, awareness, gander, guard, hawk, heed, notice, observance, observation, picket, scrutiny, sentinel, sentry, supervision, surveillance, tout, vigil

watch *verb.* **1** case, contemplate, eyeball, follow, gaze, inspect, listen, mark, observe, pipe, regard, rubber, scan, scope, see, spy, view, wait **2** attend, be vigilant, be wary, be watchful, care for, keep, look after, look out, mind, oversee, patrol, police, protect, shotgun, superintend, take heed, tend, wait

water *verb.* bathe, damp, dilute, doctor, drool, flood, hose, irrigate, moisten, soak, sodden, spatter, spray, sprinkle, steep, thin, wash, wet

wave *noun.* crush, curl, flood, foam, loop, movement, outbreak, rash, ridge, ripple, rippling, rocking, sign, surge, tendency, tide, tube, upsurge

wave *verb.* beckon, coil, curl, flow, fly, motion, pulse, ripple, shake, sign, signal, stir, surge, swing, swirl, switch, wield, wobble

wax *verb.* augment, become, build, come, develop, dilate, enlarge, expand, grow, heighten, increase, mount, multiply, rise, run, swell, turn, upsurge

way *noun.* **1** course, custom, design, expedient, form, groove, kick, manner, mode, modus, move, plan, procedure, scheme, system, technique, vehicle, wise **2** bearing, boulevard, channel, course, distance, door, drag, entry, gate, lane, line, opening, passage, route, row, stretch, trend, walk **3** bag, custom, detail, feature, form, gait, groove, kick, manner, personality, practice, respect, sense, shot, state, style, tone, wont

weak *adjective.* **1** anemic, exhausted, feeble, flimsy, frail, lackadaisical, limp, makeshift, powerless, prostrate, rocky, sluggish, tender, uncertain, undependable, weakened, weakly, wobbly **2** dud, hesitant, impotent, indecisive, insecure, nerveless, nervous, pigeon, powerless, soft, spineless, tender, uncertain, undependable, unreliable, unsure, wobbly, zero **3** dim, distant, dull, feeble, gentle, imperceptible, inaudible, indistinct, low, muffled, pale, poor, reedy, slight, small, soft, stifled, whispered **4** feeble, flimsy, green, incredible, ineffective, inept, lame, limited, poor, slight, slim, small, spineless, unbelievable, unconvincing, unsure, untrained, wanting

weaken *verb.* droop, dwindle, fade, fall, halt, impair, lessen, limp, lower, minimize, moderate, reduce, relax, sap, soften, temper, tire, wilt

weakness *noun.* appetite, debility, delicacy, fault, flaw, fondness, gap, imperfection, impotence, inclination, indecision, instability, lapse, liking, passion, penchant, taste, vice

wealth *noun.* abundance, commodities, dough, estate, fortune, funds, goods, luxuriance, possessions, property, resources, riches, richness, security, substance, treasure, velvet, worth

wealthy *adjective.* affluent, booming, comfortable, fat city, in clover, independent, loaded, moneyed, on velvet, opulent, prosperous, stinking rich, substantial, upscale, uptown, well-heeled, well-off, well-to-do

wear *noun.* abrasion, attrition, corrosion, damage, depreciation, deterioration, diminution, disappearance, employment, erosion, friction, impairment, inroads, loss, service, usefulness, utility, waste

wear *verb.* **1** array, attire, bear, carry, cover, display, don, dud, effect, exhibit, get on, harness, put on, rag out, show, sport, turn out, wrap **2** chafe, consume, crumble, decline, deteriorate, dwindle, fade, fray, gall, graze, grind, impair, scrape, scuff, shrink, tire, weary, weather

weary *adjective.* beat, bored, dead, disgusted, drooping, drowsy, exhausted, fatigued, impatient, indifferent, jaded, overworked, sick, sleepy, taxed, wearing, whacked, worn out

weary *verb.* bore, burden, distress, drain, droop, exasperate, exhaust, fade, fail, fall off, flag, harass, pain, plague, sap, sink, strain, tire

weather *verb.* acclimate, become toughened, brave, expose, get through, grow hardened, harden, make it, overcome, resist, rise above, season, stand, suffer, surmount, survive, toughen, withstand

weep *verb.* bemoan, bewail, blubber, break down, complain, deplore, drip, howl, keen, lament, let go, moan, mourn, squall, wail, whimper, yowl

weight *noun.* **1** adiposity, avoirdupois, ballast, beef, burden, density, G-factor, gravity, gross, heftiness, load, mass, measurement, net, ponderosness, pressure, substance, tonnage **2** access, clout, consideration, drag, effectiveness, efficacy, forcefulness, grease, influence, magnitude, moment, pith, power, prestige, pull, ropes, string, substance **3** albatross, charge, cumber, cumbrance, deadweight, duty, encumbrance, excess baggage, incubus, load, millstone, onus, oppression, pressure, responsibility, strain, task, tax

weird *adjective.* creepy, curious, dreadful, eerie, flaky, ghastly, ghostly, haunting, magical, mysterious, odd, ominous, peculiar, queer, secret, spooky, strange, supernatural

welcome *adjective.* acceptable, accepted, agreeable, appreciated, congenial, contenting, delightful, desirable, desired, esteemed, genial, good, gratifying, honored, invited, pleasant, pleasing, refreshing, satisfying, wanted

welcome *noun.* acceptance, blow, entertainment, entree, friendliness, glad hand, handshake, hello, high five, hospitality, howdy, low five, ovation, reception, rumble, salutation, salute, tumble

welcome *verb.* accept, accept gladly, accost, admit, bid welcome, embrace, entertain, flag, greet, hail, hug, meet, offer hospitality, receive, salute, show in, tumble, usher in

welfare *noun.* abundance, advantage, benefit, contentment, ease, euphoria, felicity, good, happiness, health, interest, luck, profit, progress, satisfaction, success, thriving, well-being

well *adjective.* **1** beefy, blooming, chipper, fine, fit, flourishing, great, hale, hardy, hearty, husky, right, sane, sound, strong, trim, whole, wholesome **2** advisable, agreeable, bright, comfortable, fine, fitting, flourishing, good, pleasing, profitable, proper, prosperous, providential, prudent, right, satisfactory, thriving, useful **3** ably, accurately, adequately, capably, competently, correctly, effectively, efficiently, expertly, pleasantly, profoundly, properly, rightly, smoothly, soundly, strongly, successfully, suitably **4** abundantly, adequately, appropriately, considerably, easily, entirely, extremely, far, freely, greatly, properly, quite, rather, readily, right, smoothly, somewhat, suitably

well *noun.* abyss, bore, chasm, derivation, fountain, fountainhead, hole, mouth, origin, pit, pool, repository, root, shaft, source, spout, spring, springs

wet *adjective.* clammy, dank, dewy, drenched, dripping, drizzling, foggy, moistened, pouring, saturated, slippery, snowy, soaked, soaking, sodden, sopping, stormy, watery

wet *verb.* bathe, damp, dampen, deluge, dip, drown, hose, irrigate, moisten, rinse, soak, sop, splash, spray, sprinkle, steep, wash, water

wheel *noun.* circuit, circulation, cycle, disk, drum, gyration, hoop, pivot, pulley, revolution, ring, roll, roller, rotation, round, spin, trolley, turn

whip *noun.* bat, belt, birch, bullwhip, cane, crop, goad, horsewhip, lash, prod, push, rawhide, rod, ruler, scourge, strap, switch, thong

whip *verb.* **1** beat, birch, bludgeon, cane, cudgel, flog, hide, lash, lather, punish, scourge, strap, strike, switch, tan, thrash, trash, wallop **2** beat, blank, blast, cook, curry, do in, dust, kill, lick, overcome, overrun, settle, skin, subdue, top, trim, tube, wallop **3** avert, dive, divert, flash, fly, jerk, pivot, pull, rush, seize, sheer, shoot, snatch, surge, tear, turn, veer, wheel

whisper *noun.* buzz, confidence, disclosure, gossip, hint, hum, innuendo, insinuation, low voice, mumble, murmur, mutter, report, secret, secret message, sigh, sighing, word

whisper *verb.* breathe, buzz, confide, gossip, hint, hiss, insinuate, intimate, mumble, murmur, mutter, say softly, sibilate, sigh, speak confidentially, spread rumor, talk low, tell

white *adjective.* alabaster, ashen, blanched, bleached, bloodless, chalky, clear, ghastly, gray, immaculate, ivory, light, neutral, pallid, pearly, silvery, spotless, wan

whole *adjective.* **1** accomplished, all, completed, concentrated, conclusive, every, exclusive, exhaustive, fixed, fulfilled, gross, integral, outright, plenary, rounded, unabridged, undivided, unqualified **2** completed, developed, faultless, flawless, good, mature, mint, plenary, preserved, replete, safe, solid, sound, thorough, unhurt, uninjured, unscathed, untouched

whole *noun.* aggregation, all, assembly, being, body, ensemble, entity, integral, oneness, organism, organization, piece, quantum, result, sum, summation, supply, system

wholesale *adjective.* broad, bulk, complete, comprehensive, extensive, far-reaching, general, in bulk, in quantity, indiscriminate, large-scale, mass, overall, quantitative, sweeping, total, wide-ranging, widespread

wholesome *adjective.* beneficial, decent, edifying, ethical, fit, good, hale, healthful, helpful, moral, normal, nourishing, respectable, restorative, right, sanitary, sound, strengthening

wicked *adjective.* **1** amoral, arch, base, contemptible, depraved, foul, gross, guilty, heartless, immoral, indecent, iniquitous, nasty, reprobate, sinful, vicious, villainous, worthless **2** acute, agonizing, distressing, dreadful, fierce, galling, harmful, hazardous, injurious, mighty, offensive, perilous, severe, treacherous, ugly, unconscionable, unpleasant, vexatious

wide *adjective.* advanced, baggy, deep, dilated, extensive, full, large, liberal, loose, open, outspread, radical, spacious, sweeping, tolerant, universal, vast, voluminous

widespread *adjective.* boundless, common, comprehensive, diffuse, epidemic, general, outspread, pervasive, popular, prevailing, prevalent, rampant, ruling, sweeping, universal, unlimited, unrestricted, wholesale

width *noun.* amplitude, area, compass, cross measure, diameter, distance across, expanse, extent, girth, measure, range, reach, scope, span, squatness, stretch, thickness, wideness

wife *noun.* apron, bride, consort, dame, dowager, helpmate, housewife, lady, madam, mama, mat, mate, matron, partner, rib, roommate, spouse, squaw

wild *adjective.* **1** agrarian, barbarian, barbaric, dense, deserted, escaped, fierce, indigenous, lush, native, natural, overrun, primitive, rampant, savage, unbroken, untouched, vicious **2** avid, boisterous, chaotic, crazed, eager, extravagant, foolhardy, impetuous, incautious, irrational, lawless, loose, nuts, riotous, rough, turbulent, unbridled, unruly

wilderness *noun.* back country, badland, barrens, boondocks, boonies, bush, desert, forest, hinterland, jungle, no-man's land, outback, primeval forest, sticks, waste, wasteland, wild, wilds

will *noun.* **1** appetite, conviction, decision, decree, design, determination, fancy, inclination, intention, liking, longing, power, preference, prerogative, temper, volition, wish, yearning **2** bequest, bestowal, declaration, decree, device, directions, dispensation, disposition, estate, heritage, inheritance, insistence, instructions, last wishes, legacy, order, property, testament

will *verb.* authorize, bid, bring about, command, decide on, decree, demand, determine, direct, effect, enjoin, exert, insist, intend, ordain, order, request, resolve

willing *adjective.* amenable, content, desirous, eager, energetic, forward, inclined, intentional, minded, obedient, on, pleased, prepared, prompt, responsible, unasked, voluntary, willful

win *verb.* **1** beat, breeze, bulldoze, conquer, edge, gain, gain victory, lock, overcome, overwhelm, prevail, shut down, sink, snow, succeed, triumph, upset, walk over **2** accomplish, annex, approach, attain, bag, collect, derive, earn, effect, gain, harvest, have, net, pick up, procure, realize, receive, secure **3** allure, argue into, attract, carry, charm, convert, convince, disarm, draw, get, induce, influence, overcome, prevail upon, prompt, slay, sway, wow

wind *noun.* air, blast, blow, breath, breeze, dirt, draft, draught, flurry, flutter, gale, gust, puff, skiff, tempest, typhoon, whiff, whirlwind

wind *verb.* coil, cover, curl, curve, deviate, encircle, fold, loop, ramble, roll, screw, snake, spiral, swerve, turn, twist, weave, wrap

winding *adjective.* circuitous, convoluted, crooked, curving, devious, flexuous, indirect, intricate, involved, mazy, meandering, roundabout, serpentine, sinuous, spiraling, tortuous, turning, twisting

wing *noun.* annex, arm, branch, clique, detachment, division, ell, group, part, projection, prolongation, protrusion, protuberance, section, segment, set, side, unit

winning *adjective.* acceptable, agreeable, amiable, captivating, charming, cute, delightful, dulcet, enchanting, endearing, fascinating, fetching, gratifying, lovable, pleasing, sweet, taking, winsome

wisdom *noun.* caution, circumspection, comprehension, discernment, discrimination, enlightenment, erudition, experience, judgment, knowledge, penetration, poise, practicality, prudence, reason, savvy, sophistication, stability

wise *adjective.* aware, careful, cunning, discerning, discreet, educated, informed, intuitive, keen, knowledgeable, politic, rational, reasonable, sensible, sensing, sharp, sound, taught

wish *noun.* ambition, aspiration, hope, inclination, intention, invocation, itch, liking, longing, pleasure, prayer, preference, request, urge, want, whim, will, yearning

wish *verb.* aspire, beg, choose, command, crave, envy, expect, fancy, hope, itch, like, need, order, prefer, request, solicit, want, will

wit *noun.* **1** badinage, banter, burlesque, fun, gag, jest, joke, lark, levity, pleasantry, prank, pun, raillery, repartee, sally, satire, trick, wittiness **2** banterer, card, comedian, comic, epigrammatist, farceur, funnyman, funster, gagman, humorist, jester, joker, jokester, punster, quipster, trickster, wag, wise guy **3** awareness, cleverness, comprehension, discernment, discrimination, esprit, grasp, ingenuity, insight, lucidity, perception, practicality, prudence, reason, sense, soundness, wisdom, wits

withdraw *verb.* **1** blow, depart, detach, disengage, eliminate, exit, extract, get away, leave, quit, recede, recoil, retreat, secede, shrink, switch, take off, vacate **2** abolish, abrogate, ban, bar, disavow, dissolve, invalidate, nullify, recall, repress, repudiate, rescind, retire, reverse, stamp out, suppress, veto, void

witness *noun.* attestant, attestor, beholder, bystander, corroborator, eyewitness, gawker, looker-on, observer, onlooker, proof, rubbernecker, signatory, signer, spectator, testimony, viewer, watcher

witness *verb.* **1** attend, be present, behold, eyeball, flash on, look on, mark, note, notice, perceive, pipe, read, see, sight, spot, spy, view, watch **2** affirm, announce, argue, attest, authenticate, bear witness, bespeak, betoken, certify, confirm, corroborate, countersign, depose, endorse, indicate, sign, subscribe, vouch for

witty *adjective.* amusing, bright, crazy, entertaining, epigrammatic, facetious, fanciful, funny, ingenious, intelligent, jocose, keen, lively, penetrating, piquant, scintillating, slapstick, whimsical

woman *noun.* babe, bird, bride, chick, dame, debutante, gal, girl, love, mate, matron, moll, partner, pigeon, she, spouse, sweetheart, tootsie

wonder *noun.* admiration, awe, bewilderment, concern, consternation, curiosity, fascination, incredulity, jolt, perplexity, perturbation, shock, skepticism, start, stupor, surprise, suspicion, wondering

wonderful *adjective.* astounding, awesome, divine, fabulous, fine, incredible, magnificent, marvelous, miraculous, prime, remarkable, staggering, startling, strange, super, surprising, tremendous, wondrous

wooden *adjective*. awkward, clumsy, gauche, gawky, graceless, heavy, inept, inflexible, maladroit, obstinate, ponderous, rigid, stilted, ungainly, ungraceful, unhandy, unyielding, weighty

word *noun*. account, bulletin, byword, declaration, dispatch, expression, gossip, intelligence, introduction, notice, proverb, remark, rumor, saying, speech, talk, tidings, utterance

work *noun*. **1** attempt, commission, effort, endeavor, exertion, functioning, grindstone, job, muscle, obligation, production, rally, stint, sweat, toil, trial, trouble, undertaking **2** art, bag, contract, do, dodge, employment, job, line, manufacture, obligation, profession, racket, responsibility, skill, specialization, stint, vocation, walk **3** act, application, article, composition, creation, deed, end product, function, handicraft, handiwork, oeuvre, opus, output, performance, piece, product, production, workmanship **4** buck, dig, drive, hustle, labor, manage, plug, ply, pursue, report, scratch, slave, specialize, strain, strive, sweat, toil, try **5** accomplish, achieve, act, cause, create, effect, execute, function, handle, manage, maneuver, move, perform, ply, progress, serve, take, wield

worker *noun*. artisan, breadwinner, craftsman, employee, hand, help, laborer, mechanic, operative, page, peasant, peon, proletarian, slave, stiff, tradesman, wage earner, working man

working *adjective*. alive, busy, dynamic, effective, employed, engaged, functioning, going, hot, in force, live, moving, occupied, operative, practical, running, useful, viable

worldly *adjective*. **1** carnal, earthly, earthy, human, lay, materialistic, mundane, natural, physical, practical, profane, secular, sublunary, telluric, temporal, terrene, terrestrial, ungodly **2** avaricious, callous, cool, cosmopolitan, covetous, grasping, greedy, hardened, hip, knowing, materialistic, opportunistic, power-loving, practical, self-centered, selfish, uptown, urbane

worn *adjective*. beat, destroyed, deteriorated, exhausted, fatigued, frayed, gone, hackneyed, jaded, old, overworked, ragged, ruined, tattered, timeworn, totaled, useless, weary

worried *adjective*. afraid, bothered, clutched, concerned, distracted, distraught, distressed, disturbed, fearful, frightened, nervous, perturbed, solicitous, tense, tormented, troubled, uneasy, upset

worry *noun*. anguish, apprehension, concern, disquiet, distress, fear, irritation, misery, pain, perplexity, pest, plague, torment, trial, trouble, uncertainty, uneasiness

worry *verb*. attack, be at, bite, bother, chafe, despair, disquiet, distress, disturb, goad, hector, needle, plague, stew, tease, torment, trouble, upset

worship *noun*. adulation, awe, benediction, chapel, devotion, exaltation, glorification, homage, idolatry, invocation, love, praise, prayer, regard, respect, ritual, service, veneration

worship *verb*. admire, adore, adulate, bow down, celebrate, chant, dote on, esteem, exalt, glorify, idolize, love, magnify, praise, respect, revere, reverence, sing

worth *noun*. account, aid, assistance, avail, benefit, dignity, equivalence, excellence, goodness, importance, mark, meaningfulness, moment, quality, rate, stature, usefulness, utility

worthwhile *adjective*. beneficial, constructive, gainful, good, important, justifiable, lucrative, meritorious, paying, priceless, productive, profitable, remunerative, rewarding, serviceable, useful, valuable, worthy

worthy *adjective*. admirable, decent, desirable, divine, ethical, good, honest, model, moral, pleasing, precious, priceless, reputable, respectable, true, valuable, winner, worthwhile

wound *noun*. anguish, bruise, cut, damage, distress, gash, grief, harm, heartbreak, hurt, insult, lesion, pain, shock, slash, torment, torture, trauma

wound *verb*. **1** bruise, carve, clip, cut, damage, gash, harm, hit, hurt, lacerate, nick, pierce, scrape, scratch, slash, slice, stick, total **2** bother, cut, distress, disturb, do in, get, hurt, kick around, offend, outrage, pain, shake up, shock, sting, traumatize, trouble, upset, zing

wrath *noun*. displeasure, exasperation, hate, huff, indignation, ire, irritation, mad, madness, offense, passion, rage, resentment, rise, stew, storm, temper, vengeance

wreck *noun*. crash, crate, debacle, debris, derelict, destruction, disruption, heap, hulk, jalopy, mess, relic, ruins, shipwreck, skeleton, total, waste, wreckage

wreck *verb*. batter, beach, break, crash, dash, disable, do in, impair, mar, sabotage, shatter, shipwreck, sink, smash, strand, total, trash, wrack

wretched *adjective*. afflicted, bad, base, cheap, contemptible, depressed, faulty, flimsy, forlorn, hapless, miserable, pitiable, pitiful, poor, unfortunate, weak, woebegone, worthless

write *verb*. address, author, commit, copy, correspond, create, ghost, letter, pen, pencil, print, record, reproduce, rewrite, scribe, sign, tell, turn out

writer *noun*. biographer, columnist, contributor, correspondent, critic, dramatist, editor, ghostwriter, hack, ink slinger, journalist, newspaperman, novelist, playwright, poet, reporter, scribe, wordsmith

writing *noun*. document, editorial, letter, literature, manuscript, opus, pamphlet, paper, piece, poem, prose, record, review, signature, thesis, tract, treatise, work

wrong *adjective*. **1** askew, astray, awry, bad, defective, erratic, erroneous, fallacious, false, faulty, miscalculated, misconstrued, misguided, out, perverse, rotten, untrue, wide **2** amoral, bad, base, criminal, crooked, dissipated, felonious, illegal, illicit, indecent, iniquitous, shady, sinful, unlawful, vicious, wanton, wicked, wrongful **3** amiss, awkward, bad, disproportionate, funny, gauche, improper, inapt, incorrect, misplaced, rotten, unacceptable, undesirable, unfit, unfitting, unhappy, unsatisfactory, unseemly

wrong *noun*. abuse, blunder, delinquency, error, grievance, harm, immorality, imposition, injury, libel, misdemeanor, offense, sinfulness, slight, spite, transgression, wickedness, wrongdoing

wrong *verb*. abuse, aggrieve, cheat, damage, discredit, dishonor, harm, hurt, illtreat, impose upon, malign, maltreat, misrepresent, mistreat, offend, oppress, outrage, persecute

Y

yard *noun*. backyard, barnyard, clearing, close, corral, court, courtyard, enclosure, fold, garden, grass, lawn, lot, patch, patio, playground, quadrangle, terrace

yarn *noun*. adventure, alibi, anecdote, chestnut, fable, fabrication, fairy tale, lie, line, narrative, old chestnut, potboiler, prose, sea story, song, string, tale, tall story

yell *verb*. bellow, cheer, complain, hoot, howl, lament, roar, scream, screech, shout, shriek, shrill, squawk, wail, weep, whoop, yelp, yip

yes *adverb*. affirmative, amen, aye, certainly, definitely, exactly, fine, gladly, good, granted, naturally, okay, precisely, surely, true, undoubtedly, willingly, yea.

yield *verb*. **1** admit, afford, beam, bear, blossom, discharge, earn, furnish, generate, give, net, offer, pay, provide, return, supply, tender, turn out **2** abandon, bend, bow, break, buy, collapse, defer, fold, go, knuckle, leave, relax, relinquish, resign, sag, submit, succumb, surrender **3** accede, accept, acknowledge, acquiesce, admit, agree, assent, bow, break, comply, concede, concur, consent, defer, fail, permit, surrender, waive

yielding *adjective*. elastic, flexible, malleable, mushy, pappy, plastic, pliable, pulpy, quaggy, resilient, spongy, springy, squishy, supple, tractable, tractile, unresisting

young *adjective.* adolescent, boyish, budding, burgeoning, childish, childlike, developing, fledgling, girlish, green, growing, infant, junior, punk, tender, tenderfoot, undeveloped, unfinished

youngster *noun.* boy, chick, fledgling, girl, junior, juvenile, kid, lad, lass, punk, pup, pupil, puppy, sapling, sonny, squirt, student, youth

youth *noun.* adolescence, bloom, boyhood, childhood, girlhood, greenness, ignorance, immaturity, inexperience, innocence, juvenescence, minority, prime, puberty, salad days, springtide, teens, virginity

youthful *adjective.* active, adolescent, boyish, budding, buoyant, childish, childlike, enthusiastic, girlish, green, inexperienced, infant, juvenile, keen, new, tender, vernal, young

Z

zeal *noun.* ardor, bustle, determination, devotion, diligence, dispatch, eagerness, enterprise, fervor, hop, inclination, intensity, mania, passion, readiness, spirit, vehemence, verve

zenith *noun.* altitude, apex, apogee, cap, climax, crest, crown, culmination, elevation, eminence, height, high point, payoff, peak, pinnacle, roof, summit, vertex

zero *noun.* aught, blank, bottom, cipher, duck egg, love, nada, nadir, naught, nil, nix, nobody, nothing, nullity, oblivion, ought, rock bottom, scratch, shutout, void, zilch, zip